BUSINESS

A Student's Guide

BUSINESS
A Student's Guide

THIRD EDITION

Desmond W Evans

A textbook specifically written for the Advanced GNVQ Business syllabus and comprehensively revised to meet all the new 1995 programme specifications

Contributors

Susan Curtis
Lecturer in Economics, Crewe & Alsager Faculty, Manchester Metropolitan University

Barry Curtis
Manager of Social Sciences & teacher of Business Studies, South Cheshire College

PITMAN PUBLISHING

PITMAN PUBLISHING
128 Long Acre, London WC2E 9AN

A Division of Pearson Professional Limited

First published in 1993
Second edition 1994
Third edition 1995

A CIP catalogue record for this book can be obtained from the British Library.

ISBN 0 273 61770 2

Typeset by M Rules
Printed and bound in Great Britain by Bath Press, Avon

The Publishers' policy is to use paper manufactured from sustainable forests.

CONTENTS

INTRODUCTION FOR THE STUDENT

The third edition of *Business: A Student's Guide* is dedicated to all students and staff who are pursuing GNVQ Business at Advanced Level.

A whole army of educational administrators, curriculum designers, publishers, textbook writers, teachers and their support staff have worked hard to develop and now to revise a stimulating and exciting – GNVQ – way of preparing students who wish to make a career in the world of business or public administration.

I very much share their enthusiasm for the GNVQ Business Awards and, with the much appreciated help and support of my wife, my publishers, contributors and many organisations who have made illustrative material available, have 'campaigned' hard to produce a textbook which follows directly and comprehensively the GNVQ specification for the mandatory Advanced Level Units. The text also provides both helpful build-up tasks and a series of evidence-building activities at the end of each Element which cover all the Elements and Performance Criteria of the Advanced Level in Business. Also, the Portfolio of Evidence Activities provide opportunities for Core Skills assessment.

The following notes are intended to assist you in making the most of this third edition, which has been comprehensively revised to meet the 1995 new programme specification. I wish you every success, both in your course of study and in your future career!

HOW TO MAKE THE BEST USE OF THIS TEXTBOOK

Structure and contents

Business: A Student's Guide 3rd edition comprises eight Units, which correspond to the mandatory units of Advanced Business, and share their titles. Each of the text's Units follows exactly the sequence of Elements and Performance Criteria of the specification, and contains information and material which relate to the GNVQ Unit Elements in these ways:

- **to provide the detailed knowledge and understanding which relate to the Units' specifications** and which provide a source of reference in preparation for the externally assessed Unit Tests
- **to supply insights and explanations of current business procedures, practices and approaches** through the inclusion of models, diagrams, examples and specimen documents etc.
- **to encourage lively discussion and debate** about current business issues and developments
- **to include opportunities for both individual and group assignments and activities** from which you will practise and acquire skills you will need throughout your business career, and which may also be used to build evidence for your portfolio.

Element and Performance Criteria references

To assist you in studying each mandatory unit of your Advanced Level programme as you progress through it, each of the text's Units is supplied with **references to the Performance Criteria** to which each portion of text refers on a page-by-page basis, including diagrams and charts. Sometimes the reference extends over a single paragraph and sometimes over several pages if the subject matter stays the same.

Study tips

- Use the GNVQ PC specifications and introduction at the beginning of each Unit as a quick way of checking areas of the text relevant to your study topic of the moment. Also, remember to use the index at the back of the text to locate specific items such as: *grievance procedures* or *charge cards* etc.
- Make a regular practice of reading and re-reading those referenced sections of each Unit of the text which correspond to the topics of your weekly studies. This will help you to assimilate and remember important points and information.
- Use the text to help you in writing up your notes of classwork and your own research studies; these will help you to recall essential facts and techniques.
- Make a habit of checking back over examples and models, such as the *job description* or the *marketing break-even chart* as they occur in your studies, so that you acquire a thorough grasp of the content and format of business documents and techniques.
- Take notes of the main points which occur in class discussions or group presentations on topics from the text, since some very useful ideas and responses are bound to emerge.

Unit tasks and activities

In addition to providing you with a helpful source of knowledge and understanding of current business practice, *Business: A Student's Guide* 3rd edition also supplies a range of tasks and activities which relate directly to specific sets of Performance Criteria (and are thus handily referenced) and which will enable you to practise and perfect newly acquired skills and competences. Your teacher/lecturer may decide to employ these activities as 'rehearsals' or 'practice goes' prior to your undertaking centre-devised activities, or may use them as the means of your building up evidence for your portfolio.

Tips on undertaking tasks and activities

- Always take the trouble to read the content of each activity scenario and instructions carefully – if you misunderstand what you have been asked to do, you will waste a lot of precious time!
- Whether singly or as a group member, make notes on how you plan to tackle the task or activity and how it progressed in the event and remember always to complete the planning section of your planning and review log before starting out on each activity – but remember to follow your teacher's directions in this regard as well.
- When you are undertaking an activity which requires you to carry out research locally, remember that you have a network of willing and easily contactable assistants – your parents, relatives, neighbours and friends who are already working, and may have accumulated many years of know-how and experience. So tap into it by arranging to talk to them about the activity you are pursuing and to ask them 'how it is done' where they work, as well as what tips and advice they can provide on good practice. This certainly does not mean that you get such 'assistants' to do your assignment for you, but it does mean that you should make sensible use of such handy sources of expertise.
- A number of activities may require you to make arrangements to meet local business or public sector managers or officers. Always take the trouble to prepare your questions or

interview material well beforehand, to be punctual and polite. This includes the sending of 'thank-you' letters which may well keep a useful door open for another similar visit. And always remember, if you pick up information about an organisation during a visit or attachment, to obtain the permission of your contact manager before you share it with your class. Business people are rightly anxious to avoid confidential or sensitive information 'leaking' without their knowledge or approval, and carelessness could wreck an invaluable local contact not only for you but for your GNVQ successors.

- Before you submit activity evidence for assessment, take the time to check it through carefully for your use of English and completeness. Cross-check each item of evidence against the Performance Criterion it meets and ensure that you have given it a clear and unique PC reference. Similarly, make sure your submitted activity covers sufficiently the range items to which it refers. Also, make sure you have filled out accurately the forms which accompany your evidence.

Careful storage of your portfolio and notes

Make a habit, right from the outset of your studies, of keeping your portfolio as it builds up in a safe place along with the notes you accumulate for each Unit. Use a ring-binder or folder to transport study materials daily to school or college and **transfer its contents daily** to your main files. Where especially precious pieces of evidence are concerned, take a photocopy of them before parting with them for whatever reason.

This text and other sources of evidence

Lastly, keep in mind always that a textbook, such as this one, which embraces a very wide range of business-related topics can, at best, provide only a limited amount of information, some of which is conveyed in overview, survey or summary form.

If you wish to do well in your GNVQ Advanced Level Business studies, you will undoubtedly need to make full use of the reference and learning resources of your school/college library, public library and other information databanks. For this reason, each Unit includes at its close a select listing of *Further Sources of Information* to help you in finding more detailed and specialised sources of information.

Acquiring the study habit

Textbooks are very much like milestones; they can point the way along main routes and highways along which to travel, but they can't do the journeying for you!

So the pains you take to acquire the study habit will prove well worthwhile in both the short and long term. The pace of technological change and product/service innovation in the world of business is now so hectic and permanent that every business executive – whether he or she realises it or not – is engaged in a career-long process of study to acquire and develop continually changing and evolving skills and expertise!

All being well, *Business: A Student's Guide* 3rd edition and the above notes will act as good milestones. But your own journey now awaits you. I very much hope it will prove enjoyable and rewarding, even if it is sometimes strenuous and uphill. Good luck and good studying!

Desmond W Evans
April 1995

ACKNOWLEDGEMENTS

I should like to thank Barry and Susan Curtis for writing *Unit 5: Production and employment in the economy*. Their contribution was much appreciated. Thanks are also due to Barbara Darby who wrote Units 6 and 7 for the first edition, parts of which have been reproduced in the third edition, as well as to the team at Bradford and Ilkley Community College – namely Stan Goleb, Peter Horton, Mike Leake, Peter Rooney and Graham Wood – for input to the second edition which has been carried forward. No author can succeed without an encouraging editorial back-up, and I thank Grace Evans and Lisa Howard, without whose hard work and expertise this third edition would not have been produced in time to reassure its existing and potential users of its 'bang-up-to-date' currency and relevance.

I should also like to thank the production and design team, typesetters and printers for their hard work in getting this edition into the market-place in such a timely way.

I also gratefully acknowledge the generous help and support of executives and staff of the following organisations for the textual illustrations and case study material etc. they made available.

ACAS: Advisory Conciliation and Arbitration Service
Aldus Pagemaker Limited
RG Anderson, *Data processing,* Macdonald & Evans Limited
Barclays Bank
The Body Shop International and Body Shop Supply Company
British Standards Institute
British Telecom
M Buckley and Longman Group Ltd
R J Bull, *Accounting in Business,* Heinemann Butterworth
Business Equipment Digest Magazine
Canon (UK) Ltd
Cave Tab Limited
CBI *Quarterly Industrial Trends Survey*
Centaur Limited
Chichester & District Angling Society
The Corporation, Chichester College of Technology
The Department of Trade and Industry, *A Summary of the UK Economy,* Mentor Publications, Dublin
John Dunn, *Accounting: An Introduction for Professional Students,* Pitman Publishing
J R Dyson and Pitman Publishing
Employment Gazette
EOC
Fellowes Manufacturing UK Limited
Fretwell-Downing Data Systems Limited
GEC Plessey Telecommunications Limited
H T Graham & R Bennett, *Human Resources Management,* M & E handbooks, Longman UK Limited
The Guardian
Hargreaves, *Starting a Small Business,* Butterworth Heinemann
John Harrison, *Finance, First Levels of Competence,* Pitman Publishing
John Harrison & Ron Dawber, *Clerical Accounting,* Pitman Publishing
Headway Computer Products
Heinemann Professional Publishing
Her Majesty's Stationery Office
J Hopkins, *Finance for BTEC,* Pitman Publishing
Peter Hingston of Hingston Associates
ICI
The Independent: Images change as joblessness affects all social classes (John Arlidge) article
Institute of Chartered Accountants
Institute for Employment Research Alan Jones & Associates
D Keenan & S Riches, *Business Law,* Pitman Publishing

Kodak Management Information Systems Limited
Lake Publishing Company
J Lambden & D Targett, *Small Business Finance,* Longman Group Limited
Marshall Editions Limited
Midland Bank plc
Minolta UK Limited
Muirfax Systems Limited
National Westminster Bank – and especially Ms Marion O'Connor
New Earnings Survey 1992
Sheila Robinson, *Frank Wood's Business Accounting AAT Student's Workbook,* Pitman Publishing
G L Thirkettle, *Wheldon's Business Statistics,* 8th ed., Macdonald & Evans
Times Newspapers Limited: *Road to the Busy Aisles,* Leading Tabloids Chart, Mars Marketing Article, *Amazing rediscovery: the phone*
Torus Systems Limited
Waterlow Business Supplies
A West, '*A Business Plan*', Natwest and Longman Group Ltd
West Sussex County Council
Western Riverside Waste Authority
G Whitehead, Heinemann Professional Publishing Limited and Longman Group Ltd
Frank Wood, *Frank Wood's Book-keeping and Accountancy* and *Frank Wood's Business Accounting,* Pitman Publishing

The unit specifications of the Advanced General National Vocational Qualification in Business shown at the beginning of each Unit in this book are reproduced by kind permission of the National Council for Vocational Qualifications.

Throughout this text I have endeavoured to demonstrate that a chief executive, manager, supervisor, assistant or operative may be either male or female. Sometimes, simply for the sake of syntax and simplicity, I have employed the generic 'he'. Similarly, I have sometimes used chairman, in preference for 'chair' or 'chairperson'. This use does not in any way imply an under-estimation of the valuable contribution which women make – at every level of activity – in both the private and public sectors of our economy.

Desmond Evans

The Purpose of Industry

'The purpose of industry is to create goods and services to meet human needs.

It is not to make money for its own sake.
It is not to make profits for shareholders, nor to create salaries and wages for the industrial community.

These are necessary conditions for success but not its purpose.'

Dr George Carey, Archbishop of Canterbury
Derby Cathedral May 1992. Service of Dedication to mark the advent of the Single European Market

UNIT

1

BUSINESS IN THE ECONOMY

Element 1.1
Analyse the forces of supply and demand on businesses

Element 1.2
Analyse the operation of markets and their effects on businesses and communities

Element 1.3
Examine the effects of government policies on markets

PERFORMANCE CRITERIA AND RANGE

Element 1.1: Analyse the forces of supply and demand on businesses

PERFORMANCE CRITERIA

A student must: *page*

1. explain **demand** for goods and services 5–32
2. explain how businesses decide on goods and services to **supply** 14–35
3. **analyse** the demand and supply interaction 17–35
4. explain the **effects on business decisions** of changes in the conditions of **demand** and **supply** 26–35
5. report research findings about **demand** and **supply** interaction and the price and sales for a particular product 38–9
6. suggest future changes in **demand** and **supply** of particular products 38–9

RANGE

Demand: satisfying customer needs and wants, effective demand, spending and income, demand curves, price and income elasticity, causes of change in demand (income, tastes, advertising, prices of other goods)
Supply: profit motive, public service motive, opportunity cost, choice of products, availability of finance for business, relationship between price and quantity supplied, elasticity of supply, supply curves, changes in supply, effect of customers, effect of competitors
Analyse in terms of: market price for a product, market volume for a product
Effects on business decisions: shifts in demand curves, shifts in supply curves, changes in market price and quantity sold, economies of scale, changes to breakeven position

EVIDENCE INDICATORS

A report which analyses two products and explains:

- causes of change in demand and supply for those products. The report should analyse how the interaction of demand and supply influenced business decisions about those two products
- the importance to businesses of the relationship between price, quantity demanded and quantity supplied
- the importance of customers and competitors in terms of their effect on demand, prices, supply and the consequences of shifts in demand and supply in terms of output or sales.

The report should indicate that equilibrium between supply and demand will determine both the price and sales of a particular product, and indicate the effects on price and sales of changes in demand and supply. It should suggest possible future changes in demand and supply for the two products.

Element 1.2: Analyse the operation of markets and their effects on businesses and communities

PERFORMANCE CRITERIA

A student must: *page*

1. explain **types of markets** 40–3
2. **compare competition** within markets 44–9
3. **analyse** behaviour of businesses in different markets 44–9
4. **evaluate** the **social costs** of market operations 49–55
5. **evaluate** the **social benefits** of market operations 49–55

RANGE

Types of markets: competitive, non-competitive; monopoly, oligopoly
Compare competition: for customers and sales, for market share, for product superiority, for price, between businesses to shift demand curves, effect on consumers
Analyse in terms of: competitive pricing strategies (skimming, expansion pricing, penetration pricing, destruction pricing, price wars); price makers, price takers; non-pricing strategies
Evaluate social costs in terms of: effects on the environment (depletion of natural resources, pollution), effects on health, effects of employment
Evaluate social benefits in terms of: effects of employment, investment, training

EVIDENCE INDICATORS

The report explains two markets, one competitive and one non-competitive, in terms of numbers of suppliers in the market (private or public sector monopolies or oligopolies); size of suppliers; and strength of demand in the markets. It should compare two businesses in one market showing shifts in demand curves and explaining why the shifts have occurred. The report should also describe how the competition effects

- consumers' choice and the quality of products
- pricing and non-pricing strategies to improve market position
- the costs and benefits to the wider community.

Element 1.3: Examine the effects of government policies on markets

PERFORMANCE CRITERIA

A student must: *page*

1 explain the **reasons for government intervention** in markets 56–65

2 explain the **ways** governments can influence markets 65–75

3 **evaluate** the effects on markets of **government policies** 72–81

RANGE

Reasons for government intervention: to increase competition, to regulate competition, to counteract anti-competitive activities, to ensure fair and honest trading, to protect consumers, to protect environmental and social interests, to stimulate consumer demand, to improve levels of employment, to control inflation, to stimulate growth

Ways: regulation, deregulation, control of monopoly, monetary policy, fiscal policy, legislation, public ownership, privatisation

Evaluate in terms of: business confidence, changes in employment opportunities, growth, consumers' disposable income, effects on demand, trading conditions

Government policies: interest rates, personal income tax, corporate tax, Value Added Tax (VAT), public services wage levels, public spending, investment, regional assistance, single market

EVIDENCE INDICATORS

Notes which explain the reasons why governments intervene in markets.

Summary notes of the ways in which at least two government policies affect local or national markets. The notes should be supported by a record of a discussion on 'Why governments try to intervene in markets'. Arguments for and against government influence should be recorded.

INTRODUCTION

Unit 1 provides a detailed examination of the economic environment in which both business and public sector enterprises operate. It provides a thorough treatment of the principal economic concepts such as: needs, wants, scarcity, supply, demand, price, elasticity and so on and relates them to the macro-economic activities of the developed economies of the UK, European Community, USA and Japan as well as Third World States.

In addition, Unit 1 analyses the ways in which the forces of supply and demand impact upon businesses, and the ensuing effects.

Unit 1 also analyses how markets operate within an economy and the effects they have on businesses and communities in terms of generating profits, ensuring access to goods and services and providing employment etc.

Lastly, Unit 1 examines the ways in which government policies affect markets and how the various mechanisms – taxation, interest rate changes, subsidies etc., are employed to steer markets into approved directions.

Element 1.1
THE EFFECTS OF SUPPLY AND DEMAND ON BUSINESSES

Introduction: the economic cycle of business

PC 1.1.1

'It is the business of the wealthy man to give employment to the artisan.'

Hilaire Belloc

Within the doggerel verse of the above quotation lie a number of ideas which inform an introduction into the world of business. Hilaire Belloc well understood, for example, the need for money to flow around in a kind of circle within an economy as a means of creating further wealth. He also understood the importance of enabling those without personal wealth to prosper from gainful employment of hand and brain.

Thus, with Hilaire Belloc's help, we can identify three important components of business enterprise:

1 The importance of putting money to work by investing in buildings, plant and the equipment needed to make a product or provide a service.
2 The need to employ the skills and energies of a workforce – sometimes referred to as human resources, manpower or labour – and in so doing both to promote business enterprise and to enable people to live and prosper.
3 The need to create a cycle of business activity in which invested money facilitates the purchase of materials and people's work in order to create added value in a product or service.

To complete this basic economic cycle of business activity, the following activities also need to be identified:

4 The selling of the created product or service at a profit to either home or overseas customers.
5 The reinvestment of accumulated profits in purchasing more materials and labour to sustain the making and selling cycle and to enable the business to grow.
6 The spending of the wages and salaries of the employees on numerous needs and wants which in turn sustain the business cycles of many other enterprises in the economy.

PC 1.1.1

Fig 1.1 **The cycle of business activity in an economy**

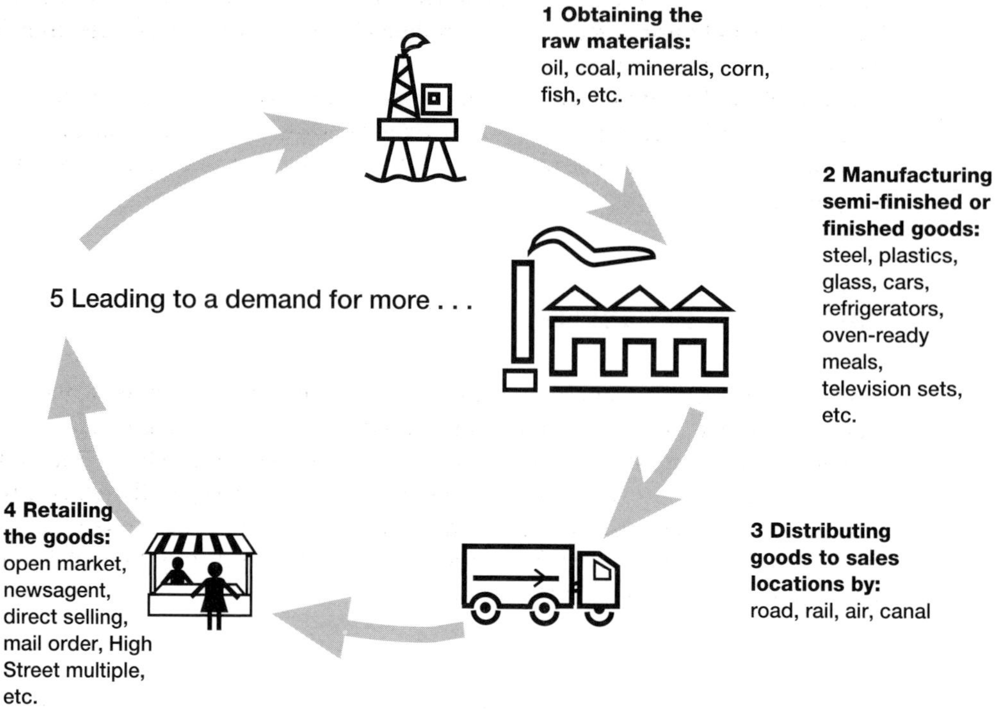
1 Obtaining the raw materials:
oil, coal, minerals, corn, fish, etc.
2 Manufacturing semi-finished or finished goods:
steel, plastics, glass, cars, refrigerators, oven-ready meals, television sets, etc.
3 Distributing goods to sales locations by:
road, rail, air, canal
4 Retailing the goods:
open market, newsagent, direct selling, mail order, High Street multiple, etc.
5 Leading to a demand for more . . .

The diagram in Fig 1.1 illustrates the circular nature of business enterprise.

PC 1.1.1

■ Primary, secondary and tertiary business sectors

As Fig 1.1 illustrates (see also Unit 3 on Marketing) in many national economies the cycle of business extends across three major sectors.

Primary sector

The primary sector comprises the getting of raw materials, the growing of food and the catching of fish. Industries in this sector include: mining for oil, coal, iron and other minerals; forestry, agriculture, fish farming and land reclamation, etc.

In the primary sector are also included the energy-making utilities like coal, oil and nuclear-fuelled power stations, gas-making plants and hydroelectric schemes.

Secondary sector

This sector refines, processes and manufactures and includes industries like petrochemical refineries, steel-making mills, factories for making equipment and machinery for industry and goods for consumer purchase.

Tertiary sector

In this sector are the businesses which distribute and retail the manufactured goods; they include transport companies which deliver goods by air, sea or land, wholesalers breaking bulk from warehouse to retail store, retailing chain stores and multiples, franchised shops, newsagents and supermarkets, etc.

Also included in this sector are the service industries which sell commodities like information, training, legal advice and finance cover provided by insurance companies, banking services, on-line database providers, office cleaning companies and telephone companies, etc.

■ Operating across the sectors

PC 1.1.1

Many businesses inhabit only one of the above sectors and sell on to the next. Extractors of iron ore, for example, may sell it on to a steel mill, or manufacturers of lawn-mowers may sell them on to wholesalers. Some firms, however, choose to operate in two or even all three sectors by, say, owning farms which grow wheat, mills which process it into flour, bakeries which produce bread and cakes and shops which retail the end-products. Such companies are said to be vertically integrated and they benefit from the profits generated at each stage of the process.

■ Adding value and creating wealth

PC 1.1.1

A key concept in a free market is that of adding value to a good or service. For example, a seam of coal lying some two miles offshore and several hundred metres below the North Sea is virtually without value until British Coal extracts it, brings it to the surface, washes it, and transports it, say, to a coal-fired power-station. This process adds value to it, since it becomes a saleable commodity. Moreover, the same coal has more value in the power-station's yards than it does at the pit-head because of the costs of transportation. Thus a key concept in the business cycle is:

Investing capital in plant, equipment and human resources → **To add value to a product (or a service)**

The same process is evident in the manufacture of, say, a house or office block from assembled parts and fixtures. And it is important to note that additions in value to products or parts arise not only from a manufacturing process – pre-stressed concrete pillars from sand, cement and steel rods – but from their location. Saloon cars protectively waxed and standing in fields around motor car factories have one value but another when polished and gleaming in dealers' showrooms.

Thus the making, distribution and selling of appliances, furniture, food, clothing and the myriad of other items which support both consumer and industrial needs and wants is a process which creates wealth by adding value.

The same concept is applicable to the wide range of services which support business in all three sectors of the economy. For example, a computer software applications company will invest in computers, disks, printers and allied products and hire expert systems analysts and programmers to write software programs which will, for example, coordinate and record a firm's entire accounting procedures. The fruits of their labours will be installed on disks which are easily transported and stored in dealers' shops. While the intrinsic value of the disk and manual of the accounts package may be a pound or two, such programs sell for hundreds of pounds because of the added value they embody in supplying a system which enables accountants to work faster and more accurately. In this way, value is added in a servicing context, whether it be legal advice from a solicitor, business start-up help from a clearing bank or the sale of a property by an estate agent.

PC 1.1.1

■ The concept of profit

Perhaps the most central concept in the business activity cycle is that of making a profit. For hundreds of years, the concept of profit has had a bad press. In the Middle Ages it was associated with usury – the setting of crippling interest rates on loans given; in the nineteenth century it was linked to the greed of some textile-mill and coal-mine owners who paid bare subsistence wages, part of which were tokens which could only be spent in company shops selling poor quality, high-priced goods. Nearer to our times the profit concept has been adversely affected by unscrupulous landlords securing high rents for derelict slum properties, and in the excessive mark-ups which characterise some companies in the defence, perfume and food industries.

However, the concept of making a profit from the added value given to products or services should not be 'rubbished' by the activities of the greedy and unscrupulous. Without a mechanism allowing goods and services to be sold at a profit, raw materials and semi-finished goods could not be bought in, machines and plant could not be acquired or renewed and employees could not be paid. Moreover, the shareholders in a business enterprise – individuals or companies putting up risk capital to float a business or aid its expansion – could not be paid any dividends or returns on their investments.

PC 1.1.1

WHY BUSINESSES NEED TO MAKE PROFITS

Businesses in every sector of the economy need to make profits:

- To buy in more finished goods or raw materials in order to sustain their cycle of business activity.
- To meet the bills they incur in operating the business – energy, labour, business rates and professional services (e.g. legal) etc.
- To pay employees and directors and to fund employers' contributions to pension and health schemes.
- To create surplus cash to plough back into the business in the form of new or replacement premises, plant and equipment.
- To build up emergency reserves to guard against any future hard times.
- To finance growth and expansion – by buying existing companies or creating new ones.
- To service loans taken out from banks or credit houses.
- To pay government taxes.
- To contribute if so desired to charitable and community projects.

Relating the concept of making a profit to the above checklist provides it with a legitimacy which far outweighs the bad press given to it as a result of the actions of a few discreditable companies and entrepreneurs.

■ The business activity cycle and its infrastructure

PC 1.1.1

The process of transforming extracted or grown raw materials into goods for consumption in either industrial or consumer markets could not proceed successfully without an infrastructure to support it. This infrastructure is illustrated in the second business cycle diagram (Fig 1.2 on page 11) which overlays the first.

PC 1.1.1

THE MAJOR COMPONENTS OF THE BUSINESS CYCLE INFRASTRUCTURE

The major components supporting the business cycle are:

The organisations supplying energy to industry and commerce

In order to keep the wheels of industry turning, vast amounts of energy are needed. This energy is supplied by coal, oil, gas and nuclear-fuelled power-stations which generate electricity sold on to the regional electricity boards. Similarly, British Gas and oil companies like British Petroleum and Shell UK plc sell on their products in both industrial and commercial markets.

Workforces

Ever since the industrial revolution began some 200 years ago, people have moved to where work is to be found, for example, to the South Wales collieries, to the shipyards of the Tyne, the factories of the Midlands or the textile mills of the North-West. The assembly of workers who become skilled in specific industries is a key factor in developing a modern economy, as the development of the Japanese Nissan car factory in Sunderland illustrates, where a new workforce was trained to work in a new industry.

Access to finance

Central to the business infrastructure are the banks and credit houses which lend out venture capital to businesses. This service industry provides a specialist brokerage by bringing together – at a fee – people or institutions with spare cash to invest and businesses seeking to borrow money to finance general growth or a special project.

Support from service industries

Industry and commerce today rely enormously on the services of specialist firms to supply services such as:

• insurance cover • legal advice • software applications • contract cleaning • refuse collection • laundry services • telecommunication channels, and so on.

Trade unions and associations

Established by industry-specific groups of employees over the past 150 years, trade unions provide a source of collective support for a wide variety of employees in diverse occupations. Full-time officers negotiate with companies and employer associations over pay and conditions of service. Their influence and position is strong in times of full employment but correspondingly weak in periods of recession.

Employers' confederations

Just as trade unions emerged to safeguard the interests of workforces, so confederations of employers in engineering, shipping and retailing, etc. evolved to secure a consensus of policy and approach across entire industries or commercial sectors. They also negotiate with relevant trade union officials. Both employers and trade union leaders act as consultants to governments over industrial and commercial policy-making.

Government agencies

The government of the day plays an important part in the infrastructure which supports business activities. Through its various departments, it provides statistical and factual data to inform marketing and corporate strategies. It supports the activities of exporters (who help governments to balance the payments for imported goods and services). It also funds agencies like Training and Enterprise Councils (TECs) which coordinate with Further Education and private sector trainers the vocational training and education of employees.

Furthermore, governments (and the EC Commission) inject finance into regions whose economies are ailing as the result of, say, the decline of industry which has become uncompetitive.

Also, through its central bank, the Bank of England, and through the Treasury, government exerts a significant influence on business activity – say, by raising the bank rate (the interest which the Bank of England charges the clearing banks for loans) – which dampens demand for goods and services, or by decreasing the amount of corporation tax paid by companies, thus leaving them with more money to purchase equipment and raw materials and so to build demand.

All governments seek to promote an economy in which business flourishes but inflation is held down; where the currency is kept strong but its goods offered for sale abroad at keen prices. No mean achievement for any government today!

PC 1.1.1

DISCUSSION TOPICS

1 What do **you** see as the essential purposes of industry and commerce?

2 What advantages do you think a business enterprise might secure which elected to operate in all three sectors (primary, secondary, tertiary) of the economy?

3 What reasons can you supply to explain why developed economies tend to move in cycles or waves from expansion to recession and then back to expansion? Can the recession phase – with all its accompanying human suffering and deprivation – ever be eliminated? How would **you** go about eliminating it?

4 Do you believe that some companies in developed economies make excessive profits? Or is there no such thing as excessive profit in a free, competitive economy?

Fig 1.2 **The cycle of business activity in an economy including infrastructures**

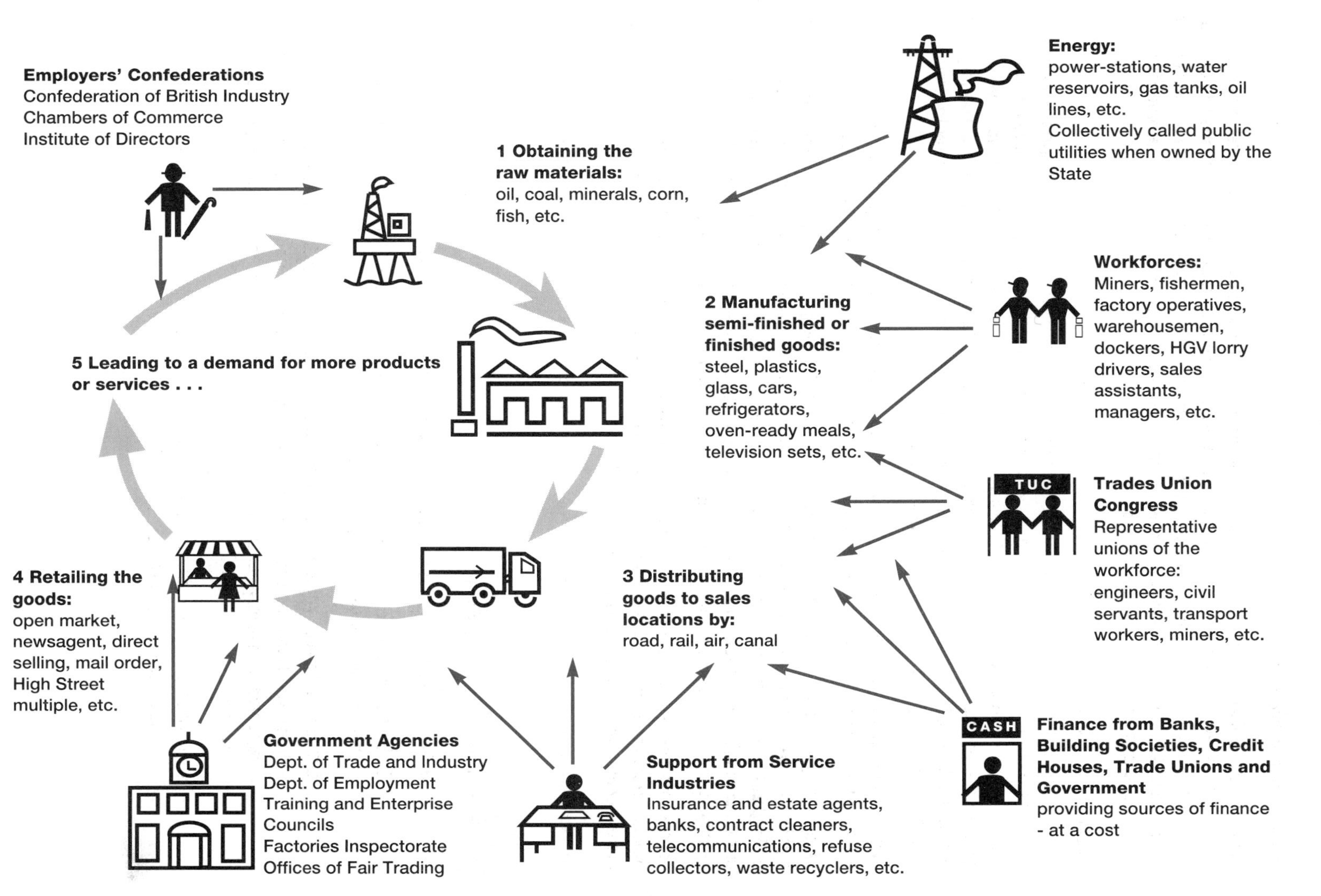
Employers' Confederations
Confederation of British Industry
Chambers of Commerce
Institute of Directors
1 Obtaining the raw materials:
oil, coal, minerals, corn, fish, etc.
Energy:
power-stations, water reservoirs, gas tanks, oil lines, etc.
Collectively called public utilities when owned by the State
2 Manufacturing semi-finished or finished goods:
steel, plastics, glass, cars, refrigerators, oven-ready meals, television sets, etc.
Workforces:
Miners, fishermen, factory operatives, warehousemen, dockers, HGV lorry drivers, sales assistants, managers, etc.
5 Leading to a demand for more products or services . . .
TUC
Trades Union Congress
Representative unions of the workforce: engineers, civil servants, transport workers, miners, etc.
4 Retailing the goods:
open market, newsagent, direct selling, mail order, High Street multiple, etc.
3 Distributing goods to sales locations by:
road, rail, air, canal
CASH
Finance from Banks, Building Societies, Credit Houses, Trade Unions and Government
providing sources of finance - at a cost
Government Agencies
Dept. of Trade and Industry
Dept. of Employment
Training and Enterprise Councils
Factories Inspectorate
Offices of Fair Trading
Support from Service Industries
Insurance and estate agents, banks, contract cleaners, telecommunications, refuse collectors, waste recyclers, etc.

PC 1.1.1

PC 1.1.1

Current types of economy: market, mixed and command

Macro-economics – economic systems viewed from both a national and international perspective – are inextricably linked to the political systems through which nation states run their affairs.

Over the past two thousand or so years, three major and contrasting ways of structuring a state's economy evolved as follows:

PC 1.1.1

■ The market economy

This economy (and its over-arching political system) is based upon the twin concepts of capitalism and free enterprise. Essentially, such an economic ideology supports these views:

- the market operates most efficiently and vigorously when it is free to operate according to the forces of supply and demand
- free competition (unrestricted by interventionist government policies) tends to result in the creation and continuance of markets which are healthy – since fierce competition benefits both consumers and industrial organisations. Weak and inefficient companies do not survive, and so scarce resources – materials, land and people – are employed most efficiently
- by minimising as far as possible its impact upon the free market economy, the government does not waste its resources on projects which may prove abortive, nor does it 'skew' the market by supporting lame-duck firms or obsolescent regional economies
- the free market is allowed to fix its prices for labour, materials, premises and equipment on the basis of 'what the market will bear', as opposed to 'how much the government is willing to pay in subsidies'

The essence of capitalism in an economic sense is to encourage the free range of entrepreneurial vigour and enterprise, with a minimum of government intervention and control. However, in such a market economy approach, the needs of the socially inadequate, poor and sick, disabled and disadvantaged may take very much of a back seat, since it tends to breed societies in which 'you get what you can pay for'! But, such an economic system also tends to avoid the waste, 'feather-bedding' and over-manning created by powerful but unaccountable bureaucracies.

PC 1.1.1

■ The mixed economy

A state operating within a mixed economy seeks to achieve an ongoing balance between a free-market entrepreneurial system interwoven with a government involvement in economic affairs. The government of such an economy will retain money created within the economy from the winning of raw materials, their manufacture into finished products and ultimate sale (allied to the sale of services such as insurance) to spend on providing those goods and services to which it committed in its last election manifesto and economic plan.

Such spending in modern, developed economies tends to concentrate upon: defence, health, social services, education, state pensions and public housing. In many Western states today, governments themselves spend about a half of the total income which their national economies generate. They tend to obtain the finance involved from direct and indirect taxation of both individuals and companies, and also by borrowing money from national and international banks and financiers.

The command economy

PC 1.1.1

Unlike either the market or mixed economies, the command economy seeks to control entirely all the resources available to it: land, transport and telecommunication infrastructures, labour and managerial resources, all buildings and premises – mines, refineries, factories, offices and shops etc.

All the resources of production, distribution and sales are organised from a central planning secretariat. In the former communist United Soviet Socialist Republics (USSR), and its eastern European allies (COMECON), as well as in the People's Republic of China, such central economies were directed and governed by a series of successive five-year plans. Also, such centralised economies accorded with the communist ideology in which the State owns all the resources within its boundaries.

In theory the command economy planners were able to ensure that the laudable principle of 'To each according to his needs, from each according to his ability'. In practice, without the disciplines of a free market regulating supply and demand, goods and services which people did not want were over-supplied, while chronic shortages occurred in essential, staple products. Moreover, as the economies of the USSR and its European allies became progressively more subordinate to communist political beliefs, they slipped into a completely introspective and archaic pricing structure for goods and services, so that their currencies became non-convertible – no state wanted payment in USSR roubles or Democratic Republic of Germany (DDR) Ostmarks. However, such states were able to offer their citizens a life-long expectation of full employment, in contrast to the all too frequent dumping of employees on to the scrap-heap of long-term unemployment which characterises Western capitalism in its phases of recession and slump.

DISCUSSION TOPICS

PC 1.1.1

1 Which of the three above economic systems would you consider most suitable to a state which possesses:

(a) a developed, industrialised economy?

(b) an emerging, Third World economy?

(c) an under-developed, highly populated economy?

2 Do you think that there will always be a variety of economies operating in different nation states across the world, or is there likely to be eventual harmonisation into a true world economy? What evidence can you provide to support your views?

3 What do you see as the problems which the emergent democratic states of the former USSR have to overcome in transforming their economy from a command to a mixed one?

PC 1.1.1

REVIEW TEST

1 Explain briefly the stages of the business activity cycle in an economy.

2 Describe briefly the main activities of the primary, secondary and tertiary business sectors.

3 Explain what is meant by the infrastructure which supports businesses in an economy. List five activities which form part of an economy's infrastructure.

4 List four examples of service industries.

5 Explain clearly how a market economy differs from a command economy.

6 Why have many western states preferred to create mixed economies?

PC 1.1.1 1.1.2

The effects of supply and demand on business

The concepts of supply and demand lie at the very heart of business. They govern the dealings of the market-place. As Mrs Thatcher once remarked, 'You can't buck the market!' They also form – in free, market economies – the foundations of all private sector business activities. So deeply have these twin activities become rooted in our way of life, every public-house economist and the proverbial man on the top of a London bus will observe sagely from time to time: 'It's all a matter of supply and demand!'

But how do supply and demand occur? For what do these concepts stand, exactly? To supply answers to these two questions, it is necessary to go right back to the origins of human beings living in social groups, and to understand first three more economic concepts, namely:

NEEDS WANTS and SCARCITY

PC 1.1.1 1.1.2

■ Needs

In order to survive, human beings must satisfy basic and essential needs – for warmth (either in the form of heating or clothing), for food and drink and for safety (in the form of a secure haven). Until these fundamental needs are met, mankind usually has little interest in goods or services which lie at the margin, such as jewellery, entertainment or prettily decorated drinking vessels etc.

PC 1.1.1 1.1.2

■ Wants

However, once they have been satisfied, man promptly moves up a gear into another level of activity, where wants emerge into his consciousness. At this stage, an assertion has to be accepted which has more to do with human nature than abstract economic theory:

Human beings are governed by a desire to satisfy a seemingly endless series of wants.

As the stone-age cave paintings all over Europe illustrate, early on in his social and economic evolution man began to adorn his habitations with colourful paintings, to fashion jewellery and to weave cloths of pleasing design. Markets emerged in which wines were exchanged for skins (or slaves!) between Celts and Phoenicians and a whole series of wants were progressively identified in the classical world, including beautiful sculptures, gardens, perfumes, garments and hairdressing fashions.

Over the past two thousand years, hundreds of industries have been created to satisfy markets which only consider wants – rock music on CDs, package holidays to the Mediterranean or adventure holidays to the Amazon, fast cars with computerised diagnostics and four-wheel drive, Broadway musicals, telephone banking, computer games, cosmetic surgery and so on – the list is only limited by man's imagination and temporary satisfactions!

■ Economic scarcity

PC 1.1.1 1.1.2

While man's needs and wants were relatively modest, his numbers reckoned in the low millions instead of billions, and his technology limited to his muscle-power, both needs and wants were relatively well met – though winter starvation was common in Europe only a few hundred years ago.

In today's over-populated and materialistic world, however, very many needs and wants are governed by economic scarcity. In other words, while man's needs and wants combine into an infinite shopping list, there is a finite limit to their supply. Some nation states are currently blessed with:

- extensive and varied natural resources – oil, gas, coal
- fertile, well watered agricultural land in a kind climate
- a technologically advanced society
- low numbers in the population to feed, clothe, house and educate and keep well

Such nation states find it comparatively easy to satisfy both needs and wants, since their resources – in the form of either goods or services – are in plentiful supply. Moreover, if such states are able to export surplus production or services to others, then their affluence improves markedly, and, like Japan today, they are able to sustain a trading surplus (with the rest of the world) of some $100 billion each year.

However, the harsh reality of the current world economy is that there is a wide gap – if not a chasm – between the distribution of scarce resources among the rich and poor countries of the world. The leaders of most states have continually to make choices about what they spend their available income on, and how they allocate what resources they can keep in their internal markets. For example, in the USSR of the 1920s and 1930s, Joseph Stalin elected to build a steel industry, almost from scratch, so as to keep pace with other developed nations such as Germany and the USA. But, given the poverty of the USSR, Stalin could not provide both steel and consumer goods at the same time. And so the people went without. German militarists during the same period offered their citizens 'guns or butter', and guns were selected as a means of reversing their sense of ignominy after their defeat in the First World War.

For Third World countries the uncaring laws of economic scarcity seem to have been designed to keep them in both a trough of despair and a poverty trap. They have to sell their produce (usually food or raw materials) on world markets, since they themselves lack the expensive technology to transform them into goods to which considerable value has been added. Gourmet mushrooms grown in Afghanistan high valleys sell there for 40p a pound. In high-class London restaurants they make £15.00 for a half-dozen on a plate! Similarly, there are large differences in price between the bauxite ore at a Latin American pithead and the alloy wheels on a Ferrari Testarossa! And, sad but true, developed Western nations have a vested interest in keeping world prices for raw materials (latex, copper and cotton) as well as foodstuffs (cocoa-beans, bananas and rice) as low as possible, since this improves significantly their buying-in and selling-out margins.

Just as scarcity in the distribution of raw materials, technological know-how and the power of strong financial reserves create the differences in the economies of nation states as they trade around the world, so they also shape the economic activity of the individuals in their populations.

PC 1.1.1 1.1.2

■ Scarcity and market segmentation

Markets for many goods and services become highly segmented (broken up into distinct, separate parts) simply because of the differences in spending power of various socio-economic groupings of consumers. The motor-car industry provides a good example. A vast array of models, from Rolls-Royce to Citroen 2CV, has been produced to suit the pockets of motorists, ranging from the chairman of a multinational to a research student finishing off a PhD. Indeed, most people are continuously engaged in juggling their incomes to pay for a mix of wants and needs – mortgage, food, heating, retirement, holidays and hobbies as one month or week succeeds another.

PC 1.1.1 1.1.2

DISCUSSION TOPICS

1 What evidence can you think of which either justifies or refutes the assertion that 'Human beings are governed by a desire to satisfy a seemingly endless series of wants.'?

2 Given that raw materials, a fertile land and a kind climate are not equally or fairly distributed among the nations of planet Earth, what economic steps can a country not blessed with them do in order to develop its economy?

3 Can you see any economic advantage to the developed countries of the world in providing more extensive financial aid to Third World countries? For example, should the massive debts they have incurred with the developed world states be written off, or is their poverty trap unavoidable?

4 Can you envisage a situation in which there is an equalisation of the economies of the world's nation states? If so, how? If not, why not?

5 To what extent are individuals able to resist the impact of economic scarcity in their own countries? How do supply, demand and scarcity affect the market for labour?

■ Demand, supply, price and price elasticity of demand

PC 1.1.1 1.1.2 1.1.3

Demand

The demand for a product is the amount or quantity of that product that consumers are willing to buy.

The market demand for a product is the total amount that will be bought in a specific market over a specified time period, e.g. the number of cars bought in the UK in January.

INDIVIDUAL ACTIVITY

List five other examples of market demand. Make them as varied as possible.

PC 1.1.1

Factors influencing demand

Demand for a product is dependent upon several factors. Changes in any or all of the following factors can increase or decrease demand:

- price of the product
- price of other products
- size of household income
- tastes and fashion
- expectations
- potential market size
- distribution of wealth.

These factors will now be considered in more detail.

Demand and price

Changes in demand caused by changes in price are represented by movement along the demand curve. An example is shown in Fig 1.3.

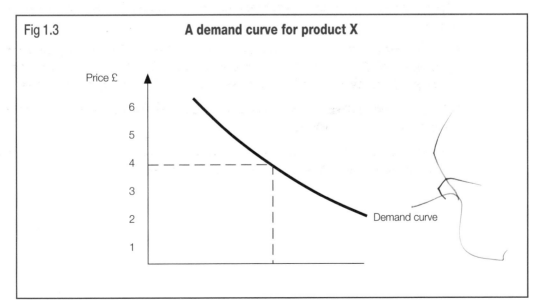

Fig 1.3 **A demand curve for product X**

PC 1.1.1 1.1.3

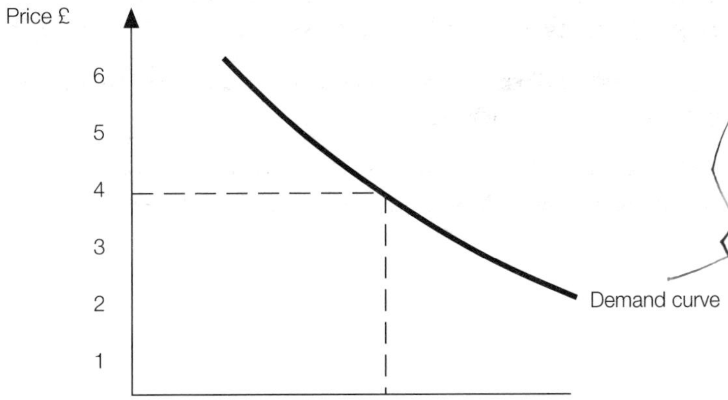

PC
1.1.1
1.1.3

INDIVIDUAL ACTIVITY

1 If we want the quantity demanded to increase to 10 what price should we set?

2 Think of a product for which demand increases as the price increases and explain why this happens.

An increase in demand due to factors other than price would move the curve upwards (D_2) and a decrease would move it downwards (D_3) (see Fig 1.4).

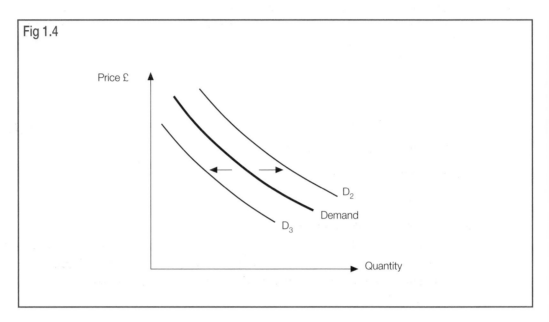

Fig 1.4

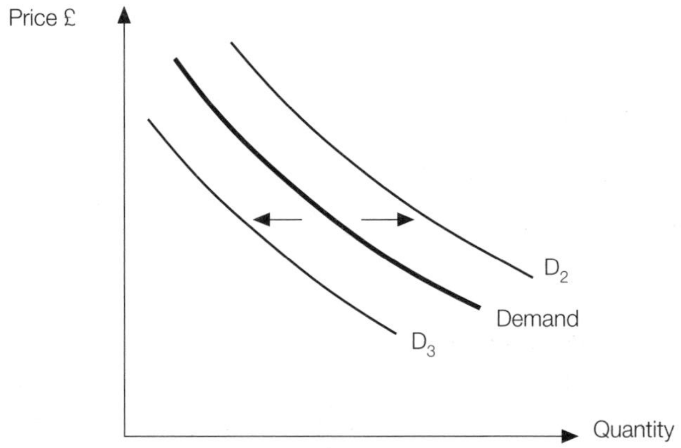

Demand and income

As household income increases, the demand for products will change.

1 The demand for normal goods, such as clothing, will rise.

2 The demand for basic goods, such as milk, will reach a maximum.

3 The demand for inferior goods will decrease.

PC
1.1.1
1.1.3

INDIVIDUAL ACTIVITY

1 Think of two examples of normal goods, basic goods and inferior goods.

2 Briefly explain why demand for these products increases or decreases with a change in household income.

Demand and fashion

Tastes and fashion can change for psychological, social or economic reasons. It is therefore very difficult to predict their effect on demand.

INDIVIDUAL ACTIVITY

1 Think of two examples where demand has increased owing to changes in tastes or fashion and two where demand has decreased.

2 Could these changes have been predicted?

PC 1.1.1 1.1.3

Demand and expectations

The things that people expect to achieve or acquire throughout their lives affect their demand for particular products. Expectations change as a result of changes in economic and social conditions. For example, in the United Kingdom home ownership has become an expectation for many people in the last 20 years.

INDIVIDUAL ACTIVITY

1 List some of your life expectations.

2 How do these affect the products that you demand?

PC 1.1.1 1.1.3

Demand and the distribution of wealth

A society in which the majority of people have a middle income will demand different quantities of certain products than a society where the majority of the population are on lower incomes. In this way the distribution of wealth affects demand.

INDIVIDUAL ACTIVITY

Study the income distributions of country A and country B shown in Fig 1.5. How will demand differ between the two countries?

PC 1.1.1 1.1.3

Fig 1.5

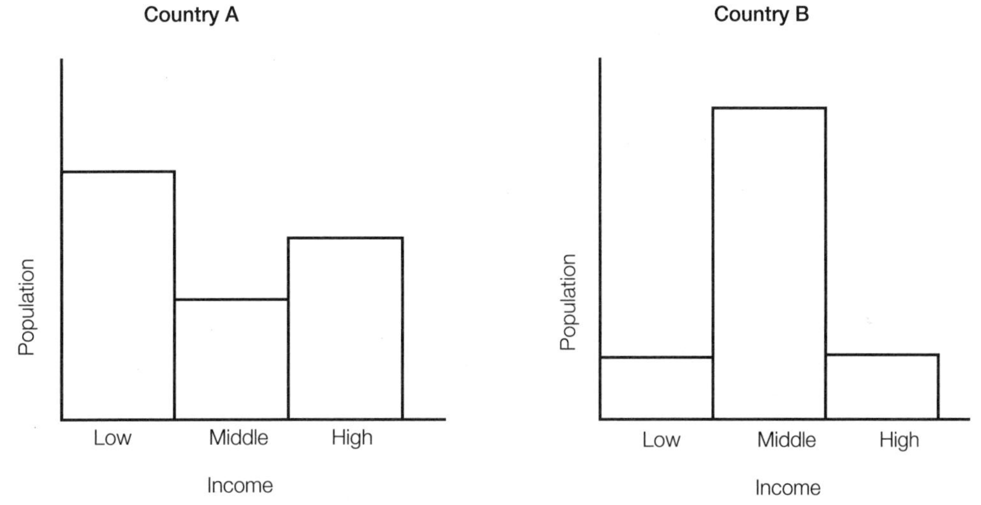

PC 1.1.1

GROUP ACTIVITY

Choose any product and explain fully how each of the factors discussed have influenced or could influence demand for it.

PC 1.1.2

Supply

The supply of a product is that quantity which existing or potential suppliers are willing to produce for the market.

The quantity supplied may vary as suppliers can increase or decrease the amount they allow on to the market, and firms can enter or leave the market.

Factors influencing supply

The factors which influence the quantity supplied are all related to prices and costs. These are:

- the price obtainable for the product
- the price of other products
- the cost of producing the product
- changes in technology
- changes in weather

PC 1.1.2 1.1.3

INDIVIDUAL ACTIVITY

1 In what way are changes in technology and the weather related to prices and costs?

2 Why would a supplier provide more products if the price obtainable rose from £5 to £7?

The supply curve

The supply curve illustrates the relationship between the price of a product and the quantity supplied at that price.

Example

The supply schedule for product Y is as follows:

Price per unit (£)	*Quantity supplied at this price (Units)*
100	10,000
150	20,000
300	30,000
500	40,000

PC 1.1.2 1.1.3

INDIVIDUAL ACTIVITY

1 Plot the supply curve for product Y on the graph shown in Fig 1.6

2 How does an increase in price affect the quantity supplied? An increase in supply caused by factors other than price would move the curve to the right and a decrease would move it to the left.

3 Plot a new supply curve showing the likely effect of an expansion in supply due to improved manufacturing processes.

Fig 1.6

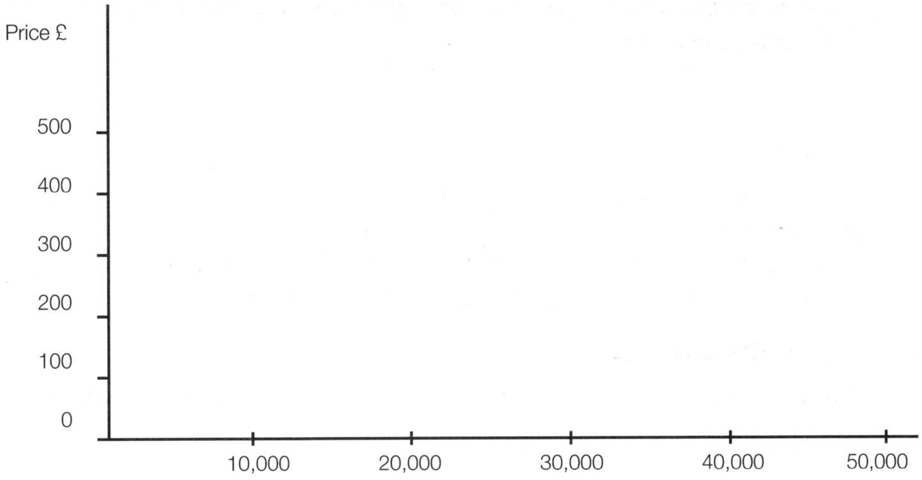

Price

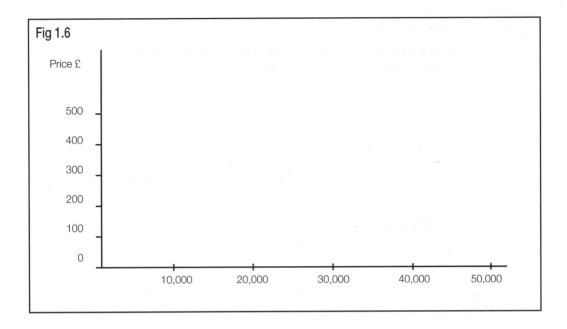

Price is the common factor influencing both the demand for and the supply of a product in a market economy. PC 1.1.1 1.1.2 1.1.3

Price determination

As firms decide which products to supply and consumers decide which products to buy, both suppliers and consumers influence the price of products.

The quantity demanded and the quantity supplied will be equal at a certain price. This price, P_1, is known as the equilibrium price (see Fig 1.7).

Fig 1.7

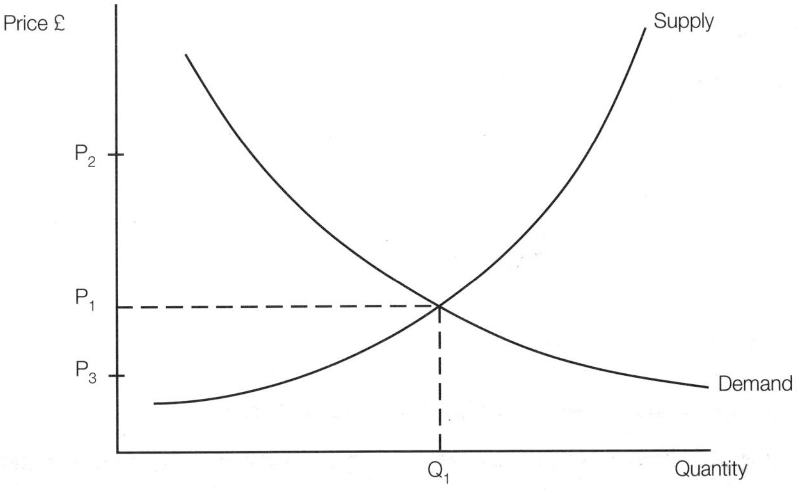

PC
1.1.1
1.1.2
1.1.3

INDIVIDUAL ACTIVITY

Referring to Fig. 1.7 answer the following questions:

1 What will happen if the price is set above the equilibrium price at P_2?

2 What will happen if the price is set below the equilibrium price at P_3?

3 In a market economy how are the situations in (1) and (2) rectified?

Price regulation

When prices are regulated or set by government policy, the market forces of supply and demand are no longer the main determinants of price.

Maximum price legislation

The graph in Fig 1.8 illustrates the effect of setting a maximum price.

PC
1.1.1
1.1.2
1.1.3

Fig 1.8

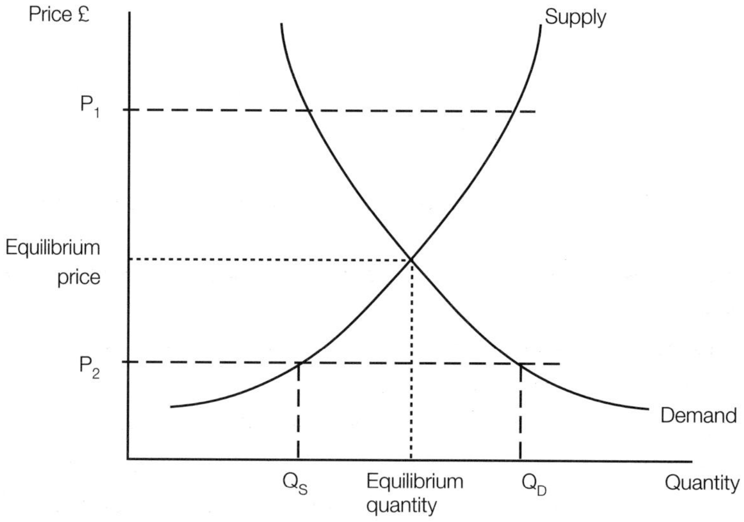

If the maximum price is set at P_1 there is no effect as suppliers can still choose the equilibrium price.

If the maximum price is set below the equilibrium price at P_2, then the quantity demanded, Q_D, is higher than the quantity supplied, Q_S, and a shortfall results.

Minimum price legislation

The graph shown in Fig 1.9 on page 23 illustrates the effect of setting a minimum price.

Fig 1.9

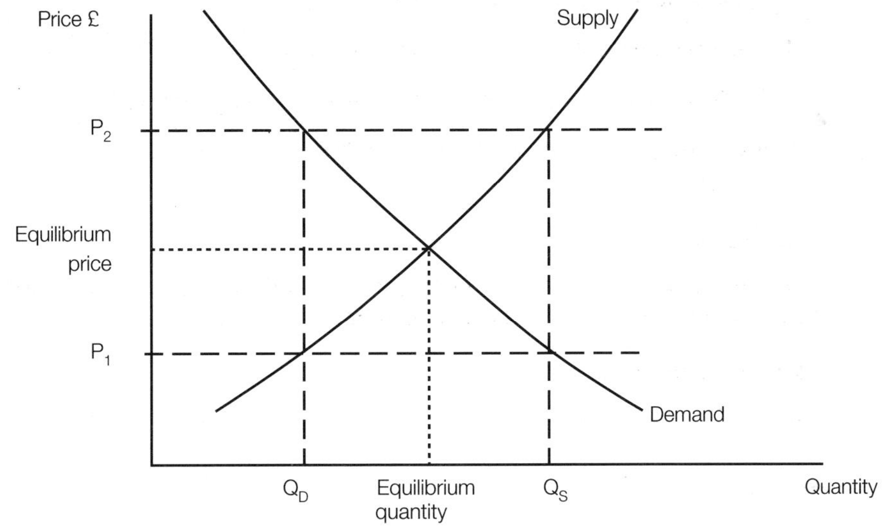

CHECKLIST OF DETERMINANTS OF PRICE

PC 1.1.1 1.1.2 1.1.3

A number of economic factors combine to determine the price of a good or service in the market-place:

- its relative scarcity, when it is in demand – the quantity available compared with the number of willing purchasers
- its relative abundance when there is a scarcity of interested potential buyers
- the nature and extent of competitors in the market
- whether the size of the market allows for economies of scale in production
- its sales price, compared with the price being asked for similar, competing products
- the cost of the raw materials and/or component parts used in its manufacture
- the cost of its manufacture, distribution and sale
- the loading upon it of Customs and Excise or VAT tax
- the likely duration of the demand for the good/service (where research and development costs having been recouped a lowering of the sales price is feasible)
- whether the good/service is a continuous widespread need or a temporary, faddish want
- the position of the good/service in its product life-cycle – does the price reflect the need to recover R&D and production tooling-up costs, or have these been recovered?
- how affordable it is in terms of the finance available (from either consumers or industries) to pay for it; in times of recession prices tend to fall because 'money is tight'
- the relative availability of credit-purchase schemes or bank loans (the 'buy now, pay later' effect) which makes expensive goods or services more readily 'affordable'
- the pressures exerted by governments such as, for instance, the increase of interest rates which makes money more expensive to borrow and thus increases production costs

PC 1.1.2

INDIVIDUAL ACTIVITY

Think of examples of products which have been in short supply. How were these shortages dealt with?

A minimum price, P_1, below the equilibrium price has no effect, but a minimum price above at P_2 leads to a higher quantity being supplied, Q_S, than quantity demanded, Q_D, giving a surplus.

INDIVIDUAL ACTIVITY

What has been the effect of minimum price selling for European agricultural products?

PC 1.1.1 1.1.2 1.1.3

GROUP ACTIVITY

The Potato Market

Price (Price per kilo)	*Amount demanded (Kilos per week)*	*Amount supplied (Kilos per week)*
7	30	62
6	35	60
5	41	57
4	45	53
3	49	49
2	53	45
1	57	41

Using the data shown in the table above:

1 Draw the supply and demand curves for the potato market.

2 State what the equilibrium price would be and why.

3 Say what would happen if the government set a minimum price of 4 pence per kilo.

4 State what the new equilibrium price would be if demand per week increased by 8kg at all prices and supply remained the same.

PC 1.1.1 1.1.2 1.1.3

Price elasticity of demand

The price elasticity of demand (PED) for a product is a measure of how much the quantity demanded is affected by changes in price. Demand is said to be elastic if it increases and decreases greatly due to only small changes in price.

Calculating the price elasticity of demand

The PED for a product can be quantified using a simple calculation.

$$\text{PED} = \frac{\text{The percentage change in quantity demanded}}{\text{The percentage change in price}}$$

shortened to $\text{PED} = \dfrac{\%\Delta Q_D}{\%\Delta P}$

The percentage change is worked out as follows

$$\%\Delta Q_D = \frac{(\text{New } Q_D - \text{Old } Q_D)}{\text{Old } Q_D} \times 100$$

$$\%\Delta P = \frac{(\text{New P} - \text{Old P})}{\text{Old P}} \times 100$$

Example

If the price of product A increases from £1.50 to £1.75, the demand decreases from 1,000 units to 600 units.

The PED for product A can be calculated.

$$\%\Delta Q_D = \frac{(600 - 1{,}000)}{(1{,}000)} \times 100$$

$$= 40\% \text{ decrease in quantity demanded}$$

$$\%\Delta P = \frac{(1.75 - 1.50)}{1.50} \times 100$$

$$= 16.7\% \text{ increase in price}$$

$$\text{PED} = \frac{40\%}{16.7\%} = 2.4$$

The price elasticity of demand for product A is 2.4.

INDIVIDUAL ACTIVITY

Calculate the PED for product B whose quantity demanded decreases from 1,000 to 800 when the price changes from £2 to £4. Which is the more elastic, product A or product B?

PC 1.1.1 1.1.2 1.1.3

Interpreting price elasticity of demand

A product is said to be elastic if its PED is greater than 1 and inelastic if its PED is less than 1.

INDIVIDUAL ACTIVITY

Referring to Fig 1.10 on page 26, which demand curve shows an elastic product and which an inelastic product?

Can you also calculate the changes in total revenue for both (a) and (b)?

PC 1.1.1 1.1.2 1.1.3

Fig 1.10

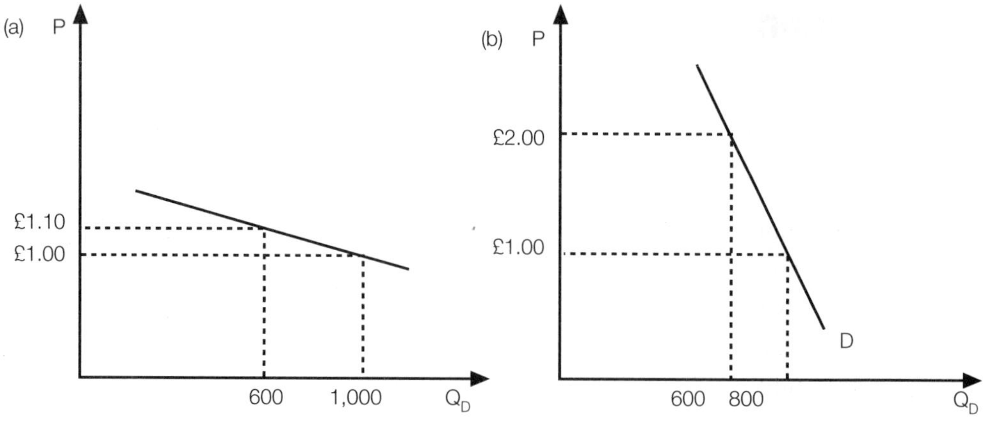

Price increases from £1.00 to £1.10

Price increases from £1.00 to £2.00

The price elasticity of demand for a product allows interested parties to predict the effect of a price change on the quantity demanded. They can then determine the optimum price to maximise revenue.

PC 1.1.1 1.1.2 1.1.3 1.1.4

Factors influencing price elasticity of demand

1 *Strength of consumer demand*

Stronger for essential items or those purchases influenced by habit or fashion.

2 *Household income*

Changes in income will affect the proportion spent on each product, e.g. the gas bill for a person on a State pension may be 30 per cent of income over a given period; for a company chairman it may be 3 per cent.

3 *Availability and prices of substitute products.*

PC 1.1.3 1.1.4

INDIVIDUAL ACTIVITY

1 Explain how the above factors would affect the price elasticity of demand.

2 List five products which are inelastic and explain why.

3 List five products which are elastic and explain why.

PC 1.1.3

DISCUSSION TOPIC

Discuss how the Government has used, or could use, PED in setting their policy on VAT.

Supply and demand: market-place decisions and interactions

PC
1.1.1
1.1.2
1.1.3
1.1.4

There are a number of factors in the market-place which bear upon the *demand for* and therefore the *supply of* a good or service. These major factors are:

- the amount of the good / service which can be readily brought to the point of sale at any given time
- the size of the demand which exists (or which can be created) for the good / service
- the asking (sales) price for the good / service
- the ability of the would-be purchaser to pay the sales price
- the willingness of the would-be purchaser to pay the sales price.

Supply shortages, buoyant demand and price increases

PC
1.1.1
1.1.2
1.1.3
1.1.4

All of the above major factors are flexible and bear upon each other. For example, during a wet summer, soft fruits like strawberries may rot where they grow and a shortage in supply may ensue. But the number of strawberry-lovers remains constant. The strawberry (in its punnet on the market) thus becomes a product with a scarcity value because the growers cannot grow more within the strawberry season. Demand therefore now exceeds supply. In such a market, the economic law which obtains is that the price for strawberries will rise. The seller will seek to maximise profits by testing out how much more consumers are willing to pay in order to enjoy their summer treat of fresh strawberries. Prices per punnet will thus rise until their sales begin to flatten out into a plateau. Would-be buyers begin to balk at the higher prices being demanded. In other words, a new equilibrium or balance has been negotiated between the seller and the buyer because the strawberry is in short supply.

Over-supply, satisfied demand and price decreases

PC
1.1.1
1.1.2
1.1.3
1.1.4

The reverse scenario can exist, however, in the same soft-fruit market when ideal growing weather, allied to too many growers in the industry, combine to produce a glut, say, of apples, which do not keep well. In order to shift their perishable produce promptly, retailers will begin to offer such apples at a discount on the normal price for the season, and shoppers will begin to shop around for the best price they can get. In this way, a steep fall in the price of apples occurs since there is a significant over-supply. The market (which has a finite size) becomes swamped with such produce and 'the bottom falls out of the market'.

In order to avoid such a calamity, growers will sometimes destroy a proportion of such crops in the fields so as to maintain the price (and profit margin) of the remainder when it does get to market.

PC
1.1.1
1.1.2
1.1.3
1.1.4

Fig 1.11 **The market mechanism**

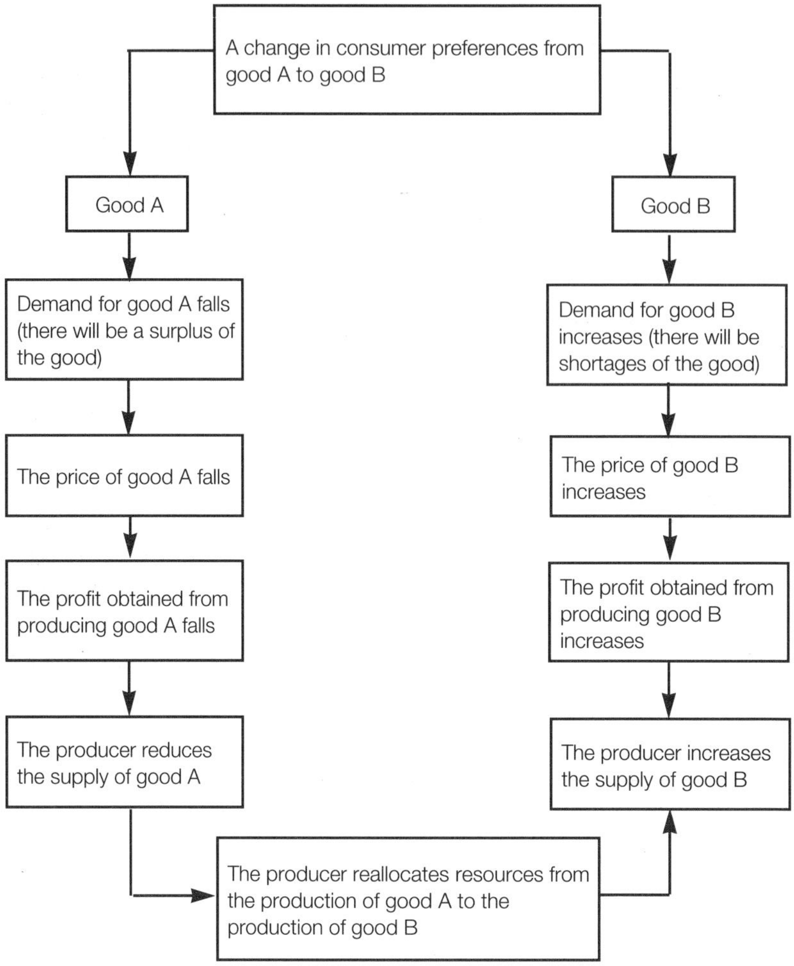

(Source: *Economics*, S Ison, M&E Handbooks)

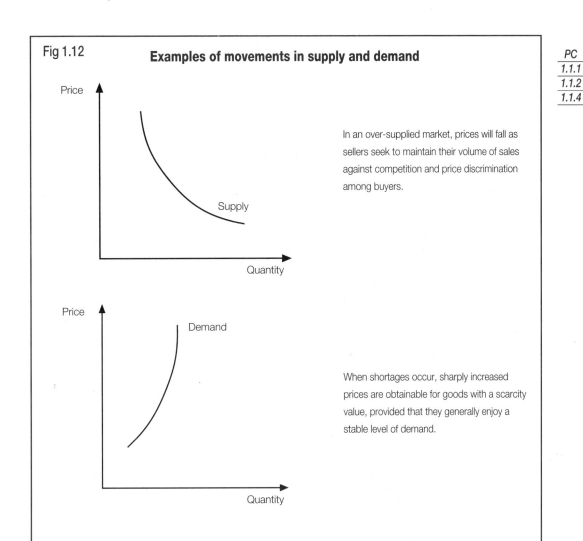

Fig 1.12 **Examples of movements in supply and demand**

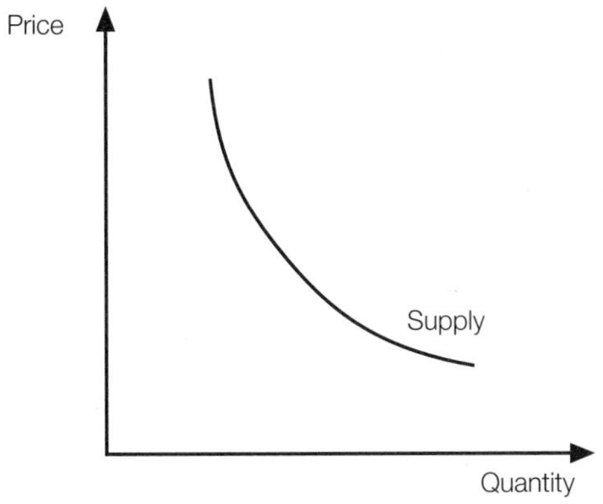

In an over-supplied market, prices will fall as sellers seek to maintain their volume of sales against competition and price discrimination among buyers.

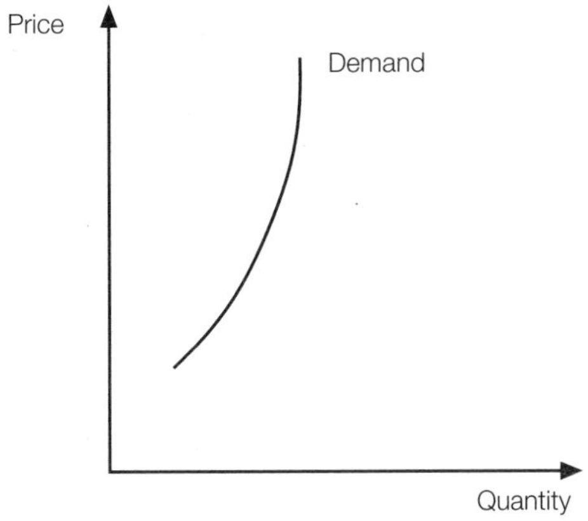

When shortages occur, sharply increased prices are obtainable for goods with a scarcity value, provided that they generally enjoy a stable level of demand.

PC 1.1.1 1.1.2 1.1.4

■ Price equilibrium in the market-place

PC 1.1.1 1.1.2 1.1.3 1.1.4

The above examples serve to illustrate the existence of market forces in the form of these variables:

- how much product is available in how large a market
- how open competition is – fierce, or monopolistic
- how sensitive is the demand for the product when its price is rising or falling.

When the market is open and not rigged (by, say, one supplier controlling all access to the product), and when buyers are able to access information easily about price movements in the market-place, then the pendulum of price equilibrium for the product will swing either to an upper or lower level, depending on whether supply exceeds demand or vice versa.

PC
1.1.1
1.1.3
1.1.4

■ Supply and price equilibrium

The factors leading to a movement along and a shift in the supply curve

A movement along the supply curve for chocolate bars

The quantity of chocolate bars supplied will

fall if:

- the price falls

rise if:

- the price rises

A shift of the supply curve for chocolate bars

The quantity of chocolate bars supplied will

fall (shift to the left) if:

- there is an increase in price of another product
- there is an increase in the price of a factor of production
- there is a deterioration in the technology used in the production of chocolate
- there is the introduction of a tax on the product

rise (shift to the right) if:

- there is a reduction in the price of another product
- there is a reduction in the price of a factor of production
- there is an improvement in the technology used to produce chocolate
- there is the introduction of a subsidy on the product

INDIVIDUAL ACTIVITY

Draw up a table similar to the one above relating to a shift in **demand** for chocolate bars.

PC
1.1.1
1.1.3
1.1.4

Fig 1.13 **The equilibrium price and quantity**

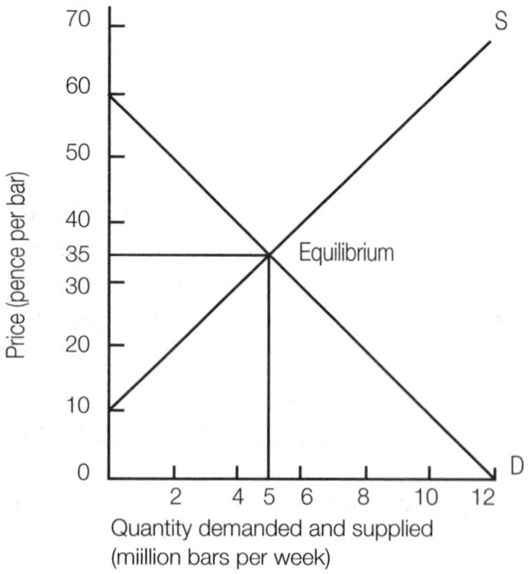

Price (pence per bar)
70
60
50
40
35
30
20
10
0
S
D
Equilibrium
2
4
5
6
8
10
12
Quantity demanded and supplied
(miillion bars per week)

(*Source: Economics*, S. Ison, M&E Handbooks)

■ Supply, demand and production

PC 1.1.1 1.1.2 1.1.3 1.1.4

Producers of goods and services are always very conscious of what it costs to bring their products to the market-place. In normal circumstances, they will seek to obtain the highest return possible on the capital they have invested in making the product.

Factors bearing upon the return achievable (the profit margin) often depend on:

- the perceived value of the product, such as its high-technology design and structure (like a Tornado fighter-plane)
- the complexity and cost of producing it, which results in few competitors participating in the industry (as in sea-based oil platform construction) so that little competition exists
- whether the perceived market is large or small (long production runs bring about economies of scale and facilitate cheaper manufacturing costs per unit)
- whether the existence of fierce competition impacts upon the sales price because products of similar design and build costs are easily brought to the market

And all of the above are closely affected by the state of the economy in the boom–recession cycle, which will have a strong bearing on demand in both consumer and industrial markets.

■ Low volume high cost; high volume low cost

PC 1.1.4

Given that such factors are important determinants in the supply/demand equation, manufacturers tend to need (and get) higher prices for goods which are expensive to produce and for which the available market is small, for example, the manufacture of operating tables as opposed to kitchen ones. In the case of the manufacture of kitchen tables, as they are relatively easy to make, and since the potential market is huge, a higher number of companies will enter the market attracted by the lure of high profits. But as the Kiwi Fruit case history below illustrates, such markets may prove hard to survive in.

CASE HISTORY

PC 1.1.1 1.1.2 1.1.3 1.1.4

The Kiwi Fruit: from gourmet's delight to grandma's fancy!

Some ten or so years ago, pleasantly green slices of fruit with interesting little black pips in them (each slice the size of a small cucumber in circumference) began to appear on plates of gourmet food – especially cuisine minceur – in London restaurants. The kiwi fruit had arrived from New Zealand! Because of its environmentally friendly appearance, delicate flavour and low-calorie make-up, the kiwi fruit quickly came to dominate the up-market trade in exotic fruits, finding its way not only into Belgravia mixed salads, but also into King's Road Chelsea fish garnishes. Demand for this delicacy combined with its scarcity value enabled fruiterers and supermarkets to ask for, and obtain, 50+ pence per little plum-shaped kiwi.

However, no sooner did the kiwi fruit take off in European supermarkets than other profit-hungry Antipodean and Channel Islands fruit-farmers moved in smartly on 'a nice little earner'!

Thus, increased supply began to shift the kiwi fruit off its gourmet delicacy podium downwards on to the 'Get us a couple of kiwi fruit, love, for a bit of colour' platform, and from its place on the top shelf of the supermarket gondola next to its passion and star fruit companions down to a spot next to the satsumas and Granny Smiths. The price of a kiwi fruit fell in a relatively short time – from 50+ pence to 11+ pence each.

The brighter kiwi fruit growers quickly came to realise that it was time to get out of kiwis and back into a better paying alternative crop. Thus the kiwi fruit market settled into a more mature and equilibrial state. Prices moved back up a little, and became more stable. The case history of the kiwi fruit illustrates the important role played by suppliers in the market-place, since prices are not only demand-created. Manufacturers will invade or quit a market, depending upon whether a satisfactory return on investment is achievable in the long as well as the short run. In this way mature markets, which may have been volatile at their outset, become established but stabilise when a price structure is established which both buyer and seller come to accept as 'fair and acceptable' given the extent of the work done in adding value – whether in growing, making or distributing.

PC
1.1.1
1.1.2
1.1.3
1.1.4

CHECKLIST OF FACTORS INFLUENCING THE QUANTITY OF A GOOD PRODUCED

From the supply viewpoint	From the demand viewpoint
Cost to research and develop	Utility of the product – how suitable will it be for its intended use
Cost to make	Features and specifications – 'what's it got that competing products haven't'?
Relative complexity of manufacture	Its cost relative to directly competing products
Size of the estimated market and whether it is likely to grow, and by how much annually	Its safety features
Nature and extent of the competition – currently and in the future	Its environmental friendliness
Likely demand for the product	The nature and extent of attached warranties and guarantees
Price the market will bear for each unit of production	Its product life and reliability – how long before another one is needed?
Long-term prospects for the product	How easily obtainable are parts and spares?
Profits achievable – in both short and long terms	The cost of repairs and maintenance

The extent of the quantity of a good made (the length of its production runs and product life cycle) depends on how well the product meets both the needs of its manufacturer and its purchaser as illustrated in the twin listings above.

Demand, quantity, price and elasticity

PC
1.1.2
1.1.3
1.1.4

Economists use the term *elasticity* to describe the ways in which the demand for a good or service and the quantity produced, are or are not, affected by upward or downward movements in their prices.

For example, goods which form part of the essentials of life – flour, water, heating or petrol – are much more likely to remain at a given level of demand, even though their prices may increase, since consumers will make economies in other purchasing areas in order to continue to be able to afford these items, since they are essential to them.

On the other hand, the demand for other goods which are 'wants', as opposed to 'needs', such as snack sweets, mouth fresheners or hobby magazines is much more likely to fall if their prices are increased, since consumers can do without them, and these goods may only be able to command a given level of demand as long as their prices continue to lie within pricing bands which are regarded as either trouser pocket change money, personal indulgence money, whim or impulse purchasing money and so on.

Such goods are said to be *elastic* in demand terms, since demand for them is affected by changes in their prices. Such a sensitivity is termed:

Price elasticity of demand

Price elasticity of demand can also occur when there is a reduction in price which leads to a corresponding increase in the purchase of the goods or services concerned.

Where the demand for goods or services is relatively insensitive to movements in prices, then they are said to be *inelastic*.

Factors affecting elasticity / inelasticity are:

- the degree of availability of alternative, substitute products to which a purchaser may switch – say from one brand of toothpaste to another – which has become cheaper because of a price increase in the favourite brand
- the relative purchase cost of the goods compared with money available – price movements measured in pennies for a newspaper affect demand much less noticeably than an increase of hundreds in the cost of a foreign holiday as far as most consumers are concerned
- consumer purchasing habits and patterns – fans of a particular rock group may continue to purchase its tapes or CDs at the same levels of demand even though the marketing pundits of the music publishing company hike their prices 'through the roof'; brand loyalty impinges upon the price–quantity relationship
- conspicuous consumption – people able to afford a Ferrari so as to demonstrate their financial power position are likely to continue to buy such status symbols even though the price demanded is increased by several thousand pounds.

PC
1.1.1
1.1.2
1.1.3
1.1.4

GROUP ACTIVITIES

In groups of two or three research into one of the following activities and then report back to your class in a suitable form:

1 Research into the 'poverty trap' of a selected Third World country and find out why and how this trap tends to be reinforced by supply and demand conditions in world trade.

2 Research into the sale of the following products in three or four outlets and then produce a report which explains how and why they differ in terms of their response to supply, demand and price elasticity:

- petrol for private vehicles
- pineapples
- beach holidays in southern Europe
- (retail) refined sugar

3 Find out what laws and activities the government has in place in order to discourage the setting-up of illegal business cartels and monopolistic dominations of the market-place.

4 Find out how 'the economic laws' of supply and demand affect what is offered for sale in your school/college shop and refectory.

5 Undertake a survey of your class-mates to find out what they consider as 'needs' and 'wants' in their own personal buying habits. See if any common items are identified.

PC
1.1.3
1.1.4

■ Costs and cartels

As you will have realised, manufacturers, distributors and retailers of products in markets which are price sensitive often have to work within tight margins and overcome problems which are caused, say, by increases in imported raw materials.

Where a product embodies a *price elasticity of demand* sensitivity, then it may not be possible to pass on price increases to customers – they would simply switch to an alternative. Such costs often, therefore, have to be absorbed through improvements in the production process, use of advanced technology, more cost-effective use of labour and so on.

For this reason, many companies operating in the same market would prefer to 'come to gentlemen's agreements' on what prices to charge to purchasers. Given the chance, they would like to establish cartels based upon price-fixing agreements.

However, such business practices are illegal under the Restrictive Trade Practices Act of 1976 and would be promptly investigated by the Office of Fair Trading.

By the same token, consumers and industrial purchasers are protected under European Community law against unfair business practices within the 1992 Single Market, including individual governments supplying an unfair advantage to 'home-grown' products by protectively subsidising them so as to skew the market in their favour.

DISCUSSION TOPICS

PC
1.1.1
1.1.2
1.1.3
1.1.4

1 How far should governments allow businesses to go in meeting people's endless 'wants' when the world's economic resources are limited?

2 Can demand for a good or service ever be artificially created? Can you think of any examples?

3 What corrective actions could a supplier of, say, fast-moving consumer goods like magazines, clothes and foodstuffs take when spotting that demand for a given product is falling?

4 Why do, say, farmers or fruit-growers prefer to destroy their produce in the fields rather than take it to market at times of a glut?

5 Why, exactly, are cartels and monopolies deemed to be against the public interest?

REVIEW TEST

PC
1.1.1
1.1.2
1.1.3
1.1.4

1 Explain simply the difference in economic terms between a 'need' and a 'want'. How are both linked to the economic concept of scarcity?

2 List five factors which influence demand for a good.

3 What main economic factors influence the price of a good or service in a competitive market?

4 What kind of lifestyle and social factors influence price?

5 In what ways does the distribution of wealth in a society influence demand?

6 List four factors which influence the supply of a good.

7 Explain briefly how the price for a good is determined in a market economy. List five price-determining factors

8 What do you understand by the term 'price equilibrium'?

9 What is meant by the specialist economic term 'price elasticity of demand'?

10 What factors influence price elasticity of demand?

11 How is the quantity of supply of a good affected by rises and falls in the price buyers are willing to pay for it? Explain the reasons for the answer you give.

12 Explain briefly how the needs of producers bear upon supply and demand in a free market.

13 Explain clearly why the laws of most developed economies prohibit price-fixing, and the creation of cartels and monopolies in their economies

KNOWLEDGE TEST

Element 1.1
Analyse the forces of supply and demand on businesses

1 Which of the following definitions best describes the concept of economic scarcity?

A a situation In a country where wants exceed needs
B the extent of availability of given resources in a country
C a shortage of luxury goods in a country
D a lack of goods to buy and sell in a country

2 Demand for a product/service is most accurately described as:

A a situation in which consumers demand goods/services which are in short supply
B the total amount of goods or services available for sale in a market
C the amount or quantity of a product or service which people are willing to buy
D the price a person is willing to pay for a good or service

3 Mark the following statements as either True or False by ringing T or F:

A	The price of a good will not influence demand for it.	T	F
B	People's tastes and lifestyles have a bearing on demand for a given good or service.	T	F
C	Demand for specific goods or services depends on how a nation's wealth is distributed.	T	F
D	The existence of competition in a market will not affect demand for its goods.	T	F
E	An increase in demand causes an increase in supply.	T	F

4 As household income increases, which of the following statements is a true description of what is likely to occur in demand terms?

A The demand for basic goods will continue to rise with further rises in income.
B The demand for poor quality, inferior goods will decrease.
C The demand for non-essential goods will increase.
D The demand for imported goods will decrease.

5 Which of the following statements is true?

A The quantity of goods supplied depends upon the price which can be obtained.
B The amount of a good supplied depends upon the quantity which existing or potential customers are willing to purchase.
C In an established market the supply of a good will steadily increase.
D The quantity of a good supplied is directly affected by changes in its price.

6 (i) The supply of goods may be affected by changes in technology.
(ii) Changes in the weather have no bearing on the supply of good.

Which of the following options best describes the above two statements?

A	(i) T	(ii)	T
B	(i) T	(ii)	F
C	(i) F	(ii)	T
D	(i) F	(ii)	F

7 Which of the following statements is true?

A An equilibrium price is reached when the quantity supplied and the quantity demanded of a good are the same .

B An equilibrium price is reached when the price of a good has been stable for an extended period of time.

C An equilibrium price for a good is reached when suppliers can no longer increase the quantity supplied.

D An equilibrium price is reached when demand for a good reaches its peak.

8 (i) The setting of a maximum price for a good will have a bearing on the quantity demanded.
(ii) The setting of a minimum price for a good will have no bearing on the quantity demanded.

Which of the following options best describes the above two statements?

A	(i) T	(ii)	T
B	(i) T	(ii)	F
C	(i) F	(ii)	T
D	(i) F	(ii)	F

9 (i) Demand for a good is said to be elastic if it increases and decreases only slightly as a result of changes in price.
(ii) Demand for a good is said to be inelastic if it does not increase or decrease markedly as a result of an increase or decrease in price.

Which of the following options best describes the above two statements?

A	(i) T	(ii)	T
B	(i) T	(ii)	F
C	(i) F	(ii)	T
D	(i) F	(ii)	F

10 Which of the following statements is true (T), and which false (F)?

A	Equilibrium prices tend to be re-established upwards when a good is in short supply.	T	F
B	An oversupply in a market will cause the purchase of a given good to increase, so as to ensure that its equilibrium price is not affected.	T	F
C	Suppliers tend to lower prices in under-supplied markets in order to ensure that there are enough goods to go round.	T	F
D	The quantity of a good supplied will fall if its price rises.	T	F

PC
1.1.1
1.1.2
1.1.3
1.1.4
1.1.5
1.1.6

PORTFOLIO OF EVIDENCE ACTIVITY

Element 1.1
Analyse the forces of supply and demand on businesses

MORGAN & FITCH: REPORT 1

Scenario

You work as a research assistant for *Morgan & Fitch* which is a long-established firm of market-research consultants. *Morgan & Fitch* regularly undertake market research in specific areas and upon particular products or services. They publish reports of their findings which are sold either through regular subscription or on a one-off basis to a wide range of companies wishing to 'stay sharp' about business and marketing developments.

Yesterday your boss, Ms Lisa Khan, provided you with the following terms of reference for a new project and eventual report:

'We've a number of clients who are reviewing their understanding and feeling for current trends in supply and demand in the market-place. They've asked me – and I'm asking you! – to research two contrasting products, and I'll give you a list to choose from in a minute, which demonstrate clearly how the interaction of supply and demand bears upon business decisions etc.

In particular, your report should focus on how important factors are such as price when it comes to generating or satisfying demand and making quantities of the product; also, you should emphasise the connection between prices charged, quantities made and profits earned. Our clients also want us to provide a section which explains how various types of customer and their needs affect the whole process of supply and demand, as well as the impact of competition. Oh, and how changes in demand and supply affect production and sales. Also, while I think about it, you had better include a piece on how equilibrium between supply and demand determines the price and sales of a product, and how future changes in demand and supply could affect the two products in terms of the decisions their producers make about them.

I understand that the report you produce is likely to be used by our clients' training people, so make sure it is clear and easily understood. You may wish to include an appendix glossary of specialist terms you employ, and I imagine some diagrammatic or graphical content will aid the process.'

LIST OF PRODUCTS TO RESEARCH AND REPORT ON

Select **two** of the following products to research and report on:

- a breakfast cereal
- a package tour holiday to a Greek Island
- a teenager's mountain bike
- an electric or petrol-driven lawn-mower
- a brand of instant coffee
- a private house mortgage
- a hi-fi stack
- a CD of a currently successful pop/rock band

Task 1

With the help of activity planning and review forms available to you, devise a plan which will enable you to research the data for your report within the time-frame given to you. Keep careful notes about the sources of likely information you intend to investigate, people you plan to visit and interview and reference material you intend to collect etc., and make sure you devise a series of deadlines within which to achieve Task 1.

Task 2

Having obtained sufficient data to enable you to produce your report, Task 2 requires you to organise it into a suitable structure and sequence. Check back through Lisa Khan's terms of reference for your report, and decide upon a structure of, say, 4–5 main sections which will form your findings, bearing in mind that you are reporting on two different products. For instance, you will need to decide whether to report on them separately or in parallel. Also, think about the type of report structure best suited to meet your reporting needs, and check out various formats using departmental or centre library resources of textbooks or examples of oral presentations etc.

Task 3

Construct your report either in writing, orally delivered or typed (audio/video), carefully following Lisa Khan's instructions. If your report is orally delivered or taped, it should include summary notes designed as a post-delivery hand-out. If written, you should consult your teacher on whether it should be hand-written or text processed.

Task 4

Proof-read your report carefully for errors of spelling, punctuation and use of English before submitting it, and make sure you also submit your completed planning and evaluation forms with your report.

Performance criteria covered

1.1.1, 1.1.2, 1.1.3, 1.1.4, 1.1.5, 1.1.6

Core skills covered

Communication:
3.2.1, 3.2.2, 3.2.3, 3.2.4, 3.2.5, 3.3.1, 3.3.2, 3.3.3, 3.4.1, 3.4.2, 3.4.3, 3.4.4

Information Technology (if report text/graphics-processed):
3.1.1, 3.1.2, 3.1.3, 3.1.4, 3.1.5, 3.2.1, 3.2.2, 3.2.3, 3.2.4, 3.2.5, 3.2.6, 3.2.7,
3.3.1, 3.3.2, 3.3.3, 3.3.4, 3.3.5, 3.3.6

Element 1.2
THE OPERATION OF MARKETS IN AN ECONOMY AND THEIR EFFECTS ON BUSINESSES AND COMMUNITIES

PC 1.2.1

The features and functions of markets

■ What is a market?

A market, whether for goods or services, may perhaps best be considered as a meeting-place, where sellers and prospective buyers can interact – to inspect goods or services closely and compare what is on offer, to consider asking prices, to assess ability to pay and, eventually, to arrive at a deal. Indeed, this describes pretty exactly the kind of markets which have existed in many British shire towns and cities since medieval times! Of course, such a definition is somewhat simplistic, since in today's many different economic markets, buyers and sellers may never physically meet (say in the context of mail order business, or stock market transactions), nor may they be able to handle products physically (such as virtual reality computer games or fire insurance). Nevertheless, in order for such goods or services to be exchanged for money, a meeting of minds is most certainly required, where both parties are happy to strike a deal and do business.

PC 1.2.1

■ Markets mobilise resources

Another key feature of any market is *movement*: of money, say from one country to another, of goods by road, rail and air, of human resources, whether within a country or across borders and of information through satellite 'super highway' telecommunications networks. Indeed, the *Single Market* of the *European Union*, created in 1992, is based entirely upon the concept of freedom of movement of people, money, goods, services and information.

PC 1.2.1

FOUR DIFFERENT MARKET STRUCTURES

Economists have identified the following four different market structures which may exist within an economy:

The Competitive Market	This market is developed in free or market economies in which private (but also sometimes public) sector businesses are free to enter or leave the market-place at will, and to produce or buy in a range of goods or services to sell to targeted groups of customers (e.g. consumers, company purchasing managers or public sector central purchasing officers etc.)
The Monopoly Market	Such a market comes into being when one business (or public sector agency/utility) achieves such a dominant position that competitors, in effect, no longer exist. Note that some of the recently 'privatised' public sector utilities – water, gas, electricity – still enjoy a monopolistic position in their markets; this is why an official regulator has to set the prices for their products annually. Note also that the *Monopoly & Mergers Commission* holds a watching brief on the dominance of private sector companies in their markets.
The Non-Competitive Market	The markets for the utilities referred to above are – for the time being – non-competitive; other types of non-competitive markets include rail transport (for the time being) public lending libraries, leisure centres (in areas where the private sector is not competing) etc.
The Oligopoly Market	An oligopolistic market exists when only a very few suppliers serve it, and thus tend to be large and powerful in market terms. Examples in the UK include the markets for: sugar, airline package-tour travel, telephone-line networks and coal.

■ Types of market

PC 1.2.1

In a developed economy a number of markets exist which interact and impact upon each other:

- **the factor market** which is concerned with the buying and selling of raw materials, semi-finished goods and component parts used in manufacturing
- **the industrial market** which exists among businesses which tend to be involved in supplying products for consumers to purchase, and which themselves need to buy in goods and services to enable the manufacturing process to take place
- **the consumer market** in which the needs and wants of individuals and families are met in terms of, say, housing, food, transport and entertainment
- **the investment or money market** where lenders of money meet borrowers and where money itself (in the form of shares, bonds, gilts, futures, commodities, annuities, pensions and insurances etc. may be bought and sold)

Beneath such macro-economic markets there exist myriads of smaller, specialist markets which are born, mature and die or are renewed, depending upon the continuance of both supply and demand for a given product or service. For example, within the industrial market is a lively sub-market for forklift trucks and another for pallet shelving. Similarly, within the factor market specialist markets exist for metals such as copper, and also in their likely future prices (as in copper futures on the stock market). Markets operate at all levels of business: people are as keen to buy and sell junk and collectables at the 50p car boot sale level, as to invest in prized antiques at the multi-million pound level of Sotheby's or Christie's international auctions.

PC 1.2.1

■ Market components

Whatever the type of market, all share a common set of characteristics:

From the supplier's stand-point:

- **a sufficiently large number of potential buyers spending sufficiently large sums of money** as to make it economically worthwhile to invest in the time, cost and effort needed to bring a specific good or service to the given market-place
- **sufficiently large prospective gross and net profits** as to make possible a satisfactory return on the money invested in the enterprise; correspondingly, a supplier's interest in a market may depend on **sufficiently low start-up and operating costs**
- **sufficient access (for the foreseeable future) to the raw materials and/or sources of product supply** (at the right prices) to justify the supplier/seller's acquiring the premises, equipment and labour needed to operate the enterprise
- **sufficient 'elbow-room' within existing competing businesses** as to enable the supplier first to enter successfully into the market and then to hold (and extend) his place within it
- **suitable access to those locations** (either in the High Street, purchasing manager's office or GP's surgery) **where selling can be effected**
- **sufficient access to information about consumer/industrial/factor market trends** as to enable the supplier to 'stay sharp and current' about the market he inhabits

From the demander's stand-point:

- **access when required to products and services which are considered to offer good value** (whether in terms of price, specifications, design, useful-life, unique properties, robustness or after sales service and warranties etc.)
- **access to expert advice about a product or service** (especially technical ones) ideally from a disinterested source (e.g. *Which?* magazine)
- **the existence of competitors likely to offer goods or services at attractive prices** to the demander/consumer; note that in a monopolistic market, the lack of competition would tend to encourage suppliers to increase prices beyond a reasonable profit-generating level – especially where the product/service was *price inelastic*, that is, not sensitive to a corresponding fall in demand when prices are increased
- **access to choice across a range of similar products or services** so as to be able to evaluate the good value features listed above
- **access to flexible forms of payment for purchases**: credit card, store card, staged direct debit/standing order payments, hire-purchase, rental, leasing etc. to complement outright purchase

■ **access to efficient and affordable post-sales servicing**, maintenance or trouble-shooting expertise

When enough of the above market factors are satisfied a sufficient number of times per day, week, month or year, in the eyes of both the sellers and the buyers in the market-place, then sales will take place sufficiently frequently for a viable market to be created and to grow. Moreover, once a new market has gained a 'critical mass', more suppliers and/or more purchasers will be attracted to it – either because it offers the prospect of handsome profits, or because its goods or services are deemed to be attractive in terms of their price and quality etc. And, as already outlined, suppliers will seek to match demand and to increase their prices whenever demand outstrips supply. Conversely, purchasers will tend to shop around for the best prices, which will tend to fall when supply exceeds a sated demand – as, for example when a glut of soft fruit occurs after a warm spring and good summer.

■ Functions of markets: the business, consumer and government perspective

PC
1.2.1
1.2.2

Views of what markets exist for tend to depend upon who is doing the evaluating and what their vested interests happen to be:

The selling organisation's perspective:

■ **to provide opportunities to make suitable profits** and to enable economies of scale to be achieved through the sale of large volumes of product –which also tends to increase profits

■ **to secure over time a dominant position in a given market**, out-selling and undercutting the competition and eventually obtaining a virtually monopolistic position in the market from which to increase prices significantly and so reap much larger profits

■ **to provide** (through activity in a number of different markets) **a hedge against ill-fortune in any single market**

The consumer's and industrial purchaser's viewpoint:

■ **to supply essential, personal needs and coveted wants**, so as to enable life to go on and enjoyment to be had; moreover – as cheaply and with as little personal effort as possible!

■ **to provide** (for the industrial market purchaser) **materials, parts, services and equipment** to enable manufacturing, distribution or retailing to continue

The UK government's expectations:

■ **to help increase employment and to reduce unemployment**, so as to reduce the burden upon the state of making social and welfare payments to individuals

■ **to help to improve the nation's balance of payments** by selling more goods and services abroad, and **to reduce the *Public Sector Borrowing Requirement (PSBR)*** by creating more government income from taxation

- **to increase affluence generally and encourage a 'feel-good factor'** central to getting governments re-elected
- **to bring about a movement in resources** (especially financial) so as to re-distribute income (and therefore the benefits which stem from income) more widely among all citizens: markets create work, work brings in income, progressive taxation equalises retained income – and social instability, unrest and anti-social sub-cultures are minimised
- through the profit motive **to bring a number of socially desirable activities** (via private transport, health schemes and education etc.) which **the state does not have to finance**

PC 1.2.2

CHECKLIST OF REASONS WHY BUSINESSES COMPETE IN A MARKET

The following checklist indicates the main reasons why businesses enter into competition with others in the same market. Remember that a mix of the following reasons will form part of a business's marketing plan and corporate strategy:

- **to move into a fresh (to them) market and win new customers' business**
- **to increase their share of the market they are already in**
- **to secure extra business by bringing superior products to the market-place**
- **to create in the minds and hearts of prospective customers a superior image (from that of their competitors), so as to encourage purchases of their products or services**
- **to increase sales through effective advertising, sales promotion and merchandising campaigns**
- **to win customers through superior product quality and customer services and the offer of a more extensive range of products**

PC 1.2.2

Competition in market and mixed economies

Given the outlawing in western economies of business monopolies, both market and mixed economies are bound to include – to a greater or lesser degree – competing businesses in the markets which constantly ebb and flow within them. The following table illustrates some major plus and minus factors of competition in markets:

PC 1.2.2

COMPETITION IN MARKETS

+ factors

- more research and development investments are made as companies vie with each other to market superior products – which benefit buyers
- design and build quality are similarly improved for the same reasons
- money spent on advertising and sales promotion tends to increase in order to give a product a higher profile, and consumers thus gain more information about goods and services
- the prices of goods and services tend to fall as competitors strive to lure potential customers to their products – through discounts, price-slashing, introductory offers and sales etc. which thus become more price attractive
- guarantees and customer post-sales service tend to improve as part of the overall package which suppliers create to give their own products or services 'unique selling benefits'

- factors

- pressure to outdo competitors tends to encourage larger, more powerful firms to dominate a market and may lead to a restriction in choice of products – but this would be the case anyway without competition
- in order to stay competitive in a cut-throat market, firms tend to cut back on the range of products they market, concentrating only on big-selling, large profit-making ones, and this really does restrict product choice
- also, in a fiercely competitive market, advertising tends to become more emotive and strident and less informative
- price wars in some markets (newspapers, air-line tickets, packaged holidays etc. tend to put smaller companies out of business – again leading to the survival of 'the big boys' and to oligarchic if not monopolistic dominance by the few survivors – which is why price wars are started in the first place!
- the arrival of too many suppliers in a given market – called 'over-segmentation' – tends to lead to dramatic falls in price levels and profits, where no single supplier does enough business; as a result, some decide to quit the market – and they may be among the best suppliers

Pricing strategies in business markets

PC 1.2.1 1.2.2 1.2.3

Even the least observant of food shoppers notices fluctuations in the price of foodstuffs in the local supermarket, say, with the approach of Christmas, because of seasonal effects on the supply of salads and vegetables or price increases in soft fruit during a wet summer. However, variations in the prices charged by suppliers for goods or services involve much more than seasonal supply problems or the 'make-it-while-you-can' approach of some retailers in the run up to Christmas or Easter.

The following checklist illustrates some of the main reasons which lie behind a particular price being asked for a given good or service. Remember how important it is *to view suppliers' prices in comparison with those being asked by competitors.*

PC
1.2.1
1.2.2
1.2.3

CHECKLIST OF PRICING STRATEGIES USED TO DETERMINE A MARKET PRICE

• **Setting of a 'skimming' price**	to secure as high a price as possible initially because a product either enjoys a unique property such as a big technological advance or because little competition exists
• **Setting of a 'penetration' price**	sometimes suppliers deliberately set a price well below those of competitors in order to gain a *penetrating* foothold in a market for a new product
• **Setting an 'expansion' price**	using factors such as economics of scale (through long production runs) or high-volume markets so as to enable low prices to be charged while securing satisfactory profits
• **Setting a 'destruction' price**	very occasionally (in a price war) a seller may deliberately price a good (say a newspaper) at a loss-making price in order to destroy the competition; once this strategy succeeds, a new replacement product is launched into a market in which the competition has been 'pole-axed'!
• **The loss-leader**	where a seller offers a wide range of goods for sale (e.g. supermarkets, DIY stores, departmental stores etc.) some very popular items may be offered for sale below (or close to) their cost prices in order to entice buyers into the store (who are then likely to buy other goods, the prices of which may recover the loss made on the loss- leader)

PC
1.2.2
1.2.3

■ Penetration pricing

This strategy is usually reserved for launching a product, since it relies on undercutting the prices of competing items in order to gain a foothold in the market-place for a new product or service. Wholesalers and retailers may be invited to purchase a new product on a 'trial offer' basis and be wooed by a significant discount on the normal price for such a good.

To counter such attempts at hiving off a share of an existing market, the new product's competitors are likely to respond by announcing to the trade hefty discounts and special offers on their products – even to the point of temporarily cutting their profit margins to zero in order to kill off a potential competitor at birth.

■ Skimming pricing

The name for this pricing strategy is most probably derived from the practice of skimming the cream from the top of a churn of milk, since it describes the process of going into a market with a very high price for a product that embodies pronounced superior qualities from all others or in which little competition exists. For example, the first company to retail flat, wall-hanging television screens in the UK could expect to obtain a high price for them, representing as they would a distinct technological advance. However, competing TV manufacturers would catch up as fast as possible with their alternatives and force the skimming price to be converted into a competitive one.

Market pricing

PC 1.2.2 1.2.3

Here a product or service is offered for sale at a price very close to that of other similar items. The strategy may well be that the product has been produced and distributed at a low cost compared to that of its competitors and that a handsome profit may be obtained by going into the market at the level at which competing products are selling. The conundrum facing marketing decision-makers is whether a significantly larger profit could be obtained by cutting the sales price in such a scenario. As the break-even chart displays, this would, however, require a larger sales volume.

Premium product pricing

The term 'product positioning' has been used in this Unit, and the strategy of premium product pricing provides an interesting example of this practice. Experienced marketing staff will decide long before a product is launched which tier or layer of the market it will inhabit, whether it will be sold at the 'silver service' or plastic cutlery end of the market, or somewhere in between. Manufacturers marketing a range of products – like china dinner services or motorcars – will tend to accord to one of their products pride of place as their 'premium' product.

As such – whether or not its manufacturing costs are higher (and they usually are) – it will be priced significantly above its middle and bottom of the range counterparts, both within the in-house product range and among competing products.

In order to give such a product the right image in the market-place, careful attention will paid by copywriting personnel to appropriate colour schemes employing gold, purple or red colours and descriptors like 'exclusive', 'superior', 'extravagant', 'excellent' and so on. As will be examined later in the Unit, there are very good reasons for marketing products in a premium or 'pole' position, since they may be bought in order to supply status and exclusivity to their purchasers.

Seasonal pricing

Many products and services enjoy seasonal peaks – turkeys and toys at Christmas, chocolate eggs at Easter, sunshine holidays during July and August, and so on. Their sellers are therefore given the recurrent headache of how to attract interest during off-peak periods. British Rail, for example discounts heavily the cost of rail tickets on commuter lines after 9.00 am when the peak commuting morning rush is over.

Hotel chains commonly market autumn and winter bargain week-end offers to couples aimed at topping up hotels which may be half empty; package holiday operators regularly offer weeks in Mediterranean, North African or southern USA resorts at 'give-away prices' to help in stimulating demand at off-peak times and offsetting hoteliers' and airline companies' fixed costs.

PC
1.2.2
1.2.3

■ Milking pricing

This strategy is normally employed during the final stage of a product's life. By then, it should have earned and repaid the money invested in its development and that spent on advertising and sales promotion in order to build demand for it. Thus the milking strategy is to turn off the tap of all further investment – no more product face-lifts, no more costly sales campaigns, no more supportive discounts or free offers. The product is allowed to move along to its eventual demise at a price which, while a little lower than that enjoyed during its mature stage, nevertheless returns a good profit, given the reduced commitment to the product in terms of updating or promotional support.

■ Loss leaders and self-liquidating offers

Where an organisation markets a wide range of products – supermarket foods, DIY materials, motorists' accessories etc. – then a common pricing strategy is to advertise at regular intervals in highly visible localised promotional campaigns popular items as loss leaders. In other words, a premium brand of cornflakes, paint or engine oil may be advertised at a break-even or even loss-making price. This strategy is used to pull shoppers into the store and the cost of making such an offer is 'liquidated' or covered by the level of profits secured from other items which the store's management expects to sell to the purchaser of the loss leader.

Also, a company may advertise a 'free' give-away as a reward for spending up to a given level, or for purchasing an expensive article. (One entrepreneurial car dealer during hard times offered a free Citroen 2CV with every Citroen XM purchased!) Clearly no firm can afford to do business at a loss for long, and the costs of making such 'free' offers are built into the overall sales price of the expensive item. The offer is thus deemed to be self-liquidating.

■ Sales pricing

Traditionally, special-offer sales in consumer products occur in January and July. After the pre-Christmas boom, January is always a slow month in the High Street and so is July / August when many people are away on holiday. However, during a recession, many retailers are obliged to stage virtually continuous sales in an effort to prompt elusive customers to spend money.

Various Acts of Parliament have been enacted to protect shoppers from being duped by spurious offers during a sale. Goods for example offered at a discounted price – £X OFF! – must have been offered for sale at the higher price for a set number of days prior to the sales offer. While some sales items offer genuine reductions on initially displayed prices, many goods are especially bought in for seasonal sales – often from Third World countries – and offered for sale under a single 'special sales price'. Sales are most commonly held to enable retailers to clear out ageing stock and make room for a new season's sales lines.

■ Non-pricing strategies

In some instances, a business may devise strategies which affect the price of goods or services which are not in themselves primarily concerned simply with price (and its fellow component profit). Sometimes a business will decide to promote a particular product (say, an environmentally kind soap-powder) and fix a price to ensure that it sells widely, so that the company concerned develops a public image as a caring organisation. By the same token, the costs of making the soap-powder environmentally kind may be absorbed by the manufacturer in its long-term marketing interest of showing a large number of potential and existing customers that it has responded to their changed expectations and purchasing preferences.

DISCUSSION TOPICS

PC 1.2.2 1.2.3

Fixing a price

1 Why do consumers drive miles to buy petrol at 1p a litre cheaper, but pay 'over-the-odds' without a qualm for a bottle of wine in a restaurant? Where does customer behaviour fit into the pricing of commodities?

2 Is there ever such a thing as 'a fair price' for something, or is the only 'fair' price what a market will bear?

3 What manufacturing factors tend to result in a high price being asked for a new product when launched on the market?

4 How important today to a business are non-price aspects such as its public image or the image of a particular brand? Is 'image' a myth kept going by PR consultants and advertising agencies?

The social costs and benefits of markets

PC 1.2.4 1.2.5

One of the recurrent problems experienced in command or centralised economies (such as that of the former USSR) is that products tend to be commissioned, designed and manufactured which consumers then choose *not* to purchase – perhaps because of shoddy quality or poor market research. Such was the case in the German Democratic Republic (DDR) during the 1970s–80s, when comparatively wealthy workers (in terms of eastern block states) elected to save their ostmarks rather than spend them on available but shoddy goods. However, full employment was maintained in the DDR's centralised economy, albeit through over-manning.

In western market/mixed economies, while a much freer market competition results in more consumer choice and much higher quality of goods, social prices are also paid for access to certain goods or services. For example, the waste from making the industrial chemicals needed to manufacture paints, plastics or fertilisers (which we tend to take for granted) when redecorating a bedroom, using a car or eating bread may find their way into rivers, streams and coastal sea-waters. Worse, radioactive materials used in both energy and defence industries may be dumped illegally or leak inadvertently into either soil or atmosphere. Or, where market dictates are allowed to rule, roads, pipe-lines and factories may be constructed on and across green-field and woodland sites. Again, in heavily populated areas, mobile 'ghetto-blasters' or simply powerful, static amplifiers result in nervous breakdowns and re-location among the neighbours of an intolerant noise polluter. Or again, shopping preference or life-style changes in a given market's customers – such as the move to all-embracing supermarket and shopping mall retailing – may result in the loss of jobs and of businesses among small retailers and traditional roundsman occupations such as milk and bread deliveries.

The following table illustrates some of these major costs and benefits to society of the operation of markets in a market/mixed economy:

PC 1.2.4 1.2.5

MAJOR SOCIAL COSTS AND BENEFITS OF MARKET OPERATIONS

Benefits

- success in home markets generates general affluence and boosts exporting opportunities through economies of scale
- open market competition tends to drive down prices and improve product quality (until the 1920s cars were playthings of the very rich); it also increases access to goods and services among a much wider social spectrum of citizens
- government interaction with markets helps to limit inflation, equalise social benefits and route financial support to where it is most needed
- free market competition acts as a spur to research and development, where eventually all a state's citizens benefit – say from pharmaceutical advances in the treatment of cancers
- developments in one market may spin off into another – military technology results in non-stick frying pans!
- the training and development which individuals receive in one type of business stays with them and is transferable often into another market
- the creation of new markets (computer games, mountain biking, activity holidays etc.) helps to create new jobs and revitalise run-down regions

Costs

- the business cycle of market economies (boom – bust – boom) regularly causes unemployment in the millions in western states, some of which becomes life-long
- the drive to make profits in a market can lead to dangerously high levels of pollution and environmental damage (to the ozone layer, rain forests, oceans, tundra, atmosphere etc.)
- in some market economies an increasing gap between rich and poor leads to an unfair distribution of resources, which in turn leads to social unrest – hence the retention by most western states of a mixed economic system
- extremely large multinational companies which operate in a kind of global market economy sometimes become too powerful and are able to 'skew' the economies of small states – especially in the Third World – and to dictate world market prices
- some markets – alcoholic beverages, tobacco, transport fuels etc. – can lead to extensive health damage among active and passive consumers

DISCUSSION TOPIC

Few if any markets yet devised have managed to deliver only social benefits; all embody social costs to a greater or lesser degree. Is this inevitable, or can better market systems and operations be developed in an economy so as to optimise social benefits and minimise social costs?

PC 1.2.4, 1.2.5

DISCUSSION TOPICS

1 What factors do *you* consider essential in the creation of a market for a good or service?

2 Do you think that the government should protect UK markets from foreign domination, or let market mechanisms run their course?

3 Are the buying and selling of shares, bonds and futures on the stock-market essentially immoral, parasitic activities, or do they serve a useful purpose in the UK economy?

4 Should small businesses be encouraged to survive in the consumer market? If so, why? If not, why not?

5 Should 'the sky be the limit' for profit levels and salaries in a free market economy?

6 Should competition in the UK economy be entirely free from government restrictions and intervention (such as by the Monopolies & Mergers Commission), or not? If so, why? If not, why not?

7 Should social considerations outweigh economic ones, or vice versa, in a developed state?

PC 1.2.1, 1.2.2, 1.2.3, 1.2.4, 1.2.5

REVIEW TEST

PC 1.2.1, 1.2.2, 1.2.3, 1.2.4, 1.2.5

1 Explain simply, in your own words, what a market is in an economic sense.

2 List the four main types of market in the UK.

3 What economic factors need to be present for a new supplier to be encouraged to enter a given market?

4 List five factors which are important to a prospective buyer in a consumer market.

5 Explain briefly why the making of profits by private sector companies is so important in market and mixed economies.

6 Explain the difference between a monopoly and an oligopoly in market terms.

7 List three 'plus factors' of competition between suppliers in a free market. List three 'minus factors' of competition between suppliers in a free market.

8 Detail briefly what you see as the major social benefits and costs of market operations in the developed world.

9 Explain briefly why businesses today are much more conscious of the environment than they were, say, twenty years ago.

KNOWLEDGE TEST

Element 1.2
Analyse the operation of markets and their effects on businesses and communities

1 (i) An oligopoly market is one in which a single, large supplier controls the market.
(ii) A competitive market is one in which businesses are able to enter and leave freely, while seeking to sell goods or services which customers will buy.

Which of the following options best describes the above two statements?

A	(i)	T	(ii)	T
B	(i)	T	(ii)	F
C	(i)	F	(ii)	T
D	(i)	F	(ii)	F

2 Which of the following statements is true, and which false?

A	Private sector businesses enter markets to provide social benefits for customers.	T	F
B	A government will intervene in a market in order to seek to reduce unemployment.	T	F
C	A buyer in a market is likely to be influenced by the availability of various kinds of credit facilities.	T	F
D	A seller is more likely to enter a market in which a large number of competing businesses are already active.	T	F

3 Which of the following situations are advantages and which disadvantages arising from competition in markets?

A market dominance by a single supplier after a price war
B product information in advertisements and promotional material
C money spent on research and design
D a highly segmented market inhabited by many suppliers

4 Which of the following statements is true, and which false?

A	A skimming price is set deliberately low, so as to 'skim' a modest profit from sales when introducing a new product.	T	F
B	A penetration price is given to a product or service when its sellers wish to ensure that it stays in the market a long time.	T	F
C	A loss-leader price is used to get customers into shops and stores to buy other goods.	T	F
D	Sellers use the destruction price mechanism to end the life-cycle of a failing product.	T	F
E	A milking price strategy is traditionally used in the sale of agricultural and dairy products.	T	F

5 (i) Social costs tend not to occur in markets which possess developed price mechanisms.
(ii) Social benefits tend to occur most frequently in the markets of a command economy.

Which of the following options best describes the above two statements?

A	(i)	T	(ii)	T
B	(i)	T	(ii)	F
C	(i)	F	(ii)	T
D	(i)	F	(ii)	F

PORTFOLIO OF EVIDENCE ACTIVITY

PC
1.2.1
1.2.2
1.2.3
1.2.4
1.2.5

Element 1.2
Analyse the operation of markets and their effects on businesses and communities

MORGAN & FITCH: REPORT 2

Scenario

Having submitted your product report in good time to Ms Khan, you had been looking forward to a less pressured time at *Morgan & Fitch*, when you received the following memorandum:

MEMORANDUM

Strictly confidential

To: A N Other, Research Assistant **From:** Chuck Schulz, Director, Research Operations

Date: 22 May 199– **Copy to:** Lisa Khan, Research Operations Manager

Subject: CROSS-MARKET SURVEY AND REPORT FOR TRANSGLOBAL INC

I am extremely pleased to inform you that M & F has recently been retained by Transglobal Incorporated, the multi-national conglomerate organisation, to undertake a series of market investigations to assist them in gaining an updated view of market trends in the UK.

As a result of your marked success with your recent product report, I have selected you to do this one! This is what TI want:

1 A survey of two contrasting UK markets (they have supplied a suggested list to select from), one of which is competitive and the other non-competitive. I guess they want to get a feeling on the main differences etc. They want us – you – to produce a profile of the two markets in terms of their respective size, the number of suppliers in the market, the amount of product sold annually, the nature and strength of demand currently and the nature of current competition in each market.

TI propose the following types of business, but say you can move outside of them if you find better alternatives:

Competitive markets	**Non-competitive markets**
national daily newspapers	home water services
soft drinks (e.g. colas)	home electricity supply
trainer footwear	council-run leisure centres
sweet snacks	industrial gas supply
pocket CD players or audio cassettes	Post Office Counter services

2 TI also want you to select **two** businesses within **one** of the markets you survey in order to report on how they compete and seek to increase demand for a given type of (similar) product and why any changes in demand occurred and also how competition affects customers' choice and the quality of the goods they purchase.

3 Lastly, TI want a survey on how two different businesses behave in two different types of market – you could use the markets you researched in 1 above – in terms of how they employ pricing and non-pricing strategies to improve their performance and market position. They also want some feedback on how these two businesses generate both social costs and benefits to the community at large in the course of doing business.

There's quite a lot of work here, but the TI account is big bucks! As they said when I was at military college Stateside: *I know you can do it, you know you can do it, so let's do it !!*

Task 1

Make sure you are clear on Chuck Schulz's briefing and then decide upon which markets and businesses you will survey. Remember that access to information is the key to your selections. Draw up your activity plan, building in review and evaluation opportunities and devise a timetable for research and visits etc.

Task 2

Review and assess the data you have assembled for each of the three parts of your report, and decide what you will include and what you will dispense with. Design a structure for your report which stays relevant to Chuck Schulz's terms of reference, and which is suited to TI's three-part survey request. Decide what illustrative material you will include.

Task 3

Compose a suitable report of about 5–7 pages of A4. Before you start, check with your teacher on whether you should hand-write or word-process your report. Remember to proof-read your report before submission.

Task 4

Complete your activity planning and review forms and hand them in with this activity.

Performance criteria covered

1.2.1, 1.2.2, 1.2.3, 1.2.4, 1.2.5

Core skills covered

Communication:
3.2.1, 3.2.2, 3.2.3, 3.2.4, 3.2.5, 3.3.1, 3.3.2, 3.3.3, 3.4.1, 3.4.2, 3.4.3, 3.4.4

Information Technology (if report text/graphics processed):
3.1.1, 3.1.2, 3.1.3, 3.1.4, 3.1.5, 3.2.1, 3.2.2, 3.2.3, 3.2.4, 3.2.5, 3.2.6, 3.3.1, 3.3.2, 3.3.3, 3.3.4, 3.3.5, 3.3.6

Application of Number:
3.1.1, 3.1.2, 3.1.3, 3.1.4, 3.1.5, 3.1.6, 3.1.7, 3.2.1, 3.2.2, 3.2.3, 3.2.4, 3.2.5, 3.2.6, 3.2.7, 3.2.8, 3.2.9 - insofar as these PCs relate to transforming raw data into analytical survey diagrams, charts and tables, etc.
3.3.1, 3.3.2, 3.3.3, 3.3.4, 3.3.5

Element 1.3
THE EFFECTS OF GOVERNMENT ON MARKETS

PC 1.3.1

The background to government intervention in markets

During the past one hundred years, the involvement and influence of successive UK governments upon business and the national economy has grown steadily – to the point where, today, the government itself spends almost half of every pound earned by private sector enterprises and consumers.

How did such a large-scale involvement come about? For much of the nineteenth century, economic theorists held strongly to the view that government intervention into the world of business should be minimal. Prevailing economic theory held that the economy of Britain was more likely to grow and prosper in a free-market environment in which open competition was actively encouraged and business entrepreneurs were given a free hand to 'speculate and accumulate'.

However, the government did intervene from time to time, as for example in 1856, when the Limited Liability Act for companies was introduced so as to encourage wider investment without the risk of investors and directors being imprisoned for the debts incurred by a failed limited company, having surrendered all their possessions to help pay creditors.

Despite such liberalising moves, however, there was a wide gulf in Victorian England separating the rich from the poor and the educated from the barely literate. As a result, strong pressure was exerted between 1860 and 1910 for both Liberal and Conservative governments to:

- make education available to all (Education Act 1870)
- introduce secondary education (Education Act 1902)
- extend the authority and roles of local government in areas such as public health and medical officers to inspect and improve amenities (Public Health Act 1848)
- construct a rudimentary 'safety net' for the very poor (Poor Law Act 1834)

■ The growth of social expectations (1850–1990)

PC 1.3.1

Thus during the last 50 years of the nineteenth century, largely as a result of pressure groups like the Trades Union Congress and Salvation Army and the development of a more educated public opinion, successive governments were encouraged to lay the foundation stones for:

- universal, free education – to 16 plus, paid for out of national taxation
- a comprehensive national health service paid for out of a national insurance levy from all in employment together with employers' contributions
- a social services 'umbrella' to assist all those in need of support as a result of poverty arising from ill-health, prolonged unemployment, disability, family break up etc. paid for out of national taxation and insurance contributions.

■ The mounting costs of enlarged social expectations

Indeed, the extent to which governments over the past 150 years have progressively taken up the responsibilities of education, health and social welfare are evidenced in the amounts spent upon them today. For example, the National Health Service costs *over £100 million per day* to run. In mid-1993, *over £16 billion per annum* was being spent by the government to provide income support to one person in six of the UK population (including claimants' dependants) as a result of hardship arising from the deep recession of 1990–93. Spending on education more than doubled between 1981 and 1991 from £13.4 billion to £29.5 billion (before taking inflation into account).

Defence spending has similarly spiralled over the past 150 years. Twice in the twentieth century Britain (with her allies) fought in two world wars, and, during the Cold War era between 1945 and 1991 when the threat of nuclear war hung over the capitalist west and communist eastern blocs, UK governments felt obliged to channel billions into defence, devoting in 1991 over £27 billion (some 15 per cent of all government expenditure) to the national security provided by the armed services.

■ An 'earth-mother' role for government evolves

What in effect took place in Britain over the past 150 years was a radical change in how its citizens viewed the role of government. 'They' – the government of the day – in the eyes of the populace became progressively responsible for ensuring:

- that parents secured a good education for their offspring
- that 'free' (paid out of taxes) health treatment was promptly and universally available
- that a reliable and affordable transport infrastructure was first constructed and then efficiently maintained
- that citizens could move about safely and sleep securely, thanks to a vigilant and efficient police force
- that a welfare-state safety-net would catch and care for all falling upon hard times, such as becoming homeless.

In this way, the role of government has expanded since 1850, when its workforce of civil servants numbered only a few hundred to its present day 'earth-mother', cradle-to-grave, over-arching social role which requires a mammoth central, local and public corporation bureaucracy employing 5 million people or almost one person in four of the UK working population!

PC 1.3.1

CHECKLIST OF ACTIVITIES ADMINISTERED BY CENTRAL/LOCAL GOVERNMENT AND FINANCED OUT OF GOVERNMENT INCOME

- Defence
- Health
- Education
- Social Security
- Provision of an Independent Legal System
- Housing and Community Amenity
- Fuel and Energy
- Transport and Communications
- Mining and Mineral Resources
- Agriculture, Forestry and Fishing
- Services and Support for Commerce and Industry
- Recreational and Cultural Affairs
- Tax Collection
- Police Services
- Fire Brigades
- Planning
- Environmental Protection
- Consumer Protection
- General Public Services

As the above checklist (by no means exhaustive) readily illustrates, there are today few areas of national or local activity which remain outside of an arm of government interest and involvement.

The reasons for government intervention in markets

PC 1.3.1

PC 1.3.1

SUMMARY OF THE REASONS FOR GOVERNMENT INTERVENTION IN MARKETS

As a result of the growth of the social as well as economic role of successive governments over the past 150 years, today's UK governments tend to intervene in markets to:

- **increase and encourage competition** and avoid the inefficiencies of monopoly (either private or public)
- **regulate competition** – internally by ensuring that markets do not become price-fixed, rigged or monopolised, and externally by imposing tariffs and quotas on certain types of imported goods from certain foreign countries
- **ensure honest, fair trading** through the work of government regulating agencies which monitor the activities of: banks, trading companies, advertising media, etc. and which support self-regulating bodies
- **protect consumers** through enacting legislation (e.g. *The Consumer Protection Act 1987*) and through the work of its 'watchdog' bodies (e.g. local *Trading Standards Offices*)
- **protect the environment** through various governmental inspectorates such as *HM Pollution Inspectorate*
- **encourage consumer demand** for goods and services (and thus to stimulate the economy) by carrying out fiscal and monetary policies (e.g. lowering direct and indirect taxes or reducing bank rates, or subsidising business developing new technologies)
- **minimise the risk of inflation** by taking counter measures to those above
- **improve employment levels** by providing financial incentives for businesses to locate in regions of high unemployment; by funding the training and work experience of trainees through the national network of TECs

In addition to effecting 'steers' within the UK economy aimed at achieving specific political policies, any UK government will seek to intervene in business markets for a variety of reasons – so as to stimulate a buoyant and growing economy within a framework of honest and fair trading, which also protects individual consumers from unfair practices and which, increasingly, protects the national environment.

In particular, a UK government will seek to:

- **encourage free market competition which stimulates economic growth**. However, differences in political ideology between the current Conservative and Labour parties result in differing boundaries of intervention. For example, the current Conservative government is implementing a policy of privatising the state railway system, which a future Labour government is likely either to limit or reverse, given its view of the social importance of a widely affordable and accessible railway network.
- **act to prohibit the creation by business organisations of unfair practices** – monopolies, cartels and 'cosy oligarchies' which illegally operate price-fixing and price-hiking

agreements between themselves to the detriment of the consumer, thus rigging the market. Note in this regard the responsibilities of the *Monopolies and Mergers Commission* and the *Office of Fair Trading* which act as vigilant watchdogs.

- **promote honest and fair trading among business organisations**. In this respect, governments act in two ways: firstly by bringing to the statute book laws which ensure that businesses trade fairly and honestly. For example, the *Trade Descriptions Act 1968* requires that goods and services are correctly described and prices honestly displayed (e.g. sales goods price reductions). Similarly, the *Consumer Protection Act 1987* and the *Consumer Credit Act 1974* provide a range of measures aimed at, for instance, enabling a customer to cancel a credit purchase contract or to obtain redress if a good or service purchased proves defective; secondly, they act to encourage bodies which co-ordinate self-regulation in given markets, such as the *Advertising Standards Authority* which monitors advertising, and the *Independent Television Commission (ITC)*, which similarly checks television commercials.
- **protect environmental and social interests**. As a result of the perceptible damage done to the world's eco-systems this century, many developed countries are slowly but surely acting to protect the planet from further damage. For example, California will, by the turn of the century, have effectively stopped its millions of motor cars from emitting polluting exhaust fumes. Also, the Department of Transport in the UK is acting to fine heavily exhaust-belching car and lorry owners through a series of random checks. Governments also intervene in markets for social reasons. For instance, as a result of pressure from the women's movement and resulting government fiscal policies (e.g. separate taxation options for married couples) women are now finding it easier to obtain loans and financial services from banks and building societies *in their own right*. In both of the above examples, legislation was the weapon used to bring about change.
- **prevent economically harmful 'dumping' and price-undercutting by foreign exporters.** No government can afford to allow its domestic economy to be undermined by an unchecked inflow of goods which have been produced (sometimes by exploiting local labour overseas) at costs which allow for retail prices to be set well below those of internal competitors. Such imports can close, for example, home textile factories or bankrupt home computer manufacturers. However, economic-block (e.g. European Union) and international agreements (e.g. the latest GATT 1995 accord) prevent participating states from introducing tariffs and quotas for imported goods and services in order to protect various home markets.

PC 1.3.1

■ Government interventions into business markets: beliefs and ideologies

The way a given government intervenes in any market and the extent to which it does so depends in no small part upon the type of economy it supports. For example, for many years now the economy of the USA has been encouraged to develop along free market (or market economy) lines. Free, capitalist-based competition has enabled markets to evolve, not only in traditional private sector areas – cars, white-goods, food etc. – but also in telephone and utility service areas (electricity, gas, water) long before the UK followed suit with its own rash of privatisations.

When, say, USA Republican and UK Conservative administrations are in power, it is likely that a much freer rein will be given to both young business entrepreneurs and mature national conglomerates to do business in a relatively unregulated way. On the other hand, when governments are elected with a more social complexion, they tend to intervene more directly and more frequently in business markets and activities by imposing regulations and obligations which, in effect, enforce a degree of social engineering. For example, in Sweden and Austria, successive socialist governments in the 1970s and 1980s imposed swingeing taxes upon businesses (and individuals) which paid for free nurseries and crèches and youth hostels, and also to supply holidays for poor teenagers, as well as high levels of health care and social housing. In communist states with fully centralised economies, free enterprise is prohibited and the state determines entirely how its revenues are spent. In short, the way a government intervenes in its economy or markets depends entirely upon its political beliefs and ideology.

■ The world economy and governments' domestic market regulations

PC 1.3.1

As a result of much improved transportation and telecommunication technologies over the past thirty years, nation states across the world are much more tied to what is, in effect, a single global economy. Economic partnerships exist today between many sets of trading countries which maintain loops or circles in which raw materials or food stuffs are extracted or grown in one country to be exported to another for processing or consumption: finished goods are then sometimes re-exported to such partners. It is becoming, therefore, increasingly difficult for states (even those which are virtually economically self-sufficient) to impose domestic regulations upon their internal markets which inhibit the free flow of trade. For this reason, many developed western states have moved over the past ten years closer to a free market economy and further away from a mixed economy which was also highly interventionist.

■ The common ground of economic influence sought by all governments

PC 1.3.1

Whatever the political complexion of a given government, it will seek to improve the economic well-being of its electorate by:

- **seeking to obtain full employment**

  people suffering the hardship of joblessness are most unlikely to vote for the party they perceive as responsible for their predicament; moreover, such people are net receivers of government money in the form of unemployment benefit, income support and mortgage relief etc. While unemployed, they are not making any contribution towards the increase in the nation's wealth, and thus the enlargement of the government's revenues, which it wishes to employ to achieve its political aims. Furthermore, people inhabiting the outer fringes of society, in terms of deprivation and demoralisation, may turn to crime or acts of anti-social behaviour which may destabilise the localities they inhabit

- **seeking to win and maintain economic growth**

  only by creating wealth on a continuous, rolling basis is a country able to sustain the levels of affluence which its populace has either come to expect, or to which it aspires. A steady growth in a country's economy enables government to:

  - ○ achieve the social, political and economic objectives it was elected to deliver
  - ○ build new road, rail and air arteries in the transport infrastructure, so as to further strengthen the economy

PC 1.3.1

CHECKLIST OF REASONS FOR UK GOVERNMENT INTERVENTIONS INTO DOMESTIC MARKETS

The following checklist illustrates the major reasons for UK governments' interventions into UK domestic markets:

- **to bring about increases in market competition and consumption**, so as to stimulate and develop the economy
- **to create regulated markets in which no single business acquires a dominant, monopolising role**: where a given company – say by acquisition or merger – appears likely to obtain more than a 25% market share, its activities may be referred to the *Monopolies and Mergers Commission*, which has powers to prohibit such enlarging moves as being against the public interest
- **to regulate the impact of overseas competition** upon a market by the imposition of tariffs and quotas – for instance the number of Japanese motor cars which may be imported (i.e. not manufactured in the UK) into the United Kingdom annually
- **to protect individual consumers from unfair or illegal business practices** by the enactment of consumer protection laws
- **to ensure that environmental and planning laws are followed** – say for controlling polluting emissions from factories making industrial chemicals, or for preventing illegal building or expansion within an industrial or retailing complex
- **to encourage social policies and interests** – such as the printing of health warnings on cigarette packets, the timing of adult advertisements on TV or the purchase of lead-free petrol as a result of government subsidies on pump-prices
- **to promote the economic development of impoverished regions** through a range of financial grants, subsidies and 'tax-holidays' offered to businesses agreeing to expand or set up within them, so as to stimulate local economies and employment

  - facilitate financial investment by companies in order to replace worn-out plant and premises
  - improve and sustain educational, health and security provisions by means of increased revenues from corporate and individual taxation.

When a nation's economy slides into reverse – in say, a recession or slump – a decrease in government revenue inevitably results because of a steep decline in trading income. Further, unemployed people do not provide the government with income from taxes but they do require increased financial support from social services funds. Thus the government of the day may be obliged to borrow money – either at home or abroad – and, as a result, create a downward spiral of an ever-increasing national debt, which burdens the economy and diminishes hopes of recovery.

Such deficit economies have a limited life, since the international value of the currency involved also spirals downwards relative to others, which makes the purchase of imports ever more expensive. This in turn tends to fuel inflation – hence the term 'stagflation', to identify economies with a declining trading performance allied to inflation caused by governments 'bailing themselves out by printing money', instead of achieving the much harder goal of improving economic performance and re-establishing an economic equilibrium, where imports are largely paid for by exports.

However, within the overall world economy, there are inevitably winners and losers in terms of creating and sustaining economic growth. Some economies are blessed with raw materials like copper, bauxite and oil which are in constant, world-wide demand. Others can grow and export efficiently crops of wheat, coffee or rice, or supply timber, wool or cotton to buoyant world markets. Yet others capitalise on superior technological know-how and production processes to sustain a marketing edge on their competitors, while others may rely on cheap labour costs and high volume outputs. Nevertheless, in world markets, it generally 'takes money to make money', and in the world's economic performance league, it is Third World countries that are currently suffering from having their margins relentlessly squeezed by the economic muscle of states with developed economies. As a result, they are unable to generate sufficient operating surpluses to plough back into their own economies and thus strengthen them on a long-term basis.

Controlling inflation – the enemy of all economies

PC 1.3.1

In addition to seeking virtually full employment and sustained economic growth, all governments strive to maintain and control inflation. As you already know, inflation occurs when too much money is available to spend – a high demand for goods or services enables suppliers to increase prices while maintaining the level of sales, for a time. However, the downside of inflationary spirals includes:

- a general loss of international competitiveness, as goods cost more to produce for export
- a progressive downward movement in the value of people's investments and savings, since their worth (buying power) may be decreasing at 10–20 per cent each year
- consumer-led purchasing of foreign goods which leads to adverse balance-of-payments problems
- an increasing downturn in saving and investment as more money is needed to maintain families and firms in a 'hand-to-mouth' situation
- an eventual slide into recession as companies start to fail to sell from an over-stocked position, and begin to lay workers off and cut production, as confidence in the economy plummets.

Such a situation occurred in the UK in the late 1980s, following upon a sudden inflow of money into the economy as a result of significant tax reductions. The economy – especially in its consumer segment – overheated and sucked in large volumes of foreign goods. Building societies were offering young men loans so they could take their girlfriends out for curry suppers! Interest rates zoomed upwards in order to keep overseas investment in the UK at a time when the innate value of the pound sterling was being undermined, but this had the effect of making bank loans much dearer for UK businesses, and thus depressed the economy further. Moreover, in order to redress this worsening situation, Sir Norman Lamont, the then Chancellor of the Exchequer was obliged to use the interest rate lever in order to continue to restrict the supply of money to the private sector and so reduce inflation. Only gradually – at a half point at a time – were interest rates allowed to fall, as inflation was brought slowly under control between 1991 and 1993. Base rate fell from a peak of 14 per cent to some 6 per cent during this period, while inflation also dropped from 10.2 per cent in 1990 to 1.3 per cent in 1993. But, unemployment rose from 1.6 million in 1990 to 3 million in 1993, and the government's Public Sector Borrowing Requirement (the amount it needs to borrow in order to balance its income and expenditure) changed from a surplus of 1.5 per cent of the UK Gross Domestic Product in 1989/90, to a deficit of some 8 per cent of GDP in 1993/4 – amounting to a need to borrow about £1 billion each week!

Indeed, the social costs of such strong economic medicine are that it tends to throw millions out of work, force the closure of thousands of businesses each year and oblige building societies to repossess homes from people unable to maintain mortgage payments. At the same time, the welfare costs of unemployment benefit, income support and social services place huge financial burdens on the government.

Achieving economic growth without fuelling inflation has, for successive UK Chancellors, proved as difficult as squaring the circle! Hence the sequence of 'stop–go' government economic policies since 1945, where violent yanks on the UK's 'brake lever' have been deemed necessary every few years in order to restrain a demand-led economy from accelerating into inflation.

PC 1.3.1

Sustaining a healthy balance of payments

All trading nations import goods and services as well as exporting them; some states with large reservoirs of natural resources may enjoy a natural healthy balance, where they are able to sell abroad far more than they need to import. Others, such as Japan and the UK, rely largely on human resources and skills to refashion imported raw materials into exportable goods. Such states also tend to develop 'invisible exports' such as banking insurance and telecommunications services which they can profitably sell overseas.

Whatever a country's economy produces, it will, sooner or later, need to balance the books of its international trading. By selling its own goods or services to a country from which it is importing, a state facilitates 'payment by exchange' – the cost of the goods (of an equal value) reciprocally bought and sold can be effected without the currency having to leave either country.

Where states do not possess a currency which is internationally accepted – like the rouble of the former communist USSR – then payments for goods purchased abroad would have to be made in a respected currency such as the US dollar, German Deutschmark or Japanese yen. Otherwise such a state would need to resort to barter – rare furs for engineering plant.

Severe economic penalties face states which fail to balance their payments books over a prolonged period:

- a balance-of-payments deficit is run up which has an adverse effect upon the rate of exchange at which other states will buy the currency of the weak economy – a crisis of confidence builds up regarding the overall economic well-being of the country concerned
- the government of such an unfortunate country is obliged to borrow money – at high interest rates – in order to pay for imported goods. Or, if it has any, it will need to draw upon its reserves. In the case of the UK, these would be held in gold (or a stable currency) by the Bank of England
- Once such a country's credit-worthiness and reserves have been depleted, it will have to 'put the bar down' on all imports, including medicines and essential equipment spare parts, and set up strict import and exchange controls. A final strategy open to it – as happens sadly all too frequently in Third World countries – is for the government to meet with its overseas creditors in order to seek a rescheduling of the debts incurred, to reduce annual repayments over a more extended period

The balance of payments in the UK is recorded statistically as follows:

	1992
	£
Visible trade	– 14 billion
Invisible trade	+ 2 billion
Balance of payments, current account	– 12 billion

While the UK's invisible balance of trade has been in surplus through the 1980s, its visible balance has worsened since 1983, peaking at £ –24 billion in 1989, and still £ –14 billion in 1992.

Policy steers towards social equalisation

PC 1.3.1

Ever since the French Revolution of 1789, Western governments have taken mind of the revolutionary consequences of too wide a gulf separating the rich from the poor. 'Ability to pay' has characterised the imposition of *progressive direct taxes* in the UK (which in the early 1970s rose to a dizzy height of 98 per cent on personal income above £150,000 per annum! Currently the first PAYE tax band (after single and married persons' allowances) levies 20 per cent on the first £3,200 of income, 25 per cent on additional income up to £24,300 and 40 per cent on all income over £24,300.

Other efforts by successive governments to equalise the relative affluence of its citizens are evidenced by zero-rated VAT on children's clothes and food, and by the creation of a floor of some £5,245 below which no PAYE tax is levied upon a married person. Current Conservative Party views hold that a ceiling of 40 per cent on all income over £24,300 encourages able entrepreneurs to create wealth from which all members of society benefit.

The imposition of indirect taxes, such as VAT are considered by some economists as being more equitable, since they are only levied from those who choose to purchase such a taxed good or service. However, the purchase of petrol (for a car) by a rural resident whose bus service has long been discontinued, may be deemed a need rather than a want! Similarly, the levy of 8 per cent VAT on fuel purchases aroused widespread hostility in 1993.

Other means of encouraging the equalising of UK citizens' wealth take the form of stamp duties on house purchases, inheritance taxes and capital gains taxes on the profit made from the purchase and sale of shares etc.

■ The levers available to government to influence the UK economy

PC 1.3.2

Given that governments of all persuasions see advantage in the creation of full employment, low inflation, a healthy balance of payments and sense of equal opportunity in a generally affluent society, they will naturally use the levers and controls which are available to them as the government of the day. The levers or 'influencers' they employ tend to be:

- control of public expenditure
- control of the money supply
- raising or lowering the base rate of the Bank of England, which effectively controls the interest rates offered by the clearing banks
- seeking to control the rate of exchange at which the pound sterling is bought and sold on international stock exchanges
- raising or lowering consumer and company direct and indirect taxes and national insurance contributions
- providing grants and subsidies to particular industrial sectors (such as information technology and telecommunications) and subsidising businesses in regions suffering economic hardship
- borrowing money from individuals, corporations or institutions (in the form of government gilts and bonds offered for sale) in order to balance its public spending books in the short term

- seeking to influence public and business opinion through mass media advertising campaigns to 'buy British', or 'think green', to 'save electricity' or to 'buy British Telecom shares'.

PC 1.3.1 1.3.2

DISCUSSION TOPIC

Some political and economic commentators believe that governments are far less able to influence the workings of the UK economy than they would have us believe. The proverbial man in the street blames all his economic ills on the incompetence of the government of the day. To what extent do you consider governments *are* able to influence the direction of an economy such as the UK's mixed economy?

PC 1.3.2

■ The control of public expenditure

Of all the levers and 'influencers' available to a government, that exercised over its own expenditure would seem the easiest to control. Each year the Treasury requires what are called spending ministers of state – those running departments like education, defence and social services to supply estimates of the costs of their spending plans for the coming financial year. Similarly, Treasury civil servants estimate – for the Chancellor of the Exchequer – the amount of government revenue or income which can be expected to be raised in the same year from direct and indirect taxation, the sale of government products and services, and interest on any government investments etc.

Budgets and autumn statements

Chancellors of the Exchequer make their pronouncements upon the control of public expenditure in their annual budgets and autumn statements. Traditionally the budget took place in March each year and the autumn statement in November. The March budget tended to concentrate on the govemment's fiscal and taxation strategies, and the autumn statement on its spending plans. However, from 1993 onwards the government announces both its spending and taxation plans every autumn.

The budget deficit problem

In some years, as in 1987, the amount of money flowing into the government's coffers exceeded that which it spent out. As a result, it was able to pay off some of the long-term debts which it holds, referred to as the national debt. Sadly, however, there have been very few such repayments made over the past twenty or so years, since most UK governments have worked within an economic or budget deficit framework, ending up each year spending more than has been received as revenue.

Indeed, in 1993, this deficit was running at the rate of £1 billion pounds each week, or £50 billion per annum! As a result, when Sir Norman Lamont resigned his Chancellorship, and Kenneth Clarke took over, his main concern was to reduce this enormous drain upon the public purse by supervising necessary but unpleasant cuts in public spending and increases in taxation such as 8 per cent VAT on fuel (April 1994), since no government can continue to spend at such a rate without passing on an unmanageable debt to its future adult citizens. Moreover, such a debt requires a significant amount of wasted money being spent on servicing the loans which the government is obliged to secure, and makes overseas investors very nervous about the pound's future, thus tending to devalue it, unless a corrective economic policy is seen to be forthcoming.

Governments as paymasters

It is also worth remembering that the government is the paymaster of some 5 million UK public sector workers – civil servants, teachers, servicemen, postmen, railwaymen, nurses and doctors etc. – and can exercise significant fiscal power by limiting their pay rises. In 1994, for example, the government limited all public sector employees, pay rises to 2.7 per cent – a figure which was at the time below the level of inflation.

In addition to making cuts in, say, the amount of income support, child or unemployment benefit in order to reduce government expenditure, a government may choose to postpone or cancel capital building projects, such as schools, hospitals or roads, or naval vessels or aircraft due to be built or refitted.

Keynes and public spending in a recession

Governments do not always cut back on public expenditure, even in times of recession. President Roosevelt in the world slump of the 1930s elected to follow the advice of economists like J M Keynes (to use public spending as a way out of the slump) by building roads, dams and public buildings.

■ Public spending control and politics

PC 1.3.2

While, at least in theory, all governments have the power to exercise tight control over public spending, in practice they find it very hard to control. The reasons stem from the politics involved. Whereas backbencher MPs tend to find it easy to support public spending cuts in general and in the abstract, they find it much harder when such cuts become specifically targeted, affecting, say, large numbers of their own constituents. By the same token, spending ministers tend to protect their budgets fiercely from any Treasury onslaught, as if any reduction would undermine their power and influence in cabinet and appear as a slight upon their public image. Perhaps this is why public spending rose so sharply between 1989 and 1993 during the recession.

DISCUSSION TOPIC

PC 1.3.2

Why do you think public expenditure rose sharply during the 1989–93 recession? Would you expect it normally to rise or to fall during a recession? What evidence can you provide to support your views?

■ Control of the money supply

PC 1.3.2

Most economic theorists agree that when too much money is available in an economy to purchase goods or services – by both consumers and businesses – the effect over a period of time is inflationary. Freely available finance, especially when on offer at low lending rates from banks or building societies, helps to create a surge in demand. As we have already seen, when demand exceeds supply, prices tend to increase until a price equilibrium is established at a higher level. In short the goods and services cost more to acquire, and thus the currency of the economy buys less.

PC 1.3.2

■ The interest rate lever

In order to combat such inflationary trends, govemments have at their disposal the major lever of interest rate adjustment. A government wishing to depress demand and so to encourage a deflationary spiral can instruct the Bank of England to increase the base rate. This is the rate at which it will lend money to the clearing banks. If the rate the Bank of England charges is higher than the prevailing market rate, the clearing banks will promptly adjust their own rates upwards. By raising or lowering the base rate, the government is able to increase or restrict the amount of money which consumers or businesses borrow to spend on goods or services, and thus help to encourage growth or cut-backs in the economy.

Ever since the Second World War, successive Chancellors of the Exchequer have sought – without much success – to promote a smoothly growing UK economy. In reality, they have tended to use 'hikes' in interest rates or 'give-away' tax cuts as crude levers to promote growth or cut back, depending whether the economy was in an expansionist or recessionary wave of the economic cycle. Hence the terms 'boom or bust', 'stop and go' were used to describe governments' economic policies over the past fifty years.

While the use of the interest rate lever or weapon may be justly regarded as crude, it is nevertheless effective. In 1990 inflation in the UK was running at some 10.2 per cent per annum. During that year, the interest rate peaked at 15 per cent dropping to 14 per cent when the UK entered the Exchange Rate Mechanism of the European Community. By employing a prudent policy regarding the use of the interest rate mechanism, the Chancellor at that time, Norman Lamont, was able to bring down interest rates from 14 per cent in January of 1991 to 6 per cent in 1993, with a corresponding drop in the rate of inflation from 10 per cent to 1.3 per cent. The downside of this policy, however, was the sharp rise in unemployment, bankrupted businesses and private house repossessions by building societies. Since 1993, inflation has been creeping slowly but steadily upwards (to some 3.4 per cent in early 1995) as the slow recovery in the UK economy begins to release more money and spending power into industrial and consumer markets.

PC 1.3.2

DISCUSSION TOPIC

Do you think that a government is entitled to use the interest rate lever as a means of control in the UK economy? Or do you think that such mechanisms should be employed – as in Germany – by a central bank which is independent of government?

PC 1.3.2

■ The taxation lever

Perhaps the most effective lever at the government's disposal at any time lies in its ability to increase or decrease the taxes paid by individuals or businesses.

Direct taxation

PC 1.3.2

Few employed people are unaware of the proportion of their gross wages taken from their pay-packets in the form of Pay As You Earn (PAYE) direct tax. At present PAYE taxation is paid in three tranches after personal and married persons' allowances have been deducted:

		Income Band
20% rate:	first	£3,200
25% rate:		£3,201–£24,300
40% rate:		£24,300 and over

Corporation Tax – the tax which companies pay on their profits – currently runs at 33 per cent for the full rate of tax, with small companies paying 25 per cent on profits up to f250,000.

In addition to PAYE and Corporation Tax, both employees and companies are obliged to pay National Insurance Contributions to the government. Some economists regard such payments as a form of taxation, in that the money goes into a 'global pot', from which the National Health Service and Social Services are funded. Currently employees' contributions* range from 2 per cent on weekly earnings of £59 per week to 8.2 per cent on earnings over £440 per week, with the employer also contributing between 3.0 and 10.2 per cent pro rata. (*In the government's 'contracted in' scheme.)

In general terms, the more direct tax a government takes from individuals and companies, the more deflationary the impact upon the economy, since less money remains for consumers to spend on cars, hi-fi stacks, washing machines and holidays, and for company directors to spend on raw materials, capital equipment, premises and employees' pay.

However, if the government decides to spend *itself* the extra revenue it obtains from increased taxation, this of itself is likely to fuel inflation! Further, when direct taxes become too high, they engender serious disincentives – for employees to work overtime or to seek financial advancement, and for companies to invest in new equipment or to expand. Thus a policy of high taxation may only work in the short term in order to damp down demand. When the highest rate of direct taxation on individuals reached an incredible 98 per cent in the early 1970s, many highly successful entrepreneurs moved abroad and took their financial interests with them. Punitive levels of direct taxation may therefore cause harm to an economy by creating poor morale and disincentives in national workforces and flight to greener pastures by national wealth creators. High taxation also tends to lead to significant growth in a country's black economy, where people work and pay for work without declaring it, thus diminishing the income from taxes due to the government.

DISCUSSION TOPIC

PC 1.3.2

States which levy high taxes also tend to have a high profile of intervention – through the funding of social services, health services, education, leisure activities, state pensions, state housing and the like. States which levy low taxes, tend to have a lower profile through the encouragement of private enterprises to supply such services at a cost to the individual, paid for as health insurance, school fees and personal pensions schemes etc.

Which system do you think preferable when thinking of a country's population as a whole? What do you see as the pros and cons of either approach to direct taxation?

PC 1.3.2

Indirect taxation

Indirect taxation in the UK takes two main forms: value added tax (VAT) on specified goods and services and customs and excise duties payable on specific goods, such as alcoholic beverages, transport fuels, betting and tobacco products.

Value added tax

VAT, introduced in 1973 to replace purchase tax (called in the USA a sales tax), is levied upon a wide range of goods and services. VAT in the UK is currently levied at 17.5 per cent of the sales price. Certain products, such as food, children's clothing, books and newspapers are currently exempt from VAT (zero rated) on social grounds, but future governments may well take a less liberal view as the need to reduce the Public Sector Borrowing Requirement (PSBR) becomes more urgent.

There is both an input side and an output side to VAT, since all sole traders or companies engaged in business (except for those making and selling zero-rated goods) are, in effect, unpaid tax collectors for the government. An enterprise, say, in the primary sector selling on raw materials to a manufacturer will add VAT to the sales price. The manufacturer of the finished goods will likewise add VAT to the price of the goods to the distributor and the retailer to the eventual consumer. VAT levied during manufacture is regarded as an input tax, and on the eventual sale as an output tax. Where a business incurs VAT charges on goods or services bought in as a necessary part of running costs – say petrol, cleaning materials, stationery and office equipment etc. – such costs may be set against the VAT collected on all 'vatable' sales, which must be remitted to HM Customs and Excise quarterly.

Excise duties

In addition to VAT, the government, through its Customs and Excise arm levies taxes on a number of products or pursuits, such as alcoholic drinks, petrol, tobacco products and betting and gambling, notably horse-racing.

Council taxes and business rates

Other sources of revenue for the government are the locally collected Council Tax and Uniform Business Rates. For decades until 1990, local taxes for individuals had been based upon the levy of a local rate from householders who either owned or were purchasing their homes. (Council house tenants were exempt.) The amount of rates paid was worked out by means of a formula which computed a notional income arising if the owner-occupier were to rent out his or her house. Over many years this form of indirect taxation operated on the basis of a not too unreasonable 'ability to pay', but was also seen to be unfair, since some residents using local facilities paid nothing and others, such as widows and old-age pensioners, were penalised if they remained in larger houses. The Thatcher Government therefore decided to introduce a Community Charge in 1990 (promptly called a poll tax by its opponents) on all 18-plus adults, with special reductions for students, pensioners and people on income support etc.

This tax proved wildly unpopular – especially in Scotland and in poor districts – where reassessments gave rise to steep increases in charges payable. Also, widespread resentment resulted from the very wealthy and the very poor in many cases paying identical Community Charge taxes. So unpopular was this tax, although in many ways inherently fairer than its antecedent, local rates, that the Conservative government was obliged to restructure it as a 'Council Tax' in 1992–93 by going back to a system based on the estimated value of owner-occupied accommodation.

Uniform business rates

PC 1.3.2

During the same period, companies and partnerships also saw the new, nationally fixed uniform business rate increase the valuation of their business premises sharply in many instances, sometimes by as much as 300 per cent on the former local business rates valuations. Many small businesses cited this increase as a major factor contributing to their collapse during the 1990–93 recession.

Miscellaneous indirect taxes

Over the past two hundred years, successive Chancellors and their ingenious senior civil servants have devised a number of other forms of indirect taxation. Eminent among these are:

- Stamp duty – a tax levied on the sale of property
- Inheritance or wealth tax – a tax levied (above a nil rate band currently up to £154,000) of some 40 per cent
- Capital gains tax – a tax charged upon individuals at their PAYE rates – on profits made from the sale of assets over and above a base level of £6,000 per annum
- Motor vehicle tax – a tax levied on cars and trucks which are then licensed to use public roads for a period of six months or one year, depending on the licence purchased
- Television and radio licences – a tax levied on the users of TV and radios who also are obliged to purchase annual licences.

When the revenue from direct and indirect taxation is totalled and then divided by the number of adult UK citizens, it is not difficult to see how the government comes to spend some 40 per cent of the entire gross domestic product of the UK!

The pound sterling's exchange rate

PC 1.3.2

Like every other currency which is generally accepted among international trading nations as a convertible currency (in effect, acceptable by foreign states for goods purchased) the pound sterling has a rate of exchange *vis-á-vis* other currencies, notably the US dollar, the Deutschmark, the Japanese yen and the French franc.

The gold standard

Until 1931, the pound sterling (along with major currencies like the US dollar) enjoyed a value which was fixed to that of gold. Such an arrangement proved a great stabilising influence, since there was very little change in value between currencies – as long as they could maintain the link to the value of gold. However, the world slump of 1929 resulted in the UK no longer being able to maintain the value of its currency in this way.

The US dollar standard

With the emergence of the USA in 1945 as the world's dominant economy, the link with gold was substituted by a link with the US dollar – a marker as to the pound's international value which still exists today. After the pound came off the gold standard, it was allowed (largely) to float in the international markets regarding its value relative to other major currencies. Sadly, the cost to the UK economy of the Second World War and the repayment of debts incurred to the USA greatly affected post-war economic reconstruction, and the pound drifted inexorably downwards in the 1950s and 1960s relative to the value of the US dollar and Deutschmark.

PC 1.3.2 1.3.3

The European Community and its exchange rate mechanism

With the creation of the Common Market between 1951 and 1957, a movement began to harmonise the economies of the participating European states. By 1986 the twelve member states of the evolved European Community had progressed far along a path of not merely creating a free-trade area, but of moving towards a form of unified federal government.

Crucial to such an evolution was the creation of a single market and a single currency. The EC Single Market – in which internal tariff barriers were scheduled to be progressively removed by 31 December 1991 – was duly established.

The creation of a community operating within a European Monetary Union, however, proved far more complex. In 1979 the Exchange Rate Mechanism (ERM) was set up and progressively joined by nine of the twelve member states during the 1980s (the UK, Greece and Portugal remaining outside it).

Essentially, the ERM was designed to provide a stable relationship between participating currencies. Economically strong participators such as Germany and France opted to link their currencies within a narrow band of pegged, related values, while less strong member states were permitted to let their currencies float between a wider band of related values. All participating currencies would be given a corresponding ECU value (European Currency Unit). The hope was that, in this way, EC states could, with little economic pain, proceed to a single currency and monetary union. Also, by obliging member states to link their currencies to the robust Deutschmark, it was hoped that EC inflation would remain low and that a climate of financial prudence and responsibility would prevail. It is worth noting that the 'mechanism' aspect of the ERM included the support by strong states of weaker ones in this way: when a currency of a member state was in danger of hitting the bottom of its band, the strong states were committed to intervening and buying the currency on international markets as a means of maintaining its exchange rate value.

John Major took the UK into the ERM in October 1990, and – as events proved – made the fatal mistake of over-valuing the pound sterling against the Deutschmark, pegging it within a band of some 2.78–3.13 DM. Since 1990, world financial markets have, in effect, revalued the pound downwards, valuing it in March 1995 at some 2.22 Deutschmarks!

'Black Wednesday'

By October 1992, it had become clear that the pound sterling could not be maintained within its ERM band parity, and on 'Black Wednesday', 16 September 1992, international speculators struck, and within a matter of hours, forced the government to come out of the ERM after a devaluation of the pound by some 15 per cent.

During the hectic trading period on the London and international stock exchanges, the Chancellor, Sir Norman Lamont, through the customary intervention of the Bank of England spent some £7 billion on buying pounds in order to seek to maintain their value. But this incredible amount of buying proved in vain, and devaluation was accepted as inevitable. The Conservative government was very bitter at the time about the alleged failure of the German Bundesbank to buy pounds according to the ERM agreement.

Return to a floating pound

With the return of the pound to a floating role (at a position some 15 per cent cheaper than it was within the ERM) UK exporters were given a heaven-sent opportunity to increase their sales both with the EC and internationally, and this opportunity was heralded by many politicians as a god-send in aiding the UK recovery from recession – hence the label 'White Wednesday'. Indeed, UK government agencies advertised widely in Germany the opportunities to German business of moving their factories to Britain so as to take advantage of low costs and prices.

The limitations of exchange rate interventions

As the above case history of the pound's October 1992 exit from the ERM amply illustrates, government intervention in international exchanges either to maintain the value of the pound or to encourage its reduction (by either buying or selling sterling), while it may work within small movement margins, cannot of itself combat the concerted efforts of an alliance of international currency speculators. Such efforts are especially doomed when such speculators are convinced that the pound is over-valued by as much as 15 per cent, and are prepared to gamble billions (by selling pounds and then buying them back at a lower value) to back their judgement!

PC 1.3.2 1.3.3

SUMMARY OF UK GOVERNMENT MONEY MEASURES USED AS INTERVENTION 'LEVERS'

In addition to its law-making and support of self-regulating business bodies, a UK government has the following fiscal or money measures at its disposal when intervening in markets in order to bring about, say, an increase in consumption, a reining back of demand or the development of a given economic sector:

- **direct taxation** – the increase or decrease in the levels of: corporation tax, PAYE or NIC payments, taxes on share dividends etc.
- **indirect taxation** – increases or decreases in VAT, Customs & Excise duties (say on alcoholic beverages, tobacco or imported gifts) road fund licences, airport taxes etc.
- **creation of new taxes** – such as the VAT on fuel and the air-travel tax introduced in 1994
- **government spending** – increases or decreases in the money which a government may spend on transport, defence, education, social services, health etc. which has a major influence on the national economy in terms of circulating money, creating or destroying jobs, stimulating or curtailing company growth etc.
- **providing grants, subsidies, tax rebates** – a UK government can energise a particular region, industrial sector or type of worker by making available finance in one of many forms, such as a study/training grant, factory-building subsidy or corporation tax rebate in order to stimulate local employment, specialised workers or regional redevelopment
- **the sale of state-owned assets** – in order to save the costs of running a state service and to capitalise on the assets the service possesses (e.g. the national telephone exchange and line network) a government may sell it off to individual and institutional buyers (e.g. British Telecom, British Gas, regional water and electricity companies etc.) – such sales are termed privatisations

PC
1.3.2
1.3.3

■ Privatisation and government market intervention

For over fifteen years, a succession of Conservative governments has implemented a party policy of privatising various state services and utilities.

EXAMPLES OF PRIVATISATION

State-run service/utility	Privatised equivalent
Post Office Telephones	British Telecom
Regional Gas Boards	British Gas
Regional Water Boards	privatised counterparts e.g. Southern Water
Regional Electricity Boards	privatised counterparts e.g. North West
Civil Airports Authority	British Airports Authority
British Leyland	The Rover Group
etc.	etc.

Currently, British Rail is undergoing a transitional phase prior to privatisation of its services and moves to privatise the Post Office have, as a result of public opinion, been mothballed for the time being.

The government's rationale for dismantling the nationalised, public sector industries which still existed in 1979 comprised the following set of convictions:

- public sector, nationalised industries result in a drain on the public purse, which privatisation would end, since they would be financed through the issue of shares in the private sector, as well as from profits earned
- public sector monopolies (e.g. gas, water, electricity, telecommunications, steel, transport etc.) tend to become over-manned and inefficient (through a lack of competition); they would therefore benefit from the more rigorous approach of the private sector
- public sector industries tend to possess large trade union memberships, which are not traditionally minded to vote conservative.

Also, by obliging local county, district and borough councils to put out to tender various services formerly run in-house (street-cleaning, refuse collection, school-dinner catering, road mending etc.) Conservative governments were able to reduce the costs of local government work forces, where council departments did not secure tenders and therefore reduced staff numbers. Where they did win tenders, the operational costs were usually reduced as a result.

PC
1.3.2
1.3.3

■ Voluntary self-regulation

Some industries and professions, such as advertising, medicine – in terms of its doctors – television, newspapers and solicitors prefer to regulate themselves, rather than have to submit to statutory control. For example, a doctor who acts unprofessionally will be investigated by the British Medical Association and may be struck off its register, thus becoming unable to practise. Similarly, the Independent Television Commission may fine

DISCUSSION TOPICS

PC 1.3.2 1.3.3

1 How successful do you consider the privatisations of the past fifteen years to have been?

2 To what extent has the privatisation of the gas, water and electricity nationalised services resulted in the creation of competition in the market-place for these services?

3 Has privatisation of nationalised industries reduced or increased prices paid by the public for the goods or services purchased?

4 What services and utilities should remain under state control? Why? If none, why none?

heavily commercial television companies which break the code of practice to which they agree to abide. The Football Association has similar powers, as for instance when it disallowed Swindon Town Football Club's promotion to the Premier Division. Regulatory and voluntary codes of practice, such as that of the newspaper industry's Press Council, act as a means of avoiding government legislation, which might prove far more constricting and demanding. In 1994 the newspaper industry – largely as a result of intrusive and harassing photographers – narrowly avoided the enactment of a privacy bill as a result of public annoyance with door-step squatting *paperazzi*.

The impact of government policies and interventions upon markets

PC 1.3.3

In western democratic states almost all governments espouse policies which will:

- increase general economic affluence
- increase full-time employment
- lessen the gap between the rich and the poor in society
- reduce taxation
- improve education and training
- provide better health care
- improve the environment, or prevent its further damage

As has been outlined above, various types of democratic government make use of economic, fiscal and legislative inducements or deterrents (e.g. advertising laws, regional development grants or tax holidays for re-locating firms etc.) in order to achieve the policies they devise. Such policies may have significant impacts upon business organisations and markets in the following ways.

The effect of the disappearance of traditional industries on a region (e.g. ship-building in Northern Ireland and Tyneside) may be offset by government-induced relocation of existing industries (such as business park and shopping mall development) or by persuading overseas industries to set up shop – as did Nissan in Sunderland. The privatisation of nationalised industries is beginning to encourage competition in what were monopolistic markets – domestic telephones are now sold in small-trader shops across a host of brands, and companies such as Cellnet and Vodaphone compete in the mobile phone market.

Also, the Conservative government's policy of creating markets for education and health (in order to promote competition leading to better services and to save money in areas of huge government spending) has resulted in schools, FE colleges, general practitioners' surgeries and hospitals become much more financially independent and responsible for their activities.

PC 1.3.3

EXAMPLES OF THE IMPACT OF GOVERNMENT INTERVENTION ON MARKETS

This process of deregulating both private and public sector industries and services has acted as a two-edged sword, as the following examples indicate:

- The price of gas has gone down by some 15 per cent over the past five years.
- Old-age pensioners are paying much more in some UK regions for their water supply than they did prior to privatisation.
- Some housing estates receive a much worse bus service since the introduction of private bus companies.
- Telecommunication services have expanded significantly since British Telecom was created.
- UK regions, such as the North East, Wales and Merseyside have benefited from government business relocation and job-creation policies and financial support (as also from European Union financial aid).
- The leisure and entertainment and tourism markets have blossomed as a result of a succession of deregulatory laws – for example on Sunday opening hours for pubs, horse-racing on Sundays and flexible opening hours for public houses generally.
- Since the 1988–93 recession, more part-time jobs are being advertised and fewer full-time ones, as a result of government 'flexible jobs' policies; however, EU regulations recently gave part-time employees the same employment rights as their full-time counterparts.
- True competition in many privatised industries – water, gas, electricity, telecommunications, rail services etc. – is either in its infancy or has yet to happen, despite billions of pounds of income having been secured on its promise.

In other words, deregulation has resulted in some successes and some failures so far. In essence, the current market economy approach is intended to bring about:

- more personal self-reliance and thus less dependency upon the state among individuals, which should result in a lowering of state social expenditure, as private pensions and health insurance companies replace state equivalents
- increasing rewards for business entrepreneurs who create markets, money and employment and thus increase general affluence
- decreases in personal and corporate taxation, since the state provides fewer services
- a sharper, more competitive national economy, since over-manning, the rescue of 'lame duck' businesses and subsidising of state-run industries have been eradicated

However, such intended aims are not always met. In the recessions of the 1970s large numbers of heavy industry businesses went bankrupt and the UK's industrial base was badly weakened as a result. In competing countries, however, temporary government support enabled similar industries to recover and take over what were UK export markets in areas such as textiles, locomotive construction and heavy machine engineering.

A recent civil service enquiry into increasing poverty in the UK came across a situation in a council housing estate, where the scheduled bus services run by its local council were radically reduced by private bus companies when they took over the service. Insufficient use made frequent service no longer cost-effective and so routes and time-tables were cut right back. As a result, a number of residents who had managed to find work were unable to get to their workplaces, and so had to fall back on unemployment benefit and income support etc. In this instance, well-meaning deregulation proved counter-productive.

On the credit side, government interventions into business markets aimed at encouraging entrepreneurs and business expansion have made significant strides since the late 1970s. For example, the management buy-out of the truck-making DAF UK Limited, the creation of the privatised Rover Group and British Telecom, the introduction of new industries to the south Wales valleys, Tyneside and south Yorkshire have all resulted in significant commercial success.

By the same token, government intervention in local labour markets through the creation of a network of 82 *Training and Enterprise Councils (TECs)* has enabled small firms to take on employees and trainees they otherwise could not have afforded to. The TECs have also provided pump-priming finance for business start-ups, loans to enable redundant professionals to retrain and free job-finding resources and support for longer-term unemployed people – all of which has much assisted local businesses and economies over the past decade.

PC
1.3.1
1.3.2
1.3.3

DISCUSSION TOPICS

1 Can a business market ever exist free from government intervention? If it can, what are likely to be the results?

2 Are current UK markets better or worse off as a result of government deregulations? Remember that a market comprises: employers, employees, sellers and buyers, products and services.

3 In what ways do government policies affect: supply and demand, price structures, efficiency and effectiveness and social fairness in UK markets?

4 Were successive Conservative governments right or wrong in privatising a wide range of nationalised industries since 1979?

5 What benefits society more in the long run – a government which largely keeps out of the business market-place, or one which views the close management of the national economy as part of its legitimate activities?

PC 1.3.3

The effects on markets of European Union (EU) policies

Since the Treaty of Rome was signed in 1957, the influence of the European Union has grown strongly, embracing all economic sectors and activities. The crops grown by UK farmers are now monitored by EU satellite cameras, the production of foodstuffs and manufactured goods have to conform to an encyclopaedia of regulations and EU articles, and business-related services such as finance and insurance also now have to comply with EC regulations.

The economic policies of the EU include:

- the establishment of a tariff-free internal market among member states – the Single Market of 1992 was established by the Single European Act 1988; the creation of an open financial services market further underpins this development (*Directive 92/12/EEC and the Investment Services Directive 1990*)
- the free movement of individuals and enterprises among member states in order to work or set up businesses, together with a progressive harmonisation of trade and professional vocational qualifications (see *Certificates of Experience*)
- working towards monetary union based around the ECU – the European Currency Unit. The Exchange Rate Mechanism (ERM) was established to harmonise the relative exchange rates of member states within a set of wide and narrow bands allocated respectively to less and more economically powerful states (see the *European Monetary System 1979*)
- the progressive creation of a unified system of company law and underpinning regulations to integrate and harmonise areas like contracts, product advertising and descriptions, quality, health and safety standards etc. (*Directives 89/666/EEC, 88/627/EEC,* and especially the *European Company Statute COM/91/174*)
- the removal of unfair barriers to trade (*Article 30*) and the implementation of fair competition laws (*Single European Act 1988, Articles 85/1 and 86*)
- the harmonisation of working conditions for employees – the Social Chapter of the Maastricht Treaty (Articles 117–122 of Maastricht Treaty)
- the progressive harmonisation of Value Added Tax percentages for goods and services of a common type (*Directive 91/680/EEC*)
- the further development of a Common Agricultural Policy (CAP) and the establishment of common food and animal transportation and slaughtering laws (*Directives 77/94, 79/112, 89/109/EEC, 89/397/EEC 91/628/EEC and 92/5/EEC*)
- the standardisation of procedures and practices for governments procuring goods and services so as to eliminate bias towards a member state's own businesses and utilities (the *Supplies, Works, Services, Utilities and Remedies Directives*)
- a unified policy for consumer protection (*Directives 84/450/EEC, 85/374/EEC, 88/314/EEC and 87/102/EEC etc.*)
- a common environmental policy for protecting the natural resources of all member states (*The Single European Act 1988,* and some 338 directives covering areas like water pollution, dangerous chemicals and the protection of rural areas etc.)

- an open systems policy for unifying information technology and computer systems (*the Open Network Provision Directive, and 92/38/EEC on television signal broadcasting by satellite*).

(*Source: The Single Market: The Facts*, published by the Department of Trade and Industry, August 1992)

Other policy areas covered by EC Directives, Articles, regulations include:

- transport
- standards
- intellectual property
- pharmaceuticals
- health and safety
- collaborative research and development.

As may be seen by the above (by no means exhaustive) checklist, European Union business and economic policy has – over a period of some thirty years – been supplied with an impressive set of 'teeth' in the form of directives, articles and statutes. These enable the European Commission and the judiciary of member states to enforce laws which aim to create a unified set of standards of business activity and to construct a legal and bureaucratic infrastructure which will lead, inexorably, to 'an ever-closer union' of member states.

As the above series of EC directives and Articles illustrate, the European Community's Commission in Brussels has intervened directly and with highly visible results across an extensive range of commercial and industrial markets in all member states. Much of this intervention has been undertaken in order to harmonise EU business practices – in, say, the labelling and description of goods, the working conditions of employees (see the *Social Charter*), and the standardisation of computer operating systems, so as to promote easier inter-Union communications.

Similarly, EC legislation ensured that the *Single Market* introduced on 1 January 1993 provided the businesses of each member state with a single, flat playing-field on which to 'play' when all tariffs and barriers were removed from all markets within the EU.

In order to avoid the creation of an over-zealous Brussels bureaucracy, however, the concept of *subsidiarity* was agreed upon by member states, which in effect states that, where a matter is being effectively handled by the government of a member state, then no additional legislation by EC institutions (the Brussels Commission, the European parliament, the Council of Ministers) should be introduced.

UK government policies and international markets

PC 1.3.3

■ As a member of the European Community

Currently about a half of all of the UK's overseas trade is with other members of the European Community. Indeed, the transition away from trading predominantly with British Commonwealth countries like Canada, Australia and New Zealand, to Germany,

France, Italy and the Netherlands has been remarkable since the United Kingdom joined the European Economic Community in 1973. Understandably, UK economic policy is now to promote strenuously the expansion of UK businesses into the European Single Market through fiscal incentives (such as the fortuitous devaluation of the pound sterling in September 1992) and government-sponsored export drives and initiatives from the Department of Trade and Industry in particular.

PC 1.3.3

■ As a member of the General Agreement on Tariff and Trade (GATT)

Since joining, the UK has naturally been obliged to harmonise its own international trade and economic policies with the unified positions adopted by all member states as European Community policy. A recent example of this was in the 1993 series of negotiations of the Uruguay Round of talks on the General Agreement on Tariffs and Trade (GATT). GATT was established in 1948 as a forum for some 25 states which wished to encourage mutual trade by reducing as much as possible the tariff barriers erected by members to protect their own national industries from external competition. Such protectionism was found to be counter-productive to sustaining general economic prosperity in the long run.

Following upon the setting up of GATT, series or rounds of trade negotiations were held every few years. The Uruguay Round started in 1986 and a new set of tariffs and agreements was finally agreed in principle in January 1994.

In the spring of 1993 the USA imposed additional tariffs on steel imports to protect its own industry (in deep recession) and came into conflict with the French who were being intransigent over allowing USA cereals into France at the levels the USA wanted. At the time, general agreement on the Uruguay Round was very close, and other member states, including the UK, put pressure on both the USA and France to make concessions so as to avoid a total GATT break-down. This would have had the effect of a melt-down on the recession-hit economies of the GATT member states, since ensuing protectionism and tariff barrier hikes might well have led to a world slump.

In the summer of 1993, at a Tokyo summit of the G7 Group (the seven most economically powerful states in the world) President Clinton led the Group into a set of agreed compromises which saved the GATT negotiations and rescued the prospect of bringing an end to the international recession and to creating an economic climate in which some 40 million unemployed people could be got back into work.

PC 1.3.2 1.3.3

■ Promoting UK exports

Against this GATT background it is not difficult to see why successive UK governments are constantly negotiating with trading partners of all complexions to:

- reduce tariffs and quotas
- encourage reciprocal amounts of trading (so as not to upset balance of trade and payments equilibriums)
- open up new markets and seize upon new trading opportunities.

■ The Organisation for Economic Cooperation and Development

PC 1.3.3

To support such international trading policies, the Organisation for Economic Cooperation and Development (OECD) which includes EC states, USA, and Japan focuses upon helping poor, Third World economies to develop trading links with GATT and G7 member states.

■ Intervention to prevent unfair subsidising of imported goods and dumping

PC 1.3.2 1.3.3

The counterpart for UK governments to encouraging trade with foreign countries lies in preventing unfair trading practices such as dumping and excessive overseas governments' subsidies of imported goods. Such practices lead to significant influxes of foreign imports into the UK which are offered for sale at prices well below those which UK manufacturers can match. For example, in order to gain a foothold in an affluent nation's economy some foreign governments may well provide significant financial support for the production of personal computers, the growing of foodstuffs or the extraction of raw materials.

By the same token, goods like cotton garments, motor-vehicle tyres, and timber may be produced in countries where labour, production and partial distribution costs are significantly lower than in countries like the USA, Japan or EU states. Such products – given the chance – may well be dumped into overseas markets. To prevent such practices, governments usually restrict their importation by imposing swingeing import duties and quotas (ceiling totals of goods which may be imported in any year). It is often difficult to see in some national economies where justified intervention ends and unwarranted protectionism begins.

■ International trade and regional policy

PC 1.3.2 1.3.3

The government of the United Kingdom as a member state of the EC receives finance from the European Regional Development and Social Funds which are specifically targeted on regional areas whose economies have suffered, for example, from structural economic decline resulting from the demise of a traditional industry such as mining, shipbuilding or fishing. Such funds are often used to pump-prime the creation of new industries – information technology, telecommunications, tourism etc. – which will attract foreign currency either through exports or an increase in overseas tourists. They are also employed to provide reskilling and retraining programmes for local inhabitants made redundant from obsolete occupations.

PC
1.3.1
1.3.2
1.3.3

REVIEW TEST

1 Why has the role of the UK government in the economy grown so dramatically during the past 150 years?

2 List three main arguments both for and against the privatisation of state-run industries.

3 What are the major economic policies which virtually all democratically elected governments seek to achieve? Explain briefly the rationale for each one.

4 What is meant by the term social equalisation? Why should a government be concerned to sustain a policy of social equalisation?

5 In what ways can a government influence the activities of a mixed economy?

6 What is likely to happen in a developed economy if its budget deficit is allowed to increase uncontrollably?

7 What do you understand by the term Keynesian economics?

8 Explain what part is played in the UK by the Public Sector Borrowing Requirement.

9 What case can you make for preferring a system of indirect as opposed to direct taxation?

10 What do these abbreviations stand for: ERM, ECU, OECD, GATT, G7?

11 List five ways in which Britain's membership of the European Community since 1973 has affected the government's relationship with the UK economy.

12 List five different economic policies which currently impact upon the UK economy.

13 What is meant by the term 'dumping'? What can a government do to prevent it?

14 How does GATT seek to develop international trade?

KNOWLEDGE TEST

Element 1.3
Examine the effects of government policies on markets

1 (i) A government will intervene in a market to prevent regulation occurring.
(ii) A government will intervene in a market to route economic support to an economically weak region of the country.

Which of the following options best describes the above statements?

A	(i)	T	(ii)	T
B	(i)	T	(ii)	F
C	(i)	F	(ii)	T
D	(i)	F	(ii)	F

2 Which of the following statements is true, and which false?

A The UK government is currently entitled to impose import tariffs. on goods from an EC member state if home markets are threatened.

B As a result of privatisation, domestic consumers must seek redress in the Small Claims Court if they are overcharged on a water, gas or electricity bill.

C Enterprise Zones no longer exist in the UK.

D As a result of signing the Maastricht Treaty, the UK must introduce the EC Social Charter by June 1998.

3 Which of the following policies do democratic governments seek to achieve when interacting with markets?

A To counteract anti-competitive activities

B To encourage the growth of oligopolies

C To protect the consumer

D To shield multinational companies from currency fluctuations

4 Which of the following do governments tend to see as arch-enemies of its economy?

A Unregulated growth of its export sales

B Annual net inflows of consumer goods from overseas

C Yearly increases in inflation

D Surpluses in its balance of payments

5 (i) The five main clearing banks meet monthly to agree upon the interest rates which they will levy on industrial and commercial loans.

(ii) The Bank of England works as the government's agent in ensuring that increases or decreases in the UK bank rate are adopted by the clearing banks.

Which of the following options best describes the above statements?

A	(i)	T	(ii)	T
B	(i)	T	(ii)	F
C	(i)	F	(ii)	T
D	(i)	F	(ii)	F

6 Which of the following statements is true, and which false?

A The Chancellor of the Exchequer announces the UK annual budget in March of each year, and changes in taxation the following November.

B JM Keynes advocated using public spending as a means of getting an economy going again after a recession.

C All governments seek to control the money supply in their economies.

D High levels of personal, direct taxation can be counter-productive in terms of increasing a government's revenue.

7 (i) The UK's exit from the EU's Exchange Rate Mechanism in September 1992 resulted in an increase in its exports.
(ii) EU policy is to introduce a single currency by the year 2000.

Which of the following options best describes the above statements?

A	(i)	T	(ii)	T
B	(i)	T	(ii)	F
C	(i)	F	(ii)	T
D	(i)	F	(ii)	F

PC
1.3.1
1.3.2
1.3.3

PORTFOLIO OF EVIDENCE ACTIVITY

Element 1.3
Examine the effects of government policies on markets

BRAINS STORM AT INSTITUTE OF MARKETING MANAGERS' SEMINAR!

Scenario

You and a number of professional acquaintances (all members of the Institute of Marketing) are currently attending a two-day seminar being run by the Institute with the aim of improving and developing members' understanding of the ways in which the UK government seeks to influence markets – both locally and nationally. After a series of presentations on the subject, you have been divided into groups and given a brief to brainstorm on this subject.

Each group member has been asked to abide by the rules of brainstorming, to take personal notes of the session and to produce afterwards a summary of the reasons why governments intervene in markets.

The organisers of the seminar also want each group to produce a recorded discussion on the subject: *The reasons for government interventions in markets*. The discussion should include arguments for and against government influence upon markets.

Task 1

Before embarking on any of the following three Tasks, make sure that you fill out the appropriate parts of your activity and review plan and complete it before handing it in with your Task activities.

Task 2

Having decided upon the size and composition of your brainstorming group, undertake the session which forms part of the IM's seminar. Remember that in brainstorming you should not disagree with someone's point or suggestion but note it down. Also, you should note down the main 'for and against' points about the subject of government interventions.

Your brainstorming session should last about 30 minutes, and the ensuing writing up of your notes about another 30 minutes.

Task 3

Having gained the benefit of the brainstorming session, Task 3 requires your group to take part in the discussion: *The reasons for government intervention in markets*. You should arrange for a member of your group to act as chairperson, and also for someone outside of the group to check and monitor the recording equipment your group uses. Your recorded discussion should last between 15–20 minutes.

Note: Your group may use either audio or video-recording equipment, and should arrange for each participating group's recordings to be played back in a general class session, so as to enable students to compare notes etc.

Task 4

This Task involves you on an individual basis in writing up notes of the above discussion.

Remember to cover the main points made during the discussion, and to include details of arguments both for and against government intervention in markets.

Having obtained your data from the discussion, produce a suitably formatted summary on about two sides of A4, either hand-written or text-processed after consultation with your teacher.

Performance criteria covered

1.3.1, 1.3.2, 1.3.3

Core skills covered

Communication:
3.1.1, 3.1.2, 3.1.3, 3.1.4, 3.1.5, 3.2.1, 3.2.2, 3.2.3, 3.2.4, 3.2.5, 3.4.3, 3.4.4

Information Technology:
3.3.1, 3.3.2, 3.3.3, 3.3.4, 3.3.5, 3.3.6 – if the notes are produced via software

GLOSSARY OF MACRO-ECONOMIC SPECIALIST TERMS

The term macro-economic simply describes a national or international economy within which individual businesses function. The following glossary explains some of the major terms you will encounter when researching business activities on a nationwide scale:

Balance of trade: the position which results from a nation's imports and exports being measured against each other; an adverse balance of trade is where the cost of imports exceeds the earnings secured from exports.

Bank of England: the UK's central bank which acts as the government's banker and controls the levels at which clearing banks lend out money.

Bank rate: the level of interest charged by a country's central bank for providing loans to commercial banks who use it as a means of setting their own lending rate – at a number of percentage points above it.

Capital: another collective term for the various components – buildings, equipment, raw materials, finished and semi-finished goods and money and transport fleets of lorries and cars available to an enterprise which are used as the 'building blocks' of business.

Commodities: this term serves as a combined label for both items or products which are manufactured and more intangible services such as legal advice.

Competition: the existence of entrepreneurs or businesses which vie with each other to supply the needs of a perceived market: note the term 'perfect competition' – a concept in which many businesses produce similar commodities at an equal advantage and in which newcomers can become established readily.

Corporation tax: a tax which is imposed upon businesses by the Inland Revenue in order to secure money for redistribution; also used by the government as a kind of regulator to discourage inflation, since high rates of corporation tax slow down growth and thus affect demand.

Demographic trends: this term describes movements and changes in a nation's population caused by factors such as the distribution of age-groups, immigration and emigration, employed and unemployed ratios, racial mix, levels of education, gender split and so on.

Elasticity: demand for some products is closely affected by the price at which they are sold in relation to the prices of competing commodities; where a change in price produces significant changes in demand, a commodity is termed 'elastic', when demand is almost unaffected, it is called 'inelastic'.

Free market economy: an economy in which prices are allowed to fluctuate according to variations in supply and demand and the availability of resources; compare this with a centralised or command economy such as existed in the Soviet Union, which set prices centrally for commodities and controlled the distribution of resources.

Gross domestic product (GDP): the total in pounds sterling of all the internal or domestic goods and services produced by a nation.

Gross national product (GNP): the total in pounds sterling of a what a nation produces, including income from overseas earnings such as insurance and other 'invisible' exports.

Inflation: a condition in which the spending power of money declines because too much money is chasing too few commodities.

Labour: a term used to describe the workforce in an enterprise or available for work in an economy; sometimes referred to as human resources.

Mixed economy: an economy which is partially 'free' and partially controlled by the state through the public ownership of certain industries such as energy and transport.

Monopoly: legally a situation in which a single business controls 25 per cent or more of a specific market; note the existence of the Commission for Monopolies and Mergers, the government agency which rules on whether a monopoly has been created and imposes strict penalties on guilty parties.

Opportunity cost: whenever a new proposal is considered to produce a product or service, an estimated cost will be drawn up; thus an opportunity cost is the cost of not being able to do something else with the sum devoted to the new project.

Output: a measurement of work achieved by an individual operative, a factory or a national economy; output may be measured in pounds sterling gained by the sale of goods made within a timescale, or the number of units produced, or the number of man-hours taken to achieve a set task, etc.

Production: the process of making a good or product; economists have traditionally viewed the production process as requiring capital, land, labour and business ingenuity or enterprise.

Profit: profit is generally defined as the difference between the amount received from the sale of a commodity and its cost of production – after overheads and other running costs are taken into account; other factors impinge on such a profit, such as directors' remunerations, dividends awarded and taxes due.

Resources: in economic terms, resources may be: money, materials, labour, land and know-how; the comparative availability of such resources, say, between competing trading nations,will significantly affect their ability to bring goods to the market which will sell and secure profits. For example, scarce resources such as uranium or a world-class pharmaceutical chemist will command high prices where an established demand exists.

Supply and demand: a central concept in macro-economics which serves as a kind of shorthand for market-place transactions in which the makers of commodities and their prospective purchasers between them evolve a market price for an item, being that at which they are respectively willing to sell and buy.

INDIVIDUAL ACTIVITY

Keep a notebook handy for jotting down specialist terms like those above and make a point of looking them up in a dictionary of economic or business terms – or ask your teacher to explain them.

Also, make a point of browsing through the business and financial pages of a good quality newspaper in your library during your studies, since seeing terms like those described above used in a current business context will help bring them to life and help you to absorb their meaning.

PC
1.1.1
1.1.2
1.1.3
1.1.4

CASE STUDY

The Safeway way

Read the following case study carefully, and then carry out the assignments which follow.

Road to the busy aisles

Why the group is big in Britain

America's Safeway Stores first signalled an interest in the United Kingdom in 1954 when it registered Safeway Food Stores, a UK subsidiary, with a nominal capital of £100, Derek Harris writes.

Not until seven years later, however, did the Americans strike out from their toehold. The subsidiary's capital was hoisted to £2 million as Safeway decided that Britain was ready to follow the American grocery retailing path to big, self-service, one-stop stores, at which a customer would do a bumper weekly shop.

After months of speculation as a Safeway team sized up the expanding UK retail scene, it was announced in the middle of 1962 that an association was being negotiated with the supermarket offshoots of John Gardner of London. There were eight supermarkets, plus warehousing, trading under two different fascias, Gardner and Prideaux, reflecting an earlier merger.

The arrangement was finalised on September 20 1962. The Gardner parent company was given £1 million in cash and a third interest in the new company. Safeway Food Stores was in business, with a mainly British directorship and management.

While the negotiations were going on, the British Safeway had started developing its first store, at Bedford, with selling space of 20,000 sq ft. It is hard to grasp the impact then of such trading methods on Britons. When the Bedford store opened in 1963, police had to be brought in to control the crowds.

As the Gardner stake in Safeway dwindled until its interests were bought out by Safeway, expansion was pursued. The first Safeway store in Scotland opened in 1965 in Glasgow. By 1969, Safeway sales were breaking the £20 million barrier. The following year, it opened a state-of-the-art central distribution centre at Aylesford in Kent.

In 1975 Terry Spratt, formerly the Prideaux manager, became chairman and managing director of the UK Safeway operation. By 1982, expansion had increased the work-force to more than 10,000.

The next year was marked by the opening of the 100th Safeway store. Profits exceeded £20 million.

The watershed years for Safeway were 1986 and 1987. Its American parent, which had run into problems, sold the UK operation.

In February 1987, the Argyll Group, which traded mainly as Presto, bought the UK Safeway with its 132 stores for £681 million. Argyll wanted to pick up the Safeway magic: its trading techniques, management expertise and methods. That year, seven big Presto stores were converted to Safeway outlets. As they were converted, staff were retrained to Safeway standards.

When Safeway opened its first store in Wales, at Colwyn Bay, in 1987, sales exceeded £1 billion for the first time.

Eventually, 140 transformed Prestos swelled the Safeway chain. The combination of conversions from Presto stores, plus greenfield store openings, meant that by the middle of 1989 Safeway owned 250 stores, and 275 by November. In that year, too, Safeway appointed a director with responsibility for environmental issues on store and product fronts, and set up an environment policy committee.

Safeway had already begun to collect awards for its fresh food and "green" policies. By 1990, Safeway was accounting for 72 per cent of Argyll's £4.1 billion turnover.

Twenty-three new Safeway stores opened during the year. By the end of 1990, Safeway had 310 stores operating and its new Coventry outlet became the 200th store with laser scanning checkouts. Coventry, with its 24-hour petrol station, rated "flagship" status as it came into operation just before Christmas, with nearly 40,000 sq feet of selling space.

The following year, Argyll, mainly through the Safeway expansion, became the third force in food retailing after J Sainsbury and Tesco. Operating profits rose by 27 per cent to £285.3 million. By now, 50,000 people were on the Safeway payroll – 30,000 more than when Argyll acquired Safeway. That year, at Bellshill in Scotland. Safeway opened Europe's biggest food distribution centre, which from May 1991 supplied nearly 300 stores with three temperature-graded goods – ambient, chilled and frozen.

The retailer has been working to close the UK's food and drink trade gap in a project co-sponsored with farmers and manufacturers aimed at creating more sales opportunities for British food suppliers.

Now 322 Safeway stores include more than 50 in-store pharmacies, nearly 270 bakeries, more than 40 coffee shops, ten post offices, seven dry-cleaners and more than 30 petrol filling stations

ASSIGNMENTS

Group activities

In groups of two or three, read the above history of Safeway's start-up and development in Britain and then carry out the following assignments:

1 Identify what you think were the key factors in Safeway's growth in Britain, from a company with a nominal capital of £100 in 1954, to 1992, when its turnover was in excess of £2.95 billion. Present your conclusions in a written discussion which compares Safeway's approach with that of other food stores you are familiar with in your own locality.

2 From your reading of the article, consider the extent to which Safeway's retailing approach differs from that of other food retailers. First list the differences your group identifies and then, in a class discussion, identify what you believe to be the essential ingredients for successful food retailing in today's consumer food market.

3 If your group were part of the top management team at Argyll, what would be the main planks of your development strategy for Safeway until the end of the present decade? Produce your answer as an illustrated oral presentation including a clear rationale and give it to your class. As a class, decide which group devised the strategy most likely to succeed.

Individual activities

4 Research into Safeway's recent financial performance and compare it with that of other major food retailing multiples. Present your findings as a short, written briefing, highlighting the aspects you think most significant.

5 Find out how companies like Safeway organise their nationwide operations and how they seek to maximise efficiency and effectiveness through their organisational structures. Present your findings in an oral presentation to your group.

Discussion topics

1 Given the economies of scale which an operation like that of Safeway can achieve, which can be translated into very competitive sales pricing policies, is there a future for the 'corner shop' grocer and general store? If so, what sort of business and marketing plans would be likely to prove successful for such stores in an age of vast shopping malls and supermarkets?

2 If you were in charge of Safeway, would you decide to go for vertical integration from food growing to food retailing? If so, to what extent, and with what products initially?

What do you see as the comparative advantages and disadvantages of vertical integration for companies like Safeway, as opposed to a policy of sticking firmly to tertiary sector food retailing only?

PC
1.1.1
1.1.2
1.1.3
1.1.4

CASE STUDY 2

British Rail – the privatisation plans

British Rail was founded in 1948 with the amalgamation and nationalisation of loss-making private railway companies. The present government plans to reverse nationalisation and privatise BR during its present term of office. A White Paper was published in 1992, giving details of the privatisation plans for BR.

In recent years BR has been making huge losses. This presents a problem for privatisation. Who would want to buy an organisation making such large losses? Other major utilities which were privatised (such as gas, water and electricity) had some prospect of being turned into profit-making businesses. The prospects for BR are not as good because it is obliged to run loss-making services for a mixture of social, economic and political reasons.

For example, in the year ending March 1991, a decline in fare revenues and a fall in profits from the property holdings, resulted in losses of £93m, twice the previous year's losses. This was even after the government increased its subsidy to BR by 20 per cent from £500m to over £600m.

However not all BR's divisions make losses. InterCity, in spite of the economic recession, made profits of £50m before interest payments. The Railfreight division usually makes profits but made losses of £55m in 1990/91.

The two divisions which make the greatest losses are (i) Regional Railways (ii) Network SouthEast. Regional Railways made losses of £503m in 1990/91. This is the provincial train service burdened with the obligation to run a network of loss-making services considered to be socially desirable but not commercially viable.

Network SouthEast is the London commuter service. It made losses of £155m in 1990/91. This division has a virtual monopoly in commuter transport and could become commercially viable if fares are increased by over 50 per cent. Naturally such an option is not politically attractive.

With this pessimistic analysis, the government will not consider selling off BR as a single entity. To do so would simply change a public monopoly into a private monopoly.

The move to privatise BR can be divided into two phases (a) the deregulation of Britain's railways (b) privatising the railways. BR's statutory monopoly of train operations will end. At present other trains run on BR's tracks only with its permission. After privatisation other trains will have automatic access to the tracks and a statutory regulatory body (similar to Oftel in telecommunications i.e. a type of 'Ofrail') will ensure that BR charges fair prices for use of tracks.

The second stage is privatisation through a graduated sell-off or franchising-out of certain BR divisions.

1 **InterCity** – all of this profit-making division will be offered for sale complete with tracks and trains. InterCity will have to give other operators access to its tracks which will be a source of revenue but not necessarily competition as the main competitors for InterCity are planes and cars.
2 **Railfreight** – even though it made losses in 1990/91 it is regarded as having great potential for profits. As it owns very few tracks, it would depend on the official regulatory body to get fair treatment on track charges.
3 **Network SouthEast** – as it is currently making heavy losses, it cannot be sold in the near future. The government will retain the tracks and franchise out train services to private owners. This could attract private buyers as 45 per cent of the costs of running train operations relate to infrastructure (i.e. tracks and stations etc.). New private owners will have to pay for use of the tracks but these costs will be reduced by any subsidies available to keep fares at a reasonable level for commuters. Franchises will come up for renewal every few years.
4 **Regional Railways** – this division is so dependent on subsidies, it cannot be sold in a privatisation sale. Its tracks will be owned by the state. Private sector companies will be invited to submit tenders for five-year contracts to operate services.

The government's plans for privatising BR will be met with both criticism and praise. Long-suffering users of the present system will hope that changes will be for the better. Critics of the proposed changes will point to the many questions left unanswered – who will be responsible for safety? Will fares increase? Will uneconomic lines be closed? Will continued subsidies be available for loss-making services? Will the breakdown of private trains entitle other users of the same track to compensation for delays?

Reproduced from *A Summary of the UK Economy* '92/93' (editor D.C. McCarthy) Mentor Publications Dublin.

ASSIGNMENTS

Discussion topics

1 What arguments can you produce either in favour of or against the privatisation of British rail?

2 Given that most European governments subsidise their railway networks, what sort of services do you think a private operator would need to concentrate upon in order to make a profit out of railway transportation? Give reasons for selecting the services you identify.

3 What sort of freight services would a private operator need to develop in order to compete successfully with road haulage companies?

4 What safeguards would the government need to introduce into its privatisation bill in order to support those citizens with low incomes or on income support (and who do not possess motor-cars) who rely on rail transport within their local districts? What is likely to happen if a private operator decides to stop an uneconomic service or close an uneconomic line?

Or are such considerations no longer a government problem after privatisation?

5 To what extent is privatisation likely to lead to the profitable parts of BR being taken up by entrepreneurs (along with the profits generated), leaving the British taxpayer to continue paying for the unprofitable parts which cannot be sold? Can you suggest ways to resolve this dilemma?

6 How important in the privatisation of BR debate is the very high cost – and who will bear it – of replacing items of capital equipment such as track, buildings and bridges, trains and rolling stock?

Group activities

In groups of two or three:

1 Find out how privatisation plans are likely to affect BR's services in your locality and report back with an oral presentation to your class.

2 Find out how one of the following countries runs its railway network and how its management differs from that employed to run BR:

Germany
France
USA

Brief your group orally on what you discover.

3 Discuss the sort of checks and balances you would want to have written into the powers given to a public watchdog organisation – Ofrail – with the brief to ensure that key public needs and interests are protected after privatisation. Brief your class on your decisions in a general debate.

FURTHER SOURCES OF INFORMATION

Sources of economic and business information

A welter of government, public and private sector, European Community and international agency information is published at regular intervals of economic trends, outcomes, forecasts and results to assist both business and government economic analysts and financial services managers. The following list of such information sources is by no means exhaustive, but includes some of the most respectable and frequently quoted:

Her Majesty's Government (UK)

United Kingdom National Accounts (annual publication), CSO* referred to as 'The Blue Book'

Public Expenditure Analyses (annual publication), HM Treasury referred to as 'The Brown Book'

Financial Statement and Budget Report (annual publication), HM Treasury referred to as 'The Red Book'

The Employment Gazette, Department of Employment, HMSO (published monthly)

Social Trends, Economic Trends, Financial Statistics, CSO

Annual and Monthly Abstract of Statistics, CSO

Labour Market Statistics and Quarterly Reports, Department of Employment

Bank of England Monthly Factsheets and Quarterly Bulletins

Monopoly and Mergers Commission Reports

Overseas Trade Statistics of the UK

*Central Statistical Office

European Community sources

European Commission Publications, e.g. Eurostat, Annual Economic Reports etc.

European Central Bank (ECB)

European Parliament, UK Information Office

DTI: Single Market Bulletins and Booklets, e.g. 'Europe Open for Business'

Office For Official Publications Of The European Communities, Luxembourg

EC and international government-funded agencies

The Organisation For Economic Cooperation and Development (OECD)

The General Agreement on Tariffs and Trade (GATT)

The International Monetary Fund (IMF)

The World Bank

The World Resources Institute International

Labour Organisation (ILO)

UK private sector and professional institute information services

The Market Research Society

Phillips & Drew Monthly Economic Forecasts

Mintel Information Sources

Datastream, Dataline, Extat and ICC Eurocompany Information Services

Clearing Banks' Economic Reviews, e.g. Natwest, Royal Bank of Scotland

Building Society Quarterly and Annual Reports

UK Financial and Economic Publications

Financial Times

The Times, Daily Telegraph, Independent. European newspapers (and their Sunday publications)

The Economist (weekly magazine)

Further reading on business in the economy

The Organisation in its Environment, 4th edn, J Beardshaw and D Palfreyman, Pitman Publishing, 1990 ISBN: 0 273 03268 2

Economics, N Palmer, Folens Publishers, 1986

Introductory Economics, 5th edn, G F Stanlake, Longman, 1989. ISBN: 0 582 03695X

An Introduction to Positive Economics, 6th edn, R G Lipsey, Weidenfeld & Nicolson, 1983. ISBN: 0 297 78265 7

The Economy in Focus 1992/93, A Anderton, Causeway Press Limited, 1992. ISBN: 1 873929 013

Applied Economics: An Introductory Course, 5th edn, A Griffiths and S Wall, Longman, 1993 ISBN: 0 582 21430 0

Economics Made Simple, 14th edn, G Whitehead, Made Simple Books, 1992. ISBN: 0 7506 0526 X

Business and Enterprise Studies Made Simple, G Whitehead, Made Simple Books, 1990 ISBN: 0 7506 0730 0

European Studies, A A Scott, Pitman Publishing, 1992. ISBN: 0 273 03813 3

The Single Market: The Facts (Europe Open for Business Series) 10th edn, Department of Trade & Industry, HMSO, 1993

Business in Europe Series, Department of Trade & Industry, HMSO, 1993

Europe on the Move Series, Office for Official Publications of the European Communities, 1990 on

Public Administration in the UK, D Farnham and M McVicar, Cassell, 1982. ISBN: 0 304 30338 0

A Summary of the UK Economy Series, D C McCarthy (Ed.), Mentor Publications, 1992–93 on

Economics and the Banks' Role in the Economy, 2nd edn, G Lipscombe, Pitman Publishing, 1991 ISBN: 0 273 03250 X

UNIT

2

BUSINESS ORGANISATIONS AND SYSTEMS

Element 2.1
Investigate business organisations

Element 2.2
Investigate administration systems

Element 2.3
Analyse communication in a business organisation

Element 2.4
Analyse information processing in a business organisation

PERFORMANCE CRITERIA AND RANGE

Element 2.1: Investigate business organisations

PERFORMANCE CRITERIA

A student must: *page*

1 explain **objectives** of **business organisations** 99–101
2 explain the **differences** between **types of ownership** 101–11
3 **compare organisational structures** 111–22

RANGE

Objectives: manufacturing, providing services, financial (profit, profit improvement, not-for-profit); market share, public service
Business organisations: private sector, public sector; charities
Differences: type of liability (limited, unlimited), use of profit (owners, shareholders, government), sources of finance, control of organisation, legal obligations
Types of ownership: sole trader, partnership, private limited company (Ltd), public limited company (plc), franchise, co-operative, public (state, local authority)
Compare in terms of: size, location, type of product, functions, meeting business objectives, changes (to organisational structures, to location, to functions)
Organisational structures: simple, divisional (by function, by product, divisions of multinationals); matrix; centralised, decentralised; flat, hierarchical;

EVIDENCE INDICATORS

A report which explains and compares three business organisations with different types of ownership, one from the public and two from the private sector. For each organisation there should be an explanation of the broad financial objectives, explaining profit and not-for-profit motives. The report should include a more detailed explanation of how the financial, legal and controlling differences can influence the objectives of each type of organisation.
For the same three organisations, the report should compare organisational charts illustrating their different structures. Notes supporting the charts should comment on the differences between the structures and note recent or planned changes to either structures, location or functions.

Element 2.2: Investigate administration systems

PERFORMANCE CRITERIA

A student must: *page*

1 identify **administration systems** which support functions of business organisations 126–37
2 explain **suitability** of one **administration system** in an identified business organisation 132–7
3 identify how **information technology** developments can change **administration systems** 138–41
4 suggest **improvements** to an **administration system** 144–5

RANGE

Administration systems: purpose, processes, procedures, equipment (hardware, software)
Suitability in terms of: fitness for purpose, value for money, security, health and safety
Information technology: hardware, software, networks, commercial administration packages
Improvements: in service, in procedure, in equipment, in training

EVIDENCE INDICATORS

A report on an administration system used in one business organisation. The report should explain:

- the suitability of the system for the purpose of supporting one or more functions of the organisation
- how information technology is changing or has changed the administration system and suggest ways in which the administration system could be improved.

Element 2.3: Analyse communication in a business organisation

PERFORMANCE CRITERIA

A student must: *page*

1 identify **communication** in and between business organisations 146–9
2 identify and explain the **objectives of** internal and external **communication** 147–8
3 **analyse** the effectiveness of **communication** in a business organisation 149–58
4 explain possible **positive** and **negative effects** of changes to **communications** 159–61
5 suggest changes to improve **communications** in a business organisation 161–6

RANGE

Communication: internal, external; communication channels (restricted, open); using electronic technology; to meet special needs
Objectives of communication: provide information, give instructions, keep people up to date, make checks, receive feedback, negotiation, confirmation
Analyse in terms of: ease of use, access; efficiency of user (health, stress); interaction between people, interaction between organisations; confidentiality, security
Positive effects: improved speed of communication, improved access to communication, potential for communication to wider audience
Negative effects: incompatible equipment, cost, exclusion from communication, threat to security

EVIDENCE INDICATORS

A report which investigates at least two examples of internal and two examples of external communication in a business organisation. The report should explain how the business organisation uses its communications to achieve its objectives. The report should analyse at least one internal and one external electronic communication for its effectiveness in enabling access to information and interaction between people.
The report should include two proposals for changes to communications in the business organisation. The proposals should be justified in terms of their possible beneficial effects on the business organisation. This section should be supported by notes explaining at least two possible positive and two possible negative effects of changes to communications in the business organisation.

Element 2.4: Analyse information processing in a business organisation

PERFORMANCE CRITERIA

A student must: *page*

1 explain the **purposes** of **information processing** 167–9
2 describe **information processing** in one business organisation 169–209
3 **analyse** the effectiveness of **information processing** in one business organisation 169–209
4 explain the **effects of the Data Protection Act** on **information processing** 209–10

RANGE

Purposes: receiving information, storing information, using information, communicating information
Information processing: manual; single-purpose systems (word processing, number processing, spreadsheets, databases, graphics processing); multi-purpose systems
Analyse in terms of: fitness for purpose, cost and value for money, efficiency, information retention, security
Effects of the Data Protection Act: on individuals: access to information, security, ownership, accuracy, on business: ability to sell information to others, cost of meeting the Act

EVIDENCE INDICATORS

A report which explains the purposes and effectiveness of information processing in business organisations and describes the systems used for processing numbers, text and graphics in one organisation.
The report should include:

- an account which illustrates the effects of the Data Protection Act on an individual's rights to personal access to information, the security of that information, and the ownership and accuracy of the information held by an organisation about the individual.

INTRODUCTION

Unit Two explains how businesses are organised, what kinds of administrative systems they employ, how they use communications and telecommunications media in the course of their business activities and how they process information.

The past ten years have seen enormous changes taking place in the ways in which organisations – both private and public – operate. The ways in which people work have been radically altered as a result of advances in electronic office equipment, based upon the ever-present desk-top computer. Also, revolutions in telecommunications – global ethernet highways, mobile phones, data processing via satellite etc. – have likewise made information far more widely and instantly accessible.

As a result, organisations large and small have had to adapt their administrative systems, from traditional paper-based documentation to on-line, real-time and networked computerised counterparts. Also, IT and the 1988–93 UK recession have brought about significant changes in the ways in which people work – flexibly, part-time, and from home with modem connected to the office etc.

Moreover, there are yet more changes in the ways in which organisations operate in the pipe-line, as inter-active information and communication systems based on CD-Rom and multi-media software become more widely established. The next generation of computers will also be able to learn from their experiences and inputs! Unit Two, therefore, provides the student with an informed overview of current practices and future trends in a world where 'change is the only constant', and in which employees are increasingly required to undertake career-long self-updating and development in order to stay current.

Element 2.1
INVESTIGATE BUSINESS ORGANISATIONS

The objectives of organisations

PC 2.1.1

All organisations are created to meet specific objectives. A sole trader's objective is quite simply to earn his or her living, a partnership's to similarly provide an income for its partners. However, larger private or public limited companies have the prime objective of generating a satisfactory return on the investment provided by their shareholders. In the public sector, a borough, district or county council and various forms of publicly owned agency will have objectives involving meeting particular citizens' needs cost-effectively and caringly. Again, voluntary, charitable organisations will set themselves objectives for improving levels of aid and support for their targeted clients.

The following checklist illustrates the main reasons for organisations' operations in both private and public sectors:

CHECKLIST OF OBJECTIVES OF ORGANISATIONS

PC 2.1.1

Organisations tend to be created and developed in order to:

- extract materials or make goods and sell them on at a profit (primary and secondary sectors)
- acquire goods or services and sell them to customers at a profit (tertiary sector)
- increase profit levels by careful management and development of products and markets
- trade in the market-place in order to expand the business first and then to make profits from an enlarged customer base (i.e. increase market share and dominance)
- provide grants and allowances for people in various walks of life (e.g. the Paul Hamlyn Trust for employees working in publishing)
- supply aid and support to deserving causes (e.g. Oxfam, MIND, Help the Aged charities)
- provide local or national communities with a range of services cost-effectively (e.g. local councils and government agencies)
- extend knowledge or appreciation of a given area (e.g. libraries, museums, art galleries)

PC 2.1.1

EXAMPLES OF MAJOR TYPES OF ORGANISATION IN THE UK

Private sector	
Sole trader	the proverbial one-man or woman small trader
Partnership	a group of 2–20 people working together and sharing profits
Private limited company	a company run by directors who are usually also the shareholders
Public limited company	a company run by a set of managers for investing shareholders
Co-operative	a loose group of businesses which ally to gain, say, better buying terms
Franchise	a semi-independent business running as an outlet aided by a well-known business – The Body Shop, Kwik-Print, Bolloms etc.
Multiple	for example national high street chain-stores: Boots, John Lewis, Next etc.
Conglomerate	large companies operating divisions or subsidiaries in quite different areas like garages and hotels: LEX, Trafalgar House, BAT etc.
Multi-national	companies operating internationally: Hanson, IBM, Shell etc.
Privatised utilities	for example British Telecom, Regional Water and Electricity companies, British Gas etc.
Public sector	
Local councils	County, District, Unitary, Metropolitan and Borough
Dispersed government agencies	Health Authorities, Inland Revenue Offices, Births, Marriages and Deaths Registries, National Rivers Authority etc.
National government departments	Department of Employment: Whitehall and Job Centres; Ministry of Defence: camps, ranges, barracks etc. Department For Education & Training: schools, universities etc.
Public utilities	very few left now: remnants of British Rail, parts of the Post Office
Voluntary sector	
Charities	vetted by the Charities Commissioner and committed to being non-profit making
Charitable trusts	created to undertake community work or 'good works' which the government does not wish to become directly involved in e.g. educational examinations boards, cultural and environment-protecting bodies etc.

PC 2.1.1

■ Mission statements, corporate strategies and business plans

For the past decade or so, many business organisations have compressed their main objectives into two or three sentences and used the American term *mission statement* as a label for this basic and essential summary of the reason for their existence (see also Unit 8). A typical mission statement for a young, but ambitious road haulage company might be:

FAST-TRAK CARRIERS PLC

Mission Statement

- The mission of *Fast-Trak Carriers plc* is to construct within the next five years a national network of depots and fleet of vehicles capable of promising and achieving next-day deliveries anywhere in the United Kingdom.
- In achieving this goal, Fast-Trak will generate a net profit of at least 10% per annum on its turnover and by the end of the coming five years will have secured 15% of the national road haulage market.
- Fast-Trak is fully committed to maintaining the highest standards of quality, security and customer service and regards its workforce as its most important asset.

As the above example illustrates, good mission statements tend to express their goals and objectives in terms of finite, factual outcomes to be achieved: *national network, within the next five years, anywhere in the UK, 10% net profit, 15% of the national market* etc.

The final paragraph illustrates the type of mission statement objective which 'makes the right noises', but which it is not possible (as expressed) to measure. Effective mission statements provide *measurable* goals.

The objectives a business organisation commits to achieve over a period of 3–5 years are set out in more detail in a comprehensive corporate strategy (see also Unit 8), which also includes summaries of the business plans of a business's departments, as well as a marketing plan. In this way, organisational senior managers are provided with a blueprint against which to measure and monitor actual outcomes as against targeted ones.

Types of business and public sector organisation

PC 2.1.2

Figure 2.1 illustrates a kind of pathway up through which enterprising business people tend to travel as their businesses grow and prosper – from small-town sole trader to transcontinental conglomerate!

■ The sole trader

PC 2.1.2

Modestly situated at the foot of the inverted organisational pyramid is the sole trader. Sometimes referred to as a 'one-man-band' kind of business organisation, it is often just that. Usually, however, it is a family concern with either husband or wife taking a leading part. The small trader may rent modest premises such as a corner grocery shop or

PC 2.1.1

Fig 2.1 **An organisation's pyramid of relative influence and importance**

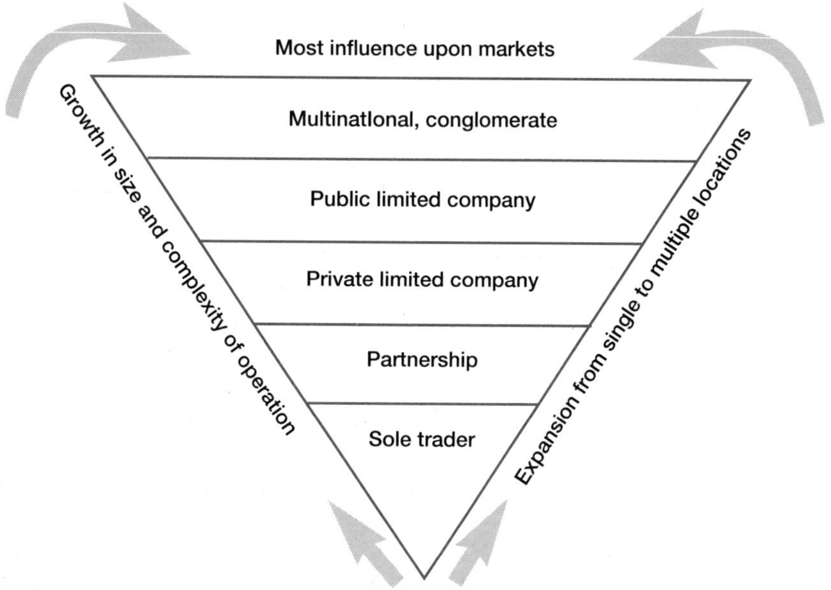
Most influence upon markets
Multinational, conglomerate
Public limited company
Private limited company
Partnership
Sole trader
Growth in size and complexity of operation
Expansion from single to multiple locations

'From small acorns mighty oak-trees grow.' Anon

newsagents, may work from home, or journey as a roundsman selling fresh fish or greengrocery products.

As a rule, sole trader businesses tend to be launched on very modest capital and operate on tight margins between the selling price of goods and services and the cost of operations. This is in no small part due to the inability of the small trader to benefit from bulk purchasing discounts. Though nowadays associations of small retailers group together to buy collectively and thus secure better terms.

In legal terms, it is very simple to become a sole trader, provided that the trading name and trade mark employed are not in existing use and comply with the Business Names Act 1985.

Sole traders currently need to register for VAT if annual sales are likely to exceed £44,000. Also, they are obliged in law to maintain proper records both for the payment of taxes and as an employer once staff are taken on. Prudent sole traders also take out public and employee liability, fire and theft insurance policies.

The trading edge in a local community enjoyed by the sole trader is summarised in Professor Schumacher's aphorism: 'Small is beautiful!' Communication is so easy if limited between a sole trader and his or her customers; decision-making is prompt if only a 'committee of one' has to be consulted. Similarly, business opportunities – to buy in stock at a bargain price, to spot a newly emerging fad or trend and to capitalise upon it – tend to be quickly spotted and taken. And it is much easier to keep a close eye and tight rein on sales and gross profits. All these benefits stem from running a small business enterprise with just a few people.

However, unless the business has been set up as a private limited company, the sole trader or business proprietor is entirely and personally liable for all debts that the business may incur once trading has commenced. Moreover, all the sole trader's personal assets and possessions could be sold from under him or her in order to pay off creditors in a bankruptcy action.

Given the modest cost of purchasing an existing but mothballed private limited company (about £100), it is astonishing that many sole traders still suffer in this way.

■ The partnership

PC 2.1.2

Often a business enterprise is created because of the shared expertise of two or more people and the fact that they can work well together. Customarily, partnerships are formed by between two and twenty partners (though there are exceptions). The relationship and respective job roles of partners is set out in articles of partnership, which will also make clear the respective share in profits due to each partner (according to the amount of capital brought into the partnership or the agreement made with other partners).

Like the sole trader, a partnership is required to maintain proper records and to comply with the relevant clauses of the Partnership and Companies Acts. Also in common with the sole trader, the business partner's liability for the debts incurred by the trading activities of the partnership is unlimited – though such liability is shared out pro rata to the partnership articles.

A typical business partnership evolves an effective division of labour – say, where one partner makes and the other sells, or where one partner oversees production while another coordinates administration. Alternatively, a partnership may comprise some active partners who run the business and one or more 'sleeping partners' who have invested in it and who secure an annual share of any profits made. Examples of business partnerships include management consultants, chartered accountants, retailers, architects and solicitors.

■ The private limited company

PC 2.1.2

In the mid-nineteenth century, the concept of limited liability was introduced into Great Britain. Initially it was aimed at limiting the liability of shareholders in failed companies but soon came to be used by the owners (as directors and shareholders) of small businesses as a means of separating their business and personal assets and liabilities. This was possible since, if a business went bankrupt, then its creditors could only seek repayment of monies owed from the sale of any assets which remained intact. The company as a legal entity had unlimited liability, but that of its directors was limited to the amounts they had invested in it.

Today private limited companies may be set up with a share valuation of a few hundred pounds divided among directors. If such businesses are launched on the basis of extensive loans from a bank, and if both premises and equipment are rented, then in the event of business failure very few if any realisable assets are likely to survive.

For this reason, detailed credit-worthiness references are required when a private limited company seeks to purchase goods or services on account. By the same token, a bank as a prospective investor in the business and as the lender of pump-priming, start-up finance will require security for any such loans. The securities the bank will want take the form of agreements to surrender to the bank the assets specified should the loan be defaulted upon. A bank will also set prudent limits on any overdraft facilities which are unsecured.

PC 2.1.2

Fig 2.2

Company directors' responsibilities

To shareholders:
- making a profit
- achieving the corporate plan
- maintaining an effective company
- sustaining statutory meetings and minutes
- ensuring all activities are legally transacted

To employees:
- insuring them against injury and accident
- maintaining PAYE and National Insurance payments
- maintaining data confidentiality
- observing employment law practices
- providing first-aid/medical facilities

For finances:
- keeping faithful records for auditing annually
- securing safely stocks and shares certificates
- recording directors' pay and withdrawals
- maintaining VAT records

For buildings:
- keeping them safe for public and employee use
- insuring them against fire, flood and other damage
- maintaining records of wiring conduits, cabling, etc.
- carrying out regular fire drills and emergency evacuation practices
- ensuring compliance with occupational use regulations, e.g. personal space, rest rooms, lavatories, etc.

. . . a director's life is not all

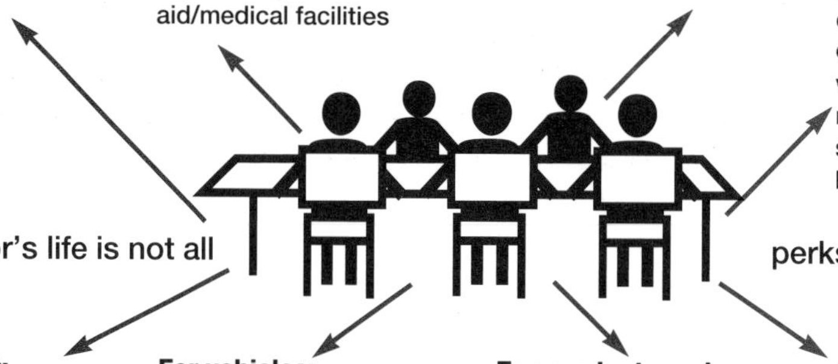

perks and junkets!

For equipment:
- ensuring regular maintenance and safety checks are made
- withdrawing from use defective plant and equipment
- complying with safety regulations
- safe disposal of waste

For vehicles:
- ensuring vehicles are safe to use and adequately maintained
- ensuring vehicles are covered under appropriate insurance
- maintaining road tax and MOT certificates
- fitting HGVs with tachographs

For products and services:
- complying with UK/EC safety and 'fitness for purpose' specifications
- ensuring goods are fairly described in advertisements
- maintaining production records and drawings of designs and blueprints

For records:
- keeping safely all deeds, share certificates, audited accounts, board of directors' minutes, contracts, production records, personnel records, etc. for the statutory periods set by law

In this way, lenders to private limited companies seek to minimise the risks they take, which they claim justify the comparatively high rates of interest they charge on such loans.

Private limited companies are required by law to draw up articles and memoranda of association. Such documents detail the precise nature of the business to be undertaken, the names and addresses of directors, the trading name and registered office of the company (usually located at the offices of its chartered accountant) and the value and allocation of shares issued. The directors will be responsible for supplying annual accounts for auditing by the company's appointed accountants prior to their despatch with an annual tax return to the allocated Inland Revenue Office. In addition, an annual return (Companies Form No 363) to the Registrar of Companies is required. This return updates any changes in directors and provides details of mortgage debts and issued share capital. It provides little or no information as to the trading performance of the company.

The various Companies Acts, and in particular the Act of 1985, define the legal liabilities of company directors of private (and public) limited companies. These include the calling of regular (usually annual) shareholders meetings, responsibility for tax and VAT returns and responsibilities under various Acts such as:

- The Factories Act 1961
- The Health and Safety at Work Act 1974
- Offices, Shops and Railway Premises Act 1963
- Employers' Liability (Compulsory Insurance) Act 1969
- Data Protection Act 1984.

The trading edge of private limited companies lies in their protection from hostile takeovers (their shares are not available for sale on public stock exchanges), the privacy they enjoy from competitor scrutiny (they do not have to publish detailed annual accounts), and their ability to react swiftly to changes in market trends. On the downside, however, it takes them time to establish credit-worthiness, and they tend (as smaller businesses) to have limited collateral with which to secure loans to expand. They are unable to benefit on the whole from volume discounts, and they often suffer – quite inexcusably – from the unwillingness of larger companies to pay up on time for purchased goods, which can so harm their cash flow that they fail.

■ Public limited companies

PC 2.1.2

Just as a private limited company is denoted as, say, Anvil Engineering Limited, so a public limited company uses the abbreviation plc to show the nature of its incorporation: Project Office Furniture plc.

The major difference between a private and public limited company is that the public version has its shares available for anyone to purchase on a stock exchange – it is in this sense 'public'. In order to become a public limited company, a company needs to have £50,000 worth of its shares purchased and a quarter of them must be fully paid up. That is to say, their owners must have paid to the company the full asking price. Sometimes, as in the various government privatisation share issues, shares can be bought in tranches at intervals until their full cost is paid off. Such shares are deemed partly paid.

When a company becomes public, it may elect to issue different types of share. Some, called preference and debenture shares, have a higher status than ordinary shares and their owners are paid first – either pre-set annual dividends or according to company performance. Also, if the company is involuntarily wound up (goes broke), such preferential shareholders are high up the ladder of creditors likely to receive some payment.

DISCUSSION TOPICS

PC 2.1.1 2.1.2

1 Is 'small' really 'beautiful', or is Professor Schumacher's axiom merely a myth when it comes to operating a successful business?

2 Should there be a ceiling on the amount of net profit a company makes on a given turnover ? Or is the sky the limit in a free economy ?

3 What in your opinion is the ideal balance of power between business managers and employees? Should all companies, for example, be obliged to include representatives of the workforce on their boards of directors? Has the right to strike been made too difficult to action by trade unions, or were they irresponsible in the 1970s thus deserving of a harder-line treatment today?

4 Are there too few large companies today in the UK controlling too much of the national market in their sphere of activities ? Are small shopkeepers and sole traders doomed ?

PC 2.1.2

■ Conglomerates and multinationals

A further development among plcs is for them to become multinational or conglomerates – or both. Marks & Spencer plc, for example, has set up stores in France and also trades in Canada. The Hanson Corporation has been very active acquiring and building up companies in the USA, while organisations like International Business Machines Incorporated – IBM – is well established in all four corners of the world. Sometimes there are straightforward reasons for a plc becoming a multinational. In the oil business, for example, it makes good sense for a company like Royal Dutch Shell or British Petroleum to control the operation from extraction to petrol-tank filling, which may well start on an oil rig in the China Seas and end up in a filling station in Ealing Broadway, London!

Another reason for the growth of multinationals lies in the benefits which accrue from having a business operation in, say, a Third World economy where abundant raw materials or foods are to be found, and to be able to buy in very cheap labour and allied services on the spot. While controlling the costs of distribution to richer countries such multinationals are able, for example, to sell pineapples, bananas, hard woods or guano at premium prices but with low production and distribution costs.

The term conglomerate is used to describe organisations which operate quite different types of business. The Lex company in the 1960s, for example, was a network of garages and motor car dealerships. Its directors then decided to use accrued profits to move into the hotel business. The reason for successful plcs expanding into quite different business sectors has much to do with spreading the risk of their business activities. Just as a stockbroker will vary the portfolio of an investor between government gilts, equities and unit trust certificates, so some plcs deliberately choose to distribute their capital around totally different sectors on the basis that they are unlikely to go through a bad patch all at the same time.

The trading edge of multinationals lies particularly in their ability to use the differences in the value of various national currencies and the economic growth and recession phases of different countries to their own advantage. Also, their huge size gives some of them the buying power and influence of many a nation state! The downside lies in the distance between multinational centres and complexes (though this is now very much offset by electronic mail, fax and teleconferencing), and the problems in creating any sense of international corporate identity. Also, critics consider that multinationals wield too much power through their financial muscle but exercise too little responsibility, not being accountable to any unified group of voters or government.

While a deliberate policy of expanding into a number of different business areas as a conglomerate protects a firm from the risks associated with operating in a single market, it takes an extraordinarily able holding company board of directors to coordinate the whole enterprise. As a result, what starts off as a business diversification programme often ends in asset stripping an acquired company (selling it off in component parts) to get rid of a problem purchase.

PC 2.1.2

■ Public corporations and utilities

So far, this survey of different types of business organisation has examined private sector organisations. In a mixed economy, however (one in which the operation of a free market is offset by a degree of government control and operation of certain industries), the role of what are called public corporations or sometimes utilities is very important.

In the UK, the following industries have either been or still are run as government-controlled public corporations:

- coal mining; gas and electricity manufacture, distribution and retailing; nuclear-fuelled power-stations;
- steel-making;
- rail transport, road haulage;
- docks, harbours and airport authorities; telecommunication services;
- water services.

As the above checklist shows, in the UK this century various governments have been most interested in controlling energy supplies, transport and communication services, together with key areas of heavy industry. Part of the reason for such government involvement lies in the enormous costs involved in designing and building, say, a nuclear-fuelled power-station or in maintaining a national railway network. Also, governments have been concerned to ensure that no single conglomerate or multinational should gain control of such an important economic resource as, say, energy production.

Nationalisation and privatisation

PC 2.1.2

Since 1946 consecutive Labour and Conservative governments have followed a zig-zag policy of delivering certain companies into public ownership (called nationalising them) and subsequently selling them back into private ownership. British Steel is one such industry whose development has been affected by such 'yanks on its tiller'. In various post-war administrations, as part of their belief in the benefits of public ownership, Labour governments nationalised some nineteen industry areas including:

- The Bank of England
- The Coal Industry
- British Road Services
- The Iron and Steel Industry
- Civil Aviation
- British Rail
- The Gas and Electricity Industries.

With the election of Mrs Thatcher in 1979, the Conservatives developed a central policy of privatisation of nationalised industries. As a result, companies like British Telecom and British Gas were established by selling shares in them to the public at large, backed up by City financial institutions. Other utilities like electricity and water were also privatised in the 1980s in the same way, and private companies now supply these essential services to the UK's regions.

While public corporations have some degree of independence from government intervention, ultimately they lie under government control and may aid a government's policies in these ways:

- they are employers of large workforces and thus give government influence over the number of people in work
- through their pricing policies they enable governments to influence supply and demand on a significant scale
- if a government so chooses, industries and consumers can benefit from subsidised prices for, say, energy and travel
- they provide a means of developing social policies – like maintaining a coal mine or steel mill in an area of high unemployment.

The critics of public corporations – those wishing to return them to the private sector – identify these shortcomings in them:

- they suffer from overmanning – too many employees producing too little – and are therefore inefficient
- they breed bureaucracy – their managers adopt work cultures associated with the less attractive characteristics of central government civil servants
- because they often work as state monopolies they lose touch with the competitiveness of free market companies
- they absorb – like blotting-paper – ever-increasing sums from the public purse sometimes with little or no increase in profitability or output.

PC 2.1.2

Charitable and non-profit-making organisations

As well as the organisations of the private and public sectors, there is a third area occupied by organisations called the voluntary sector.

This sector is characterised by organisations such as:

- Registered charities: like Oxfam and Save the Children
- Charitable trusts: which often run schools, homes for the elderly or small hospitals on the income from willed monies and endowments
- Companies limited by guarantee: which are not established to make a profit, such as national examination boards and certain schools and colleges.

Such organisations are normally exempt from paying taxes, since they generally are performing socially valuable work while administering their activities at low costs. The Registrar of Charities exercises a careful control on what kind of activity may be so registered so as to prevent unscrupulous organisations from siphoning income due for tax into such an organisation, or evading tax payment altogether.

DISCUSSION TOPICS

1 If Professor Schumacher is right and 'small' really is 'beautiful', why is it that so many national chain store and multiple businesses emerge in the consumer market and so many multinationals in the industrial field ?

2 What do you see as the major problems and challenges facing a company as it grows in size?

3 Is limited liability in the consumer's interest?

4 To what extent do multinationals and large conglomerates become immune to government control? Should their activities be more closely monitored? If so, how?

5 Should all public corporations be privatised ? Or only some? What do you see as the pros and cons in the nationalisation–privatisation argument?

6 To what extent should a government become involved in business enterprise? What do you see as the advantages and disadvantages of government intervention in an economy?

INDIVIDUAL ACTIVITIES

PC 2.1.2

1 Find out how a typical partnership agreement is drawn up. Report back to your group on what you discover.

2 Research into the structure and content of private limited company articles and memoranda of agreement (a solicitor will help you find out about formats and customary clauses). Brief your group on what you discover.

3 Find out where the responsibilities of company directors are set down and draw up a short fact-sheet on them to share with your group.

4 Research into one of the following organisation's activities and range of wholly owned subsidiaries and/or divisions and give a suitably illustrated oral presentation to your group:

The Hanson Trust Limited
Imperial Chemical Industries plc
Barclays Bank
Unilever plc

5 Find out how the work of the Charity Commissioners protects the general public.

CHECKLIST OF CENTRAL AND LOCAL GOVERNMENT DEPARTMENTS AND AGENCIES WHICH INTERACT WITH BUSINESS ORGANISATIONS

PC 2.1.2

The Inland Revenue; collector of the government's taxes (see Treasury).

HM Customs & Excise; collector of Value Added Tax and other duties.

European Community; through its Commission, the EC issues and monitors Community legislation with significant impact upon industry and commerce, covering a host of areas from cheese-making to VDU screen use.

Government departments of:

Agriculture, Fisheries & Food; works with, inspects and develops the agricultural industry.

Trade & Industry; supportive of industry and commerce; directs government policy and resources and assists exporters, etc.

Employment; helps industry to train and develop its human resources – see also Training & Enterprise Councils.

Treasury; publishes detailed economic analyses and surveys; produces annual budgets and tax policies, etc.

Transport; co-ordinates transport policy and EC directives on transport administration and law.

Bank of England; issues currency and acts as the government's banker; monitors activities of national and private banks.

Central Office of Information; publishes regular reports, forecasts, surveys and statistics often useful to industry and commerce.

Health & Safety Commission; health, safety and care of employees and customers on premises, etc.

Factories, Public Health Inspectorates; corps of inspectors set up to carry out in-situ inspections of factories, restaurants, shops, etc. to ensure that relevant health and safety requirements are in place.

Registrar of Companies; maintains a national registry of private limited companies and details of shareholdings, etc. Monitors use of trade names and marks.

Office of Fair Trading; public watchdog on trading practices and legality of activities.

Monopolies and Mergers Commission; set up to monitor any potential establishment of monopolistic business activities, with powers to stop acquisitions and mergers if deemed 'not in the public interest'.

Industrial Tribunals; listen to industrial/employment law disputes and adjudicate – for example, on unfair dismissal or sexual/racial discrimination.

Advertising Standards Authority, and Independent Television Commission; monitor advertising standards and regulations and investigate complaints.

County and District Councils; implement various Acts of Parliament bearing upon business, including public health, trading standards, planning consents, collection of business rates and taxes on premises, etc.

The above checklist – by no means exhaustive – indicates both the range and depth of government involvement in trade and industry. This interest varies from the rigorous collection of VAT payments to support for exporters at foreign trade fairs. Much of what the government agencies do lies in monitoring and checking to make sure that the relevant Acts of Parliament are in fact being adhered to. To some this smacks of Big Brother interference, but many employees and consumers have good reason to be grateful to vigilant equipment or kitchen inspectors, or watchful trading standards officers whose actions may prevent the loss of a limb, or an eye, or a nasty attack of salmonellosis.

INDIVIDUAL ACTIVITY

By arrangement with your teacher, investigate one of the above government departments, agencies or arms and produce a summary of its main activities and involvements with business on about two sides of A4 typescript, keeping your points short and sharp.

Collate your group's individual briefing sheets into bound booklets and issue one to each member of the group as a source of reference.

GROUP ACTIVITIES

PC 2.1.2

1 In pairs, arrange to interview two or three sole traders in order to find out what they see as their major preoccupations and essential activities and report back with an oral briefing of 5–10 minutes to your class.

2 Arrange in pairs to meet with members of a business partnership – solicitors, accountants, small traders etc. – and find out how some of the partners view the partnership type of business structure and why they prefer it to, say, a private limited company.

3 In groups of three, research into the duties and obligations which directors of private limited companies have to discharge and then report back to your class with an illustrated short presentation.

4 In pairs, select one of the Acts listed on page 105. Research into it and then design a factsheet on one side of A4 which summarises its main features. Circulate this factsheet to your class members as a study aid.

5 In pairs, find out why large public limited companies such as the IBM Corporation and ICI plc decided to decentralise their activities and to give more autonomy to their wholly owned subsidiary companies. Report back to your class in a short oral presentation.

6 In groups of two or three carry out your research into the activities of one of the following:

The Bank of England, The Monopolies and Mergers Commission, Oftel, The Training Education and Enterprise Directorate (TEED), The Charities Commission, The Department of Trade & Industry (DTI),

and produce a factsheet outlining clearly why it was established and how it interacts with UK business/economic/charitable activities.

■ What factors affect the way an organisation is structured?

PC 2.1.3

Private sector organisations

The main factors which are likely to affect the way organisation is built or structured are:

- its **size**: 1 or 100 or 1000 or 10 000 employees?
- its **location**: in one office block? ten supermarkets within a region? fifteen factories spread across the country?
- its **nature**: mining? growing? manufacturing? distributing? retailing? providing a professional service?
- its **clientele**: three or four international companies? twenty to thirty major distributors or factors? two to three hundred retailing companies? ten thousand mail-order customers? two million High Street shoppers?
- its **past shape**, its **current structure**, its **future needs**: the structure a company had as a family business may not suit the chain store which bought it out; to grow or even to survive a company may need to change shape by acquiring different businesses or by transforming the traditional nature of its activities, i.e. by diversifying its range of products or acquiring a varied range of companies to spread its risk of failure – not all companies will do badly simultaneously.

PC 2.1.3

Public sector organisations

The structural characteristics which private sector organisations experience are largely mirrored in the public sector – the number of employees, the location of the organisation's buildings, what sort of activities it carries out, etc., will have a similar effect upon the structure or shape. These are additional factors in the public sector, however:

- the **extent of the duties and obligations** posed upon it by government and statute, which the public authority must carry out;
- the **boundaries of its authority**: national, regional, county, district, borough, parish;
- the **amount of income it has to spend** either supplied by central government or via local rates;
- the **impact of government policies**, for example, to reduce public spending. (Note a recession in the economy may have a similar effect on the size of private companies);
- whether the organisation or part of it is in **direct contact with the public or not**. (Note that there is some similarity between the manufacturing and retailing private sector factors, where activities are either machine intensive or people intensive);
- **changes in technology**. For example, county councils during the past twenty years have developed sophisticated computer services departments. (As indeed have private organisations);
- **changes in society's expectations.** Citizens expect to be told more about local and central government activities so more meetings are open to the public and more councils now have public relations units and officers;
- **increasing complexity of the work** to be carried out. Many County Councils now have senior Policy and Resources Committees to help Chief Executives in making policy decisions.

PC 2.1.3

CHECKLIST OF PROS AND CONS OF DIFFERING ORGANISATIONAL STRUCTURES

Sole trader

PROS:
- Communications are uninvolved and the chain is short.
- Decision-making is simple – often a 'committee of one'.
- Swift responses to market shifts are readily made.
- Profits are not diluted by having to be divided among several partners or directors.

CONS:
- As the business expands, the 'one-man (or woman) band' cannot handle all jobs efficiently.
- Obtaining unsecured loans and purchasing on account status is not easy.
- Securing competitive buying discounts is also difficult.
- The business is susceptible to general market dips and downturns.
- The proprietor is responsible for all debts incurred without limit to liability.
- Sole traders are sometimes under-capitalised and the business is therefore unable to grow very easily.

Private limited company

PROS:

- The business becomes a legal entity in itself and its directors' personal possessions are not at risk if the business fails.
- The business is protected from hostile takeover in that no one can purchase any shares that share-owning directors do not wish to sell.
- The generally larger size of a private limited company enables specialist departments/units to be set up, managed and run by specialist personnel.
- Private limited companies are legally obliged to publish or release very little information which could be of use to their competitors.

CONS:

- Once it becomes an employer of staff, its legal requirements become much more complicated with many Acts and regulations to comply with.
- As the company grows, its directors build structures which may set up departmental barriers to communication, and rivalry among different employee groups may emerge.
- Contact and understanding of customers' needs and wants diminishes as senior staff become more remote from the customer interface.
- Its directors may take too much money out of the business in the form of pay or 'perks' and it may become vulnerable.

Public limited companies

PROS:

- Being quoted on the Stock Exchange and being able to offer shares for sale publicly enables plcs to acquire readily capital for further development if they are doing well – money makes money.
- High volume sales and turnover enable the plc to buy at large discounts and thus sell very competitively while maintaining sufficient profit margins.
- The possession of multiple outlets or business centres helps the plc to dominate the market and thus to control prices.
- The collateral provided by its many capital assets assists the plc in securing loans to fuel its further expansion.
- Its operating profit levels enable the plc to afford more back-up and technical support staff.

CONS:

- It is possible for the plc to be taken over by another company which manages to secure 51 per cent of its shares.
- Net profits shrink because overheads are allowed to proliferate – too many people and activities have to be supported.
- Its size and the dispersion of its premises and employees make communication more costly, complicated and time-consuming – the 'what-did-he-say, pass-it-on' syndrome emerges. Employees cannot relate to the whole enterprise.
- Distribution, advertising and administration costs escalate.
- Decision-making becomes time-consuming and emasculated because of 'decision by committee'. Bureaucracy sets in.
- Becoming slower moving because of size and structure, the plc is vulnerable to the speedier and more dynamic activities of small, young businesses.

Moral: Small is often 'more beautiful' than big; and flat, simply tiered structures more effective than deep, many-layered ones.

PC 2.1.3

Fig 2.3 **Organisational structures vary according to the nature of the business**

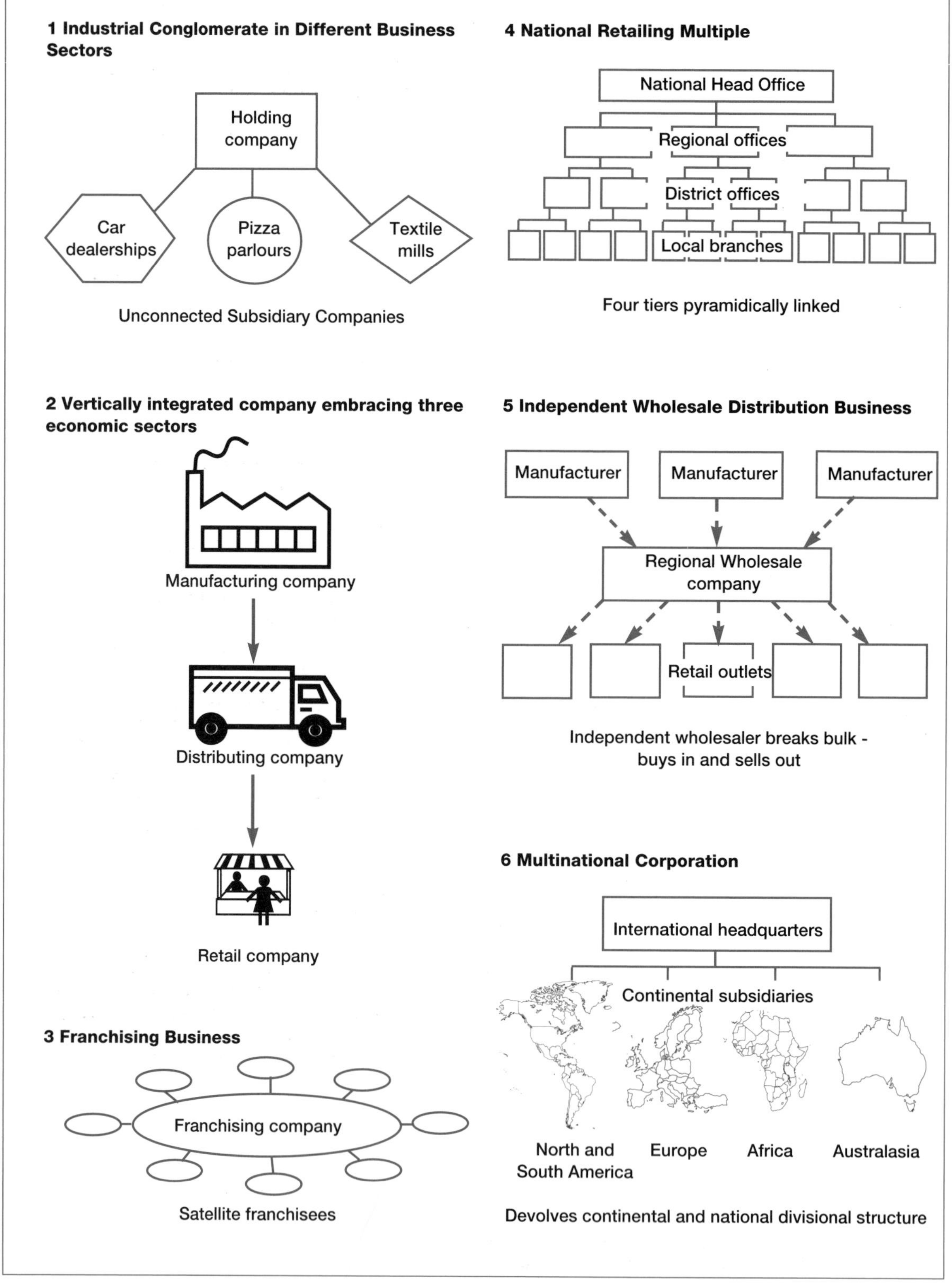
1 Industrial Conglomerate in Different Business Sectors
Holding company
Car dealerships
Pizza parlours
Textile mills
Unconnected Subsidiary Companies
2 Vertically integrated company embracing three economic sectors
Manufacturing company
Distributing company
Retail company
3 Franchising Business
Franchising company
Satellite franchisees
4 National Retailing Multiple
National Head Office
Regional offices
District offices
Local branches
Four tiers pyramidically linked
5 Independent Wholesale Distribution Business
Manufacturer
Manufacturer
Manufacturer
Regional Wholesale company
Retail outlets
Independent wholesaler breaks bulk - buys in and sells out
6 Multinational Corporation
International headquarters
Continental subsidiaries
North and South America
Europe
Africa
Australasia
Devolves continental and national divisional structure

PC 2.1.3

Fig 2.4 **Examples of different types of organisational structure**

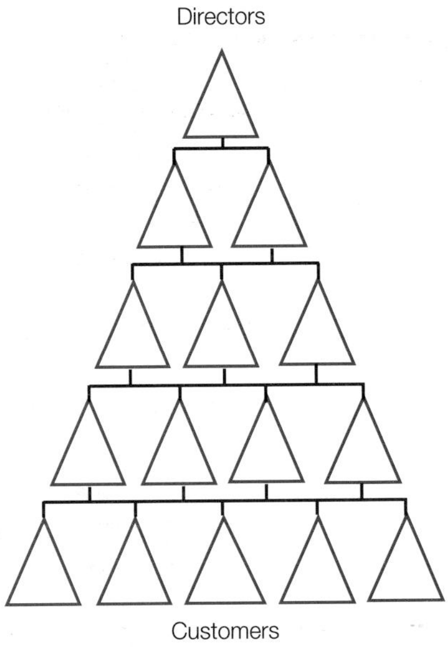
Directors
Customers

1 The Complicated Organisation: The steep pyramid

- Many tiers of management in the organisation
- Operating from many remote locations
- Distance of directors from customers
- Complexity of channelling and routing messages, orders, complaints, information, etc.
- Problems of maintaining a sense of corporate identity among employees
- Likelihood of bureaucratic inertia leading to delays in decision-making

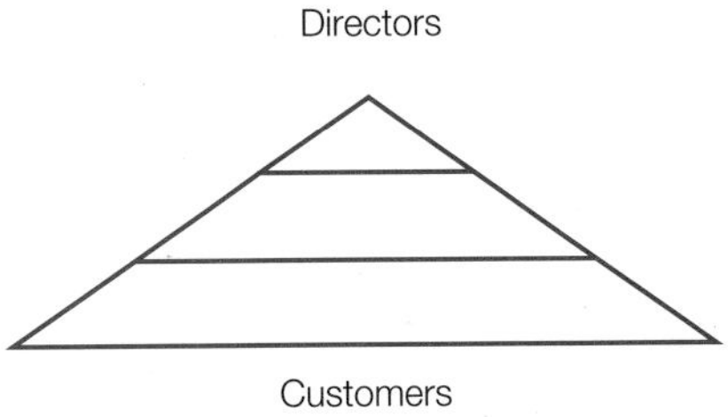
Directors
Customers

2 The Simple Organisation: The flat pyramid

- Few tiers in the organisation's management and communication structure promotes faster, more effective data interchange
- Single-site operations make it easier and faster to serve customers
- Proximity of directors to customers aids good customer relations and marketing
- A simple structure makes it easier to create and sustain employee morale and sense of corporate identity
- Single-site autonomy promotes faster decision-making
- Bureaucracy is less likely to set in

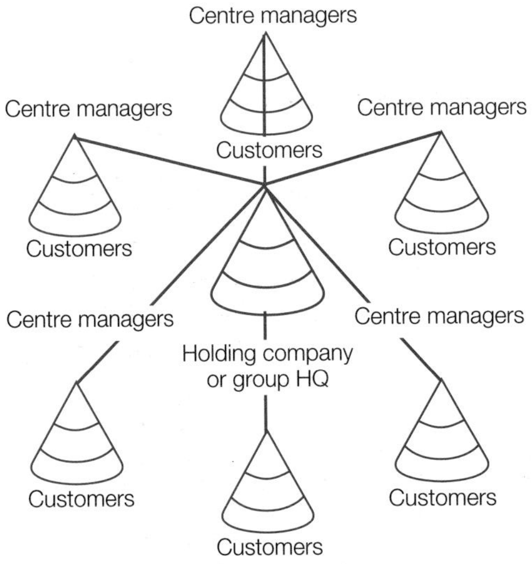
Centre managers
Customers
Centre managers
Centre managers
Customers
Customers
Centre managers
Centre managers
Holding company
or group HQ
Customers
Customers
Customers

3 Central and Satellite 'Cone' Structure

Learning from the lessons implicit in the above two differing organisation structures, many businesses – including IBM Inc. – are developing structures which devolve management autonomy and authority away from centralised to decentralised centres of either production, distribution or retailing.

Satellite divisions or subsidiaries (or branches) have more 'on-site' authority and freedom to be entrepreneurial.

PC
2.1.3

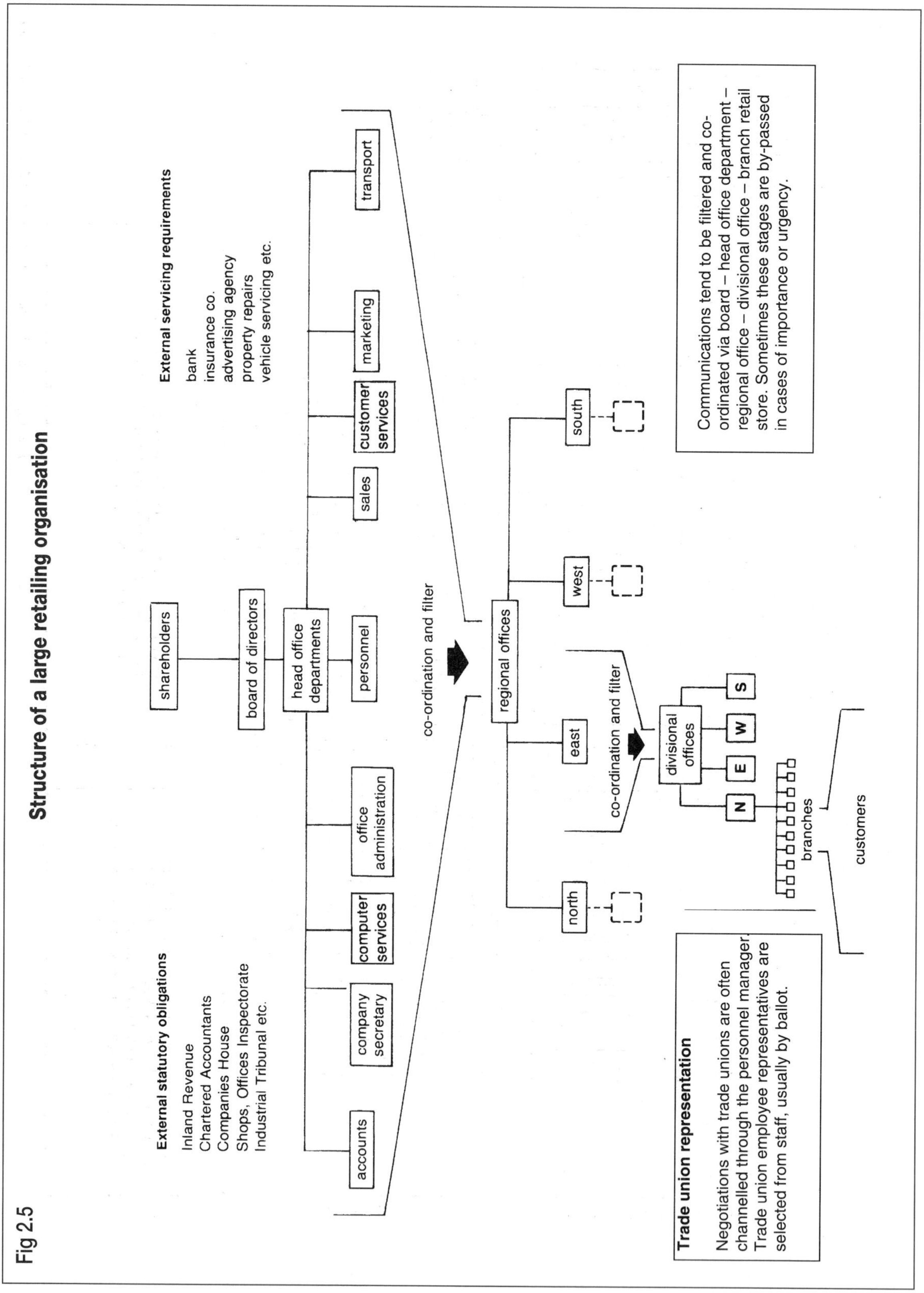
Fig 2.5
Structure of a large retailing organisation
shareholders
board of directors
head office departments
accounts
company secretary
computer services
office administration
personnel
sales
customer services
marketing
transport
External statutory obligations
Inland Revenue
Chartered Accountants
Companies House
Shops, Offices Inspectorate
Industrial Tribunal etc.
External servicing requirements
bank
insurance co.
advertising agency
property repairs
vehicle servicing etc.
co-ordination and filter
regional offices
north
east
west
south
co-ordination and filter
divisional offices
N
E
W
S
branches
customers
Trade union representation
Negotiations with trade unions are often channelled through the personnel manager. Trade union employee representatives are selected from staff, usually by ballot.
Communications tend to be filtered and co-ordinated via board – head office department – regional office – divisional office – branch retail store. Sometimes these stages are by-passed in cases of importance or urgency.

Fig 2.6

Organisational structure of West Sussex County Council

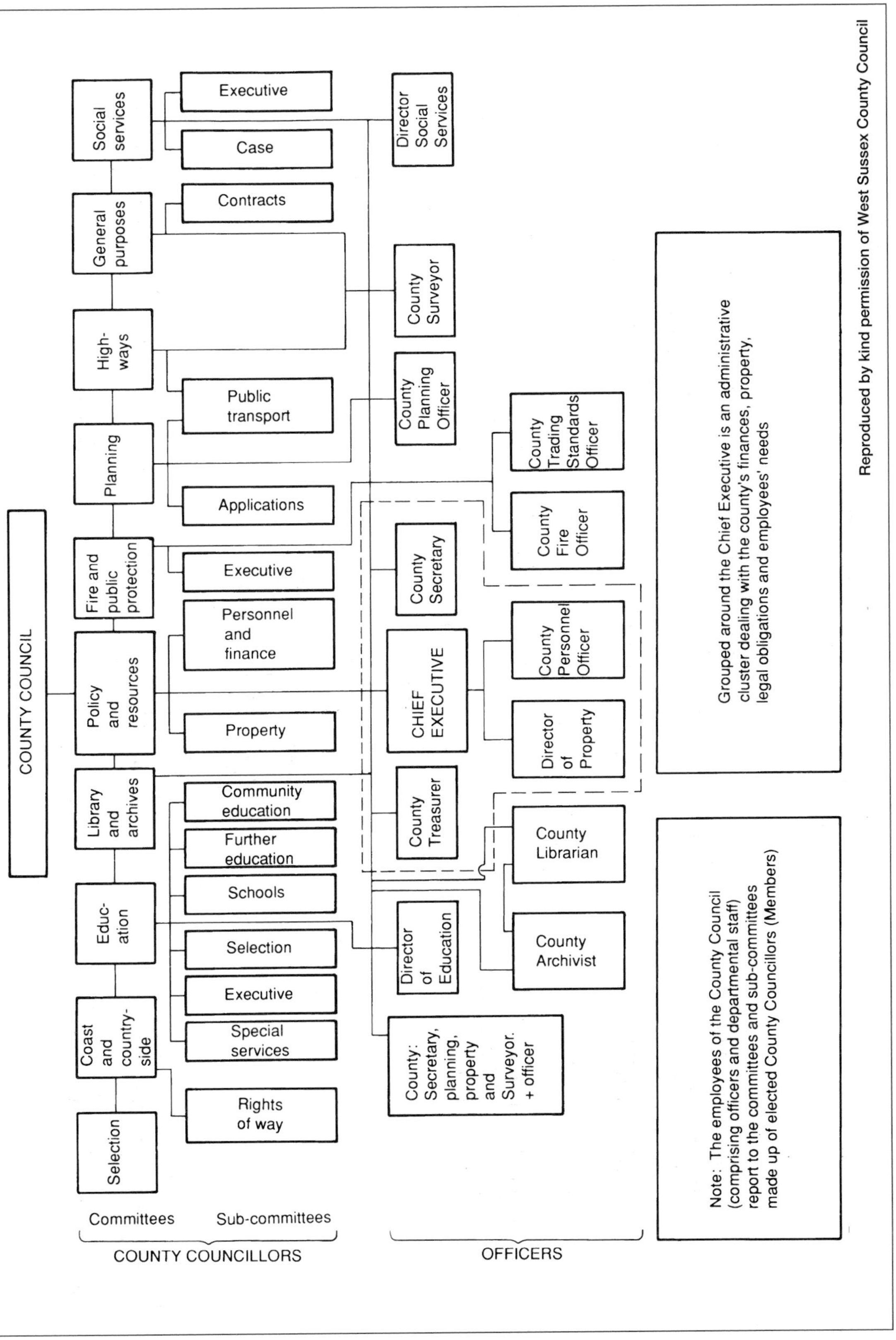
COUNTY COUNCIL
Selection
Coast and countryside
Education
Library and archives
Policy and resources
Fire and public protection
Planning
Highways
General purposes
Social services
Rights of way
Special services
Executive
Selection
Schools
Further education
Community education
Property
Personnel and finance
Executive
Applications
Public transport
Contracts
Case
Executive
Committees
Sub-committees
COUNTY COUNCILLORS
County: Secretary, planning, property and Surveyor. + officer
Director of Education
County Treasurer
CHIEF EXECUTIVE
County Secretary
County Planning Officer
County Surveyor
Director Social Services
County Archivist
County Librarian
Director of Property
County Personnel Officer
County Fire Officer
County Trading Standards Officer
OFFICERS
Note: The employees of the County Council (comprising officers and departmental staff) report to the committees and sub-committees made up of elected County Councillors (Members)
Grouped around the Chief Executive is an administrative cluster dealing with the county's finances, property, legal obligations and employees' needs

PC 2.1.3

■ Hierarchies

Apart from the structures which are determined by an organisation's general activities – whether in the private or public sector, whether selling goods or services – most organisations are internally structured.

Perhaps the most significant aspect of organising people into groups which have specific aims and functions is that either intentionally or unconsciously a 'pecking-order' is established. Few groups operate successfully without leaders and followers. Organisations are no exception. When organisations are composed of 'layers' or gradings of personnel they are termed hierarchies. A popular way of expressing this concept is the organisational pyramid.

The structuring of organisations into hierarchies is in many ways inevitable – although some organisations are evolving other structures, such as the franchise system (see diagram on p. 114). The need for important decisions to be made by people with expertise and experience, in consultation very often with those affected, together with the need to provide a person with sufficient authority to execute a decision, results in the 'pyramid effect'; by this means a small number of senior managers or officials are given the responsibility of directing an organisation's activities. It should be pointed out, however, that they are also, by dint of office, made accountable for its success or failure!

The layer-sandwich structure of the pyramid is termed an organisational hierarchy. In this, people work at different levels and receive instructions and action requests from senior staff, either to carry out themselves or to manage through staff reporting to them (Fig 2.7).

PC 2.1.3

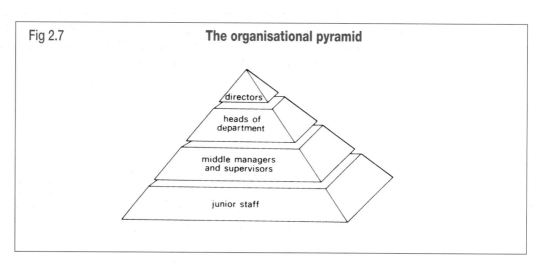

Fig 2.7 **The organisational pyramid**

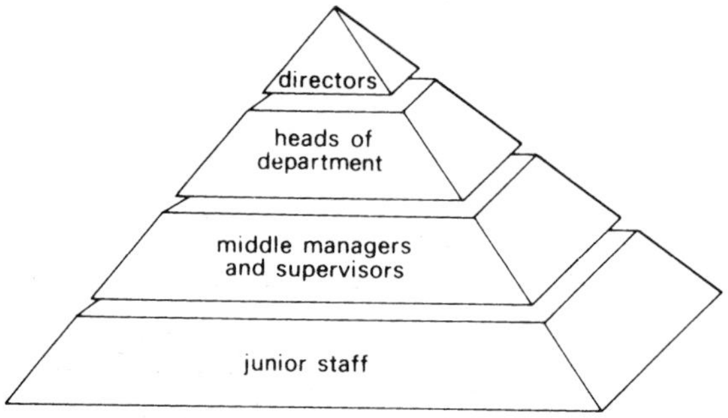
directors
heads of department
middle managers and supervisors
junior staff

PC 2.1.3

Fig 2.8 **The stepped hierarchy**

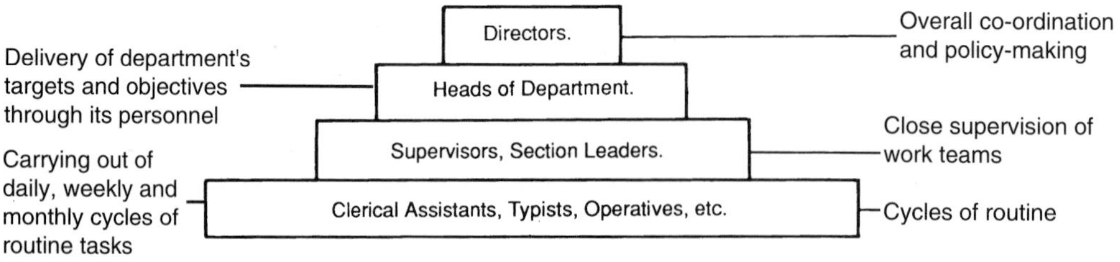
Directors.
Heads of Department.
Supervisors, Section Leaders.
Clerical Assistants, Typists, Operatives, etc.
Overall co-ordination and policy-making
Delivery of department's targets and objectives through its personnel
Close supervision of work teams
Carrying out of daily, weekly and monthly cycles of routine tasks
Cycles of routine

PC 2.1.3

THE NATURE OF THE BUSINESS DEFINES ITS SHAPE

The shapes and structures into which business organisations eventually evolve are influenced by a number of factors including:

- **Economic sector;** The sector of the economy they inhabit – primary, secondary or tertiary.
- **Type of market**; The market(s) in which they operate – industrial or consumer, product or service selling.
- **Type of process**; The constraints and demands of the business operation – foundry or beauty salon.
- **Type of customer**; The type of customer the business serves – central purchaser of a conglomerate, or housewife at a Saturday food market.
- **Degree of complexity of business activity**; The degree of complexity of the business operation – from, say, a multinational designing and manufacturing computers, to the sole trader making and selling dried flower arrangements at weekly craft fairs.
- **Extent of line of management control required**; The extent of the line of the management control the business – ranging from international central holding companies like BT or ICI, with their many divisions and wholly owned subsidiaries on different continents, to the fast food regional franchiser supporting virtually independent retailers with a limited range of services.
- **Number and location of employees**; The number of employees (and the extent of their dispersal) being involved in the business operation and the number of tiers they inhabit in the overall organisational pyramid.
- **Number of different customers served and their location**; The number of customers who are served – ranging say from a few dozen wholesalers in a national agricultural herbicide/pesticide market to millions of consumers buying in national retail chain stores. Also, the requirements of running an exporting business, as opposed to a purely domestic one.

PC 2.1.3

Fig 2.9 **Hierarchies in county councils: members and employees**

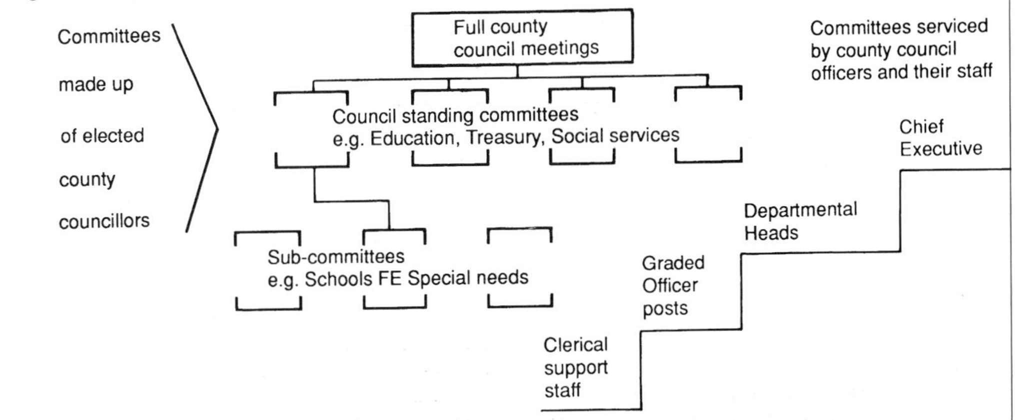

PC 2.1.3

Specialist divisions

As the examples on pages 116 and 117 show, the other source of the pyramid effect in organisations is the division of the total operation into specialist departments, all of which are answerable to a more senior co-ordinator.

Fig 2.10

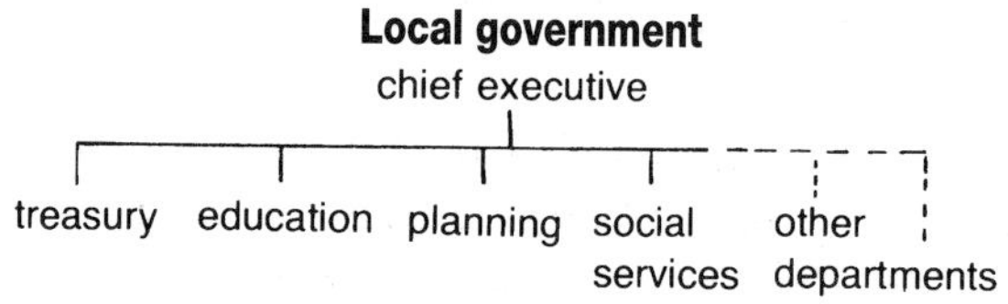

Local government
chief executive
treasury
education
planning
social services
other departments

Fig 2.11

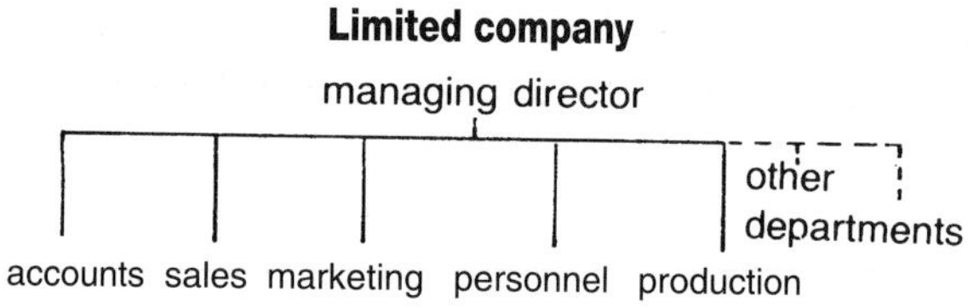

Limited company
managing director
accounts
sales
marketing
personnel
production
other departments

Each department will have its own pyramid structure of head, senior, middle and junior staff, and career hopes and expectations will cause employees to seek to climb the pyramid.

There are problems in communication, administration and effectiveness – which are attributable to the size and the complicated grading of authority in some hierarchic structures. To avoid such complications many organisations deliberately limit size and grant extensive independence to departments.

PC 2.1.3

■ Organisational structures: management styles, culture and change

As the above diagrams illustrate, business and public sector organisations tend to create for themselves a structure suited to the nature of their activities, legal liabilities and ownership. They also tend to 'grow' or evolve different structures as they expand or as the nature of their business changes. By the same token, organisational structures depend in no small part on the culture which becomes established. For example, in espionage and terrorist networks, small, isolated cells are created which link only to the centre, so that no single cell can betray others. Organisations which require the prompt following of orders and instructions – like the armed services or police – create clear lines of command and break their employees up into smallish units.

Where organisations employ large numbers of highly educated and articulate professionals – solicitors' partnerships, software companies, universities etc. – employees are given much personal freedom (within an hierarchic framework) in order to work freely and creatively. Thus an organisation's management style – laissez-faire or close supervision – is very likely to arise directly from what it does and the kind of people it employs.

A basic and important description of all organisations is that they are *dynamic*. In other words, they respond to change – in order to survive. Thus change in all its forms – technological, political, life-style and social – inevitably impacts upon the way an organisation pursues its activities and shapes itself. For example, ten years ago supermarkets and multiple stores jostled for 'pole positions' in the High Street. Today, as a result of changes in consumers' shopping and motoring habits and expectations, they are to be found out of town, in warehouse or mall clusters, surrounded by acres of parking spaces! Similarly, the irresistible growth of information technology has led to many organisations adding computer services to their departmental structures.

Organisations and responsiveness

PC 2.1.3

Changes to organisational structures and how they do business are also caused by customers' rising expectations. Hotels nowadays will arrange rental cars for customers. Dry-cleaners and film-processing retailers offer 'within-the-hour' services, and supermarkets bake a wide range fresh bread on their premises. Such responsiveness to customers' demands may entail a business in developing not only appropriate training provisions for staff, but also constructing additional premises.

PC 2.1.3

DISCUSSION TOPICS

1 Has government privatisation of many public utilities resulted in the construction of more effective organisations?

2 'The small trader is doomed!' What do you think is likely to happen to small businesses in the UK over the next ten years?

3 Charities have lost their way; today they are run like businesses and less of the money they collect gets to where its donors intended. To what extent has organisational change affected charities for the worse?

4 'Flat pyramid structures came about during the last recession when large firms thought they could strip out their middle-management tiers in order to save money. As a result, they now employ people at the sharp end who are under-trained, under-managed and ill-informed, while their top managers haven't a clue what's going on!'

5 Given the choice, most people would rather work for themselves, than in a large organisation! Why?

PC
2.1.1
2.1.2
2.1.3

REVIEW TEST

1 List five different types of organisational objective.

2 List five different types of private sector organisation and three public sector ones.

3 What is the function of an organisation's mission statement?

4 Explain briefly the difference between a private and public limited company.

5 List three main responsibilities of a company director.

6 Explain briefly the difference between a conglomerate, a multiple and a multi-national kind of business.

7 Why are there so few UK public utilities in being today?

8 Explain briefly what a franchise is in business organisational terms.

9 List three factors which affect the way an organisation structures itself.

10 What does *vertically integrated* mean in organisational terms?

11 List three advantages to a company which becomes a plc.

12 Explain simply what is meant by the term: *organisational hierarchy*.

KNOWLEDGE TEST

Element 2.1
Investigate business organisations

1 (i) An organisation may have as a legitimate business objective increasing its market share at the expense of its levels of profit.

(ii) Charitable organisations are not permitted to make profits.

Which of the following options best describes the above statements ?

A	(i)	T	(ii)	T
B	(i)	T	(ii)	F
C	(i)	F	(ii)	T
D	(i)	F	(ii)	F

2 Which of the following statements is true, and which false?

A A sole trader is entirely liable for the business debts he or she incurs.

B A partnership is not liable to pay VAT.

C Company directors have limited legal liability for the debts their companies incur

D The shares of a private limited company may be bought and sold on a stock exchange.

3 Which of the following factors is likely to affect the way in which an organisation is structured?

A Where its head office is located.

B Its size in terms of numbers of employees.

C The fact that it does business with HM government.

D The kind of customers it serves.

4 Which of the following would you expect to find in the public sector?

A a conglomerate

B a utility

C a franchise

D a QUANGO

5 (i) The term *organisational hierarchy* describes the tall multi-storey office-blocks currently popular among multi-national companies.

(ii) The term *flat pyramid* was coined to describe modern, low-cost business developments in inner-city re-development areas.

Which of the options below best describes the above statements?

A	(i)	T	(ii)	T
B	(i)	T	(ii)	F
C	(i)	F	(ii)	T
D	(i)	F	(ii)	F

PC
2.1.1
2.1.2
2.1.3

PORTFOLIO OF EVIDENCE ACTIVITY

Element 2.1
Investigate business organisations

MIDSHIRE COUNTY COUNCIL'S ANNUAL ECONOMIC INTELLIGENCE REPORT

Scenario

You work as a local government officer in the *Economic Intelligence Unit of Midshire County Council's Planning Department*. Every year, the County Planning Officer, Mr Ted Sharple, co-ordinates the production of the Council's *Annual Economic Intelligence Report*. This report takes the form of a round-up and up-dating of business developments and trends across Midshire, and is published for both business executives' and public sector managers' support and briefing.

This year, Mr Sharple has decided to focus on current business and public sector organisational characteristics in the county and the sort of changes to which they are being subjected and for what reasons.

He therefore briefed you earlier today as follows;

'I should like you to undertake a sort of fact-finding survey and to produce a report which my editing staff can use during the production of the Annual Economic Intelligence Report*. This is what I want you to do.*

1 *Select three organisations fairly typical of our locality, two in the private and one in the public sector.*
2 *Research into the organisational structure and activities of each, concentrating on: what their respective financial aims are, and how they differ; how what each does impacts upon its structure and the nature of its operations; and how the different ways in which either organisation operates – financially, legally and in terms of how the organisation is controlled – influences its goals.*
3 *Part of the report should include an organisational chart for each organisation, and an accompanying explanation which explains the reasons for the different organisational structures and any likely future changes.*

I should like you to adopt a sort of 'compare and contrast' approach, so you'll have to think about a suitable report structure and format. It's quite possible that we can use your report as the basis of a profile on 'bang-up-to-the-minute' approaches and trends in the county, so give it your best shot!'

Task 1

Before embarking on this activity, make sure you have filled out the appropriate parts of your planning and review forms, and developed your action plan.

Task 2

Carry out the interview visits and research activities needed to secure the information Mr Sharple has asked for. While you do this, make sure you update your planning and review forms.

Task 3

Review the data you have collected and collate it into separate topic areas. Next, consider how best to structure and sequence your material into a suitable report for Mr Sharple, and set down a writing plan you can follow.

Task 4

Check first with your teacher and then either hand-write or word-process your report, using any suitable graphic illustrations you have obtained. Make sure your report meets Mr Sharple's terms of reference before you start writing. Remember to complete your planning and review form and to submit it with your report.

Task 5 (Optional)

Deliver a 5–10 minute oral presentation to your class which summarises the main points of your report.

Performance criteria covered

2.1.1, 2.1.2, 2.1.3

Core skills covered

Communication:
3.2.1, 3.2.2, 3.2.3, 3.2.4, 3.2.5, 3.3.1, 3.3.2, 3.3.3, 3.4.1, 3.4.2, 3.4.3, 3.4.4

Information Technology:
3.1.1, 3.1.2, 3.1.3, 3.1.4, 3.1.5, 3.2.1, 3.2.2, 3.2.3, 3.2.4, 3.2.5, 3.2.6, 3.2.7, 3.3.1, 3.3.2, 3.3.3, 3.3.4, 3.3.5, 3.3.6

Element 2.2
INVESTIGATE ADMINISTRATION SYSTEMS

One of the most important characteristics which distinguishes a sole trader from a national chainstore or conglomerate is the development of effective administrative systems. Of course, a small trader in his or her way can be just as efficient as a multi-million pound company. But it is naturally much simpler and easier to administer a business run by one or two people than one which encompasses many thousands of employees spread across hundreds of branches or dozens of factories.

In order to administer an organisation cost-effectively and to enable it to deliver profits annually, the senior management of large businesses have developed over the past century a range of administrative approaches and systems, the main features of which are set out here.

PC 2.2.1

Administrative systems and approaches used in business

■ People systems

As Element 2.1 illustrated, as organisations grow, the people who work in them tend to be organised into specialist divisions, departments or units. For example:

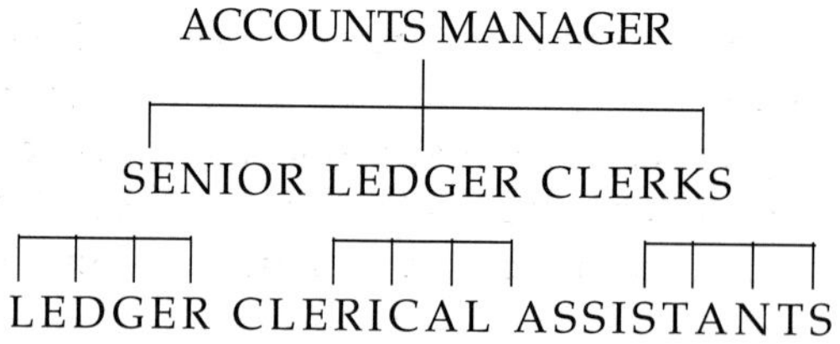
ACCOUNTS MANAGER
SENIOR LEDGER CLERKS
LEDGER CLERICAL ASSISTANTS

In this way specialist functions are created which – because of the increasing size of a business – attend solely to a single, specific part if it: research and development, production, personnel and so on.

In order to enable working instructions and requests to be passed on from senior managers to junior operative or support staff, a 'reports-to' function was also introduced in which a *line manager* has a number of subordinate staff reporting to him or her in the following chain-of-command structure:

Line management function

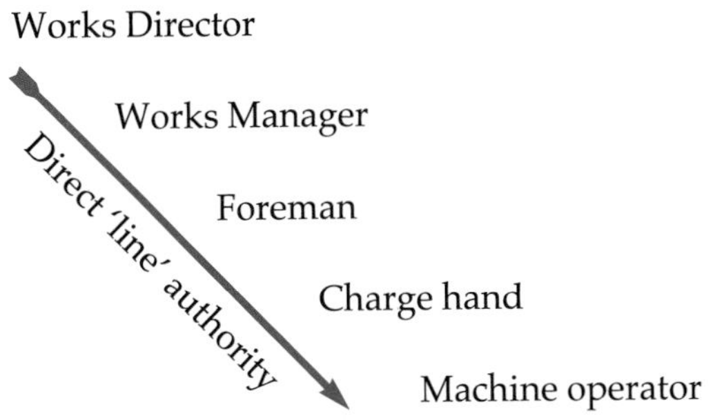

In order to link different types of employee function into an overall system, the concept of *staff relationships* was added to that of line management control. For example, a secretary or personal assistant working directly to, say, a senior manager is said to be in a staff relationship in terms of his or her work role and job function, since such an employee works outside of the line of command relationship. This being the case, he or she cannot *require* or *order* one of the manager's subordinates to do something, but must adopt an approach like: 'Mr Hargreaves has asked me to remind you that he needs the debtors' report by eleven o'clock this morning.'

Line and staff relationships

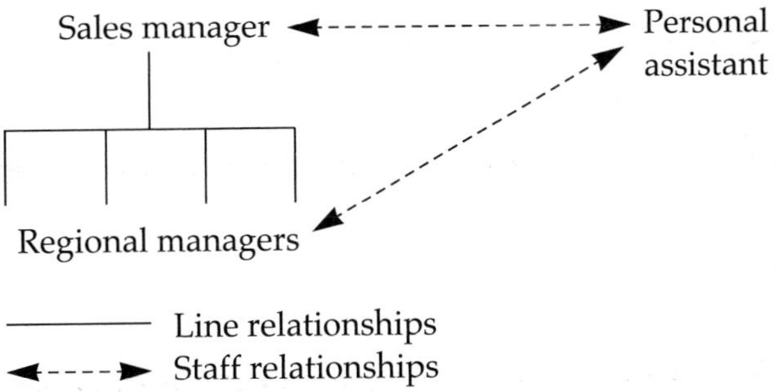

A third working relationship in large organisations is called *functional*. It occurs when certain specialist types of staff work across the entire organisation, such as personnel when maintaining employee records, or management services staff when monitoring production workers' systems of working. Very often such staff report directly to a managing director and are expected to liaise productively with heads of the various specialist departments

Teams and task groups

In addition to organising their staff into line management tiers and staff or functional relationships, many large organisations employ a range of team-based people systems to address problems, come up with suggestions or creative proposals:

- **Quality Circle**: a group of employees from different departments and positions in the hierarchy who come together in order to find ways and means of improving quality
- **Task Force**: similarly, a group of specialists may be brought together, say, to design an innovative product or manage a take-over bid
- **Committee**: some organisations – notably local government – use the creation of a committee of staff to co-ordinate specific tasks or to make recommendations to a more senior body.

PC 2.2.1

Procedures

In addition to organising people so as to enable them to manage and administer operations effectively, larger businesses also tend to develop set procedures which all employees are required to observe and to implement as appropriate. The following table provides illustrations of commonly occurring types of business procedure:

PC 2.2.1

Procedure:	Actioned by:
• logging the arrival and stay of a visitor to a firm's premises	receptionist for security and HASAW purposes
• documenting an account sale	accounts department sales ledger staff, so as to keep track of debtors and issue timely request for payment
• keeping up-to-date records on all employees' pay, promotion, transfer and training etc.	personnel department staff to assist manpower planning etc.
• logging and analysing customers' complaints about products or services purchased	customer services staff, so as to assist the improvement of product quality and customer satisfaction

Centralising and standardising procedures

Business organisations also introduce standardised working procedures when they have numerous branches or outlets dispersed throughout the country – banks, building societies, chainstores etc. This enables remote head office senior managers to control from a distance how 'sharp-end' operations are carried out and to simplify the collection and analysis of statistical data to aid management decision-making.

PC 2.2.1

Equipment

In today's highly technological working environment, people working to set procedures make very extensive use of office machines and equipment to save time, minimise errors and communicate with co-workers. The chart on page 129 illustrates how rapidly office equipment has advanced during the past 150 years.

From paper to electronic pulse

PC 2.2.1

For some one hundred years – from 1840–1940, mechanical office equipment was developed to enable administrative personnel to process information on paper sheets and forms. During this time specialist departments – sales, accounts, production – devised various sets or sequences of forms to record essential data, and used carbon paper or NCR (no carbon required) treated sets of forms to provide informational duplicates to interested colleagues or customers.

However, the development of electronic typewriters and the now famous silicon chip in the late 1960s came to revolutionalise utterly the way in which people in organisations used equipment to help to administer operations. Indeed, the past thirty years has seen a transformation as a result in the ways in which organisations acquire, process, store and disseminate information – first using stand-alone computers and now highly sophisticated email networks and highways. No would-be clerical assistant or business manager can expect to function effectively today without some form of expertise in, for instance, word-processing, database manipulation, spreadsheet design and interrogation or desk-top publishing and graphic display.

Fig 2.12 **The evolution of IT information systems in the office**

PC 2.2.1

1870s – 1970s
The stand-alone typewriter was the office workhorse – from mechanical manual to electric, to electronic and electronic with memory

1970s – 1980s
The dedicated, stand-alone wordprocessing personal computer was introduced (Could only perform WP tasks with 'built-in' software)

1980s – 1990s
'Connectivity' or 'convergence' evolved: local and wide area networks (LANs and WANs) interlink computers, printers, fax, telex, view-data, copiers, etc.

1990s – on
Open Systems Connection introduced internationally – protocols are developed to enable computers of different manufacture, using different operating systems, to communicate with each other

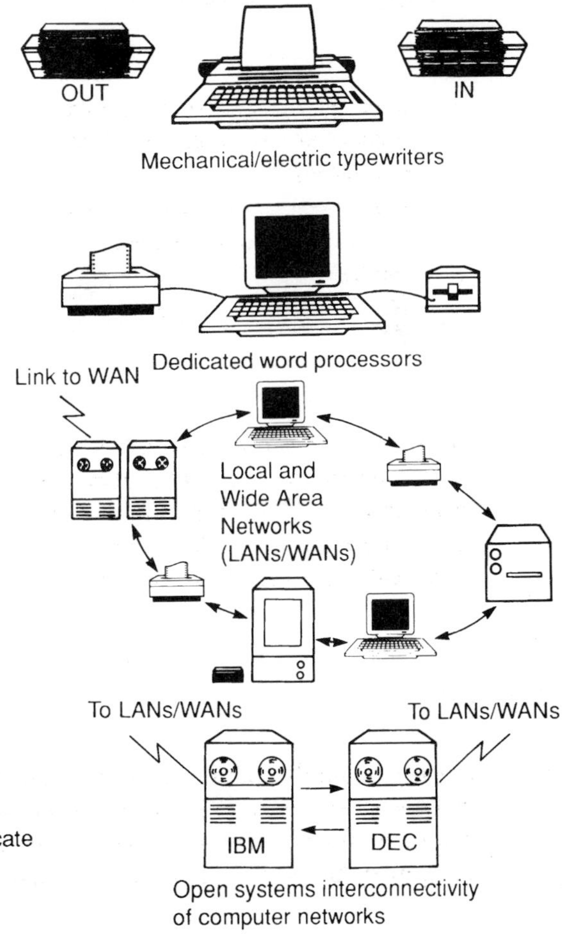
OUT
IN
Mechanical/electric typewriters
Dedicated word processors
Link to WAN
Local and
Wide Area
Networks
(LANs/WANs)
To LANs/WANs
To LANs/WANs
IBM
DEC
Open systems interconnectivity
of computer networks

PC
2.2.1
2.2.2

THE EVOLUTION OF INFORMATION TECHNOLOGY IN BUSINESS

1714	Henry Mill typewriter patent.
1837	Samuel Morse (USA), telegraph line.
1839	Wheatstone & Cook, London, telegraph.
1843	Facsimile transmission invention – patented by A Bain.
1868–1874	Scholes invents mechanical typewriter (USA) which Remington market.
1876	Alexander Bell – first voice transmission by telephone.
1882	Vertical filing system introduced into businesses.
1897	First cathode ray tube invented by K F Braun.
1901	Guglielmo Marconi sends first radio signal from Cornwall to Newfoundland.
1913	First vacuum tube amplifier (valve) developed by H D Arnold and first long-distance telephone cable laid.
1920	Electric typewriters introduced.
1925	John Logie Baird produces first real television transmission.
1936	BBC transmits first world TV programmes.
1946	ENIAC – Electronic Numerical Indicator and Calculator developed – the dawn of the computer age in Pennsylvania!
1947	Brattain and Barden invent the solid state transistor to replace the valve.
1949	EDSAC computer with memory storage developed in Cambridge, England.
1950s	Long-distance direct dialling available in UK.
1956	IBM Corporation develop the computer disk-drive.
1958	First international message routed by satellite.

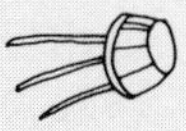

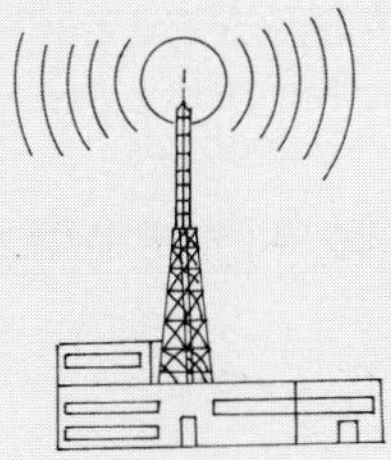

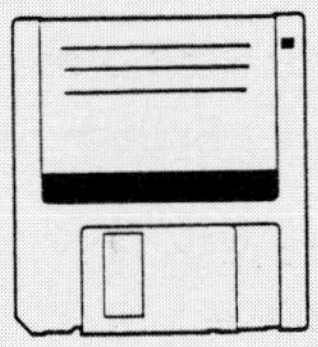

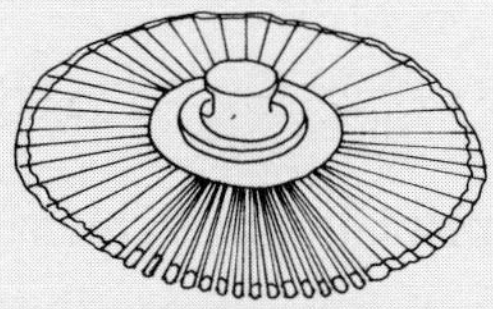

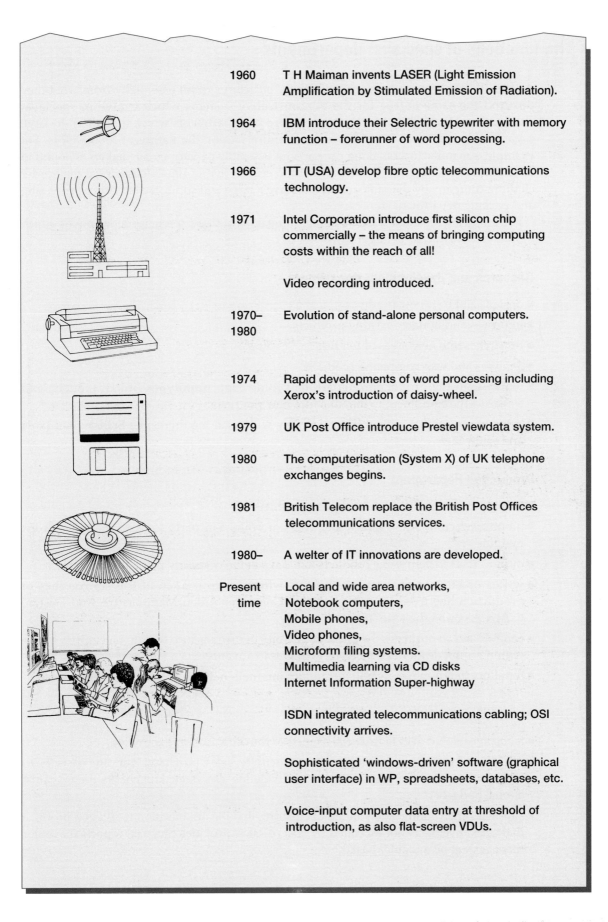

1960	T H Maiman invents LASER (Light Emission Amplification by Stimulated Emission of Radiation).
1964	IBM introduce their Selectric typewriter with memory function – forerunner of word processing.
1966	ITT (USA) develop fibre optic telecommunications technology.
1971	Intel Corporation introduce first silicon chip commercially – the means of bringing computing costs within the reach of all! Video recording introduced.
1970–1980	Evolution of stand-alone personal computers.
1974	Rapid developments of word processing including Xerox's introduction of daisy-wheel.
1979	UK Post Office introduce Prestel viewdata system.
1980	The computerisation (System X) of UK telephone exchanges begins.
1981	British Telecom replace the British Post Offices telecommunications services.
1980–Present time	A welter of IT innovations are developed. Local and wide area networks, Notebook computers, Mobile phones, Video phones, Microform filing systems. Multimedia learning via CD disks Internet Information Super-highway ISDN integrated telecommunications cabling; OSI connectivity arrives. Sophisticated 'windows-driven' software (graphical user interface) in WP, spreadsheets, databases, etc. Voice-input computer data entry at threshold of introduction, as also flat-screen VDUs.

PC
2.2.1
2.2.2

■ The functions of specialist departments

As has already been outlined, organisations' structures result essentially from what they do. And the same is true for the administrative systems which evolve in specialist departments. Naturally, the number and type of departments which a medium-to-large organisation creates as it grows depends entirely upon the nature of its business. For example, a manufacturer making car parts for assembly by various car-makers is bound to have a developed distribution department to ensure 'just-in-time' deliveries; a mail-order clothing company by the same token will have a large and sophisticated order processing and packing department etc.

The following section explains the major functions of those specialist departments which most commonly occur in larger firms.

Research and development department

- designs and tests new products
- improves and updates existing products
- researches into new areas of interest
- analyses and tests competing products
- works with the production department to develop **prototypes** (initial models) and construct the equipment to manufacture new products
- helps to ensure that new products comply with legal requirements, **British Standards** and safety laws.

Production department

- manufactures the company's range of products
- monitors factors like wastage and costs of bought-in parts so as to maintain profit margins
- designs tools to help make products and buys in the necessary plant and equipment
- writes or buys in computer programs which control much of the set routines of production-line manufacturing – **Note:** 'Computer-Aided Manufacture And Design' (CADCAM) and the term 'robotics' .
- controls and co-ordinates the rate and quantity of manufacture so as to meet given orders within pre-set deadlines – plans its activities in advance
- monitors trends in production techniques internationally so as to remain competitive.

Accounts department

- is responsible for overall financial aspects of the organisation's activities
- records and monitors all areas of financial activity: sales, purchases, running costs (heat, light, payroll, etc), manufacturing costs, dividends issued, etc and checks these against annual budgets.
- supplies timely information aimed at ensuring that the organisation works at a profit, ie that sales revenue is not exceeded by cost of sales; provides financial reports for senior management on a regular basis

- produces information for senior managers and shareholders at regular intervals – in the form of financial reports including balance sheets and profit and loss accounts
- maintains financial information required by law, such as the details of income upon which tax must be paid.

Marketing department

- ensures that the organisation remains competitive by providing information about what products and services the market wants and what sort of prices it will pay
- maintains a market research function to explore new markets and new product opportunities; monitors the success/failure of its own products and competing products
- works with R & D and production departments in the design of attractive and 'sellable' new products, as well as the updating and improving of existing ones
- designs and develops advertising materials and campaigns aimed at increasing sales
- monitors local and national trends in consumer demand or industrial marketing needs
- provides advice on the termination of existing products and the introduction of new ones at appropriate intervals; in large companies, maintains computerised models of markets and uses them to predict what will sell.

Sales department

- prepares an annual sales plan which breaks down how many of what type of product will be sold at what profit in the year; divides the plan up into regions, districts and branches, or sales representatives' territories
- supplies point-of-sale material and advice to customers to help sell products
- monitors discreetly the sales of competing products in customers' outlets
- supplies market intelligence to the marketing department on current sales activities; sales representatives provide weekly sales reports to senior sales department personnel
- aims to secure new business with new customers and to increase sales with existing customers on a given target basis.

Personnel department

- ensures that the organisation has the human resources needed to achieve its aims
- co-ordinates employee selection, promotion and termination; supervises appraisal schemes
- provides a staff training and development service
- maintains the organisation's employee records, including pension, sickness benefit and superannuation payments
- supervises industrial negotiations on pay and conditions of work with trade unions and associations
- provides a confidential employee counselling service and runs welfare and social activities in many instances
- monitors personnel activities in competing companies so as to avoid key staff being lured away by increased offers on pay and fringe benefits, etc.

PC 2.2.1 2.2.2

Fig 2.13 **Specialised but integrated departments**

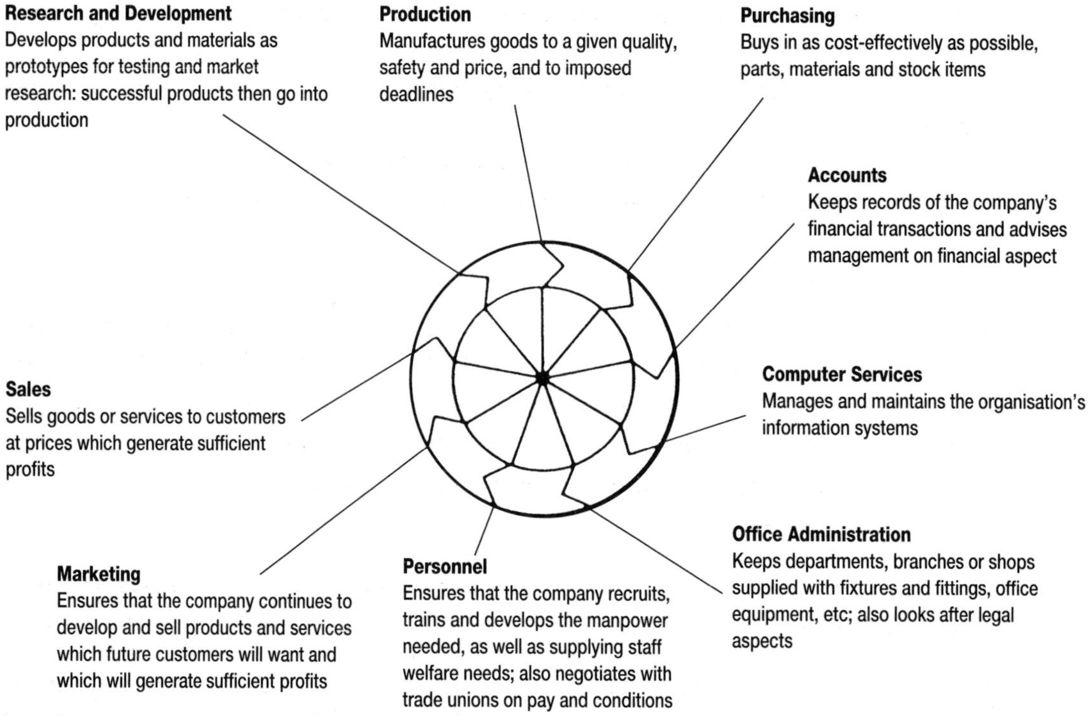
Research and Development
Develops products and materials as prototypes for testing and market research: successful products then go into production
Production
Manufactures goods to a given quality, safety and price, and to imposed deadlines
Purchasing
Buys in as cost-effectively as possible, parts, materials and stock items
Accounts
Keeps records of the company's financial transactions and advises management on financial aspect
Computer Services
Manages and maintains the organisation's information systems
Office Administration
Keeps departments, branches or shops supplied with fixtures and fittings, office equipment, etc; also looks after legal aspects
Personnel
Ensures that the company recruits, trains and develops the manpower needed, as well as supplying staff welfare needs; also negotiates with trade unions on pay and conditions
Marketing
Ensures that the company continues to develop and sell products and services which future customers will want and which will generate sufficient profits
Sales
Sells goods or services to customers at prices which generate sufficient profits

All departments need to work together to keep the company wheel turning!

Office administration department

- provides a service for other departments in areas such as centralised purchasing of stationery and office supplies, and advice on what equipment to purchase for office use
- co-ordinates the internal or external design and printing of forms and schedules
- oversees a centralised reprographics service for bulk photocopying/printing for other departments
- provides word processing/desktop publishing/text production services, if required
- maintains the organisation's insurance requirements
- monitors any leasing arrangements
- where an organisation has dispersed branches or retail outlets, supervises their administration with the help of branch inspectors.

Computer services department

- acquires and maintains company computing equipment
- secures or creates computer software needed by all departments: in larger organisations many computer functions are supplied via custom-designed software
- maintains computer records of organisational information and archived data: large companies have a single database of information which is constantly extended and updated and accessible according to security clearance: back-up duplicate records are essential!

- co-ordinates and supports national and international computer-based communications on behalf of staff
- maintains a watching brief on new developments in information technology to ensure competitiveness and efficiency
- may run staff training schemes for new staff in various computer/data-processing functions
- installs new/updated versions of **software** as they are released; ensures **hardware** is able to match growth in company's activities and increased use by staff.

Transport department

- co-ordinates the organisation's transport needs, from directors', managers' and sales representatives' cars to acquisition and maintenance of fleets of lorries and/or vans
- keeps service records and renews insurances, vehicle registrations etc
- designs cost-effective delivery routes via computer for delivery fleets
- negotiates purchases and leasings with car/HGV dealers
- provides training as needed.

Note: Some business organisations have separate purchasing departments and training departments, while some amalgamate marketing and sales. They may also have a press or public relations office to promote their company image and publicise the company's products in a general way, perhaps by sponsorship of a sports event. Generally, the larger the organisation, the more specialised departments it is likely to create. Remember that the number of departments and the work they do depends directly upon the nature of the organisation's activities, its size and the degree to which it can afford to employ specialist as opposed to generalist employees and managers.

Centralised support services and functions

PC 2.2.1 2.2.2

Most organisations reach a point in their development when it makes sense to bring together the fragmented, departmentalised functions or services, such as filing or computing. Such activities, which are made use of throughout a company's departments, are restructured so as to report directly either to a managing director or an office administration manager with an overall servicing brief.

The chart on page 136 illustrates some of the major services which tend to be centralised in larger organisations. Note that some centralised services, like the personnel function may be run from a department which in many respects is structured just like any other department, with a hierarchical system of responsibility. At other times, units may be set up quite outside the departmental structure and this may create its own problems in communication and inter-personal relations.

PC
2.2.1
2.2.2

Fig 2.14 **Centralised company support services and functions**

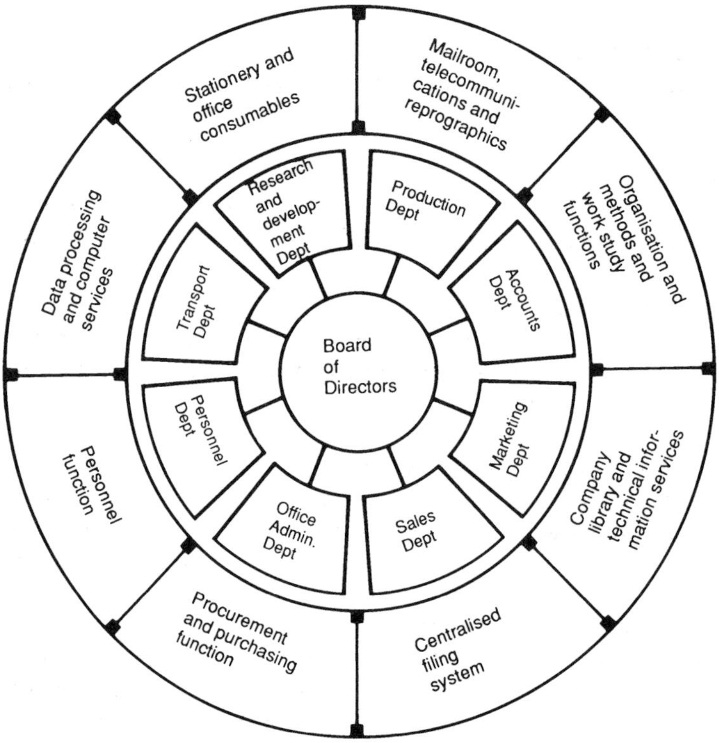

Stationery and office consumables
Mailroom, telecommuni-cations and reprographics
Organisation and methods and work study functions
Company library and technical infor-mation services
Centralised filing system
Procurement and purchasing function
Personnel function
Data processing and computer services
Research and develop-ment Dept
Production Dept
Accounts Dept
Marketing Dept
Sales Dept
Office Admin. Dept
Personnel Dept
Transport Dept
Board of Directors

Advantages

- Easier for directors to exert overall control and direction.
- Uniform, company-wide policies quicker and easier to introduce.
- By providing extra support, encourages departments to do their own work faster.
- Security and continuity improved (see DP and tiling especially).
- Rationalisation secures lower costs and a higher level of service equally available to all departments.
- Gathers into a single group staff who can develop an expert company-wide service.

Disadvantages

- Departments compete for a service which is finite.
- Being external to the departments, the services suffer from 'the distancing effect' and intermittent contact inhibits communication.
- Uniform policies and procedures stifle departmental initiative and innovation.
- 'Things' take longer to happen!
- Face-to-face contact and 'the personal touch' suffer.
- Possible lack of consultation about policy changes
- Increase in costs of running support services – at expense of, say, production and sales activities.

- Note: Some centralised services are set up as departments, e.g. personnel. Centralised services need excellent administrative and communication skills in their staff if they are to work well

PC
2.2.1
2.2.4

EXAMPLES OF FREQUENTLY CENTRALISED SERVICES

1 **Office administration**
Used frequently in national retail and distribution organisations to administer branches and depots.

2 **Personnel function**
Provides a comprehensive service from staff recruitment to pensions fund administration, including training, welfare, industrial relations, and legal advice to management.

3 **Organisation and methods/work study**
O & M provides a service which monitors office practices and procedures in order to improve efficiency. Work study in factories vets production processes so as to maximise efficiency and minimise costs and wastage.

4 **Data processing and computer services**
Provides an around-the-clock, non-stop service, backing up and maintaining an organisation's computing and information processing needs. DP also provides a computer program-writing service for departments needing to administer specific tasks via computers.

5 **Mailroom and telecommunications**
With the widespread use of information technology in organisations today, the function of the mailroom to administer internal and external mail is being superseded in many instances by telecommunications services located at key access points. Such services include fax, telex, BT data transmission services (like SATSTREAM), Internet and email. Thus, area networking is bringing such services to every computerised desktop!

6 **Filing and records**
Many organisations run a centralised filing and records system which loans out paper-based files on request and logs respective users. Advantages include better control, security, avoidance of duplication and fewer lost documents – at the cost of accessibility, time taken to obtain documents and slower pace of updating.

The computerisation of information enables the organisation's database to be kept constantly up to date and made available to all terminals from a mainframe or mini-computer (subject to security clearance). This makes centralised paper-based filing and records systems obsolete, save where legal requirements oblige papers to be kept. Also, computer output microfilm (COM), linking microfilm technology with computers, greatly reduces the need for archiving paper documents.

7 **Library and technical information services**
Many large organisations, like ICI, IBM (UK) and Shell, include scientific/technical libraries in their range of centralised services. Such services offer computerised databases of information from remote locations to all company desktop terminals. Also, optical scanning equipment and computer networks, enable staff to access and to look at paper-originated documents (stored in the form of electronic files on their desktop computer screens.

8 **Procurement and purchasing**
Both public and private sector organisations make significant economies by centralising their purchasing functions and take advantage of bulk purchasing discounts by doing so.

PC 2.2.3

Developments in information technology and administrative systems

In 1971, an American company, Intel, introduced to an unsuspecting world the first silicon micro-chip, which was to form the driving-force of the emerging desk-top personal computer. During the next ten years it found its way into typewriters, wordprocessors, computers and all kinds of gadgets which used small yet powerful electronic circuitry. However, during the 1970s, office equipment using the new information technology was used in stand-alone mode, since the technique of local area networking (LAN) was in its infancy in laboratories. This meant that the IT-based equipment was used for the most part to generate more A4 and fanfold, tractor paper more quickly.

By 1981, the UK government realised that a momentous information revolution was under way, and therefore announced 1982 as the Year of Information Technology, and despatched exhibition pantechnicons of IT equipment to schools and colleges to raise young people's consciousness.

By the end of the 1980s, brilliant teams of computer scientists and software writers had developed from a concept of inter-connectivity a means of linking the regiments of PCs which were sprouting overnight on office workers' desks like mushrooms. At first tv-type coaxial cable was used to send messages around a circuit on to which individual PCs were 'hooked' and able both to send and receive electronic mail (email) messages – initially up to a distance of about 150 metres. Today, after a few short years, email can be sent and received without wires by radio-wave, not simply around a multi-storey office block, but criss-crossing the world !

The chart below illustrates how advances in information technology have changed the ways in which business administration systems are designed and used:

PC 2.2.3

IT AS AN AGENT OF CHANGE TO BUSINESS ADMINISTRATION SYSTEMS

1850–1950	The age of mechanical office equipment: manual typewriters, calculators, ink-duplicating machines, lino-type printing machines etc.
1950–1960	Electrically-driven typewriters appear, and the invention of the solid-state transistor in 1947 results in the demise of the glass, evacuated valve, and smaller 'works' in machines; calculators arrive in Europe from the USA which are electronic and battery-driven. Satellites carry the first international tele-messages in 1958 and herald a new age in global telecommunications.
1960–1970	IBM market their Selectric typewriter in 1964 which included a resident memory and was a fore-runner of the dedicated wordprocessor which arrived in Europe in the early 1970s. Fibre optics are invented in 1966 which will make possible the carrying of thousands of more telephone conversations along much smaller telephone lines.
1970–1980	This decade marks the development of the desktop, personal computer which ousted the mystical mainframe computer gurus who hoarded computer know-how, and which, together with the development of MODEMS (modulating – demodulating systems) and LAN/WAN networking technology, made possible revolutionary changes in the ways business administrative systems were designed and used.

The 1980s also saw great strides made in telecommunications. First, pocket mobile message bleepers were developed for use within short distances of, say, a hospital or school. Then truly mobile phones were introduced using a honeycomb of message relay 'beacons' across the country to enable callers to contact their offices while driving.

Also, the versatile and flexible note-book computer and pocket (Psion) personal computers were developed, which link massive memory power with pocket-book ease of carrying.

1990–Present During the past several years, software applications have been developed to make full use of the 486/586 computers. Microsoft developed its Windows, graphical user interface operations system which uses drop-down menus, touch-active ikons and mouses to simplify software operations.

Also, great strides have been made in electronic file storage and fast access (Canonfile), as well as interactive, computerised programs stored on optical disk (CD-ROM) which are displayed on tv-type computer screens. Multi-media systems were introduced using this technology which provide information in the media of: film, VDU-screened text, sound and dialogue, music, film-slide-type still pictures and any kind of graphic – picture, cartoon, line-drawing etc. Moreover, multi-media technology enables its user to use a kind of decision-tree selection system to browse through a wealth of information, what, where and in what order, at will.

In terms of reprographics, colour-copiers are now priced within the reach of the smallest business, and documents can be reproduced – from concept to bound copy – totally automatically; fax is cheaper than posting a letter, and all can be controlled and programmed from a secretary's desktop PC console!

DISCUSSION TOPICS

PC 2.2.3

1 'The helter-skelter rush into IT-based office administration systems has brought about as many disadvantages as advantages to businesses and their employees.'

2 'Despite all the efforts of IT-responsive organisations to create the 'paperless office', there is today far more paper overwhelming business offices and mailrooms than ever!'

3 'Simply too much information bunging up the administration – that's the result of the IT thing!'

4 Without access to high-powered, low-cost PCs and easy-to drive business software, many small businesses today would be unable to compete with their larger competitors.

5 In the long run, IT will create more office support and administrative jobs, rather than flatter organisational pyramids.

PC 2.2.3 2.2.4

■ How advances in IT changed administrative systems

Given the above rapid pace of change in office technology, it was inevitable that business managers would take advantage of IT advances to improve their administrative systems. The motivation behind the introduction of such change was:

to make savings on:

- time
- operational costs
- human resource costs

and **to make improvements in:**

- effectiveness
- efficiency
- quality
- productivity
- customer service

As the above examples show, information technology is currently being used in a host of different applications spanning industry and commerce as both an agent of change and to support it in administrative terms. Moreover, the resulting changes are also affecting the ways in which people shop as consumers, for example ordering take-away meals via interactive 'tele-computers', and in which they lead their lives – by working from home as a 'telemuter' linked in to the office by phone, fax and modem.

Some of the major ways in which the advent of IT has led to improvements in administrative effectiveness and efficiency may be summarised, broadly, as follows:

PC 2.2.3 2.2.4 2.2.5

IT IMPROVEMENTS TO ADMINISTRATIVE SYSTEMS

Business administrative systems and procedures have been improved as a result of the widespread introduction of IT in the following areas:

- **Faster processing of high-volume data**
- **Quicker retrieval of stored data**
- **Improved dissemination of information**
- **Fewer errors and mistakes in displayed data for reference**
- **Better security for sensitive and confidential data**
- **Much improved analysis and presentation of data**
- **Simpler and clearer administrative procedures made possible**

PC
2.2.3
2.2.4

EXAMPLES OF IT-BASED CHANGES IN ADMINISTRATION SYSTEMS AND WORK METHODS

Time saving

Using an integrated accounts package to process all the transactions of the sales, purchase and general ledgers of an accounts department – with the aide of 'speed-of-light' calculations and data transfers.

Using a note-book computer and modem to transmit a sales order or urgent request from a distant territory to a head office mainframe computer.

Using email LAN/WAN networks to exchange files of data and information virtually instantaneously across the country and the globe.

Operational cost-saving

Using a LAN network and the creation of electronic files from paper originals (by the use of scanning) to copy a team of workers simultaneously with, say, an important in-coming paper letter.
Using EDI (electronic data interchange) to support cost effective ordering and just-in-time deliveries, say in a factory context, where two firms' computers directly and continuously 'talk to each other' about production runs and order needs.

Using group-ware computer software to enable a team of workers (who may be remote from each other) to work together on a project by providing common access to files and work in progress via networked, special software.

Human resource cost-saving

Making savings in the numbers of clerks, assistants and support staff needed, through the introduction of IT systems in bank cash machines, computerised self-interrogation databases (used in some doctors' surgeries), self-booking of holidays, hotels etc (via Prestel/Viewdata) etc.

Using a remote telephone to check for messages on an office telephone answering machine.

Encouraging managers to administer themselves through a networked computer rather than a secretary etc.

Improvements in efficiency and effectiveness

Creating and storing files electronically, rather than as paper, which takes less space and supplies much faster retrieval, as well as much improved security.

Constructing a unified database of information on a mainframe computer which is constantly updated and supplies for all staff accurate and current information according to access status.

Using electronic systems like BACS and SWIFT to transfer money electronically to business people at home and abroad.

Using computerised systems to improve productivity – in, say, processing mail-order sales, re-ordering of supermarket goods automatically at the check-out, monitoring sales of specific goods hourly (Marks & Spencer's electronic sales feedback system), using a software database to log and analyse customers' responses and complaints (e.g package holidays, house insurance).

PC
2.2.1
2.2.2
2.2.3
2.2.4

REVIEW TEST

1 Explain the difference between line, staff and functional relationships in an organisation.

2 What is the difference between a Task Force and a Quality Circle?

3 How did the invention of the silicon chip change office equipment design?

4 What is the difference between a stand-alone and a networked piece of office equipment?

5 What is a multi-media computer application?

6 Explain the main functions of these departments: R & D, Personnel, Computer Services.

7 List three main advantages of a centralised administrative support unit.

8 List five examples of the ways in which IT has changed business administrative systems.

9 List three types of saving made possible by the use of IT-driven administration systems.

10 List five types of improvement which IT has introduced into business administration.

PC
2.2.1
2.2.2
2.2.3
2.2.4

GROUP ACTIVITIES

1 Find out how an integrated accounts software package has developed the process of keeping a business's accounts.

2 Find out how a scanner makes electronic files.

3 Investigate the way in which email works in LAN/WAN networks.

4 Find out how electronic data interchange EDI works among manufacturers.

5 Check out the electronic money transfer services available to businesses via clearing banks.

6 Investigate the way in which a supermarket re-orders goods as they are sold.

7 Look into the electronic analysis of sales carried out by companies like Marks & Spencer.

8 Find out how notebook computers and modems interconnect with remote computers.

KNOWLEDGE TEST

Element 2.2
Investigate administration systems

1 (i) A line management relationship is said to exist between an organisation's managers when they are all of equal status, in a line.
(ii) An employee in a staff relationship with a manager cannot normally require that manager's staff carry out an instruction.

Which of the following options best describes the above statements?

A	(i)	T	(ii)	T
B	(i)	T	(ii)	F
C	(i)	F	(ii)	T
D	(i)	F	(ii)	F

2 Which of the following would you expect to find in a business organisation?

A an expeditionary force
B an advisory committee
C a quality circle
D a focus group

3 Put the following inventions into a chronological sequence, starting with the earliest and ending with the most recent.

A stand-alone word-processing
B laser printing
C manual typewriting
D mobile telephone

4 Which of the following specialist departments is normally responsible for designing an organisation's administrative systems?

A Production
B Office Administration
C Personnel
D Research & Development

5 A business manager is able to communicate from a distance with his or her office with the help of a notebook computer and a:

A PIN
B personal tracking system
C cellphone
D MODEM

6 (i) A scanner is used to convert paper files into electronic ones
(ii) WAN stands for Widely Available Network.

Which of the following options best describes the above statements?

A	(i)	T	(ii)	T
B	(i)	T	(ii)	F
C	(i)	F	(ii)	T
D	(i)	F	(ii)	F

7 Which of the following statements is true, and which false?

A IT has enabled fewer people to process more data more quickly.
B IT has resulted in an unexpected increase in UK employment since 1988.
C IT has led to a significant decline in the use of paper in administrative systems.
D IT has led to the development of administrative systems which are faster in use and more secure.

PC
2.2.1
2.2.2
2.2.3
2.2.4

PORTFOLIO OF EVIDENCE ACTIVITY

Element 2.2
Investigate administration systems

UNIVERSAL'S ADMINISTRATION AUDIT

Scenario

You work as a trainee supervisor for the Management Services Unit in the holding company of a large conglomerate called Universal Trading Group plc, which has subsidiary companies undertaking all kinds of business across the UK and abroad. Your boss, Jimmy Chang, Unit Manager has been charged with carrying out a series of efficiency and effectiveness audits across the Group. Accordingly, he has shared out the workload, and this is what you have been charged to deliver:

1 A detailed audit of a specific administration system within one of the group's companies - which you have been given the freedom to select.

   Your audit is to take the form of an investigation and subsequent report, and should take into account: the system's suitability for the purpose it has been designed to carry out, and how it provides support for the business function(s) it administers. Also, Jimmy Chang is keen for your audit to be carried out on a system which uses information technology, and to discuss how this has (or has not) changed the ways in which things are done.

2 Your report should also consider how information technology is affecting the system, and how current changes in IT are impacting upon the system.

3 Lastly, your report should indicate briefly any ways in which you consider the administrative system might be improved or further developed.

Task 1

As a customary preliminary, plan your approach to this activity and fill out the appropriate parts of your planning and review log.

Task 2

With the help of your family, contacts and/or teacher, decide upon a local business organisation (which you can readily visit etc.) and which will simulate a subsidiary company for this activity. Before making contact with the staff who will help you to obtain the information you need, prepare a visit plan and questions to ask etc., and make sure that you have also made appropriate requests (through letters and phone calls) to support your fact-finding.

Task 3

Having secured the necessary information, made observations and conducted interviews and so on, review your assembled evidence and plan a suitable structure and format for your report. Then compose it - either hand-written or text-processed - as agreed with your teacher. Your report should comprise about 4–5 pages of A4, excluding any illustrations or graphics.

Task 4

In consultation with your teacher, you may produce the final part of your report which deals with possible improvements as an oral presentation to your class of about 5–7 minutes.

Performance criteria covered

2.2.1, 2.2.2, 2.2.3, 2.2.4

Core skills covered

Communication:
3.2.1, 3.2.2, 3.3.1, 3.3.2, 3.3.3, 3.3.4, 3.3.5, 3.4.1, 3.4.2, 3.4.3, 3.4.4

Information Technology:
3.1.1, 3.1.2, 3.1.3, 3.1.4, 3.1.5, 3.2.1, 3.2.2, 3.2.3, 3.2.4, 3.2.5, 3.2.6, 3.2.7, 3.3.1, 3.3.2, 3.3.3, 3.3.4, 3.3.5, 3.3.6

Element 2.3
INFORMATION AND COMMUNICATION IN BUSINESS ORGANISATIONS

In most business organisations, the processing of information and the exchange of communication – between co-workers themselves, workforce and customers, managers and contacts – go hand in hand. Indeed, business consultants tend to view most of the activities which a business organisation carries out as the processing of information of one sort or another. Information residing in the memory of a computer or lying in a filing cabinet may contain information of key importance. However, until it is either viewed, read, discussed or analysed through one type of communications medium or another, it has no value.

PC 2.3.1

■ Theory and process

Ever since the 1930s, management and communication specialists have sought to explain the complex processes of human communication with the help of models. Two such American researchers, C Shannon and W Weaver devised a model identifying the key processes of communication to explain their work in telephone and radio telecommunications in the late 1930s.

Basically, the Shannon and Weaver model illustrates a one-way system, since they were interested in how an electrical signal was transmitted along a wire or radio wave and what happened to it during transmission. Their concept of noise allowed for the distortion and interference of static upon the message's signal which might prevent its clear reception. Today, the concept of 'noise' in human communication models refers to anything interfering between the transmission and reception of the message. For example, an urgent memorandum might lie undetected upon an executive's desk if blanked out by a canopy of white paper documents. Or the distraction of a noisy office might prevent a manager from grasping the crucial points of an orally delivered report.

Other communication theorists have emphasised the importance of the two-way nature of communication in which the success of the process depends heavily upon the sender receiving feed-back. Naturally, the sender needs frequent reassurance that his points are being received and understood – hence the regular confirmations we all make over the telephone to assure our contact that we are still paying attention: 'Yes, of course . . . no, no . . . Absolutely!', etc.

Fig 2.15 PC 2.3.1

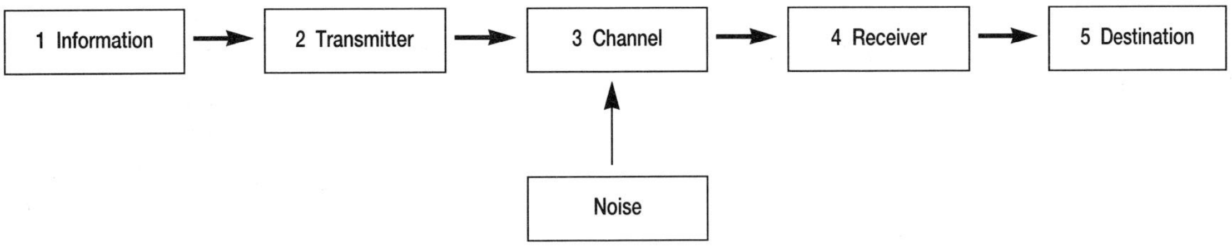
1 Information
2 Transmitter
3 Channel
4 Receiver
5 Destination
Noise

Source: C Shannon and W Weaver Model

The objectives and media of communication in business PC 2.3.2

Simply, an organisation carries out two types of communication which, while using similar media, often have quite different intents and objectives:

■ Internal communications PC 2.3.2

The purposes of most internal communications may be summarised as follows:

- to transmit instructions or requests down (and up) the lines of command, say from managing director to accounts manager to ledger clerk
- to brief staff on new developments, processes, policies or arrangements etc.
- to request information (from specialists or more junior staff) needed to help make decisions, analyse situations or provide feedback on previously instigated actions or policies
- to persuade, to reassure or to motivate staff as and when circumstances require and to encourage the development of individuals and teams
- to provide confirmations, responses and information upwards
- to make proposals or suggestions and to transmit ideas up, down and across an organisation.

■ External communications PC 2.3.2

- to provide information (to customers) about products or services
- to handle incoming enquiries about products or services
- to provide information required (say by statute to the Inland Revenue)
- to promote corporate and brand images

- to advertise and promote sales items
- to liaise and maintain productive contacts with the organisation's network of associates, local public sector agencies and customers etc.
- to effect inter-connected administrative arrangements – as between a purchasing and selling company.

PC 2.3.2 2.3.3

The media employed to effect internal and external communication

Element 2.4, covered later in this Unit, provides a detailed examination of the equipment and media employed in information exchange systems in businesses. However, the following checklist illustrates some of the major media and systems currently in use:

PC 2.3.2 2.3.3

CHECKLIST OF THE MEDIA AND EQUIPMENT USED TO COMMUNICATE IN BUSINESS

Textual Media

- computerised text and graphics processing equipment allied to dot-matrix, bubblejet or laser printer
- photocopied A4 paper sheets (black and white or colour)
- computerised display screens for showing enlarged versions of VDU screened data (say at presentations)
- electronic typewriters and dedicated wordprocessors
- overhead projection equipment, foils and pens
- facsimile transmitters (fax) and teleprinters
- interlinked computers using satellite and radio-wave technology to exchange data (now usually in digitised format)

Spoken word

- interviews, discussions, briefings
- meetings, seminars, conferences
- telephone link-ups, video-conferences
- video/audio-based tapes, cassettes, CD-ROMS for training etc
- bleepers, mobile phones, voice-paging systems, computerised PABX internal telephone systems, public address system

Graphic/visual communication

- computer-created graphs, charts, diagrams, cartoons
- photographs, film-slides, films, OHPs
- desktop published clip-art and designs
- virtual reality and multi-media programs – as encyclopaedias and training environments etc.
- signing for people with special needs

Tactile communication

- Braille, textured surfaces and signing
- touch-sensitive VDU screens
- embossed keyboards

Measures of the effectiveness of business communication: recipients, structures, style, routes and feedback

PC 2.3.3

No communication can be deemed to have worked in a two-way transmitting and receiving mode unless the transmitter is provided with some form of feedback.

Examples of communication feedback:

- a letter is received in response to one sent
- a listener provides non-verbal communication signals (nods, smiles, frowns) in response to a person talking to him or her
- a customer orders a new product after receiving a mailed sales leaflet
- an outside caller rings back in response to a message left on his/her answering machine

etc.

But before feedback can be transmitted, any communicated message first has to be understood, which implies that the following have been correctly created or understood:

Recipient

- The profile and/or background of the targeted recipient in terms of being an expert or a learner, highly educated or not, young or old etc.
- The essential content of the created message has been logically structured or sequenced and is complete in itself, so as to be promptly understood.
- The style and tone of the message has been so designed as to be suited to its context and the nature of its intended recipient(s) – which may mean that it is either formal or friendly, objective or persuasive etc.

Routes

- A highly effective message – in structure, style and format terms – can prove to have been totally ineffective if the wrong route is used to send it to its recipient. An email or fax message will reach someone about to leave the country, but a second-class letter probably won't.
- Fast routes, however, tend to be costly – telegrams, guaranteed overnight mail delivery, courier delivered packets etc.; therefore there is a trade-off between the need for speed and the cost to be borne.
- Also, when people need to be simultaneously informed of a matter, an oral group meeting is likely to be better than individually produced and despatched memoranda – especially if prompt feedback is desired.
- Aspects such as security and confidentiality also directly affect the type of route chosen for a message, where a memorandum in an envelope might be much better than an announcement in a meeting.

As the above section indicates, communicating effectively in business is not a matter of luck and a following wind. Success comes only after acquiring expertise and experience in practice. Furthermore, the people-factor in organisations usually punishes communication mistakes. No one likes to be made to feel small in front of peers, and so they usually find a way of getting back at the perpetrator. No one works well in the dark, starved of information by an insecure hoarder-manager. High-profile errors and typos stick out like sore thumbs in 10,000 advertising leaflets, and insulted customers take their business elsewhere 96% of the time!

On the other hand, effective communication sells goods and services, builds teams, reduces labour turnover, increases productivity and reduces the chances of industrial accidents.

PC 2.3.2 2.3.3

Fig 2.16 **Relationships affect communication styles**

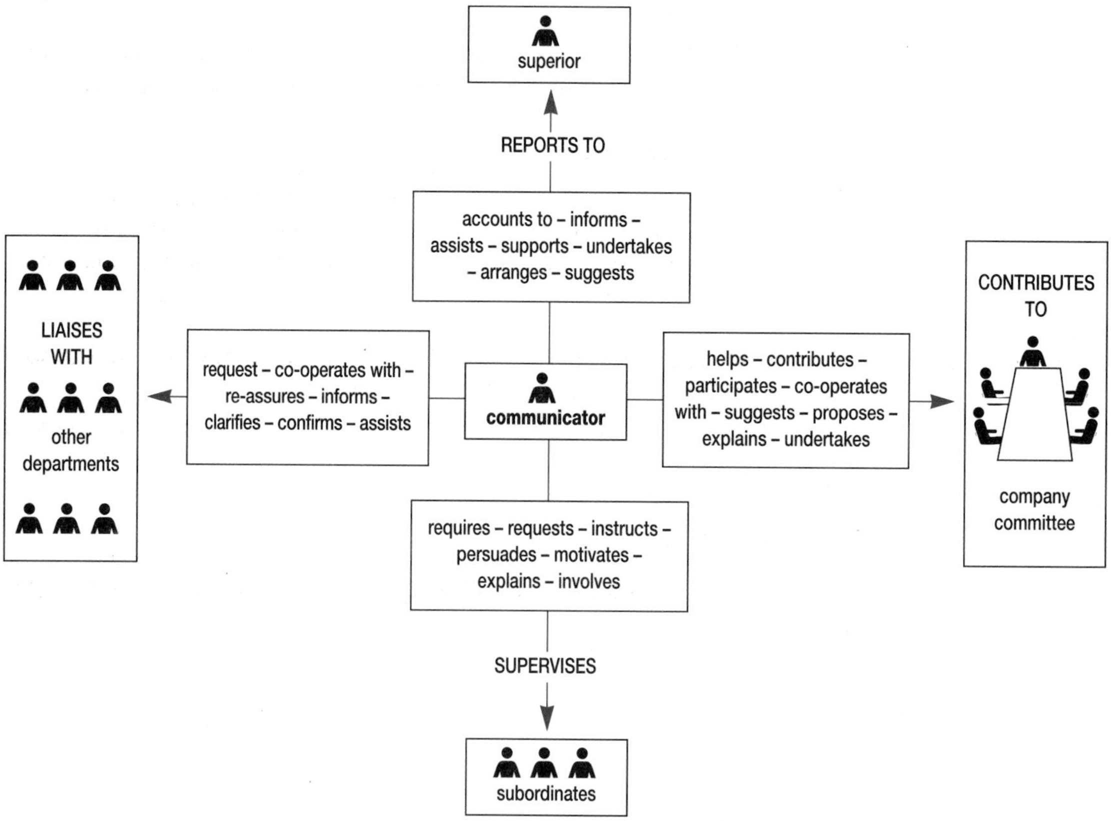

Effective communication in organisations depends on relationships and contexts which influence manner, tone and style

PC 2.3.3

■ Analysing business information needs

The kinds of information needed by business and public sector organisations are many and varied. For example, businesses typically need information answering questions such as:

- What do our customers want?
- What are our competitors up to?
- How are our sales going?

PC 2.3.2 2.3.3

DIFFERENT TYPES OF INFORMATION USED BY ORGANISATIONS

Type of information	Examples	Typical applications
1 Number-based in chart form (sometimes called quantitative information):	Tables, graphs, pie-charts, ratios, formulae	Sales performance analysis, share of market, level of profits, wastage rates, proportion of bad debts, etc.
2 Oral or written word based: rational, logical, analytical treatments of researched information (sometimes called qualitative information)	Investigatory reports, factsheets, briefings, abstracts, summaries, specifications	Problem-solving reports, product specifications, technical updatings, operating manuals, etc.
3 Audio-visual information (sometimes called graphic information):	Videos, over-head viewfoils, audio-cassettes, slides, films, colour graphic charts, photographs	Presentations, opinion-leading advertising, training, briefings, etc.
4 Persuasive information: Influencing, promoting, convincing (sometimes called subjective information)	Advertisements, sales literature, posters, newsletters, oral presentations, meetings, press-conferences	Sales and marketing, public relations, team-building, internal communications, etc.

Accurate, up-to-date, easy-to-digest information is the life-blood of all organisations, without which purpose, direction and effective management are all soon lost!

- Are we making enough profit?
- Where should we be in three years' time?

In order to respond to such questions effectively, organisations need to have available to them information which is:

- up-to-date
- accurate
- relevant
- reliable
- significant (from a statistical viewpoint)

For example, if a manufacturer of sweet snacks surveys customers' current preferences across a representative area of the country and a cross-section of consumers, the following responses may be obtained:

- Three-quarters of the respondents preferred snacks with a low-sugar, low-calorie content.
- Two-thirds disliked 'gooey centres', preferring 'chewy' ones.
- Ninety per cent preferred to buy snacks which, if consumed between meals, did not make them feel guilty.

If such a survey had been conducted only two weeks ago, among a sufficiently large sample (so as to make it 'statistically significant'), and if it had been compared with similar surveys carried out over the past two to three years, then the information it contained would meet the conditions outlined above. It would provide up-to-date, statistically significant data. When the costs of introducing a new product on to a production line and bringing it to the market are considered (and they may run into hundreds of thousands of pounds), then the importance of high quality information is readily appreciated.

It is in this way, as an aid to effective decision-making, that information is power in organisations.

PC 2.3.3

■ Sources of information

As the chart in Fig 2.17 illustrates, a medium to large manufacturing company needs to obtain, analyse and respond to an enormous amount of information across some eight departments and embracing both internal and external sources.

Primary sources of information

Primary sources of information are those that provide data which is usually original in its content and specific to a particular organisation's needs. For example, a firm wishing to develop a new product, say, a blend of coffee, may well identify a sample of targeted customers, who might be young professionals in the 22–30 age range. This group might be invited to test the new blend over a period of time, during which they return questionnaires and attend marketing feedback sessions. The information gleaned by such an activity is technically said to come from a **primary source**. Primary sources of information are valued because they are tailored to meet specific needs, are confidential to the organisation and represent the very latest in available data.

Other primary sources of information could include a selection of customers (who have recently purchased an upgraded product), regional groups of dealers or retailers belonging to specified turnover sizes and so on.

Secondary sources of information

All departments make extensive use of sources of secondary information. Basically this is information obtained and compiled by others which, nevertheless, has a value to the organisation. For example:

- Reviews of new software and updates in monthly computer user magazines.
- Surveys of economic indicators and trends published by the Department of Trade & Industry.
- Regular updatings on legislation and EC directives published by the specialist press, such as *Croner's A–Z of Business Information Sources*.
- Revisions and introductions of specifications by the British Standards Institute.
- Changes to personal taxation and/or VAT rates following upon the annual government budget and accountants' interpretations and advice on such changes.

and so on.

Fig 2.17

Sources of information that organisations seek out

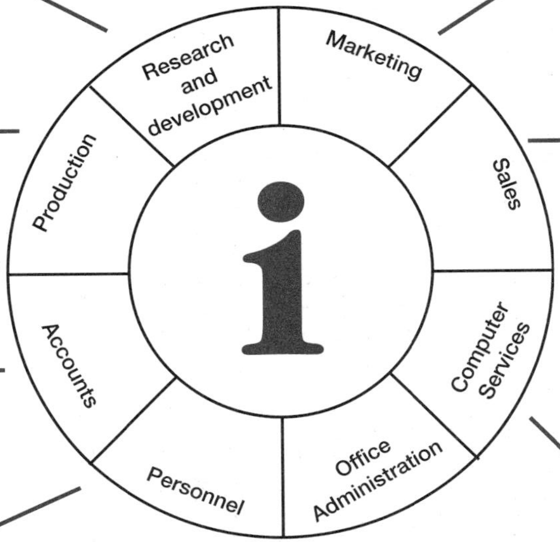

Research and Development
- Latest abstracts/reports on new processes and developments from technical libraries and information consultants
- Results of product tests, upgradings, etc.
- Information on competitor activities

Production
- Accurate data on forward orders to enable production runs to be planned cost-effectively
- Feedback on production costs, wastage rates, etc.
- Up-to-date data on costs of bought-in raw materials, parts, etc.

Accounts
- Continuous flow of data on purchases, sales, running costs and incurred expenses
- Performance of any investments, reports on subsidiary companies
- Management accounting information, e.g. rate of gross profit on sales made

Personnel
- Going pay rates locally for company-similar jobs
- Changes in employment/industrial law
- The manpower audit profiles of all employees

Office Administration
- Latest costs of office equipment and consumables
- Changes in HASAW/working conditions law, e.g. working with VDUs
- Tendering, contracting, leasing terms for cleaning, maintenance, etc.
- Costs of commercial offices, warehouses
- Services of support bureaux, e.g. printing, colour copying

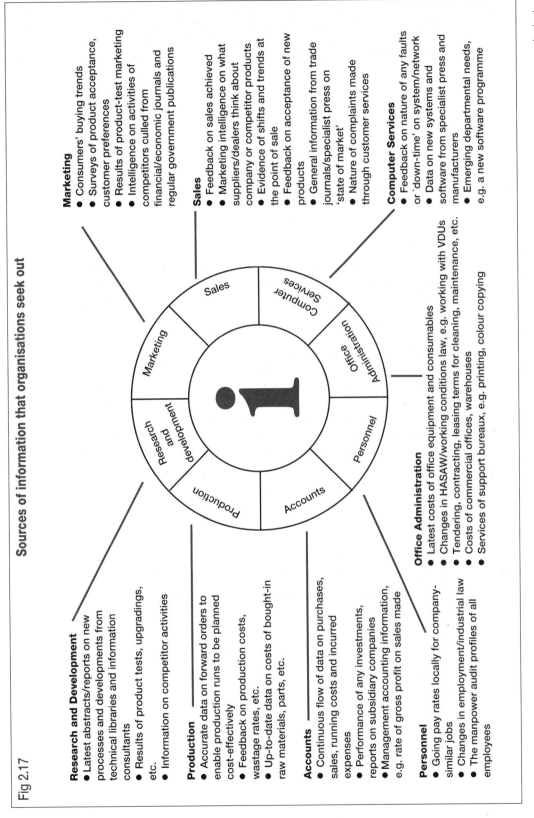

Marketing
- Consumers' buying trends
- Surveys of product acceptance, customer preferences
- Results of product-test marketing
- Intelligence on activities of competitors culled from financial/economic journals and regular government publications

Sales
- Feedback on sales achieved
- Marketing intelligence on what suppliers/dealers think about company or competitor products
- Evidence of shifts and trends at the point of sale
- Feedback on acceptance of new products
- General information from trade journals/specialist press on 'state of market'
- Nature of complaints made through customer services

Computer Services
- Feedback on nature of any faults or 'down-time' on system/network
- Data on new systems and software from specialist press and manufacturers
- Emerging departmental needs, e.g. a new software programme

PC
2.3.2
2.3.3

PC
2.3.2
2.3.3

MAJOR SOURCES OF SECONDARY BUSINESS INFORMATION

• Government department official publications	published by HMSO
• Professional institute magazines e.g.	*Banking World* *Management Today*
• Specialist trade journals	*PC User* *Marketing Weekly* *Business Equipment Digest* *The Grocer*
• Specialist 'state of the art' reports published by information consultants like Frost & Sullivan Inc., e.g. Note: Multinational companies and other large organisations may commission such reports for their own, exclusive use.	'The Implications for the Food Industry of the EC Legislation on Labelling, Presentation and Advertising of Foodstuffs For Sale': (Document 89/395) published 20 June 1992
• National/international newspaper cuttings and clippings, e.g.	*Financial Times* *New York Herald Tribune* *The Times*
• Annually published yearbooks and handbooks, e.g.	*Annual Abstract of Statistics* *Post Office Guide* *Kompass* (listings of UK and European companies and products) etc.

Secondary information and technical libraries

Large organisations maintain their own technical libraries which stock standard references, subscribe to relevant trade, institution and professional association journals and provide connections to national and international computer databases. Their librarians may also produce abstracts on demand of specialist articles and papers for company research scientists, marketing executives and so on.

PC
2.3.3

Desk research: sources of in-house information

External sources of primary or secondary information may be supplemented as a general rule by accessing information from within the organisation. All organisations are obliged to store certain types of information, such as annual balance sheets for up to 30 years. In addition to information which has to be retained by law, organisations also store details for their own convenience and assistance:

- Plans, designs and specifications of products developed and produced.
- Account customer records and purchasing patterns.
- Listings of suppliers and buying terms.
- Registration records of equipment sold to customers – for warranty and customer service reasons.
- Inventory of plant and equipment and details of date of purchase.
- Personnel records – salary progression, promotion, relocations, etc.

And so, whenever an executive is given an investigation to undertake, he or she will probably start at the office desk by sifting through the data which is readily available from within the organisation – hence the term 'desk research'.

INDIVIDUAL ACTIVITIES

PC 2.3.2 2.3.3

First carry out your researches and then report back to your group in an illustrated oral presentation:

1 The major primary and secondary sources of information currently in use in your department either at work, in your college or in your school.

2 The regular publications produced by one of the following government departments/agencies to aid commerce and industry:

a The Department of Trade & Industry

b The Department of Employment

c The Bank of England

d The Treasury

e The Central Office of Information

3 The different types of data and information available in your local reference library which would be useful to your local business community.

4 Make arrangements to interview the manager of one of the following local businesses:

a A major car dealership;

b A building society branch;

c A supermarket;

in order to find out what sort of top priority information they need to be able to run the business successfully, and what information they are most interested in at present.

How people in business use information

PC 2.3.3 2.3.4

How businesses and public sector organisations use information depends very much upon the level of operation of executives or officers. Consider, for example, the diagram shown in Fig 2.18.

In its rough and ready way, the chart illustrates the different timespans of decisions and the extent of their impact in an organisation. It is also useful to highlight the different types of information which tend to be employed at various levels in the organisational pyramid.

At corporate director level

Information needs to be presented in summarised, analytical form – say, as the comparative breakdown of last month's sales in the seven regions of a national company. This data will be expressed as 'Actual to Target'. Other information may be expressed as a forecast of market share over the next three years, or as a quarterly set of trading accounts.

Much of senior management's information needs tends to be of the quantifiable type, which covers the entire scope of company activities. Such data is usually provided in reports, surveys, abstracts, reviews, analyses and so on. It is as though the managers are continually monitoring the firm's pulse-points, and measuring present against past performances, while seeking to meet anticipated future needs. And indeed, it is just such constant monitoring that informs and influences the rolling corporate plans produced by senior management annually, which deal with the coming (financial) year in detail, and the subsequent two years in overview.

PC
2.3.3
2.3.4

Fig 2.18 **The time-span of decisions in organisations**

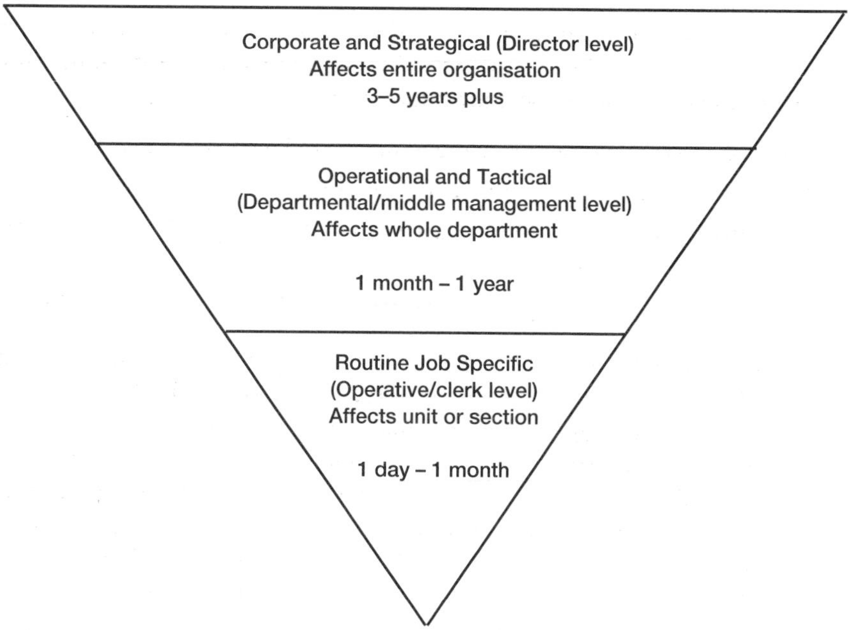
Corporate and Strategical (Director level)
Affects entire organisation
3–5 years plus
Operational and Tactical
(Departmental/middle management level)
Affects whole department
1 month – 1 year
Routine Job Specific
(Operative/clerk level)
Affects unit or section
1 day – 1 month

PC
2.3.3
2.3.4

At the operational and tactical level

Middle and departmental managers also need number-based information to enable them to monitor how they are matching up to targets allocated in annual business plans; they also tend to require direct, word-of-mouth feedback from operatives or office support staff on daily events and activities, so as to be kept 'in the picture'.

While directors and public service executives concentrate on long-term cycles of activity – the strategic dimension – middle managers are primarily concerned with: this month's sales compared with last month's; next month's projected production; output for the third quarter of this year compared to the same quarter last year and so on. Their management activities are said to be tactical, and rarely span more than a year.

At the job-specific, routine level

Inevitably, the job-role of the clerical assistant or factory operative is limited – say, to the maintenance of a section of a company's accounts, or to the assembly of a small part of a washing machine. Consequently, much of the informational needs at this level take the form of orally delivered instructions, short-life data schedules or amendments to operating routines.

At the operative level of activity information tends to be limited to current daily or weekly cycles of activity and to remain within a tightly controlled framework of routines and procedures, where there is limited scope for the use of discretion.

■ Business information systems and the decision-making pyramid

PC 2.3.3 2.3.4

If a business information system is to be effective, it must meet the needs of, the organisation at each level of activity. By the same token, its designers must take fully into account the needs of its users for information which may be:

- Historical – reviewing past achievement and keeping records
- Current – monitoring processes as they occur
- Futuring – anticipating and forecasting what is likely to happen next month or next year.

The need for 'after the event' or 'historical feedback'

In order to assess the success (or otherwise) of a project or operation, organisations need to have set up procedures for monitoring the activities they undertake. For example, both the shareholders of a company and the Inland Revenue receive at 12 monthly intervals a set of company accounts which provide an in-depth profile of the company's financial position on a particular day of the year – usually at the end of its annual trading period. The information provided by the set of accounts summarises the overall sales achieved by the firm, the costs it incurred in making the sales, the amounts of money it owes to others and the amounts others owe to it, as well as the computed value (at the time the accounts were produced) of the stock it has in hand, the value of its plant and equipment as well as of any property and other assets it owns.

Other examples of the evaluation of information which is 'historical' – by the time it is available – are:

- reviews of sales achieved compared with targets set
- running expenses incurred in maintaining a sales force on a regional basis
- the number of sales the company has achieved in a specific trading period and their value in pounds sterling etc.

Unless procedures are established for monitoring the success or cost-effectiveness of activities as soon as possible after their occurrence, a company has no way of knowing whether it is on or off track in meeting preset budgets, targets or planned costs – hence the common question among sales representatives, factory foremen and accountants: 'How did we do?'

The need for operational information

While some kinds of information serve to summarise events which have already happened, other kinds are needed to monitor activities **as they occur**.

Take, for example, the involved process of developing and manufacturing a new model of saloon motor car. In order to be in a position to sell the model at a preplanned level of output per month and to maintain a precalculated profit, the following operational costs have to be analysed very closely as they arise in the overall development and production process:

- Research and developmental costs.
- The buying-in costs of raw materials or finished/semi-finished parts.
- Labour costs in the production phase.
- Overhead charges to be apportioned from the expense of providing: energy, light, heat, rental and rates charges, etc.

- Value-added taxes to be borne at each phase of the production to sales process.
- The costs of distributing the product to bulk-breaking wholesalers or to retail outlets.
- The expenses incurred in printing and mailing catalogues price-lists, sales brochures, merchandising displays, trade journal and newspaper advertising, etc.
- Providing customer service facilities (such as the availability of customising add-ons like CD-players or mobile phones).

As the above checklist illustrates, bringing a motor car to the market is a highly complex operation. It requires systems – nowadays extensively computerised – which make continuously available various measures and ratios of quantitative (number-based) information for teams of accountants and allied staff to analyse.

For instance: If 500 sheets of lightweight alloy have been calculated to produce 20,000 wheel-trims, how many were actually produced to company quality standards and what was the percentage wastage rate?

Similarly, if a pre-launch mailshot to established dealers expects a positive response from 8 per cent, what was the actual percentage of dealers who placed orders compared with the planned response level?

Only by introducing detailed methods for obtaining information relating to such operational activities can a car maker keep within the levels of costs allowed, and produce the percentages of overall profit which have been planned.

And this is why the question 'How are we doing?' is asked at regular intervals by all involved in making and selling operations.

Assuring the organisation's future

While detailed information is needed to assess past performance and compare it with similar preceding data like:

this month – last month
this year – last year (first quarter)
etc.

and while it is important to monitor information relating to ongoing operations, perhaps the most important information an organisation needs to obtain and sift is that which will inform the crucial question: 'Where are we going?'

If this question fails to be answered, or prompts the wrong answers, then as night follows day, the commercial undertaking concerned is headed for the slippery slope descending to Carey Street, 'Queer Street', or in other words, bankruptcy!

For this reason, large investments of time and money are devoted to gaining just this kind of futuring information:

PC 2.3.4

INFORMATION NEEDED TO ASSURE THE FUTURE

Research and Development:
- What technologies and scientific processes currently or newly developed are most likely to affect the products or services we sell?
- What should be our developmental priorities?
- In what general directions is research going?
- Are we keeping pace in our field?

Marketing:
- What introductions or changes do we need to plan for now in order to ensure that our goods or services remain in high demand in three to five years' time?
- How do we maintain a competitive edge over our competitors in terms of these future offerings?

Production:
- How can we refine and improve our manufacturing processes so as to increase output, reduce waste and remain cost-effective?
- What new plant do we need? What training and development does the factory workforce require?

Personnel:
- What kind of workforce does the organisation need in the coming five years in terms of age, qualifications, skills and experience?
- What manpower planning steps need to be taken – recruitment, early retirement, retraining, fast-track development, etc. – to generate the right employee profile in good time?

Finance:
- Are the levels of profit currently being produced sufficient to ensure that the corporate development plan for the next three years can be financed?
- Should the company:
  - obtain further capital by a rights issue of shares (i.e. offer new shares in the company to existing or new shareholders)?
  - or restructure its activities so as to improve both cash-flow and profits in key sectors?

As the above examples illustrate, senior executives in organisations devote expensive time and energy to acquiring the information needed to answer such crucial, corporate questions.

■ Modelling and forecasting

PC 2.3.4

The advent of high-capacity, networked computers in the 1980s gave corporate futuring – anticipating future possibilities which could affect the organisation's success – a powerful thrust.

Researchers were able to create computer models of:

- specific national and international markets;
- trends in consumer lifestyles and purchasing patterns;
- comparative costs in complex products related to the use of alternative parts and/or processes;
- design options to meet high/low build schedules, costs and quality specifications.

PC 2.3.3 2.3.4

DISCUSSION TOPICS

1 The Information Revolution is placing ever more reliance upon impersonal computers and their support equipment to minister to our everyday needs – like personal finance, shopping, travelling and recreation – as well as in our daily working lives. Are we in danger of creating an impersonal and uncaring world in which only electronic logic rules?

2 How many different types of information can you identify? Or is information incapable of being broken down into different types?

3 'Would that the infernal Information Revolution had never reared its ugly head! Contemporary society and its business concerns are becoming buried beneath an avalanche of information – most of it unasked for, time-consuming to absorb and, in the event, trivial and unnecessary!'

Do you agree with this jaundiced view of the 1990s?

4 'The ability to communicate effectively is the thing most people lack, but fortunately I possess!'

5 'Despite all the IT gadgetry which surrounds business workers, there are more technophobics around than senior managers care to believe!'

Such models provide answers to questions like:

- What happens to product sales if consumers continue to be influenced by environmental issues at the present rate?
- By how much should the price of our vacuum-cleaner increase if our energy costs rise by 8 per cent next year, and the costs of our bought-in electric motors by 6 per cent?

In a similar way, computers enable likely future trends to be forecast as a result of analysing historic and current results. For example, market-makers and stockbrokers use highly sophisticated software to record the hourly, daily, weekly and monthly fluctuations of the stock market so as to gain insights into the likely future movements of particular shares. Such information influences the prices at which they are prepared to buy or sell.

Government departments and public sector organisations also make extensive use of computer modelling techniques. Civil servants in, say, the National Health Service need to explore the impact upon the provision of geriatric wards and day-care centres of the current trend of people living ten to fifteen years longer than they did fifty years ago. Similarly, staff in the Department of Social Security need to secure realistic estimates of the likely costs in income support for single parents across the country should the current divorce rate remain at some 40 per cent of all marriages.

GROUP ACTIVITIES

PC 2.3.3 2.3.4

In a group of two or three, first undertake your researches and then report back to your group in a ten to fifteen minute illustrated oral presentation:

1 The kind of 'historical snapshot' information about a company's business activities and financial state provided in its annual balance sheet.

2 The historical information published by a company in its annual report to its shareholders.

3 The sort of data which project planners assemble when using PERT – Programme Evaluation and Review Technique – in order to manage a project.

4 The information used to design a business plan prior to opening a small business.

5 The sort of information a company like *Laura Ashley*, *Halfords* or *Body Shop* would include when drawing up their corporate plan for the coming three years.

CASE STUDY

PC 2.3.3 2.3.4

Clean sweep at Colorama

Kathy Wilkins joined the head office of Colorama plc on the first of September 19-- as the company's new Office Administration Manager. Colorama are a national company which manufactures a wide range of wallpaper and interior decoration fabrics. There are four factories strategically dispersed across the UK and a head office located in Walsall. Currently Colorama employs some 2000 employees, 120 of whom work at head office.

The major role of the Office Administration Department is to provide a support service – in-house printing, stationery supplies, office equipment, purchasing, contract management for cleaning etc. company tenders co-ordination and so on.

Kathy Wilkins was appointed as the result of her unremitting hard work and personal commitment to the job. She had come from a smaller company and been doing a similar job. She was considered hard but fair. Her former company – and former colleagues – had benefited from her drive and determination. Colorama was in a much bigger league, however. During the DIY boom of the mid 1980s, the company had ridden on the crest of the home improvement wave and acquired three of its four factories between 1985 and 1988. A favourite watchword of the MD's was 'What we lack in whizzkids we make up for in continuity!'

During past two years, though, sales had proved disappointing and Colorama's image was fast becoming staid and 'old-hat', as younger and more aggressive companies ate into Colorama's markets – in no small part as the result of having installed fast and cost-effective computerised management information and communications systems.

Kathy saw her central role as helping the company to catch up with its rivals in this regard. About four months after her appointment, she sent this email memo through the Office Administration's newly installed local area network (LAN) communications system to all Departmental staff:

Unclassified	Page 1	12 January 19--

From: Katherine Wilkins

To: All Departmental Staff

Subject: Use of LAN Office Communications System

You will recall that at my first Staff Meeting in September of last year, I informed the Department of my dissatisfaction at the poor performance I perceived on arrival. I told you all then that a fundamental change in attitude and performance was needed and that a new computerised communications network would be installed as a company pilot scheme to improve our administrative procedures and systems.

To this end, a great deal of effort was put into installing a LAN system against the clock. Colorama has also invested significant finance in securing LAN training for all Departmental staff since November.

I am therefore appalled to see in my daily movements around the Department that the LAN system is being scarcely used at all. I detect a widespread apathy regarding the use of the email system – apart from offensive and sexist messages being sent. And I see little or no use of the electronic diary and desk-top management features. What I do see is the same old wasteful use of photocopying practices and the same time-consuming practice of text-processing and photo-copying of endless paper memos and reports.

Clearly my policies and instructions are being flouted. You are therefore reminded of the obligations implicit in your conditions of service concerning adherence to company policies and routines and to supply a degree of commitment related to your remuneration. Unless I detect an immediate improvement from each member of staff, I shall take firm and immediate steps to rectify matters.

KATHERINE WILKINS
Office Administration Manager
11:23 All Group C 12/01/9

Within three hours of Kathy Wilkins having sent out her email memo on the LAN network, she was called into the MD's office. A stormy interview ensued. She was told there was no room at Colorama for any Catherine The Greats. Kathy's answer was that she considered her memorandum fully justified and had a right to get the fullest support from top management regarding its requirements needed to overcome what she identified as 'Colorama's cosy and cushy complacency'. If her resignation was required it was immediately available.

CASE STUDY QUESTIONS

Either: Discuss the following questions as a class
Or: Provide individual written answers for each one

1 Did Kathy go wrong in her approach to what she saw as the response to the installation of the LAN network?

2 If Kathy's email memo goes wrong, where does it and how does it?

3 In Kathy's place, what would you have done to resolve the situation?

4 How would you have handled the interview with the MD?

5 If you think that the memorandum is less than appropriate, rewrite it as you think it should be.

6 Did she choose the right medium in which to send the message?

REVIEW TEST

PC
2.3.1
2.3.2
2.3.3
2.3.4

1 List the five main stages in Shannon & Weaver's communication model.

2 List five objectives of internal communication and five of external communication.

3 Detail four different media for producing textual communications.

4 Cite five different kinds of oral communication media.

5 Why is feedback so important in effective communication?

6 Why should a transmitter of a message take its recipient's profile into account?

7 In what main ways do relationships at work affect communication styles?

8 List four main features which information needs to possess in order to be of use to business workers.

9 Explain the difference between primary and secondary sources of information.

10 What measures would you use to evaluate the effectiveness of communication in a business organisation?

11 What are likely to be the main effects of poor communication practices in a large organisation?

12 Explain the difference between the informational needs of a manager working at a corporate strategy-making level and an operational level in a large business organisation.

13 List three examples of how the introduction of IT equipment has improved communication outcomes in current business organisations.

PC
2.3.2
2.3.3
2.3.4

INDIVIDUAL ACTIVITIES

1 Research into the ways in which IT equipment is able to be used in a restricted, limited access way according to the entry level and security status of various users. Report back to your class in a 5–10 minute oral presentation.

2 Find out how a medium-to-large organisation uses open communication channels – in-house newspapers, notice-boards, circulated bulletins, public address systems etc. and for what particular purposes. Report back to your class in a 5–10 minute oral briefing.

3 Research into the effectiveness of email in team project work. Summarise your findings in a bullet-point sheet and post in your base-room.

4 Find out how companies are beginning to use the Internet 'super highway' and report back to your class in a 5–10 minute oral presentation.

5 Research into the ways in which three international IT manufacturers (e.g. IBM, Apple and Toshiba) are working to promote OSI – open systems integration, so as to enable equipment of various makes to be inter-compatible.

KNOWLEDGE TEST

Element 2.3
Analyse communication in a business organisation

1 Which of the following are key communication objectives of a business organisation?

A To provide annual statistical returns for the Central Office of Information
B To route instructions to employees promptly and clearly
C To ensure that all employees have ready access to all company information at all times
D To ensure that all external communications are personally checked and signed by the appropriate head of department
E To maintain contact with its external network of customers and associates

2 (i) An example of a tactile communications medium is a touch-sensitive VDU screen.
(ii) Processed data sent at high speed via satellite tends to be digitised.

Which of the following options best describes the above two statements?

A (i) T (ii) T
B (i) T (ii) F
C (i) F (ii) T
D (i) F (ii) F

3 Which of the following statements is true, and which false?

A High speed message routes tend to be expensive to use.
B Email messages can be sent to teams of workers simultaneously.
C A disadvantage of using fax machines to send messages is that they are not confidential.
D Quantitative information is that which can be measured objectively.

4 (i) A technophobe is a person who is highly computer literate.
(ii) Incompatibility of equipment is a problem affecting wide area networking among computer users.

Which of the following option best describes the above statements?

A	(i)	T	(ii)	T
B	(i)	T	(ii)	F
C	(i)	F	(ii)	T
D	(i)	F	(ii)	F

5 Which of the following statements is true and which false?

A Information overload is a common cause of stress among middle managers.
B The Data Protection Act was introduced to ensure the security of sensitive and confidential company information.
C An example of an open medium of communication is a bulletin board.
D 'Information super-highway' is a term coined to describe an international form of communication via electronic mail.

PORTFOLIO OF EVIDENCE ACTIVITY

PC
2.3.1
2.3.2
2.3.3
2.3.4
2.3.5

Element 2.3
Analyse communication in a business organisation

BUSINESS TODAY

Scenario

You work as research assistant for Business Today, a monthly magazine which enjoys a wide circulation among up-and-coming business managers. Your editor, Amitra Patel, is planning to include in an issue to appear the month after next a feature about current trends in business communication - especially communication processes and practices in which IT equipment is employed.

Ms Patel briefed you yesterday as follows:

'I'd like you to find a suitable business organisation – say near where you live – which you can readily access. Then you should make arrangements to research into four different kinds of communication process in use – say two internal and two external. Oh, and make sure that at least one of each is IT-electronic equipment based. The main thrust of your research should be to find out how the business you survey employs its communication equipment and systems to help it to achieve its goals and objectives.
Also, a particular focus of your investigations should be to find out whether the IT equipment used improves employees' access to information – or not, and whether it improves contact and interaction between staff – or not.

I'd like a suitably formatted report of your findings which I can use to help me plan the approach of the feature, which will be a big, middle-page spread.

And before I forget, to save time after you've met and talked to the staff who are involved in the systems you survey, I'd like you to make an audio recording of your discussions, supported by summary notes which outlines two plus and two minus outcomes which change has brought about in the organisation's communication practices. And lastly, I'd like you to suggest two changes which the organisation might profitably make in their current communication practices which would improve their operations.'

Ms Patel has a way of making a tall order seem like the granting of a favour, so you smiled graciously, uttered 'No problem!' and got stuck in!

Task 1

First, make out your planning and review activity plan and liaise with your teacher before contacting a local business organisation.

Task 2

Having made contact with your chosen organisation, explore the types of communication processes you can most readily research and, with the help of your contact staff, select four as briefed by Ms Patel, which meet her terms of reference. Carry out your researches conscientiously and keep careful notes on what you discover, as well as collecting any documents about them which can be made available.

Task 3

Once satisfied that you have amassed enough information, sift your data into suitable topic areas and then plan and produce a report which meets your brief. A suitable report is likely to be some 5–6 sides of A4 long.

Task 4

Using the notes you took during and immediately after your discussions with the staff you visited, make an audio recording (of about 3–5 minutes) which summarises your observations of outcomes and suggested changes. Also, remember to produce a suitable summary of about one side of A4.

Performance criteria covered

2.3.1, 2.3.2, 2.3.3, 2.3.4, 2.3.5

Core skills covered

Communication:
3.2.1, 3.2.2, 3.2.3, 3.2.4, 3.2.5, 3.3.1, 3.3.2, 3.3.3, 3.4.1, 3.4.2, 3.4.3, 3.4.4

Information Technology:
3.1.1, 3.1.2, 3.1.3, 3.1.4, 3.1.5, 3.2.1, 3.2.2, 3.2.3, 3.2.4, 3.2.5, 3.2.6, 3.2.7, 3.3.1, 3.3.2, 3.3.3, 3.3.4, 3.3.5, 3.3.6

Element 2.4
INFORMATION PROCESSING IN A BUSINESS ORGANISATION

The first three Elements of this Unit have examined how business organisations are structured and function, and how they devise and employ administrative and communication systems to enable them to reach their objectives. To complete your detailed examination of *Business Organisations and Systems*, Element 2.4 provides an analysis of how businesses use information processing to *deliver* their administrative and communication systems. It also surveys current electronic office and telecommunications equipment and its applications, so you can carry out your own analysis of actual information processing in a business organisation, to find out how it contributes to the effectiveness of the activities of its workforce.

The systems approach to information

PC 2.4.1

A very useful place to start is to consider how information is processed – both in theory and in practice. Some fifty years ago, a meeting of minds occurred between biologists and computer scientists. The biologists had already long established that living organisms existed within a kind of open system, in which their life-cycles depended upon taking up nutrients from their environments, processing and storing them, and using arising energy to reproduce in due course – so that the continuance of the species was assured. In this way a continuing spiral of evolution was created. Similarly, living creatures sought to maintain the 'user-friendliness' of the eco-systems they inhabited – by obtaining feedback on, for them, good or bad events and then acting appropriately – by seeing off a competing male, gorging on available food or fleeing a stronger adversary etc.

Computer scientists and management specialists like Kenneth Boulding in the 1950s took on board this cyclical process – and used it to develop a concept called *the systems approach*, as Figure 2.19 illustrates. They came to see the processing of information as a major function of all organisations, in which messages arrive in the form of *inputs* – letters, phone calls, conversations etc., are *processed* – absorbed and responded to, and then *stored* for subsequent access and reference, in, say, a file in a computer's memory. The arising responses are then distributed as *outputs*, say in the form of an answering letter or memo to communicate a decision. To complete the process, *feedback* is sought to ensure that an instruction, for example, has been understood and carried out.

PC 2.4.1

Fig 2.19 **Organisational systems model**

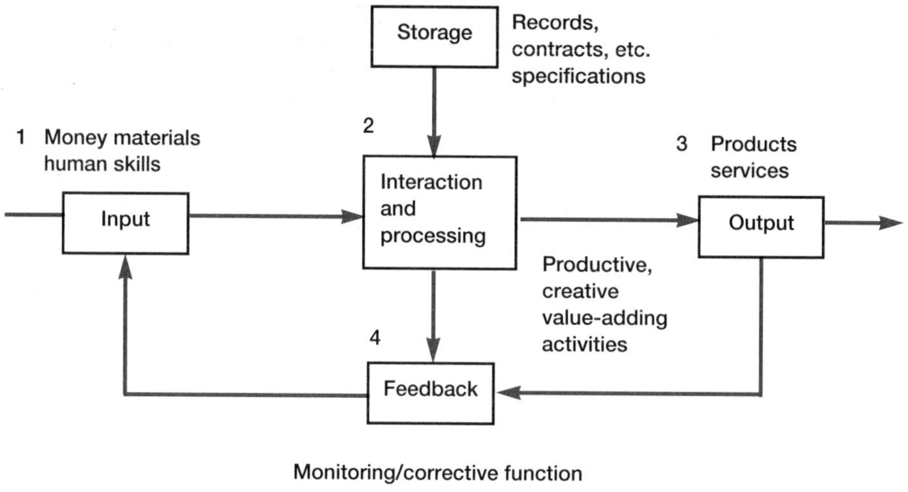

1 In order to function and maintain itself, an organisation needs continual inputs of money, materials and human skills. In the above systems management model, this process is called **the input phase**.

2 The ingredients of finance, materials and human skill are then mixed together in a number of ways, depending upon the work of the organisation – in, say, the process of manufacturing a product, writing software programs, or supplying legal advice and services, etc. This activity is called **the process phase**. The storage of records, files, prototypes and so on is included in this phase.

3 The process of making, designing or advising may result in making a 36-piece china tea-set, writing a desktop publishing program or drawing up a new will. Whatever their form, in systems management these end results are termed **outputs**.

In the process of transforming inputs into outputs, value is added, which forms the source of profit and of further money inputs so that the system can continue.

4 In order for the system to work effectively, the process phase needs to be continuously monitored. Thus feedback is supplied – either that all is going according to plan, or that faults, break-downs, incorrect data, bottle-necks, etc. have occurred which threaten the system.

Figure 2.20 illustrates the essential principles which all computers embody in processing data, which also mirror the systems model.

The approach of systems management, embodied in the INPUT – PROCESS – OUTPUT – FEEDBACK model above is particularly suited to the design and management of business information systems. Indeed, from its earliest development, computerised data processing has been explained by using virtually the same model to illustrate the way in which computers work (see Fig 2.20).

The diagram in Fig 2.21 fleshes out the INPUT – PROCESS – OUTPUT computer model with a number of examples of input, process, storage and output media and processes.

PC
2.4.1
2.4.2

Fig 2.20 **The computer as a system for processing information**

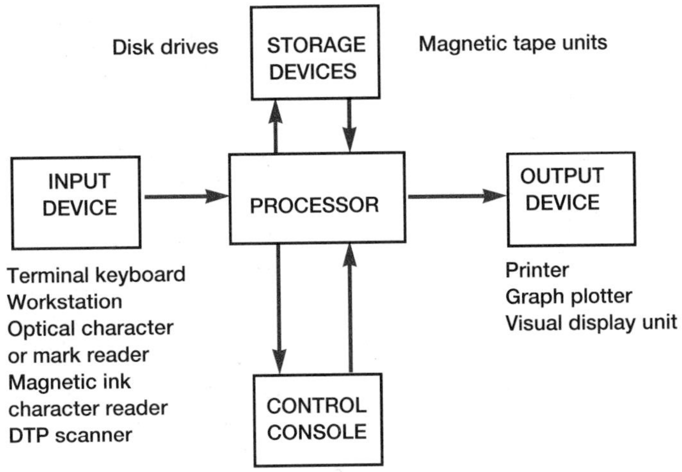

Disk drives
STORAGE DEVICES
Magnetic tape units
INPUT DEVICE
PROCESSOR
OUTPUT DEVICE
Terminal keyboard
Workstation
Optical character or mark reader
Magnetic ink character reader
DTP scanner
Printer
Graph plotter
Visual display unit
CONTROL CONSOLE

From *Data Processing* by R G Anderson. © Longman Group UK Limited 1990

PC
2.4.1
2.4.2

Fig 2.21 **A systems model of the information processing function in the office**

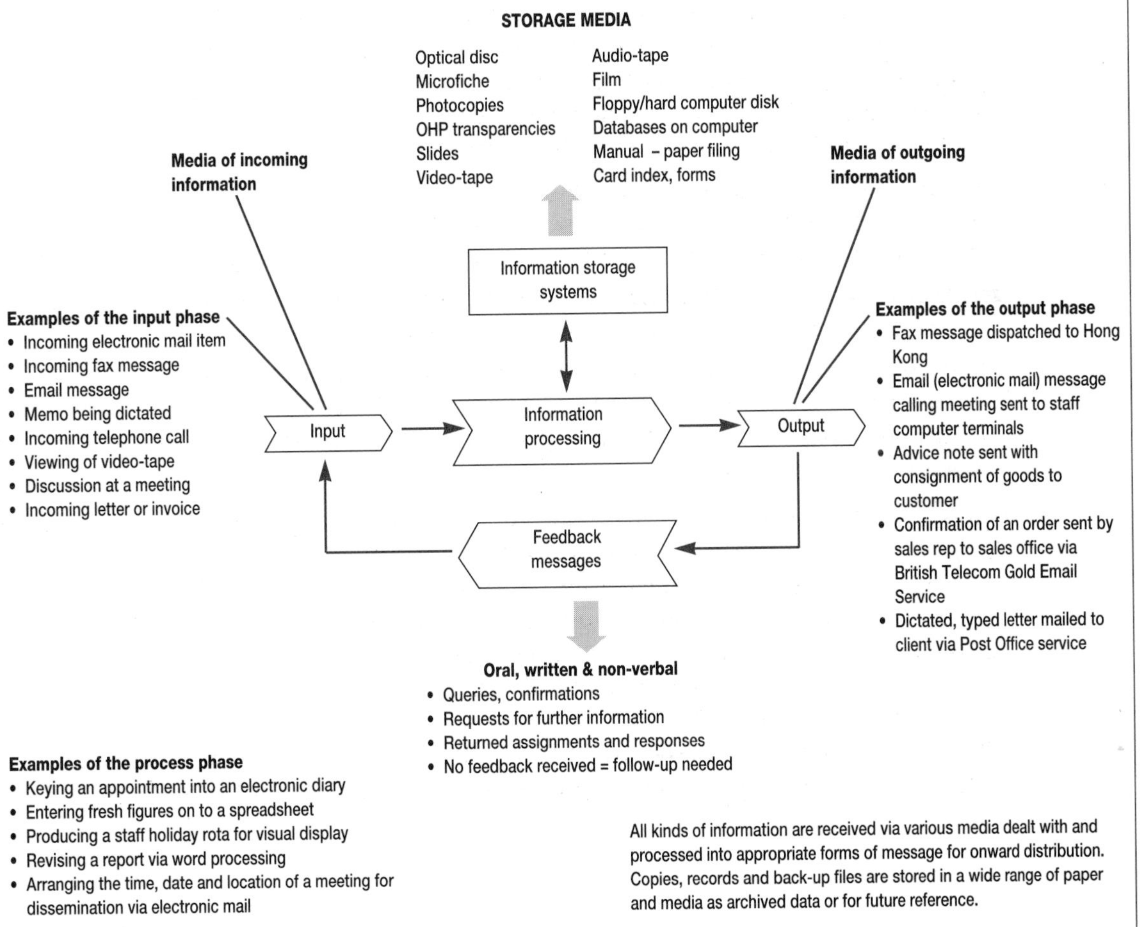

STORAGE MEDIA
Optical disc
Microfiche
Photocopies
OHP transparencies
Slides
Video-tape
Audio-tape
Film
Floppy/hard computer disk
Databases on computer
Manual – paper filing
Card index, forms
Media of incoming information
Media of outgoing information
Information storage systems
Examples of the input phase
• Incoming electronic mail item
• Incoming fax message
• Email message
• Memo being dictated
• Incoming telephone call
• Viewing of video-tape
• Discussion at a meeting
• Incoming letter or invoice
Input
Information processing
Output
Examples of the output phase
• Fax message dispatched to Hong Kong
• Email (electronic mail) message calling meeting sent to staff computer terminals
• Advice note sent with consignment of goods to customer
• Confirmation of an order sent by sales rep to sales office via British Telecom Gold Email Service
• Dictated, typed letter mailed to client via Post Office service
Feedback messages
Oral, written & non-verbal
• Queries, confirmations
• Requests for further information
• Returned assignments and responses
• No feedback received = follow-up needed
Examples of the process phase
• Keying an appointment into an electronic diary
• Entering fresh figures on to a spreadsheet
• Producing a staff holiday rota for visual display
• Revising a report via word processing
• Arranging the time, date and location of a meeting for dissemination via electronic mail

All kinds of information are received via various media dealt with and processed into appropriate forms of message for onward distribution. Copies, records and back-up files are stored in a wide range of paper and media as archived data or for future reference.

PC 2.4.2 2.4.3

■ From paper to computerised systems

Since the introduction into western Europe of movable-type technology in the fifteenth century, the communication of ideas has been largely paper-based. Even Victorian etchings and early photographs were distributed in a paper medium.

It is not unnatural, then, that businesses should have developed over the past five hundred years information systems which relied on complex cycles of document exchange. Consider, for example, the eight main stages (each one capable of being transacted by means of a paper document) of making an account sale (see Fig 2.22)

As the diagram at Fig 2.22 illustrates, instructions and authorisations are effected by the physical movement of paper documents – from mailroom (in) to sales department to warehouse to despatch, to accounts department and back to mailroom (out).

As a consequence of the limitations of the paper-based system, a number of complications inevitably arise:

PC 2.4.2 2.4.3

THE DOWNSIDE OF PAPER-BASED INFORMATION SYSTEMS

- The same information has to be repeated a number of times on different forms at various stages in the process.
- Copies of issued forms have to be sent around the organisation to maintain essential communications among those involved.
- The process of issuing dockets, notes and forms is expensive in both time and money and keeps the customer waiting.
- Records of the transaction need to be kept, and over a period of time, storing paper is costly in terms of floor space occupied, and document recovery time. Currently 1 in 10 of all paper documents filed becomes lost for ever!
- Maintaining paper-based information systems is labour-intensive, and therefore costly.

The illustration in Fig 2.23 further emphasises the complex processes involved in maintaining a paper-based, double-entry bookkeeping system. In the chart, five stages are explained:

1 The original document data entry phase
2 The input to the Books of Original Entry phase
3 The posting to the Ledger phase
4 The extraction of the Trial Balance phase
5 The preparation of Final Accounts phase.

PC
2.4.2
2.4.3

Fig 2.22 **The account sale process using a paper-based system**

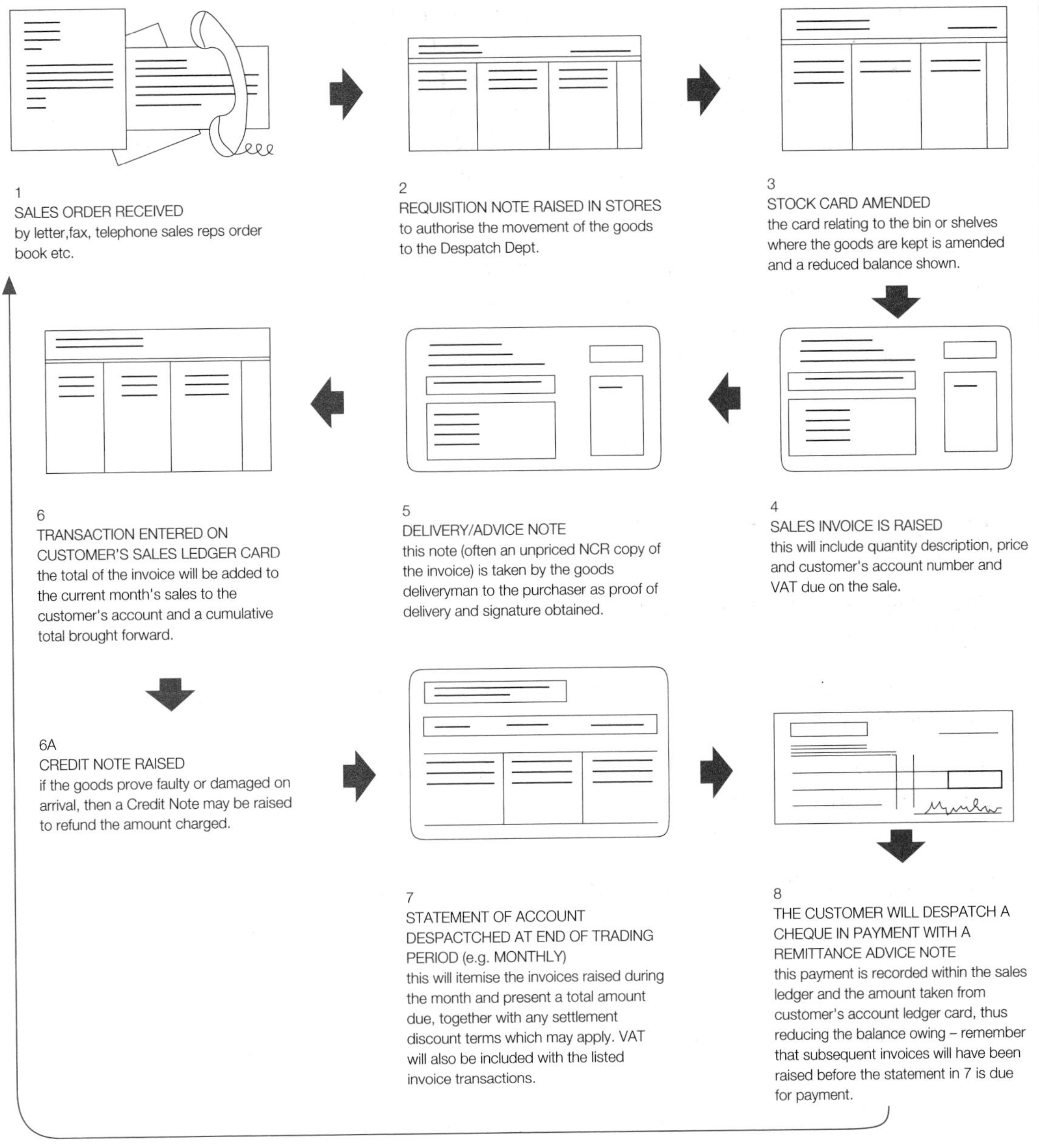
1
SALES ORDER RECEIVED
by letter,fax, telephone sales reps order book etc.
2
REQUISITION NOTE RAISED IN STORES
to authorise the movement of the goods to the Despatch Dept.
3
STOCK CARD AMENDED
the card relating to the bin or shelves where the goods are kept is amended and a reduced balance shown.
4
SALES INVOICE IS RAISED
this will include quantity description, price and customer's account number and VAT due on the sale.
5
DELIVERY/ADVICE NOTE
this note (often an unpriced NCR copy of the invoice) is taken by the goods deliveryman to the purchaser as proof of delivery and signature obtained.
6
TRANSACTION ENTERED ON CUSTOMER'S SALES LEDGER CARD
the total of the invoice will be added to the current month's sales to the customer's account and a cumulative total brought forward.
6A
CREDIT NOTE RAISED
if the goods prove faulty or damaged on arrival, then a Credit Note may be raised to refund the amount charged.
7
STATEMENT OF ACCOUNT DESPACTCHED AT END OF TRADING PERIOD (e.g. MONTHLY)
this will itemise the invoices raised during the month and present a total amount due, together with any settlement discount terms which may apply. VAT will also be included with the listed invoice transactions.
8
THE CUSTOMER WILL DESPATCH A CHEQUE IN PAYMENT WITH A REMITTANCE ADVICE NOTE
this payment is recorded within the sales ledger and the amount taken from customer's account ledger card, thus reducing the balance owing – remember that subsequent invoices will have been raised before the statement in 7 is due for payment.

PC
2.4.2
2.4.3

Fig 2.23 **Example of paper-based double-entry book-keeping system**

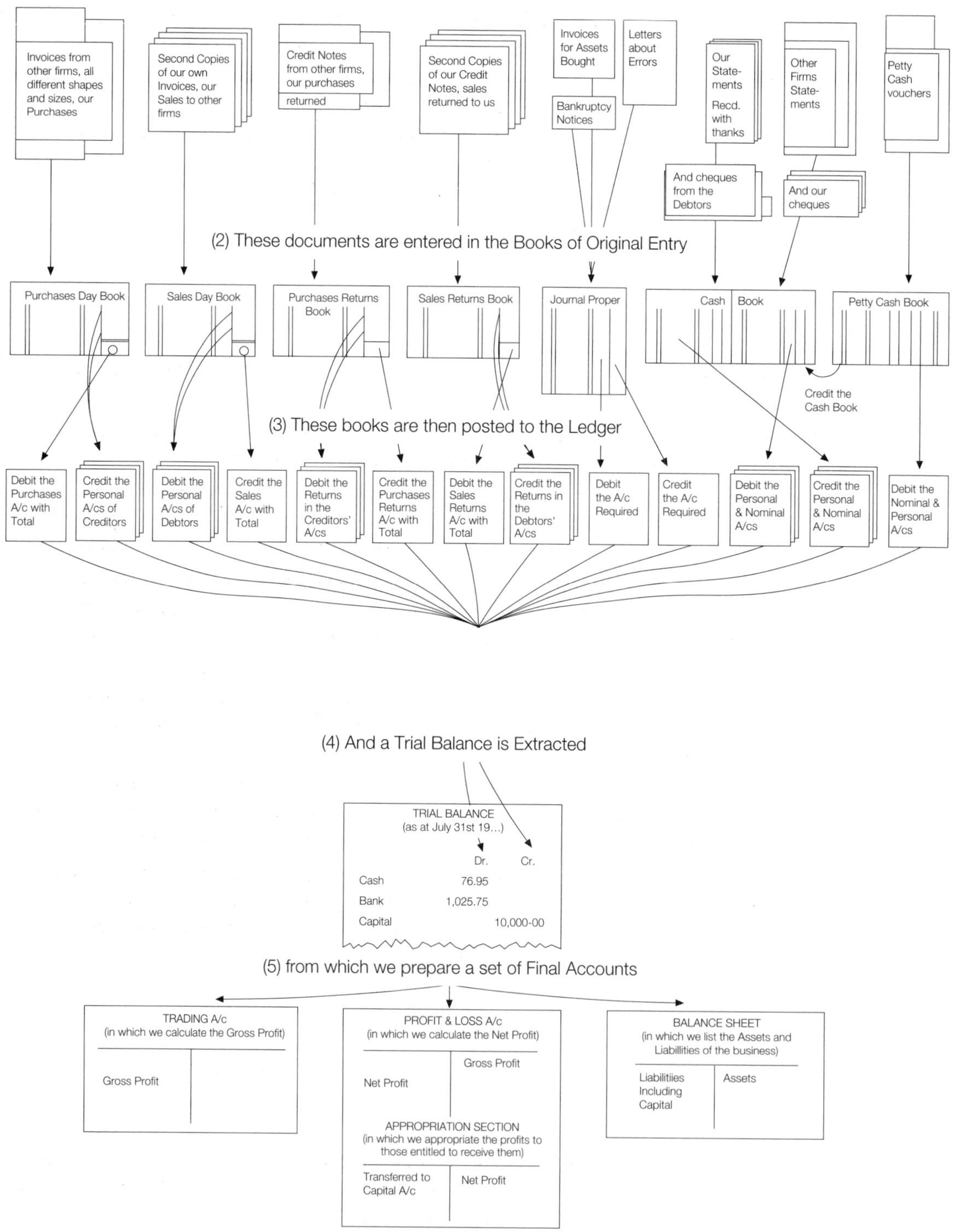

Invoices from other firms, all different shapes and sizes, our Purchases
Second Copies of our own Invoices, our Sales to other firms
Credit Notes from other firms, our purchases returned
Second Copies of our Credit Notes, sales returned to us
Invoices for Assets Bought
Bankruptcy Notices
Letters about Errors
Our Statements Recd. with thanks
And cheques from the Debtors
Other Firms Statements
And our cheques
Petty Cash vouchers
(2) These documents are entered in the Books of Original Entry
Purchases Day Book
Sales Day Book
Purchases Returns Book
Sales Returns Book
Journal Proper
Cash Book
Petty Cash Book
Credit the Cash Book
(3) These books are then posted to the Ledger
Debit the Purchases A/c with Total
Credit the Personal A/cs of Creditors
Debit the Personal A/cs of Debtors
Credit the Sales A/c with Total
Debit the Returns in the Creditors' A/cs
Credit the Purchases Returns A/c with Total
Debit the Sales Returns A/c with Total
Credit the Returns in the Debtors' A/cs
Debit the A/c Required
Credit the A/c Required
Debit the Personal & Nominal A/cs
Credit the Personal & Nominal A/cs
Debit the Nominal & Personal A/cs
(4) And a Trial Balance is Extracted
TRIAL BALANCE
(as at July 31st 19...)
Dr.
Cr.
Cash 76.95
Bank 1,025.75
Capital 10,000-00
(5) from which we prepare a set of Final Accounts
TRADING A/c
(in which we calculate the Gross Profit)
Gross Profit
PROFIT & LOSS A/c
(in which we calculate the Net Profit)
Gross Profit
Net Profit
APPROPRIATION SECTION
(in which we appropriate the profits to those entitled to receive them)
Transferred to Capital A/c
Net Profit
BALANCE SHEET
(in which we list the Assets and Liabillities of the business)
Liabilitiies Including Capital
Assets

As the above diagrams of the paper-based account sale and double entry book-keeping system readily illustrate, a major disadvantage of all paper systems lies in the *amount of paper sheets generated* to complete the process – since every interested party needs to receive a copy and the *slow speed* of carrying out the process, since the copies have to be physically routed around an organisation or through the post etc. Also, paper-based filing systems have always been notorious for the numbers of *mis-filed paper documents* which are never found again!

The advent in the late 1980s of networked computers – in which large numbers of PC-type terminals may be linked to a central single or series of file-serving mini computers effectively rendered traditional, paper systems obsolete. Moreover, the development in the mid 1990s of the information superhighway, linking terminals together and to on-line databases internationally carried the revolution even further.

PC 2.4.3

MAJOR FEATURES OF NETWORKING COMPUTERISED INFORMATION SYSTEMS

- Powerful central file-servers enable network users to access simultaneously the same software application e.g. *Word for Windows* × 24 users at once.
- The same file server provides access to different software applications simultaneously e.g. 12 × *Lotus Excel*, 15 × *Lotus 123 for Windows*, 25 × *Borland dBASE for Windows* etc.
- Communications hardware enables each network user to access from his/her desktop terminal: national/international telephone networks and any internal computerised PABX system; other users (nationally and internationally) on LAN/WAN and superhighway networks; internal users via email.
- Sophisticated electronics also empowers users to generate documents on the desktop terminal and route them to an intelligent photocopier, *capable automatically* of printing, collating and binding as many copies of, say, a management report as needed.
- The latest generation of networked terminals embodies a dual television and VDU screen, which facilitates both conventional colour Windows GUI work and interactive, CD-ROM-driven multi-media work, not to mention the ability to display either off-air television or video-cassette programmes.
- Also, a software development called *groupware* provides a facility which enables the members of a team or project group to access files and work on them *simultaneously* – say in the development of plans for a building, or electronic circuits – from remote locations connected to the network.
- Needless to say, today's multi-purpose terminals are able to access – via their mini or mainframe file-servers and land-line/satellite/radio-wave connections – a growing number of on-line databases anywhere in the world, such as *Lexis*, the international database for lawyers and solicitors, or the *ICC Eurocompany Information Service*.

■ Fretwell-Downing data systems business management system

PC 2.4.2 2.4.3

As the diagrammatic presentation of the software package in Fig 2.24 reveals, the package is both flexible and cost-effective. Items like updated pricelists, trial balances, outstanding purchase order details, and so on, may be printed on demand, and until needed, occupy a minuscule storage space within the computer's hard disk.

Managers and support staff can call up any data for checking in a trice on their desktop VDUs (on-line review) and have more time to audit and monitor the sales and purchase order process since so many tasks – like posting to the sales or purchase ledgers – are automatically effected through the software's commands.

PC
2.4.2
2.4.3

Fig 2.24 **A computerised accounting system**

The Business Management System (BMS) uses the latest business computer technology to provide a highly flexible approach to the tasks of order processing, stock control and accounts. The relationships between the principal modules of

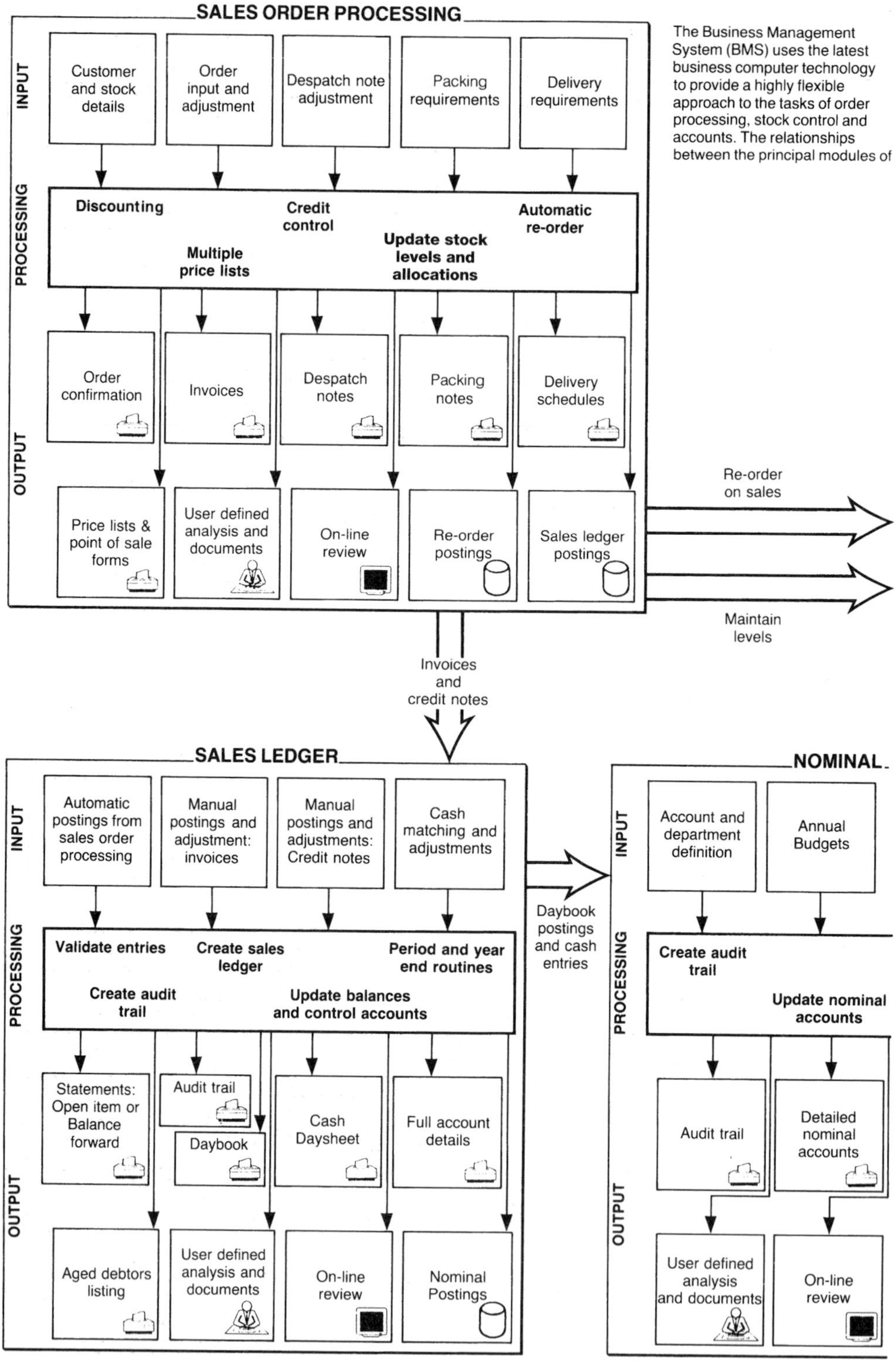

Fretwell-Downing Data Systems Ltd

Sales Order Processing with Invoicing, Purchase Order Processing, Stock Control, Sales Ledger, Purchase Ledger and Nominal Ledger are illustrated here. The choice of modules and their specific components within the BMS framework can be geared to precise user requirements.

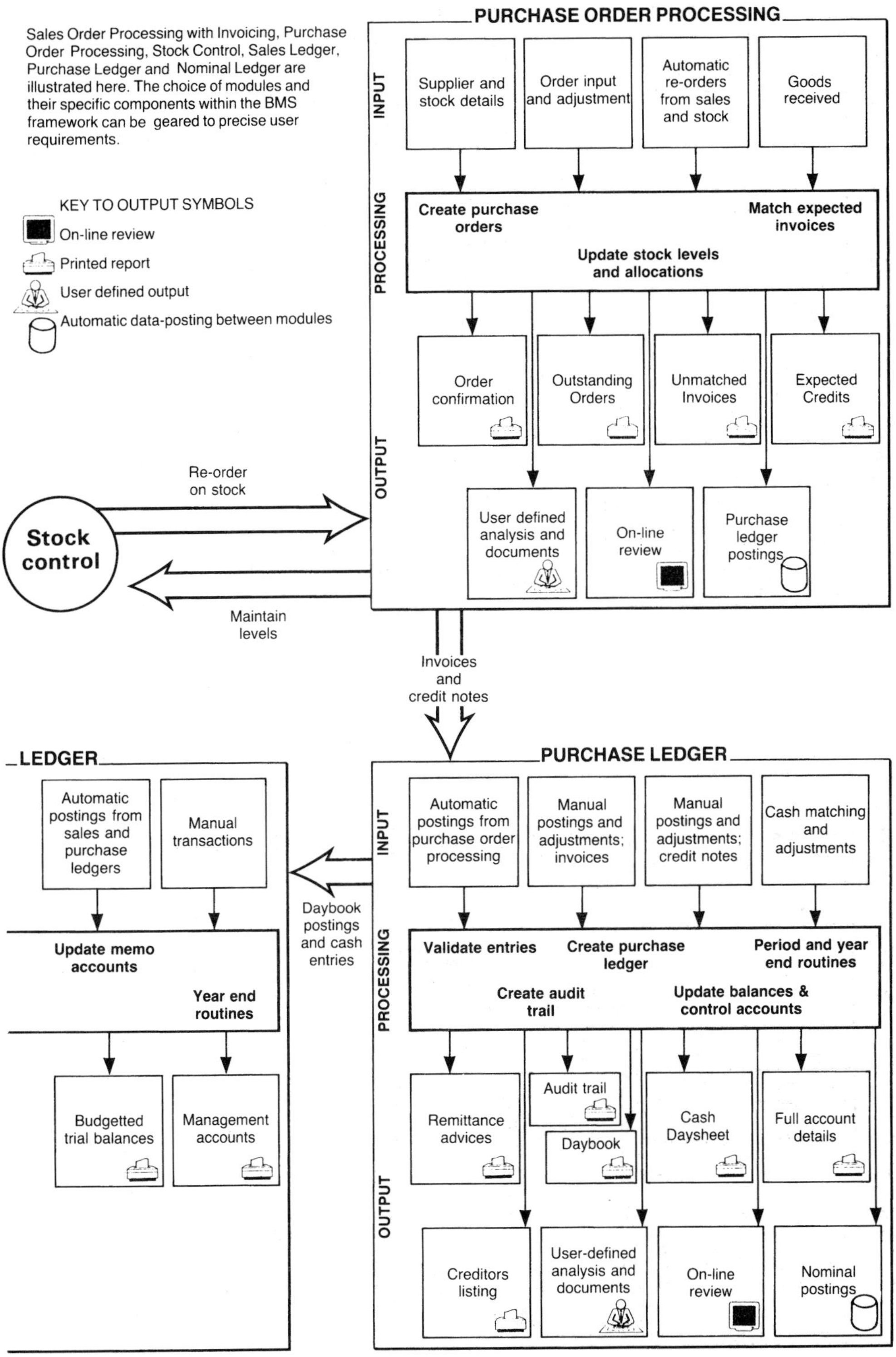

KEY TO OUTPUT SYMBOLS
On-line review
Printed report
User defined output
Automatic data-posting between modules
PURCHASE ORDER PROCESSING
INPUT
Supplier and stock details
Order input and adjustment
Automatic re-orders from sales and stock
Goods received
PROCESSING
Create purchase orders
Match expected invoices
Update stock levels and allocations
OUTPUT
Order confirmation
Outstanding Orders
Unmatched Invoices
Expected Credits
User defined analysis and documents
On-line review
Purchase ledger postings
Re-order on stock
Stock control
Maintain levels
Invoices and credit notes
PURCHASE LEDGER
INPUT
Automatic postings from purchase order processing
Manual postings and adjustments; invoices
Manual postings and adjustments; credit notes
Cash matching and adjustments
PROCESSING
Validate entries
Create purchase ledger
Period and year end routines
Create audit trail
Update balances & control accounts
OUTPUT
Remittance advices
Audit trail
Daybook
Cash Daysheet
Full account details
Creditors listing
User-defined analysis and documents
On-line review
Nominal postings
Daybook postings and cash entries
LEDGER
Automatic postings from sales and purchase ledgers
Manual transactions
Update memo accounts
Year end routines
Budgetted trial balances
Management accounts

PC
2.4.3

THE UPSIDE OF COMPUTERISED INFORMATION SYSTEMS

- Software applications may be designed to promote 'one-touch football', in other words once-only entry of data which is automatically relayed to any part of the information process where it is needed.
- Accuracy is built in; provided the software has been rigorously tested, and provided that data is entered correctly, the subsequent manipulations of the data within the computer are not prone to human error.
- Security of sensitive information is good; while no program is hacker-proof, password systems and levels of access are much more secure than metal filing cabinet locks.
- Access to files and records is far faster than in paper-based systems.
- The equivalent of wall-lengths of vertical or lateral paper filing systems is available in the 40cm square processor housing the hard disk memory of a personal computer.
- The advent of computerised networks (see Fig 2.26) made it possible for files and data to be transmitted not only between office block floors, but also continents in seconds and in safety!
- Provided sufficient investment is made in data entry resourcing, the system may be developed into an overarching database, housing all an organisation's records and in-house informational needs.
- The worldwide development of specialist computerised databases is extending fast and the day when 'all you need to know' can be called up on your VDU is not far distant.

PC
2.4.2
2.4.3

Software – types and purposes

Essentially, four different types of software are used by people in business:

- **tailor-made software especially written to perform a specific job within a particular organisation;** such software may be designed by a large company's in-house computer services team of systems analyst and programmers who produce a package which meets a brief given, say, by a marketing or production manager; sometimes specialist outside firms are contracted to develop such programs
- **specialist commercially designed and marketed software** which enables very specialised work to be carried out, such as the tracking of sales orders or access to downloadable fonts and other printer's devices used by skilled graphics designers
- **general-purpose commercially designed and marketed software** – which now forms the basis of networked applications provision in the mix of wordprocessing, spreadsheet, database, presentation, desktop publisher and organiser
- **utility software,** in the form of file managers, virus protectors, spelling, thesaurus and grammar checkers, file searchers and recoverers etc.

Note: The rapid increase of PC users – whether working from home or in offices – who 'drive' what are now highly sophisticated and powerful information processing tools has led to software and hardware manufacturers nunning 24-hour help-lines so that people who become bewildered, 'stuck' or lost can obtain immediate, expert assistance. Needless to say, after an initial free, post-purchase provision, such services usually cost!

PC
2.4.2
2.4.3

INDIVIDUAL ACTIVITY

First undertake your researches, and then report back to your group in an illustrated oral presentation:

1 Examine carefully the type of information which your organisation uses (firm, school or college) in terms of the inputs–processes–outputs–feedback systems model.

Then design a diagram to illustrate the system and include the mechanisms of boards, committees, task groups or working parties, etc. which are employed to link the system's parts.

2 Find out what the acronym EDI stands for and how it is currently revolutionising the purchasing–supply interface of large manufacturers.

3 Reread the account sale process using a paper-based system in Fig 2.22 on page 171 and then with the help of family and friends, obtain examples of the documents referred to used by local businesses. Post them on your base-room noticeboard as a group briefing.

4 Find out what an 'audit-trail' is in an accounts software package and why the Inland Revenue insists on its presence and effective working.

5 Find out what management accounting reports are routinely used in a manufacturing company and why.

PC
2.4.2
2.4.3

TYPICAL FILES CREATED AND STORED ELECTRONICALLY

Department	*Application software package*	*Type of file*
Sales	Database	List of account customer particulars and purchasing limits
	Spreadsheet	Records of salesforce, actual to target sales
	Sales tracking (the progress of prospective sales is closely monitored)	Sales representatives' records
	Word processing	Sets of mailmerged sales circular letters – easily updated
R & D/Production Marketing	Project management	Introduction of a new product – from prototype to launch
Marketing	Graphics and modelling software	Analysis of market penetration/client types/market share, etc.
	Desktop publishing	Advertising copy – display ads, leaflets, brochures, etc.
Personnel	Database	All employee records
	Database	Training/staff development notes Promotion/pay increase records
Accounts	Spreadsheet	Management accounting reports and ratios
	Integrated accounts package	All ledgers – sales, purchasing, nominal, etc. plus payroll
Transport	Database	Fleet servicing records
	Tailor-made	Optimum journeys and routes to distribute goods

All departments All staff	Unified database	Specifically designed data files relevant to the organisation's work
Manager/PA – Secretary	Local area network operating software Integrated modular management package (allows data to be merged from one application to another)	Email messages, notes to self, diary, appointments and meetings schedulers, etc. Letters, reports, tables, calculations, graphs and charts, database records, etc.
Created by technicians and secretaries for managers	Desktop publishing	News sheets, bulletins, invitations, reports, etc.
PA/secretary	Word processing	Letters, memos, reports, minutes, abstracts, press releases, pricelists, etc.

Note: The above chart indicates the extent to which business/public service application software packages have mushroomed since the original dedicated wp software of the mid 1970s. As the section on convergence which follows indicates, the arrival of computer networks meant that such files could also be shared amongst the different users on the network.

PC 2.4.1 2.4.2 2.4.3

DISCUSSION TOPICS

1 How valid do you think the systems model is as a means of explaining how organisations function? Does it oversimplify the way that organisations work, or is it a fair reflection?

2 In the 1970s, over-eager supporters of IT were proclaiming the imminent arrival of 'the paperless office'; in the 1980s they modified the slogan to 'the less paper office'; today, most managers complain that they are being deluged by more paper to wade through than ever.

Does this trend suggest that IT has failed to deliver a promised freedom from 'bumf', or that, deep down, we much prefer to rummage around the A4 paper sheets on our desks than to gaze for hours at a colour VDU screen ?

3 The preceding pages of this Unit have emphasised the 'downside' of paper-based information systems and the 'upside' of their computerised counterparts. Can you think of any 'upside' points in favour of paper systems, and 'downside' ones against computerised alternatives?

Fig 2.25 **The information flow handled by software applications**

PC 2.4.2 2.4.3

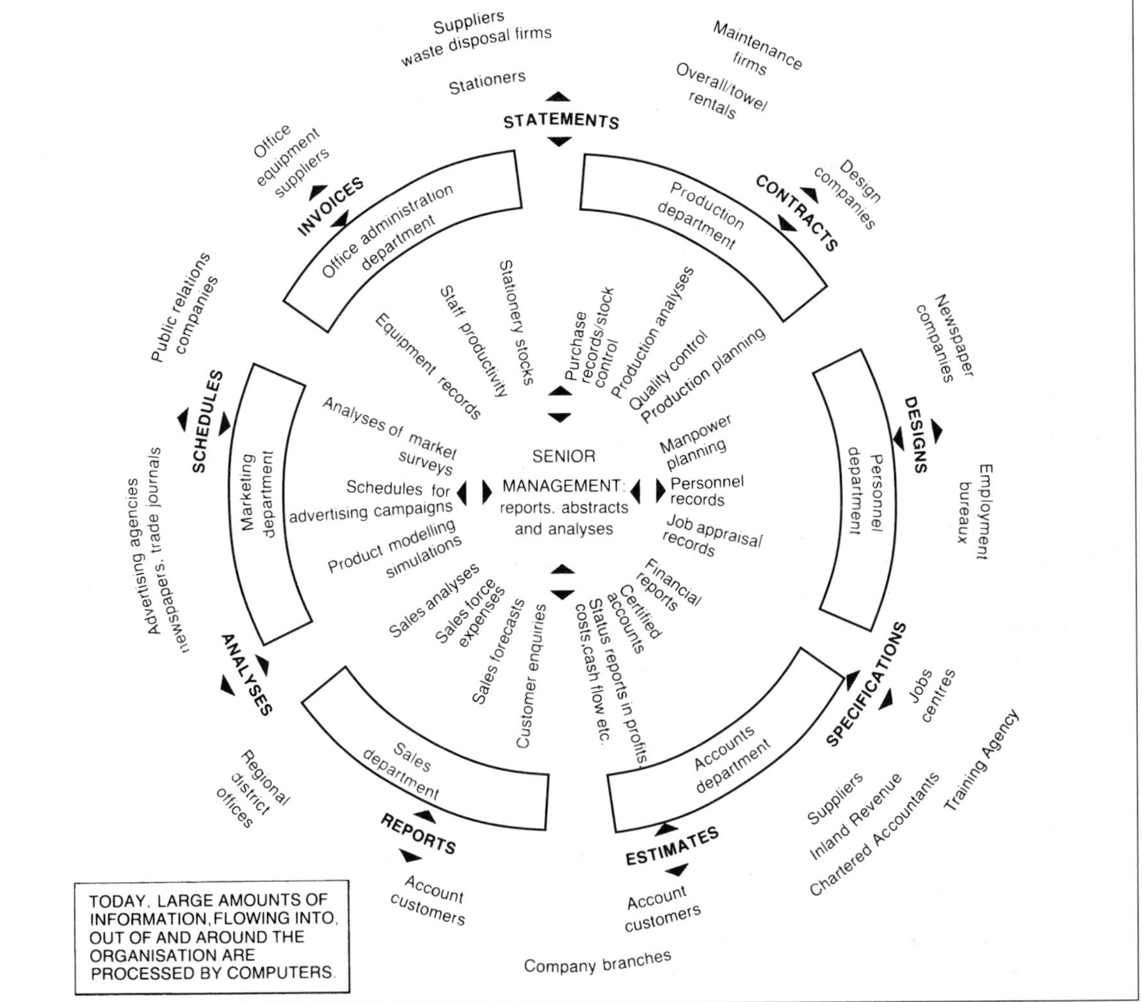

Local and wide area networks – the key to the information superhighway

PC 2.4.2 2.4.3

The advantages of improved speed, security and lower costs of computerised information systems became rapidly apparent in the early 1980s. Yet there remained the stubborn problem of how to move information around the managers and support workers who needed to interact with it without having to revert to paper in the form of hard-copy printouts, or as distributed source documents.

Fig 2.26

LAN installed in a multi-storey head office linked to a remotely located branch office

The manager station
One PC acts as a manager station holding details of the shared resources and authorised network users of the other PCs connected to it. Storing this information centrally permits changes to be made at a single location and accurate presentation of available resources.

Network domains
A system of domain management is necessary if more than about 50–100 stations are involved in order to control the network effectively. Each domain is a portion of the total network representing a single department or a floor of a large building. Each domain has its own manager station.

Internetworking
The use of packet switched data networks based on the international X25 standard provides an ideal basis for internetwork links for companies based on multiple sites.

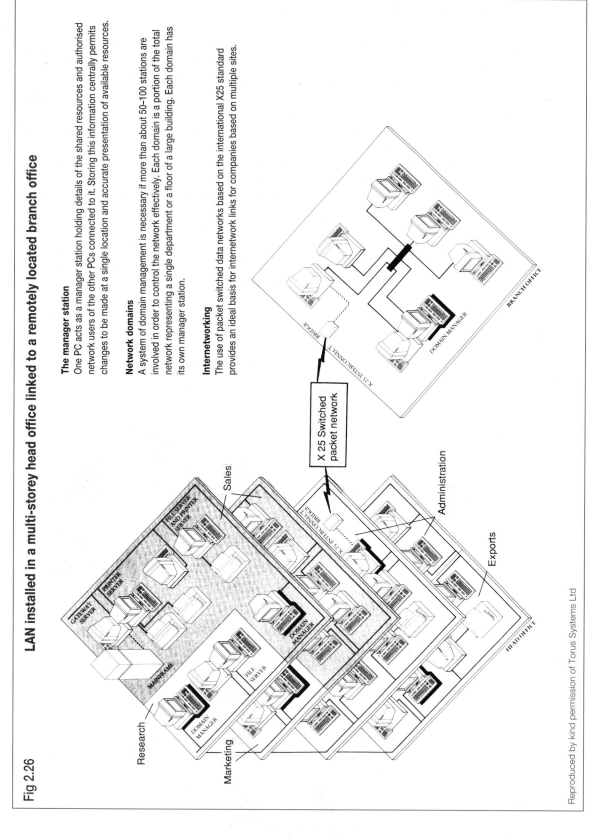

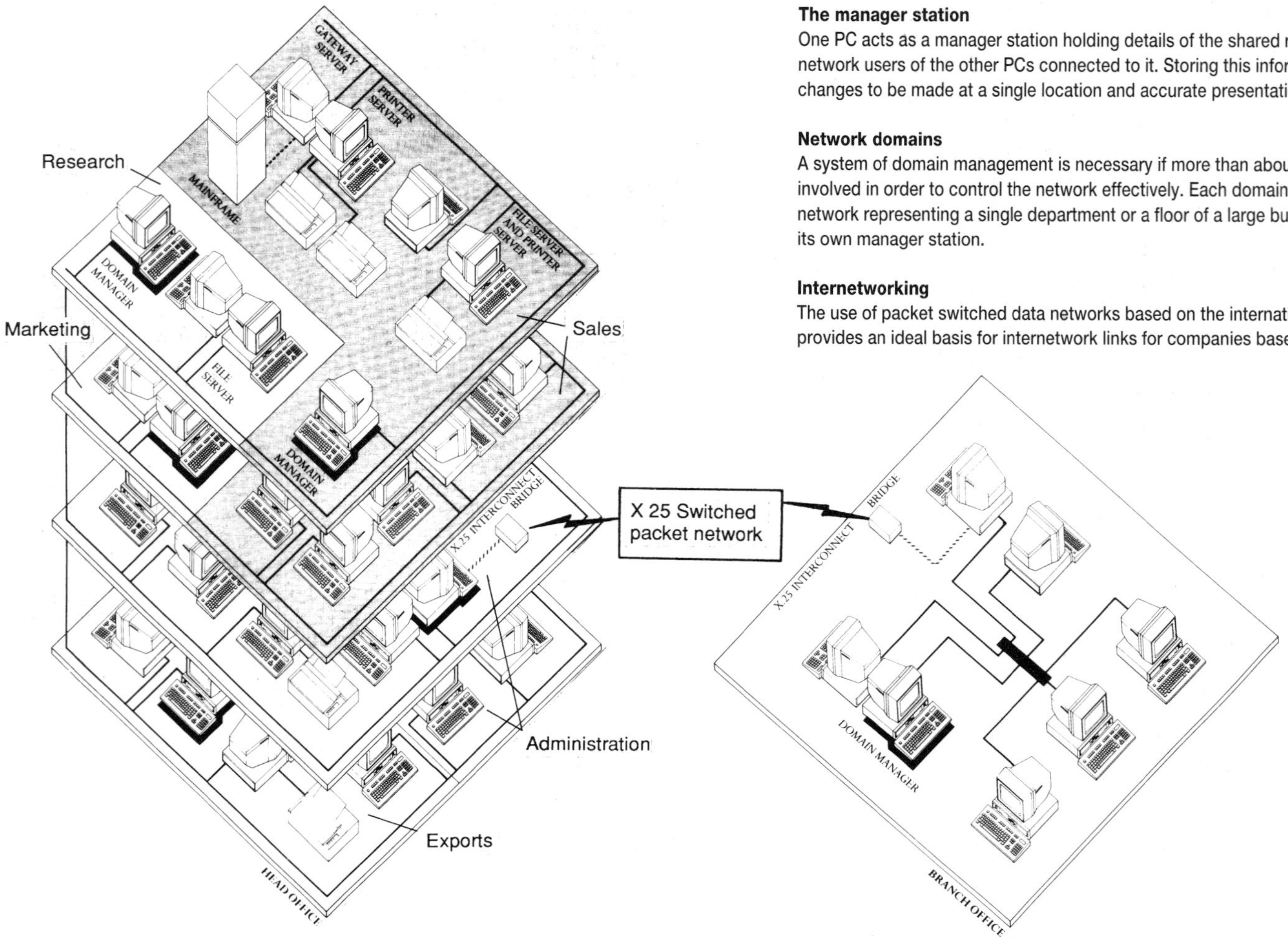

Reproduced by kind permission of Torus Systems Ltd

■ LAN – messaging at the speed of light!

PC 2.4.2 2.4.3

This problem was solved ingeniously by computer scientists who developed cabling systems interconnecting desktop terminals which were capable of transmitting messages in electronic form, either up and down a 'bus' (a kind of electronic high-speed motorway with spurs leading to connected terminals), or around a kind of ring-main to which terminals were linked. Such systems came to be called Local Area Networks partly because, initially, the furthest a terminal could be from its host file-server (a kind of central processing unit) was some 200 metres. The two transmission systems moving the messages around the network which became most popular are Ethernet (line bus system) and Token Ring ('ring-main' system). The unique attraction of the LAN system in terms of information interchange is that its electronics circuitry enables messages to zip around the network at virtually the speed of light!

As the diagrams in Figs 2.27 and 2.28 illustrate, LANs may be networked in a number of ways – along a line, as a ring or as a star. Whatever their structure, the principle of their operation remains the same. 'Messages' intended for one or several LAN terminals are directed around the network – virtually at the speed of light – by the central processor or file-server. The speed at which the message pulses travel around the LAN is in the order of 10 million (10 megabits) per second. Each terminal in turn interrogates the message to see if

Fig 2.27 **Examples of LAN connection layouts**

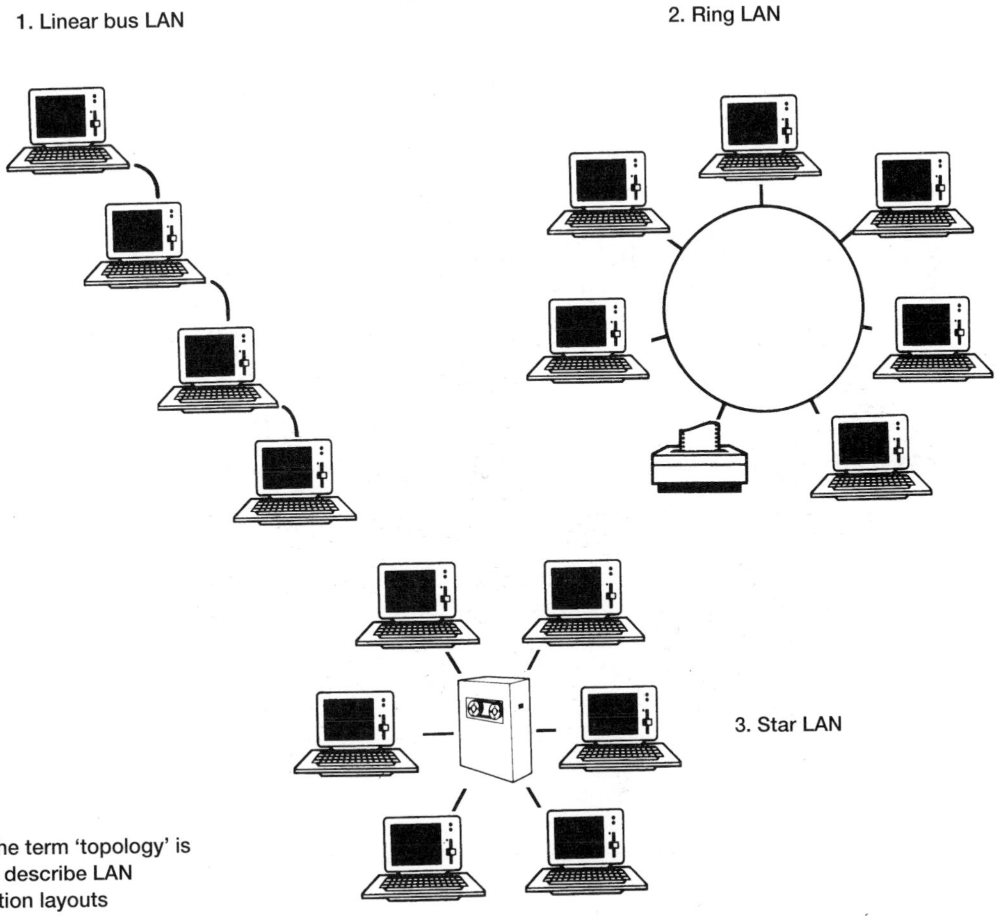
1. Linear bus LAN
2. Ring LAN
3. Star LAN

Note: The term 'topology' is used to describe LAN connection layouts it is the intended recipient. If it isn't it passes it on. Only the one bearing the correct 'address' retains the message and displays the fact of its arrival on its VDU as, for example, 'New Mail For You'.

In the initial stages of the development of LANs, computer terminals were interconnected by a kind of coaxial cable. Nowadays technology has made possible LANs and WANs which are linked by radio signal, thus removing the geographical restrictions of having to provide a kind of cable ring-main connecting the system.

PC 2.4.2 2.4.3

■ The file-server: multi-tasking and multi-serving workhorse

At the heart of the LAN/WAN system is the file-server, the nerve-centre of the system. A file-server may take the form of a mainframe or mini-computer, or in smaller networks it may be a terminal similar to all the rest, but possessing a large hard-disk memory of 100 plus megabytes.

The attractiveness of the LAN network lies in the flexibility and versatility of its operation. Because of the speed at which it can send information around the system to all or some users it can:

■ **multi-serve**

In other words, simultaneously attend to the **individual** needs of 250 or more users, whether they are in the process of booting-up their terminal, using a software package, importing artwork via a scanner or printing out completed work. The file-server manages to do this by sending high-speed, interrupted message parts to each terminal. But so fast are the interrupted pulses, that each user 'sees' them as a continuous stream.

■ **multi-task**

As a result of its powerful memory and drive, the file-server is able to download multiple versions of any of the software application passages stored on its hard disk. As a result, each of four adjacent users could be word processing, desktop publishing, working with a spreadsheet or designing a colour graphic.

Just as the file-server attends to the needs of multiple network users using software packages, so a network print-server ensures multiple access to a network printer with a minimum of delay.

The LAN's ability to multi-serve and multi-task provides its users with the following facilities:

USER FEATURES PROVIDED BY A LOCAL AREA NETWORK

- Sending or receiving electronic mail (email) messages; messages may either be emailed to individuals or simultaneously to designated groups.
- Any file produced by a user whether by word processing, spreadsheet, graphics or DTP package, etc. may be 'clipped' to the email note and transmitted with it.
- Files produced by a remote user which are stored centrally on the file-server may be called up (with authorisation) by any other user.
- Created files may be imported or exported to any software application package being used on a given terminal, e.g. from a spreadsheet on to a report being word processed.
- By employing a package like an electronic diary, a user may call a meeting of, say, five members of a project team on the first possible day and time when all are available; the computer interrogates each user's electronic diary to check for a common available slot. Similarly, if kept in open mode, any diary may be called up by any user wishing to arrange to see a colleague. Sophisticated LANs also enable users to book meeting rooms and audio visual aids equipment!

■ From LANs to WANs and the information superhighway

PC 2.4.2 2.4.3

All the above features of the network system are available in wide area networking, which works on entirely the same principle, save that the terminals may be thousands of miles apart and electronic messages may need several power boosts to keep them going along the route. One company which makes extensive use of the WAN system is IBM Incorporated. As a multinational computer manufacturer, IBM has offices and factories all over the world. Wherever IBM has a terminal installed, its user, whether production manager, marketing executive or research scientist is able to communicate with a co-worker – perhaps on the other side of the world – in a matter of seconds. Not only does IBM's WAN system permit its staff to communicate swiftly, it also enables messages to be sent to a WAN electronic address overnight, to be 'opened' by its recipient in the same way as incoming letter post. Moreover, recent developments in telecommunications have made it possible for interconnected WAN users to work simultaneously via their visual display screens on, say, the design of an architectural plan, the wording of a joint diplomatic communiqué or set of spreadsheet figures. The devlopment of the Internet Superhighway is also enabling computer users across the world to inter-communicate and to access on-line databases of business, educational and leisure information and activities.

Fig 2.28 **Example of a converging network**

PC 2.4.2 2.4.3

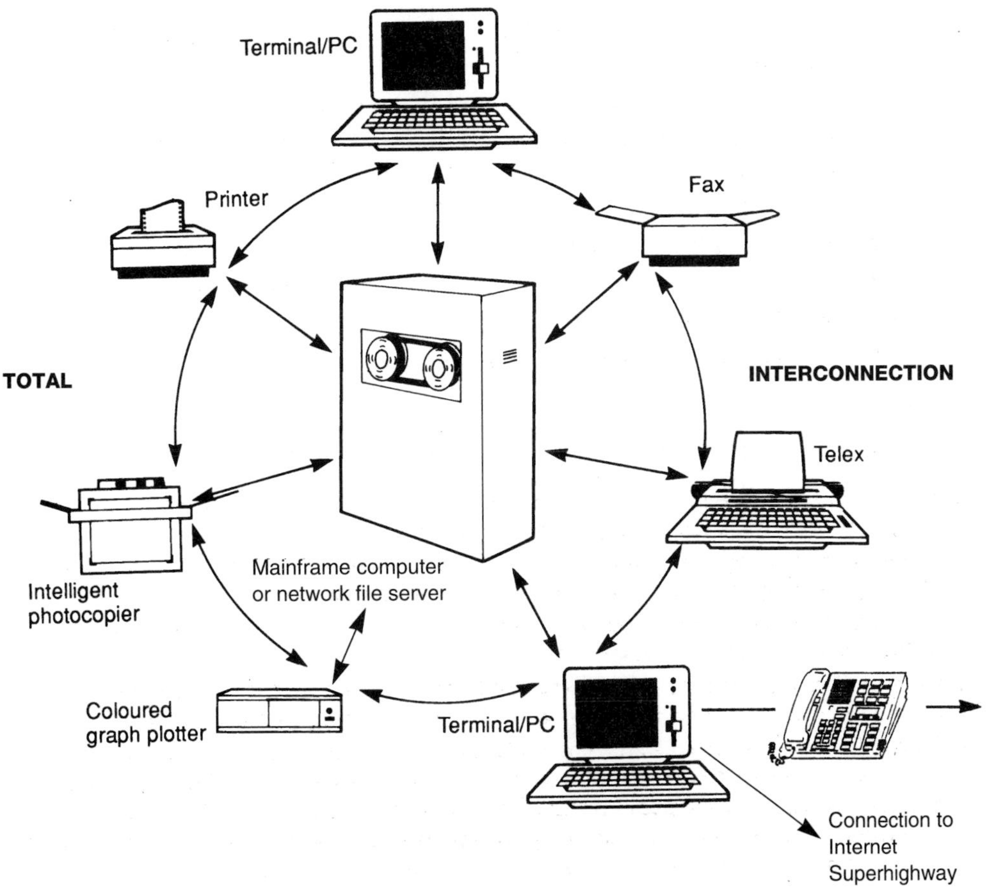
Terminal/PC
Printer
Fax
TOTAL
INTERCONNECTION
Telex
Intelligent photocopier
Mainframe computer or network file server
Coloured graph plotter
Terminal/PC
Connection to Internet Superhighway

Fig 2.29

Connectivity at the workstation – the information nerve point

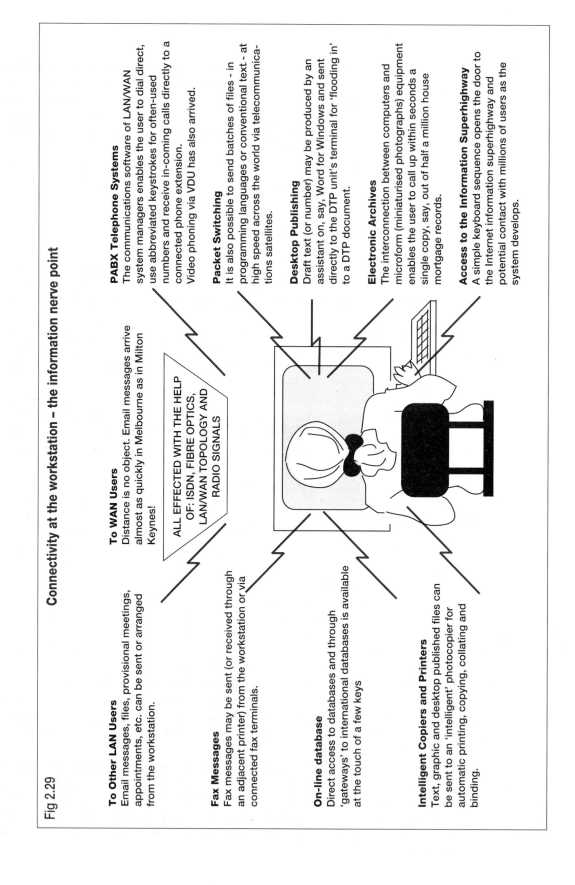

To Other LAN Users
Email messages, files, provisional meetings, appointments, etc. can be sent or arranged from the workstation.

To WAN Users
Distance is no object. Email messages arrive almost as quickly in Melbourne as in Milton Keynes!

PABX Telephone Systems
The communications software of LAN/WAN system managers enables the user to dial direct, use abbreviated keystrokes for often-used numbers and receive in-coming calls directly to a connected phone extension.
Video phoning via VDU has also arrived.

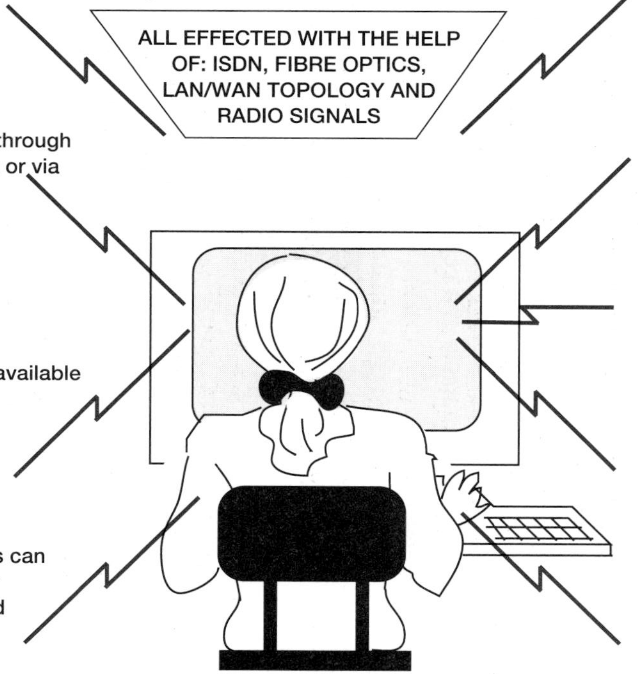
ALL EFFECTED WITH THE HELP OF: ISDN, FIBRE OPTICS, LAN/WAN TOPOLOGY AND RADIO SIGNALS

Fax Messages
Fax messages may be sent (or received through an adjacent printer) from the workstation or via connected fax terminals.

Packet Switching
It is also possible to send batches of files - in programming languages or conventional text - at high speed across the world via telecommunications satellites.

Desktop Publishing
Draft text (or number) may be produced by an assistant on, say, Word for Windows and sent directly to the DTP unit's terminal for 'flooding in' to a DTP document.

On-line database
Direct access to databases and through 'gateways' to international databases is available at the touch of a few keys

Electronic Archives
The interconnection between computers and microform (miniaturised photographs) equipment enables the user to call up within seconds a single copy, say, out of half a million house mortgage records.

Intelligent Copiers and Printers
Text, graphic and desktop published files can be sent to an 'intelligent' photocopier for automatic printing, copying, collating and binding.

Access to the Information Superhighway
A simple keyboard sequence opens the door to the Internet information superhighway and potential contact with millions of users as the system develops.

PC
2.4.2
2.4.3

■ LANs and connectivity

PC 2.4.2 2.4.3

The commercial introduction of the local area network in the 1980s formed only a part of what computer scientists came to call the 'process of convergence'. As you will be aware, the verb to converge means to come together, and that is exactly what systems analysts and computer engineers brought about – a coming together or interconnection of all the electronic office equipment available to an organisation's personnel. The label for this process which caught on was 'connectivity', but whatever the label, this electronic wizardry transformed yet again the capacity to communicate – on a local or worldwide basis – from each and every desktop workstation, as the diagram in Fig 2.28 above illustrates.

■ Open systems, connectivity and the office worker

Anyone who has ever purchased a ball-point pen knows (usually through bitter experience) that you have to buy a refill made by the same company that made the pen. Others simply don't fit. Indeed, wily manufacturers take steps to ensure that they don't fit, since they are in the refills as well as the new ball-point market!

For the past ten to fifteen years, a similar kind of situation has obtained among computer and peripheral equipment manufacturers. The problem area that emerged as the kink in the pipe of increasing computer sales and improving business information systems was the computer's operating system, or rather systems.

Equipment designed for use with one operating system would not 'fit' or talk to similar equipment using a different operating system. Various manufacturers since earliest days had constructed IT equipment to work either on DOS (short for Disk Operating System), UNIX, CP/M (control program/monitor) or other operating systems none of which could talk to each other.

The result was that organisations became wedded to a particular system where computers using, say, DOS, could not communicate with others using UNIX. Such isolationist developments were preventing the open communications essential for establishing a worldwide infrastructure vital to the further development of IT. And so international interested bodies – makers, dealers and users, etc. – set about introducing network designs which would conform to an International Standards Organisation/Open System Interconnection (ISO/OSI).

At present the process of OSI is still being haggled over by profit-conscious computer manufacturers, but the future of truly open and intercommunicating networks looks bright, since many competing manufacturers have come to see the market potential of a much more interactive and more widely spread climate of 'connectivity' which will encourage more users to use more systems more frequently.

Easy connectivity (see Fig 2.29 on page 184) between computer, printer, photocopier, facsimile transceiver (fax), PABX telephone switchboard, telex, viewdata (Prestel), optical character readers (OCR scanners), etc. – whether in-house or worldwide – will bring an enormous range of communications media and opportunities literally to the keying-in fingertips of each office workstation user!

And a further development in the incredible surge of telecommunications technology which is central to the development of open systems and connectivity is ISDN, short for Integrated Services Digital Network. This telecommunications technology enables a variety of digitised (data converted into streams of numbers or digits) messages to be transmitted simultaneously either along a fibre optic cable or as radio signals. A single cable network is therefore able to handle:

- telephone calls
- digitised DP data transmissions
- email on LAN/WAN systems
- teleconferencing
- video telephone calls
- fax/telex transmission

etc.

PC
2.4.2
2.4.3

THE INFORMATION AND COMMUNICATION SUPPORT AVAILABLE FROM ISDN – INTEGRATED SERVICES DIGITAL NETWORK

- Files expressed in a computer language like COBOL for high-speed, batched packet-switching.
- Two-way telephone conversations, including the newly introduced videophones which operate through PC workstations.
- Fax and telex transmissions.
- Electronic mail messages and files on LAN/WAN systems.
- Closed-circuit television transmissions or video-cassette playbacks (which can be distributed simultaneously to, say, 200 retail branches as part of a training programme).
- Audio and teleconferencing – live hook-ups linking remotely located colleagues and/or clients via phone or TV monitor.
- Shared screening and co-working on computer software applications files between remote locations – two electronic engineers 15,000 kilometres distant are able to modify, say, the design of a microchip.
- The interrogation of specialised databases – like the legal LEXIS database which provides case precedents and judgements, etc. and interaction with CD ROM libraries of information (a mixture of film, slides, computer package, textual and graphic data – all displayable on the VDU and capable of being browsed through at will).

Throughout the 1990s, ISDN will revolutionise the information available – either through a home TV/computer console or a workplace, desktop workstation.

The diagram (Fig 2.30) of Plessey's GPT ISDX System Architecture provides a 'see-at-a-glance' explanation of the Integrated Services Digital Network which will dominate office communications in the 1990s.

ISDN can distribute not only telephone conversations but also fax, telex, viewdata, electronic mail and digitised inter-computer packet switching. As the Plessey diagram shows, all an organisation's messaging in-house, local, national and international, can now be distributed at high speed and high volume thanks to ISDN technology.

Fig 2.30 Example of the range of IT and telecommunication services supported by an 'all-in' ISDN system

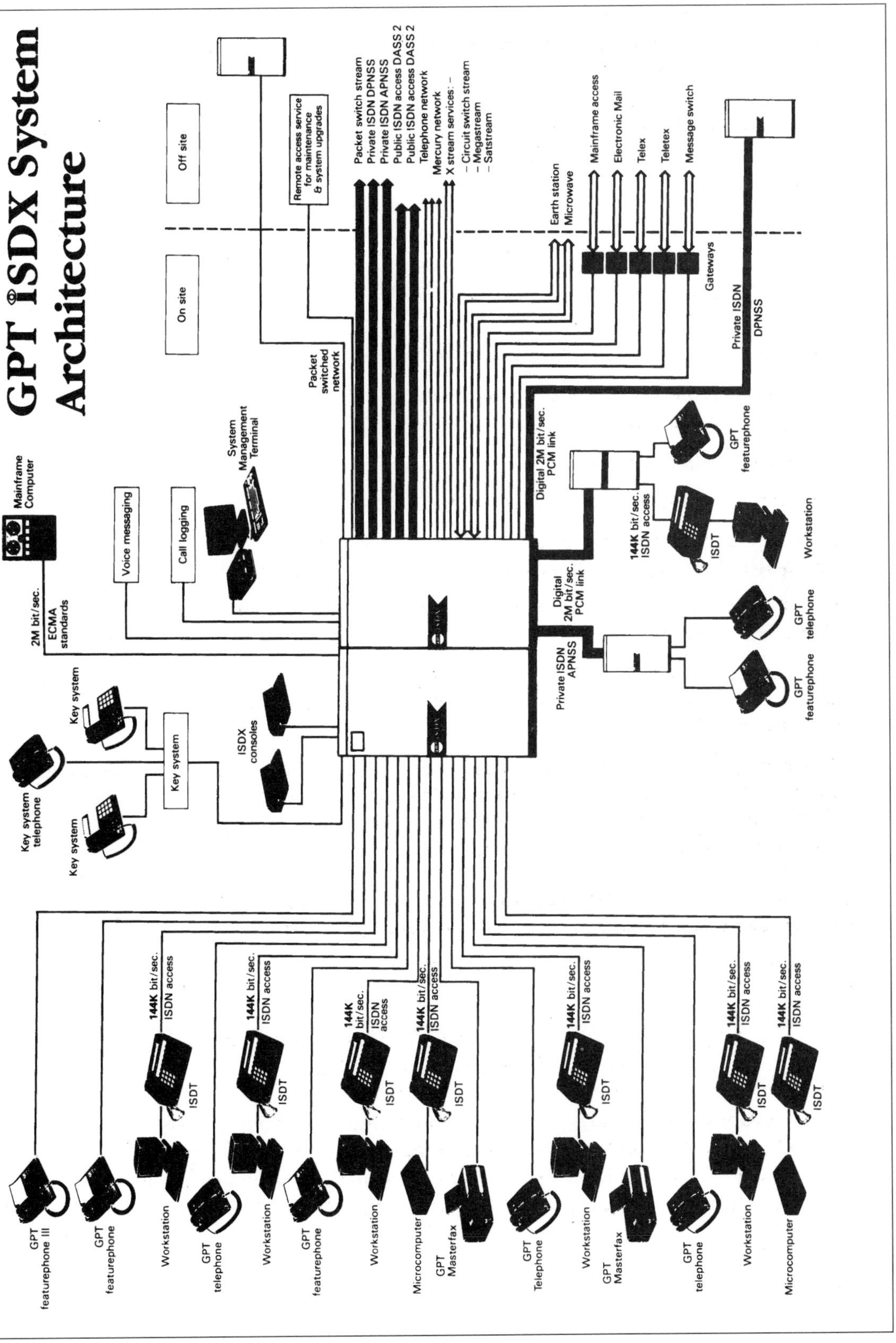

PC
2.4.2
2.4.3

The IT equipment used in information systems

As we have already seen, business information systems today rely increasingly on the connectivity of computerised, electronic equipment. In order to understand how current information systems work, it is necessary to be thoroughly familiar with the operating principles of the equipment involved.

This section, therefore, examines in detail the following equipment:

- Facsimile transceivers
- Telephone systems
- Photocopiers
- Printers
- Computerised filing and microform record systems.

Facsimile transmission

Known universally today as fax, this telecommunications system has become extremely popular with the managers and secretaries in all kinds of organisational departments, largely as a result of the speed and versatility which IT technology has given to it over the past decade. Fax can transmit to local, national and international locations all kinds of messages – handwritten notes, word processed printout, maps, diagrams, or even photographs and can accept messages in the same range of media. Transmission is effected in the space of a few seconds or minutes, depending upon the length of the document and can be undertaken (through BT and international telephone networks or through private telecommunications circuits) directly or at cheap, off-peak times in order to minimise costs.

Fax transceivers are given a rating depending on the speed at which they can transmit. A Group 3 fax transceiver can take as little as 20 seconds to transmit or receive a typical A4 page business letter. A Group 4 series carries out the same task in about six seconds.

Feedback confirmation of the safe arrival of a fax message and the facility to transmit messages confidentially are further important features of fax. The latest transceivers can also handle high-quality, plain-paper faxes.

How fax works

The way in which facsimile transmission works may be compared to the way in which a photocopier takes a copy of a document and the way a telephone line carries an oral message, which becomes an electronic signal along the telephone line and is converted back into speech at the receiver's end. In a similar way, the fax transceiver converts the text or image of the original for transmission into a series of electronic pulses or signals so that they may be transmitted over a telecommunications network of either telephone lines or satellite communication radio signals.

At the reception end (another fax transceiver), these signals are converted back into their original form, as either text, photograph or diagram etc.

The diagram (Fig 2.31) illustrates the principal routes of fax transmissions.

PC
2.4.2
2.4.3

Fig 2.31 **Three routes for fax transmission**

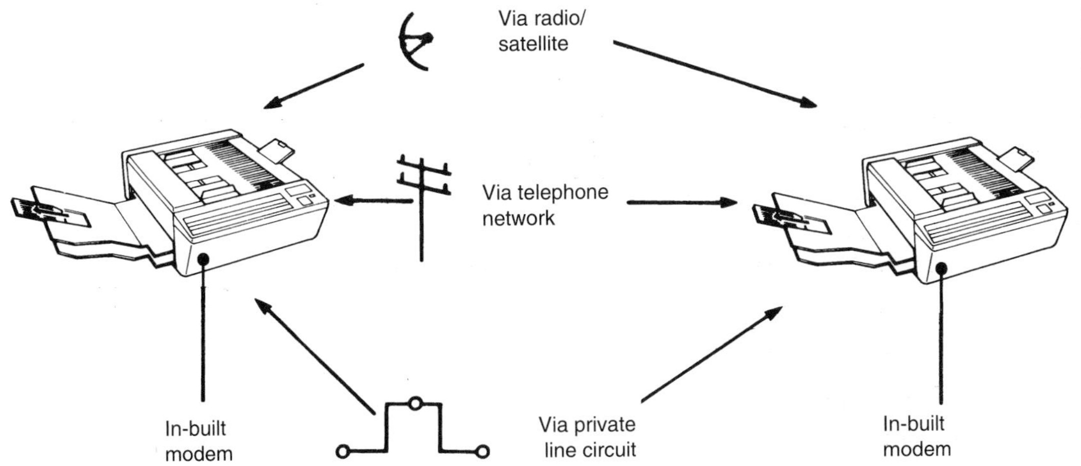
Via radio/
satellite
Via telephone
network
In-built
modem
Via private
line circuit
In-built
modem

Sending a fax message

1 Initial checks are made to ensure the transceiver is powered up and has paper loaded.

2 The document is fed into a document feeder for encoding. Note: if multiple documents are being transmitted care must be taken with their alignment.

3 A test copy is taken whenever the light/shade tones of a document need to be checked prior to transmission. The fax transceiver can regulate this aspect just like a photocopier. Also, fax transceivers generally provide a dual means of document transmission (fine or standard) according to the variety of shades in the original.

4 The document's recipient (another fax transceiver) is contacted by dialling the appropriate fax number. Note: fax transceivers for extensive use incorporate a feature which provides for 50–100+ fax numbers to be accessed through abbreviated codes.

5 Transmission may be effected either automatically or after telephone verbal contact with the recipient, to talk through any relevant matters or to arrange for confidential message reception etc.

6 The fax transceiver returns to a state of readiness for document acceptance once the transmission is completed.

7 A print-out of a message confirmation report detailing the date, time, transmission time, receiver machine identification code, number of pages and confirmation of the message's safe arrival may also be obtained from the transceiver.

Delayed transmission

In order to save costs or avoid busy peak transmission times, most fax systems allow the user to 'stack' a number of messages for onward transmission until a predetermined transmission time – say overnight UK time. At the appropriate moment a timer is activated to set the transmission sequences into operation. This function is usually set up at the end of the office day when no further messages are to be sent by normal means.

Status reports

A very useful feature of fax transmission is the intermittent (say after 50 transmissions) issuing of a status report which lists the number of calls made, their date, time and transmission duration, their destination and the number of pages transmitted. This provides a means of monitoring the fax bills when they arrive.

Receiving a fax message

1 A check must be made to ensure that the fax transceiver is switched on to an automatic reception mode (i.e. AUTO RECEIVE).

2 Care must be taken to ensure that sufficient paper is loaded into the transceiver to print out the anticipated number of incoming messages while fax is on auto receive. Note: fax transceivers can also be set up for the manual reception of an individual message (see 5 above).

3 At the end of each document's reception, the transceiver guillotines it and stores it in its document stacker. The date, time, and sender machine code number are printed out on each incoming message.

4 Reception polling: this device enables the receiving transceiver to accept an incoming message once a password command has been transmitted to the sending fax, and so enables a message to be despatched and received confidentially. Polling transmission techniques also allow messages to be sent to a preselected number of fax transceivers simultaneously, once passwords have been exchanged.

Facts on fax

Specifications

All fax transceivers are built to meet international (CCITT) specifications and are given a group rating. Group 1 is now almost obsolete. Group 2 operates at about 5–6 minutes to process a typical A4 sized letter. Group 3 does this in about 20 seconds. Group 4 machines do the same job in about 6 seconds. Group 4s can 'talk' to Group 3s, but at Group 3 speeds only. Many fax transceivers possess a variety of resolution facilities – 'fine' for delicate work, 'standard' for normal documents and some have a 'half-tone' facility for photographic work. The size of fax rolls of paper for printing upon is a compromise between UK, European and USA paper size standards in order for respective users to be able to accept each other's documents. Increasingly 'flat and cut A4 sheet' fax machines are being marketed.

Paper and printing

For a long time fax transceivers used thermal copying paper which did not give a particularly good copy. Recently office equipment manufacturers have developed the means of printing out fax messages to letter quality standards on laser/ink-jet printers.

Fax and the future

The future of fax is assured. It is extremely versatile, being able to transmit handwritten notes, typed/printed text, images and diagrams and photographs in seconds. One major telephone company reckons to be able to guarantee a fax transmission to anywhere in the world within two minutes, given that there are no faults in the telecommunications network! Fax equipment is becoming cheaper to buy (machines now under £300) and run. Worldwide users now far surpass telex in number. It is user-friendly and simple to operate.

Fig 2.32 **Examples of status and message confirmation reports**

(Status Report Print Out)

Below you will find an example status report and an explanation of its components.

Example Status Report

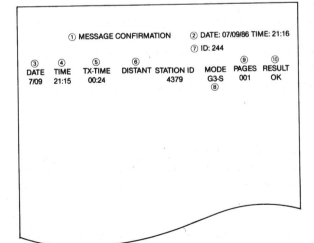

① STATUS REPORT

② DATE: 20/09/86 TIME: 17:24

③ TOTAL TIME TX = 00:09' RX = 00:01'

④ ID: 0081 3 432 3211

⑤ DATE	⑥ TIME	⑦ TX,RX-TIME	⑧ DISTANT STATION ID	⑨ MODE	⑩ PAGES	⑪ RESULT	⑫
09/09	13:12	00'36"	6294	G3-S	001	OK	0000
09/09	13:27	01'09"	6294	G3-S	003	OK	0000
09/09	15:54	04'32"	6294	G3-S	006	OK	0000
09/12	15:01	00'24"	03 432 1519	G3-S	001	OK	0000
09/17	11:28	00'44"		G3-R	000	NO	9081
09/18	10:26	00'08"		G3-S	000	STP	9080
09/18	18:28	00'35"		G3-S	000	NO	9081
09/19	09:02	00'00"	0PPP432-1519	G3-S	000	NO	9999
09/19	09:04	00'00"	0PPP432-1519	G3-S	000	NO	9999
09/19	09:05	00'34"	03 432 1519	G3-S	001	OK	0000
09/19	09:08	00'00"	0PPP432-1519	G3-S	000	NO	9999
09/19	09:10	00'34"	03 432 1519	G3-S	001	OK	0000
09/19	09:12	00'00"	0PPP432-1519	G3-S	000	NO	9999
09/19	09:13	00'00"	0PPP432-1519	G3-S	000	NO	9999
09/19	09:15	00'00"	0PPP432-1519	G3-S	000	NO	9999
09/19	09:16	00'00"	0PPP432-1519	G3-S	000	NO	9999
09/19	09:25	00'38"	6294	G3-S	001	OK	0000
09/19	09:33	00'47"	03 432 1519	G3-R	001	OK	0000
09/19	15:48	00'09"		G3-R	000	STP	9080

Explanation of Status Report Components

① Title of Report
② Date and time report is made
③ Total transmission and reception time
④ TSI/CSI data (Your 9550's telephone number)
⑤ Date of each facsimile transaction
⑥ Time at which each transaction started
⑦ Time taken for each transmission (TX) or reception (RX) transaction
⑧ Identification of the remote machine
⑨ Communication mode for sending (S) and receiving (R) operations
⑩ Number of pages transmitted or received for each transaction
⑪ Result status of transaction
⑫ Four-digit code used by servicing engineer

Example codes for possible result problems:
STP (stop button pressed)
BUSY (partner fax did not answer)
NO (problem with partner machine or telephone line)

(Message Confirmation Report Print Out)

Below you will find an example Message Confirmation Report and an explanation of its components.

Example Message Confirmation Report

① MESSAGE CONFIRMATION ② DATE: 07/09/86 TIME: 21:16

⑦ ID: 244

③ DATE	④ TIME	⑤ TX-TIME	⑥ DISTANT STATION ID	MODE	⑨ PAGES	⑩ RESULT
7/09	21:15	00:24	4379	G3-S ⑧	001	OK

Explanation of Message Confirmation Report Components

① Title of Report
② Date and time of report
③ Date of the communication mode
④ Time at which communication began
⑤ The length of time the communication took to complete
⑥ Remote machine identification data
⑦ TSI/CSI data (Your 9550's telephone number)
⑧ Communication mode ("S" = Transmission, "R" = Reception)
⑨ Total number of pages transmitted
⑩ Result status of communication

Reproduced by kind permission of Muirifax Systems Ltd

Its confidential transmission service and message integrity features are making fax increasingly popular with senior managers, and its incorporation into LAN/WAN systems is offering a versatile and express service to a fast increasing number of organisations.

PC
2.4.2
2.4.3

A TYPICAL FAX FEATURES CHECKLIST

- Storage of telephone numbers via a predetermined code.
- Automatic call initiation.
- High speed automatic dialling facility.
- Automatic storage of last number called.
- Call Progress Monitor.
- Tone detection: Ring, Busy, Equipment Engaged, Unobtainable.
- Repeat attempt facility.
- Auto-clear from originating end.
- One touch auto-dialling and auto-polling.
- Automatic copying of transmitted documents.
- Delayed transmission facilities.
- Reception and transmission polling.
- Provision to supply status and management reports on fax transmissions and receptions.

■ Telephone services in organisations

Nowhere in today's office has IT brought about more changes than in the telephone systems linking in-house, local, national and international calls. Indeed, the current global network of telephone lines not only carries several hundred billion telephone calls around the world each year, but it also routes similarly huge amounts of data between computers and their users via modems and multiplexing (a means of enabling telephone lines to transmit varying data voice and computer language based – much faster).

It is therefore becoming increasingly difficult to view the telephone system – as it once was – as a totally distinct medium of communication. Indeed, British Telecom is currently installing an **Integrated Services Digital Network (ISDN)** in the UK which joins together voice-based telecommunications via Private Automatic Branch Exchanges (PABXs)* and the **Public Switched Telephone Network (PSTN)** with computer digital data switching networks, like BT's **Packet Switched Services (PSS)** – Datel, Satstream and Kilostream. In this way, communications in the media of voice, telex, fax, videotex, Confravision and digitally processed data will become fully exchangeable through a unified telecommunications network, instead of in today's piecemeal fashion in which some equipment cannot 'talk to' similar equipment of a different make and design, because they are not compatible.

Telephone services and the office

Essentially, there are two kinds of telephone service available in any office. Firstly there is the private line which connects its user directly to the PSTN exchange which is known as a Direct Exchange Line. Some senior managers have such telephone lines connected to a personal desktop handset so as to be able to make confidential business calls in complete privacy.

Secondly there is the extension line which connects the user to a central switchboard. In large organisations several switchboard operators are kept busy routing incoming calls to desired extensions and obtaining telephone numbers for staff wishing to make outgoing calls. At the turn of the century such connections were made by plugging large sets of

*Note increasingly Computerised Automatic Branch Exchanges (CABX) are replacing their PABX counterparts.

cables into a board by means of jack plugs – 'trying to connect you . . .' Today such arm-aching activity has been replaced by pressing touch-sensitive buttons on a desktop computerised switchboard no bigger than a ring-binder which may control as many as 50–100 extensions!

For many years small firms like accountants', solicitors' and doctors' practices used systems which linked some 8–12 handsets. Any one user could accept an incoming call and route it if need be to a companion extension. By the same token, any one user could access an outside line. Such systems, however, offered no protection from unauthorised use.

As a result, large organisations preferred to employ systems which allowed centralised control. For example, current computerised systems provide a number of monitoring features:

- **Outside line access limited to local call-making only:** usually by dialling 9 on any extension given this facility
- **Call barring:** outside calls may only be made through the switchboard operator or not at all.
- **Call interrupting:** audio or visual prompts are activated in handsets when calls go on for longer than a pre-arranged time (say 5 minutes)
- **Call override:** a switchboard operator or senior manager may break into a call if the caller is urgently required.

Fig 2.33 **The four stages of the telephone network**

PC 2.4.2 2.4.3

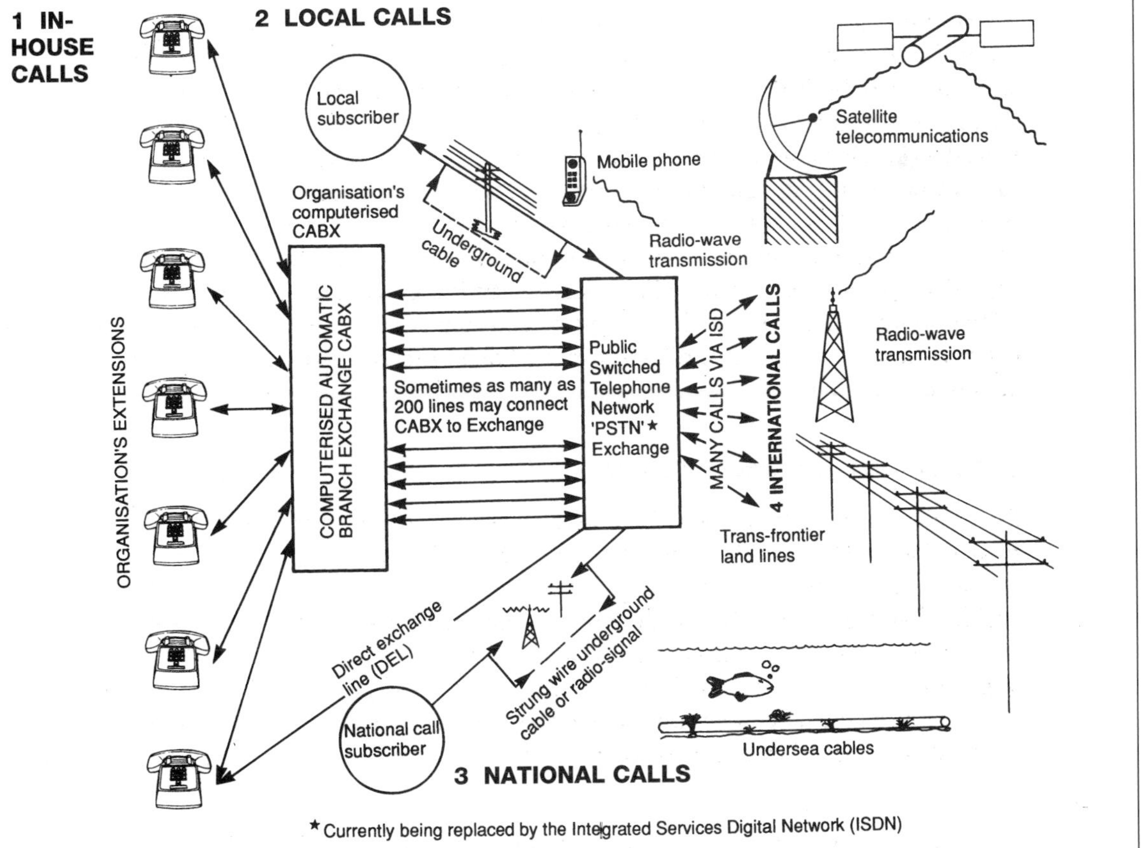

* Currently being replaced by the Integrated Services Digital Network (ISDN)

- **Call logging and reporting:** sophisticated equipment exists to monitor all incoming and outgoing calls by extension number and to calculate ongoing costs and the time a handset is active; such measures help to keep down telephone costs and to enable accounts departments to allocate to each department an accurate proportion of the single, all-in telephone bill it receives quarterly.

Following upon the privatisation of British Telecom a number of UK telecommunications manufacturers like Plessey and Ferranti introduced a range of C/PABX (sometimes simply referred to as PBX) computerised telephone systems capable of supplying the needs of 8–250+ extension users. Such manufacturers vied with each other to include yet more sophisticated features in order to win orders and to provide a better service. Some of the more commonly occurring ones are described below.

PC
2.4.2
2.4.3

EXAMPLES OF BRITISH TELECOM TELEPHONE SERVICES TO BUSINESS

Audio conferencing – Providing regional/national/international telephone hook-ups for meetings etc.

Call cost indication – Informing user of the cost of a telephone call just completed.

Citicall – Information service on stocks and shares.

Yellow Pages – 1.4 million listed business services in district directories, and as an electronic database.

Credit authorisation – Acceptance of credit payment for phone calls, etc.

Pay card sales – Sale of units of phone call time via a plastic card: many public phone boxes accept this form of payment and erase time used from the inserted card (cards sold in units of 20, 40 and 100).

Freefone service – Businesses accept sales enquiries by phone and pay for the incoming calls – up to a preset time limit.

Mobile radiophone and car/train phone service – Mobile, cordless telephones connected by radio to BT telephone network; equipment is sold by Cellnet and Vodaphone for national use via BT's Cellnet system to route messages over more than short local distances.

Ship's telephone service – Long-established passenger phone service routed via radio signals and/or satellite.

Star services – Eight services provided by System X exchanges: call waiting warning signal; abbreviated call coding, up to 27 numbers' repeat last call; charge advice; call diversion; 3-way calling; call barring.

Telephone credit cards (national and international) – Internationally placed calls are accepted and placed by the operator upon the citing of your credit number; especially useful for sales representatives.

Radio paging – Individuals are 'bleeped' anywhere in UK by radio signal and asked to get into telephone contact. Note: some pagers only emit certain tones, others will communicate short messages on an LCD strip.

Data sources: British Telecom and The Telecom User's Handbook; and Telecommunications Press

PC
2.4.2
2.4.3

MAJOR TYPICAL FEATURES OF A LARGE COMPUTERISED PABX SYSTEM

This table is based upon the Ferranti GTE OMNI System and is kindly made available by Ferranti GTE Ltd)

Some of OMNI's system features

Administration message recording – to provide usage reports
Dictation access – providing a link to dictation services
Group hunting – seeking out any one of a working team's extensions available to take an in-coming call by trying each in turn
Intercom groups – linking users via intercom speakers
Music on hold – playing a soothing tune over the phone while a caller is waiting to be connected
Paging and code calling access – ability to activate pagers used by roving staff
Standby power – facility to keep system going in event of power failure
Call barring – ability to restrict the range of connections availability on any extension

Some attendant features

Automatic recall re-dial – system keeps trying to connect to a busy number
Break in – facility to break into an active conversation in case of urgency
Call waiting – provision to alert extension user of another call awaiting attention
Camp on busy – ability to wait, having dialled a number until it becomes available and then to ring dialler's extension having effected the connection
Conference – linking of several extension users so all can converse with each other over the phone system can also include outside callers

Some extension features

Abbreviated dialling – often used numbers are given a short 1/2 digit code to save time
Boss–secretary – direct interconnection
Call forwarding follow me – instruction for incoming calls to be routed from a customary extension to others near to a roving staff member
Call hold – facility to keep line open to caller while specific staff member located
Direct inward dialling – facility to enable incoming calls to be routed directly to selected extension by adding its number to normal organisation's number
Direct outward dialling – facility to access PSTN directly
Do not disturb – cuts phone off while meeting etc. taking place; avoids irritating interruptions
Extension to extension calling – for direct in-house phone calls

Other major features included in computerised PABX systems are:

Amplifying speech – to enable an incoming call to be heard across a room
Night service – enables incoming calls to be answered by late staying staff after switchboard staff have left
Call parking – the ability to divert an incoming call to another extension
'No answer' transfer – facility to re-route a call to another, specified extension

Note: Many of the above features of computerised switchboards are available to the general public with the introduction of BT's System X digital exchanges.

■ Summary

Information Technology has made a tremendous impact upon telephone systems. The number of potential contacts – customers, government officials, organisation managers, etc. – who may call up a given executive has increased greatly as a result of national and international direct dialling and the extension of private line circuits. Similarly, the ways in which such callers may be handled by a computerised PABX system have become much more sophisticated.

No two computerised PABX or key system circuits are the same and so it becomes most important for all new personnel to acquire an informed understanding of typical routines and features and once in a post to acquire an absolutely thorough mastery of the system employed by the organisation.

PC 2.4.2 2.4.3

■ Mobile phones for mobile people

The early 1980s saw a rapid uptake among managers, executives, professionals and self-employed businessmen of the mobile phone and its 'sidekick' the radiopager.

The system developed by both Telecom-Securicor and Racal-Vodaphone under licence is called a cellular telephone network. As the diagram (Fig 2.34) illustrates, it enables different types of mobile telephone (powered by either car or inserted batteries) to transmit a radio signal which is, in effect, like the dialled telephone call. This radio signal is picked up at the perimeter of the cell (the area picked up by one British Telecom exchange) in which the user finds himself and relayed to a telephone exchange where it connects with

PC 2.4.2 2.4.3

Fig 2.34 **How cellphones work**

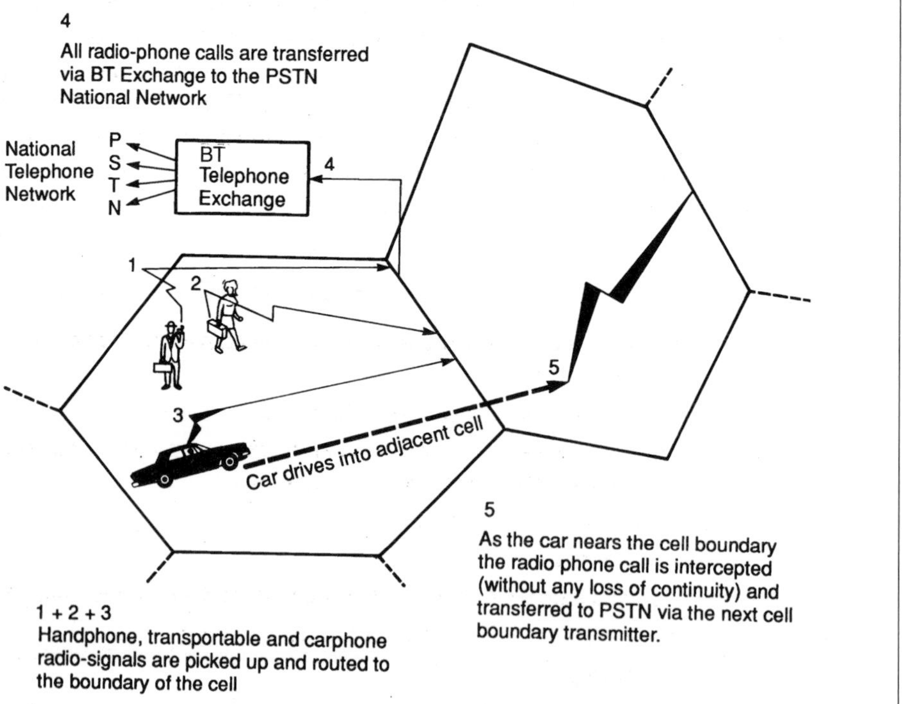
4
All radio-phone calls are transferred via BT Exchange to the PSTN National Network
National Telephone Network
P S T N
BT Telephone Exchange
4
1
2
3
5
Car drives into adjacent cell
5
As the car nears the cell boundary the radio phone call is intercepted (without any loss of continuity) and transferred to PSTN via the next cell boundary transmitter.
1 + 2 + 3
Handphone, transportable and carphone radio-signals are picked up and routed to the boundary of the cell

the national PSTN system. As the mobile telephone user moves from one cell to another in his car, the radio signal of the continuing telephone call is relayed on to the next cell in the network.

A further development of mobile telephoning in the 1990s is that of telephone points. Within densely populated urban areas, mobile phones can link into networks of a form of relay station – called a phone point – which may be situated in a restaurant or shop. These relay stations route the mobile phone call into the nearest PSTN exchange, and hence into national and international systems.

PC 2.4.2 2.4.3

GROUP ACTIVITIES

First undertake your researches and then report back to your group on:

1 How an organisation controls the costs of acquiring and maintaining its office equipment systems.

2 The current range of services provided by British Telecom, Mercury or Cable and Wireless plc for one of the following:

a personal call networks (PCNs)

b teleconferencing

c private line packet switching

3 How Integrated Services Digital Network (ISDN) systems work and how they are likely to develop in the near future.

Radiopaging

A less expensive form of contacting mobile staff is through radiopagers. These are small devices which are sometimes called bleepers, which pick up a radio signal which causes them to emit a bleeping sound. Such a signal alerts the person carrying the radiopager to telephone his office, say, from an internal extension in a large hospital, or from a payphone in the world at large if he does not possess a cellphone. The latest type of radiopager includes a LCD panel which can accept transmitted brief messages via radio signal, such as: CONGRATS! GLOBAL CONTRACT IN THE BAG! or, MOST URGENT YOU RING 0171-345-9876 DIRECTLY. British Telecom offers a range of services to enable customers to transmit such messages over the UK as a whole to remotely located radiopager holders – even veterinary surgeons knee-deep in Farmer Giles' water meadows!

PC 2.4.2 2.4.3

CHECKLIST OF USEFUL TELECOMMUNICATIONS DIRECTORIES

Effective fax and telephone systems users ensure that they have easy access to the following internal and external directories:

- Up-to-date Directory of Internal Telephone Extensions
- Personal Directories of Frequently Used Phone and Fax Numbers (note the ability of PCs and fax transceivers to store these through macro abbreviations)
- BT/Mercury Local Telephone Directories
- Thomson Local Directories
- Thomson Yellow Pages (Local Commercial Businesses) and electronic database
  Note: also now available as a national computerised database
- National BT Fax Directory
- Directory of Private Line Numbers (if organisation is leasing a private telephone network system)

PC
2.4.2
2.4.3

INDIVIDUAL ACTIVITY

Choose one of the above external directories, find out what range of information it provides and provide a suitable briefing about it to your group.

PC
2.4.2
2.4.3

DISCUSSION TOPICS

Information issues

1 With the rapid expansion of national and global telecommunication systems, which can now bring the world to any manager's desk, what steps should organisations take to protect their executives from the information overload which prevents them concentrating on the organisation's key objectives?

2 Is the abundance of data nowadays readily available to large and small organisations a help or a hindrance to effective decision-making? Can a manager know too much as well as too little?

3 Is the trend of routing all kinds of communication to staff's desktop terminals likely to result in the loss of valuable face-to-face direct communication? If it did, would it matter?

PC
2.4.2
2.4.3

■ Reprographics: printers, photocopiers and publishing systems

Just as IT has revolutionised the creation of information on the ever-present PC work-station, so it has transformed the ways in which this information is transformed into the printed word, number or graphic.

Computer-connected printers: dot-matrix, ink-jet, laser

Currently there are three types of printer connectable to the desk-top PC:

- laser
- bubble/inkjet
- dot-matrix

Dot-matrix

The oldest of the three in development terms is the dot-matrix. This type of printer relies on the traditional ink-impregnated ribbon (just as did the manual and electric typewriters). Various combinations of pins hit the ribbon to produce letters or numbers etc. Originally the text appeared in a ragged, crude format, since only eight pins were used. Later, twenty four pins were used. Nowadays the dot-matrix is a humble, low-cost printer used primarily to print documents limited to in-house use, or to effect label runs for mail-shots.

Ink-jet

The inkjet printer was developed in response to users demands for a smoother 'letter-quality' printer which could reproduce the print quality of an electronic, daisy-wheel-driven typewriter. It works by emitting 'squirts' of ink through nozzles which produce the shapes of letters or symbols etc. Once the ink hits the paper, it is almost immediately heat-dried.

Laser

The laser printer soon emerged in the 1980s as the 'Rolls-Royce' of printers, as a result of its superior technology which produced a much clearer, sharper print, and which could also handle images, grey tones and complex patterns (as employed in desktop publishing) with equal excellence. Moreover, the letters and other high-profile documents it produced approached the quality of the professional printer's photo-typesetting equipment.

The technology involves a drum or roller moving over the blank paper sheet, and accepting or rejecting deposits of toner. Where the toner lands, printing occurs, where not, white space is left. The laser printer not only prints at a resolution higher than 300 dots per inch (or 90,000 dots per square inch!), it also churns pages of A4 out at up to 200-plus per minute on professional printers' models. A typical desktop laser printer will produce an A4 sheet every 6–8 seconds.

Laser printers also accept printer-driver instructions which include fonts which have had the 'ragged' edges of their characters smoothed out by *Adobe Postscript*-type utility packages.

Printers and paper

All the above printers will accept A4 cut sheet paper if appropriate feeders are fitted to them. Depending on their width, they will also accept continuous stationery up to some 400 mm or 16 inches in width. Dot matrix and ink-jet printers accept most types of office paper, but laser printers require high quality bond paper for best results.

Printers and costs

As you might expect, there is with electronic printers a direct relationship between quality output and cost. The following factors affect such printing costs:

- Capital cost or leasing cost of the printer.
- Cost of maintenance contract (can be significant).
- Renewal costs of: toner cassettes, cartridges and laser drums or black/colour ribbons or print wheels.
- Cost of electricity to drive the printer.
- Cost of paper used and amount used per month.

Note: some printer and photocopier suppliers levy monthly charges based on the number of pages/copies printed.

When costed out at an all-in price per sheet, such costs vary considerably depending on the above factors and type of printer employed, with laser printers proving most expensive to run.

Photocopiers

Despite the fact that the paperless office has been 'round the corner' for thew past 25 years, the photocopier is still the informational work-horse of most business organisations!

As a result of the IT revolution, they have progressed from slow, manually-driven types which could only cope with single sheets, to systems versions, able to 'devour' reams of paper and copy A4 sheets at rates exceeding 200 copies per minute.

The following table illustrates some of the major features of the mid-range departmental copier.

PC
2.4.2
2.4.3

THE MID-RANGE OR DEPARTMENTAL COPIER

Such copiers have become increasingly popular since they occupy little space – not much more than a desktop – yet provide a very much larger range of features, while the cost of the modest single sheet copier is a few hundred pounds, the middle range copier (sometimes referred to as a departmental copier) will cost anything from £1500–£10,000. As with all office equipment, the buyer tends to get what he pays for. The following checklist illustrates some typical features of the mid-range copier:

- Able to copy from A6 postcard and A5 to A3 paper sizes.
- Automatic enlargement and reduction.
- Automatic document feed – for copying sets of different originals.
- Bypass feed to do a quick single-sheet copy in the middle of a long job.
- Automatic exposure control – to adapt to originals of varying quality.
- At least a 20-copy stacking bin which automatically collates copies into sets of reports, minutes, etc.
- User control system – either a security lock or insertable type of credit card which meters copies made.
- At least two automatic paper feed trays (A4 and A3). Note: some models automatically activate the appropriate paper 'cassette' tray according to the size of original.
- Capacity to hold at least 1 ream (500 sheets) of copy paper – many will hold 2000 sheets or more.
- Automatic enlargement and reduction features both by predetermined ratios (according to paper sizes A5, A4, A3, etc., or by percentage from, say 50 per cent to 150 per cent of original by single percentage steps – sometimes referred to as 'zoom magnification'.
- Emergency override switch to halt the photocopying process in the event of a mistake or machine fault.

Such is the pressure of competition to sell photocopiers – a market leader sold over half a million worldwide in one year alone – that even the above range of features in the middle tier of copiers is being increased by such sophisticated facilities like:

- Editing board and stylus – rather like a computer's VDU and light-pen, this additional equipment enables the user to edit existing originals on a screen electronically and to blank out unwanted portions (image overlay), to join together parts of different originals without tell-tale lines showing and to adjust margins for right or left hand sheets in a bound document.
- Automatic double-sided copying (sometimes called duplexing) – a feature which prints simultaneously on both sides of the paper from two originals placed side-by-side (tandem copying).
- Colour printing – the incorporation of red, blue, sepia, etc., colours one to a single sheet (not to be confused with full-colour copiers which can reproduce colour photographs) at the touch of a button.
- Copying of three-dimensional objects, such as jewellery for insurance purposes and bound books without showing dark areas where light has been let in.
- Automatic electrical power saving mode operated when the machine is not in active use (to save electricity and costs).

Given the present pace of copier design development, such features and facilities are being extended and improved virtually every month as a new or upgraded model is introduced.

■ Desktop publishing (DTP)

PC 2.4.2 2.4.3

Desktop publishing (sometimes referred to as electronic publishing) has been one of the fastest growing IT developments of the past decade. Its rapid uptake was the result of a number of factors and influences, principal among which was that the equipment was already in existence – PC desktop computer with hard disk, laser printer, scanner and mouse. What was the vital additional ingredient was of course the software to do the creative job.

In a nutshell, a desktop publishing system provides its user with the means of producing page-by-page and document-by-document highly attractive and well printed copy – that is a mix of:

- text in a wide variety of typefaces and sizes,
- photographs, drawings, graphs and charts all capable of being enlarged or reduced to fit a predetermined space,
- lines, rules, shading, cross-hatching and frames which either make reading easier or create visual appeal as part of the overall page design,
- imported artwork (known as clip-art) from the DTP software which can be quickly positioned on to a given page.

Previously, such printed matter had to be given to a printing house to set and print. The development of DTP, however, has had a profound effect upon the production of

Fig 2.35 **Desktop publishing kit**

PC 2.4.2 2.4.3

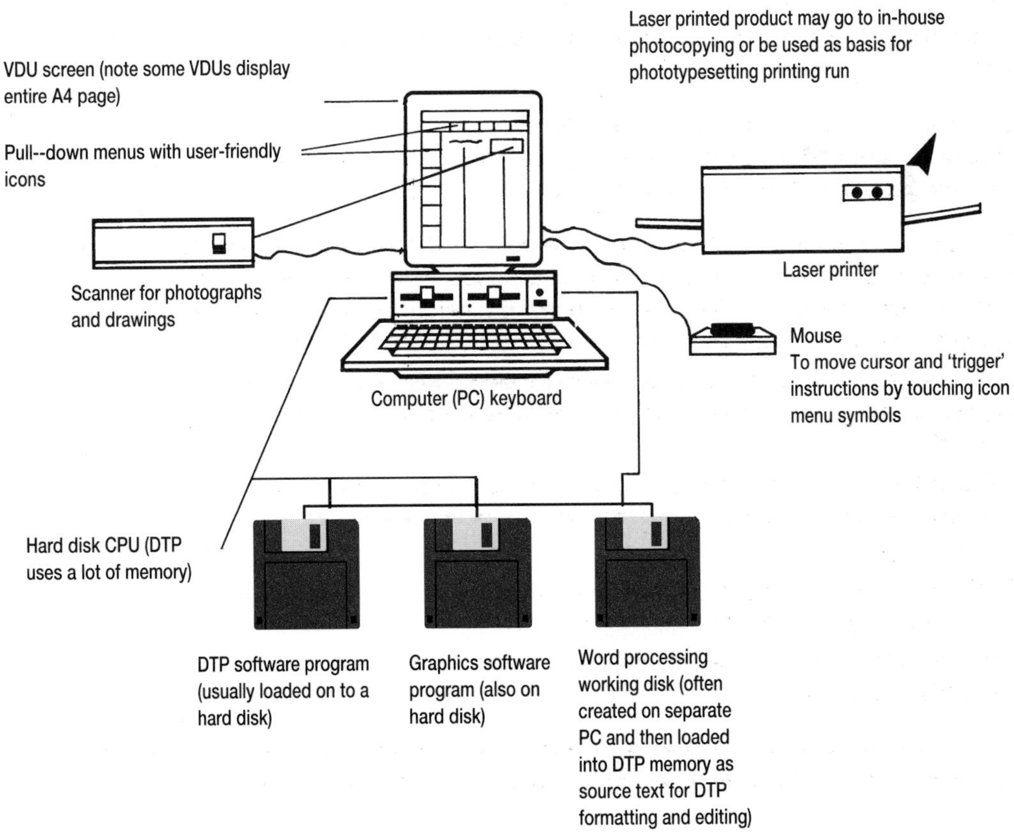

VDU screen (note some VDUs display entire A4 page)
Pull--down menus with user-friendly icons
Laser printed product may go to in-house photocopying or be used as basis for phototypesetting printing run
Scanner for photographs and drawings
Laser printer
Mouse
To move cursor and 'trigger' instructions by touching icon menu symbols
Computer (PC) keyboard
Hard disk CPU (DTP uses a lot of memory)
DTP software program (usually loaded on to a hard disk)
Graphics software program (also on hard disk)
Word processing working disk (often created on separate PC and then loaded into DTP memory as source text for DTP formatting and editing)

organisational documents and the presentation of information, as it has brought the printing house – with many of its visual and graphics devices and effects – right into the heart of office information processing.

Indeed, at the end of the 1980s some 50 per cent of everything we read was produced by a DTP system!

How desktop publishing works

Perhaps the best way to view DTP is as a kind of enhanced word processing and visual image combining system. Desktop publishing creates an electronic page of text on the PC's visual display screen using aspects of the mix outlined above. The text for this mix is usually originated by means of a current commercial word processing package and, in a similar way, previously devised charts and graphs, etc., may be installed into the DTP system from a graphics software package. Photographic or drawn images are installed by means of a scanner. Once all the desired ingredients have been 'loaded' into the DTP system, the process of designing each page of the document may commence.

PC
2.4.2
2.4.3

GROUP ACTIVITIES

In groups of two or three first undertake your researches then report back to your group as indicated.

1 Investigate the current costs (and how they break down) of leasing for a two-year period a departmental group photocopier.

Compare the comparative costs of outright purchase as opposed to leasing, if the department you work in typically produced: (a) 20,000 or (b) 12,000 A4 copies each month.

2 Find out about the range of printing features available in a mid-range laser printer relevant to in-house desktop publishing.

3 Ascertain what services are available from a local reprographics bureau – e.g. colour copying, photocopying, photo-enlarging, report binding, 3-colour printing, etc. and what they cost. Devise a short fact sheet to communicate your findings.

4 Produce a 'what you get for what you pay' chart to compare and contrast the features of mid-range 24-pin dot matrix, ink-jet and laser printers which would be of use to a departmental manager seeking to update his printing facilities.

PC
2.4.2
2.4.3

■ Micrographics, microform and microfilm

An important method of records management takes the form of the miniaturisation of original documents on to frames of film/photographic media. In the USA, this process is called micrographics. For years in the UK it has been known as microfilming, but perhaps it ought to be called 'microform' since this term reflects the various photographic forms that the miniaturisation can take.

Essentially, microform records are produced by the reverse of the process which enables us to have enlargements made of photographs which start out as contact prints. In microforming, special cameras take photographs of, say, A4 documents and reduce them by up to 105 times. In many popular processes, the reduction ranges between 24 and 48 times. As a result, an entire textbook could be transferred on to a set of microfiche cards or 100 feet roll of microfilm!

Fig 2.36 **Diagram of Kodak's information management system, KIMS 5000**

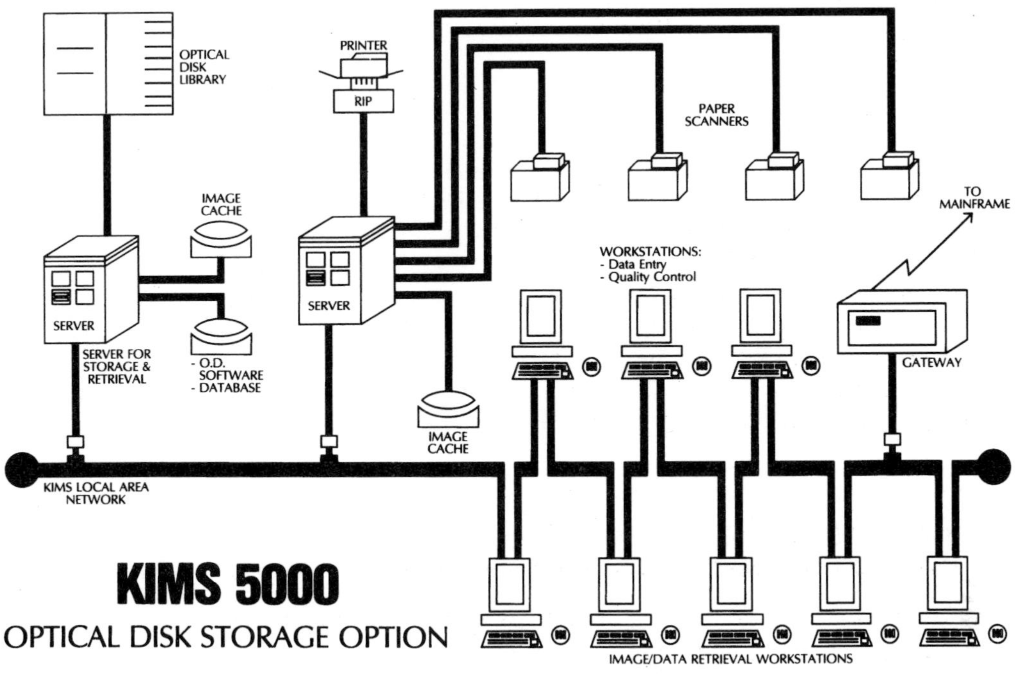

PC 2.4.2 2.4.3

Furthermore, at higher ratios of reduction it is possible to store the Bible on a strip of microform known as Ultrastrip no more than 20 cm long!

Microform and the computer

The widespread expansion of computer-based records management in the 1970s and 80s caused microform equipment manufacturers to work hard to develop an integrated technology which would preserve their investment – and that already made by many large organisations. As a result, three major areas of joint technology were introduced:

Computer output microform (COM)

COM is a system which enables computer-created data to be transferred during its creation *direct* on to microfilm at speeds which emulate those of a laser-printer. The use of such equipment is perhaps best described by means of an example. A large manufacturing company may run its sales invoices for national accounts customers in batches at intervals throughout the month and in so doing potentially create vast piles of copy invoices for its own records. COM enables such company records to be produced directly on to microfilm and thus to save as much as 95 per cent of the storage space needed and, as the process is simultaneous with the production of the paper invoice for onward despatch, at no extra cost in time.

Computer input microform (CIM)

CIM is a process which enables a computer to read the data held on microform and to transfer it into a computerised electronic file for distribution and examination, etc. In this way it provides a facility very much like that of an OCR scanner.

Computer aided retrieval (CAR)

It is not uncommon nowadays for international companies to hold millions (if not billions) of microform records of past activities in research, production, accounts, sales, and purchases, etc. While the vast majority may remain dormant for years, occasionally – say in the unhappy event of an airline disaster – it may prove necessary to locate quickly the records of parts, specifications, sources of supply and personnel involved in manufacturing an aero engine or wing part which go back 5–10 years. In such cases CAR is invaluable, since it links the memory and classification power of the computer with the vast records storage capacity of the microform media.

Frequently computer and microfilm frame are linked by 'blip' squares – tiny boxes to record serial numbers, etc. – which are printed on to each frame. As documents are microfilmed, a unique number is imprinted on to each frame which is also built into an indexing system on computer file. Thus the calling up of a given serial number enables the computer to find the file-roll or fiche in question and to display the desired frame in a matter of seconds!

Records management and optical disks

While great strides have been made in integrating computers and microform systems – even to the extent of including a microform reading and printing facility on LAN/WAN systems – the development of the optical disk offers even more economical records and archive management systems. For example, a single 35 cm (14-inch) optical storage disk (rather like an LP record in appearance) is capable of holding the equivalent of 1,000 computer floppy disks or 250,000 sheets of typescript A4! Some CD-ROM disks are 'WORM'-produced (Write Once, Read Many times), and the convenience of holding vast quantities of data in such a small space, and within a medium which is considered very safe from accidental damage or corruption is already proving very attractive to personnel managers, lawyers, librarians and scientists, despite the comparatively high cost of optical disks and associated equipment. A new interactive video (IV) technology, also called multimedia technology, is rapidly becoming established as a highly effective self-learning and training medium. It allows the user to access sequences of text, video film, graphics and photographs etc. and to interact with them.

Summary

Microform technology has rightly earned a central place in the records management systems available to managers of all kinds of data. Its plus factors include:

- Enormous savings in the space (and hence cost) needed to store paper documents.
- Data security and completeness: with microform storage, individual files and records do not go astray and are not easily destroyed by accident.
- Costs: once the capital costs of installing equipment are recovered, the actual cost per frame of microforming can be measured in fractions of a penny.
- Information in microform is cheap and easy to send to widely distributed branches, offices or sites.

■ Linked to a computerised management information system (MIS) microform can handle millions of records safely and swiftly.

As with any modern technology, a period of rapid technological change inevitably means that minus factors occur:

■ To acquire a fully versatile microform facility is expensive in terms of cameras, lenses, reader-printers, and computer-linked equipment.
■ A high standard of indexing and cataloguing skills is needed to manage a large system.
■ Some processes, such as obtaining printouts and film copies, are time-consuming.

PC 2.4.2 2.4.3

■ Computerised filing systems

Computerised, electronic filing of records is fast becoming the established norm. Indeed, in organisations using a LAN/WAN system, many communications are only ever made in electronic file form. One of the most important features of a computerised information system is its ability to handle enormous amounts of stored and archived information.

Basically, computerised records systems operate in two modes:

1 Centrally held files (in electronic form) are stored on a mainframe or mini-computer and are available for access by organisational users within a carefully controlled security system which restricts access to authorised personnel by means of passwords, etc.

2 Files are held in desktop PCs and distributed throughout the organisation. If such PCs are linked on a LAN/WAN system, then a file created, say, in the export section of a

PC 2.4.2 2.4.3

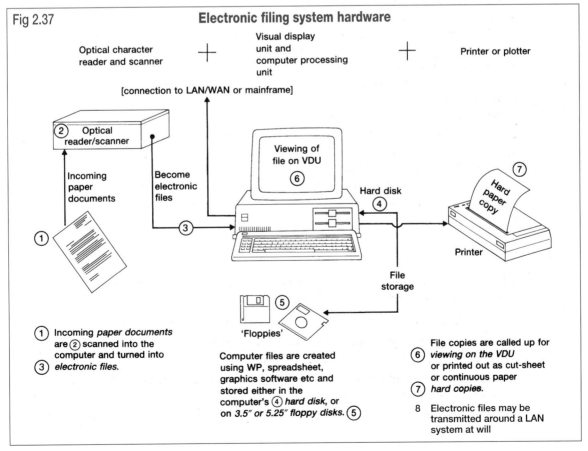

Fig 2.37 **Electronic filing system hardware**

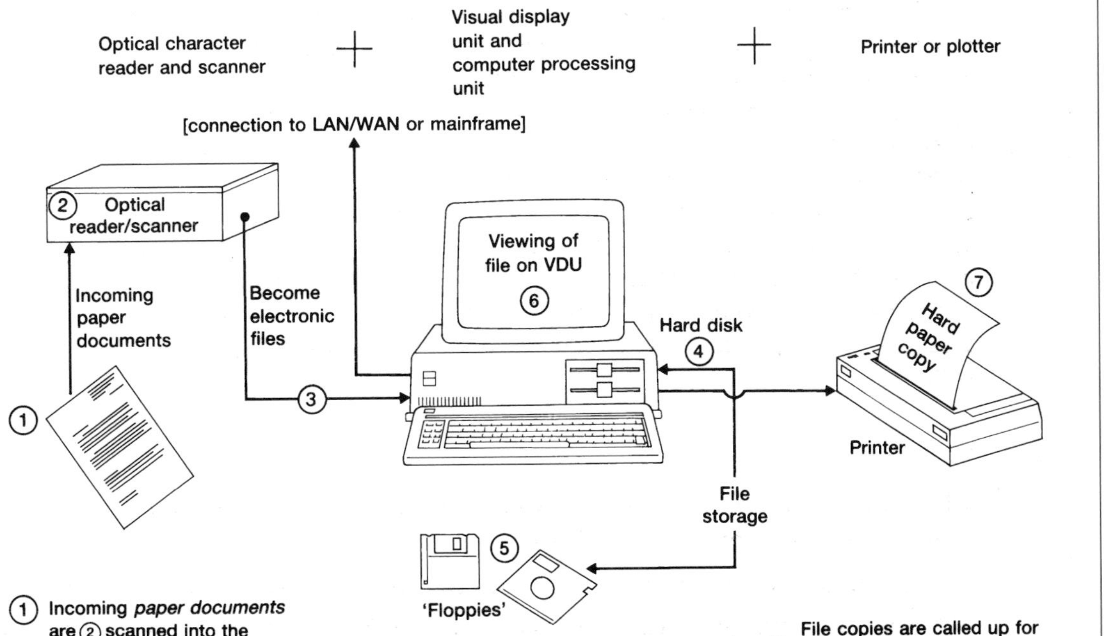
Optical character reader and scanner
+
Visual display unit and computer processing unit
+
Printer or plotter
[connection to LAN/WAN or mainframe]
② Optical reader/scanner
Incoming paper documents
Become electronic files
①
③
Viewing of file on VDU
⑥
Hard disk
④
⑦
Hard paper copy
Printer
File storage
⑤
'Floppies'

① Incoming *paper documents* are ② scanned into the computer and turned into ③ *electronic files*.

Computer files are created using WP, spreadsheet, graphics software etc and stored either in the computer's ④ *hard disk*, or on *3.5″ or 5.25″ floppy disks.* ⑤

File copies are called up for ⑥ *viewing on the VDU* or printed out as cut-sheet or continuous paper ⑦ *hard copies.*

8 Electronic files may be transmitted around a LAN system at will

sales department may be made accessible to another PC user in, say, accounts. However, files maintained in decentralised systems tend to be used only by that part of the organisation.

There are distinct advantages in maintaining a centralised records system (sometimes called a unified information database). Note also the growth of computerised management information systems (CMIS).

- All the information is held in a database which is continually being updated. Its value and credibility ratings are therefore high.
- Careful control may be exercised over the data input process so that 'garbage in' is less likely to occur.
- All information accessed at all levels may be guarded by a co-ordinated security system.

Disadvantages of the centralised system are

- The costs of producing and maintaining the centralised database are comparatively high.
- Access to information and its updating may be adversely affected by the 'bureaucratic tendency' which tends to slow up entrepreneurs and go-getters in the organisation.
- Managers may not be able to influence the ways in which data is obtained and organised and so not have available the information they most need to do their jobs well.
- Centralised systems are vulnerable to data loss through computer or energy failure and so expensive back-up and fail-safe systems are needed.

PC
2.4.2
2.4.3

Filing features of desktop PCs

Nowadays, intelligent PCs (as opposed to dumb network terminals) commonly embody as much as 240mb of memory. This capacity (equivalent to some 100,000 pages of A4 typescript) has revolutionised record-keeping in many offices. The memory storage available to managers and support staff through desktop PCs has led to the following significant changes in office procedures:

- Incoming letters and similar documents may now be transformed into electronic files by means of Optical Character Readers (OCR scanners) linked to the LAN system and distributed as computerised files to interested staff. Only the most important of the incoming paper letters – tenders, written job offer acceptances etc. are kept in paper filing systems, since a printout of the electronically transformed letter is available at any time.
- Retained paper file copies of correspondence sent out are no longer kept, nor are paper informational file copies distributed internally.
- Documents which were originated in paper form may be archived in microform and the need for paper documents minimised by a computer output microform system allied to computer aided retrieval (CAR).
- Managers' job roles have been modified. They now do much more file creation (using WP, spreadsheet or database software etc.), and file distribution (directly via email) and therefore have to maintain personally their own records management system.

Fortunately, today's software applications packages (supported by utility packages like Xtree Gold and PC Tools) enable individual users readily and simply to:

- create and erase directories and subdirectories (the electronic counterpart of filing cabinets and suspended file wallets);

- move a subdirectory to different directory;
- keep a check on how many megabytes of memory space are still available within a given hard-disk drive and the amount currently being used up within each create directory;
- find *an individual file among, say, hundreds* by setting up a search for the file based upon either its known filename or a particular keyword or phrase likely to have been used in it, such as appraisal, depreciation, European Community, etc. In seconds the user is provided with a short list of files to scan which may also be undertaken by means of the utility program, before going into a major applications package.

■ Filing and applications packages

PC 2.4.2 2.4.3

In addition to support from a DOS-supporting utilities package, major software applications packages greatly assist the filing process through their branching-tree system for creating directories and subdirectories:

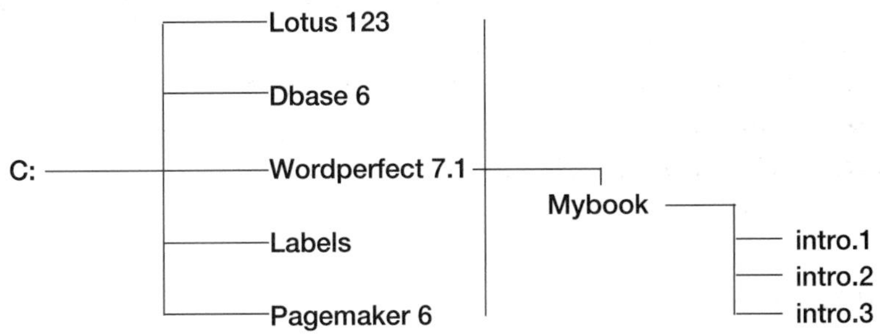

In the above example, five software applications packages have been installed in the computer's C Drive. Within the Wordperfect 7.1 a subdirectory has been created called 'MYBOOK' – perhaps a novel being written. The author has so far created a number of files within MYBOOK which have been labelled INTRO.l, 2, 3 etc. By moving through the branching tree displayed on his VDU, the user may call up the desired file – say, INTRO.3 – within seconds, either to view and modify on screen, or as a preliminary to securing a hard copy printout.

■ Electronic file security

While such electronic files occupy a tiny physical space, they need to be backed up regularly as part of a file maintenance system. This may be effected either by taking a floppy disk copy and keeping the disk safely in a remote location, or by tapestreaming (making a back-up copy) from the hard disk on to a magnetic tape disk. Either way, such precautions are an essential if loss through file corruption or overwriting etc. are to be avoided.

■ Electronic filing and optical disk technology

Further impetus has been given to electronic filing by the introduction of optical disk storage systems. Canon (UK) Limited marketed in the early 1990s a system – their Canonfile 250 – which was based upon document scanning input and a 5.25-inch magnetic optical disk capable of storing 13,000 A4 sheets of typescript. The Canonfile has a remarkably compact footprint – 57 × 42 centimetres and is capable of scanning documents at 40 A4 pages per minute. Retrieval is effected by four alternative methods – index cell, which identifies an 'attached' visual symbol, a filename using up to 32 characters, a file number using up to nine digits or date. Additionally, documents may be easily cross-referenced. A print facility enables up to 99 copies of a retrieved document to be printed automatically.

At present, optical disk storage systems are expensive – R&D costs have to be recovered – but as with most IT innovations, competition will shortly ensure that prices tumble and purchasers multiply.

PC
2.4.2
2.4.3

ADVANTAGES AND DISADVANTAGES OF ELECTRONIC FILING SYSTEMS

Advantages

- **Speed of set up** – files are made of created documents at the press of a key.
- **Small storage requirements** – electronic files occupy tiny spaces within a hard disk.
- **Speed of access** – practised terminal users can call up one of many thousands of records in seconds.
- **Ease of distribution** – with the aid of LAN/WAN systems, electronic files may be transmitted across office blocks or continents in seconds.
- **High standard of security** – with proper back-up and file maintenance, electronic files are very secure.
- **Long-term cost-effectiveness** – once the comparatively high costs of equipment purchase have been recovered, operational costs are low: document creation, storage and distribution may be carried out by a single employee.

Disadvantages

- **Partial use of system** – problems occur at the interface between paper and electronic systems, where electronic filing is only partially used in an organisation.
- **High costs of installation** – effective electronic filing requires a terminal on each desk linked to a LAN.
- **Acceptance of electronic culture** – older staff feel much more comfortable using paper-based filing systems; it takes time and determination to introduce electronic filing across the board.
- **User disciplines** – computer 'crashes' can be dire if backing-up procedures are overlooked; staff using electronic filing have to be most conscientious in their records housekeeping.

PC 2.4.2 2.4.3

DISCUSSION TOPICS

1 What case could you make as an influential senior manager of an organisation for introducing a policy aimed at removing as a matter of priority as many paper-based information systems as possible in order to replace them with computerised ones?

2 If you had been given the go-ahead to 'go for' the computerised information system option, how would you tackle its introduction so as to avoid alienating your staff in, say, a national head office?

3 The uncontrolled use of IT systems in terms of posture at PC terminals, interacting with VDUs and using keyboards for long periods is proving increasingly hazardous to employees' health. If you were responsible for your organisation's HASAW obligations, what steps would you take to ensure that all employees worked in a healthy and protective environment?

Legal requirements affecting business systems: the Data Protection Act 1984

PC 2.4.4

While business systems are primarily designed and integrated so as to bring logic and order into an organisation's activities, the over-arching system must make provision for the legal requirements with which *all* business enterprises have to comply.

The Data Protection Act 1984 was introduced to protect employees and individuals from the unauthorised use or exchange of information held in computerised databanks, following upon the rapid growth of information technology applications in business in the early 1980s.

Essentially, organisations which hold on computer personal data – about employees, customers, patients, pupils or students etc. – who are living and who are identifiable from the data held must:

- register with The Data Protection Registrar details of the data stored and the uses to which it is put
- keep to specific principles relating to this type of retained data, which must be fairly and legally obtained and processed, used only for legal purposes, be accurate and correctly maintained, be deleted once its purpose has been fulfilled, be protected by adequate security systems.

Individuals and employees have particular rights under The Data Protection Act, which include:

- right of access to information being held by an organisation about the individual which is personal data within the definitions of the Act
- the right to be given a copy of such data being held in a computer system.

A fee fixed by the Registrar is levied by organisations which supply data in this way, and provisions are established for individuals who have been affected by incorrect or inaccurate information, as a result of negligence or lack of due care by the organisation, to receive compensation through the courts.

There are some exemptions to the Act, which concern payroll and accounting practices. Also, some categories of data being held do not fall within the scope of the Act. These include:

- crime prevention and prosecution activities
- privileged data (as between a lawyer and client)
- data held for statistical or research purposes
- data covered by the Consumer Credit Act
- data held by regulatory public bodies for the protection of the public against dishonest, fraudulent and malpractice in financial matters
- data held in connection with physical/mental health or social work – on the order of the Secretary of State.

The Act also provides for a series of disclosure clauses which the government may deem to be in the public interest.

The effect of the Act has been to reassure the public that a state of Big Brotherdom would not be allowed to develop, where sensitive or private information held on computer could be used in such a way as to damage the affected person's reputation, business, private relationships or credit-worthiness etc. or could be used or moved around inter-connected computer networks without an individual's knowledge or permission. Note that the Act does **not** include information retained in paper-based systems.

PC 2.4.4

THE EFFECTS OF THE DATA PROTECTION ACT 1984 ON INFORMATION PROCESSING

The main impact of the provisions of the Data Protection Act 1984 upon information processing was to:

- cause computer services professionals to review from the bottom up how they obtained, stored and disseminated information about people – whether employees, customers, patients or inmates
- bring about much tighter security systems for such computerised information, where, previously, databases could be accessed via unattended terminals etc.
- encourage computer managers to consider carefully what sort of information about people was really necessary to computerise and to consolidate dispersed sources of such information into single, easier to control databases
- to review who was entitled to access what kind of personal information about people
- require market research and sales data companies etc. to review whether the information they traditionally sold to sales organisations in the form of individualised details about consumers, their addresses and socio-economic grouping etc. could still be legitimately traded without contravening the Act
- review how the additional costs of meeting the registration and recording requirements of the Act could be financed

Finally, whether data exchange – from one computerised database to another – was legal when the information concerned was within the scope of the Act.

The positive and negative effects of changes in information processing upon individuals and businesses

No change as fundamental and far-reaching as that of IT-based information processing in business occurs without pain. Moreover, when the pace of the change is as rapid, then the pain can be severe. And it is worth recalling that the pace of all technological change has increased dramatically during this century. In the nineteenth century for example, radio-waves were known about for many years before Guglielmo Marconi's famous transatlantic transmission from Cornwall to Newfoundland in 1901. Thereafter it took another thirty or so years for television to be developed and another thirty or so for the first transatlantic satellite tv transmissions. By contrast, the *Internet* information superhighway has come about only fifteen or so years after the introduction of local area networks; also, personal computers virtually replaced typewriters within a similar period after the introduction of the micro-chip in 1971. The following section indicates some of the major positive and negative effects of changes upon individuals and businesses of developments in information processing over the past ten years.

THE POSITIVE EFFECTS

The positive effects of the IT-driven information processing change may be summarised as follows:

- Computerisation allied to telecommunications has caused businesses large and small to review their systems and informational needs and to redesign them as appropriate. This has led to improvements in effectiveness and efficiency through savings made in time, operational and human resources costs, and the development of better systems and processes.
- Such systems re-developments have also led to improved levels of customer service and satisfaction: individuals can access cash-point machines or pay for services on credit at any time; holiday availability can be checked and firm bookings made instantly at a travel agent's shop; shoppers can order goods via home computer stations and have them delivered.
- Much of the drudgery of tedious re-typing of textual drafts and the filing of piles of paperwork has been eliminated.
- People at work can communicate far more rapidly and extensively.
- Complex processes and detail-work is now undertaken in what is mostly an error-free environment – electronic transfer of money by banks, route navigation in motor-vehicles or marine shipping etc.
- Records in immense volumes can be created and stored swiftly and securely, and retrieved just as promptly – as for example in national building societies' archives.
- New ways of learning, training and re-skilling have been opened up and disabled people are being helped to fresh career opportunities via IT.

THE NEGATIVE EFFECTS

- People at work (and working from home) are tending to take less part in face-to-face communication.

- The production of too much information is swamping some business people.
- The introduction of IT-based information processing has led to the destruction of millions of jobs in the developed world.
- Far more effort has to be made by business executives to keep pace with developments in information processing affecting their work.
- When the technology breaks down, whole airports, factories and hospitals etc. can be disrupted.
- Personal privacy and freedom are in danger of being eroded by IT-based intrusions.
- Some workers' health can be adversely affected by, for example, repetitive strain injury (RSI) when using a keyboard, or VDU glare etc.
- Further developments are said to be likely to lead to two-tier societies in which IT-literate and numerate people come to possess far more power, opportunity and earnings potential etc. than their counterparts who are unable to interact with the technology.

DISCUSSION TOPIC

Select one or two of the positive and negative effects listed above and discuss them further within your class, making notes of the main points which emerge.

HOW INFORMATION PROCESSING CHANGES IMPACT ON WORK PRACTICES

As a result of the above changes in information processing developments, the following changes have occurred in business working practices:

- New jobs and work roles have developed in the area of computer services in specifying systems and equipment to be acquired, maintenance, software design and user support etc.
- Additional training and staff development programmes have been devised and delivered to enable existing staff to learn new skills and techniques related to IT.
- Jobs have been re-designed in order to transform, say a paper, manual systems filing clerk into an electronic counterpart, or a traditional printer into a desktop publishing technician.
- New processes have had to be introduced to protect computerised information systems from hackers, viruses, Internet 'surfers' and other unauthorised accessors,
- New administrative and communications systems have been developed to cope with entirely different ways of processing information.
- Managers have had to manage the process of this change in terms of taking older, less responsive staff with them along the road of IT development.

Setting up a business information system

PC 2.4.3

In large organisations it often falls to a computer specialist called a systems analyst to design a computerised information system, which is usually the result of a change in technology employed or procedures in use. Also, in a mature organisation, the system required is most likely to be a relatively small component part of the network of systems in use.

Small businesses, however, rarely possess the luxury of a systems analyst, and so it often falls to an individual manager within a department to design an information system to meet a need by using commercially available software as opposed to a custom-designed, 'bespoke' piece of programming. Nevertheless, the principles of setting up an information system large or small follow the same sequence:

PC 2.4.3

STEPS IN SETTING UP AN INFORMATION SYSTEM

1 **Clarify desired outcomes** What the system is to achieve needs to be painstakingly clarified and agreed by both designer and end-user.

2 **Undertaking of a feasibility study** Before any large-scale work is commenced, careful examination must be made of whether the desired outcomes are possible, and if so, by the use of what resources, at what cost and with what return or advantage, etc.

3 **Submission of formal proposal** All information systems cost money – to design, implement and maintain. Therefore it is prudent to obtain outline approval from senior management at the outset of any systems project.

4 **Research and analysis** Methodical collection of the small nuts and bolts of relevant data must be collected and analysed. Usually this process takes the form of a project which is managed by systems analysis staff. The project would establish who (exactly) currently does (exactly) what (exactly) when and how frequently, etc.

5 **Designing the new system** With the assistance of the techniques and program logic (if a customised program is being written) a careful sequence of activities and/or processes is set down. Such a design will systematise aspects such as the type of data to be created or classified, the needs of its main users and how to route the data to them, means of storing and accessing the data, the form the data should take for different types of user – e.g., management summary or full report and the formats in which to present the data, etc.

6 **Testing the new system** Prior to its announcement and implementation, a freshly designed system must be field trialled and tested – for bugs and other design defects, user acceptance, and delivery of the originally desired outcomes.

7 **System documentation** The principal steps or phases of the system need to be set down as a user operations manual for ready reference by all who will be involved in the new system.

8 **Personnel training and orientation** The introduction of new systems inevitably means changing established ones, which can cause some stress and discomfort among staff. Therefore training programmes also need to be designed and introduced if the whole process is to succeed.

9 **Ongoing monitoring and refinement** Once the system has been introduced, care must be taken to ensure that it is regularly checked for positive/negative feedback. Most systems are capable of improvement once in operation, and almost certainly, the dynamics of business will ensure that the system ages and becomes obsolete sooner or later !

PC
2.4.1
2.4.2
2.4.3
2.4.4

■ Summary

Managing a business information system

Any system involving human beings is likely to be highly unpredictable and prone to Murphy's Law, which states that if anything can go wrong it will, but at the worst possible moment.

The development of western civilisation may be seen as an attempt to impose a rational view and meaning upon an illogical and inscrutable universe. Business information systems attempt a similar interpretation.

It is therefore timely at the end of this Unit to emphasise a number of cautions and caveats:

- Human beings are not always rational or logical. It therefore pays to have systems in place which can cope with the irrational side of human nature, especially contrariness in the light of clear and fully disseminated instructions.
- Business activities tend not to occur in obliging tidy designs (like textbook diagrams) but in patterns of surge, turmoil, and inactivity. Effective systems therefore have to cope with problems like overload, interference, lack of use and ignorance of available support.
- While computing is catching up, the human brain is still infinitely more versatile and imaginative. It is therefore dangerous to prefer computerised information systems to human ingenuity, intuition and lateral thinking, despite the growing popularity of expert systems (software which offers rules and approaches derived from analyses of the outcomes of previous occurrences).

Nevertheless, no business large or small can function for long in the absence of systematised procedures. The following checklist therefore suggests the main criteria to be kept in mind when seeking to manage a business information system:

PC
2.4.1
2.4.2
2.4.3
2.4.4

CRITERIA FOR MANAGING A BUSINESS INFORMATION SYSTEM

1 **Credibility** Most important of all. If employees cannot see the advantages of using a given system, they won't. They'll continue to use the old one, which, for all its faults, actually works.

2 **Accuracy and currency** Managers have to ensure that the information available in the system is accurate and up-to-date. Once in place and accepted, users tend to trust the data in the system. If it is corrupted by error or lack of updating, then the costs this can cause to an organisation will be enormous, since they may be compounded many times.

3 **Flexibility** The principal danger of established information systems is that they keep churning out data which has become old-hat and superseded. It is therefore vital that the system in use is capable of being quickly and simply modified to take changes into account, and that a manager is assigned the duty of monitoring which systems reports are used and which are not, the latter being promptly removed in regular systems housekeeping.

4 **User-friendliness** To be universally accepted and used, an information system needs to be even more user-friendly than the informal 'it grew like Topsy' processes it replaced – or staff will simply revert to the old ways. Staff (given the chance) will unerringly opt for the 'shortest way out' in doing a job, whatever tools they may have been supplied with.

REVIEW TEST

PC
2.4.1
2.4.2
2.4.3
2.4.4

1 Explain simply how the systems concept applies to information processing.

2 List three downside aspects of paper-based information processing.

3 List three upside aspects of computerised information processing.

4 Provide an example of an advantage of paper-based information processing and a disadvantage of its computerised counterpart.

5 List five main features of networked information systems.

6 List three different business applications for which spreadsheet and database software could be used.

7 List four different types of software application program commonly used in business.

8 What is meant by the terms 'connectivity' and 'convergence'?

9 Explain these acronyms: OSI, GUI, PABX, ISDN, OCR.

10 What is the difference between multi-tasking and multi-serving?

11 What is an on-line database?

12 What is packet-switching?

13 Explain simply how facsimile transceiving works.

14 List five commonly occurring features of a computerised PABX system.

15 List three business services currently provided by British Telecom.

16 Explain briefly how the cellnet mobile phone system works.

17 Explain the differences in how dot-matrix, inkjet and laser printers work.

18 List five useful functions of a departmental photocopier.

19 Explain briefly the main features of the DTP process.

20 Explain the difference between: COM, CIM and CAR.

21 What is multi-media software in the context of IT?

22 List three main advantages of computerised filing systems.

23 What are the main advantages of optical disk technology in a business context?

24 Explain the main purposes of the Data Protection Act 1984.

25 List four positive and four negative effects of change upon business information processing.

PC
2.4.3
2.4.4

DISCUSSION TOPICS

1 The Information Revolution is placing ever more reliance upon impersonal computers and their support equipment to minister to our everyday needs – like personal finance, shopping, travelling and recreation – as well as in our daily working lives. Are we in danger of creating an impersonal and uncaring world in which only electronic logic rules?

2 How many different types of information can you identify? Or is information incapable of being broken down into different types?

3 'Would that the infernal Information Revolution had never reared its ugly head! Contemporary society and its business concerns are becoming buried beneath an avalanche of information – most of it unasked for, time-consuming to absorb and, in the event, trivial and unnecessary!'

Do you agree with this jaundiced view of the 1990s?

4 Do you think the Data Protection Act 1984 goes far enough in protecting people's rights to privacy?

KNOWLEDGE TEST

Element 2.4
Analyse information processing in a business organisation

1 Which of the following statements are true, and which false?

A A main purpose of information processing is to break large inputs into a series of more manageable bits of data.
B Information processing involves keeping other members of the workforce informed.
C The more information a person receives at work, the more likely he or she is to function effectively.
D The computerisation of information processing has lead to increasing problems in guaranteeing its security.

2 (i) Electronic Data Interchange (EDI) is a system devised to keep firms making electronics parts in touch with each other.
(ii) An network file server carries out the same purpose as a dumb terminal.

Which of the following options best describes the above two statements?

A	(i)	T	(ii)	T
B	(i)	T	(ii)	F
C	(i)	F	(ii)	T
D	(i)	F	(ii)	F

3 Which of the following best describes the use of different forms of information in computerised software?

A multi-tasking
B multi-purpose
C multi-media
D multi-serving

4 (i) A unified database is a single set of information installed on a computer network for all staff to access according to security clearance.
(ii) An integrated accounts package is so termed because it integrates readily with spreadsheet and database packages.

Which of the following options best describes the above two statements?

A (i) T (ii) T
B (i) T (ii) F
C (i) F (ii) T
D (i) F (ii) F

5 A tailor-made software
B general-purpose software
C facility software
D specialist software

Which of the above is the odd-man out in terms of software types used by business organisations?

6 (i) A WAN is a less powerful type of LAN.
(ii) It is not yet possible to send a message confidentially via fax.

Which of the following options best describes the above two statements?

A (i) T (ii) T
B (i) T (ii) F
C (i) F (ii) T
D (i) F (ii) F

7 Which of the following statements is true, and which false?

A computerised PABX telephone system installed in a large business complex enables its users to:

A Bar calls
B Translate calls
C Interrupt calls
D Anticipate calls

8 (i) The mobile phone cellnet system works by guiding mobile users to a series of points from where they can make calls.
(ii) It is now possible to receive short, displayed messages on pagers.

Which of the following options best describes the above two statements?

A (i) T (ii) T
B (i) T (ii) F
C (i) F (ii) T
D (i) F (ii) F

9 Which of the following statements is true, and which false?

A The Data Protection Act 1984 was drawn up to prevent confidential information from being illegally accessed by 'hackers'.

B Modern departmental photocopiers now enable text to be edited as well as copied.

C Centralised computer systems are vulnerable to power-cuts.

D Optical disk technology was developed to enable users to see their files faster and more clearly.

10 (i) Recent changes in information processing developments have led to a decrease in face-to-face communication.

(ii) As a result of information processing changes many routine jobs can be done more quickly and with less drudgery,

Which of the following options best describes the above two statements?

A	(i)	T	(ii)	T
B	(i)	T	(ii)	F
C	(i)	F	(ii)	T
D	(i)	F	(ii)	F

PC
2.4.1
2.4.2
2.4.3
2.4.4

PORTFOLIO OF EVIDENCE ACTIVITY

Element 2.4
Analyse information processing in a business organisation

BUSINESS COMPUTING TODAY

Scenario One

You work as a journalist for *Business Computing Today*, a monthly magazine for business computer managers which provides non-jargonised articles and features about the latest trends and developments in information processing applications to help busy executives keep current.

Your editor wants you to research and write a piece aimed at providing a 'state-of-the-art' overview of the purposes for which businesses are at present employing information processing systems – especially in situations where technological advances have led to the installation of new equipment and systems. You have also been asked to survey the effectiveness of such systems.
Your brief is to cover:

- installation costs, running costs, staff re-training costs etc.
- value for money as perceived by senior management and users
- improvements (or otherwise) in work routines and processes
- changes in users' work loads and expectations of management

In addition, your editor has asked you to profile a single business organisation in terms of the systems it employs to process text, number and graphics.

Scenario Two

The next job your editor has given to you is to write up a recent case involving the application of the Data Protection Act 1984, and how it impacted upon both an individual and organisation, in terms of the individual's right to access certain data, and the organisation's obligations to keep such data accurately and accessibly.

Scenario Three (optional)

You have been asked to take part in a group discussion (at a regional one-day seminar for IT journalists) on:

> **Pluses and minuses of changes in information processing – for the employee and the organisation**

Each journalist has been asked to take part in a 30 minute discussion, to take notes of the main points which emerge, and to write up a piece which includes a treatment of two plus and two minus points. The aim of the discussion is also to enable participants to suggest some changes which could be introduced with benefit to businesses – based on their own recent findings and investigations. The best pieces will be published in the *IT Journalists Bulletin* (i.e. on your base-room notice-board).

Task 1

Before undertaking the work arising from the above three scenarios, make sure that you complete the appropriate parts of your activity planning and review log.

Task 2

Research the subject matter relating to Scenario One, using the resources of your centre and public reference libraries, including specialist journals and magazines. Then compose a suitable article to meet the brief of your editor. Your article should comprise some 4 sides of A4, either hand-written or text-processed as you are advised.

Task 3

Next, make arrangements to visit a suitable local business organisation in order to research into the ways in which they process the information referred to in Scenario One. Having secured your information, write a piece which explains your findings clearly in about 750 words. Remember to angle it to the readership of *Business Computing Today*.

Task 4

Research a suitable Data Protection Act 1984 case as required for Scenario Two (you may need to contact local newspapers here) and then compose a short article of about 500 words outlining your findings.

Task 5 (optional)

Take part in the journalists' group discussion as described in Scenario Three, and then produce the piece asked for in about 400–500 words.

Note: Remember to keep careful notes in your activity and review log of the way in which you approached the above five tasks and evaluated your success in completing them etc.

Performance criteria covered

2.4.1, 2.4.2, 2.4.3, 2.4.4

Core skills covered

Communication:

3.1.1, 3.1.2, 3.1.3, 3.1.4, 3.1.5 (if scenario 3 is undertaken)
3.2.1, 3.2.2, 3.2.3, 3.2.4, 3.2.5, 3.3.1, 3.3.2, 3.3.3, 3.4.1, 3.4.2, 3.4.3, 3.4.4

Information technology:

3.1.1, 3.1.2, 3.1.3, 3.1.4, 3.1.5, 3.2.1, 3.2.2, 3.2.3, 3.2.4, 3.2.5, 3.2.6, 3.2.7, 3.3.1, 3.3.2, 3.3.3, 3.3.4, 3.3.5, 3.3.6

CASE STUDY 1 PC 2.4.2 2.4.3

The Henry Perkins Legacy

Henry Perkins (Builders) Limited is a private building company which was established in 1932 in Dilchester, a thriving market town in the middle of a rural area. The district was much favoured by wealthy couples buying retirement properties, London commuters looking for week-end cottages to acquire cheaply and renovate, and, because of its proximity to ports and the motorway network, young industrial companies in the field of electronics and light engineering.

Until recently, the company had been controlled by the iron grip of the 'Old Man', Henry Perkins, a staunch traditionalist who believed that 'the old, tried and tested ways are best,' disliked things he called 'newfangled' and stood no nonsense from his family or employees.

The workforce currently numbers 52 site employees, with some 30–40 self-employed sub-contractors, depending on the number of contracts with work in progress, and an office staff of 13, which is organised as shown in the diagram below.

Three months ago Henry Perkins died peacefully in his sleep at the age of 72, leaving his two sons David and Andrew and his daughter Julie as directors of a prosperous business run on distinctly old-fashioned lines. At a recent meeting of directors, David, eldest son and now managing director gave this report:

'As we agreed, I've spent the past week reviewing our administrative procedures and, broadly speaking, this is the picture. We have at any given time about 100 active account customers, 30 or so large concerns and 70 small works customers. We're kept busy on the accounts side, which is virtually a paper-based system, because we have to maintain careful costing records of jobs over several months or more and because a lot of our purchase ledger work is involved in keeping track of frequent orders, even though some are quite modest.

'Our accountants do our payroll every week, but I can't say they're as cheap as they were. And we're getting more complaints from the site men about mistakes in their payslips and their bonuses and what have you.

Fig 2.38 **Henry Perkins (Builders) Limited organisation chart**

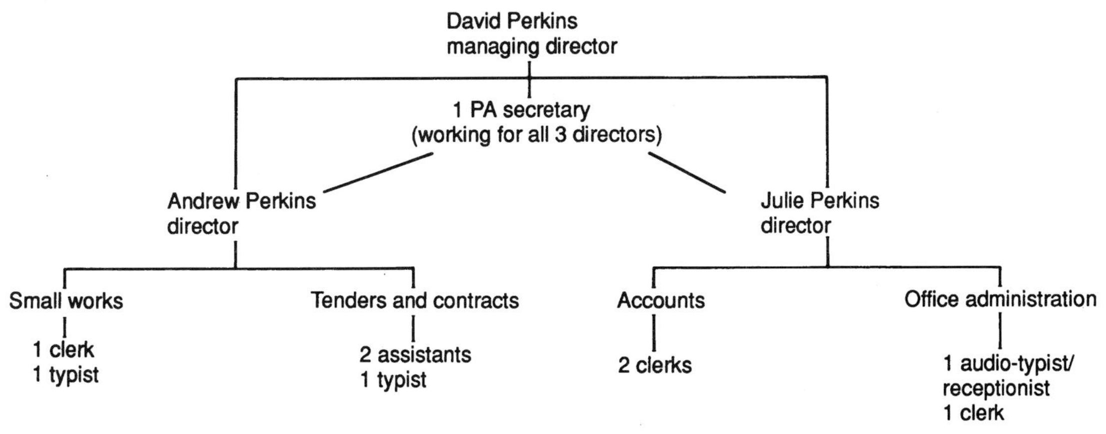

'On the stock control side, we still seem to be losing money on materials which just seem to disappear. We need a better system for controlling what leaves here and what unused materials ought to be coming back! And our filing system could do with a complete overhaul. I spent half an hour yesterday looking for the Robertson contract, and eventually found it in the Robinson and Parker file. There must be some better way of handling contracts we are regularly referring to while they're active.

'Then there's our company image. If you look at our letterheads and stationery, we look as if we're still in the "jobbing builder pulling handcart age", instead of doing most of our work for the council and the business park. And don't forget that a lot of the people moving into the area have worked for big outfits. I don't think our existing electronic typewriters and vintage copier can deliver the quality of text processing we need now, never mind the time taken to get a mailshot out.

'Lastly, there's what I think the experts call our "informational database". We're always getting in each other's way, or kicking our heels to get at our reference files, suppliers' price lists, contract stipulations, stock sheets and so on. We ought to take a fresh look at how we could organise this aspect better – we're not only wasting time and money, but getting under each others' skin at times.

'Well, that must be enough for starters. Dad did us proud in his way and we've him to thank for seeing us through some sticky times. But time doesn't stand still. If we're to remain competitive, we must undertake a root and branch overhaul of our administration, and be prepared to take a few chances with computers and information technology before our competitors steal a march on us – especially with our tendered contract work increasing.'

ASSIGNMENTS

In groups of three or four, undertake the following assignment:

Consider carefully the information in the case study and organisational chart. Then, as a group, prepare to give an oral presentation (using appropriate visual aids) to the board of directors of Henry Perkins (Builders) Limited on the following:

A specification of the type of computerised business information system (both hardware and software) which you would recommend for installation. Your presentation should be pitched at an informed, non-technical level, and show clearly how your recommendations would be of practical use to the business, both currently and in any middle-term future expansion.

Your presentation should concentrate on a single range of equipment and provide costings.

Each member of the group should play an approximately equal part in the presentation which should last some fifteen minutes. Observer members of the class should assess each presenting group's performance and, in a class wash-up, decide which presentation was best and why.

PC
2.4.2
2.4.3

A bit of a sort out!

National Car Accessories Limited was founded in 1967 by Phil Sturrock, a live-wire entrepreneur who had begun with a single car accessory centre on the outskirts of Manchester at a time when interest in cars was booming and 'add-ons' were all the rage. In 1978, and some fifty established branches later, National acquired a three-storey building near the centre of Manchester, close to good road and rail communications. The head office building was constructed in the 1950s around a steel girder framework and each floor comprises a series of smallish offices separated by plasterboard partitions.

Having successfully weathered the recessions of the 1970s and 1980s, National now has a network of 120 branches spread across southern Scotland and the north of England. Phil Sturrock remains the company's majority shareholder and managing director, and the company has the following head office departments: Purchasing, Sales, Marketing, Accounts, Personnel, Transport and Branch Administration.

The Marketing Department is headed up by Mrs Jean Watson, Director, and is situated on the western half of the top floor of the building.

The Marketing Department is currently organised as shown in Fig 2.39 below.

Section responsibilities

The three major sections of the Department have the following responsibilities:

Product development
Making sure that National is stocking brand-name and own brand products which are 'up-to-the minute' in design and appeal; close liaison is maintained with a large number of manufacturers, both in the UK and overseas.

Advertising
The Advertising Section is responsible for sustaining effective merchandising within the stores, and for press, promotions and exhibitions, advertising and public relations. Two executives take care of these twin arms.

The Advertising Manager also coordinates the desktop publishing and reprographics work. National recently acquired a DTP system to produce its own masters for stores leaflets and sales brochures, etc. At this time, morale in the unit is low because the two reprographics assistants are being overloaded with photocopying demands from all and sundry.

Fig 2.39 **Layout of National's marketing department**

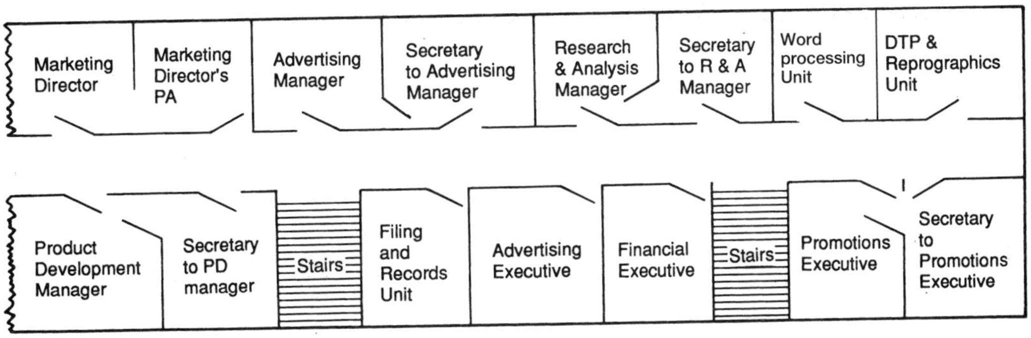

Research and analysis

Phil Sturrock always claims he got where he is by 'keeping a close eye on the competition and keeping one step ahead of the beggars!' So he maintains a keen interest in analyses of buying trends and product popularity and surveying what groups of motorists buy what types of product etc.

The Research and Analysis Manager is also responsible for the department's Filing and Records Unit and Word Processing Unit. The former is really a store for past survey records and statistics and marketing data is dispersed through all the department's offices. While the Word Processing Unit is available to everyone in theory, there is much 'behind-the-scenes' grumbling that undue priority is always given to R & A work by the typists.

Financial executive

Andrew Wilson reports directly to Jean Watson and provides advice and information on money aspects of marketing. He has to rely on the Director's PA and the Word Processing Unit for his text processing etc. and claims that his particular needs are largely underestimated.

Secretarial support staff

The Director and three managers have each a personal secretary; the director's enjoys the title of 'PA' but the other three secretaries resent this because they consider they do just as much demanding work!

Equipment distribution

National Car Accessories Head Office has not exactly moved with the times, largely because every last penny of profit has been put into acquiring and equipping new stores. However, the success of National's rapid growth in the past five years is putting tremendous pressure on Head Office staff – with increasing staff turn-over and morale problems.

In the Marketing Department, the following equipment distribution obtains:

Current equipment distribution

PAs/secretaries to managers: stand-alone 286 personal computers and bubble-jet printers (PA has fax transceiver; Product Development secretary has telex access).

DTP: scanner, PC + laser printer + 'Pagewrite' software recently acquired to do in-house masters for sales leaflets and brochures.

Copying: A3/A4/A5 departmental b/w copier.

3 LCD electronic memory typewriters.

Filing and records: largely manual. One PC holds details of press advertising on disk and is 'stand-alone'.

Senior management have woken up to the shortcomings in providing the 'tools to do the job' – witness the acquisition of the DTP equipment and a PC installed in the Filing Unit. The following conversation took place earlier this week after a Board of Directors' meeting:

PHIL STURROCK: 'You can see from my review this morning that something must be done as a matter of urgency! Over the years some of our managerial staff have been "featherbedded" by under-utilised secretaries, while others have had to cope as best they can on a goodwill basis by getting their work done a bit here and a bit there. It's high time we had a bit of a sort out on how we are using our secretarial and clerical support staff and on what equipment and systems they could do with to get the job done. If it's going to cost money, so be it! We'll grow no more until we get this right!'

JEAN WATSON: 'I think you're right. We've managed fairly well so far, but this time it's Head Office that needs investing in and not the branches. I'll set up a Task Force Team in my Department and let you have a written report and recommendations within a fortnight – well before the next Board Meeting.'

PHIL STURROCK: 'Right, And while you're at it, give a thought to your Departmental layout. If we're going into this, we might as well go the whole hog!'

Fig 2.40 **Current organisational chart of marketing department**

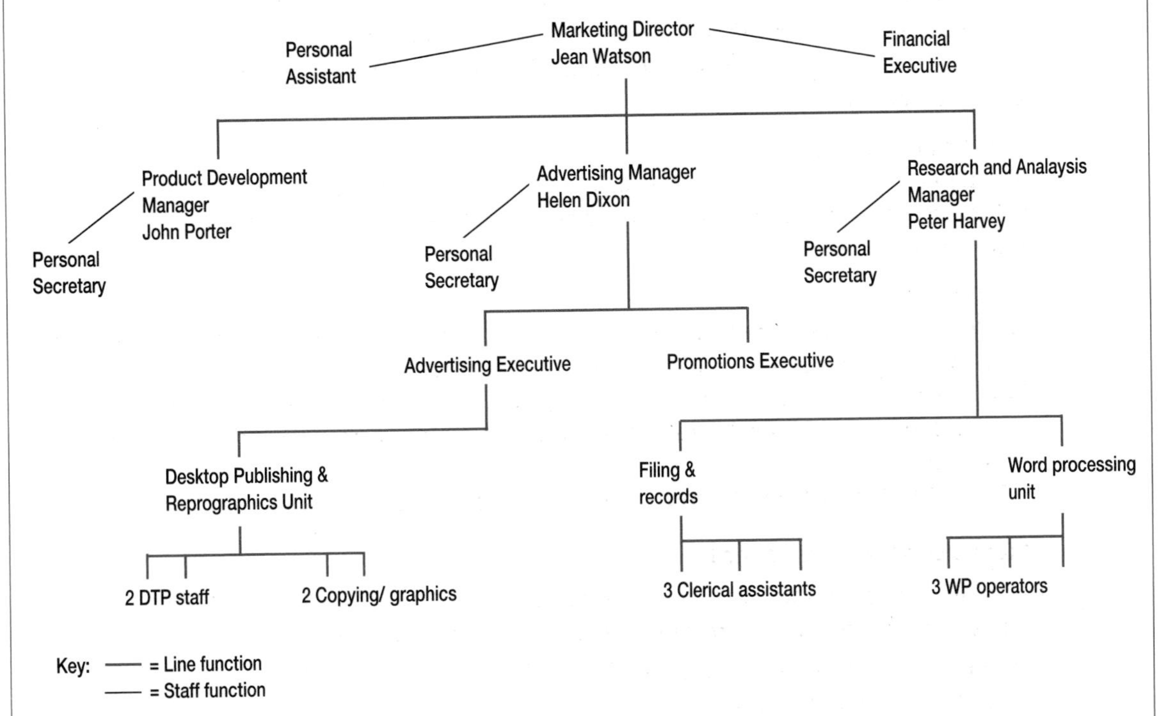

ASSIGNMENTS

1 As the manager of National Car Accessories newly introduced Computer Services Department, Phil Sturrock has asked you to consider the information currently available (the above case study), and to produce for him a feasibility study outline, which would indicate how you would introduce the sort of information system needed to enable the Marketing Department (see Fig 2.40 on page 225 for current organisational chart) to work effectively.

2 What do you think may be the human problems likely to arise in the department if the sort of changes which Phil Sturrock envisages are put into effect? How might they be minimised?

3 In pairs, draw up an organisational chart and floor layout which illustrates the changes you would make. You may assume that the building's structure would allow total flexibility within the floor space occupied by the department, other than the location of the stairs and double swing door access to them.

4 What changes would you make to the ways in which the Marketing Department works in the light of the shortcomings which Phil Sturrock reviewed? How would you reorganise:

a the current structure of the Marketing Department's secretarial and office support services?

b the layout of the department so as to optimise access and ease of communications between managerial and support staff?

c the range and type of equipment and systems the Department should have, so as to be able to market the 120 stores and their products more efficiently?

5 Can you identify any new/additional staff needs which the department would have in your development plan? What would be the comparative advantages of advertising for new staff or providing updating training for existing staff? Which option would you take? Why?

6 What particular training needs do you think the managers and executives would need, assuming a large-scale reorganisation of work patterns and organisational structure was put into effect?

7 Where would be the best place to start in introducing a reorganisation of some 21 staff within such a department? What sort of approach is likely to prove most effective?

FURTHER SOURCES OF INFORMATION

Analysis and Design of Information Systems, J A Senn, 2nd edn, McGraw-Hill, 1989. ISBN: 0 07 056236 9

Analysis and Design of Information Systems, L Seymour Smith, Stanley Thornes, 1990. ISBN: 0 7487 0409 4

Information Technology: An Introduction, 4th edn, P Zorkoczy, Pitman Publishing, 1994. ISBN: 0 273 60591 7

New Office IT: Human and Managerial Implications, R J Long, Croom Helm, 1990. ISBN: 0 7099 4130 X

The Electronic Office and IT, H Armour, Hutchinson, 1988. ISBN: 0 09 173008 2

The ABCs of Novell Networks, J Woodward, Sybex Publ., 1989. ISBN: 0 895588 694 6

Planning IT: Creating an Information Management Strategy, D Silk, Butterworth, 1991. ISBN: 0 7506 0326 7

Understanding PC Software, R A Penfold, Bernard Babani Publ., 1991. ISBN: 0 85934 248 4

Inside Information, J Megarry, BBC Publications, 1985. ISBN: 0 563 21102 4

Webster's New World Dictionary of Computer Terms, 3rd edn, 1988. ISBN: 0 13 949 23 3

Dictionary of Computing and IT, 3rd edn, Meadows, Gordon, Singleton and Feeney, Kogan Page, 1987. ISBN: 1 85091 262 9

UNIT

3

MARKETING

Element 3.1
Investigate the principles and functions of marketing in organisations

Element 3.2
Propose and present product developments based on analysis of marketing research information

Element 3.3
Evaluate marketing communications designed to influence a target audience

Element 3.4
Evaluate sales methods and customer service to achieve customer satisfaction

PERFORMANCE CRITERIA AND RANGE

Element 3.1: Investigate the principles and functions of marketing in organisations

PERFORMANCE CRITERIA

A student must: *page*

1 discuss **marketing principles** and **marketing functions** 231–41
2 explain how the **marketing principles** underpin the **marketing functions** 241–8
3 explain an organisation's need to have a **customer focus** while meeting its **own needs** 249–54
4 **analyse marketing activities** in business organisations 256–7
5 explain **growth of organisations** which relates to marketing 253–7

RANGE

Marketing principles: anticipate market needs and opportunities. satisfy customer expectations, generate income and/or profit, maximise benefit to the organisation, manage effects of change and competition, co-ordinate activities to achieve marketing aims, utilise technological developments, enhance customer perception (of the organisation, of the product)
Marketing functions: manage change, co-ordinate marketing planning and control, implement marketing mix (product, place, promotion, price), ensure survival of business, branding
Customer focus/organisation's own needs: market orientation versus product orientation; cost of customer service versus productivity, cost of customer service versus profitability, cost of customer service versus accountability
Analyse marketing activities in terms of: assessing market needs (marketing research), satisfying customer requirements, managing effects of change, managing effects of competition, co-ordinating role (marketing, planning, control), generating maximum income and/or profit (sales, sales channels), optimising customer perception (customer service, marketing communications)
Growth of organisations through: product development, markets (market development, market share, new market, new customers, retained customers)

EVIDENCE INDICATORS

- A record of a discussion about marketing principles and marketing functions, with supporting notes which explain how the principles identified in the range underpin the marketing functions. The discussion and supporting notes should explain the ways in which business organisations manage to balance the interests of customers with their own interests.
- A report which analyses marketing activities in two contrasting business organisations, one profit-making and the other not-for-profit. The introduction should explain how the two organisations achieved growth using product development and market development.
- The report should focus on how the businesses assess market needs by marketing research and how this information is used by marketing personnel. It should conclude by analysing the marketing and selling activities used by both organisations to generate maximum income and, where appropriate, to maximise profit.

Element 3.2: Propose and present product developments based on analysis of marketing research information

PERFORMANCE CRITERIA

A student must: *page*

1 identify **marketing research methods** and explain their **suitability** for selected products 258–73
2 analyse **marketing research information** from different **sources** for its contribution to **marketing decisions** for selected products 260–73
3 propose and justify **product development** with reference to **marketing research information** 276–7
4 present proposals for **product development** to an audience 276–7

RANGE

Marketing research methods: interview, observation, questionnaire, survey, panel discussion, telecommunications, focus groups, field trials, piloting; qualitative research methods, quantitative research methods
Suitability: accessibility, fitness for purpose, validity, cost, time, reliability
Marketing research information: sales trends, changes in sales of new products, changes in sales of existing products, changes in market share, changes in profitability of businesses in the market, product substitution, customer behaviour, buying patterns, customer preferences, competitor activities
Sources: government statistics, other published statistics, primary market data, secondary market data
Marketing decisions: product (type, features, packaging), place, promotion, price, timing, sales methods
Product development: innovation, modification, technological breakthrough

EVIDENCE INDICATORS

A presentation to an audience of proposals for the development of one product. Proposals should be based on an analysis of marketing research information from at least two different sources. Proposals should include:

- changes to the type of product
- features of the product
- packaging of the product
- the sales outlets (place)
- product promotion
- selling price
- the timing of marketing communications and sales

The proposals should be justified with reference to marketing research information.
The presentation should be supported by notes and numerical information which explain and illustrate qualitative and quantitative research methods.

Element 3.3: Evaluate marketing communications designed to influence a target audience

PERFORMANCE CRITERIA

A student must: *page*

1. explain the suitability of **advertising** and **publicity** for promoting products and the image of an organisation 278–97
2. identify and give examples of **public relations** to promote products and organisations 297–8
3. evaluate **sales promotion methods** for their effectiveness in reaching a **target audience** 298–301, 303–4
4. evaluate the effect of marketing communications on **product performance** 307–8
5. explain growth in **direct marketing methods** in terms of customer needs and new technology 307–8
6. explain effects on marketing communications of **guidelines and controls** 301–5

RANGE

Advertising: newspaper, magazine, TV, poster, radio, cinema
Publicity: sales literature, signage, vehicle livery, stationery, point-of-sale (POS)
Public relations: press releases, sponsorship, lobbying, community relations
Sales promotion methods: competitions, coupons, special offers, free mail-ins, loyalty incentives
Target audience: socio-economic group, age, lifestyle, gender
Product performance: sales levels (volume, value, growth), repeat sales, brand loyalty, customer loyalty, product life cycles, product awareness
Direct marketing methods: direct mail, telemarketing, selling off-screen, selling off-page
Guidelines and controls: Advertising Standards Authority, Code of Advertising Practice Committee (CAP), codes of practice

EVIDENCE INDICATORS

A report which evaluates the advertising, publicity, public relations and sales promotion methods of two business organisations. For one of the organisations, the study of the marketing communications should include recent growth in direct marketing, with an explanation of changing customer needs and changing technology which encourages direct marketing methods.
The report should:

- explain why the organisations use particular types of marketing communications to promote their products and image
- evaluate how marketing communications help organisations reach a specified target audience
- evaluate the effect of marketing communications in the two organisations in terms of product sales, product awareness, customer and brand loyalty and length of the product life cycle
- identify marketing communications which may contravene the Advertising Standards Authority's code of practice and explain why these marketing communications may need controlling.

Element 3.4: Evaluate sales methods and customer service to achieve customer satisfaction

PERFORMANCE CRITERIA

A student must: *page*

1. compare **direct** and **indirect sales methods** for their suitability to meet the **needs of customers** and **organisations** 309–15
2. describe **sales campaign methods** 313–15
3. explain and give examples of **responsibilities of sales persons** 315–19
4. explain the importance of effective **sales administration** to an organisation and its customers 315–19
5. evaluate **customer service** in terms of the **needs of customers** and **organisations** 320–38

RANGE

Direct sales methods: TV, radio, factory, telesales, door-to-door, pyramid, catalogues
Indirect sales methods: distribution channels (national, international), direct factory, retail, wholesale, distributor, agents
Needs of customers: quick and easy purchasing, clear and accurate information, clear refund procedure, easy exchange of goods, complaints procedure, special service to meet special needs
Needs of organisations: to make a profit, to retain or improve market share, to secure customer satisfaction
Sales campaign methods: sales letters, sales memos, sales conferences, sales meetings
Responsibilities of sales persons: presenting appropriate image, customer care, point of sale service, product knowledge, after-sales service, sales administration. knowledge of Sale of Goods Act, knowledge of Trades Descriptions Act, communicating effectively
Sales administration: order processing, credit clearance, credit control, customer accounts, delivery schedules, security, prospecting
Customer service: to meet the needs of external customers (sales, complaints, information, problems); to meet needs of internal customers (help, information)

EVIDENCE INDICATORS

A report comparing the sales methods used by business organisations, including the suitability of different sales methods to meet the needs of both organisation and its customers. The report should describe the methods used by one organisation for one sales campaign.
The report should explain the responsibilities of sales people in providing customer service; specifically their responsibilities in conforming with the Sale of Goods and Trades Descriptions Acts. It should explain the importance of sales administration in terms of the needs of customers and the business organisation. The report should conclude with a summary which evaluates the customer service provided in an organisation in terms of meeting the needs of internal and external customers and the organisation's own needs.

INTRODUCTION

This Unit explains in detail the main concepts and principles which form the marketing function in business and public service organisations – from the process of obtaining information on what a market wants, to product design and development, marketing communications associated with selling and promoting a product, sales methods and techniques and customer service.

In particular, Unit 3 explains how marketing principles and techniques relate to a business's overall operations and form a kind of umbrella over-arching all the activities of its specialist departments by having a responsibility to secure the future viability of the organisation. It also examines the importance of customer orientation and centredness to a business's success, and the ways in which trends and patterns of consumption in a market are analysed, so as to inform product development.

The role of marketing communications is also examined – advertising, sales promotion, public relations etc. – where businesses devise a range of strategies to encourage the sale of their products or services, and what controls exist to monitor such activities.

Lastly, Unit 3 surveys the relationship between sales and customer service in terms of promoting customer satisfaction, so as to keep customers happy – and loyal – and to ensure the development of business.

Element 3.1
PRINCIPLES AND FUNCTIONS OF MARKETING IN ORGANISATIONS

'Marketing is producing the right goods or services at the right time, in the right place, for the right customer, at the right price and the right return.'

A classical definition

■ 'Marketing is everything!'

PC 3.1.1

Behind this sweeping statement lies the truth that marketing an enterprise successfully involves every aspect of its various activities. In another way it might be said that the marketing function of an organisation is the cement which holds all its parts together. The marketing of an organisation is essentially forward looking, it is concerned with securing the organisation's future in terms of the products or services it sells, the kind of customers it wishes to serve and the profits it wishes to make.

Once viewed in this light, it is easier to see that marketing is vitally interested in each of these departmental functions of the organisation:

Research and development

So as to check that avenues of research are being directed into fruitful areas, centring around products or services which will satisfy a demand and for which a market already exists or can be created.

Production

So as to make sure that whatever is being produced is being made to a design which has been field-tested by a sample of customers for whom it is intended; that it is being made at an agreed price (so that it does not become too expensive), and that it will be available at the right time and in sufficient quantity.

Sales and sales promotion

So as to ensure that the product or service is distributed and packaged with a maximum appeal and availability to the customers at whom it is targeted; that wholesalers and dealers are well briefed on its selling points and provided with appealing point-of-sale merchandising, and that local advertising will aid its launch and raise public awareness of its existence, and where it may be readily purchased.

Accounts

So as to provide company accountants with feedback on, for instance, what retail price the market will bear for the good or service, what the likely annual costs of advertising and sales promotion are likely to be, and what the estimated growth in demand for the product or service will be, and so on.

Personnel - staff training and development

So as to supply information on what new features and specifications are central to a new product, so that company staff may be suitably trained in, say, new production procedures, sales techniques, advertising approaches and customer service aspects.

If the marketing function is broken down by identifying areas of involvement in an organisation's major departments, as illustrated above, it is then easy to see why marketing is seen to be involved in everything an organisation does.

PC 3.1.1

■ Definitions of marketing

Because of its central role in an enterprise's activities, many definitions of marketing have been conceived over the years. Here are some of the more enduring ones:

Marketing is getting the right goods (or services) to the right place for the right customers at the right time and at the right price.

Much depends here on what is meant by 'right'. But this definition does emphasise the amount of effort needed in successful marketing. Design a product the consumer does not like and failure results. Fail to get your new-style Christmas card into the shops by October and, 'forget it'! Fail to make your targeted group of customers aware of your product and sales won't even begin to take off. Over-price your product or service and it will simply age on the shelf !

Marketing is selling goods that won't come back to customers who will!

Such a definition emphasises the importance of a product's quality, utility (being good at what it has been designed for) and the nurturing of the organisation's customers so as to foster their goodwill and brand loyalty – 'Thanks, but I've always worn Nordica ski boots.' This definition centres upon an extremely important aspect of marketing which is called customer orientation, by which is meant focusing all the organisation does upon meeting the customer's needs and expectations.

Marketing is the effective exchange of goods or services between suppliers and buyers, so that the needs and wants of consumers and industry are satisfied.

This definition concentrates upon the economic aspect of marketing. It emphasises the creation of a market-place where seller and buyer meet to exchange commodities – goods (or services) for money, and it also highlights the difference in an economy between satisfying essential needs like food, housing, heat and light and wants – the endless stream of products and services for which mankind seems to have an insatiable appetite – the

PC
3.1.1

Fig 3.1

The marketing function

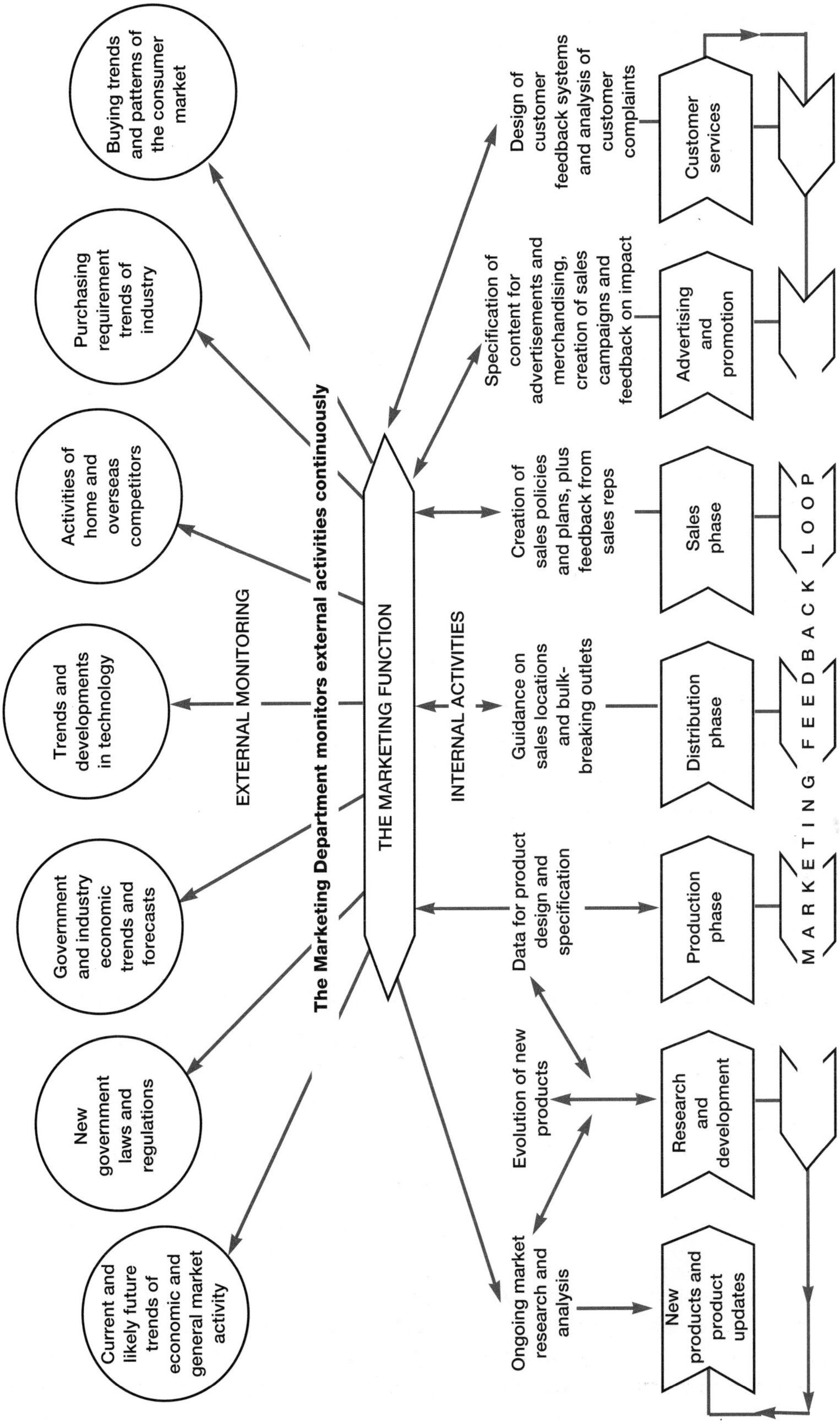

Current and likely future trends of economic and general market activity
New government laws and regulations
Government and industry economic trends and forecasts
Trends and developments in technology
Activities of home and overseas competitors
Purchasing requirement trends of industry
Buying trends and patterns of the consumer market
EXTERNAL MONITORING
The Marketing Department monitors external activities continuously
THE MARKETING FUNCTION
INTERNAL ACTIVITIES
Ongoing market research and analysis
Evolution of new products
Data for product design and specification
Guidance on sales locations and bulk-breaking outlets
Creation of sales policies and plans, plus feedback from sales reps
Specification of content for advertisements and merchandising, creation of sales campaigns and feedback on impact
Design of customer feedback systems and analysis of customer complaints
New products and product updates
Research and development
Production phase
Distribution phase
Sales phase
Advertising and promotion
Customer services
MARKETING FEEDBACK LOOP

The marketing function integrates the product/service creation and renewal cycle, as its external monitoring activities and internal operations direct and inform the process.

latest marque of Porsche or Ferrari, the newest release of Prince or Madonna, a videophone or a holiday in Sri Lanka etc.

The idea of the purchaser being satisfied also implies that the supplier has got the design, specification, packaging, price, and warranty of his product right because the buyer has no complaints or dissatisfactions.

Marketing is all about identifying – and then providing – what customers will want in one to four years' time.

The impact of this definition is upon the crucial importance of finding out what the market will want – not today, but some years into the future. It highlights the marketing challenge in, for example, the car-making industry where the lead time from beginning to design a new model to wheeling it into showrooms all over the world is some three to four years. In order to ensure that the enormous financial investment involved is secured, market analysts take extreme care to survey all interested parties in depth so as to take their preferences, desires, dislikes, ideas, proposals, past experiences, etc. into account. In this way, market researchers try to ensure as best they may that their design will meet not current, but future customer requirements and expectations – not to mention incoming government regulations and new laws.

Marketing is the art of getting – and staying – one step ahead of the competition!

In this definition the competitive nature of a free market is emphasised. The refrain which all good marketing executives keep constantly in mind is:

Never forget that the public has a choice!

In order to make that proverbial jump to become a brand or industry leader, many companies spend high proportions of their income on activities listed below:

PC 3.1.1

EFFECTIVE MARKETING REQUIRES INVESTMENT IN:

- Testing (to destruction) the products of a competitor – food-mixers, trainers, cameras, etc., in order to establish precisely how they work, what new technologies they employ and what their likely production costs are.
- Surveying and sampling consumer and industrial markets – and what are called niches or segments of markets – slices of the buyer pie – so as to find out in minute detail what makes them tick and what kind of good or service they are most likely to choose and why.
- Interviewing and consulting wholesalers, distributors, retailers and mail-order houses to ascertain the trends in buyer behaviour and the ever-changing moods and whims of the market.
- Seeking intelligence on how well competitors are doing, how a newly launched product is selling or what the demand is for, say, a novel mortgage offer to first-time buyers, or the discount being offered on a new, fitted kitchen.
- Trying to find out what new models, upgrades, revamped packages of services, etc. competitors are developing in order to leap-frog them and go one better themselves.
- Determining what new needs or wants are emerging in the High Street, such as electric bikes, pocket phones, Nicam TV, or teenage fashions, in order to come to the market ahead of the competition and thus establish a 'pole-position' before too many alternative models arrive to provide the inevitable choice a free market supplies.

SUMMARY OF MARKETING PRINCIPLES

PC 3.1.1

Marketing means many things to many people, depending upon what type of organisation they work for and what type of work they do. Nevertheless, the following checklist provides a useful summary of the most important principles which underpin marketing.

- At the heart of all marketing activities is **the responsibility of ensuring the future viability and continuance of the organisation** – by ensuring that it continues to offer products or services which people will want to buy.
- To achieve this basic objective, **marketers need to anticipate market wants and needs** – by continually researching trends and patterns of consumption and preferences.
- They also have to work with research and development, production and cost-accounting colleagues, so as to ensure that **new goods or services brought to the market can be sold at a suitable level of profit**.
- In order to ensure the successful launch and extended life of a product, marketers also have to **devise and execute effective market communications strategies** in the form of advertising and sales promotion, merchandising and public relations, **within a marketing mix** which defines the product, price, sales location (place) and promotion.
- Marketers also work closely with quality assurers and customer service personnel so as to **maintain and enhance customer relations** by delivering high-quality product information, support and post-sales services.
- Lastly, **marketers produce a 3–5 year rolling plan annually – the marketing plan**, which demonstrates how the mission statement goals of the organisation will be delivered in marketing terms – by securing, say, new business from the introduction of new products, or increased sales of existing ones; this plan also informs the organisation's all-inclusive corporate rolling plan.

DISCUSSION TOPICS

PC 3.1.1

1 How would *you* define what marketing is?

2 Do you agree that consumers' buying trends and habits can be successfully analysed so as to tailor products and services to particular groups? Or do you think that it all boils down to trial and error – or luck?

3 Having produced your definition of marketing in 1 above, how would you distinguish between what is marketing and what is selling? Is there a meaningful difference, or do they both merge into each other?

4 'The best definition of marketing that I know is: developing and introducing strategies which enable the organisation to survive!'

Do you agree? Or is this too simple a view of marketing?

PC 3.1.2

From marketing principles to marketing functions

■ 'You get what you pay for!'

We have already identified the important activities of the market research function in evaluating existing and possible future markets for a business organisation. The ongoing work of a company's research and development department has also been touched upon as a means of creating entirely new products or of improving and refining existing ones. Both functions need to be integrated in order for a successful product development strategy to be identified and pursued.

The existence in both industrial and consumer markets of tiered segments or subdivisions of a market has been examined and reasons for their existence given, such as supplying 'the luxury end of the market' or meeting what computer salesmen call 'entry level' or basic model demands.

To achieve successful product development, careful thought needs to be given to what exactly a targeted group of prospective customers requires of a given product, and how these requirements can be met, while at the same time generating profits to a preset level.

Thus the process of product development usually follows these steps.

■ 1 The conceptualising stage

- Expert staff – R&D, Marketing and Sales – meet to brainstorm around a central idea for a new product, say, a longer-lasting dry battery or a faster alpine ski.
- The motivation for developing a new product may alternatively stem from the launch of a competing product which embodies a technology rendering all alternatives obsolete.
- Or, a company's market researchers may have identified an entirely new market niche emerging for which no product or service currently exists, say, in the field of foreign holidays in Russia or TV satellite-driven European modern language courses.

During the conceptualising stage, a large company may examine 200–300 proposals for making a film, publishing a thriller or recording a pop tune before narrowing the field to five possibles and, ultimately, one certainty.

■ 2 The design phase

- Once a decision has been reached to invest in a chosen new product, then groups of expert personnel – draughtsmen, designers, toolmakers and marketeers – join together to plan the eventual appearance of the product (or service). At the design phase, answers have to be found to such pertinent questions as:

Q What is the overall budget for product development? And that for production itself? PC 3.1.2

Q What return upon investment (profit) is sought from the sale of the product: during its first year; over the span of its lifetime?

Q What does its end-user require in terms of its design, range of applications and overall appearance?

Q What are the implications for its overall costs of: development, production, distribution and promotion? Has a Rolls-Royce been conceived when a Ford Escort would do?

Q How does the development of this product fit into the company's corporate marketing plan? Is it seen as a major contributor to future profits or a low-priced, short-term stop-gap while a superior product is being developed?

Q How do the costs of development and production affect the price at which the new product can be successfully launched and then profitably sold through its lifetime?

Q To what extent will the prices at which competing products are being sold affect the price which can be obtained for the new product?

Q Will the new product embody sufficient superior features so as to enable it to be marketed at a higher price than competing products?

Such questions – and their answers – result in compromises and accommodations by the design team in order to produce a product prototype which they consider will prove attractive to its target market while returning a satisfactory profit on the investment given to it.

In an ideal business world, new product launches are always successful because easy answers are found to questions like those above. In reality, product development is likely to be adversely affected by:

1 a shortage of finance to fund ideal R&D, market research and pre-production activities

2 the existence of competing products/services marketed by larger, more affluent organisations being produced via economies of scale at sales prices which are very hard to compete with

3 the limitations of the firm's existing research scientists, designers and production managers

4 the restrictions imposed by:

available production capacity

existing warehousing facilities

available outlets and dealers willing to stock the new product

5 the likely extent of demand for the product generated by advertising and sales promotion campaigns – limited by the budget allocated to them

Unless strategies are devised to overcome such obstacles, then the launch of the new product or service is likely to fail because:

- the product's design specification was compromised by a lack of investment
- once produced, the product proved too expensive for its overall perceived worth in the eyes of its buyers
- production, warehousing and distribution capacity could not keep pace with the demand generated by advertising, sales promotion and the intrinsic demand for the product itself, thus alienating prospective customers

As the above scenarios indicate, coordinating the development of a product is by no means simple. And the executives responsible know their jobs may be on the line if hundreds of thousands or millions of pounds of investment 'go down the tubes' as a result of their mistakes and miscalculations.

In order to minimise the impact of any possible mistakes, extensive care is taken in the pre-production phase of product development as explained below:

PC 3.1.2

■ 3 The pre-production stage

At this stage there are likely to be several alternative versions of the embryonic product in development, each one embodying some variation within a unified design concept. The following factors are particularly important at this stage:

1 That the operation of the product and its appearance are well-accepted by end-users and dealers.

   For this reason, product development staff are likely to field-test the product's central features and packaging across a number of representative regions and customer groups, so as to obtain feedback to confirm that selected features and appearance meet with approval.

2 That the costs of the product's design and ultimate production-line build quality remain in line with projected cost estimates.

   During the prototype testing phase, a manufacturer's cost accountants and design engineers are likely to monitor closely the relationship between the development design and the production prototype and their respective costs. For example, what a designer commits to a blueprint or CADCAM computer model may prove too costly for the firm's toolmakers to tool up for. Producing the housing for an innovative combustion engine may be beyond a factory's metal-casting resources, so designers and production staff have to work out a compromise, and so on. Alternatively it may prove that the selected sources of raw materials and/or bought-in parts prove too costly and other sources need to be secured.

3 That the prototype evolving into the production model is suited to existing forms of transport and showroom/shop display.

   For example, publishers and booksellers dislike textbooks which are printed in an A4 format because they do not fit into existing bookshelves. By the same token a product in development could prove awkward to package in a shrink wrapping or polystyrene knock-proof shell.

4 That the product in its eventual form and design conforms to legal requirements governing HASAW, consumer protection and a host of either factory-based or general consumer legislation.

   For this reason all versions and marks of drawings and plans are carefully stored and, in certain industries such as aviation, all design specifications are coded and signed off by the responsible staff as a means of implementing design safety checks.

■ 4 The production stage

Despite all the efforts and attention given to a product during development there are almost always snags which only seem to manifest themselves once a product is in production. For example, the marketing of a computer software application is almost never 'bug-free'; somewhere within some thousands of lines of programming lurks an error which sooner or later surfaces. For this reason Version 1 issues of software are soon followed up by their 1.1 and 2.0 successors. PC 3.1.2

Therefore, R&D and development staff are likely to be needed to trouble-shoot problems during early production runs. By the same token, the production experts – foremen and operatives – may be able to suggest ways and means of cutting production costs or increasing output without further costs.

Three important factors in the production process should be noted:

1 That the overall design creates a minimum of waste – of raw materials, manpower or time.

   All three cost money and force unwanted contributions on to the costs of producing the product, thus eating into forecast profits.

2 That the product can be built to stringent quality standards.

   Since the Second World War, total quality management (TQM) and 'just-in-time' policies for the delivery of required production materials, as well as the operation of processes meeting British Standard 5750 and ISO 9000 have been introduced into UK factories, warehouses, shops and offices as a means of ensuring that products and services are able to meet and beat overseas and national competition. Thus every new product has to incorporate design and build features which are capable of satisfying a company's quality assurance personnel.

3 That the production runs or batches of the product are planned and executed so as to ensure the optimum cost-effectiveness of production resources.

   Works and factory managers devote much time and effort to the future planning of production runs which are smooth, uninterrupted and which operate at the lowest cost of heat, light and manpower. Rush orders which have to be turned out during a weekend when double-time may be charged are frowned upon when a factory has spare plant capacity during a normal working week. For such reasons, communication and liaison between sales and production are vital in keeping costs down while ensuring that sales are made and deliveries are on time.

■ Product planning: costing and breaking even

At the earliest stage in marketing a new product, a product planning schedule is drawn up which provides – as accurately as possible – estimates of the costs which will be incurred in its:

- development
- production
- distribution and promotion.

As the chart in Fig 3.2 indicates, costs are inevitably incurred at each of the six stages of marketing a product or service. And in order to ensure that a profit still ensues, cost accountants must monitor closely the staged costs which are attributable to a given product. Such costs are deemed direct and indirect. Direct costs will include items like the cost of raw materials, specific production processes like firing a batch of chinaware and the work of production operatives on the production line. Indirect costs will embrace factory heating, running a head office and maintaining a salesforce, etc. The cost accountants apportion a percentage of such overheads as fairly as possible to each product in a manufacturer's range.

PC
3.1.1
3.1.2

Fig 3.2 **Where costs are incurred in marketing a product**

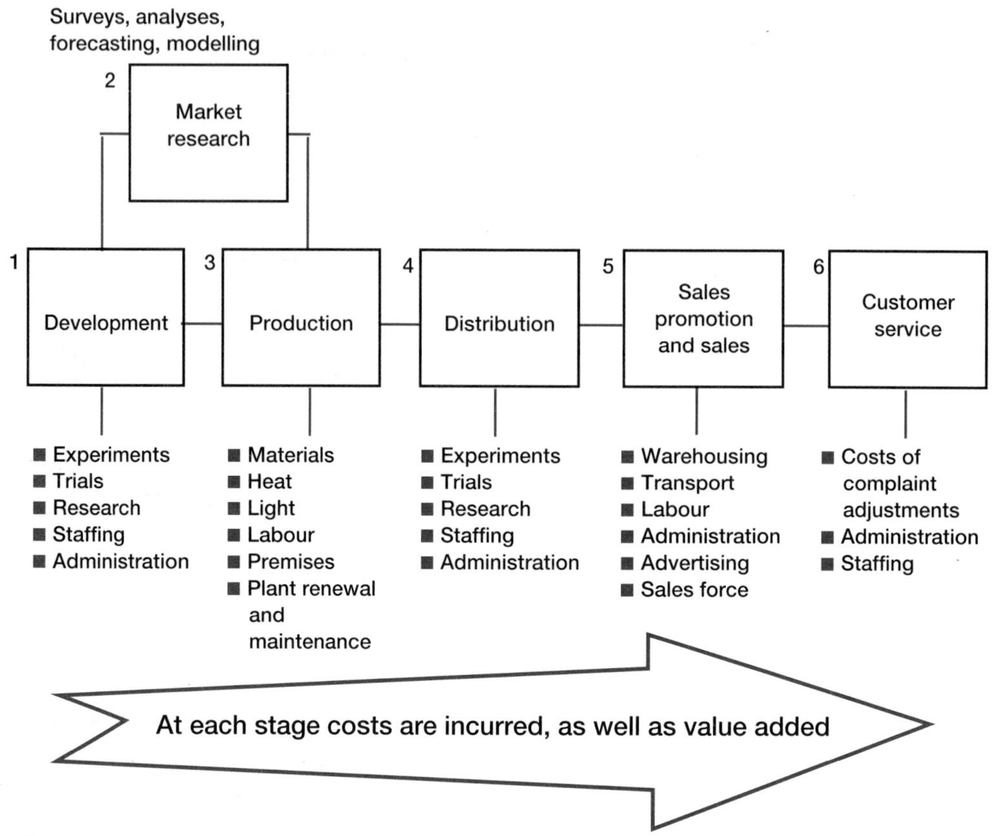

Fixed and variable costs

Also, the nature of costs incurred in marketing a product or service differ in two essential ways. Some costs – such as the agreed rental of factory or office premises over a financial year remain fixed, as do those for business rates, and charges like road tax, and insurances.

The costs of other inputs, such as bought-in raw materials, the fuelling of plant or vehicles and company payroll will vary according to the amount of work done. At peak times more staff may be recruited, more raw materials employed and more plant run over longer periods, while at times of low demand personnel may be laid off, plant left idle and stocks of raw material run down.

Thus the manufacture of each product incurs both fixed and variable costs. A firm's cost accountants as outlined above will apportion fixed costs to each product and will then estimate the amount of variable costs which will be incurred according to the number of products made. The diagram in Fig 3.3 illustrates how a break-even chart is drawn up to provide indications of costs, revenue and a break-even point at which income from sales matches costs incurred.

As the break-even chart (Fig 3.3) illustrates, it is possible for market researchers to plot anticipated fixed and variable costs for a given product against expected income from sales. By adjusting the levels of total costs and sales prices, different amounts of profit will emerge for the number of units sold. In this way, a long production run may generate acceptable profits from a low-priced unit and a short run from a higher priced alternative – if it can be sold!

Break-even charts are thus very helpful in deciding how to pitch sales prices, control manufacturing costs and yield required profits.

Fig 3.3 **A tool for calculating sales needed to generate a profit from given costs**

PC
3.1.1
3.1.2

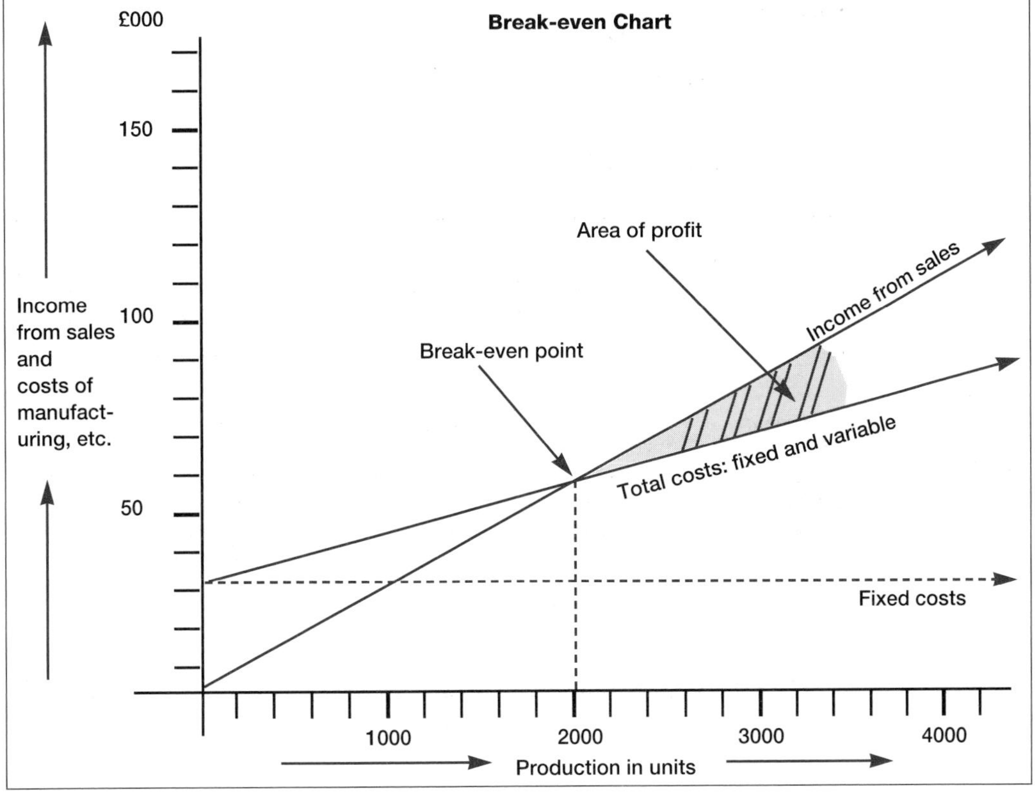

Break-even Chart
£000
150
100
50
Income from sales and costs of manufact-uring, etc.
Area of profit
Income from sales
Break-even point
Total costs: fixed and variable
Fixed costs
1000
2000
3000
4000
Production in units

PC
3.1.3
3.1.4

GROUP ACTIVITIES

Product development

In groups of two or three, undertake **one** of the following activities.

1 You work in the Research and Design Department of the British Bicycle Company plc. Your company's market research unit has recently identified what they consider to be an exciting new market niche – a bicycle in both male and female versions for 18-plus-year-olds who are about to enter higher education at a university or college of HE.

Kim Turner, your Marketing Director has, as a result, given you the following brief:

'I'd like you to brainstorm around the design concept for the two bikes in terms of features which a student would really appreciate and find irresistible! We intend to target the bike at mums and dads as a kind of present to a son or daughter for having passed A-levels or BTEC GNVQ Level 3, etc. A rough shot at the recommended retail sales price is some £250–290, so it can't have **all** the bells and whistles!

I'd like you to produce a rough design with explanatory notes justifying the features you think should be emphasised. Oh, and I'll need it by today week for a meeting with yourselves, Market Research and Production.'

First, survey your local bicycle retailing scene for an update on what is available, and then carry out Kim Turner's instructions.

2 First research into **one** of the following and then deliver an oral presentation to your group on why you think the product involved lost its place in the market-place.

   a The Ford Edsel motorcar

   b Sir Clive Sinclair's CS motorised vehicle

   c Sir Freddie Laker's 'Laker Airlines'

   d The BSA motorcycle

3 Make arrangements to interview one or two senior cost accountants in a manufacturing company in your locality. Ask them to explain to you the procedures they follow to cost the development of a product up until the time it goes into regular production.

4 Arrange to interview the manager responsible for quality in **either** a manufacturing or a service industry company. Find out how quality aspects impinge on product development and production-line working.

For both activities 3 and 4, report back orally to your class.

PC 3.1.1 3.1.2 3.1.3

A CASE STUDY IN PRODUCT DEVELOPMENT

1992 – and all that!

Your Head of Department has recently found that an increasing number of enquiries are coming into the Departmental Office about full-time courses which blend business studies with European languages. The impact of the EC 1992 Single Market seems at last to be impacting upon school pupils and FE college students who are pursuing one or more European languages to GCE Advanced level, and to university undergraduates who are pursuing degree courses in arts subjects, including a European language.

The following represents the most commonly requested features of the sort of business/EU language course requested:

1 It must not exceed 15/16 months of study

2 Intending students must have at least a GCE A-level C grade or equivalent in any EU language they wish to study, and have attained either a BTEC National/GCE A-level/GNVQ Level 3 award.

3 The course should result in qualifications in both the business studies and language course areas which, ideally, should be recognised in EU countries as well as the UK.

4 A period of work experience attachment in an EU country should be part of the course, and achievement in it should count to the overall course assessment.

5 The prospective students for this course are in a hurry to find worthwhile first posts and therefore don't want to study within the traditional three terms per academic year framework.

Your HOD has asked you to research into what programmes and syllabuses are being currently promoted by the major national examination boards and to what NVQ/GNVQ levels. S/he also wants you to discuss your outline proposals with representatives of local commerce and industry to see find out what they think would be most appropriate. Having ascertained what is available, your brief is then to:

1 Design a suitable course using, as appropriate, available national assessment programmes or units which meet the above criteria. Your design should form part of a briefing paper which also justifies the recommendations you make.

2 Work out an appropriate cost for the course fees:

a for UK nationals;

b for overseas students paying full-cost fees.

Your familiarity with break-even costing techniques will help here, and your teacher will help with existing cost components and formulae used in your school or college.

3 Draw up a plan for the effective promotion of the course to the target students you identify.

4 Design a course brochure/leaflet which you believe will prompt recruitment.

As a group, consider how you could obtain feedback on your course design without having to wait some 16 months for the results of a first intake.

5 Give an oral presentation to your class of about ten to fifteen minutes, suitably supported by AVA materials as a briefing on what course you designed, and your rationale for it.

6 In a general class discussion, consider the differences between marketing a manufactured product like an electric kettle, and an abstract service such as this vocational education course.

Fixing a price

[see also Element 1.2]

PC 3.1.2

One of the most difficult aspects of effective marketing of goods and services is arriving at a sales price for a given commodity.

Moreover, a product (or service) may be sold at a range of differing prices during its lifetime as part of an organisation's marketing plan for it, and its overall place in a corporate marketing strategy.

With certain products, there is very little room for manoeuvre. For example, in a mature market for, say, toothpastes or shampoos, a wide range of products jostle for position and consumers purchase to a large extent within a narrow band of prices. If the price of a particular brand moves up significantly, its users are very likely to move across to an alternative. In such markets products are said to be prone to a high elasticity of demand.

With other products, however, where preferences are deeply rooted – say in a favourite pipe tobacco or pop group – a significantly increased price may not result in a fall in demand for the tobacco or compact disk. In such circumstances, the products concerned display an inelasticity of demand. This may also be true of essential items like petrol or sugar provided that all suppliers increase their prices in unison. However, to prevent such price-fixing or setting up of what are called business cartels, legislation has been introduced making it illegal for suppliers to create and manipulate a monopolistic market for goods or services.

At this stage it is important to note that for many markets and their products, goods or services are introduced which are claimed to embody distinct differences from their competitors and so to warrant a higher or lower price – they are deliberately **positioned** to appeal to a targeted market segment.

PC 3.1.2

■ Determinants of a product's price

Wherever a product is positioned in a market, the following factors will affect the price at which it is offered for sale:

- **Unique properties**

  A product may possess a unique property and be marketed as a market leader, say, because of a technological breakthrough. In this case, the product can command a very high price; for instance just after the Second World War the first biros brought on to the UK market sold for a week's wages because of their novelty value.

- **Development costs**

  Products with high development costs tend to be sold initially at high prices (compared to other competing goods) since they embody updated features and incorporate the latest technological advances; thus they have more appeal than 'elderly' products which have been around for a long time. Also, most companies are keen to recoup their development costs sooner rather than later so as to be able to invest them in other developments if this is at all possible.

- **Sales prices of competitors**

  Unless a new product possesses some really superior features, it is likely to be 'boxed in' by the pricing patterns of established alternatives; indeed it may have to significantly undercut the prices of well-accepted brands in order to gain a toe-hold in the market-place.

- **The general state of the market**

  Demand for products and services ebbs and flows according to the state of the economic tide. At times of buoyant activity and demand, high prices may be secured for – trainers, garden furniture or Nicam television-sets; in periods or recession, during a wet summer or after the World Soccer Cup or Olympics, prices will fall as retailers chase after sales during a sharp drop in demand.

- **How the product is perceived by the supplier**

  If a product is perceived by its supplier as a premium product – the best they can produce and more than a match for its competition – then it will be deliberately priced at the top end of the continuum. 'Get-in-and-get-out' products consciously made down to a price will correspondingly inhabit the other end of the market.

■ Major approaches to pricing

PC 3.1.2

The cost-plus price

Users of this approach calculate as closely as possible the costs of producing the product and getting it to its point of sale and then include an additional amount to represent the profit to be generated (Fig. 3.4).

The advantage of such a model is that it is likely to arrive at a sales price which truly reflects the accumulated costs of its development, production and sales support. However, when a desirable profit percentage is added on, the resultant price may well prove more than the market will readily bear. It is also rather unsophisticated in that it makes no allowance for, say, spreading particular costs over the lifetime of the product. For example, a more astute pricing policy may add a relatively small charge for development costs on to the price components at the launch of a product in order to help it gain acceptance, and then progressively increase such a charge in stages (and through modest price increases) as demand grows.

Top-down pricing

The alternative to 'cost-plus' pricing may be termed 'top-down'. Users of this pricing strategy tend to start at the retail user price end of the process by posing the question: 'At what price would a product or service sell well in this market?'

The pricing strategies of competitors are carefully evaluated and a new product/service commissioned either to undercut them or match them while supplying superior features. Thus products emerge which have been made to a specific selling price. The quality of the materials used, design and workmanship will have been costed so as to remain within tightly fixed limits.

Many holiday package tour operators price in this way, by estimating what a significant segment of the market, say, blue-collar workers, will pay for a Mediterranean, beach-based holiday and then negotiating with hoteliers, coach firms and airlines to meet specific end-user prices.

Fig 3.4 **The cost-plus pricing model**

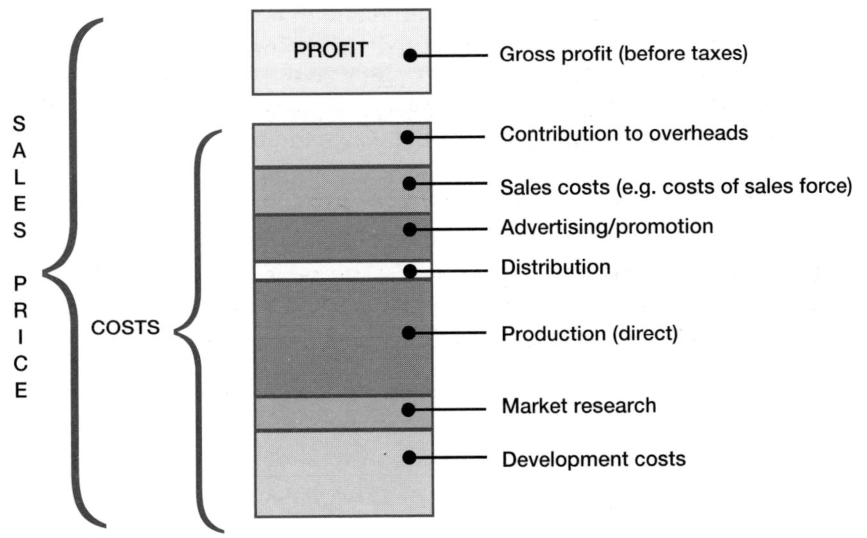
SALES PRICE
COSTS
PROFIT
Gross profit (before taxes)
Contribution to overheads
Sales costs (e.g. costs of sales force)
Advertising/promotion
Distribution
Production (direct)
Market research
Development costs

Fixed rate of profit return

Some firms seek to obtain a minimum fixed rate of profit on each product as a return on their investment. This may be because they need to generate a known total profit each year in order to:

- pay a sufficient dividend to shareholders
- service loans from banks or credit houses
- cover all operating costs
- allow for depreciation and replacement of premises, plant and equipment
- provide for future developments.

While this approach is sound in terms of its good housekeeping it may well come to grief and need intermittent reappraisal if:

- the equilibrium of the market is jolted say by a sudden rise in interest rates
- a strong competitor introduces a hostile, price-slashing campaign to increase market share, or block out a newly-launched product
- an innovative product causes a major change in buying habits among end-users

and so on.

In many ways, a market is like the open sea – at times placid and at times stormy; thus prices, like the trim of a yacht's sails seldom remains constant; they are continually being raised and lowered in response to market conditions.

For this reason, an overall pricing strategy must be flexible and designed to operate within upper and lower limits.

Pricing for segmented markets

Some firms vary the price of identical products according to the type of customer they target and the nature of the sales environment. Much higher prices are commanded for, say, tins of coke or cans of lager in mountain-top, ski-resort cafes than in city-centre supermarkets. Thus a wholesale supplier may choose to price a product accordingly.

Also, economies of scale play an important part in this strategy, together with the concept of marginal costing. Once fixed costs have been absorbed and total costs are running into profit, the actual cost of producing additional units of production is very small. Therefore, if additionally produced goods can be sold – even at prices lower than their premium-market counterparts – they may still make a significant contribution to overall profits. Thus, such a segmented pricing policy is adopted by many manufacturers spanning the maker's brand, the retailers 'own' brand and unbranded versions of the same good.

Mark-ups and discounts

A further factor complicating a pricing policy for a manufacturer is the percentage of mark-up (representing a profit taken) which first a wholesaler and then a retailer add on to a manufacturer's selling price. While such mark-ups or margins are outside the control of the manufacturer, he has to allow in his pricing policy for sufficient space to exist between ex-works prices and ultimate retail prices so as to allow both wholesaler and retailer to live. Failure to do so may of itself result in a new product flopping disastrously, if these margins prove unattractive, given the price the good can be effectively sold for.

Manufacturers and wholesalers may also mask price movements with special price reduction offers, additional contents (say, an extra 10 per cent in a hair conditioner) and self-liquidating offers like 'three for the price of two' built into an overall retail price. Such offers may be introduced to liven up a sluggish demand for a product or to counter competitors' activities.

On the other hand, they may precede a reduction in the price of a product geared to the premium end of the market which is not sustaining its share of this market.

Another ploy in changing price structures surreptitiously is to alter the size of a product's container and therefore of its contents, thus enabling a price to change while retaining a profit margin.

■ Pricing strategies and the product life cycle

PC 3.1.2

In order to examine the various price strategies applied to a product during its lifetime, it is necessary to explain what marketers see as the key stages in the life cycle of a product or service (Fig 3.5).

The major proposition of the product life cycle model is that no product or service goes

Fig 3.5 **The product life cycle**

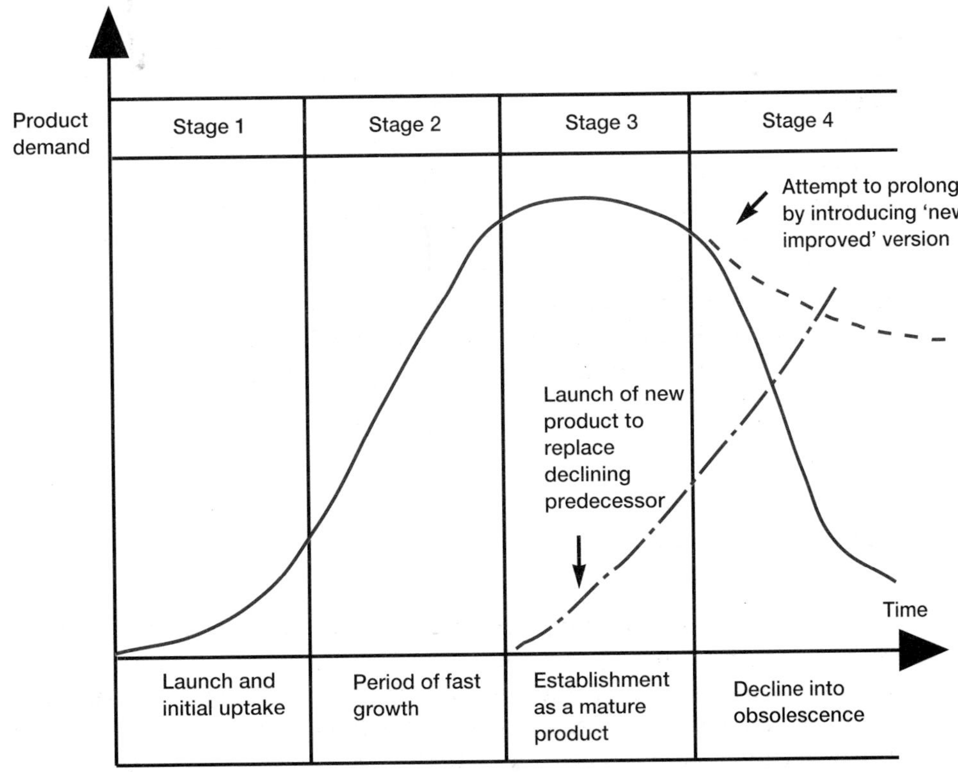
Product demand
Stage 1
Stage 2
Stage 3
Stage 4
Attempt to prolong life by introducing 'new improved' version
Launch of new product to replace declining predecessor
Time
Launch and initial uptake
Period of fast growth
Establishment as a mature product
Decline into obsolescence

on for ever finding a demand in the market-place. Technology moves on, fashions change, fresh fads and crazes arise in all industrial and consumer markets.

And to reinforce such general observations, market research has demonstrated that a product's life typically moves through four stages:

Stage 1: Launch and initial uptake

A successful product tends to start life slowly until sales promotion, determined selling and customer acceptance have done their work. Penetrating a well-established market may be slow going at first, since all sales organisations object to losing market share to a cocky newcomer!

Stage 2: Fast growing demand

Provided that the product has intrinsic worth and appeal, and is effectively supported in advertising and sales promotion terms, then sales are likely to come thick and fast in Stage 2 – especially since the new product benefits from 'bang-up-to-date' design features and packaging.

Stage 3: Consolidated maturity

Once the initial excitement for the product wears out, and it becomes 'newish' rather than 'brand, spanking new', then the rate of climb in demand tends to level off. In fact the product will by then have peaked. Marketing staff during this stage may seek to extend the duration of a high plateau of sales by introducing forceful advertising campaigns which stress the product's status and reliability. And in order to stave off as long as possible the inevitable arrival of Stage 4, they may relaunch the product by giving it a low-cost, cosmetic face-lift. Car makers do this by adding fresh trim and colour schemes to existing bodies, engines and subframes. Washing powder manufacturers tend suddenly to discover a magic new ingredient making the powder wash 'even whiter' than before, and buy extensive peak TV commercial advertising time to prove it!

Stage 4

Despite every promotional blandishment and face-lift, the product begins to look weary and time-worn. Prospective buyers look and inspect but move on to younger models which are more attractive.

Eventually a decision is taken to stop production and the life cycle ends. However, if the marketing department has stayed sharp, the demise of one product is not allowed to take place until its lively and energetic successor is well on its way up the ladder of its own Stage 2! In this way, organisations maintain their profits and market share over decades and dozens of successive product life cycles.

Marketing and customer orientation

PC 3.1.3

A simple, yet very apt marketing and sales slogan asserts: **The customer is king!** Another affirms baldly that, **No one ever won an argument with a customer!**

What both intend to communicate is the supremacy of the customer in any market where competition exists to provide an alternative place where people can shop and buy and feel good while doing so.

Historically, markets were either utilitarian or manufacturer-orientated. For example, in the middle ages consumer goods tended to be made so as to perform a specific task by a few craftsmen within a local guild. Designs were simple and there tended to be restricted choice and little to differentiate, say, one jug from another. At the dawn of the mass production age in the mid-nineteenth century, manufacturers tended to design and make goods to their own specifications and then to offer them to customers on a 'take it or leave it basis'. Before the twentieth century very little market research into consumer expectations or preferences took place.

However, with the rapid rise of mass-production techniques, mass-media advertising and the growth of more affluent consumers in mass markets, the notion of consumerism was born, where business entrepreneurs came to realise the extent of the spending power of consumers in mass markets. As a result, during the 1930s–50s in the USA in particular, marketing concepts emerged which were based upon a perception of the customer as the most important person to a business enterprise. The indifferent assertion of the American car-maker Henry Ford: 'You can have any colour you like – as long as it's black!' had characterised production-orientated marketing up till then. The cost-savings made by using a single colour to spray Model T Fords on the production-line had been justified by the low price of the car as a result. The return to peace-time across the western world post 1945, however, led to millions of people wishing to acquire the better life victory had promised – not least through the acquisition of fast-moving consumer goods. Economic reconstruction also led to increased competition, as old multi-nationals and young small traders alike jostled for their 'slice of the peace-dividend cake'.

■ Quality becomes an issue

PC 3.1.3

Increased consumer choice and a resurgent world economy in the 1940s began a process of quality improvement, ably spear-headed by Dr W Edwards Deming in Japan. The re-building of the Japanese economy after Hiroshima brought Dr Deming, a statistical quality control expert, to Japan with the help of the US government, to lead a team whose aim was to assist Japanese manufacturing to recover, and thus support the re-democratising of its people. As a result of this team's work on imparting techniques to reduce wastage in manufacturing processes, and to devise fault-free production systems, Japanese industry took off on an upward spiral which has resulted in 'made in Japan' becoming a watchword of top quality design and build. Also during the post war decade, Dr J M Juran, Dr Armand Feigenbaum and Malcolm Baldridge – all Americans – further developed stringent quality assurance systems into a concept of *total quality management* (TQM) to embrace every part of an organisation's activities, in which internal customers were as important as external ones.

The impetus for the tremendous costs involved in establishing a quality management system in large business organisations was, of course, the spur of competition and the growing awareness in the 1960s and 1970s among consumers of the power of their choice-making abilities.

PC
3.1.3

CASE HISTORY

The six year anti-corrosion warranties on car bodies

In the 1950s and 1960s, car sales boomed as millions of people earning good money came into the market. To meet a rapid rise in demand, car-makers both in Europe and the Far East churned them out as if there was no tomorrow. But in terms of body rust, tomorrow soon dawned with a cold light.

The avid purchaser of a new car soon became unhappy and then outraged at the speed with which flaky paintwork and rust-red, crumbling holes disfigured the shining bodywork of his or her pride and joy. This was because of the minimalist efforts made in factories to subject the pressed steel used to make car bodies to rust-proofing techniques. At least one Asian car-maker had to change its name as a result of producing what became known as 'rust-buckets'.

The change came about when one shrewd manufacturer started to include a six-year anti-corrosion warranty for its car-bodies as standard. In a short time all its competitors were obliged to follow suit, despite incurring additional production costs – such was the demand for longer-lasting car bodies.

This particular case history illustrates well how a customer-orientated approach leads to success, and indifference to customer satisfaction leads to major corporate image problems.

PC
3.1.3

■ Quality in the 1990s

As a result of the Japanese-led production of long-lasting, defect-free goods, European businesses came to realise in the 1980s that, unless they could improve their own quality assurance systems, they would undoubtedly lose much trade to the Japanese. As a result, many companies worked hard to improve their quality processes under the banner of British Standard 5750 and International Standard Organisation 9000 and European standard EN29000. All these standards have the aim of encouraging organisations to deliver outcomes to a detailed standard – all the time – through the conscientious pursuit and monitoring of stringent procedures. Some organisations also embraced Total Quality Management and committed to a continual process of improvement.

There emerged, as a result, a number of businesses, large and small which were rightly entitled to the description *world class*, since their products conformed to the highest standards of *fitness for purpose*. Also during the early 1990s a number of organisations applied for and won the government's *Investors In People* award which encourages firms to improve the training and development of their workforces.

■ The customer-organisational focus

There has emerged, then, over the past fifty years among forward-looking compan heightened awareness of how being customer-orientated and quality-conscious contribu to increasing profits and the meeting of pre-set goals:

CUSTOMER ORIENTATION AND ORGANISATIONAL OBJECTIVES

Focus on customer expectations:

- more market research on what the customer wants
- greater investment in developing improved products
- better design and build through meeting demanding quality management standards
- more detailed and informative product information for customers
- better systems for distributing products safely and quickly to customers
- improved guarantees, warranties and product support through a strong commitment to customer services

Organisational objectives:

- gaining the information needed to become a market leader
- acquiring a reputation for 'being in the market to stay'
- becoming acknowledged as a world class company
- building a reputation for customer satisfaction
- increasing sales and profit through the continuous availability of the product range
- holding on to customers and winning repeat business as a result of a caring approach to customers

INVESTING IN CUSTOMERS LEADS TO ANNUAL DIVIDENDS OF SALES AND PROFIT!

DISCUSSION TOPICS

PC 3.1.1 3.1.2 3.1.3

1 What do you think is meant by the phrase: *Marketing is everything*?

2 How can an organisation ensure its survival through its marketing plan?

3 American market research recently demonstrated that some 96% of customers who considered that a complaint they made was poorly handled never used the business in question again. Do you think that customer orientation is sufficiently widely established in your locality? If not, what steps could be taken at a local level to improve it?

4 Is the customer *really* always king?

...ivities in business organisations

PC 3.1.3

... everything' and forms an over-arching umbrella spanning the entire ...ise, then what is the nature and scope of its various parts and activities? ...ction provides an overview of marketing activities in organisations.

MARKETING: THE OVER-ARCHING UMBRELLA

Market research
A key role of marketing is to monitor continually – by surveys, interviews, analysis of competing products etc. – the trends, developments and changes in taste in the targeted market.

Research and development
Effective marketing relies on the availability of high-quality products and services to sell; therefore an essential part of the marketing effort lies in the continuous process of developing new products and improving existing ones.

Production
Marketing is also concerned to ensure that products can be made in quantities which will satisfy generated demand and at costs which will enable satisfactory profits to be made.

Customer service
The long-term growth of a business depends a great deal on repeat business and brand-loyal customers; for this reason, marketing is becoming increasingly concerned to ensure that customer service receives sufficient investment and resource support.

Selling the product
No product or service is sold in a market vacuum, and so marketing has also to ensure that products and services are brought to potential buyers' attention by 'shouting louder' than the competition in appealing advertisements and sales promotion campaigns.

Financial aspects
Marketing is intimately concerned with accounting decisions in a business which affect: product development costs, production costs, promotional costs, distribution costs and customer service costs, since all these contribute to overall product marketing costs, and if left uncontrolled could quickly erode profits.

Corporate and brand image
Whether a potential customer decides to buy a product, or not, depends very much on his or her perception of (a) the firm making and/or offering it for sale, and (b) the reputation of the product for reliability and value-for-money etc., all of which are influenced by the images they communicate to the customer.

DISCUSSION TOPICS PC 3.1.1 3.1.2 3.1.3

1 Assuming that the department in which you study wishes to market a new course – say marketing for junior managers – how would you advise the head to go about it?

2 Do you agree that, as a consumer, you are now on the receiving end of better customer service? If so, why, if not, why not?

3 'Marketing is simply commonsense – it's only the johnnies who rely on it for their pay-packet who hype it up into some kind of mystique!' Is this a true or bigoted perception of the marketing function?

4 Do you agree or disagree on the importance of a business having a good corporate image, and that products do have 'brand images' – or is this another feature of the hype referred to in 3 above?

Marketing and growth in businesses

PC 3.1.5

As outlined above, the most essential function of marketing is to assure the future success of a business by ensuring that a constant stream of products or services come off the 'production-line' and into the sales arena. In some industries, such as the car industry, this entails marketing specialists anticipating what styles of cars possessing what specifications and add-ons are going to be attractive to buyers in three to four years time, since that is the lead time needed to process a new concept into a production-line model in a dealer's showroom.

■ Products don't live for ever!

Moreover, no product lives for ever. Sooner or later it will become obselete as technology moves on, or left stranded on the back-shelf as people's tastes and life-styles change. How many youngsters are pestering their parents for a hula-hoop today? Who, apart from collectors, is interested in buying 12-inch vinyl records? This kind of change prompts a firm's marketing specialists to achieve a number of important marketing outcomes – if the business is not only to survive, but to grow:

WHAT MARKETERS NEED TO ACHIEVE IF THEIR BUSINESS IS TO GROW

In order to enable the business they work in to grow, its marketing staff need to achieve the following outcomes as year rolls into year:

- **that an effective product development strategy is in place** which delivers to the sales force products or services they can sell at a profit and, usually, in high volumes
- **that sufficient finance and know-how is being invested in research and development**, by encouraging scientists, 'whizz-kids' and brain-stormers to come up with innovative ideas for entirely new products or services – such as the flexible mortgage, the mountain-bike, the pocket-sized computer-organiser etc.
- **that product development includes the existing product range** – especially when, in their mature phase, sales of such products begin to drop off
- **that an effective market research function is in place**, to ensure that the products or services being marketed can match or beat competing ones and that up-to-date and accurate feedback on market trends, changes and developments informs the R&D function
- **that access to new markets is constantly being explored and entry gained** – since a business may have reached saturation point with some of its products, where it is too costly to seek extra sales; new markets bring in new customers who are, quite obviously, a key factor in business growth
- **that loyal, existing customers are not overlooked in the battle for new business** – since their repeat business often forms the basis of secure profit

PC
3.1.1
3.1.2
3.1.3
3.1.4
3.1.5

REVIEW TEST

1 Write down your definition of marketing in about 50–70 words.

2 List four main marketing principles.

3 Explain briefly how marketing principles interact with a business organisation's specialist departments.

4 Explain briefly why effective market research is such an important part of the marketing function.

5 Explain why the needs of the customer and the needs of the business organisation may not always entirely coincide.

6 Explain briefly how the marketing function interacts with product design and development.

7 List four points at which costs are incurred in marketing a new product – from concept to launch.

8 What is a break-even chart used for? How does it work?

9 List four determinants of a product's sales price.

10 Explain the difference between cost-plus and top-down pricing strategies.

11 List the four main stages of a product life-cycle and explain what occurs during a typical life-cycle.

12 Explain what you understand by the term *customer orientation*.

13 Why did quality assurance and management systems become so important in business organisations in the period from 1980 to the present time?

14 Explain the difference between the marketing and the sales function in a business.

15 List four key activities which marketers have to succeed in delivering if their business organisation is to grow.

16 Why is it that products 'don't live for ever!'?

INDIVIDUAL ACTIVITIES

PC
3.1.1
3.1.2
3.1.3
3.1.4
3.1.5

1 Make contact with a practising marketing manager and ask him or her to give you the definition of marketing which makes most sense in the context of the job he/she performs. Then share it with your class.

2 Arrange to interview one of the following: an R&D specialist; a production manager; a sales manager; and find out how the marketing function impacts upon and interacts with the operations they manage.

3 Arrange to visit a business which believes in a customer-orientated way of doing business, and find out what this means in practice. Report back to your class in a 5-minute oral presentation.

4 Research into 3 different types of product which have been on the market for some time and produce a set of bullet-points to explain how product improvement has been undertaken to boost/maintain their sales.

5 Research into the past ten years history of your study centre and report back to your class on what it did which resulted in its growing in particular areas of its work.

KNOWLEDGE TEST

Element 3.1
Investigate the principles and functions of marketing in organisations

1 (i) The primary role of marketing is to support the sales function.
(ii) The marketing function's main concern is to assure the future success of the organisation.

Which of the following options best describes the above two statements?

A (i) T (ii) T
B (i) T (ii) F
C (i) F (ii) T
D (i) F (ii) F

2 Which of the following statements are true, and which false?

Key marketing functions include:

A managing change
B training the workforce in marketing skills
C researching markets
D vetting suppliers' goods for quality

3 (i) Customer orientation occurs when a marketing strategy includes the purchase and sale of goods from the Far East.

(ii) Marketing mix is a term which describes the blend of sales and marketing which has been given to a specific product or service.

Which of the following options best describes the above two statements?

A	(i)	T	(ii)	T
B	(i)	T	(ii)	F
C	(i)	F	(ii)	T
D	(i)	F	(ii)	F

4 An organisation will grow if its marketing function:

A develops more product ideas
B increases its market share
C sells successfully into fresh markets
D replaces existing products with new ones

Which of the above statements is true, and which false?

5 (i) Marketing is not a function of public sector organisations.

(ii) Marketing is a function of private sector organisations.

Which of the following options best describes the above two statements?

A	(i)	T	(ii)	T
B	(i)	T	(ii)	F
C	(i)	F	(ii)	T
D	(i)	F	(ii)	F

PC
3.1.1
3.1.2
3.1.3
3.1.4
3.1.5

PORTFOLIO OF EVIDENCE ACTIVITY

Element 3.1
Investigate the principles and functions of marketing in organisations

UK MRC

Scenario One

You have been asked to take part in a discussion between a focus group, a group of consumers who provide objective information and views for a market research company called *UK Market Research Consultants Limited* (UK MRC) and a team of the company's managers.

The discussion is to centre upon identifying:

a) What consumers expect to receive as customers of 'customer-orientated' businesses.

b) What business organisations expect to receive from the business they generate with such customers.

UK MRC – as a result of a commission they have been given – are keen to establish the relationship between consumers' expectations and business organisations' goals in order to ascertain where interests coincide and where not, in terms of the costs to the organisation of being in business, changes in consumer expectations, such as in quality and customer service, the needs of the business to make a profit, the limitations of any workforce employed and so on.

Scenario Two

UK MRC has also been tasked with producing a report for the same client which compares and contrasts the marketing approach of two quite different organisations – one in the private and one in the public sector. The report is to focus on:

- an evaluation of their respective marketing operations
- how each secured expansion through: market developments, expanding market share, product or service development, technological innovation etc.
- how each organisation researches the markets it is in or wishes to enter and how the data it secures impacts upon its operations
- what strategies each organisation employs to sell its products or services in order to optimise sales and profits

You have been detailed by your manager, John Turner, to research and produce an appropriate report.

Task 1

For each of the above Scenarios, remember to complete your planning and review log and to submit it with your activities.

Task 2

In liaison with your teacher, take part in a discussion lasting about 30 minutes as outlined in Scenario One above. You should either take the part of a focus group consumer or a *UK MRC* manager. Before the discussion commences, spend about 20 minutes making notes of the points you wish to raise which are relevant to the objectives of the discussion. During the discussion, take down your own notes of the main points which emerge from either set of participants and afterwards, create from them a suitable set of notes which accurately summarise the discussion – in not more than 2 sides of A4.

Task 3

Make arrangements to visit a private and a public sector organisation locally and to research into their respective marketing activities as outlined in Scenario Two above. Having secured sufficient information and views etc. compose a report to meet the needs of John Turner – in about 6 sides of A4, including any suitable graphic illustrations.

Performance criteria covered

3.1.1, 3.1.2, 3.1.3, 3.1.4, 3.1.5

Core skills covered

Communication:
3.1.1, 3.1.2, 3.1.3, 3.1.4, 3.1.5, 3.2.1, 3.2.2, 3.2.3, 3.2.4, 3.2.5, 3.4.1, 3.4.2, 3.4.3, 3.4.4

Information Technology:
3.1.1, 3.1.2, 3.1.3, 3.1.4, 3.1.5, 3.3.1, 3.3.2, 3.3.3, 3.3.4, 3.3.5, 3.3.6

Element 3.2
MARKETING RESEARCH INFORMATION AND PRODUCT DEVELOPMENT

PC 3.2.1

The use of the terms market research and marketing research sometimes cause confusion. Marketing research is the label for the activity of enquiring into and analysing the wide range of activities which make up the marketing function – product development, customer profiling, research into advertising media, the effectiveness of customer service systems and so on. Market research occupies a much narrower sphere of activity, it is the investigation into and analysis and evaluation of the key features, trends, tendencies and activities of a specific market – say for the purchase of satellite TV receivers or for polyunsaturated margarines.

The diagram in Fig 3.6 below illustrates the relationship of market research to the overall process of conceiving, producing and then selling a product or service.

At base, the market research function is to remain 'in the know' about two types of market:

a the market or markets in which the organisation is active

b the market or markets which the organisation is thinking of entering in the future.

In the first type, market research staff maintain a monitoring function for existing products. They set up regular surveys in order to check that acceptance of a product or product line is holding up, or whether industrial buyers, wholesalers, retailers or consumers are migrating or 'defecting' to competing products or services. If a company wishes to enter into a new market, perhaps as part of a corporate strategy of diversifying as a means of long-term security, then its market researchers will survey that new market in order to ascertain:

- its current size
- its future potential for growth
- its ability to generate profit both currently and in the future
- the nature and size of existing competitors and their share of the market
- a detailed analysis of the type of customers who make up the market and how they segment into 'slices of the pie' according to factors like age, income and life-style.

In order to secure the raw data from which to extract meaningful analysis, researchers of markets devise various methods for obtaining research data. These methods are divided into primary and secondary research.

PC 3.2.1

Fig 3.6 The role of market research in the marketing process

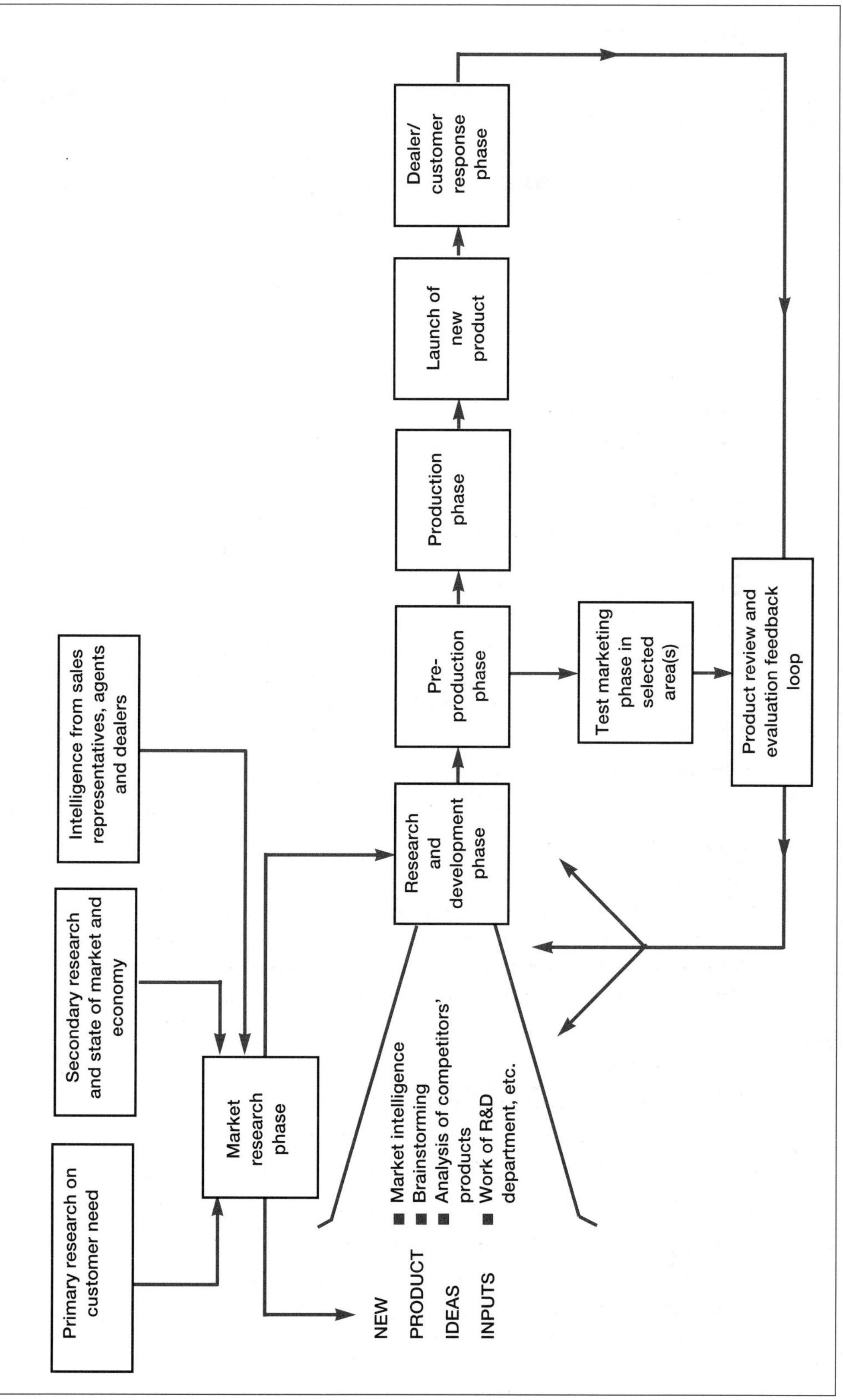
Primary research on customer need
Secondary research and state of market and economy
Intelligence from sales representatives, agents and dealers
Market research phase
Research and development phase
Pre-production phase
Production phase
Launch of new product
Dealer/customer response phase
Test marketing phase in selected area(s)
Product review and evaluation feedback loop
NEW PRODUCT IDEAS INPUTS
■ Market intelligence
■ Brainstorming
■ Analysis of competitors' products
■ Work of R&D department, etc.

PC 3.2.1 3.2.2

Primary research

This type of research tends to comprise:

- 'tailor-made' interview questions for in-depth, probing of attitudes and preferences
- 'one-off' questionnaires designed to survey specifically targeted groups of buyers and/or consumers
- carefully designed discussion topics and questions for use in group discussions with, say, a set of consumers in a common category who are test-marketing a new product
- briefing of sales personnel on what information to seek, say, about competing products, during their visits to existing and new dealers.

Such data is expensive to acquire but is essential in preparing a new product or service for a national or international market.

Secondary research

This type of research concerns the acquisition of potentially useful information from published, readily accessible sources such as:

- Government publications: HMSO Reports, Treasury Statements, briefings from the Department of Trade and Industry and British Overseas Trade Board, etc.
- Monthly, quarterly, annual reports and reviews published by organisations like: The Economist Intelligence Unit, The Market Research Society, The Financial Times Business Information Service, etc.
- On-line databases like: Datacards, Dataline, Data-ease, Exstat and Dialog
- Articles in relevant trade journals and magazines
- Cuttings from national and local newspapers
- Regular reports sold on subscription by specialist companies like: Mintel Information Services, Jordan's Business Reviews and Surveys and Phillips & Drew Monthly Forecasts.

A number of government departments – such as the Department of Trade and Industry – publish regular newspapers and bulletins (such as *British Business* and *Export Times*) sent free of charge to interested organisations to assist the process of market research. For example, during the run-up to the European Community's Single Market in 1992, the DTI was very active in regularly updating bulletins on EC directives and regulations for exporters.

PC 3.2.1 3.2.2

■ Methods of securing primary data

The following represent major ways of acquiring primary research data used in market researching.

Face-to-face surveys

A common sight nowadays is the researcher with clip-board and pen patrolling the High Street to secure direct responses (the survey questionnaire is clipped to the board) from shoppers and the proverbial man or woman in the street. Such local residents may be chosen at random, but it is more likely that the researcher has been given a particular brief to interview a specific type of consumer who is being targeted and who meets a profile involving his or her age, sex, apparent socio-economic group, occupation (e.g. housewife).

The questionnaire is likely to seek information about:

- what type of product (in a given range) is preferred and why
- what expectations the interviewees have of particular products
- the degree of satisfaction with a given product
- how the type of product might be improved, etc.

Usually the questionnaire has been designed to secure structured and valuable responses about a particular product whose identity is concealed within generalised questions. This is done in an effort to obtain impartial and unprejudiced responses.

Telephone surveys

Less expensive and time-consuming to conduct – if the respondent is a willing telephone conversationalist – is the telephone survey. Again, respondents are asked to provide answer questions which may be of the yes/no kind or the scalar variety; 'To what extent are you satisfied with . . . ?'

Such interviewees are likely to have been selected from listings which are sold to market research firms and which are compiled through individuals:

- living in particular residential areas
- having purchased a motor car of a set value
- having purchased a foreign holiday, etc.

A number of market research support organisations exist to provide national, regional and local information of this kind. One such, CACI Consultancy, with the assistance of the Official Census Database produces 'A Classification of Residential Neighbourhoods'. This database breaks down all UK residential areas into some 38 types, according to the socio-economic status, income, possessions etc. of the inhabitants. Such databases are used by researchers and sales organisations to target various kinds of consumer.

Exit profiles

Another source of primary data is for survey teams to stop customers upon exiting from a store and ask them to complete a short set of questions from a prompt card which lists the questions and range of available responses:

How often do you shop at the store?

Daily	Weekly	Fortnightly	Monthly	Occasionally
❑	❑	❑	❑	❑

How easy do you find it to park?

Very easy	Fairly easy	Easy	Fairly difficult	Very difficult
❑	❑	❑	❑	❑

Such on-the-spot responses are used to monitor (in the above example) shopping habits and acceptance levels of store facilities.

Postal surveys

Another way of securing information is by the use of mailed returns. Public inertia provides a very low response to unsolicited mail surveys (commonly 2–3 per cent). However, manufacturers and suppliers achieve higher responses in these ways:

- attaching a questionnaire to a warranty card which has to be returned to the manufacturer
- making the completion of a questionnaire a condition of continuing to receive a free copy of an informational magazine
- offering a reward in return for the completion of the questionnaire – perhaps an additional monthly copy of a magazine being bought on subscription.

PC
3.2.1
3.2.2

KEY TERMS IN MARKET RESEARCH SAMPLING

The undertaking of surveys through the completion of questionnaires and other forms of information gathering is governed by a series of statistical rules and procedures which have to be scrupulously followed if a survey may be relied upon to give accurate information. The following is an introductory checklist to some of the major terms and concepts which are used in statistical analysis:

Sample: a representative proportion of a whole.

Population: the name given to the whole, from which the sample is taken.

Random sample: one taken by selecting units/people from within the total population in an unstructured and fortuitous manner; a refinement of this process is multi-stage sampling, where a second random sample is taken of an initial larger series of random samples.

Bias: the introduction into the sampling process of data which affects the overall outcome so that it is no longer truly representative.

Sampling error: even when large samples (l,000-plus) are taken from large populations, it is possible that a degree of statistical error creeps into the resultant analyses; for this reason many samples are described as correct to + or – 3 per cent (or whatever the calculated margin of error is).

Survey: a structured enquiry into a chosen area of interest which displays common features and characteristics.

Percentile: a one hundredth part – e.g. the forty-first percentile would be 41/100.

Quartile: the divisor which divides 100 by 4 – e.g. the top quartile would be 75–100 per cent.

Index: An index is an average taken of a series of individual numbers over a period of time; indices are used to show the general movement – up or down in, for example, a basket of typical food items or pay rates over set periods of time.

Averages: a number of different types of average statistical analysis:

a ARITHMETIC or MEAN: this average is calculated by dividing a whole by its component parts – if five batsmen score 85 runs, then their arithmetic/means average is 85 ÷ 5 = 17.

b MEDIAN: the median average is the middle point in a series; for example, if there are eleven items in a series or scale, then the sixth number or item would be in the median position, with the same number of items above it as beneath it – X X X X X <u>X</u> X X X X X

c MODE: this type of average identifies a number or item which occurs most frequently in collected data; for example, if in a population of randomly selected people most were aged 38, then this would be the mode average of the population.

PC
3.2.2

CHECKLIST OF TYPES OF QUESTION USED IN SURVEYS

Market researchers employ different types of question in order to secure data. While the questions vary in the responses they seek to elicit, almost all share a common feature – they are all capable of being collated into percentage groups of the total sample being surveyed:

1 The closed question

This question is designed to obtain a single response from two alternatives

Example:	Are you a smoker?	YES ❑	NO ❑
	Can you drive a motor car?	YES ❑	NO ❑

2 The open question

This type of question is reserved for acquiring personalised responses to questions for which no simple response is appropriate. Since the responses of each member of the sample will vary, open questions are not designed for percentage analysis:

Example: How are you affected by the design and colour combination of this particular fabric?

3 The prioritising question

This question is used to ascertain relative preferences in ranking order and can be numerically analysed:

Example: Place the following features of the proposed optional extras in order of importance to you: where 1 is most important and 7 least important:

central locking system	❑
quadraphonic loudspeakers	❑
adjustable steering wheel	❑
detachable car-radio	❑
self-locking wheel nuts	❑
alloy wheel-trims	❑
metallic finish	❑

4 The scaled question

This is a semi-closed question as respondents are required to select an answer from a given scale which is expressed as a set of intervals along a continuum.

Example: Indicate how easy you found it to use the operating manual which you received with your personal computer:

Extremely easy	Fairly easy	Neither easy nor difficult	Fairly difficult	Very difficult
❑	❑	❑	❑	❑

PC
3.2.1
3.2.2

EXAMPLES OF IMPORTANT SOURCES OF SECONDARY MARKETING RESEARCH DATA

From HMSO:

Annual Abstract of Statistics
Economic Trends
Family Expenditure Survey
Financial Statistics
National Income & Expenditure (Blue Book)
Central Statistical Office Reports, e.g. Social Trends 1992
Overseas Trade Statistics of the UK
Guide to Official Statistics

From Government Departments:

British Business DTI
Commission of the European Communities: *Europe on the Move.*
Department of Employment: *Euro Action*

From Market Research Specialists:

The Market Research Society
Directory of Information Sources in the UK
Dun & Bradstreet: *Key British Enterprises*
Kompass: *UK and EC Company Information, Products and Services*
Extel: *Handbook of Market Leaders*
Eurostat: *Statistical Yearbook*
British Statistical Office Newport Gwent
Euromonitor Ltd: *The A–Z of UK Brand Leaders*
The A–Z of UK Marketing Data

From Organisations Publishing Frequent Reports and Updatings:

Jordan's Business Reviews and Surveys
Phillips & Drew Monthly Economic Forecasts
Economic Intelligence Unit – Quarterly Reviews
OECD: Regular Reports
Financial Times Business Information Service
Mintel Information Services

From Online Databases:

ICC Database – Dialog
ICC Eurocompany Information Service
Extat
Datastream
Dataline
Datacards

PC
3.2.1
3.2.2

Qualitative market research

The term qualitative market research has been coined to describe that type of research activity which seeks to establish users' and potential users' responses in ways which are not then simply collated into sets of statistics such as: 81.6% of the 2000 respondents were either *very satisfied* or *satisfied* with the sales service received.

Contrastingly, qualitative market research is concerned with customers':

- **perceptions:** say of the colour and texture of a product's packaging
- **current tastes and lifestyles:** say in the context of how they spend their leisure time and where, which could influence how a given product is advertised

- **outlook on life:** which could include views on current political and social trends, attitudes to particular showbiz personalities – who could be on a 'possibles' list for sponsoring a product, views on the use of children or eroticism in advertising and so on – all of which influence the ways in which advertising agencies and marketing personnel adapt their marketing communications, so as to influence but not offend
- **likes and dislikes:** people's tastes change markedly over time and market researchers are continually seeking to keep track of the changes in consumers' tastes, likes and dislikes; for instance, real fur is absolutely 'out' as a fashion fabric in many western countries, while organically grown vegetables are very much 'in' among certain socio-economic consumer groups
- **use of disposable income:** market researchers are also most interested in how people occupying the various tiers of society spend their money on 'wants' as opposed to 'needs', since such information is crucial to businesses in the tourism, leisure, catering and sports industries etc.

Qualitative market research tends to be undertaken via in-depth interviews, regular meetings of focus groups, regular response monitoring of randomly selected users – such as those who agree to watch certain tv programmes and supply their responses etc.

Focus groups and consumer panels

Customer attitudes and responses to products and services on offer have become increasingly important to their sellers as a result of increasing discrimination among consumers and the sophisticated mix of advertising to which they are nowadays exposed.

Market researchers have therefore devised carefully managed group discussions which examine in depth a range of attitudes to, say, a product's design, packaging, major features and cost, etc. Usually the consumers brought together share a common background and profile – they are representative of the targeted market segment at which the product is aimed.

The conduct of such a focus group meeting may, for example, involve the sample of consumers examining three or four different types of package design for, say, a blend of Kenyan coffee and putting them into a preferred ranking, while supplying reasons for their decision.

Such responses – considered in depth and arising from the group's consensus is likely to influence the eventually selected packaging design, especially if the group's choice is replicated by other groups in other regions.

Quantitative market research

PC
3.2.1
3.2.2

By contrast, quantitative market research works by obtaining data which is capable of numerical analysis – percentages, ratios, volumes, totals, moving totals, graphically measured rises and falls etc. Such research arrives at irrefutable statements such as:

'Red Triangle cement achieved a 23.4% UK market share in 199-.'

'Total sales of lager beer in the European Union for the period January–March 199- was 290.24 million ECU.'

Quantitative research tends to provide answers to questions beginning:

- How many?
- How much?
- How frequently?
- What proportion?
- To what extent?
- What percentage?
- In what ratio?
- For how long? etc.

Quantitative research presents the answers to such investigative questions in the form of:

- **tables:** of sets of figures, which very often group data over time – say each of four quarters or twelve months of a year, or in groups such as the individual components of a product range; but note that, while tables are good at storing detailed sets of figures, they are not very easily or quickly digested in presentation terms
- **graphs:** which are usually plotted on vertical and horizontal axes and often show performance of volume or amount against time
- **bar charts:** which present graph-type data in pillars or columns and use 3-D effects for visual appeal
- **pie-charts:** which displays 'slices of the pie' – proportions of a known total within a circle or pie

Note: A detailed examination of the main types of quantitative data presentation is given on pages 267–70.

PC 3.2.1 3.2.2

■ Graphs and charts chiefly used to present statistical analysis

Pie chart

A known quantity is broken down into a set of component parts and displayed as segments of a circle – hence the image of 'slices of a pie' (Fig 3.7).

Fig 3.7 **Pie chart**

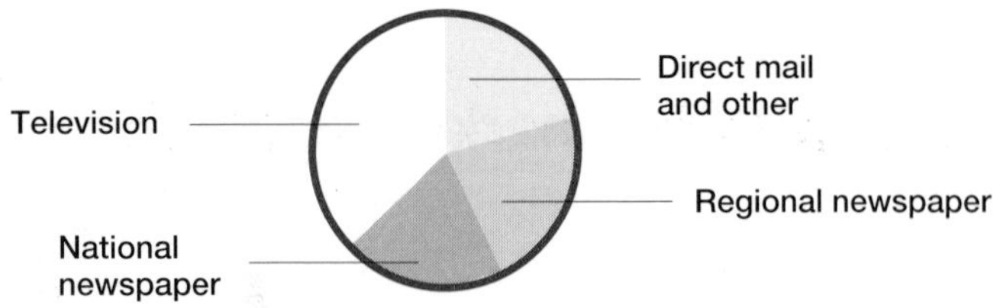

Television
Direct mail and other
Regional newspaper
National newspaper

Media advertising

Line graph

Collected data is plotted against a vertical and lateral axis; variables such as quantity are plotted vertically and invariables such as time laterally (Fig 3.8).

Fig 3.8

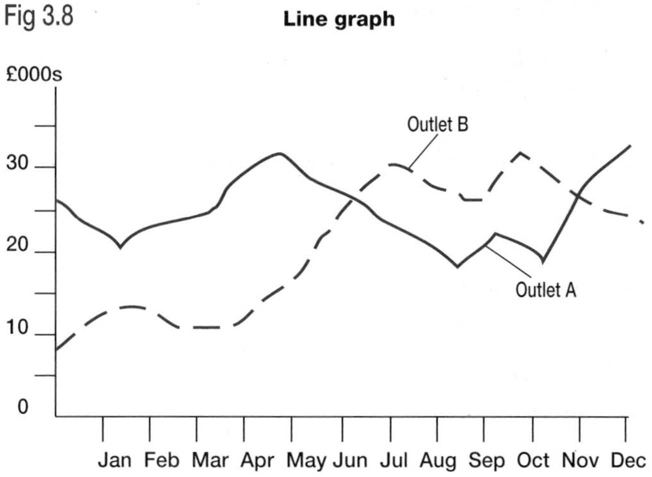

Bar chart

Bar charts are plotted in the same way as line graphs, except that amounts are shown as columns of varying height (but of an equal width) (Fig 3.9).

Fig 3.9

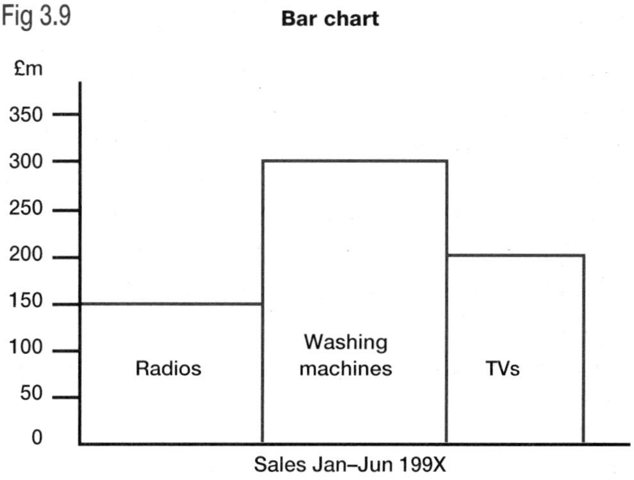

Stacked bar chart

Designed the same way as bar charts, the stacked version embodies two or more different items in its column height – quantities are 'stacked up' and displayed in contrasting colours or patterns (Fig 3.10).

Fig 3.10

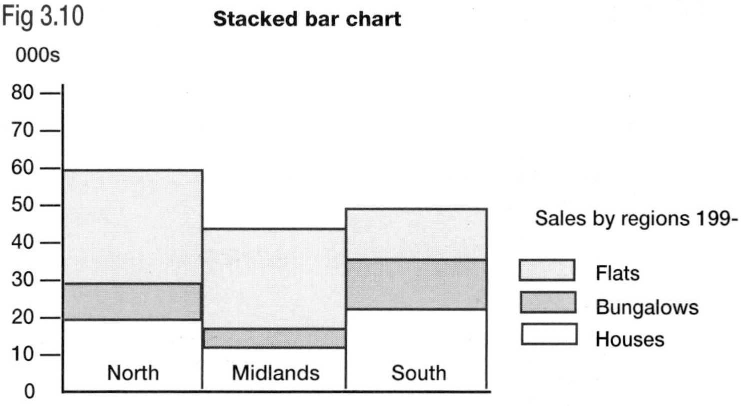

Three-dimensional bar chart

This chart is also a bar chart, may also be stacked, and is drawn to show three dimensions as a means of providing visual appeal (Fig 3.11).

Fig 3.11 **Three-dimensional chart**

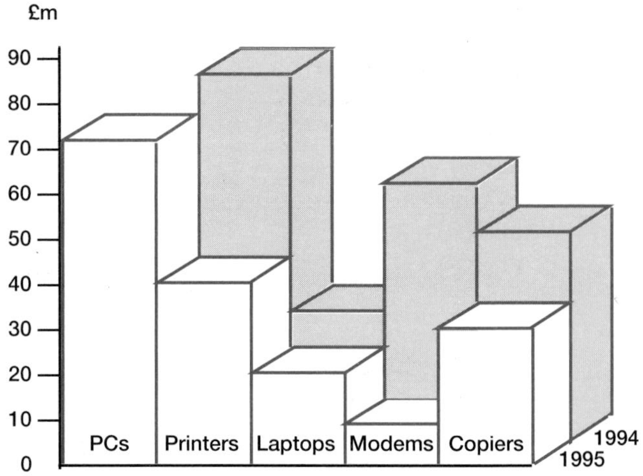

Frequency curves, frequency polygons and histograms

These three diagrams represent different ways of showing how data is distributed across a known range of intervals – say ages from 1–100.

The histogram is a set of bars of varying height, where the level of each bar shows the proportion of the total for the part of the range in which the bar is placed (Fig 3.12).

Fig 3.12 **Histogram**

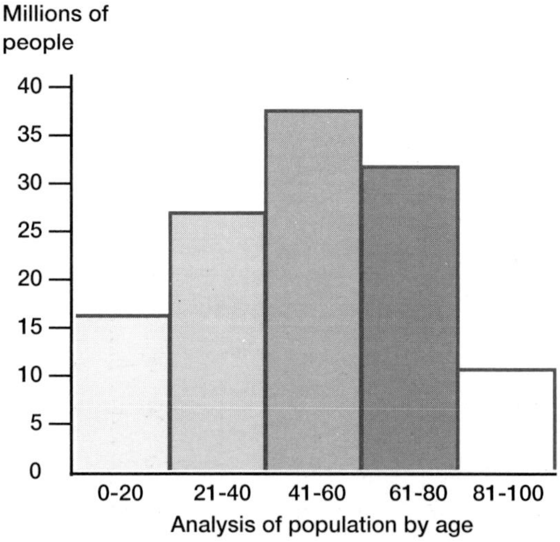

The frequency polygon is arrived at by connecting the points (as for a graph) which lie in the middle of the top of each bar (Fig 3.13).

Fig 3.13

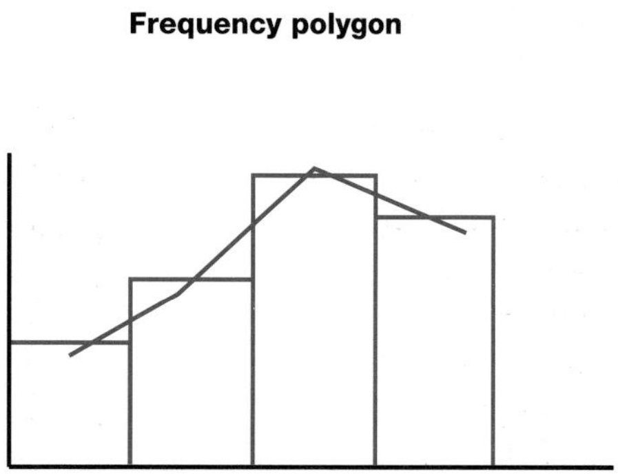

The distribution curve is very much like that of the polygon, except that it has a smoother appearance because of an increased amount of data plotted as a means of defining its shape (Fig 3.14).

Fig 3.14

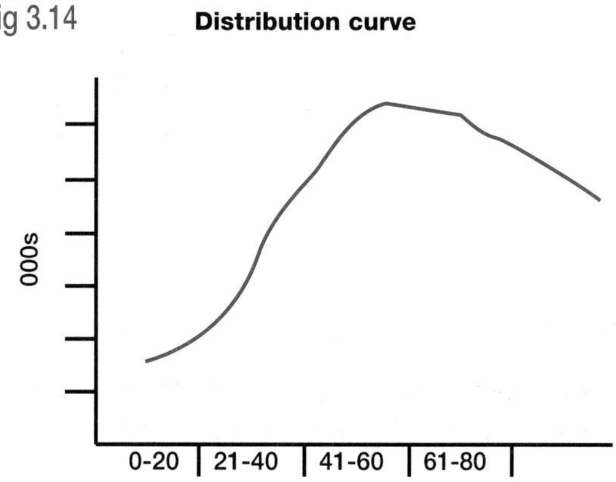

Scatter diagram

A scatter diagram is drawn along two axes, where a set of data is plotted in order to ascertain the nature of the relationship between two known variables; for example, a scatter diagram could be used to demonstrate the effect of unemployment upon the purchase of foreign holidays or the sale of ice-cream during the interval in a cinema as the heating is turned up! (Fig 3.15).

Fig 3.15

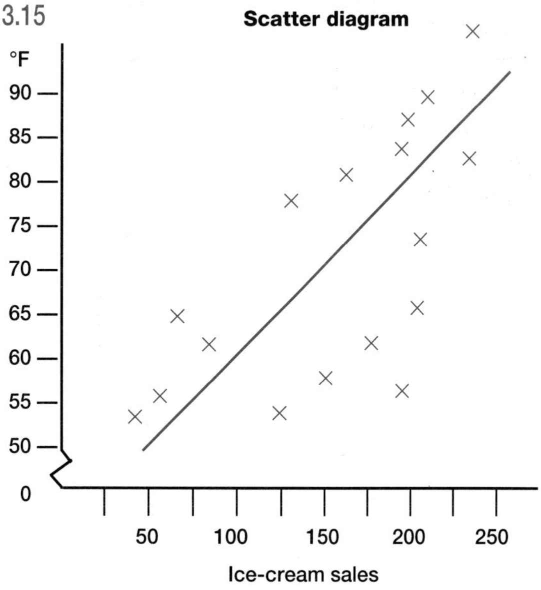

Z chart

The Z chart (Fig 3.16) is used to plot data over a moving period, say, the calendar year, as one year moves on from its predecessor; the chart shows three sets of data:

- current data – plotted week by week or month by month
- a moving total – say, January 1994 – January 1995 which becomes February 1994–February 1995 as time moves on in the 1995 calendar year
- a cumulative total – as the year progresses, each month's total is added to those preceding it

Fig 3.16 **Z chart**

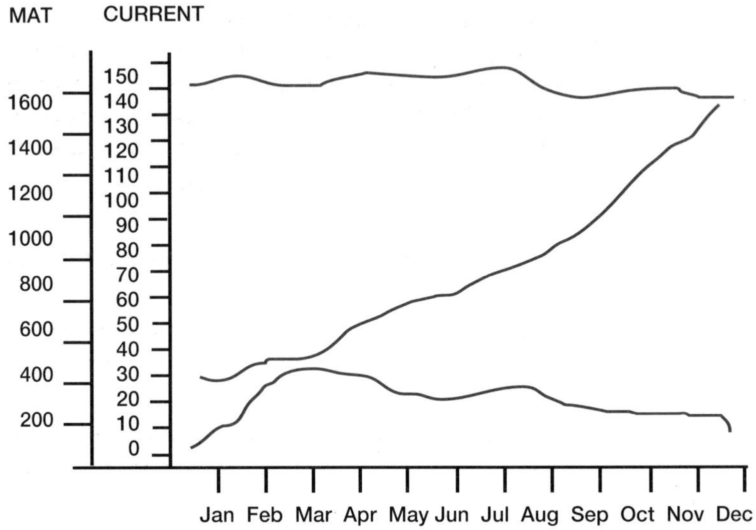

Pictograph

This chart depicts amounts in the form of appropriate icons or images of relative size in order to make the chart more visually appealing (Fig 3.17).

Fig 3.17 **Pictograph**

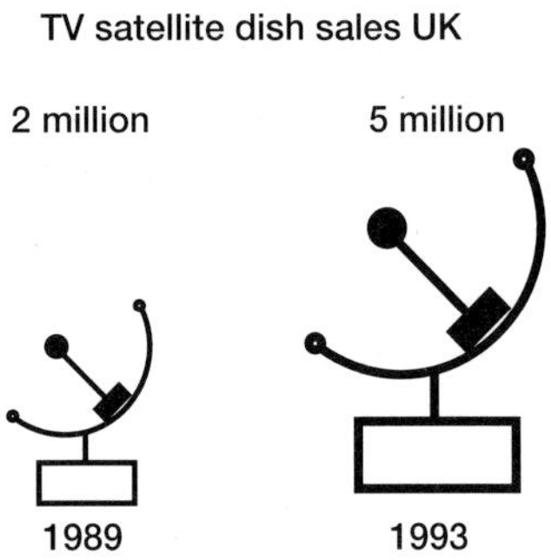

PC 3.2.2

KEY FEATURES OF GOOD QUESTIONNAIRE DESIGN

The characteristics of a good questionnaire.
The list of desirable qualities that a questionnaire should possess, given below, would seem to be a matter of common sense. Nevertheless, the drafting of questionnaires is one of the most difficult tasks of an inquiry. A pilot survey – that is, a trial survey, carried out prior to the actual survey – invariably leads to alterations and improvements in the questionnaires.

1. *Questions should not be ambiguous.* This means that the question must be capable of only one interpretation.
2. *Questions must be easily understood.* Technical terms should be avoided, except where the questionnaire is addressed to specialists.
3. *Questions should be capable of having a precise answer.* The answer should take the form of 'yes' or 'no', a number, a measurement, a quantity, a date, a place; facts are required, not opinions (except where opinions are wanted, as in opinion polls).
4. *Questions must not contain words of vague meaning.* To ask if something is large or if a man is unskilled are examples of such questions. When does something become large? What jobs are unskilled?
5. *Questions should not require calculations to be made.* Such questions give rise to unnecessary sources of error. If for the purpose of the inquiry it is necessary to know annual earnings, but the respondent is paid weekly, the weekly earnings are asked for. The calculations necessary are done by the statistician's staff.
6. *Questions should not require the respondent to decide upon classification.*
7. *Questions must not be in such a form that the answers will be biased.* The questions will not therefore contain emotionally coloured words, they will not be leading questions – that is, they will not put answers into the respondents' mouths – and, of course, they must not give offence.
8. *The questionnaire should not be too long.* If a questionnaire is too long, the respondent will not be co-operative, and this may mean inaccurate answers; often a way out is for some of the respondents to answer part of the questions and other respondents to answer other questions.
9. *The questionnaire should cover the exact object of the inquiry.* However, provided the questionnaire is not made too long, advantage can be taken of the arrangements made to obtain information on another subject of interest.

From: *Wheldon's Business Statistics* 8th edition by G.L. Thirlkettle.
Reproduced by kind permission of Macdonald and Evans.

PC
3.2.1
3.2.2

SUMMARY OF MARKET RESEARCH METHODS COMMONLY EMPLOYED

Primary Research

- surveys via questionnaires: directly proffered, posted or distributed to 'captive customers'
- exit profiles using question checklists for prompt computer data inputting
- questionnaires as part of guarantee registration returns
- telephone interview surveys
- face-to-face interviews
- focus group meetings, discussions and responses
- product testing: responses after having used a new product being test-marketed

Secondary Research

- analysis of government, industry or consumer group (e.g. *Which?*) published statistics
- scrutiny of specialist articles and features in trade magazines (e.g. *Marketing Weekly*)
- subscription to on-line specialist informational databases (e.g. *Extat*)
- use of reference texts, directories and yearbooks (e.g. *UK and Euro Kompass*)
- maintenance of a newspaper clippings library (e.g. special supplements or regular features published by, say, *The Times*, *The European*, *The Financial Times* newspapers)
- collecting sales information brochures, price-lists and catalogues etc. for competing products or services

PC
3.2.2
3.2.3

HOW MARKET RESEARCHED INFORMATION AFFECTS BUSINESS OPERATIONS AND DECISION-MAKING

The following checklist indicates some of the main ways in which the information gained from market research activities is used to give direction to or to change the range of activities a business undertakes:

- **research and development** — feedback from what customers want and how their tastes are changing etc. will prompt new product development and the modification of existing products where improvements can be introduced
- **production** — information about market trends – say into or out of recession will directly influence levels of production, emphasis on runs for specific products, ceasing production or installing additional production lines etc.
- **advertising and sales, promotion** — feedback on the effectiveness of advertising campaigns, types of packaging and merchandising, informational literature etc. will prompt either the retention of specific promotional material, or a fresh communications strategy

- **pricing and positioning** — responses about the degree of market penetration, sales volume and product acceptance etc. will influence decisions about modifying sales prices, changing target customers and re-targeting of advertising etc.
- **points of sale** — feedback from users and purchasers will also influence a company's distribution and sales location policies – perhaps to switching from direct-mail to agents and factors, or to vending-machines from small traders etc.
- **packaging** — information about product acceptance and use may influence the way in which a good is packaged – say where feedback reveals irritation with the difficulty in removing shrink-wrapped plastic covers, or dissatisfaction with the quantity of items in a pre-packed set, such as economy packs of beer or of baked beans
- **design and specification** — user feedback (often from customer services) will sometimes reveal unsuspected shortcomings in the design and build of a product or a set of specifications which are either less or more than the customer requires

Thus the essential role of market research is to ensure that product development, production, promotion and sales do not occur in a vacuum, but are constantly being modified and fine-tuned in response to what the market wants and expects to get.

REVIEW TEST

PC 3.2.1 3.2.2 3.2.3

1 Explain briefly the difference between primary and secondary sources of information in the context of market research.

2 List three different methods for obtaining primary source market research information.

3 List three sources of information in the secondary source sector commonly used in market research.

4 Explain simply how market research supports product development.

5 What is an exit profile? What is it used for?

6 What are the main advantages of a telephone survey compared with a postal survey?

7 Explain briefly what is meant by the following terms:

a a statistically significant sample

b a random sample

c bias in sampling

d a percentile

e a quartile

8 Explain the difference between a median and a mode type of average.

9 What is the difference between a closed and an open question in a questionnaire?

10 Name three statistical publications regularly published by HMSO which are used in market research.

11 Explain the difference between qualitative and quantitative market research.

12 What is a focus group? For what purpose is it brought together?

13 List three features of effective questionnaire design.

14 List four primary and four secondary sources which provide market research information.

15 Explain briefly three ways in which acquired market research information aids business decision-making in a marketing context.

PC
3.2.1
3.2.2
3.2.3

GROUP ACTIVITIES

Market research

1 Design a questionnaire which identifies among a representative group of students in your college or school the reasons which made them choose it for their course of study.

Also use the questionnaire to discover how they rated the advertising material used to promote the course, the application and interview process and their induction on to the course.

First trial your questionnaire and, having surveyed an appropriate student sample, present your findings suitably to your class.

2 Choose **one** item from each of the five categories on page 264 – Examples of Important Sources of Secondary Market Research Data – and produce half an A4 page summarising the way in which it assists the market research function.

Arrange this activity so that each class member receives a copy of the full set of summaries each group produces.

3 Make arrangements to visit one of the largest commercial companies in your locality and interview its marketing staff in order to find out what kind of information it seeks in its market research activities and how it uses it.

4 Choose **one of the items** listed below, carry out your research on it and report back to your group orally on what you discovered:

1 JICNARS, 2 ITCA, 3 BARB, 4 BOTB, 5 OECD.

5 Find out what sources of information are available locally to assist a small retail business owner in researching his or her market in your locality – in one of the following businesses:

1 newsagent, 2 antique shop, 3 carpet shop,

4 bed and breakfast guest-house, 5 sports shop

Having carried out your research, produce a briefing sheet which could be supplied to your local Chamber of Commerce for issuing to its members.

KNOWLEDGE TEST

Element 3.2
Propose and present product developments based on analysis of marketing research information

1 (i) Primary research aims to obtain data from original sources.
(ii) Secondary research aims to obtain data from published sources.

Which of the following options best describes the above statements?

A	(i)	T	(ii)	T
B	(i)	T	(ii)	F
C	(i)	F	(ii)	T
D	(i)	F	(ii)	F

2 Which of the following statements is true, and which false?

A New product ideas sometimes come from market intelligence.
B Customer surveys are sometimes included on guarantee registration cards.
C A mode averaging system is frequently employed in fashion industry market research.
D A margin of error in market research sampling is the space used by researchers in which to note down wrong answers given by interviewees.

3 (i) A prioritising question in a survey is the one which is placed first in the list.
(ii) A scaled question in a survey is a semi-closed question.

Which of the following options best describes the above statements?

A	(i)	T	(ii)	T
B	(i)	T	(ii)	F
C	(i)	F	(ii)	T
D	(i)	F	(ii)	F

4 If a market researcher were conducting a qualitative research study, he or she would be:

A seeking to assess the quality of a given product as perceived by a consumer
B building up a database of numerical statistics about a product
C obtaining consumers' views, preferences and tastes in the context of a given product
D assessing consumers' views of a business's quality assurance system

5 (i) A bar chart can display the same data as a graph.
(ii) A histogram is used to display historical marketing data.

Which of the following options best describes the above statements?

A	(i)	T	(ii)	T
B	(i)	T	(ii)	F
C	(i)	F	(ii)	T
D	(i)	F	(ii)	F

6 Which of the following statements is true, and which false?

A A Z-chart is used to plot data over a moving period.
B A distribution curve is a sort of smoothed out frequency polygon.

Which of the following options best describes the above statements?

A	(i)	T	(ii)	T
B	(i)	T	(ii)	F
C	(i)	F	(ii)	T
D	(i)	F	(ii)	F

PC
3.2.1
3.2.2
3.2.3
3.2.4

PORTFOLIO OF EVIDENCE ACTIVITY

Element 3.2
Propose and present product developments based on analysis of marketing research information

UP FOR PROMOTION AT MILLENNIUM ENTERPRISES PLC

Scenario

You work in the marketing department of *Millennium Enterprises plc*. The marketing department forms one of the holding company's head office specialist departments with a responsibility for product development across all *Millennium*'s fifteen wholly-owned subsidiaries - which span a supermarket chain, sports shop chain, fast-food restaurant network, footwear, fashion-wear and carpet factories, as well as chains of travel agencies, leisure centres and music centres.

Having worked extremely hard and well for the past several years, you are currently in line for promotion to the post of Group Assistant Marketing Manager – one of some dozen equivalent posts which are regarded as stepping stones to a senior marketing post in *Millennium*.

In order to assist the selection process, your Group Chairman, Ros Dervila, has decided that all applicants should prepare and then deliver an oral presentation which presents proposals for the development of **two products** – each of which could be marketed by one of *Millenium*'s subsidiary companies.

Your brief instructs you to select two products for which marketing research information is readily available. The products must relate to two different markets and your presentation on each product should focus on: how its specification and design might be changed if your proposal is to re-launch an existing product, what key features it would possess, how it would be promoted, how packaged, where and how sold, what pricing policy it would embody, and what type of marketing communications would support it.

Your presentation should also include data drawn from market sector statistics relevant to that occupied by your two selected products.

An important part of your oral presentation is the production of a suitable set of notes which will act as a briefing hand-out for the panel of assessors to whom you will present. This hand-out must include an example of one quantitative and one qualitative research method which would be suitable for collecting data relevant to the two products of your presentation.

Task 1

Consider first how you will tackle the tasks in the above Scenario and then complete appropriately your activity planning and review log.

Task 2

Select two suitable products for your oral presentation, bearing in mind the importance of being able to obtain suitable marketing research information directly. Then, decide upon an appropriate structure for your presentation, which should be between 7–12 minutes long. You should also consider what audio-visual aids you could employ to communicate your proposals promptly and with visual appeal.

Task 3

Having finalised preparations for your oral presentation, compose a suitable hand-out explaining the two research methods referred to in the Scenario. This should not exceed 2 sides of A4. Make sure that your hand-out is well structured and formatted suitably. Note that you are not expected to undertake your own marketing research for this activity.

Performance criteria covered

3.2.1, 3.2.2, 3.2.3, 3.2.4

Core skills covered

Communication:
3.1.1, 3.1.2, 3.1.3, 3.1.4, 3.1.5, 3.2.1, 3.2.2, 3.2.3, 3.2.4, 3.2.5, 3.3.1, 3.3.2, 3.3.3, 3.4.1, 3.4.2, 3.4.3, 3.4.4

Information Technology:
3.1.1, 3.1.2, 3.1.3, 3.1.4, 3.1.5, 3.2.1, 3.2.2, 3.2.3, 3.2.4, 3.2.5, 3.2.6, 3.2.7, 3.3.1, 3.3.2, 3.3.3, 3.3.4, 3.3.5, 3.3.6

Application of Number:
Performance Criteria from 3.1, 3.2 and 3.3 deriving from the obtaining, analysis and presentation of statistical information.

Element 3.3
MARKETING COMMUNICATIONS AND TARGET AUDIENCES

PC 3.3.1

The rise of consumerism

What changed the manufacturing-led marketing approach radically in the course of the twentieth century was the reliance of mass production upon the rapidly expanding mass-media communications industry. In order to take advantage of economies of scale – long production runs reduce costs, large volume sales recoup research and development charges – the makers of consumer products needed to build and sustain high volume markets. Thus they came to rely upon the blanket coverage and persuasive skills of mass-media advertising delivered through the press, radio, cinema and then television.

In this way a market-place dominated in the nineteenth century by production-led marketing evolved (for consumer goods and services) into a customer-led counterpart.

The following table illustrates how this worked, through a mix of economic, social and cultural change, hastened by the technological breakthroughs engendered by two World Wars.

THE RISE OF THE CONSUMER-LED MARKET, 1900s–1990s

1900–10	An era ends with the death of Queen Victoria in 1901; Britain begins to lose its supremacy as an industrial, exporting nation; the rising power of the working class is acknowledged in the founding of the Labour Representation Committee in 1900; the Board of Education is set up to run all state schools – education is provided between the age of five and fourteen.
1911–20	The First World War (1914–18) causes radical social changes: the gap narrows between rich and poor; women work as factory operatives to aid the war effort; war technology brings advances in the internal combustion engine, paving the way for faster distribution of goods with reliable lorries; the aircraft industry is born; rapid growth in retail sales outlets; rise of popular newspapers between 1900 and 1920.

1921–30	International slump forces manufacturers to find ways of making and distributing goods more cheaply; rise of cinema and 'talkies'; stars endorse ranges of products.
1931–40	Rapid development of mass media communications: 'tabloid' newspapers, photographic magazines, cinema, radio and television broadcasting; education advances improve literacy and discernment; rapid growth of advertising based on branded goods – Ovaltine, Brasso, Hoover etc; road and rail transport communications improve; long-haul airlines develop, e.g. Imperial Airways; Hitler introduces the Volkswagen, 'the people's car'; outbreak of Second World War (1939–45).
1941–50	The Second World War provides a massive boost to manufacturing design and telecommunications; war effort propaganda and public information services develop mass-media visual advertising techniques; arrival of American forces in Europe enlarges perceptions of a consumer culture across the Atlantic.
1951–60	Six years of wartime deprivation fuels an insatiable demand for consumer goods as economies are rebuilt across Europe. The UK absorbs US consumer culture, as national broadcasting develops mass audiences; Radio Luxembourg advertises and commercial radio is born in Europe.
1961–70	The 1960s mark an era of boom and full employment; commercial television develops as a highly effective medium of advertising and of influencing public taste and opinion; Ralph Nader in USA becomes the conscience of the consumer and leads a crusade for better consumer-supporting sales legislation; the concept of consumerism arrives in Europe; the rise in owner-occupied houses promotes marketing of domestic consumer goods.
1971–80	In the 1970s and 80s extensive reforms take place in consumer legislation in UK – in areas of advertising, sales ticketing, credit sales, guarantees etc; the introduction of credit cards (nicknamed 'plastic money') encourages spending sprees and a sharp increase in mailshots to people's homes, urging 'buy now – pay later'; Asian-built electronic consumer durables flood into the UK and undercut European counterparts.
1981–90	As a result of a stop-go economy alternating boom and recession between 1960 and 1993, the UK consumer market becomes highly segmented with a wide variation in spending power; goods are therefore marketed across extensive product ranges, with optional extras and add-ons; foreign competition secures large slices of UK markets, with consumer durables built to higher specifications and quality standards.
Present day	Most consumer purchasing takes place through national chain stores and out-of-town malls and hypermarkets; TV, radio and newspaper advertising increase their influence; user groups are set up to protect the interests of buyers and consumers as business enterprises merge into ever more conglomerates; a backlash starts against plastic, mass-produced goods in favour of hand-crafted alternatives; ecological 'green' lobby forces manufacturers to rethink their use of raw materials and production techniques; public opinion moves from the throw-away to the recycling society.

PC 3.3.1

MILESTONES IN TWENTIETH-CENTURY MARKETING

1900	First mass-produced Kodak camera.
1901	First British gramophone record.
1903	Birth of the *Daily Mirror.*
1905	Pathé France develops colour moving pictures.
1907	First newspaper picture transmitted by wire.
1908	Henry Ford markets first Model T Ford.
1919	RCA-Radio Corporation of America launched.
	Alcock and Brown fly the Atlantic.
1920	Magnetic tape recording developed.
	First commercial radio station KDKA broadcasts from Pittsburgh.
1924	First photographs transmitted from UK to USA.
1927	Movietone News founded – first newsreel made by Fox Films.
	USA manufactures 3.5 million motor cars.
1928	Television transmissions start development in UK and USA.
1929	First colour TV experimental transmissions.
	Germans develop magnetic tape recording.
	Motorola market first car radios in USA.
	29 million phones installed in USA.
	Pre-prepared baby foods launched.
1930	PVC discovered in USA – age of plastic dawns.
	Sliced bread launched in USA.
	First electric kettle.
1931	First UK teleprinter (telex) exchange opens in London.
	Alka Seltzer comes to the aid of the hung over.
1932	First automatic dishwasher marketed.
1934	First launderette opens in Texas.
1935	IBM successfully market their electric typewriter.
1937	Chester Carlson introduces the first Xerox photocopier.
1938	Non-stick Teflon developed by Dupont.
1938	27 per cent of British homes have a vacuum-cleaner, 3 per cent a washing machine, 18 per cent an electric cooker and 3 per cent a refrigerator.
	Nescafé first marketed by the Swiss.
	First Volkswagen sold – 'the people's car' – in Germany.
1939	ICI develop polythene – for a myriad of applications.
	Birdseye pre-cooked frozen foods launched.
1941	Aerosol sprays developed.
1945/6	BBC introduce Home, Light and Third Programmes.
1946	Bikini swimsuit launched.
	First car phones in USA.
1947	Alec Issigonis designs Morris Minor – forerunner of the Mini.
	First large supermarket opens in North London.
1953	IBM develop commercial computer market.
1955	Independent television first broadcasts in UK.
	Wimpy Bars introduce the hamburger to the English.
	Sony markets its portable transistor 'tranny' radio.
1958	BBC pilots stereo broadcasting.
1961	Pentel introduce the felt-tip pen.
	IBM launch their golfball typewriter.

1963	Polaroid film and cameras marketed. Word processing developed by IBM. Microfilm archiving technology marketed.
1966	Fibre optic technology developed.
1967	Americans experiment with laser beams. BBC launch colour television service.
1970	Early version of video disk developed in West Berlin.
1971	Intel Corporation USA market first microchip.
1975	BIC introduce first disposable razor.
1976	IBM market ink-jet printers.
1981	Post Office records 711 million private and 336 million business items of direct mail posted in UK.
1982	34 national daily and Sunday newspapers published regularly in UK. Channel Four independent television broadcasts.
1984	Breakfast TV is launched in UK.
1985	Miniaturised hi-fi 'stacks' become popular.
1988	Mobile, cellular phones become an essential 'yuppie' accessory.
1990	CDs oust plastic LPs in recorded entertainment market.
1991	Interactive TV or a mix of video, film, slide, sound and computing arrives.
1992	Nicam stereo enhances television sound reception.
1994	QVC home shopping TV channel starts broadcasting.
1995	Advertising on Internet, the information 'super-highway'.

Reproduced from data kindly provided by Marshall Editions Ltd: 'The Time-table of Technology' © 1982

PC 3.3.1

DISCUSSION TOPICS

1 In what ways did the social changes brought about by two World Wars influence the evolution of twentieth-century markets?

2 How did the development of first the popular press, and then radio and television broadcasting affect consumers' buying habits?

3 In terms of the twentieth century, the development of the consumer market could be described as the consumer's search for individuality. Yet at the same time, mass production provided millions of identical products for consumers to buy. Can these two opposites be readily reconciled ?

4 Is the most serious charge to be levelled against marketing experts this century the fact that they have actively encouraged the 'use-it-once-and-throw-it-away' mentality in society?

5 If this is the case, how do you expect marketing to change in the next ten to twenty years ?

6 To what extent and in what ways do government policies and activities affect industrial marketing strategies?

7 What promotional ploys are open to an industrial organisation whose sales in its home market are being attacked by undercutting foreign competition?

8 Since the Second World War, the UK economy has been subject to recurring cycles of growth and recession, variously called 'boom-bust' and 'stop-go' cycles. To what extent can a manufacturing company minimise the adverse effects of the 'stop' phase of the cycle, as the economy slides into a recession? Or is its marketing strategy of no use in such circumstances?

9 A great deal of effort in consumer marketing is put into understanding the buying habits and patterns of the UK shopper. Do you consider such aspects as 'understanding the psychology of the customer' and 'creating a positive buying mood in the new shopping malls' as worth investing time and effort in, or do you consider that a product that is well designed and made will sell itself? To what extent are consumers manipulated into buying products or services by 'artful' businesses?

10 How important in a consumer marketing strategy is public opinion? Consider the impact of public opinion upon stemming the manufacture of CFCs in aerosol sprays, the recycling of packaging materials by supermarkets and bodycare multiples, and the sale of unleaded petrol by filling-station chains.

11 We live in a world of rapidly increasing population and decreasing natural resources. How do you think these two trends will affect the marketing of consumer products over the next decade?

12 What are the likely outcomes for a UK company manufacturing domestic heating systems (which employ extensive copper piping) if the world supply of mined copper falls significantly? What options would be open to the company's board of directors?

13 A recession in one sector of the economy has a domino effect upon the next. What can a shopping mall carpet retailer do when faced by a sharp downturn in demand for the carpeting of newly-built but unsold houses in his locality?

14 Supposing a major car-making firm has a breakthrough in engine design and is ready to market a battery-powered saloon car which will do 0–60 mph in 10 seconds, has a range of 300 miles and thus needs recharging on average once weekly.

As the firm's marketing executives, how would you maximise the profit potential of such a motoring innovation?

15 How would you go about marketing a newly developed nitrates-based fertiliser for cereal crops which was environmentally 'green', with no adverse side-effects in the water-table?

Bear in mind that most agricultural fertilisers are sold through distributor dealers in farming areas.

16 Assume that you and three partners had just set up a local employment agency or printing services bureau. How would you set about marketing your business to potential customers?

PC 3.3.1

MAJOR FEATURES OF INDUSTRIAL AND CONSUMER MARKETS

Industrial markets

- Are highly specialised and segmented into areas of specific expertise – e.g. deep mining, satellite telecommunications, four colour printing, etc.
- Deal in products and services which are highly technical – e.g. computerised drilling machines or acquisitions and mergers consultancy.
- Buy and sell goods and services which are very costly; re-equipping a production line can cost millions.
- Therefore the decision-making process of what to buy takes a long time and involves committees and teams of expert people.
- Selling organisations have to produce extensive tenders which include specifications and prices which are binding if accepted.
- Sales promotion tends to take the form of equipment demonstration and extended loan 'on approval' to allow prospective buyers to check if a system does what its sales force say it will do.
- Industrial products and services tend to include extensive agreements on warranties, servicing and customer support activities.
- With highly expensive plant and systems on offer, sellers often design 'one-offs' or modify designs in order to tailor a product or service to a specific need.
- Highly skilled support teams are needed to help advertise industrial products, such as technical writers and illustrators.
- Because of high acquisition costs, many industrial products and services are expected to have a longer life cycle than their consumer market counterparts.

Consumer markets

- Meet not only staple needs, such as food and warmth, they also cater for 'wants' in the forms of fads, whims and fashions.
- Extensive research is conducted into identifying different kinds of consumer – from rich landowner to impoverished pensioner – and into what impels them to buy what they do, and the prices they are prepared to pay.
- Thus consumer products are designed, produced, promoted, distributed and priced with very specific buyers in mind.
- As a result advertising and sales promotional material is placed with media which are known to have high readership, listening and viewing rates among targeted customers.
- Consumer markets are highly competitive and thus product life cycles tend to be short, with continual improvements, upgradings and replacements.
- The prices of many consumer products are relatively low and therefore encourage impulse purchasing; thus product merchandising and packaging is very important.
- Also, many consumer products are made in high volume quantities and need expensive advertising/sales campaigns to sustain a required high level of demand.
- Many consumer goods and services producers design and package several similar products – like tea or pension plans – to suit various sectors of the market – they 'position' their products according to the incomes and life-styles of their customers.

PC 3.3.1

Industrial and consumer markets

Branded goods and brand loyalties

An interesting contrast between industrial and consumer markets lies in the emphasis placed upon branded goods and brand loyalties. While sellers in both markets seek to 'brand' their products – Perkins diesel engines, Otis lifts, Kelloggs cornflakes, Heinz baked beans, etc., their respective buyers possess different purchasing habits. Industrial buyers using the tender process may opt for a relatively unknown product, if it will meet tender specifications on performance, price, warranty and so on. Brand loyalty in industrial markets is less impulsive and more hard-bitten. In consumer markets, however, marketing departments go to great lengths to promote brand loyalty – with special offers, discounts, self-liquidating 'free' offers, etc. This is generally because there is, intrinsically, little to choose in terms of ingredients and performance between, say, any one of a range of petrols, toothpastes, baked beans, cornflakes or toilet papers.

Also, an intriguing feature of the consumer market, especially in retail food, clothing, DIY and motorists' outlets, is product labelling or branding. Here, some products carry manufacturers' labels which are given high promotional prominence! – Pringle sweaters, Gucci shoes, Jaeger fashions, etc. Other products carry the outlet's brand name: St Michael's underwear (Marks & Spencer), Sainsbury's cornflakes or Halfords' engine oils etc. Sometimes manufacturers seek to enlarge their sales by selling one part of their output as **premium branded goods** carrying their own house labels, another part (often from the same production run or batch) carrying the label of the outlet, and a further proportion as unbranded goods for distribution to small retailers, open markets, mail order houses and so on.

In this way, a manufacturer can achieve economies of scale by marketing **a single production design and run** at the top, middle and bottom of the consumer market spectrum. By contrast, industrial goods manufacturers tend to design and market equipment and systems, say, photocopiers, in a stepped sequence which satisfies varying levels of performance. These are then targeted at specific customers.

Finance and markets

A further area of contrast lies in the differing ways in which industrial and consumer goods are financed. In industrial markets, investment in capital goods – car-making sheet metal presses, newspaper computerised printing systems, chemical refinery plant and so on may run into millions of pounds.

As a result, the sellers of such plant and equipment very often have to work with merchant banks and finance houses in order to market financial loan packages alongside the industrial products – not merely as a service to the customer, but as an essential part of the sales-securing process. And manufacturers generally lobby government continually in order to secure some kind of subsidy on capital expenditure, say in the form of tax allowances or credits. It is for this reason in particular that manufacturing industry puts a premium on interest rate cuts, so that the costs of investment (in the form of bank loans) are less expensive.

In the consumer market, while manufacturers do not need to package loan schemes to aid the sales of washing machines or hi-fi stacks, they do have an interest in encouraging consumer demand as much as possible. For this reason, the clearing banks and High Street retailers have developed a very sophisticated credit purchasing system, based upon the plastic credit card.

Consumers applying for a Barclaycard, Access Card or TSB Trust Card, etc. are given a credit limit (£200, £500, £1,000) depending upon their income levels. Once issued with their cards, consumers are then enabled to make credit purchases up to the given limit each month. Provided they pay for the goods when billed monthly, their cost is interest-free (to the consumer). However, failure to pay within the time limit initiates an interest charge currently running at some 30-plus per cent per annum. As many consumers prove slow payers, the clearing banks make very high profits from this source of deferred payment. In addition, retailers pay a percentage of the price of each sale (2–3 per cent) to the bank running the card system as the price not only of the bank's administrative costs, but also for supplying the means of increasing sales (which would fall significantly if goods purchased had to be paid for on the spot).

Because of the increasing bank charges for servicing credit-card sales, an increasing number of retailing multiples are promoting their own in-house credit sales facilities or attempting to charge more for goods purchased on credit.

■ Consumer and industrial markets and marketing communications

PC 3.3.1

As the above section indicates, the twentieth century has seen a tremendous development of consumer-based markets across the world, developed to a very large extent by successive advances in technology. The growing consciousness since the 1960s of the fragility of the earth's environment has also led to environmentalism in which people like Ralph Nader in the USA eventually prompted various state and federal governments to ban lead petrol-based exhaust emissions and to introduce catalytic converters.

Also, this section has drawn attention to the very different characteristics of industrial as opposed to consumer markets. In the former, the costs and specifications of, say, industrial plant and equipment offered for sale are scrupulously examined, because of the costs involved and the need to assure a satisfactory return on capital invested – thus very little chance of impulse purchasing here!

On the other hand, in a consumer market, much effort is put into building brand loyalties and brand images, since experience has shown that individual consumers are susceptible to hard-hitting, repetitious advertising of trade-marks, brand logos and slogans.

PC 3.3.1

Marketing communications and the marketing mix

Essentially, the term marketing mix stands for the interplay and interrelationship of all the activities which are needed to transform a product or service idea into a reality and to sell it successfully to its intended customers.

This complex chain of operations was simplified by an American marketing expert, Professor E J McCarthy in 1975 into a set of four Ps: **Product, Promotion, Place, Price**.

Over the two decades, these four Ps have become internationally famous as a shorthand way of remembering what the central components of the mix are.

The chart in Fig 3.18 illustrates the major activities which make up each of the four Ps.

■ Managing the marketing mix

At the beginning of this Unit, emphasis was placed on the integrative nature of marketing. The comprehensiveness of the marketing function is further illustrated by illustrating the components of the marketing mix.

The product

A number of key questions are central to the product dimension to which correct answers must be found if the launch of a new product is to be successful:

- Who, exactly, is the product aimed at?
- What specific needs/wants must it satisfy?
- What are the criteria and specifications for its development, design and production?
- What is the boundary of acceptable costs within which it must be placed?
- What package of ancillary features must it embody: warranty, operations manual, servicing requirements, consumables – like copier toner cartridges, printer ribbons, etc?
- How long is it expected to last?

The price

Arriving at a suitable price for a product or product range depends upon a number of interlocking factors. Very often the fixing of a sales price is the result of a compromise between what the firm would like and what the market will bear, given the state of competition and demand. (*Note*: a detailed examination of pricing strategies is provided on pages 245–53 and also in Unit 1.)

- What are the factors which will influence the price of the product?
  - development costs, costs of raw materials and components, production costs, contribution to overheads, contribution to targeted company profits, competitors' prices, quantity likely to be sold, etc.
- What price will the market bear given the positioning of the product and the income of its identified purchasers?

Fig 3.18 **Products do not market themselves and success relies on careful planning and monitoring**

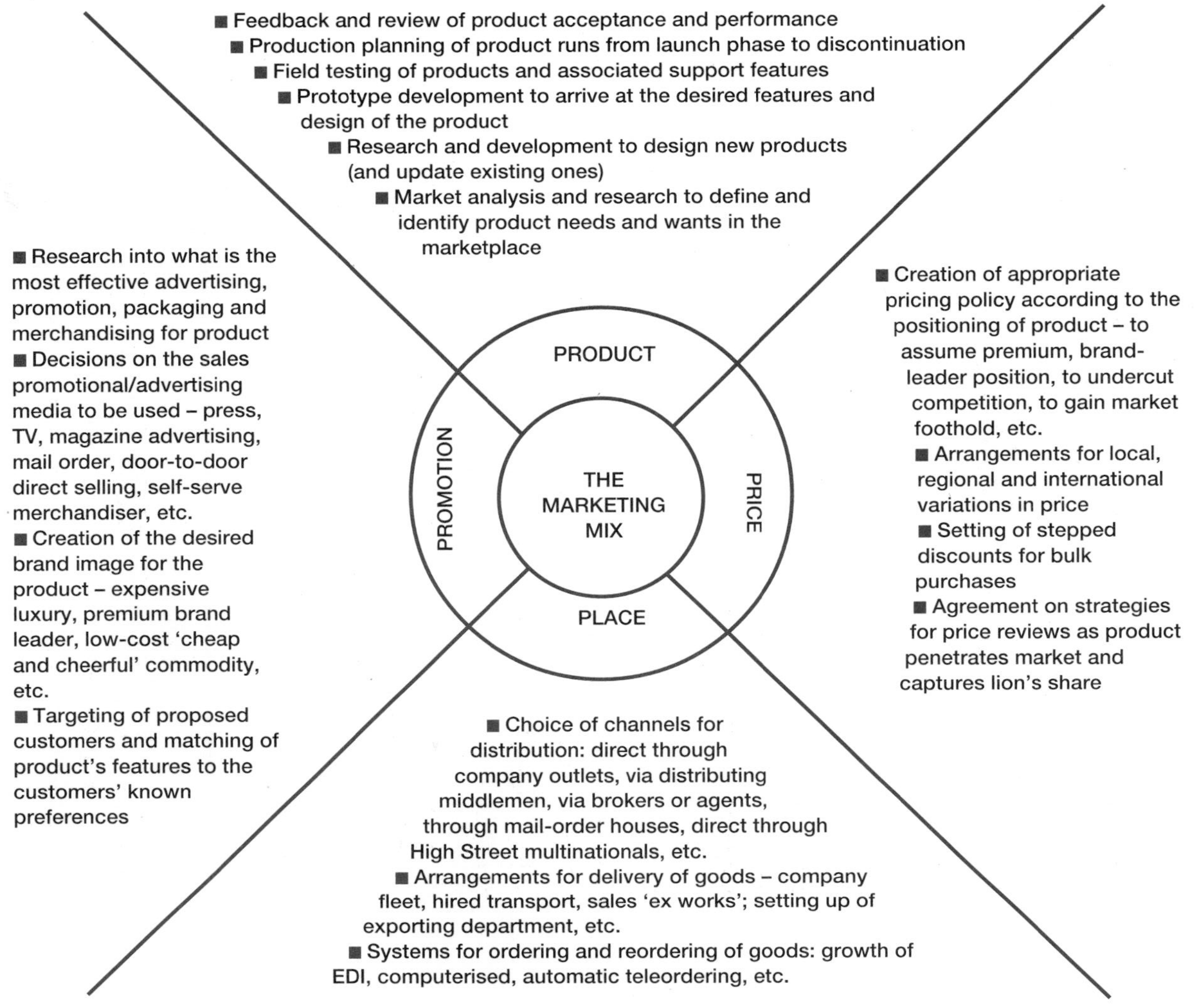
■ Feedback and review of product acceptance and performance
■ Production planning of product runs from launch phase to discontinuation
■ Field testing of products and associated support features
■ Prototype development to arrive at the desired features and design of the product
■ Research and development to design new products (and update existing ones)
■ Market analysis and research to define and identify product needs and wants in the marketplace
■ Research into what is the most effective advertising, promotion, packaging and merchandising for product
■ Decisions on the sales promotional/advertising media to be used – press, TV, magazine advertising, mail order, door-to-door direct selling, self-serve merchandiser, etc.
■ Creation of the desired brand image for the product – expensive luxury, premium brand leader, low-cost 'cheap and cheerful' commodity, etc.
■ Targeting of proposed customers and matching of product's features to the customers' known preferences
PRODUCT
PROMOTION
THE MARKETING MIX
PRICE
PLACE
■ Creation of appropriate pricing policy according to the positioning of product – to assume premium, brand-leader position, to undercut competition, to gain market foothold, etc.
■ Arrangements for local, regional and international variations in price
■ Setting of stepped discounts for bulk purchases
■ Agreement on strategies for price reviews as product penetrates market and captures lion's share
■ Choice of channels for distribution: direct through company outlets, via distributing middlemen, via brokers or agents, through mail-order houses, direct through High Street multinationals, etc.
■ Arrangements for delivery of goods – company fleet, hired transport, sales 'ex works'; setting up of exporting department, etc.
■ Systems for ordering and reordering of goods: growth of EDI, computerised, automatic teleordering, etc.

- What pricing policy does the company wish to adopt:
  a during the launch phase of the product?
  b during its various product life-cycle phases?
- How will the prices of competing products affect the company's pricing strategy?

The promotion

An appropriate promotional strategy is crucial for the effective marketing of any product or service. Essentially product promotion brings together the choice of channels and media through which to announce and present the product, the creation of a clear identity and image for the product (which will include the all-important aspect of its packaging), and the training and briefing of all those having a part in its sale and post-sales service.

- What is likely to be the most successful choice of promotional activities and media in launching the product – and then sustaining it?
- Where and how will the product be sold?
- How should it be packaged and presented?
- What sort of brand image should be created for it?
- How can its unique selling benefits best be brought to customers' notice?
- How can it best be distinguished from competing products?
- What levels of sales training and support will be needed by:
  a company sales personnel
  b dealers and/or agents?
- What level of after-sales service is appropriate?

The place

The creation of a successful 'place' strategy involves careful logistical planning – in order to get sufficient numbers of the product to a selected mix of outlets. It also involves the planning of availability, or in other words, the establishment of a networked delivery system which will ensure that no wholesale warehouse or retail store is without goods to satisfy an ongoing demand.

A place strategy also involves costings. It may be more profitable to deliver the product to relatively few regional wholesalers and let them absorb the cost of breaking down the bulk by deliveries to large numbers of retailers in repetitive penny numbers.

- What will be the most effective kind of outlet for the product?
  - wholesaler, retail shop, mail order company, departmental store, out-of-town shopping mall, door-to-door direct sales, craft fair, overseas agents, etc.
- What is the most cost-effective means of distributing the product?
  - own fleet of articulated lorries, contracting of transport, use of British Rail, use of Post Office or private sector courier services, etc.
- What production and distribution planning should be undertaken to ensure a continuous availability of the product in its outlets?

Note: there are two options open to a manufacturer of either selling to a wholesale firm and allowing it to benefit from the adding of value in the distribution chain, or of setting up its own distribution and retail networks so as to retain at each stage the profit attributable to the adding of value to the product (by being in the right place at the right time).

The second option is called **vertically integrating the organisation**.

■ How the marketing mix impacts upon the communication mix

PC
3.3.1
3.3.2
3.3.3

The four Ps of the marketing mix – *product, price, promotion* and *place* – exercise an enormous influence upon the way in which a marketing communications strategy to promote a product or service is first designed and then implemented. The four Ps do this in these ways:

HOW THE MARKETING MIX INFLUENCES THE COMMUNICATIONS MIX

Product

Products or services are not marketed on a wing and a prayer, nor targeted at potential customers by holding a wet finger in the air! They are researched, designed and marketed with very specifically targeted customers in mind – land-owners, business executives, blue-collar workers or old-age pensioners etc.

For this reason, the advertisements, tv commercials or posters used to promote the product also need to be targeted by appearing in those newspapers the targeted customer reads, between those tv programmes he or she views and so on.

Price

Similarly, goods tend to be made to a given price specification – so as to become premium, entry-level or cut-price products, depending on whether they are to be positioned at the top, middle or bottom of a given market.

This being the case, the associated marketing communications will either promote the product as 'glitzy, super de luxe' or 'easy and simple to use', or 'no frills, but works like a charm'. In other words, a brand or product image will be devised and advertised which reflects the price being charged.

Promotion

In the same way, the design of a marketing communications strategy to promote a product is influenced by the classification of its intended customers, its design and specification and its price. For example, a Rolls Royce is much more likely to be advertised in *Country Life* or the *Financial Times* than *Woman's Own* or *Sport On Sunday*. Similarly, clothes or soft drinks commercials targeting teenagers are much more likely to be shown in cinemas (where the vast majority of customers are in the 16–25 age range).

Place

Where a product also influences a marketing communications mix, since, for example, much more information can be obtained, say, from an expert sales assistant in a specialist hi-fi retail centre than from a mail order catalogue; on the other hand, a short, catchy merchandising slogan at a supermarket cash-out often prompts an impulse purchase sale.

PC 3.3.1

■ Why advertise?

'Half the money I spend on advertising is wasted; the trouble is, I don't know which half.'

Lord Leverhulme, Unilever plc.

Why small traders and large multinationals alike advertise is, quite simply, because they believe that advertising will increase both sales and profit! They also believe it will help them extend their hold on a given market or increase it. Where, however they tend to disagree is about the degree of effectiveness of their advertising budgets and whether money spent might provide better value elsewhere. For this reason, advertising agencies and marketing specialists now spend more time and effort in evaluating the impact of a sales campaign or promotional event.

However, another major impulse which prompts businesses to advertise is the fear of what might happen if they ceased doing something which – while not entirely understood or scientifically controlled – has 'brought home the gravy' for a number of years. Also, the desire of many companies not to be outdone by their competition similarly stimulates the will to advertise.

PC 3.3.1

WHY BUSINESSES ADVERTISE THEIR PRODUCTS OR SERVICES

In addition to the prompts of not wishing to dispense with a winning formula and the need to keep up with the competing Joneses, businesses advertise for the following basic reasons:

- **to promote the existence of a new or improved product or service** to potential customers who may be unaware of it
- **to focus a potential customer's attention upon superior features of a product** (as against those of a competing product) in order to encourage purchase
- **to supply information** (particularly where expensive, high-tech goods are concerned) without which a customer is unlikely to decide to buy
- **to reinforce brand recognition and brand loyalty** during an intense advertising campaign in which logos, slogans and jingles are regularly repeated – on tv and radio, on hoardings or in newspapers etc.
- **to promote a business's corporate image** as part of an ongoing soft sell which is often used to support intermittent hard-selling, specific promotional campaigns
- **to 'blow a newly launched, competing product out of the water'** by bombarding the marketing communications media with intensive, hard-hitting advertisements, which frequently cut prices temporarily, until the new competitor is 'sunk'
- **to maintain a market position;** advertising certainly does create sales, and so a company will often choose to do its business in front of a continual background of advertising and allied promotional activities, which act rather like pleasant and reassuring background music in a restaurant or store

■ The role of the advertising agency

PC 3.3.1

The general role of the advertising agency is to assist in-house managers with:

- devising the brand image of a product or service;
- monitoring the advertising activities of competitors;
- positioning new products within an existing product range;
- designing the packaging of a product;
- planning and arranging advertising campaigns on a national or local basis; this service includes liaising with mass-media offices and space sellers;
- designing point-of-sale placards, brochures and leaflets.

At the top end of the advertising agency market, a client account may be worth several million pounds a year in terms of its budget and such accounts are usually serviced by a manager and staff working exclusively to them.

■ The advertising media mix

As a result of the development of the advertising and telecommunications industries this century, a wide range of media are available for inclusion in an advertising campaign:

PC 3.3.1

CHECKLIST OF AVAILABLE ADVERTISING MEDIA TODAY

- Television commercial, radio commercial, cinema commercial, video-tape film cassette commercial, viewdata entries on Prestel
- Hot-air balloon/trailed airplane poster
- National/local newspaper display or classified advertisement
- Free local newspaper insertion/plug
- Free specialist magazines distributed to key buying decision-makers
- Roadside/sports stadium/forecourt hoarding. Public transport signs and placards – in buses, tubes and taxis
- Leaflets, brochures, pamphlets mailed or delivered by hand to homes and business premises
- Unsolicited sales letters and enclosures
- Trade and public fairs and exhibitions
- Event sponsorship: names of sponsors prominently displayed on racing-cars, sports shirts or power boats
- Give-away items: pens, matches, key-rings, etc. carrying brand names, trade-marks and slogans
- Home selling television channels
- Recorded messages left on telephone answering machines and unsolicited fax messages

The range and scope of available advertising media grows each year as technological innovations multiply and bright media people brainstorm new ways of reaching prospective purchasers.

CURRENT NEWSPAPER AND MAGAZINES IN PRINT IN BRITAIN

- 21 National Newspapers (owned by 11 proprietors)
- 1,500 Weekly Newspapers
- 7,500 Magazines

393 newspapers are circulated in Britain per 1000 of the population

Source: Ms Jane Reed, *British Journalism Review*

PC
3.3.1

EXAMPLES OF MARKETING COMMUNICATIONS MEDIA

Consumer advertising

Since we are all consumers, it is natural that the promoters of sales and advertising campaigns use communications media which have a high degree of visual or aural impact in those locations which capture and hold our attention:

- Roadside hoardings, football stadium billboards, signs and placards fixed to buildings, names on sports people's kit, etc.
- Television, radio, video film and cinema commercials
- Newspaper, magazine, free local paper display advertisements, home and office-delivered advertising mail, telephone sales, etc.

  Such widescale advertising is also reinforced by point-of-sale merchandising:
- Hanging signs and placards, stickers, counter-standing advertisements, self-service stands and shelves with advertising slogans, uniformed sales staff, advertisements on sales receipts, etc.

Such is the extent of the available media for promoting consumer goods, that companies exist solely to sell space in newspapers or on hoardings, and advertising agencies employ staff to plan a suitable mix of such media for a given sales campaign.

Industrial advertising

Most consumers are blissfully unaware of the tremendous efforts which industrial marketeers put into the promotion of their goods and services. This is because the effort is carefully targeted to known potential customers within industrial sectors by means of:

- trade fairs and exhibitions relating to a given industrial sector such as electronic data interchange (EDI)
- in-company presentations and demonstrations of products and systems
- seminars and briefings given by manufacturing companies to potential industrial customers, e.g. on the advantages of computer-aided design and manufacture, demonstrating the equipment being offered for sale
- extended visits and discussions between technical sales representatives and company buyers
- display advertising and feature articles in specialised trade journals like *Network* (for data communication) or *Business Equipment Digest* for office equipment and systems
- high-quality technical literature and briefing/updating journals
- summarising papers, updates and bulletins sent to industrial companies' technical libraries

While many large organisations in the consumer market employ advertising agencies to design and coordinate their advertising and promotional activities, because of the highly technical (and often confidential) nature of industrial goods and services, their manufacturers and suppliers tend to have developed in-house departments to undertake similar work, liaising closely with their colleagues in R&D and production.

■ Planning an advertising campaign

PC 3.3.1

Targeting the right customer

Whether the job is undertaken by in-house marketing managers or contracted out to an advertising agency, the planning and execution of an advertising campaign to promote the launch of a new product is crucial to its acceptance in its chosen market.

Given the wide variety of media options available, the agency staff need first to decide precisely at what type of purchaser the campaign is aimed.

For many years the advertising industry has classified consumers according to the socio-economic groups they belong to. *The Institute of Practitioners in Advertising* in 1970 produced the following classification:

SOCIO-ECONOMIC GROUPS: IPA CLASSIFICATION

A Senior/top managers, administrators and professionals: surgeons, barristers, business directors, generals, public utility directors and so on. (3 per cent of population)*

B Middle/senior managers and public sector personnel – county/district council senior officers, business departmental managers, partners in solicitors/accountants firms, headteachers, smaller business directors and proprietors. (13 per cent of population)*

C1 Supervisory staff/'white-collar' workers in clerical and administrative posts: supervisors, section-heads, factory foremen, assistant managers in branch offices of banks, building societies, etc. (22 per cent of population)*

C2 Skilled manual workers in industrial posts: technicians, maintenance engineers, shipwrights, oil-rig drillers, masons, electricians, etc. (32 per cent of population)*

D Semi-skilled/unskilled workers: bricklayers' hod-carriers, road-menders, farm-workers, office-cleaners, etc. (19 per cent of population)*

E Low/fixed income category: old-age pensioners, single parents, widows, long-term unemployed, etc. (11 per cent of population)*

*Source: JICNARS National Readership Surveys

Note: It is important to keep in mind that the examples given above in no way imply a superiority of one type of occupation over another; they are simply intended to provide a rough and ready insight into the spectrum of occupations which have been classified into groups as a result of the life-style, culture and spending power each represents.

Today the income of each group is likely to be distributed as follows:

Group	*Income per annum in £s*
A	50,000 plus
B	30,000–50,000
C1	20,000–30,000
C2	10,000–20,000
D	4,000–10,000
E	under 4,000

PC 3.3.1

Fig 3.19 **Leading tabloids: average sales per day**

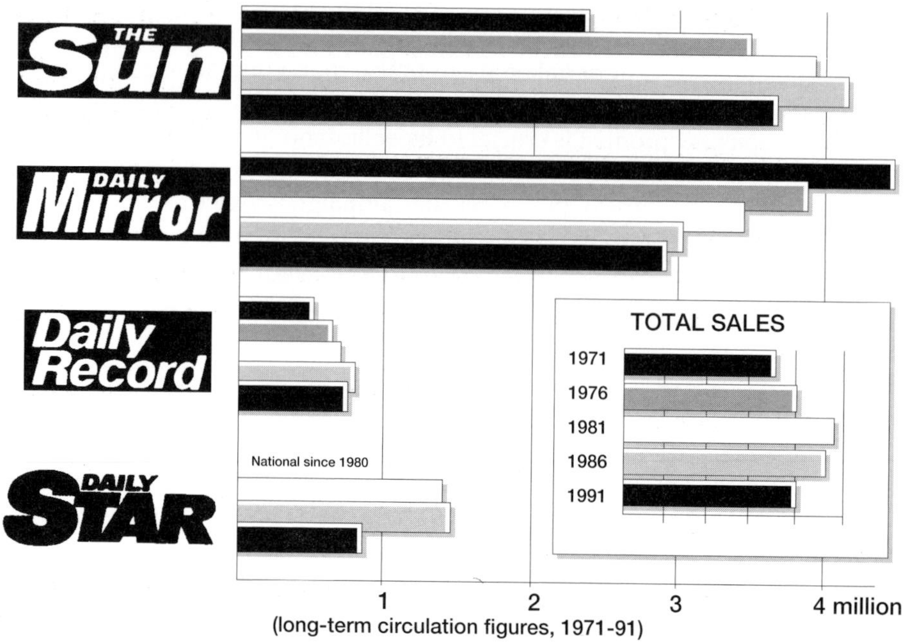
THE Sun
DAILY Mirror
Daily Record
DAILY STAR
National since 1980
TOTAL SALES
1971
1976
1981
1986
1991
1
2
3
4 million
(long-term circulation figures, 1971-91)

Reproduced from *The Times* 21 April 1992, by kind permission of Times Newspapers

Once such approximate classifications have been made, further analysis of life-styles reveals, for example, which UK national newspapers and magazines each group subscribes to or purchases on a regular basis:

Sunday Times	*The Times*	*Country Life*
Observer	*Financial Times*	*The Lady*
Sunday Telegraph	*Daily Telegraph*	*Good Housekeeping*
Sunday Express	*Daily Mail*	*Woman's Own*
Sunday Mail	*Daily Express*	*Woman's Realm*
News of the World	*Sun*	*She*
etc.	*Daily Mirror*	*Jackie* etc.

The same kind of market segmentation can be made of each group's television viewing habits, which may range from 'The Money Programme' and 'Panorama' to 'Blind Date' and 'Big Break'.

The reason for pin-pointing such reading and viewing habits is to ensure that any commercial or display advertisement placed in a given newspaper or with a specific independent television company will reach its intended audience. There would be little point, say, in promoting installed garden swimming pools among E group families; correspondingly, A and B groups may not have an interest in motor coach day-trips to the seaside. The point being that while no value judgement is being made as to whether one group may be socially superior or inferior to another, their respective life-styles and interests do vary according to what is financially affordable and what interests are demonstrated by the peer groups in each category.

Allocated budgets – cutting the cloth

Each advertising campaign will have a limitation imposed upon it by the amount of finance allocated to it. Therefore agency staff will seek to obtain best value for money. For instance an agency may, over a year, place hundreds of thousands of pounds with a TV company or national newspaper for peak viewing time or 'premium position' advertisements. As a result they will obtain a bulk buying discount, the benefits of which may be passed on to regular customers.

However well spent, the budget is subject to a number of decisions:

Q How long should the campaign run?

Q Is it to be national or limited to some regions/districts?

Q Given the targeted customers and the type of product/service which would be more effective:

- Simple posters with a strong visual message on arterial road hoardings and in forecourts?
- Run-of-paper display advertisements?
- Blanket mail shots to targeted private residences?

Q How is the product/service to be presented?

Here the decision will involve design features, colours used, type-faces employed, etc.

Q What mix of media would prove most cost-effective? e.g. a full-page colour advertisement in a single edition of a 'quality Sunday paper' followed up by three, weekly quarter-page display advertisements in selected regional evening dailies? Or a series of short commercials at peak times on regional commercial radio broadcasts and so on.

Supplying the correct answers to such questions will decide whether the campaign hits home or misfires completely, and when commissioning an advertising agency to run a campaign, a company is often buying into many years of expertise in a range of markets. Expert knowledge of viewing, reading or travelling habits among consumers may enable an agency to achieve its target exposure at a fraction of the costs incurred by inexperienced in-house managers – a point which helps them justify their fees and commissions!

Hard sell or soft sell?

PC 3.3.1

The overall approach of an advertising campaign tends to fall into the category of either a hard or soft sell:

The hard sell

- Emphasises the key selling benefits of a product or service and compares and contrasts its sales price with those of competing items.
- It may indulge in 'knocking copy' a jargon term for making disparaging comments about competing products and their 'inferior' features.
- It may 'push' a significantly discounted special offer price etc.

The soft sell

- Seeks to create a mood in tune with the product's image and to emphasise the 'feel good' effect that buying/owning the product (or service) brings.
- No mention is made of price, x per cent off, competing brands or key selling benefits.

- Colours, music, soft-focusing and textures will combine in the soft selling advertisement to promote a sense of exclusivity, comfort, pride of ownership or whatever response is being sought.
- Soft-selling advertisements are often used to maintain demand for well-established, premium-positioned products.

Advertising reinforcers

In order to gain as much impact as possible throughout a campaign, advertisers seek to reinforce the effect of a mix of media advertised messages by:

- reproducing the logo or trade-mark prominently in every advertisement within each medium
- using the same combination of colours and graphic design so it becomes embedded in customers' minds
- devising a catchy slogan or tune which the public easily memorises:

  'It's the real thing, Coke!'
- replicating in point-of-sale materials key elements of the above reinforcers to stimulate impulse purchasing
- using well-liked and respected sports people and entertainment celebrities to endorse the product
- ensuring that the campaign advertisements and promotional material embody common elements with the product's packaging so as to aid product recognition

Above and below-the-line activities

Not to be confused with 'below-the belt' blows, below-the-line is the term used in advertising to describe the myriad of promotional activities which are devised to support generally a product range or company's activities.

Above-the-line advertising relates to that which identifies a given product or service and then sings its praises. Its below-the-line counterpart includes:

- give-away badges, pens, picture cards for collection, etc.
- free entry into competitions whose prizes are provided by the advertising firm
- give-away, trial samples – at fairs, exhibitions, shows, etc.
- articles written in popular magazines about a company's history and good works
- subsidised items like sweat-shirts carrying the company logo, diaries, tax-disk holders, desktop calendars, etc.
- sponsored stunts which make the headlines – e.g. a round-Britain ride on a tandem for charity, etc.

Building brand loyalty

A number of products – notably in the food industry – are supported by ongoing special offers and discounts. Tins of baked beans, for example, may display detachable coupons worth '5p off your next purchase of Brown's Baked Beans'. Other offers involve collecting stamps or coupons printed on the packaging of a product – cornflakes, beer six-packs – or supplied with every £10 worth of petrol purchased, until the total assembled is enough to send off for a 'free' set of tumblers, table-mats or kitchen knives. Such offers are said to be 'self-liquidating' since the cost of the 'free gifts' is built into the promotional budget and increased sales of the targeted product.

In such sales promotional ways, the marketing team builds brand loyalty and heightens interest in the weekly chore of shopping.

INDIVIDUAL ACTIVITIES

PC 3.3.1

Marketing: buyer behaviour and the advertising function

1 Find out about what Abraham Maslow described as a hierarchy of human needs in his *A Theory of Human Motivation* in 1943. Give an illustrated talk to your class about Maslow's Hierarchy and then, in a class discussion, consider whether they are valid in terms of buyer behaviour.

2 Research into these advertising agency job roles:

Creative Department Manager, Account Executive, Brand Manager,

and then brief your class on what each contributes to the work of an advertising agency.

3 Find out the current scale of charges for *a* national and *b* regional TV commercials – at peak and off-peak times, and the length of TV transmission times offered for sale. Draw up a table of charges to share with your group.

4 Do the same as for 3 above, but this time for your local commercial radio station.

5 In terms of both 3 and 4 above, find out how TV and radio advertising salespeople convince prospective customers of the cost-effectiveness of using their advertising media.

6 Arrange to interview a senior member of staff in a local company which provides public relations and 'below-the-line' services to private and public-sector organisations. Find out how the costs involved in securing such services are justified and what motivates businesses to invest in indirect advertising activities.

Marketing communications and public relations (PR)

PC 3.3.2

In some ways public relations has been the Cinderella of the marketing communications industry. In the past, executives working in PR were considered by some as rather suspect, wining and dining journalists, broadcasters and other media opinion-influencers using PR as an alternative to doing real work in a real job. However, as the following section indicates, this stereotyped image is nowadays far removed from reality, given the undeniable power of mass-media news items, articles, features, profiles and documentaries to affect the ways in which the general public regards industrial and business enterprises which operate in an era when the public is rightly concerned in aspects such a air, river and arable land pollution, urban sprawl, evasion of planning requirements and so on.

■ The role of public relations

Marketing communications professionals speak of advertising and sales promotion being 'above the line', and public relations being 'below the line'. Perhaps this contributes to a misunderstanding of PR as an activity which is, somehow, 'below the salt'. What however is meant by its position 'below the line' is that, unlike the very direct and clearly budgeted activities of advertising and promotion, the work of PR is much more difficult to pinpoint in terms of successful outcomes or a return of X% increase in total product sales as a result of £Y spent on advertising etc. This is because of basic differences in the two functions.

PC 3.3.2

THE ROLE OF PUBLIC RELATIONS IS:

- to promote the corporate image of a business, so that its contacts – suppliers, dealers, customers, government officials etc. – view its activities in a positive light
- to help in keeping the name, image, logo and livery etc. in the public eye – again in a positive way – by taking part in publicised events, such as, say, the sponsoring of the annual Cheltenham horse racing festival by *The Sporting Life Guide*, and as a result, say, having banners and posters televised in the paddock, unsaddling enclosure or by the winning post
- to provide newspapers, trade journals, television news units etc. with a steady flow of newsworthy press and news releases which, in addition to supplying news which it is hoped will be published or broadcast, also manages to show the business concerned in a good light; of course, journalists are aware of this PR 'angle', but will often use a PR piece if it is objectively written, and if they are pressed by a going-to-print deadline – to fill a part-column or corner
- to provide staff who will, say, lobby members of parliament in order to persuade them to adopt a positive view of, say, the safety of a wastage-processing plant, or the need to secure a multimillion pound overseas contract
- to promote a positive corporate image by helping with community projects etc.

As the above checklist illustrates, the work of a public relations executive relies on the development of good relationships with media workers, an ability to work behind the scenes, and to act as a spokesperson when something dire happens and adverse publicity threatens to hurt a business. While the work is not easy, it is important, particularly today, when sensationalism in the tabloid press and brief sound-bites on television often skew the presentation of news, or fail to supply all the relevant facts.

PC 3.3.3

Sales promotion: media and methods

Given the current blend of paper, voice, sound and picture (still or moving) available through multi-media mass communication channels, the would-be sales promoter today has a large armoury of media and methods to call into play when planning and designing a sales promotion campaign. As has already been explained, the particular combination employed depends upon the marketing mix of strategy adopted to market a given product or service.

Sales promotion is usually directed at increasing the sale of a specific product, and often (but not exclusively) concentrates its efforts at the point-of sale. For this reason the following promotional media and methods have proved both popular and successful in recent years:

- **coupons or tokens** which, when collected and presented, supply their owner with either a 'free' gift, discount on a subsequent purchase or additional 'free' product item, such as a quarter of tea
- **discounted introductory offers:** when a new product is launched, it is often offered at a lower (penetrative) price in order to gain customer acceptance in the hope of repeat purchases etc.
- **competitions:** many shopping tasks (like the weekly food shop) are routine and become boring; as a result, manufacturers and retailers often devise competitions (in which a product item may or may not need to have been bought) in order to enliven both product and business image
- **loyalty bonuses:** another effective way of promoting goods or services is to reward the purchaser for having stuck to the same brand or make by supplying, say, a 'free' can of beer with every 12-pack purchased, or upon the presentation of, say, collected tokens taken from a product's packaging
- **free samples:** this approach is popular with low-cost items and is usually employed to promote interest in either a new or re-launched product
- **club discounts:** some businesses, such as Tesco, create customer clubs and issue membership cards entitling members to certain privileges or discounts etc. – such an approach is used to build corporate and brand loyalty by encouraging a sense of belonging and having access to certain privileges not open to all.

Packaging: a vital link in the marketing chain

PC 3.3.3

A central part of the excitement of Christmas lies in seeing the assembled Christmas presents lying around the foot of a glittering tree, wrapped in a variety of papers – loud and jazzy, quiet and elegant or foil and fun! And a key factor in the excitement they generate lies both in the appeal and promise of their exterior packaging and the concealment they give to what they enclose.

The packaging of more mundane and every-day products also plays a vital role in transforming them from routine items for sale into goods which a consumer cannot resist purchasing.

Packaging and brand image

A hundred or so years ago, many fast-moving consumer foodstuffs, such as flour, sugar, butter and eggs, were offered for sale in grocer's shops in plain blue, brown or grey bags or cartons, without any logo, trader's business or product name imprinted upon them.

But as the twentieth century revolution in mass production and mass consumer markets took off, manufacturers and retailers soon came to realise that a given product could be made to sell better if it bore the logo, name and an advertising slogan of its originators or sellers – especially if they already enjoyed consumers' respect and approval. Thus toilet soaps became Pears and Camay and Knight's Castille, while washing powders became Persil and Lux and Ariel.

As a result of such powerful advertising campaigns and the reinforcement provided by associated packaging and point-of-sale merchandising, consumers soon came to ask for a Hoover when they were referring to a vacuum-cleaner, or a Kleenex instead of a tissue, or a packet of Kelloggs, instead of breakfast cereal.

Understandably, once manufacturers realised the power of brand image in creating initial and also repeat sales, they lost no opportunity to create an indelible image upon the consumer's mind of the brand name and the key sales features of each of their products through the design of their packaging.

Moreover, as marketing became more sophisticated after the Second World War, advertising departments and agencies exploited product packaging techniques as a means of positioning products in increasingly segmented markets. For example, in the tea market, single manufacturers devised suitable names, such as Earl Grey and Silver Label, accompanied by suitable graphic designs and colour schemes, which ensured that either brand found favour with consumers in the A, B or C1 market segments or in their C2, D counterparts.

GROUP ACTIVITY

Can you think of any other product ranges which manufacturers position similarly with the help of stepped packaging techniques?

Current trends in packaging

The growing influence of environmentalism is having a profound impact upon packaging design and construction. For example, the German Bundeshaus (Parliament) recently passed a law which obliges retail stores and outlets to accept and dispose of in a 'green' way the wrappings and packagings (often in many layers) left by customers on the shop's floor, having unwrapped a product immediately after paying for it. A deliberate intention of this law was to force manufacturers into being more environmentally conscious and less wasteful in the design of their packagings.

Correspondingly in the UK, retailers like The Body Shop actively encourage their customers to use previously purchased cartons, bottles and containers as refill receptacles for their repeat purchases. Multinational companies like Canon are also now providing a free postal and packaging service to enable photocopier toner cartridges to be recycled, and motor-car manufacturers like BMW are even designing the entire motor car as a recyclable 'package'!

By the same token, manufacturers (and their advertising agencies) are creating good public relations and corporate images by using recycled materials – such as plastic, cardboard and paper – as part of their protective packaging processes.

In addition to responding to 'green' trends, packaging designers are becoming far more conscious of the fast-track life styles of consumers, who as partnered couples may both work and cherish their limited free time. As a result, packaging has become much more time-saving and user-friendly. For instance, oven or micro-oven-ready meals are packaged in trays for instant heating and from which they may subsequently be eaten. Again, boxed wine cartons are designed with inbuilt taps and combine easy dispensing with long-life insulation.

INDIVIDUAL ACTIVITY

Make a checklist of items whose packaging design also influences their sales appeal by incorporating similar user-friendly and ingenious features.

PC 3.3.3

CHECKLIST OF KEY FEATURES OF CONTEMPORARY PACKAGING DESIGN

The following checklist includes some of the most typical and commonly employed features of packaging design:

- **functional design** which assists the user – such as engine oil cartons with funnels to assist easy pouring
- **easy access** – wrappings should be easy to remove and not – like some vacuum-packed plastics – require the teeth of a large carnivore to remove them!
- **environmental friendliness**, so that precious raw materials are not wasted in today's 'throw-away' societies
- **recyclable materials** are employed wherever possible, so as to reduce waste and environmental pollution
- **reinforcement of the product's brand image** and unique sales appeal – luxury, comfort, strength and ease of use etc.
- **ease of use** in terms of the distributor and retailer – good packaging does not overlook the needs of the wholesaler who may store goods in multiple packs on pallets and move them around on fork-lift trucks; similarly, good packaging design takes into account the standardised heights of supermarket gondola shelving, delivery crates etc.
- **safety-consciousness:** highly inflammable or toxic materials should not be used in packaging, and guidance as to disposal of packaging materials should be included with those materials which embody any risk
- **compliance with legal requirements:** text, prices, specifications and contents etc. all come within the scope of the Sales Description Act and may result in legal action if the law is broken
- **and most important: visual and tactile appeal** – unless the packaging, as virtually the last link in the marketing chain, captures the consumer's eye and notice and then confirms the all-important decision to buy, all the work and effort from R&D idea to arrival at the point-of-sale will have been to no avail!

■ Trading standards and consumer protection

PC 3.3.6

The Office of Fair Trading as an arm of government acts as the nation's watchdog on the many-faceted activities of buying and selling in the consumer market-place.

At local levels, each county council operates its own trading standards department. Its role is to monitor through its inspectors the businesses within its catchment area in terms of the following major activities:

- **The Weights and Measures Act 1985**

  The role here is to ensure that all scales and balances in use are correctly calibrated so as to give accurate and 'fair measure', and also to check that vessels used to contain solids or liquids for use in the selling or distributing processes are also correctly sized and marked – such as pint beer glasses, milk bottles and churns etc.

- **The Consumer Protection Act 1987**

  The role here involves checking sales goods for safety – such as imported toys which may have dangerous materials in them, or be dangerously constructed – checking on standards of assembly, construction or processing – such as glass being found in jars and bottles in a supermarket and back-tracking this to a production batch and recall etc.

- **The Trades Descriptions Acts 1968 and 1972**

  Here the role is to ensure that local business advertisements, point-of-sale merchandising placards and labelling comply with the Act, and often, responding to consumers' complaints of alleged misleading or false descriptions on advertised or displayed products.

Note: The work of the Trading Standards Departments in local authorities is complemented by that of the Environmental Health Office, the Health and Safety Commission and the local Citizens' Advice Bureaux.

PC 3.3.6

■ The Advertising Standards Authority and Independent Television Commission

There are two principal bodies which act as watchdogs over UK advertising:

for all television advertising: the Independent Television Commission (ITC)
for all other advertising: the Advertising Standards Authority (ASA).

The roles of these twin authorities are as follows

- to monitor all advertising against established criteria for public morality and good taste, compliance with established laws and fair and accurate statements regarding the product or service advertised
- like ACAS, they provide guidelines and models of codes of practice, and many advertising agencies and television companies have incorporated them into their own manuals of operational practice.
- the two authorities may be required to pronounce on a given advertisement or TV commercial, and if they are against it, it is usually speedily withdrawn.

GROUP ACTIVITY

In pairs, research into either the ITC or the ASA and the work they do. Then provide upon a factsheet of not more than two sides of A4 a clear set of informational points based on your findings.

Decide in class which factsheet is most informative and then copy it to each class member as a revision aid.

MAJOR ADVERTISING/SALES STATUTES

1893	Sale of Goods Act
1889	Indecent Advertisements Act
1955	Food and Drugs Act (Labelling)
1967	Advertisements (Hire Purchase) Act
1968	Trade Descriptions Act
1971	Unsolicited Goods and Services Act
1973	Fair Trading Act
1973	Independent Broadcasting Act (covering TV Commercials)
1973	Supply of Goods (Implied Terms Act)
1974	Consumer Credit Act
1974	Prices Act (covering clear pricing of goods)
1978	Consumer Safety Act
1979	Sale of Goods Act (updated 1893 Act)
1982	Supply of Goods and Services Act
1987	Consumer Protection Act
1995	Sale and Supply of Goods Act

These Acts embrace a wide range of powers which ensure that goods sold deliver what they promise, that labels and advertisements supply information which is accurate and not misleading, that residents are not mailed items they have not ordered and do not want, that goods are not sold on credit under high sales pressure, that national safety standards are complied with and so on.

INDIVIDUAL ACTIVITY

Select **two** of the above Acts, research into their contents and then summarise their principal points in about 300 words. Photocopy or display your findings to share with your class.

GROUP ACTIVITY

PC 3.3.3 3.3.4

Promoting another Supersnax product!

In groups of two or three, carry out the following activity and give your oral presentation to your class in turn:

The scenario

You are a unit within the Marketing Department of Supasnax plc, a national company manufacturing a range of sweets and confections which sell in supermarkets, newsagents, general stores and cinemas, etc. Your Research & Development Department has recently developed a new snack bar with the following features:

Dimensions:	12 cm × 4 cm × 1.5 cm
Weight:	80 grams net
Calorific value:	75 kcal per 100 grams
Ingredients:	chocolate, cane sugar, artificial sweetener, caramel flavouring, raisins, oatmeal biscuit

The snack's particular characteristics which were first market-researched and then built in to the manufacture of the bar are that it is low in calories and high in food value. Your market analysts identified a market niche for a new product which weight-conscious and dieting consumers could include in their daily intake without feeling guilty or worrying about calorie counting.

This is essentially the product's 'unique selling benefit'.

It is also intended to appeal to consumers who buy snacks in health food shops, because of its high 'natural food content'.

The test market locality

As part of your promotional research, first:

Investigate your local market for sweet snack bars – like Yorkie, Snicker, Topic, etc. Then, make notes on the following aspects:

- Type of sales outlet.
- Location of sales outlets.
- Profile of the type of customers purchasing sweet snacks.
- Methods for point-of-sale promotion and merchandising.
- Price comparisons – between competing snack bars and competing outlets.

Try to find out which bars sell best and why.

Presenting a promotional plan

Then, design a presentation to your senior management for launching the newly created snack bar in your locality, which has been selected as a test market. Your presentation should include:

- an outline of your promotional strategy;
- a point-of-sale promotional placard;
- a design for a 'self-serve' box which also serves as the packaging of the snacks (in packs of 50);
- the design for the wrapper of the bar;
- a name for the snack bar;
- a suggested sales price with reasons for it based on the local situation (assume that your manufacturing, distribution and promotional cost amount to approximately 15p per bar);
- a draft sales letter to existing dealers to promote the launch of your new product;
- a draft sales letter to retailers with whom you do not as yet trade, to introduce yourselves and your new product.

As a class group, observe critically each presentation and decide which was the most effective and why.

DISCUSSION TOPICS

PC 3.3.3 3.3.4

1 How price-sensitive is the snack bar market?

2 How important in the snack bar market is a product's name?

3 To what extent do product packaging and point-of-sale merchandising appear to influence sales?

4 How do the retailers present snack bars for sale?
Do approaches vary, or are they closely similar?

5 As a sales representative for Supasnax who regularly calls on a range of local retailers (i.e. the ones you researched), what advice could you give the marketing unit on the best way to design point-of-sale merchandising material?

6 What advertising media in your locality would you recommend be used to support the launch of your new product, and why?

REVIEW TEST

PC 3.3.1 3.3.2 3.3.3 3.3.4 3.3.5 3.3.6

1 Explain briefly how the rise in the twentieth century of consumerism and the mass-media affected the development of marketing communications.

2 Identify three contrasting characteristics which distinguish a consumer from an industrial market.

3 What prompted the creation and development of branded products?

4 What are the four components of the marketing mix?

5 List three ways in which the marketing mix of a marketing strategy impacts upon its marketing communications approach.

6 How does the positioning policy of a product in its market affect the way in which it is promoted?

7 Supply four major reasons why businesses advertise their products or services.

8 Explain briefly the role of an advertising agency.

9 List five main communications media commonly used in an FMCG market today.

10 What is meant by 'socio-economic group classification'? How does it help in marketing communications activities?

11 Explain briefly the difference between a hard-sell and a soft-sell in advertising.

12 List four main activities of the public relations function.

13 List four ways in which a company may promote the sale of a consumer good.

14 Why is packaging important in the context of marketing communications?

15 What are the main duties of Trading Standards Authority?

16 What do ITC and ASA stand for?

PC
3.3.1
3.3.2
3.3.3
3.3.4

DISCUSSION TOPICS

1 'The costs of the rise of consumerism have been higher than we realise – in terms of the wasteful use of raw materials, trivialising people's spare time and hard-selling things people don't really need!' Is this a fair judgement of the impact of consumerism due in no small part to ceaseless, high-volume marketing communications activities carried out by thousands of businesses?

2 Would consumer market promotional activities work in industrial markets?

3 People learn to grow a resistance to marketing communications like growing a thicker skin! If this is so, what strategies for reaching and influencing sales-resistant customers are likely to emerge in the next few years?

4 Why do advertising and sales promotion *really* work?

5 Could an economy function without advertising and sales promotion activities?

6 How do business owners know that 'it pays to advertise'?

7 'The truth is, self-regulation of marketing communications activities simply doesn't work!' True, or false?

KNOWLEDGE TEST

Element 3.3
Evaluate marketing communications designed to influence a target audience

1 (i) Marketing communications in industrial markets is more concerned to impart technical information about a product than to promote its visual appeal.
(ii) Brand images are promoted in consumer markets in order to encourage customer loyalty.

Which of the following options best describes the above statements?

A	(i)	T	(ii)	T
B	(i)	T	(ii)	F
C	(i)	F	(ii)	T
D	(i)	F	(ii)	F

2 Which of the following are components of the marketing mix?

A Performance
B Place
C Price
D Plan

3 (i) A hard-selling advertisement will emphasise price.
(ii) A soft-selling advertisement will not mention the product.

Which of the following options best describes the above statements?

A (i) T (ii) T
B (i) T (ii) F
C (i) F (ii) T
D (i) F (ii) F

4 Which of the following statements is true, and which false?

A The public relations function seeks to influence public opinion.
B Public relations manufactures news items to assist newspapers in filling their columns.
C The public relations function is not yet accepted as a legitimate part of marketing communications.
D It is more difficult to measure the effectiveness of a public relations activity than a sales promotion activity.

5 (i) 'A self-liquidating offer' usually correctly describes the giving away of free samples to promote a newly marketed product.
(ii) A business is obliged by law, if the customer requires it, to exchange collected tokens for cash.

Which of the following options best describes the above statements?

A (i) T (ii) T
B (i) T (ii) F
C (i) F (ii) T
D (i) F (ii) F

6 Which of the following statements is true, and which false?

(i) Watchdog bodies like the Independent Television Commission can advise advertisers about the suitability of their commercials but cannot insist on their modification or discontinuance.
(ii) All advertisements must be decent according to current guidelines and controls.

PORTFOLIO OF EVIDENCE ACTIVITY

PC
3.3.1
3.3.2
3.3.3
3.3.4
3.3.5
3.3.6

Element 3.3
Evaluate marketing communications designed to influence a target audience

COMMUNICATING MARKET COMMUNICATIONS!

Scenario

You work as a research assistant for the international advertising agency, *Klein, Murphy & Fraser*. The agency is currently seeking to gain the business of an important national conglomerate business, and is currently preparing to present itself and its many aspects of expertise to a panel of the prospective client's board of directors and marketing managers.

As part of the preparations for this important event, you have been asked to produce an analytical report on the marketing communications methods, mix and media employed by two different types of business – focusing particularly on their advertising, sales promotion and public relations activities. Also, one of the selected businesses must be active in the direct marketing, in which *KMF*'s client is particularly interested, as it has invested a lot of money in direct marketing technology.

Your report aims to show how sharp and professional your agency's research and presentational skills are, and you have been briefed by your immediate boss, Jo Churchill, to make sure you include coverage of:

- how specific media and methods are used to reach targeted customers
- how different media promote goods or services in different ways
- how effective marketing communications promote brand loyalty and customers' awareness of the selling features of goods or services
- how promotional activities can be used to extend a product's life and how they have to work within statutory and/or self-regulatory controls and guidelines

Task 1

First, plan your approach to the above Scenario carefully and complete as appropriate your activity planning and review log. Remember to submit a fully completed log with your activity.

Task 2

Make a careful choice of two local (or national) business organisations whose marketing communications material etc. you are able to access promptly. Try to select organisations which are able to support this activity and seek to visit marketing executives and to enlist their help. If local support is not readily available, then approach this activity through an analysis of published material.

Having collected sufficient data, compose a report which will satisfy Jo Churchill's and *KMF*'s requirements. Your report should be about 5–6 A4 sides in length (excluding illustrative material).

Task 3 (Optional)

Give an oral presentation of about five minutes to your class which summarises the findings of your written report. Simulate part of *KMF*'s presentation to its prospective client, while your co-students simulate the panel and ask you questions etc.

Performance criteria covered

3.3.1, 3.3.2, 3.3.3, 3.3.4, 3.3.5, 3.3.6

Core skills covered

Communication:
3.2.1, 3.2.2, 3.2.3, 3.2.4, 3.2.5, 3.3.1, 3.3.2, 3.3.3, 3.4.1, 3.4.2, 3.4.3, 3.4.4

Information Technology:
3.1.1, 3.1.2, 3.1.3, 3.1.4, 3.1.5, 3.2.1, 3.2.2, 3.2.3, 3.2.4, 3.2.5, 3.2.6, 3.2.7,
3.3.1, 3.3.2, 3.3.3, 3.3.4, 3.3.5, 3.3.6

Element 3.4
SALES METHODS, CUSTOMER SATISFACTION AND CUSTOMER SERVICE

Meeting customers' and organisations' needs and wants

PC 3.4.1

Element 3.4 examines in depth the interface between the sales and customer service functions and the needs and wants of both individuals and customers and business organisations in their roles as buyers and customers.

At the outset, it is important to gain an insight into buyer behaviour, or the impulses, decision-to-buy processes and general perceptions of people in the market to but a good or service.

■ What makes people tick?

Buyers, whether industrial purchasing officers, housewives, teenagers or tiny tots, are complex mechanisms when it comes to identifying what motivates them to buy one product or service as opposed to another.

Industrial and social psychologists have undertaken extensive, in-depth studies and identified some of the major reasons for buyer behaviour. They differentiated between perceived needs or wants at a personal, family or social level. Also, they confirmed that buyer behaviour tends to alter as people move from one life cycle phase into another, say from youthful experimentation in buying to deeply entrenched, middle-aged brand loyalties.

■ Needs versus wants

Some goods sell because they form part of the essential prerequisites of staying alive – food, clothing, shelter, medicines and so on. Therefore, little prompting is needed to sell such goods. Indeed, products like fresh bread, flour, sugar, milk and eggs need very little in the way of merchandising, packaging or expensive advertising campaigns. Because they supply a basic need, they tend to sell themselves.

People's wants, however, are a very different matter. Human beings seem never to be satisfied in life. Indeed, they possess insatiable appetites which span a host of goods and services:

'Mummy! I want a mountain-bike for my birthday!'

'Darling, I've seen the most gorgeous little eternity ring at Mappins ... '

'You'll love it when you see it – silver metallic finish, Paris grey leather upholstery, 16-valve, petrol injection motor and does 0–60 in under seven seconds!'

The underlying psychological motivators which fuel such wants are examined below in detail and include: status within a peer group – 'Everyone else's got a mountain-bike', the need to feel good by showing off expensive jewellery, or to feed one's ego in a surge of overtaking power.

Moreover, in a developed consumer market where a number of suppliers exist to supply basic staple needs, then they will seek to differentiate their products from others. They will invest them with a number of benefits and qualities which project an image way beyond any basic function:

Wessex Sovereign potatoes are grown in soils rich in nutrients and come to you fresh and wholesome, graded for the size you like and scrubbed clean and sweet!

Baked in their jackets, they're just the job for the hearty appetites you have to cater for on a raw winter evening!

Such advertising copy seeks to sell the humble potato, not merely as a filling vegetable, but as a convenience food, and one which a loving mum can rely on to satisfy her family when they come in from the cold. In this way advertising develops branded goods from staple products in a needs market by working upon consumers' susceptibilities. And so the line between needs and wants becomes blurred and indistinct as producers' brands and product images take over.

PC 3.4.1

THE BUYING MOTIVATORS

The following checklist illustrates the broad range of buying motivators around which advertising and sales promotion campaigns are created:

Safety and security

People need to feel secure in their daily lives and so the safety/security factor is applied to sales features like central-locking in cars, make-up which is irritant free, tissues which have a 'wet-strength', shoes with waterproof welts, high-performing pensions schemes and so on.

The 'feel-good factor'

Many people spend their lives feeling relatively inadequate and insecure, thus a product or service which reassures them and boosts their morale and ego always finds a ready demand: contact lenses instead of glasses, well-made toupées, a well-cut dress, exclusive pens, lighters and handbags, etc.

Exclusivity

The feeling of being well ahead of the pack, or in American terms, 'ahead of the Jones' is important for many people.

For this reason they may be willing to pay large sums for this year's Jaguar or Mercedes coupé, a month's holiday in Thailand, a Chanel perfume and so on.

Peer group status

People are motivated to buy not necessarily to keep ahead of, but simply to keep up with their peers – co-workers, neighbours or friends. Thus pressures are felt and given in to for buying, say, a gas-fuelled barbecue, a water-softener, an automatic garage door, or a 90-channel satellite dish and decoder.

To win approval

Very many products and services do well because of the natural urge among consumers to look attractive either to existing or to prospective partners – witness the number of hair-stylists, fashion boutiques, fitness centres and jewellery businesses in any population centre. The approval sought may not only be obtained through physical appearance, but through learning to ride, drive, speak French or a host of other accomplishments.

The nest-making instinct

Extensive industries from house-building to Bonsai-tree cultivation rely on the deep-seated urge in people to rear offspring in comfortable or even luxurious surroundings; home-building, DIY and garden-centre firms supply a market which is highly segmented as consumers migrate upwards over time and as income increases.

Value-for-money

While people on occasion 'splash out' way beyond their normal spending power limits, most of the time they are on the look-out for high value-for-money deals which make their income go further. As a result, many firms market goods like food mixers, lawn-mowers, vacuum-cleaners and washing machines as being high on reliability, performance and effectiveness but low on purchase and maintenance costs.

The above list is by no means exhaustive but is indicative of the many psychological prompts which underpin these aspects of modern life:

- Personal esteem and self image
- Sense of personal safety and security
- Status/position in social and work groups
- Mating and child-rearing instincts
- Recreational and leisure life style
- Personal values, beliefs and outlooks
- Personal ambitions, goals, life-plans etc.

■ Unconscious buying triggers

PC 3.4.1

A further complicating factor in seeking to establish what makes a person buy something is that everyone is prompted in purchasing situations as much by unconscious motivations as by conscious ones. For instance, a man or woman who is actively seeking a life partner and is becoming anxious at a lack of success may tend to buy clothes, perfumes or colognes which are more overstated and extreme in fashion terms than he or she would normally buy, as an unconscious means of gaining attention. By contrast, the ageing husband or wife of 30–40 years standing is, more likely to opt for durability and comfort than for stunning visual appeal in a suit or dress.

■ Position in the buying life cycle

Another important aspect of buying behaviour is the phase in the human life cycle in which people find themselves. Young adults, for instance are generally far more willing to experiment – with music disks, hair-styles, food, sports and so on – while their middle-aged parents may be 'set in their ways' with extensive brand loyalties and preferences:

> **'Your father prefers Coleman's English Mustard!'**
>
> **'Always bought Pringle sweaters. Needn't bother to get me anything else!'**

For such reasons, advertisers often target brand-loyal customers so as to maximise repeat purchasing.

■ Spending power

Though left until last, probably the most important factor in influencing people's buying patterns and traits is their disposable income. It is important to keep in mind that this, too, follows a curve of distribution (Fig 3.20).

PC 3.4.1

Fig 3.20 **Consumer spending power chart**

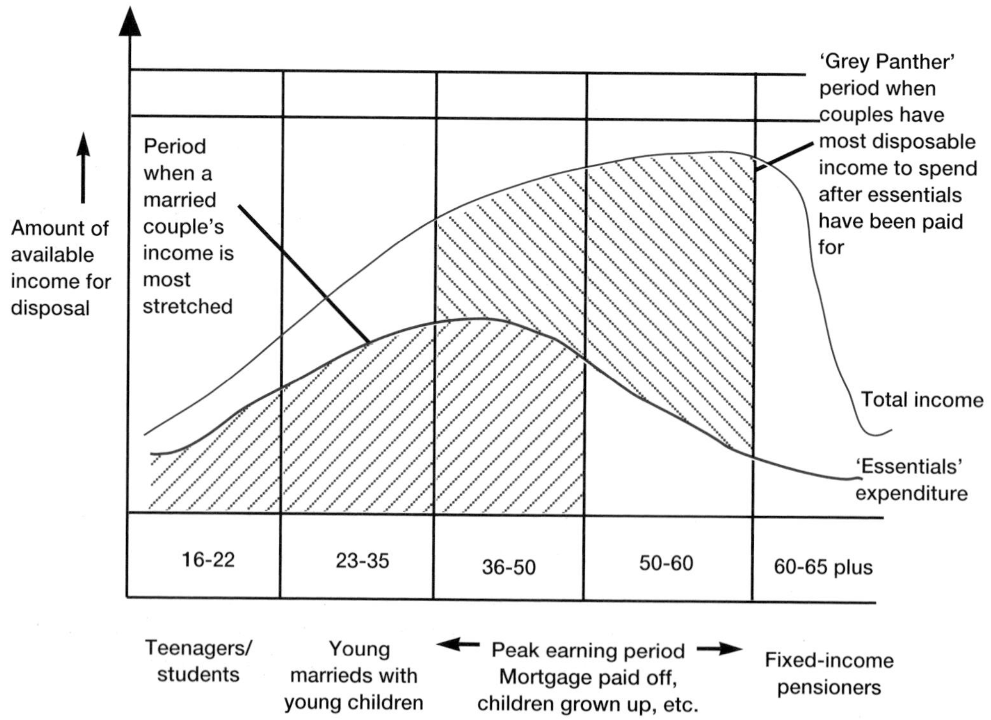

In order to keep their fingers on the pulse of buying behaviour, a company's market researchers as well as government statistical offices are continually analysing who bought what from whom and for how much; how sample companies, individuals and families spend their income; what shifts and trends in purchasing habits are detectable and in what directions as a result specific markets are moving. In analysing consumer purchasing trends, there is only one constant: human beings are fickle and, at times irrational, so their buying behaviour can never be taken for granted!

Direct and indirect sales methods

PC
3.4.1
3.4.2

The terms *direct* and *indirect* are used here to distinguish two quite different approaches to selling to customers with the motivators and spending power outlined above.

■ Direct selling

During the past ten years, direct selling techniques have been used increasingly in the fast-moving consumer goods and financial services sectors for the following main reasons.

- **Direct selling cuts out the middleman** – distributor, dealer – who want their share of the profits deriving from the value added to a product —and so enables the single supplier to increase profit margins.
- **Direct selling cuts out the red-tape and layers of bureaucracy** – by dealing with customer sales enquiries and orders directly, delays arising from processing paperwork or routing orders are cut right back.
- **Direct selling cuts operational and payroll costs** – instead of having to finance hundreds of outlets and sales personnel nationally, direct selling saves money by concentrating its operations in, say, a single centrally located warehouse complex and using a private or public service postal or delivery agency.
- **Direct selling has the capacity to pass on savings to the customer in the form of lower prices** – selling directly from a warehouse or direct from a container depot may enable goods to be sold on at lower prices to the consumer.

■ Types of direct sales method

Direct selling takes place in a host of ways, principal among which are:

■ **mail order**	by means of photographic catalogues and mailed orders
■ **factory sales**	where the buyer deals directly with the manufacturer
■ **tv/radio sales**	such as *QVC*, where goods are displayed and explained on tv and orders phoned in (soon to be supplemented by keyboarded orders as home tvs are designed with computer systems built in)

- **doorstep selling** where roundspeople carrying samples or catalogues take orders and delivery is effected within a few days
- **house parties** women's jewellery, lingerie, make-up and fashionwear etc. are often sold by agents who visit people's houses to sell to the hostess's circle of friends and neighbours
- **telesales** one of the fastest rising forms of direct selling is by phone, where a salesperson makes a stream of cold calls to private homes in order to sell double glazing, house extensions or new bathroom or kitchen fittings etc.

PC 3.4.1 3.4.2

■ Types of indirect sales method

Indirect sales methods tend to cluster around the three phases of *manufacture – distribution – retailing* in the following main ways:

- **traditional linear system** the manufacturer's role ends at the factory gate, and a wholesale distributor collects goods and takes them to a depot warehouse or cash-and-carry unit for onward sale to retailers – who either collect or accept wholesale deliveries
- **area dealerships** in the car industry, manufacturers negotiate agreements with car dealers and/or garages who restrict their sales to a single make – *Rover, Ford, Vauxhall* etc. in return for being given a territory of so many square miles, within which no other licensed (*Rover, Ford, Vauxhall*) dealer may operate
- **franchised outlets** clusters of semi-independent businesses which contract to sell only the products of the franchising business e.g. *The Body Shop*
- **agencies** an agency negotiates with one or more manufacturers or distributors to sell its product or service in return for some advantage (e.g. improved buying terms); agencies also enjoy at times territorial allocations
- **national distribution** in some businesses – newspapers, magazines, parcels etc. – large distributors may win contracts to deliver to destinations nationally, on the basis of reduced cost and increased speed (e.g. guaranteed next day delivery)
- **retail co-operatives** small traders such as general stores or market gardeners may band together either to obtain improved buying terms from wholesalers or to obtain better marketing support.

PC 3.4.2

■ Sales campaign methods

No two sales campaigns are ever alike, since they depend on:

- the profile of the targeted customer
- the nature of the product or service
- the timing of the campaign (e.g. summer, Christmas)

- the position of the product in its market
- the marketing mix strategy for the product.

Nevertheless, a range of commonly employed methods tend to be used frequently in very different types of sales campaign.

For the purchaser

Methods employed include:

- **the sales letter** to new or existing customers which provides sales information and/or credit purchase details, as well as introductory offers and try-out or sampling opportunities and full details of where the product may be obtained etc.
- **presentation packs** where expensive items are involved and, when business purchasers are being wooed, expensive, glossy A4 presentation packs containing brochures, price-lists, sample fabric or text etc. are used to promote a sale
- **give-aways** pens, diaries, T-shirts, mini-replicas etc. emblazoned with the name and logo of, say, a new product are frequently used as 'soft-sell gifts' to reinforce a newly launched product
- **merchandising packs and stands** in order for it to be as easy as possible for, say, a grocer or chemist to take on a new product range, its suppliers often provide free self-serve revolving stands or counter-top dispensers etc. to make the product appealing.

For the sales force

Nor are the hard-working sales representatives overlooked. They are supported by:

- **sales conference/meeting** where key selling points and tactics are rehearsed, product advantages explained and customer objections anticipated and counter-points supplied
- **sales packs, presentation folders** effective marketing organisations ensure that their sales force is armed with sophisticated and appealing visual materials and samples etc. to use as sales 'props'
- **free samples** many retailers like to 'try before they buy' and may demand some free samples to pass on to customers in order to gauge reactions and acceptance levels.

Sales administration and the sales force

PC
3.4.3
3.4.4

A key part of the marketing process is the selling operation. All the work, energy and combined effort of creating, developing, producing and distributing a product counts for nought unless the sales operation is successful.

PC 3.4.3

Fig 3.21 **Sales Department of a National Company**

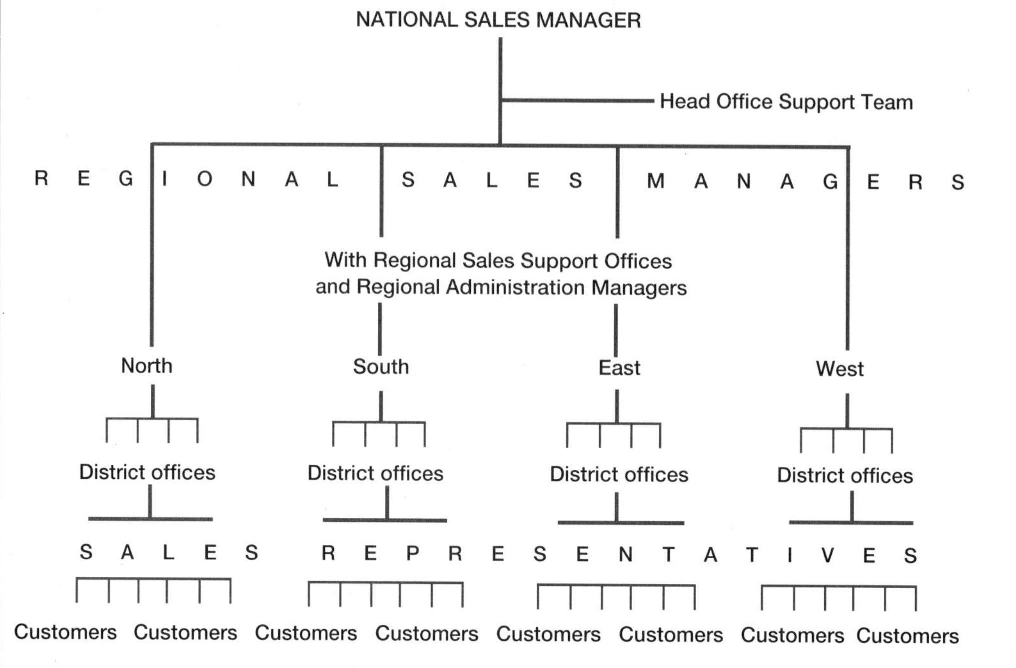

As in all organisational undertakings, effective selling requires careful planning, administration and the training of personnel.

A typical Sales Department of a national company is structured as shown in Fig 3.21.

PC 3.4.3 3.4.4

■ Structuring the sales operation

In a national company, say, a company selling motor car tyres and accessories, the breakdown of responsibilities and functions will follow these lines:

National Sales Manager

Negotiates annual sales target with senior management and the budget to support the national sales effort. (Note, this budget will include as cost centres the sales department in a head office complex, each regional sales/administration office and their respective district offices. The budget may also include regional allocations of an advertising/sales promotion budget to support sales which may be run from either regional offices or head office.) Breaks down national sales targets and budgets to regional level. Agrees with regional managers district sub-allocations. Monitors daily/weekly/monthly sales to target statistics. Keeps running costs under review and control, e.g. sales force expenses. Services large national account customers, say, Sainsbury's, Halfords or Boots.

Checks that sales forces are selling to new as well as existing customers. Liaises with marketing department regarding emergence of new markets, product development and market intelligence coming up his management line from sales representatives' customer calls.

Regional Manager

Coordinates regional sales effort, visits major customers regularly with district managers/sales representatives. Monitors sales/expenses for region in same way as national sales manager. Develops sales personnel. Supervises administrative work of regional office – but usually relies on Regional Administrative Manager.

Ensures regional advertising and sales promotional campaigns effective. Works at improving sales in low-achieving districts. Sets targets for new customers and sales of new products etc. Provides regular reports for national sales manager.

District Manager

Primarily organises the selling routines of the district salesforce. May be heavily engaged in selling also. Trouble-shoots customer complaints and problems. In many ways mirrors Regional Manager's role on a smaller scale. Provides regular reports for Regional Manager about sales performance.

Sales Representative

Works at interface with customers to achieve preset sales target. Assists in securing market intelligence from visits. Seeks to enlarge customer base by making new calls. Supports customer services by handling directly any product complaints or warranty problems, etc. Delivers point-of-sale merchandising material. Leaves samples for consideration/evaluation. Provides dealers and retailers with product update briefings and new product sales information, etc. Chases up slow-paying customers whose accounts are overdue. Provides regular reports for district manager.

■ The sales representative's role

PC 3.4.3 3.4.4

The Hollywood stereotype of the successful salesman is usually of a genial, paunchy, flamboyant Old Stager, who's 'been around', who definitely has 'the gift of the gab' but who is not too bothered by unethical or seamy business practices.

This stereotyped caricature is unlikely to sell very well in today's business climate where the sales representative is expected to be:

- **smartly dressed and in good shape**

  Buyers or 'prospects' invariably relate the desirability of the product (or service) with the visual appearance of its seller; an old but true proverb says that the salesman must first sell himself, and that includes personal appearance – well-groomed hair, freshly laundered shirt, polished shoes, etc.

- **expertly informed and up-to-date on their wares**

  Buyers are always evaluating competing products in retailing or company procurement and no sales representative can sell effectively if his or her information is sketchy, outdated or invalidated by embarrassing gaps.

- **expertly informed about sales trends and the market**

  The successful sales representative has to be expertly informed about local/regional/national/international sales trends and market characteristics; almost certainly buyers will advance counter-arguments, objections or ripostes during a sales pitch about costs, consumer trends, competitors' activities, etc. which the successful sales representative must be aware of and ready to overcome diplomatically on the basis of high-quality information rather than blind assertion.

- **skilled and sympathetic in understanding the buyer's needs and problems**

  Just as 'no one ever won an argument with a customer', so no sales representative ever built sales without first establishing and then developing rapport with the buyer.

- **able to handle objections, complaints or 'hassles' without giving offence or upsetting the buyer**

  Most sales representatives are both 'front-line troops' and ambassadors for their companies and so to the buyer, they *are* the company; one reckless remark or rude response can 'blow away' years of goodwill and high-volume purchasing.

- **a good listener, amateur psychologist and sincere exponent of their chosen field**

  Invaluable market intelligence stems from casual conversation and gossip if the sales representative has a sympathetic ear; further, abundant sales tend to follow around those sales people who have the skill of putting retailers, buyers and assistants at their ease and who are able to demonstrate a sincere enthusiasm and involvement in their sales sector and product service range.

- **expertly informed about the legal aspects of selling**

  Sales personnel need to possess a very informed grasp of the laws associated with buying and selling – so as to be able to advise customers and avoid pitfalls etc.

And as if that weren't sufficient, the successful sales person will be expected by his or her employers to possess developed expertise in self-organisation, sales administration, and follow-up customer maintenance techniques.

PC 3.4.3 3.4.4

■ Selling face-to-face

While there are many other successful means of selling: direct mail, telephone-selling, unsolicited mailing and faxing, etc. undoubtedly the most powerful is the 'flesh and blood' negotiating process where customer and sales person interact face-to-face. In some ways it may be regarded as a ritual process in which both parties are aware of the roles they are expected to play. Certainly this selling process conforms to social and cultural practices – which may vary considerably from country to country. The haggling norms of the Arab souk or bazaar would be treated very dustily in a Rolls-Royce salesroom or Paris fashion-house salon! Nevertheless, there are patterns and sequences which typify the European face-to-face selling which are listed below for you to examine:

Guidelines on face-to-face selling

A well-tried and tested formula is summarised in the acronym AIDA: **Awareness – Information – Desire – Action!**

Awareness: as the first step, this phase seeks to make the customer aware of a product or service; no 'hard sell' is undertaken, rather a consciousness-raising move: 'We're bringing out an improved version of the economy model next month. I'll leave you these brochures to browse through ...'

Information: the next step (on the next visit) may be for the salesman to brief the customer on the product's specifications and attractions, to answer any arising queries and to counter any objections or uncertainties, etc.

Desire: if phases one and two have gone according to plan,the buyer will be signalling evidence of a desire to acquire the product, evidenced by remarks like: 'Well, we might try a case or two – if the price is right! or: 'I might be able to shift a case if you could guarantee delivery before this weekend.'

Action: having created the desire to buy, the final phase is for the salesman to 'close the deal' by initiating actions which cause the customer to make a definite commitment to buy: 'I'll just put you down for the three cases, then, Mrs Harbold, if you could just sign here ... Lovely!' 'I'll just pop over to the car to telephone the warehouse. I'm sure we've got a dozen gross left at the old price. I'll make sure they despatch them this minute, and you'll have 'em first thing tomorrow!'

Other sales specialists sequence the selling steps as:

1. **Re-establishing rapport:** an initial period of small talk about 'the car, the golf, the test match score' – whatever the conscientious rep. has noted as items which interest the buyer.
2. **Lead-in to the desired sales pitch:** general and low-key exchanges about business trends provide a cue for the salesman to introduce his sales item: 'Funny you should say that, we've just modified ours. Look, here's a sample of the new version (hands it to the buyer to examine) see how the cunning devils in R & D have re-routed that circuit ... and that alone has increased its life by 30 per cent!'
3. **Delivery of major selling points, features and benefits for the buyer and his customers:** ever-watchful of the buyers' reactions, the salesman unfolds his practised sales routine, varying it according to the personality of the buyer and the overall context of the sale; depending on the product and circumstances, stress will be given to aspects such as price, performance, design features, durability.
4. **Countering/overcoming objections or buyer resistance:** short of giving away money-trees, the sales person is bound to encounter some resistance to his selling efforts such as cash-flow problems, over-stocking, lulls in trade, and existing loyalty to a competing brand. These must be countered by sales tools like special offers, a one-off extended credit deal, a sale-or return deal, or an introductory extra discount.
5. **Closing the sale:** in all sales transactions, a psychological moment arrives when the buyer is ready to say 'yes'. The practised salesman knows how to spot the verbal/NVC signals, knows when he's said enough and which technique will work to seal the bargain. *Note:* effective sales people never oversell, create overstocking, over-commit their customers financially or sulk if they walk away unsuccessful that day, for 'today's browse is tomorrow's sale!'

PC 3.4.4

SUMMARY OF SALES TRANSACTION DOCUMENTS

A detailed examination of sales documents and transactions is provided in Element 6.2. The following summary outlines the main documents involved in credit sales transactions:

- **a purchase order** provides authorisation from the purchasing organisation for a sales order to be processed
- **an advice/delivery note** details the components of an order delivered by to a purchaser's premises
- **an invoice** adds prices and allowable discounts to the data provided by the delivery note (in practice the same core data is entered onto NCR sets of forms)
- **a statement** provides a trading period (monthly) summary of what has been bought on credit and what in total is due (less any agreed settlement discount)
- **a credit note/debit note** used to make adjustments for either overcharges or allowances for, say, goods returned as defective

■ The sales person's credit monitoring role

Normally, a firm supplying goods on credit will obtain traders' and bankers' references about a would-be credit customer before delivering goods on a credit sale basis. However, it often falls to the sales representative to keep a watching brief on orders taken and accounts due for payment, as a means of credit control and management of debtors.

PC 3.4.4

SUMMARY OF THE SALES ADMINISTRATION ROLE

The main functions of sales administration are:

- **devising and delivering the annual sales plan** in terms of sales revenue, profitability and market share
- **organising the sales effort** and sales-force cost-effectively
- **managing a sales budget** allocated to the sales department
- **monitoring performance:** target sales against actual sales – by week, month, region, district, sales person etc.
- **encouraging the development of new business** by requiring cold-calling
- **'prospecting'**: unsolicited mailings etc.
- **contributing to market research intelligence** by feeding back data from sales-force reports
- **supporting the accounts function** by helping to recover money owed by slow payers via the visiting sales rep
- **tracking sales** (nowadays by computer) so as to maintain efficient deliveries and not to lose orders through slack administration

Customer service – 'delivering ever-higher transports of customer delight!'

PC 3.4.5

Only a few years ago, businesses were striving in the UK to establish and live up to quality management systems which would deliver products or services which were 'fit for their purpose'. Today, however, after a bruising recession sharply increased competition for people's business, customer expectations have markedly increased, to a point where some customer service and support managers see their roles as sustaining such an excellent service that the customer's delight and pleasure in owning a product or enjoying a service moves on to ever-higher levels of delight!

Delivering such a high level of customer satisfaction is a tall order day in, day out, and quite naturally is impossible without a high degree of planning, systems development and inter-departmental liaison and collaboration – not to mention teamwork among different clusters of staff.

This section examines the part played in business operations by the customer services function, and explains how it meets the needs and expectations of many different types of customer.

At the outset of this section, then, a working definition of what customer services is and does will be helpful:

A DEFINITION OF THE CUSTOMER SERVICES FUNCTION

PC 3.4.5

The goals of the customer service function are to satisfy customers' needs through these activities:

1. to channel feedback information from customers to R&D and Marketing personnel which will influence the design and specification of goods and services;
2. to provide information, guidance and support during the decision-to-buy phase, so as to aid the sales function;
3. to ensure that the transaction of purchase-through-to-installation proceeds smoothly;
4. to supply a prompt, courteous and effective aftersales service should the product/service prove less than satisfactory in any way; and
5. to co-ordinate a reliable maintenance service where this is appropriate.

As you will have noticed, the above definition of customer service bears a number of similarities to that of the marketing function. And indeed, both functions dovetail together and overlap in many ways, since they are both essentially customer oriented. As the diagram below illustrates, customer services, like marketing embraces the central activities of a customer-serving organisation, from the research and design stage, to the aftersales service stage. And, like marketing, the customer services function acts as a broker and intermediary between the organisation and its customers.

PC 3.4.5

Fig 3.22 **The needs and expectations of the customer . . .**

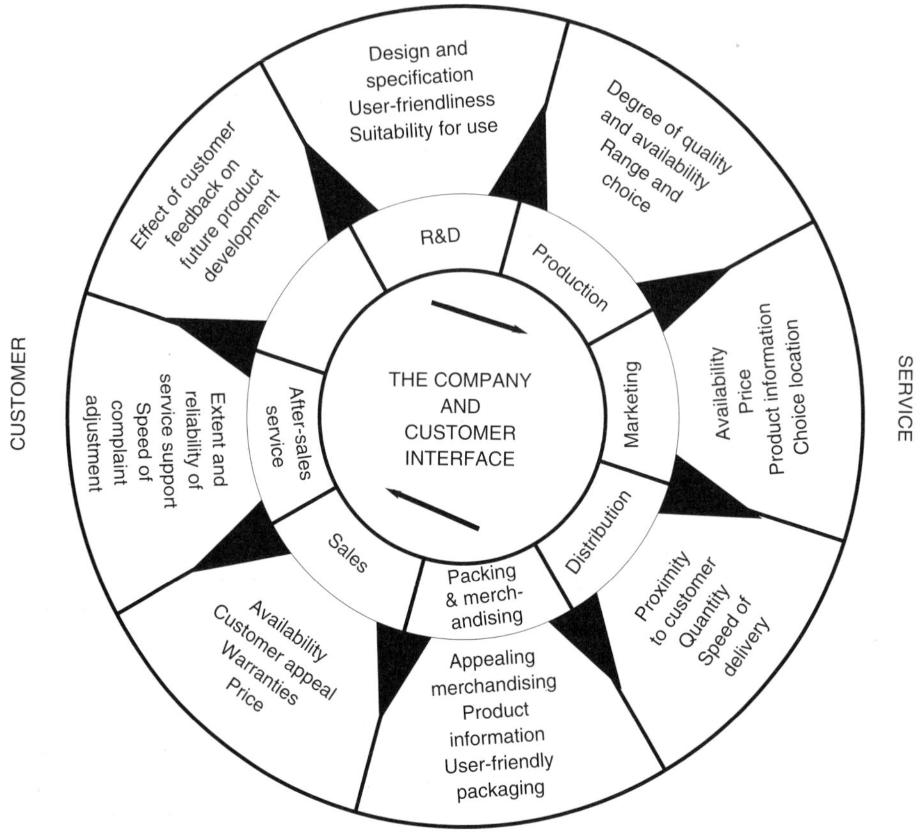
CUSTOMER
SERVICE
THE COMPANY AND CUSTOMER INTERFACE
R&D
Production
Marketing
Distribution
Packing & merch-andising
Sales
After-sales service
Design and specification
User-friendliness
Suitability for use
Degree of quality and availability
Range and choice
Availability
Price
Product information
Choice location
Proximity to customer
Quantity
Speed of delivery
Appealing merchandising
Product information
User-friendly packaging
Availability
Customer appeal
Warranties
Price
Extent and reliability of service support
Speed of complaint adjustment
Effect of customer feedback on future product development

. . . influence every stage of the business activity circle

PC 3.4.5

EXAMPLES OF HOW CUSTOMER SERVICES INTERACTS WITH OTHER DEPARTMENTS

Research & Development

Businesses selling and installing equipment such as white goods or industrial plant tend to employ service engineers who firstly fit and then maintain them; as a result, they are in an excellent position to provide customer service staff with continual feedback on users' views and any needs etc. for design modifications arising from real as opposed to prototype-testing use; such valuable data is then relayed to R&D.

Production

Similarly, feedback from customers and a company's sales-force about product design, ease of use, dimensions and specifications will be relayed to production management who may institute modifications to a product in production; feedback on warranty recalls, repairs and failure rates etc. also provides invaluable information to production's quality assurance personnel.

Marketing and market research

Specially trained customer service personnel handle complaints from customers daily and in progressive businesses log and classify them for further analysis and follow-up; in this way, a constant stream of very useful data is fed to marketing staff who may be thus caused to re-think a product's specification, position or target customer etc.

Distribution

Positive or negative feedback to customer services about late or non-deliveries of goods, breakages en route, faulty labelling etc. will cause investigation and rectification of a business's distribution and sales tracking systems.

Packaging and merchandising

In the same way, customer services will be interested to ensure that product packaging is safe, easy to remove, and simple to dispose of; feedback to the contrary will prompt modifications etc.

Sales

Constant contact with a representative sample of current customers enables customer services to supply a wealth of information to a company's sales force about, say, what customers perceive as a product's main strengths and weaknesses what they mainly use it for and how it performs etc. – all of which provides useful material for selling points and approaches.

Quality assurance

Customer service in many firms includes obtaining feedback from customers via questionnaires and surveys – say from homebound package holiday-makers; this data is then fed to market researching and quality assuring staff to inform their analyses and product improvement strategies etc.

■ Summary

As the above check-list has illustrated, the concept of customer services is far away nowadays from being the slow-moving and reluctant post-sales, complaints-adjusting function it was in the 1950s and '60s.

Its scope is all-embracing and is as much an attitude of mind in today's successful business organisations as is the new-style 'Marketing is everything!' approach.

The rest of this Unit examines in detail those aspects of customer services which, while specialised, impact upon the work of every employee and in particular, those with management aspirations.

PC
3.4.4
3.4.5

DISCUSSION TOPICS

1 If the product or service is any good, people are going to buy it anyway. If it isn't, no amount of customer watchamacallit is going to help!

2 Is it 'pie-in-the-sky' to expect an accounts ledger clerk who spends all day, every day eyeballing a VDU screen to develop a customer caring approach?

3 What strategies could a company develop to help employees who never see a customer to become more customer services oriented?

4 If the customer function is supposed to be as all-embracing as its marketing counterpart, why is it the Cinderella department in so many firms?

5 A number of package-tour operators contract out their complaining customer claims to claims adjusters, who operate quite independently. How do you view this practice?

PC
3.4.5

WHO IS THE CUSTOMER?

The following table highlights some of the main types of support which different types of customer expect to receive from their suppliers and servicers.

Type of customer	Type of support needed
Manufacturer	• High quality information from suppliers about their products and materials
	• Honouring of JIT delivery schedules and deadlines
	• Continuity of supply
	• Notice of planned price increases for parts/raw materials
	• Meeting of agreed quality specifications and standards in suppliers' goods and services
Wholesaler	• Ongoing product quality and reliability
	• Capacity to meet fluctuating orders and delivery requirements
	• Responsiveness to requests for goods to be made in 'wholesaler-friendly' batches and sizes, like modular bulkbreaking packs
	• Attractive packaging and point-of-sale merchandising
	• Strong yet easy-to-move storage and packaging materials
Retailer	• Pricing policies yielding satisfactory profit margins (see also Wholesaler)
	• Sufficient support from supplier's branded goods advertising and point-of-sale merchandising
	• A fast, efficient and reliable ordering system for obtaining goods
	• An equally good delivery system for getting the goods from the factory or distribution point to the retail store
	• A high quality of design and build which throws up negligible numbers of faulty products
	• Top-quality warranties on manufactured products to aid retail sales

- A user-friendly after-sales service to help when the retailer's customers complain

Service Sector

- A top-quality information service which details clearly the structure and sales benefits of, say, a mortgage protection policy with life cover
- Ample back-up explanatory brochures and leaflets to support the sale of banking. legal and surveying services etc.
- Clearly expressed warranties and consumer protective undertakings to support products
- A committed after-sales service like prompt handling of flood damage insurance claims

The Consumer/Customer

- The consumer's needs embrace virtually all the above listed expectations, since he or she is very often the end-user, in a nutshell, then, the consumer expects:
  - excellent design, build and fitness for purpose
  - easily understood and readily available product/service information
  - whenever possible, immediate availability of the good or service
  - a long trouble-free operational life of goods and services
  - high levels of warranty protection and support
  - caring after-sales service from the seller and his/her associated suppliers
  - a sense of customer/seller rapport – through intermittent post-sales contact (e.g. sales information about a follow-on marque of car) – which promotes a conviction that his business is valued long-term

As the above check-list illustrates, customer needs and expectations about the goods and services they purchase vary considerably. But all customers have a keen interest in:

The Universal Expectations

Pre-Purchase

- Design
- Build
- Information
- Availability
- Continuity of supply
- Stability of prices
- Helpful purchasing schemes (like hire-purchase)

At The Point of Sale

- Informative merchandising
- Demonstrations
- Warranty data
- Choice: colour/size/quality
- Resale/Trade-in Future value

Post-purchase

- Top-quality complaints handling
- Maintenance/Servicing
- Availability of spares/Add-ons
- Fault-free life-span

PC 3.4.5

■ Shaping customer services according to product types and customers' needs

It is has become self-evident to say that an organisation is shaped by what it does. And nowhere is this more valid than in the function of customer services.

When senior directors and managers meet either to restructure or review the shape of their organisations, they take pains to ensure that the type of customer services which they are providing is in tune with the range of goods or services they are selling.

For example, if a national UK company wished to diversify into selling desktop, personal computers and networked computer systems to both domestic and commercial users, it would first need to consider very carefully what the needs and expectations of its prospective customers would be in terms of customer services (see the checklist on page 325). Since personal computers are complex electronic machines, the following areas of customer support would be essential:

- Installation either by a visiting service engineer, or with the help of a well-designed manual for self-installing home-users.
- Provision of a 'Help Hotline' for commercial/domestic users who get into difficulty.
- A first-class service engineer network to support call-out visits arising from system failure. Note: many computer sales organisations 'bundle' such emergency services into the cost of purchase for the first 12 months and the customer is encouraged to take out an annual insurance to cover such calls thereafter.
- Rapid repair and return service for equipment which cannot be repaired in situ backed up by temporary replacement VDU/hard disk, etc. according to contract.

As you will readily determine, the costs of establishing such a customer support infrastructure in terms of service engineers, help-line trouble-shooters, back-up office administration, a fleet of service vans and regional repair workshops and so on are very high and could only be met from high-volume sales generating sufficient profits.

Thus the national company's directors would need to have produced a most carefully costed business plan and secured sufficient start-up investment if the diversification were to be successfully introduced. Moreover, the manufacturing company supplying the personal computers and network systems would also impose their conditions on such a development. Whenever a manufacturer has a high reputation for quality products and service to protect, it may insist on minimum standards being met and maintained by the dealerships selling its product range. For instance, a car dealership retailing a range of Japanese or German motor cars may have to maintain a stock of spare parts and accessories up to a given quantity and range, which the manufacturer deems necessary to ensure continuity of supply and availability. Dealers who are unable to meet the financial burden this imposes may have to look elsewhere for a motor car range to sell.

At the other end of the customer services spectrum are the much less technical and expensive products, like fountain pens or wrist-watches. With such products, customer expectations are such that they will usually accept that the purchased product may have to be returned to its manufacturer for attention in case of a defect occurring under warranty. And few would demand a temporary substitute during the repair/examination period.

Thus the costs of maintaining a satisfactory customer services provision are much lower. And they are kept in line with the levels of customer expectations by careful management, and monitoring of 'how much support is enough?' Customer servicing of products like, pens, watches and garments will rely on rapid turnround of repairs/warranty examinations or instant replacement policies as the most cost-effective service policies/for relatively low cost, simple design products.

The diagrams set out in Figs 3.23–3.25 illustrate such different type of customer service systems:

PC 3.4.5

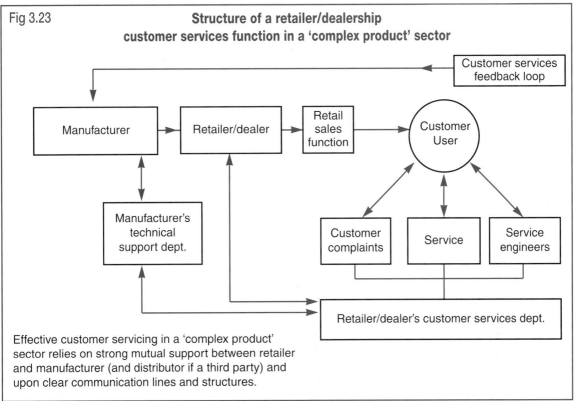

Fig 3.23 **Structure of a retailer/dealership customer services function in a 'complex product' sector**

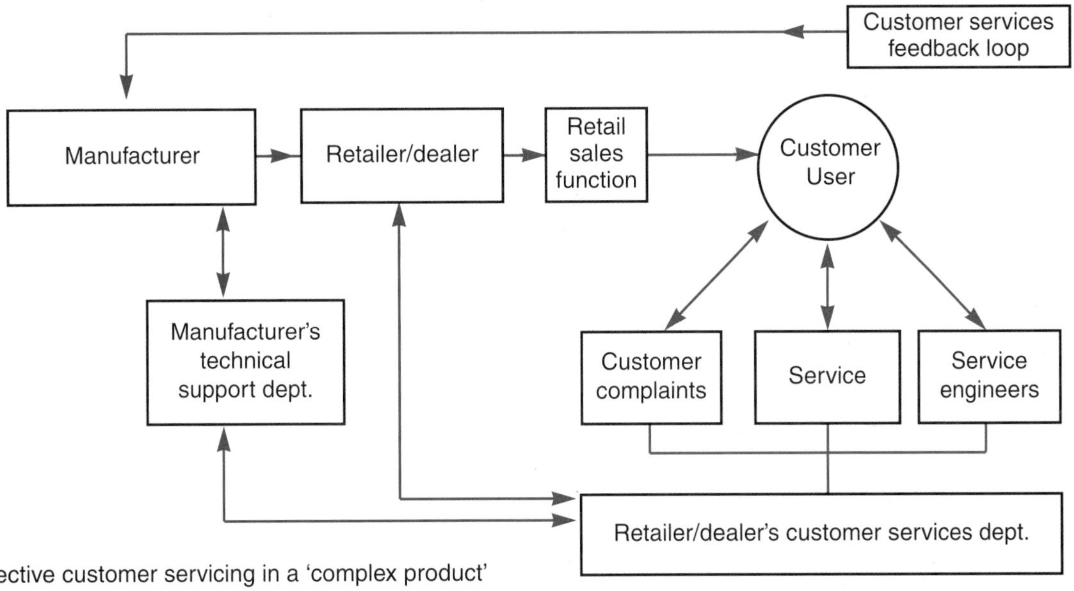

Effective customer servicing in a 'complex product' sector relies on strong mutual support between retailer and manufacturer (and distributor if a third party) and upon clear communication lines and structures.

PC 3.4.5

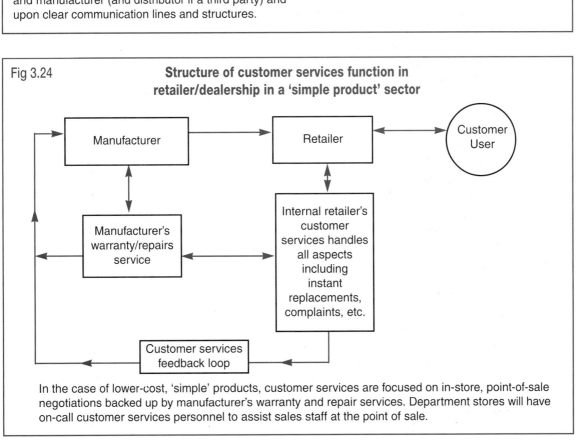

Fig 3.24 **Structure of customer services function in retailer/dealership in a 'simple product' sector**

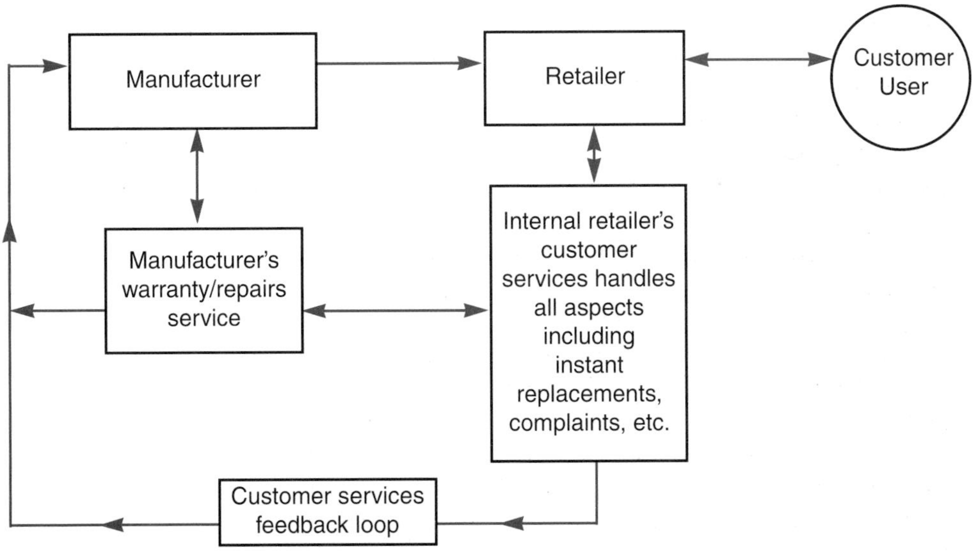

In the case of lower-cost, 'simple' products, customer services are focused on in-store, point-of-sale negotiations backed up by manufacturer's warranty and repair services. Department stores will have on-call customer services personnel to assist sales staff at the point of sale.

PC 3.4.5

■ The structure and operations of a customer services department

As you will by now have appreciated, organisations tend to structure their departments and units according to their individual and specific needs. Thus there can never be a single, correct way of structuring a particular departmental function.

However structured, there remains nevertheless a set of common denominators present in most customer service departmental structures, and Fig 3.25 has been designed to indicate them and to show their differing communication lines and contact.

Customer complaints and grievances

At the very front line of the Customer Services Department is the section dealing with complaints and grievances. Depending on the nature of the organisation's activities, these will usually include the following:

- Ordered goods which failed to arrive.
- Wrong goods delivered.
- Right model, wrong colour delivered.
- Goods found broken/faulty on unpacking:
  - 'It doesn't work!'

    'It fell apart in my hands when I lifted it out of the polystyrene packing!'
- Delivered goods which do not match specification, and/or customer's expectations.
- Delivery notes, invoices, credit notes and/or statements deemed wrongly made out or wrongly totalled.
- Omission of essential documentation like registration/warranty card or operating manual from packaged item.
- Advertising/sales promotion literature misleading or offensive.
- Product information not available or too technical.
- Sales assistant, clerk, motor-mechanic, sales representative, etc. 'rude, overbearing, arrogant, unhelpful or casual', and so on.
- 'Guarantee not worth the paper it's written on!'
- 'Your wretched call-out engineer hasn't turned up yet! Why am I paying you good money for a service you can't deliver?'

The above list though typical of the everyday stream of complaints a large organisation may receive is by no means exhaustive. What it does illustrate, however, is that complaints may occur in a number of readily identifiable areas:

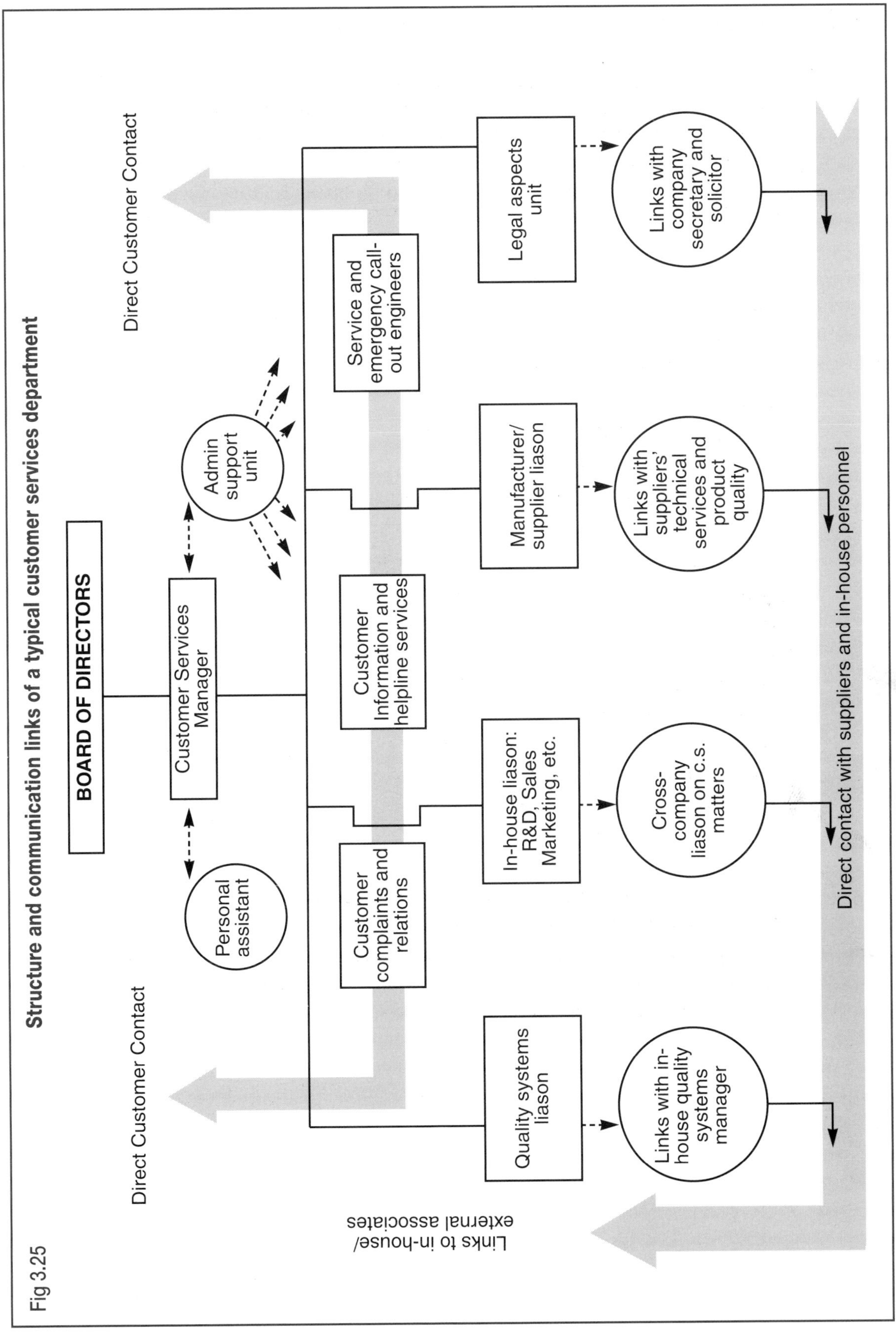
BOARD OF DIRECTORS
Customer Services Manager
Personal assistant
Admin support unit
Direct Customer Contact
Direct Customer Contact
Customer complaints and relations
Customer Information and helpline services
Service and emergency call-out engineers
Quality systems liason
In-house liason: R&D, Sales Marketing, etc.
Manufacturer/ supplier liason
Legal aspects unit
Links with in-house quality systems manager
Cross-company liason on c.s. matters
Links with suppliers' technical services and product quality
Links with company secretary and solicitor
Links to in-house/ external associates
Direct contact with suppliers and in-house personnel

Fig 3.25 Structure and communication links of a typical customer services department

PC 3.4.5

COMMONLY OCCURRING TYPES OF CUSTOMER COMPLAINTS

- Breakdowns in the sale order and delivery process.
- Breakage or damage of goods in transit or unpacking phases.
- Intrinsic product defects.
- Shortcomings in the documentation of sales – whether originating in sales, accounts or despatch functions.
- Problems arising from advertising and sales publications, whether of a legal, moral or informational kind.
- Perceived shortcomings of an interpersonal and customer relations kind arising from employee–customer direct contact.
- Warranty-associated complaints.
- After-sales service complaints connected with servicing maintenance and emergency call-out agreements.

By careful monitoring and analysis of customer complaints by type and by pin-pointing the sources of the shortcomings, customer services departments are able to make a significant contribution to the improvement of the organisation's quality management system and to improvements in customer relations. In this sense the well-worn adage 'Every customer complaint is an opportunity!' holds true.

Interpersonal and communication skills

Of all the various job roles in large organisations, that of customer services complaints and grievances trouble-shooter must surely rate among the most demanding in terms of the skills needed if complaining customers' good-will is to be retained and their upset calmed. For this reason, effective organisations provide extensive training in this area, and some rotate their staff in such posts so as to avoid chronic stress developing.

PC 3.4.5

■ A procedure for handling customer complaints

The following checklist provides a general-purpose procedure for handling customer complaints:

1 Receiving the complaint phase

1.1 The customer makes his/her complaint known by:

- face-to-face contact;
- letter;
- fax;
- phone.

1.2 The adjuster immediately makes contact with the customer on receipt of the complaint.

AIM: To ensure the customer is informed with as little delay as possible that the complaint is much regretted and that it will be looked into directly. PC 3.4.5

Preferred communications medium:

Face-to-face or telephone contact followed up by letter/fax.

2 Investigating the complaint phase

2.1 If the complaint is product-related, the customer is advised that the goods in question must be made available for examination. If service-related, then a full detail of the complaint should be requested; where serious complaints are involved a written detail should be obtained from the customer if at all possible.

2.2 The investigative process should identify the 'what, where, when and by whom' details which define the source of the complaint.

2.3 The examination of goods may be effected by a customer services visit, if the product is an installed washing-machine or television, or by the customer bringing the article back to the sales outlet, if a small item like a handbag or pocket calculator.

AIM: To establish whether the complaint is justified and, if so, the precise cause of the defect/shortcoming.

Suitable examination procedures

2.4 In-house experts – such as service engineer or garment buyer.

2.5 Referral to supplier/manufacturer of the product for examination and analysis.

2.6 Trade or association inspectors for items such as carpets and flooring materials.

3 Adjusting the complaint phase

If the complaint is found to be justified, a decision is taken on the most appropriate form of adjustment, which may include:

3.1 Immediate replacement of the item in question with another of the same type, model and price.

3.2 Where 3.1 may not be possible – such as in 'end-of-line' sales, then a product similar in price and design may be offered in exchange.

3.3 Where neither 3.1. or 3.2 proves acceptable, a refund of the purchase price of the item may prove most acceptable to the customer.

AIM: To ensure that the customer's inconvenience has been accommodated by the adjustment process and his/her goodwill retained.

Where it is felt appropriate, suppliers may elect to pay out an additional 'without prejudice' sum to the customer as a way of acknowledging the time devoted to the complaint process and the loss of the use of the product/service.

Communications media

At all events, a final letter of apology with an expression of hope that the customer will continue to purchase from the supplier is too important to be overlooked.

PC 3.4.5

4 Complaint not upheld procedure

Where the complaint is found to have been caused by customer misuse of the product or post-sale accidental damage, then the adjustment may take the form of:

4.2 A communication (face-to-face or by letter) which explains how the damage/fault occurred and points out diplomatically that it is not a product or installation-related fault.

4.3 This may be helpfully followed up by an offer to repair at cost if this is possible.

Whenever a complaint is not upheld, it is vital to demonstrate as fully as possible how the fault occurred and how it may be prevented in the future. Supportive report documentation from the manufacturer or association inspector may help the communication process.

5 Maintenance of customer goodwill

It is a matter of negotiation with the customer as to whether a supplier decides to adjust a complaint by one of the methods shown in 4 above. The customer's business over a period may be so extensive as to warrant full adjustment even if it is not merited. However, no business can afford to replace for free many items which have been abused or accidentally broken post sale.

6 The legal dimension

6.1 All suppliers of goods and services do well to be fully familiar with consumer and sales related law (see pages 301–3 in this Unit). The Sale of Goods Acts 1893 and 1979 stress the importance of an item being of merchantable quality and fit for the use it purports to meet. Similarly, the Trade Descriptions Act 1968 stipulates a number of conditions which advertising and merchandising information has to satisfy so as to avoid misrepresentation. It is also worth noting that the provision of a guarantee or warranty in no way diminishes or restricts a purchaser's rights in common law.

6.2 It is good practice to store carefully all the documents relating to a customer complaint about a sale or service. If the adjustment process should fail, they may be needed in any future action brought by either the supplier or purchaser.

7 Follow-up with own supplier

Where a product or service is found to be defective, it is important once the customer's complaint has been adjusted, to make contact with the original supplier so as to:

7.1 Check that a batch of items currently in stock does not possess the same type of fault.

7.2 Alert the manufacturer about a possible design or production fault.

7.3 Arrange for a replacement or credit note for any defective and substituted items.

If You Fail To Make A Sale, The Customer May Well Come Back Another Day. If You Fail To Handle A Complaint Correctly, The Chances Are, The Customer Never Will!

PC 3.4.5

Fig 3.26

Example of how breakdowns occur in the supplier–customer relationship

Activity	Comments	Common failures
	1 The customer supplies the salesman with a briefing.	
1 Meeting with the customer.	(a) Here the salesman relies on the information supplied by his external customer.	(i) Not all requirements are identified.
	2/3 The salesman gives a draft proposal to his secretary.	
2 Salesman prepares draft proposal in manuscript or by dictation. 3 The secretary types the draft proposal.	(a) At this point the salesman is the supplier to his secretary. The secretary should insist on the salesman providing enough information to enable the process to be completed right first time.	(i) The salesman's writing might be illegible, or his voice indistinct. (ii) The salesman might not specify a timescale for completing the typing. (iii) The secretary might be overloaded and unable to achieve the deadline. (iv) The salesman might not deliver the draft to the secretary in time for it to be typed.
	4/5 The secretary returns the proposal to the salesman.	
4 The secretary passes the draft proposal to the salesman for review. 5 The salesman reviews the proposal and signs it.	(a) Now the secretary is the supplier and the salesman is the customer. (b) Any deficiencies in the information given to the secretary will show up at this point. (c) The action of reviewing a draft proposal is an appraisal activity. If the salesman got it right when he drafted the proposal, and the secretary typed it correctly, it could be run off in final in the first instance.	(i) Typing might be delayed by interruptions. (ii) The wrong format may be used for the proposal. (iii) No spelling checks might be operated. (iv) Typing may be inaccurate. (v) For important documents it might be acceptable to run off a draft at this stage. Routine documents should be run off in final.
	6 The salesman supplies the proposal to the customer.	
6 The salesman sends the proposal to the customer.	(a) The customer requires the proposal on his desk within 48 hours of the meeting.	(i) Beware the internal mail system for urgent post!

PC
3.4.5

Fig 3.27 **Specimen letter of complaint**

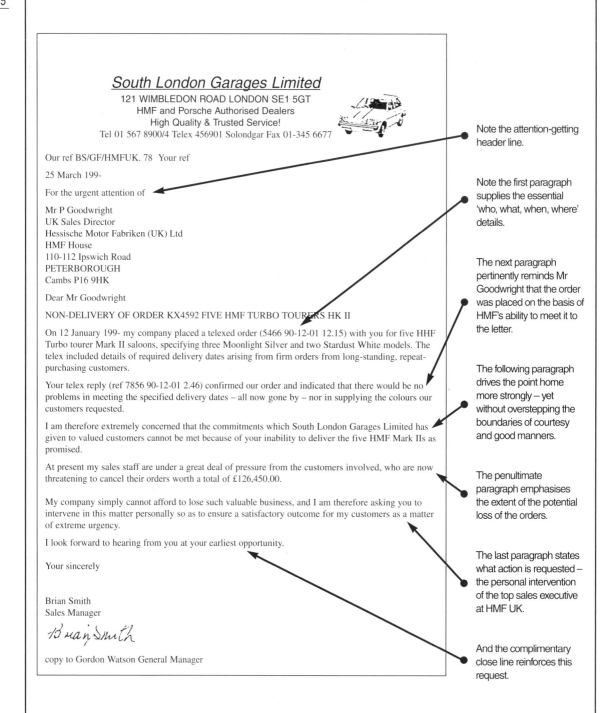

South London Garages Limited

121 WIMBLEDON ROAD LONDON SE1 5GT
HMF and Porsche Authorised Dealers
High Quality & Trusted Service!
Tel 01 567 8900/4 Telex 456901 Solondgar Fax 01-345 6677

Our ref BS/GF/HMFUK. 78 Your ref

25 March 199-

For the urgent attention of

Mr P Goodwright
UK Sales Director
Hessische Motor Fabriken (UK) Ltd
HMF House
110-112 Ipswich Road
PETERBOROUGH
Cambs P16 9HK

Dear Mr Goodwright

NON-DELIVERY OF ORDER KX4592 FIVE HMF TURBO TOURERS HK II

On 12 January 199- my company placed a telexed order (5466 90-12-01 12.15) with you for five HHF Turbo tourer Mark II saloons, specifying three Moonlight Silver and two Stardust White models. The telex included details of required delivery dates arising from firm orders from long-standing, repeat-purchasing customers.

Your telex reply (ref 7856 90-12-01 2.46) confirmed our order and indicated that there would be no problems in meeting the specified delivery dates – all now gone by – nor in supplying the colours our customers requested.

I am therefore extremely concerned that the commitments which South London Garages Limited has given to valued customers cannot be met because of your inability to deliver the five HMF Mark IIs as promised.

At present my sales staff are under a great deal of pressure from the customers involved, who are now threatening to cancel their orders worth a total of £126,450.00.

My company simply cannot afford to lose such valuable business, and I am therefore asking you to intervene in this matter personally so as to ensure a satisfactory outcome for my customers as a matter of extreme urgency.

I look forward to hearing from you at your earliest opportunity.

Your sincerely

Brian Smith
Sales Manager

Brian Smith

copy to Gordon Watson General Manager

Note the attention-getting header line.

Note the first paragraph supplies the essential 'who, what, when, where' details.

The next paragraph pertinently reminds Mr Goodwright that the order was placed on the basis of HMF's ability to meet it to the letter.

The following paragraph drives the point home more strongly – yet without overstepping the boundaries of courtesy and good manners.

The penultimate paragraph emphasises the extent of the potential loss of the orders.

The last paragraph states what action is requested – the personal intervention of the top sales executive at HMF UK.

And the complimentary close line reinforces this request.

PC
3.4.5

Fig 3.28 **Letter of adjustment**

Hessische Motor Fabriken UK Limited

HMF House 110 - 112 Ipswich Road
Peterborough Cambridgeshire P16 9HK

Tel: 0733 29634 Telex: 313123 HMF UK
Fax: 0733 827169
HMF UK Ltd A subsidiary of MMF Aktiengesellschaft
Bundesrepublik Deutschland. Registered in England 963472
Registered Office: HMFAG 241 Knightsbridge, London W3 4AJ

Your ref BS/GJ/HMF UK. 78

Our ref PG/ATY/SLGL/192

28 March 199-

Brian Smith Esq
Sales Manager
South London Garages Limited
121 Wimbledon Road
LONDON
SE1 5TG

Dear Mr Smith

Your Order KX4592 FOR FIVE HMF TURBO TOURERS MARK II

I was very concerned to receive your letter of 25 March 199- in which you complain about the non-delivery of your order KX4592, 12 January 199-, for five HMF Turbo Tourer Mark II motor cars.

As I explained in my telephone conversation with you yesterday, these vehicles are (very unfortunately) still on board the SS Hamburg at Milford Haven docks and we have not been able to secure them because of the current unofficial industrial dispute which our transport contractors are experiencing between their drivers and the port"s cargo handlers.

I fully appreciate how frustrating this must be for you, having already closed firm sales for the Tourers and that your customers are putting you and your staff under pressure for delivery.

It may assist you to know that I have located one Mark II (colour Velvet black) at our Watford deposit and three Mark Is in the Midlands (Pine green, Pewter grey and Aubergine).

In view of our inability to supply for the time being your order as placed, I should be pleased to offer you an additional 7.5% discount on the supply of the Mark Is. If you would like to take advantage of these substitutes, please telephone me directly and I shall arrange for you to have the motor-cars by the beginning of next week.

May I finally give you my sincere assurance that HMF is doing all it can to secure the release of the cargo at Milford Haven and offer my sincere apologies for the inconvenience you are experiencing. As soon as the situation improves I shall contact you at once.

Yours sincerely

P Goodwright

P Goodwright
UK Sales Director

Note: This letter would be dispatched as a vehicle of confirmation after the matter had been discussed by telephone.

Note that the subject heading and first paragraph provide essential references.

The second paragraph takes pains to communicate that the problems are largely beyond the control of HMF and its tone is conciliatory as is that of the next paragraph.

The following two paragraphs convey the best fall-back compromise the Sales Director is able to put together.

And the final paragraph emphasises the ongoing efforts being made to resolve the problems by HMF.

In real life, customer complaints and dissatisfactions are not always capable of being rectified at the drop of a hat. But the adjuster must always communicate a sense of everything being done which is realistically possible to put matters right whenever a complaint is justified. Note also that it is a matter of company policy as to whether a sales or customer services department handles customer complaints – smaller firms may not possess a separate customer services function.

PC 3.4.5

■ Customer information and helpline

Product information at the point-of-sale

Few people can fail to have experienced the annoyance when shopping around for, say, a washing machine or television set to be told by a sales assistant:

'No, sorry, we seem to be right out of the brochures on the Washco Ecology Super model. We should be getting some in . . . soon.'

or to be exposed to empty sales patter like:

'Yeah, it's a dandy one is that! We sell a lot of those . . . Picks up quite a lot of satellite channels does that one . . . Nicam? Yeah, I daresay it's got one of those. Amazing what they all put into the little darlings these days. Real snip at £399!'

The absence of information at the point-of-sale about technical specifications and features may well lose the sale, since the careful shopper will go elsewhere to do his pre-purchase research. Also, the totally uninformed salesman who tries to hide this inadequacy behind a burbling patter may also thoroughly irritate a discriminating consumer.

While the retail manager has clear responsibilities in both the above illustrated areas, it is also important that the supplier's customer services department ensures sufficient product information reaches the point-of-sale and the purchasing decision-maker. Companies in industrial markets realise the importance of supplying product information at the right time and place much better than some departmental store chains.

Customer services may also decide that it is well worth investing in sales training packs about their products for use with sales personnel. A salesman naturally feels more confident about a product or service upon which he has been extensively briefed and rehearsed.

Customer helplines

With the increasing technical complexity of many electronic appliances, more and more sales companies are finding it worth their while to maintain round-the clock telephone helplines to assist both business and domestic users in areas like computer hardware and software, vehicle breakdown, stocks and shares sales, home-delivered ready-foods and so on.

In addition, both private and public service health organisations provide phone-in services which relay information on all kinds of symptoms, conditions and treatments. Such services are provided more visually in the home by fastext services like the BBC's Ceefax and the ITV's Oracle call-up TV pages of information and leisure interest.

Customer information services are today part of the total selling package which may persuade a purchaser to select one as against another product which are both otherwise inseparable in terms of price and performance.

■ Summary

As the above section amply illustrates, to run a customer services unit or department successfully entails a great deal of administrative know-how and interpersonal communication skills.

No two customers are ever the same, and just a few can prove extremely demanding to handle in terms of achieving an outcome which entirely re-establishes customer satisfaction as well as meeting organisational requirements and policies. Nevertheless, research has clearly demonstrated (to an astonishing level of 96 per cent) that if a customer feels him or herself to have been demeaned or not to have had a complaint suitably handled, he or she won't ever use that business again – ever!

REVIEW TEST

PC
3.4.1
3.4.2
3.4.3
3.4.4
3.4.5

1 List five buying motivators which prompt consumers to buy.

2 Explain briefly why middle-aged people are termed 'grey panthers' in terms of their buying power.

3 List four different types of direct selling method and explain briefly how each work.

4 Do the same for four types of indirect selling method.

5 List four types of sales promotion, sales support 'tool' used to encourage potential business customers to place an order.

6 What is merchandising material?

7 Explain what is meant by the term 'self-liquidating offer' in terms of sales promotion.

8 List five main administrative functions of a sales department.

9 Draw up a list of six bullet points which summarise a sales person's job role.

10 What does the acronym AIDA stand for?

11 Put in correct sequence the four main credit sales transaction documents.

12 Provide a short definition of what you understand as the function of customer service.

13 Provide three different examples of the ways in which customer services liaises with other business departments in a large firm to deliver customer satisfaction.

14 Explain how a service engineer might assist the customer service function.

15 With whom does the legal responsibility for a defective product lie for a good purchased by a consumer – its manufacturer or its retailer?

16 List four types of commonly occurring customer complaint.

17 Put in to a correct sequence the seven stages in handling effectively a customer's complaint.

PC 3.4.5

DISCUSSION TOPICS

1 'Consumers have legal rights in theory, but in practice litigation is so expensive such rights really don't exist for the vast majority of the public!'

True? False? What do you think should be done to ensure that everyone has access to legal redress?

2 'In reality, both the shop assistant and the shopper have only the haziest notion of their respective legal rights and responsibilities – so buying and selling's a bit of a lottery where both sides hope for the best and a quiet life!'

How would you set about improving the above state of affairs?

3 What do you think should be included in every guarantee of goods and appliances on the consumer market?

4 How developed would you say customer services are at present in the UK, according to your own buying experiences?

5 What do you think should be the priorities for improving current UK customer services generally?

KNOWLEDGE TEST

Element 3.4
Evaluate sales methods and customer service to achieve customer satisfaction

1 Which of the following statements is true, and which false?

A Direct selling methods include sending unsolicited faxes to business people.
B Telesales is a term used to describe selling over the phone.
C Pyramid selling is illegal in the UK.
D Indirect selling methods includes selling through agents.

2 (i) Consumers are sometimes prompted to buy in order to satisfy a need for self-esteem to be boosted.
(ii) 'Keeping up with the Joneses' is an outdated motivator for consumer buying.

Which of the following options best describes the above statements?

A	(i)	T	(ii)	T
B	(i)	T	(ii)	F
C	(i)	F	(ii)	T
D	(i)	F	(ii)	F

3 (i) Direct selling cuts operational and payroll costs.
(ii) Direct selling gives consumers more choice.

Which of the following options best describes the above statements?

A	(i)	T	(ii)	T
B	(i)	T	(ii)	F
C	(i)	F	(ii)	T
D	(i)	F	(ii)	F

4 Which of the following is a direct selling method, and which not?

A Calling in on pubs and restaurants to sell insurance to customers.
B Selling via television programmes.
C Selling from factories.
D Selling surplus stock from museums and art galleries.

5 (i) Providing point-of-sale material comes under the classification of merchandising.
(ii) In reality, there is no such thing as a free gift in sales promotion.

Which of the following options best describes the above statements?

A	(i)	T	(ii)	T
B	(i)	T	(ii)	F
C	(i)	F	(ii)	T
D	(i)	F	(ii)	F

6 Which of the following statements is true, and which false?

A 'Closing a sale' is a specialist term used to describe a situation in which a sales person decides not to proceed when faced with an unwilling buyer.
B A credit note is used to provide a refund to a credit customer.
C Sales tracking software packages are used to locate business or consumer customers who might be persuaded to buy a good or service.
D A sales representative's job may include chasing bad debts.

7 (i) An important part of customer services is to progress-chase sales orders.
(ii) Customer services generally has strong links with quality assurance.

Which of the following options best describes the above statements?

A	(i)	T	(ii)	T
B	(i)	T	(ii)	F
C	(i)	F	(ii)	T
D	(i)	F	(ii)	F

PORTFOLIO OF EVIDENCE ACTIVITY

PC
3.4.1
3.4.2
3.4.3
3.4.4
3.4.5

Element 3.4
Evaluate sales methods and customer service to achieve customer satisfaction

ELECTRONIC OFFICE EQUIPMENT PLC

Scenario

You work in the Marketing Department of *Electronic Office Equipment plc*, a national public company which sells a wide range of electronic office and business telecommunications equipment to a diverse set of businesses – large and small.

You have been asked by your boss, Fiona Carlton, to undertake a project which will enable the company to improve its sales-force training and development. The project is detailed below.

Phase 1

Initially, you have been asked to research and write a report which profiles *EOE*'s sales methods in terms of (a) meeting its customers' needs and (b) meeting its own needs. Your report should also include a set of proposals which explain how a sales campaign could be planned and executed for a single product in *EOE*'s range - either using direct or indirect sales methods.

Phase 2

You have also been asked to design a wallet which forms an information pack for *EOE*'s sales-force. The aim of the pack is to provide a clear and simple set of material which explains the main features of the sales-person's role, how the sales process can be successfully effected, and what legal aspects it is important for a salesperson to be fully familiar with, The pack should also include details of how the salesperson's job interacts with sales administration and the importance of carrying out sales administration duties which play a key part in *EOE*'s efficiency and profitability.

Phase 3

Lastly, you have been asked to produce a short and simple hand-out to go in the pack which outlines the role of *EOE*'s Customer Service Department, and how it helps the company to achieve its mission and corporate plan objectives.

Task 1

At the outset of this activity, take time to plan your action and to fill out the appropriate parts of your activity planning and review log - and also to submit it with your evidence.

Task 2

Research and compose the report as requested by Fiona Carlton. Note: you may base your research on the selling methods employed by a local or national business equipment sales business - or use a mix of sources for your research data.

Produce a suitable report in not more than 5 sides of A5 (excluding illustrative material).

Task 3

Carry out a suitable programme of fact-finding, and then design a suitable sales-force briefing pack as detailed above in Phase 2. Your pack should include no more than the equivalent of 5 sides of A4 - excluding the Customer Services hand-out (see below).

Task 4

Produce a clearly set out summary of the role and functions of the customer service department in not more than two sides of A4, and seek to present your information in an visually appealing way.

Performance criteria covered

3.4.1, 3.4.2, 3.4.3, 3.4.4, 3.4.5

Core skills covered

Communication:
3.2.1, 3.2.2, 3.2.3, 3.2.4, 3.2.5, 3.3.1, 3.3.2, 3.3.3, 3.4.1, 3.4.3, 3.4.4

Information Technology:
3.1.1, 3.1.2, 3.1.3, 3.1.4, 3.1.5, 3.2.1, 3.2.2, 3.2.3, 3.2.4, 3.2.5, 3.2.6, 3.2.7, 3.3.1, 3.3.2, 3.3.3, 3.3.4, 3.3.5, 3.3.6

CASE STUDY 1

PC
3.1.4
3.1.5

'A Mars a Day'

Clever tactics and famous slogan boost sales of the black-wrapped product born in small Slough factory

MILLIONS OF MARS A DAY ADD UP TO HEALTHY ANNIVERSARY

The Mars bar is still thriving after 60 years. ***Nicholas Watt*** *reports on a success story that defies the laws of marketing*

BRITAIN'S most enduring nibble has reached its 60th anniversary. The Mars bar, chewed by children and adults alike, was launched with little fanfare from a one-room factory in Slough, Berkshire, in August 1932.

Since then Mars has defied all the laws of marketing. The caramel and nougat filling has not changed; the bar's weight has remained virtually the same at just over 60 grammes; and its black wrapping has resisted the hands of meddlesome marketing men.

The strategy has remained simple: to sell the chocolate from as many outlets as possible. This has been underlined by one of the most successful, and certainly the simplest, of advertising slogans. 'A Mars a day helps you work, rest and play,' runs the ditty launched in 1959.

It is not always a comfortable ride. Kit Kat outsells the Mars bar by £60 million. In 1991 Kit Kat's sales were worth £190 million compared with £130 million for Mars bars.

Last year food watchdogs, led by Action and Information on Sugars (AIS), tried to ban the Mars slogan on the basis that there was no scientific proof that chewing chocolate was of any benefit

Jack Winkler, of AIS, said: 'There is no scientific evidence whatsoever that Mars makes any positive contribution to working, resting or playing.' After a 14-month deliberation the Independent Television Commission ruled in favour of the slogan.

Alan Mitchell, editor of *Marketing,* said yesterday that the Mars strategy has been brilliant. 'They think very carefully and in the long term. For example, they carried out three years of tests before launching Mars ice cream in 1989. This allowed the company to set up their own manufacturing technique that was uncopyable.

'Mars also maintain constant awareness by sponsoring key events such as the London Marathon, and supporting the British Olympic team in Barcelona.'

Mars is working on an ambitious plan to follow the Japanese example of selling confectionery from public vending machines. Mr Mitchell said: 'This would give Mars control of distribution and would mean that the product would be available 24 hours a day.'

What do the food experts think of the bar? Keith Floyd, the television cook, said: 'I have been eating Mars bars

THE PRICE OF A MARS BAR

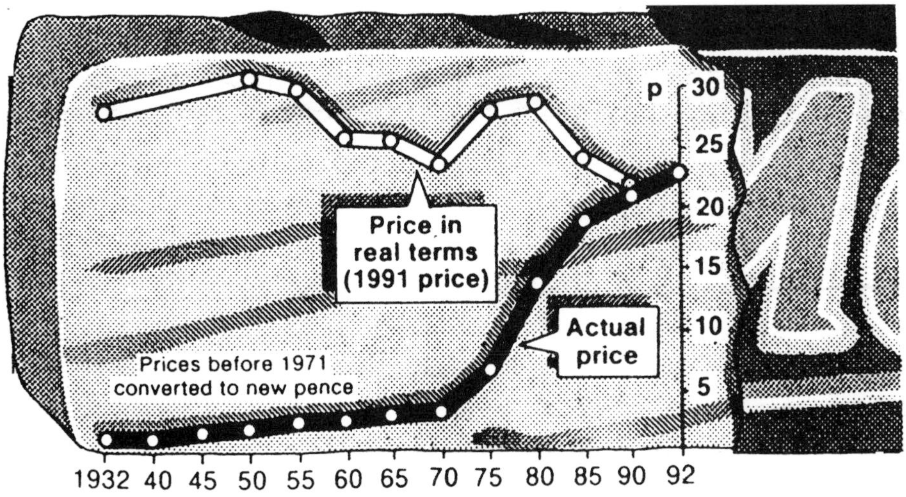

since as long as I can remember. I always keep them in the fridge in quarter inch slices which I eat with crunchy sour apples.

'Mars is one of the few things that is so quintessentially British, like HP Sauce and Bird's Eye. When I was once in real trouble in my restaurant I melted down a Mars bar and poured it on to ice cream. The customers were delighted.'

Mars was launched in Britain by the American entrepreneur, Forrest E. Mars senior, after his father, Frank gave him $50,000 and the foreign rights to the Milky Way.

Frank had launched Milky Way in America in the 1920s after his son suggested that he should put a chocolate-malted drink in a candy bar. Forrest Mars senior was attracted by Britain's reputation for devouring chocolate which was fed by a line of manufacturers, including Rowntrees, Terry's and Cadburys.

The British start was relatively modest, with the factory in Slough employing 12 people. Within a year that had shot up to 100, and in the first year two million bars were sold.

That was followed by a British version of the Milky Way in 1935 and Maltesers in 1937. Those two were temporarily stopped during the war, but production of the Mars bars continued.

Today the Mars company has 18 per cent of all confectionery sales in Britain. The factory, which is still based in Slough, produces three million Mars bars a day.

Mars does not sell just chocolate. Its other brands include Uncle Ben's rice and Whiskas and Pedigree pet food.

The Slough factory is the British side of a worldwide operation which has annual sales of $12 billion. Mars Inc is based in the Washington suburb of McLean, in Virginia, where Forrest Mars senior's two sons share the role of chief executive.

The family is highly secretive and shuns contact with the media. According to *Forbes* magazine the family is worth $12.5 billion, making it the fifth richest family in the world.

Mars received its most impressive accolade when the *Financial Times* suggested that the bar was 'a currency of our time'.

The paper's Lombard column said the Mars bar was a long-established basket of staple commodities, which include cocoa, vegetable fats, milk solids and sugar. It was also a much more reliable unit of account than gold, which is prone to speculation.

PC
3.1.4
3.1.5

DISCUSSION TOPICS

1 To what do you put down the enduring success of the Mars bar as a snack?
2 Do you think that the public would buy Mars bars from vending machines? If so, why? If not, why not?
3 What point is Nicholas Watt making when he refers to Mars bars as 'a much more reliable unit of account than gold'?
4 To what extent does the article satisfactorily explain the success of the Mars bar? Are there any other factors you can think of from your own experience – for example, having to do with consumer buying behaviour?
5 How do you see the future of the Mars bar over the next ten years?
6 What conclusions do you draw from the graph of Mars bar prices?

GROUP ACTIVITIES

PC
3.1.4
3.1.5

1 In about 300 words, write a summary of what you understand to be the main strands of the Mars marketing plan since 1932.
2 Having first undertaken your local researches into the sale of Mars bars through various outlets, devise a sales promotion plan as follows:

Aims:
- To increase the local sales of Mars bars by 10 per cent over eight weeks in local outlets.
- To maintain the increase for the subsequent two months.

Budget: £3,500

Pricing strategy:
- Discounts to established customers:
  3–7 per cent on purchases depending on volume for the promotional period.
- Discounts to new customers:
  5–10 per cent on normal RRP less 30 per cent for promotional period for orders as follows:

50–100 bars:	5 per cent
100–250 bars:	7.5 per cent
250–500 bars:	10 per cent

Your sales promotion plan should include details of:

- sales communications to *(a)* existing customers, *(b)* new customers;
- outline of design concept for point-of-sale material;
- a rationale for the expenditure of the £3,500;
- a statement on pricing policy.

CASE STUDY 2

PC
3.2.1
3.2.2
3.2.3
3.2.4

Consumer characteristics and trends

'Our Five-Year Plan!'

In groups of three or four, first study the following scenario carefully, and then carry out the activities detailed:

Scenario

Your class (and your year in your Department) have been selected for an in-depth study of consumer characteristics and trends being undertaken for a multinational company – Transglobal Incorporated – which is planning to open in the UK a string of High Street departmental stores which cater exclusively for people in the 15–25 age range.

The stores will be structured on identical lines, having these departments:

- **Clothing and Footwear**
- **Sports and Leisure**
- **Music**
- **Holidays**

- **Education and Training**
- **Bodycare**
- **'Wheels' (bikes and motor-bikes)**
- **Pastimes and Gifts (including books and videos)**
- **'Nico's' – a fast food cafeteria and meeting-place**.

Your group has been briefed to carry out a survey of the tastes, buying characteristics and trends which people **in your current age range** are likely to possess **in three to five years' time** (which is when the stores will be going 'on stream' and be progressively ready to open).

Global's commission to which you are working therefore requires you to research (in your class and department) into the following aspects of your co-students' current life styles and what they are most likely to develop into during the coming 3–5 years:

- **Clothing**: for work / leisure / party-going / informal socialising etc.
- **Footwear**: for work / leisure / dancing / training / sport etc.
- **Sports and Leisure**: what main activities will be popular and what sort of kit and equipment will be in demand.
- **Music**: what types of music will be in fashion, and what sort of equipment will be used to relay it.
- **Holidays**: what kind of holidays and breaks the target consumers will want and where, and how they will pay for them.
- **Education and Training**: what types of education and training programmes will be on offer and what sort of learning materials, personal equipment etc. will prove to be in demand to support them.
- **Bodycare**: what kinds of toiletries, cosmetics, body treatments, equipment and devices will be popular and enjoy a widespread demand.
- **'Wheels'**: what sort of transport consumers in the age-range will wish to buy – for work, social and domestic purposes. (*Note*: Global are considering whether or not to include a small car department in their out-of-town stores.)
- **Pastimes and Gifts**: what sort of hobbies, pastimes and spare-time activities the target consumers will follow, and thus what sort of items this department should stock.
- **'Nico's'**: what sort of products the cafeteria should sell and what decor it should have.

Research guide-lines

Your group's research should take the following factors into consideration:

- how your age range differs in needs, wants, pursuits and tastes etc. from younger–older age ranges
- what contrasts and what similarities in goods (or services) purchased in Global's stores will arise from the differences in gender of your age range
- how likely changes in life-style will alter the type and range of items stocked in 3–5 years' time
- what impact there will be on the stores' decor, image and stocks for sale resulting from: 'green' / environmental issues, the conscience and sense of social needs the targeted consumers will possess (e.g. cosmetics not tested on animals), goods for sale which exploit poor, Third World economies (e.g. hand-made goods requiring many hours of skilled labour being sold 'dirt-cheap')

- what sort of disposable income the targeted age-range will have to spend, and how this will affect the prices of the goods/services for sale and what policy the stores should adopt in this area
- what areas of consumer spending in the age range are likely to increase and what decrease.

GROUP ACTIVITIES

PC 3.2.1 3.2.2 3.2.3 3.2.4

1. In a group meeting discuss and decide how you will tackle the overall assignment. Think about allocating activities among group members fairly and effectively.
2. Design a questionnaire or interview set of questions which will help you to obtain the data you need.
3. Find out what other sources of data (e.g. secondary) are available which you can tap into for your report.
4. Present your findings as a group oral presentation of 15–20 minutes and support it with a suitably designed text-processed hand-out.
5. Decide which group gave the best presentation and why.

CASE STUDY 3

PC 3.4.4 3.4.5

Twenty-four hour call-out service – guaranteed!

Apex Computers (UK) Limited was formed in 1983 as the British wholly owned subsidiary of Apex Computers, a company manufacturing a range of desktop computers based in the Far East. Apex was one of the growing number of 'IBM-clone' computer producers which was able to sell its product range favourably in Europe because of its highly competitive labour and distribution costs. Largely as a result of its penetration pricing marketing, Apex over the past decade had established a flourishing business in the UK, working out of its London and Leeds distribution centres.

Its computer range carries a thirty-day parts and labour full guarantee, and purchasers are able – if they so wish – to extend this by buying additional cover as follows:

a Twelve calendar month parts and labour full cover based on a twenty-four hour call-out guarantee.

b A further two years' parts and labour cover based on a 'return faulty goods to regional maintenance workshop' guarantee.

This maintenance contract is strongly promoted as excellent value for money at £250.00 in Apex's sales literature and is widely taken up. As a result of its rapid expansion during the 1980s, Apex has subcontracted its maintenance contract work to Zenith Electronic Services Limited, a specialist service engineering company with national cover.

Approximately nine months ago, Jim Saunders, a home-based, freelance technical author bought an Apex 386 Apollo computer, together with the £250.00 maintenance contract.

Wednesday 12 May, 4.15pm in Jim Saunders' home office
'Yes, that's right, the colour on the VDU went haywire – all reds and oranges – and then it just went dead!'

'HG 464 JK 361 – You sure that's your insurance reference number?'

'Yes, quite sure.'

'And the model you purchased is a 386 Apollo Mark 2, about nine months old.'

'Absolutely! Look, I'd be grateful if you'd get your engineer over here as early as possible tomorrow, as I'm finishing off a manuscript for a publisher with a tight deadline to meet . . . Yes, I realise I'm not your only customer, it's just that . . . Yes, right. Well, if you can't say whether it will be morning or afternoon, I'll arrange to be in all day. Yes, goodbye.'

Friday 14 May, 12.30pm
'Hello? I rang you about ten minutes ago and asked for your service department. You put the music on, and I listened to "Moon River" about six times, then the line went dead. Look, its really very urgent . . .'

Friday 14 May, 12.40pm
'Put me through to your Sales Manager, please . . . Hello, is that the Sales Manager of Apex Computers? Oh. Well may I ask who I'm talking to . . . Karen Hutchins. Right, well its about my computer. I rang your Service Call-out Department two days ago and arranged for your engineer to call yesterday. I stayed in all day, but no one called, and no one's arrived yet today! I've given up trying to get through to your Customer Services people, your telephonist doesn't seem to know how to put me through, so I've rung you. Tell me, why do you advertise and sell a service you can't honour? . . . Yes, please do. I really need my computer seen to urgently. I really can't afford to lose this coming week-end. A replacement VDU. Excellent! By Red Circle carrier you say. Good, well let's hope it does arrive tomorrow. Thank you.'

Monday 17 May, 10.00am
'Yes, your Sales Manager. In a meeting? Well the Deputy Sales Manager, then. She's in the meeting too. I don't believe this is happening! Well let me talk to the Assistant Deputy Sales Manager, or whoever holds the fort when all your Sales Department's in a meeting. Shirley Waters at Guildford. You mean she's the only one who can help me . . . Yes, I realise, everyone's at a meeting!'

Monday 17 May, 10.20am
'. . . So that's the whole awful saga, Miss Waters. Yes, I'm sorry to bother you personally, but you're the only person in your whole set-up who seems actually interested in solving my VDU problem. Tell me, just for the record, what's your job role in Apex? Assistant Southern Region Distribution Manager. Amazing ! Well, thanks for your listening ear. You promise you'll call back this morning? Right, I'll expect your call about eleven.'

Monday 17 May, 11.05am
'. . . Hello, oh hello, Miss Waters. It's what? Been sitting in Red Circle's Southampton Depot since last Thursday ! I don't believe it . . . because there was no delivery address with it. But I gave them every possible detail . . . and they took down my home phone number wrongly, so they couldn't ring me back . . . Well, I'm really most grateful. This afternoon at 3pm. Right. Well, Miss Waters, I really am indebted to you. You're the only bright star in an Apex sky full of black holes!'

DISCUSSION TOPICS

PC 3.4.4 3.4.5

1 What do you see as Apex's major customer services problems? Can you suggest how the shortcomings you identify are likely to have arisen?

2 How would you judge the action Jim Saunders took? Did he take the right steps to get his computer repaired? Do you think he should have tackled his problem differently?

3 Apex's maintenance contract is costed at £100 for the first months and £150 for the subsequent two years. Do you think this is a realistic price for the sort of cover promised on their guarantee?

GROUP ACTIVITIES

PC 3.4.4 3.4.5

1 In groups of two or three, reread the case study and analyse carefully the shortcomings you identify in Apex's customer services provision. Then produce an entry in a revised Apex operations manual which sets out the procedures to be followed in arranging a twenty-four hour call-out service to repair/replace a defective computer part.

2 As Jim Saunders, compose a letter of complaint to the Director of Customer Services at Apex, who is Mr Alex Watson, Apex Computers (UK) Limited, Apex House, 115–121 North Circular Road, Tottenham, London NW3 4AJ.

3 As Mr Alex Watson, when you have received and absorbed the contents of Jim Saunders' letter (see 2 above), compose a suitable letter of adjustment.

4 As a result of the Jim Saunders incident, Alex Watson decides to hold an urgent training session with his maintenance contract customer services team.

Write the notes he will use in a ten-minute presentation to the team on the importance of effective telephone answering techniques, and then arrange to video record your version. When each group has made its video, play them back in turn, and decide which was the most effective and why.

PC 3.4.1 3.3.5

CASE STUDY 4

Amazing rediscovery: the phone

The humble telephone is back as a top marketing tool

Forget the information superhighway. The really hot interactive medium that is sweeping marketing is far more mundane and humble. The old-fashioned telephone, having shaken up insurance and banking, is breaking boundaries.

Last week, Richard Branson launched Virgin Direct. Like other direct operations, it offers a double marketing bonus of lower costs and more convenience. Last weekend, while most competitors were shut, Virgin Direct was open from 8am to 10pm.

Phone-based businesses such as Virgin Direct, Direct Line and First Direct are just the tip of a growing phone-marketing iceberg. Computer companies are running huge helpline operations to aid customers when their machines go wrong. Flora, Persil and other packaged-goods companies have 0800 customer-care lines and more and more businesses are using telesales operators to replace expensive sale people, or ton organise appointments. Some mail-order catalogues do more than 90 per cent of their business by phone. And one in five packaged holidays are now booked direct with the tour operator, bypassing the travel agent.

New, entirely phone-based operations are emerging, from share and cricket-score information lines to telephone car auctions and outfits such as the London-based Local Heroes, which uses high-tech call-routing technology to enable consumers to use only one freephone line to contact pizza shops, funeral parlours and other local services. The number of 0800 and 0345 calls last year reached 540 million, and BT will this month introduce the 0897 premium line which, for £1.50 a minute, will offer services such as legal advice and faxed sheet music.

All this, says Howard Sandom, BT's marketing manager for telemarketing, is part of an emerging phone culture. He says the phone recently overtook face-to-face meetings and letters as the main means of doing business. He predicts that over the next five years, telemarketing will soar from a £200-million-a-year business to £2 billion.

Yet Britain still has a long way to go. Its systems are not as advanced as those in America. And marketers are finding it difficult to manage the way in which telemarketing is blurring the boundaries between previously separate operations such as market research, customer service, order-taking, selling and distribution.

Worse, they are realising with a tinge of horror that carefully cultivated 'brand personalities' now need to be brought alive through the words and tone of voice of their telephone operators.

How far will the telemarketing revolution go? Some industry experts contend that logistical obstacles will limit phone-ordering to high-value items such a computers and furniture, or services like travel and insurance. But as consumer demand for convenience grows, that may change.

Colin Lloyd, chief executive of the Direct Marketing Association, says, 'The telephone will be the supermarket car-park of tomorrow. You won't need to park your car; you will have only to put your fingers on the button. The shop will come to you.'

The biggest breakthrough would be grocery home shopping. Most recent experiments have failed. But Food Ferry, which delivers the weekly grocery shop to about 1,500 Londoners' doors, is, says Jonathan Hartnell-Beavis, its director, growing at 40 per cent a year.

More could be on the way. As Bob Tyrrell, the Henley Centre's chief executive, told a media conference last week, 'Don't tell me logistics won't allow it .You can be just about anywhere in the northwestern part of the hemisphere and you will be half an hour away from a pizza. If they can do it with pizzas, why not elsewhere? Why can't I phone at 10pm and say . . . I want ten cans of dog food – now?'

ALAN MITCHELL

Source: *The Times*, 8 March 1995. © Times Newspapers Ltd, 1995.

PC 3.4.1 3.3.5

DISCUSSION TOPICS

1 What market niche is Virgin Direct exploiting?

2 To what extent are phone-based businesses responding to changes in life-styles of UK residents?

3 Are there any adverse side-effects likely to emerge from this new type of business?

4 Is telemarketing a buzz-word or a significant development in marketing communications?

5 In what ways could consumers come off worse by carrying out transactions via telephoned arrangements?

FURTHER SOURCES OF INFORMATION

Basic Marketing: Principles and Practice, 3rd edn, T Cannon, Cassell Education, 1992. ISBN: 0 304 31673 3

Elements of Marketing, 2nd edn, A R Morden, DP Publications, 1991. ISBN: 1 870 941 70 5

The Fundamentals of Marketing Practice, 2nd edn, J Wilmhurst, Butterworth Heinemann, 1984. ISBN: 0 7506 0433 6

Do-It-Yourself Marketing Research, 3rd edn, G Breen and A Blankenslip, McGraw Hill, 1989. ISBN: 0 07 00751 8

Effective Industrial Selling, M Macdonald and J Leppard, Heinemann, 1988. ISBN: 0 434 91264 6

The Principles And Practice of Selling, A Gillan, Butterworth Heinemann, 1982. ISBN: 0 7500 0109 4

Selling: Management & Practice, 4th edn, P Allen, M & E Business Handbooks, 1993. ISBN: 0 7121 0854 8

Retail Management, 2nd edn, P Cox and P Brittain, M & E Business Handbooks, 1993. ISBN: 0 7121 1825 X

The Fundamentals of Advertising, J Wilmhurst, Butterworth Heinemann, 1988. ISBN: 0 7506 0250 3

The Marketing of Services, D Cowell, Butterworth Heinemann, 1984. ISBN: 0 434 90263 2

The Customer Service Planner, M Christopher, Butterworth Heinemann, 1992. ISBN: 0 7506 0149 3

The Practice of Advertising, 3rd edn, N Hart, Heinemann, 1990. ISBN: 0 434 90796 0

Public Relations, 4th edn, F Jefkins, M & E Business Handbooks, 1992. ISBN: 0 7121 1709 1

The Marketing Dictionary, 4th edn, N Hart and J Stapleton, Butterworth Heinemann, 1992. ISBN: 0 7506 0208 2

Macmillan Dictionary of Retailing, S Baron, B Davies, D Swindley, Macmillan, 1991. ISBN: 0 333 56499 9

Macmillan Dictionary of Marketing & Advertising, 2nd edn, M J Baker, Macmillan, 1990. ISBN: 0 333 51605 2

Getting It Right the Second Time (Marketing Case Histories), M Gershman, Mercury Books, 1991. ISBN: 1 85251 160 5

Customer Service: How to Achieve Total Customer Satisfaction, M Peel, Kogan Page, 1987. ISBN: 1 85091 305 6

How To Turn Customer Service Into Customer Sales, B Katz, Gower Business Skills, 1988. ISBN: 0 7045 0616 5

Customer Service and Support, C Armistead and G Clark, Financial Times & Pitman Publishing, 1992.
ISBN: 0 273 032739

Implementing Total Quality Management, L and M Munro-Faure, Financial Times & Pitman Publishing, 1992.
ISBN: 0 273 038 48 6

Business Law, 3rd edn, D Keenan and S Riches, Pitman Publishing, 1993. ISBN: 0 273 60114 8

Total Customer Service – The Ultimate Weapon, W Davidow & Buttal, Harper Perennial, 1989. ISBN: 0 06 092009 2

UNIT

4

HUMAN RESOURCES

Element 4.1
Investigate human resourcing

Element 4.2
Investigate job roles and changing working conditions

Element 4.3
Evaluate recruitment procedures, job applications and interviews

PERFORMANCE CRITERIA AND RANGE

Element 4.1: Investigate human resourcing

PERFORMANCE CRITERIA

A student must: *page*

1 **analyse** the rights of employers and employees 358–67
2 explain **employer** and **employee responsibilities** in human resourcing 365–71
3 describe **procedures** available to **employers** and **employees** when rights are not upheld 371–80
4 explain the **roles of trade unions** and **staff associations** 380–3
5 explain employers' **methods** for **gaining employee co-operation** 384–5

RANGE

Analyse in terms of: contracts (pay, holiday pay, sick pay, procedures for disciplinary action), health and safety regulations, non-discriminatory legislation

Employer responsibilities: clarify business objectives, offer and facilitate training and professional development; negotiation of pay and conditions, disciplinary procedures, grievance procedures, implement non-discriminatory legislation (Sex Discrimination Act, Race Relations Act, Equal Pay Act)[1], implement health and safety regulations

Employee responsibilities: compliance with terms of contract, compliance with health and safety at work, non-discriminatory behaviour, work towards organisational objectives, meet customer needs

Procedures for employers: negotiation (with individuals, with trades unions, with staff associations); negotiation through Advisory Conciliation and Arbitration Services (ACAS)[2], industrial tribunals; court action

Procedures for employees: negotiation (with employer, through trades unions, staff associations) negotiations through Advisory Conciliation and Arbitration Services (ACAS)[2], industrial tribunals, court action, industrial action

Role of trade unions and staff associations: negotiating pay and conditions, giving advice and information, defending employees' rights, resolving conflict

Methods for gaining employee co-operation: representation, consultation, team working, employee share ownership, quality circles, job security

EVIDENCE INDICATORS

A report which analyses:

- features of contracts of employment concerned with pay and disciplinary procedures
- two working environments for compliance or contravention of health and safety regulations, and compliance or contravention of non-discriminatory legislation.

The report should describe the procedures available to employees and employers in upholding their rights when health and safety regulations and non-discriminatory legislation have been contravened.

A section of the report should explain the role that trade unions and staff associations can play in negotiating pay and conditions, and providing advice, information and legal representation.

The report should include a section which explains how employer responsibilities for two of the following are met in one organisation: negotiating pay and conditions; handling disciplinary procedures and handling grievance procedures. It should also explain how employee co-operation can be gained.

[1]Northern Ireland – Fair Employment (NI) Act
[2]ACAS in Northern Ireland is known as Labour Relations Agency

Element 4.2: Investigate job roles and changing working conditions

PERFORMANCE CRITERIA

A student must: *page*

1 identify **job roles** in business organisations 395–8
2 describe **responsibilities** for human resources in job roles 399–405
3 explain **reasons for change** in **working conditions** 403–9
4 **evaluate** change in **working conditions** 403–9
5 propose a **plan** for a business **implementing change** to **working conditions** 410–11

RANGE

Job roles: director, manager, supervisor, operative, assistant

Responsibilities: to identify business objectives, to work with others, to meet targets, to monitor performance, to implement change in working conditions, to provide training, to give advice, to discipline, to handle grievance

Reasons for change: labour mobility, improving productivity, improving employee motivation, adapting to technological changes, employing new skills

Working conditions: fixed short-term contracts, long-term contracts; pay, benefits; flexible (hours, location, work space, multi-skilling, job sharing)

Evaluate in terms of: costs to business, benefits for business, costs to individuals, benefits for individuals

Plan to implement change through: planning, training, monitoring progress

EVIDENCE INDICATORS

A report which identifies five individuals in business organisations who hold the range of job roles. The report should describe each individual's responsibilities in identifying and meeting targets, working with others, training, discipline and implementing change in working conditions.

The report should explain why working conditions are subject to change, and explain indepth one reason for change in working conditions.

A plan to implement change in working conditions. The plan should also identify those job roles which would have a responsibility for implementing the change.

Element 4.3: Evaluate recruitment procedures, job applications and interviews

PERFORMANCE CRITERIA

A student must: *page*

1. assess the effectiveness of **recruitment procedures** in attracting and recruiting applicants — 415–18, 423–6
2. explain how **job descriptions** and **person specifications** match applicants with vacancies — 419–23
3. produce and evaluate letters of application for clarity and quality of presentation — 431–5
4. produce and evaluate **curricula vitae** for clarity and quality of presentation — 430, 436–8
5. practise and **appraise interviewer techniques** — 438–45, 451–6
6. practise and **appraise interviewee techniques** — 438–45, 451–6
7. explain and give examples of **legal obligations** and **ethical responsibilities** in **recruitment procedures** and interviews — 445–7

RANGE

Recruitment procedures: advertising vacancies, shortlisting, dealing with references, assessing candidates, confirming employment, dealing with unsuccessful candidates

Job descriptions: job title, position within organisational structure, duties and responsibilities

Person specifications: personal attributes and achievements, qualifications, experience, competence

Curricula vitae: name, date of birth, address, telephone number, education and training, qualifications, other relevant achievements, interests, references

Interviewer techniques: opening the interview, asking questions, asking follow-on questions, using body language, closing the interview, giving feedback

Interviewee techniques: preparing, showing confidence, using body language, listening to questions, responding to questions, asking questions, being clear and concise

Appraise in terms of: own performance in demonstrating interviewer and interviewee techniques, interaction between participants, success of interview (meeting its intended purpose, meeting legal obligations, meeting ethical responsibilities)

Legal obligations: equal opportunities*, contract of employment

Ethical responsibilities: honesty, objectivity, fairness, confidentiality

EVIDENCE INDICATORS

A report based on the recruitment procedures used [illegible] business or a recruitment agency. The report should [illegible]

- two job descriptions and two person specifications with a commentary which identifies the most appropriate applicant for the vacancy
- two application letters and two curricula vitae - one should be the student's own, the other produced for a person with several years' work experience. The curricula vitae should be evaluated for the clarity of language, the quality of presentation, and their relevance to the jobs applied for
- two interview appraisal forms recording a self-appraisal and appraisal by others of the student's performance as interviewee and interviewer in two mock or real interviews. The interview appraisal forms should be supported by notes explaining the issues underlying examples of discrimination and unethical behaviour in recruitment.

* For Northern Ireland equal opportunities should include religion and politics.

he work of the human resources or personnel function and the ways ks with other specialised departments or units within a private or public ion. It examines the rights and responsibilities of both employers and enues of redress which are available to both in cases of grievance or elationship between employer, employee and trade unions and staff ass , as well as good practices in creating and maintaining productive employer-employee relations.

In addition, Unit Four surveys the main features of key job roles in organisations, together with the main responsibilities of staff working at various levels within a hierarchy. It also examines the specialist functions and operations of human resource management and its role in negotiating and administering pay and working conditions.

Lastly, Unit Four evaluates current approaches to recruitment, including the design and purpose of situations vacant advertisements, techniques of short-listing, person specifications, job descriptions, curricula vitae and letters of application. In this section, the job interview process is examined in detail – from both interviewer and interviewee perspectives, together with the associated interview documents, pointers on body language and interviewing techniques. Also, the legal and ethical aspects of recruitment are detailed and explained.

Unit overview

■ People: the ultimate resource

'An organisation's most precious asset is its people.'

A well-worn observation, which nevertheless bears repeating, is that it is not the bricks and mortar, not the factory machines, not the office systems and equipment and not the availability of money which ensure an organisation's success or failure, it is the ability, determination and morale of its people.

Over the past one hundred and fifty years, a number of terms and descriptors have been used as labels for the people who work in organisations – from labour and hands to staff and personnel. Of all these, the term human resources is probably the happiest and most accurate, since it acknowledges the contributions made by people working at every level in the organisation as a resource which costs money to provide, which is finite, and which should therefore be employed wisely. It is also a term which avoids overtones of us-ness and them-ness, which sometimes characterise poor industrial relations.

In this Unit the title Human Resources is used as a collective term for the workforce, and also to embrace many of the management and administrative activities which support employees as they go about their work, as in 'human resources management'. The other term widely in use is, of course, 'the personnel function'. Of the two perhaps human resource management has a broader meaning, while 'personnel' describes the activities of the department or unit which discharges the responsibilities set out below. For the purpose of this Unit, human resources and personnel take on the same meaning.

■ The personnel function

In many ways, the personnel function in organisations operates across a kind of 'cradle-to-grave' spectrum. It certainly spans the progression of employees from recruitment to retirement and beyond, in the management of company pension schemes and involvement in company social activities.

The following checklist identifies the major responsibilities of the personnel function in organisations:

THE PERSONNEL FUNCTION EMBRACES:

Manpower planning and skills auditing

Monitoring the organisation's human resource needs and providing for them; this function involves manpower planning, auditing the skills and expertise of the workforce and designing staff development programmes for existing employees.

Recruitment and personnel selection

Maintaining a recruitment policy which ensures a continuity of supply of personnel in all arms of the business so as to meet human resource needs caused by retirement, resignations, promotions, maternity leave, changing organisational activities and so on.

Staff training and development

Once on the payroll, all staff need to be included in a rolling programme of personal development in order to grow and to maintain their job interest; moreover, the organisation constantly needs to ensure that its workforce is up to the challenges of change – in the market-place, in technology, in terms of foreign competition, in product development and so on – if it is to survive.

Staff appraisal and performance review

Many organisations relate employees' pay to their performance in the job, and so personnel departments are required to devise and maintain systems which appraise every member of staff at least once a year and to relate such appraisals to carefully structured pay scales and bonus tables.

Industrial relations

It generally falls to the personnel department to coordinate on behalf of the board of directors company policy on pay and conditions of service. These are regularly updated in rounds of negotiations with the trade unions and associations recognised by the company and its industry. In addition, personnel will design and implement procedures for handling complaints and grievances from employees and also any disciplinary measures deemed necessary and warranted by management. It will also handle issues like voluntary and involuntary redundancy and early retirement schemes, as well as the termination of contracts of employment. In this context, personnel staff need to be expert in matters of industrial and employment law.

Employment conditions analysis

In order to sustain a competitive position in the market for employees, personnel managers need to obtain regular analyses of local and national labour market trends.

The 'rate for the job' – what employers will pay and employees accept in any recruitment process – is continuously changing due to supply and demand, boom or recession, specific local circumstances, like the winning of a massive government contract by a single engineering firm and so on.

Thus personnel managers need to keep fully abreast of employment trends and developments, like government subsidised youth training schemes, in order to ensure that recruitment advertisements are effective and that pay scales and packages are attractive enough to ensure that key personnel are happy and stay with the company or public service organisation.

Employee welfare

All enlightened organisations extend the personnel function to include support for the social and recreational needs of the workforce. Thus many personnel departments are responsible for organising outings – to the theatre, pop-concert or sports event – at subsidised prices; for the running of a works social club and allied sports facilities for retired employees, which may include Christmas parties and so on. The contribution of such welfare services to staff morale should not be underestimated. Moreover, some organisations will support their employee associations in helping aged former employees fallen on hard times through the setting up of trust funds, etc.

Pensions administration

It usually falls to the personnel department in an organisation to manage the firm's pensions programme. Normally the actual payment of pensions and maintenance of records is undertaken by the pensions company which holds the contract to manage a company's scheme – in much the same way as a bank or chartered accounting partnership will manage a company's payroll for a set fee.

In many organisations a joint body representing both employers and employees acts as a watchdog to ensure that pension payments in and out of the scheme are made within the law. Recent cases of gross misappropriation of pension funds are likely to bring about changes in the law and devolve more responsibility on to the personnel function.

Element 4.1
INVESTIGATE HUMAN RESOURCING

PC 4.1.1

The rights of employers and employees

Since ancient, Biblical times, 'the labourer' has been reckoned to be 'worthy of his hire'. In other words, a fair day's work should be rewarded with a fair day's pay. And, indeed, this concept of a mutual agreement, arrangement – in our age, a contract of employment – has characterised the underpinning relationship between the giver and the receiver of employment.

Many of the contemporary employment rights which are, today, taken very much for granted by both employers and employees alike did not reach the proverbial statute book without long and hard struggles – of nineteenth century philanthropists, like the Rowntree family, early trade unionists, like the Tolpuddle Martyrs and the founders of the first Trade Union Congress (held in 1868), as well as enlightened employers such as the Shippams of Sussex and trail-blazing politicians and social workers such as Kier Hardy and Sidney and Beatrice Webb. Between 1840 and 1980 a slow, but effective, bandwagon rolled away from the exploitation of workers and towards a much more even-handed relationship between employers and employees.

In recent times, the 1970s and early 1980s saw a significant amount of employment legislation enacted in successive UK parliaments aimed at providing:

- an employer with a clear understanding of what could reasonably be expected from a person accepting employment
- clear details of what had to be included in a contract of employment
- details of what statutory entitlements an employee had a right to expect from his or her employer in terms of job security, safety, the right to join (or not to join) a trade union, sanitary and restroom provisions, sick pay and maternity leave entitlements, maximum hours of work (particularly for juveniles), freedom from racial or gender discrimination and so on.
- similarly, the rights of employers were also reviewed in the period 1971–93; the terms under which an employee could legitimately have his or her employment terminated, be declared redundant or be summarily dismissed were redefined, as well as the procedures which trade unions would have to follow in order to call a strike, picket employers'

premises and obtain decisions from its membership – shows of hands were replaced by secret ballots for example.

The following table illustrates the major Acts of Parliament which encompass the legislation referred to above:

PC 4.1.1

LEGAL ASPECTS OF RECRUITMENT AND EMPLOYMENT

A number of statutes bear upon the recruitment process:

Disabled Persons (Employment) Act 1958

Employers' Liability (Compulsory Insurance) Act 1969

Equal Pay Act 1970

Sex Discrimination Act 1975

Race Relations Act 1976

Employment Protection Act 1975 and Consolidation Act 1978

Employment Acts of 1980 and 1982

Trade Union Reform and Employment Rights Act 1993

These Acts concentrate on issues such as the following:

- An obligation on firms of more than 20 employees to employ disabled people up to at least 3 per cent of the workforce.
- The requirement of all employers to insure their employees against accidental injury.
- The right of women to enjoy equal pay for equal work (with men).
- The prohibition placed upon job advertisers to discriminate against women in advertising or conditions of service.
- The outlawing of discrimination against employees because of their race, colour or ethnic origin.
- The rights of employees to enjoy basic job security by having a fair contract which stipulates the essentials of the employment agreement: pay rate, notice of termination of contract on either side, sick pay rights, holiday entitlement etc.
- The right for employees to be protected from unfair dismissal and to have access to predetermined procedures for airing a grievance.
- The rights of employees to choose whether or not to join a trade union – whether it is recognised by the organisation or not.
- The rights of employees to reasonable time off work for community duties like being a magistrate or for trade union representative training.

PC 4.1.1

KEY POINTS OF THE TRADE UNION REFORM AND EMPLOYMENT RIGHTS ACT 1993

As a result of the Employment and Employment Protection Acts 1975, 1978, 1980 and 1982 (see pages 361–5) and the Trade Union Reform and Employment Rights Act 1993, the whole area of employment relations is extensively underpinned by statutory rights and obligations on the parts of both employers and employees. The 1993 Act includes these notable consolidating features:

- written employment particulars – place of work, any collective agreements in place, working outside the UK – must be given to a new employee within 2 months instead of 13 weeks
- maternity leave rights and protection from dismissal arising from maternity leave have been strengthened
- employees are increasingly protected from unfair dismissal as a result of their involvement in HASAW activities
- employees' rights to join the trade union of their choice have been strengthened, and their consent must be obtained before any trade union subscriptions are deducted from their pay
- trade unions must now seek a mandate for a strike by conducting a fully-postal ballot and give employers 7 days' notice of strike action
- unlawful organised industrial action can now be legally restrained by any individual deprived of goods or services as a result of it
- ACAS is no longer required to encourage collective bargaining (by which an employer negotiates with a trade union to agree a 'collective' agreement binding upon all the union's members).

PC 4.1.1

The contract of employment

A business or public sector organisation can obtain work from others in two main ways:

- by taking on a person on as an employee
- by giving an independent person or business a fixed-term contract to deliver specified work or services.

When taking on an employee, an organisation takes on board an extensive, complex body of employment law, recommended (but not obligatory) procedures for regulating aspects such as disputes and grievances, and what can be demanding relations between, say, business owners, employed managers and operative staff. For this reason, many companies and public bodies prefer to have work done for them by individuals who are self-employed or by other organisations which operate independently such as freelance consultants, contracting builders, 'outsourced' computer services companies which carry out specific tasks, or other businesses working to specifically issued, fixed-term contracts.

■ The contract between employer and employee

PC 4.1.1

The legal force of a contract of employment stems from contract law in general, and the *Employment Protection (Consolidation) Act 1978* and the *Trade Union Reform and Employment Rights (TURER) Act 1993* in particular.

The following table details the main points of the contract, which must be delivered to a newly appointed employee within eight weeks of his or her starting work:

PC 4.1.1

CONTENTS OF A CONTRACT OF EMPLOYMENT

A contract of employment must contain details of:

- job role and job title: details of what the precise nature of the job is, and its title
- pay: hourly, weekly or monthly rate and position on any scale or spine: circumstances in which overtime may be worked and/or details of any bonus or commission entitlement
- working periods: normal starting and finishing times and total hours/week before any overtime may be claimed, etc.
- paid holidays: the number of working days each year (excluding public holidays) of paid leave entitlement
- sick leave and payment: details of the duration and nature of entitlement to sick pay, maternity leave, etc.
- pension/superannuation scheme: details of the contributory or non-contributory schemes the organisation offers; grievance procedure: clear details of the procedures in operation and the identity of the grievance officer; period of notice of termination of contract: the number of weeks/months of notice normally required on either side to effect resignation or termination

The date when a contract of employment is issued has a particular importance, since a full-time employee must wait two years from the commencement of the post to become entitled to a number of legal benefits, notable among which is an entitlement to redundancy payments on a sliding scale, where the sum paid relates to the number of years of continuous employment.

Job role

The contract of employment is unlikely to provide much more detail about a person's job other than its title and a brief description. However, most larger employers today provide a new employee with a job description (see pages 422–3) which details the scope and range of the job. However, the contract of employment will normally make clear to whom the employee reports – his or her line manager.

Pay

The employment contract must include details of the amount of pay agreed and the pay intervals – whether weekly, calendar monthly or on a four week rolling basis. Also, the contract must include details of the nature of any bonuses, commissions or piece-work rates etc. to which the employee is entitled. Of particular importance – so as to avoid misunderstandings at the outset – details of any weekend or unsocial hours working which

PC 4.1.1

Fig 4.1

Example of a contract of employment

To Ms Jane Doe,
350, Elton Road,
Manchester M62 10AS

The following particulars are given to you pursuant to the Employment Protection (Consolidation) Act 1978

1. The parties are as follows:

Name and address of Employer: Michael Snooks Ltd,
520 London Square
Manchester M42 145A

Name and address of employee: Jane Doe
350, Elton Road
Manchester M62 10AS

2. The date when your employment began was: 2 February 1987

Your employment with John Bloggs Ltd from whom Michael Snooks Ltd purchased the business and which began on 3 February 1986 counts as part of your period of continuous employment with Michael Snooks Ltd. No employment with a previous employer counts as part of your period of continuous employment.

3. The following are the particulars of the terms of your employment

as at 9 March 1987

(a) You are employed at 520 London Square, Manchester M62 145A

as a Shorthand - Typist

(b) The rate of your remuneration is £150 per week

(c) Your remuneration is paid at weekly intervals

(d) Your normal working hours are from 9.30a.m to 5p.m

Mondays to Fridays inclusive

(e) (i) You are entitled to two weeks holiday with pay after one completed year of service and to three weeks holiday with pay every year after two completed years of service.

These holidays are to be taken at a time convenient to the employer between 1st May and 30 October in each year. If an employee's employment terminates before all holiday accrued due has been taken, the employee is entitled to payment in lieu thereof on leaving the said employment. You are also entitled to the customary holidays with pay, i.e. New Year's Day, Good Friday, Easter Monday, May Day, Spring Bank Holiday, Late Summer Bank Holiday, Christmas Day and Boxing Day.

(ii) Regulations as to payment while absent during sickness or injury are available for inspection during normal working hours in the office of the Secretary/PA to the Personnel Manager

(iii) There is no pension shceme applicable to you.

(f) The length of notice which you are obliged to give to end your contract of employment is one week and the length of notice you are entitled to receive unless your conduct is such that you may be summarily dismissed is as follows:—

(i) One week if your period of continuous employment is less than two years.

(ii) One week's notice for each year of continuous employment if your period of continuous employment is two years or more but less than twelve years: and

(iii) Twelve weeks if your period of continuous employment is twelve years or more.

(g) *NOTE*

If you are not satisfied with any disciplinary decision relating to you or seek redress of any grievance relating to your employment you can apply in the first place to the person in charge of the typing pool

Details of the procedure available and to be followed in connection with your employment are posted in the staff room

Dated ninth day of March 19 87

Signed

Sarah Snooks

Company Secretary

From *Business Law*, 2nd edition, by Denis Keenan and Sarah Riches.
Reproduced by kind permission of the authors and publisher.

may be required intermittently will be included, together with differing rates of pay, such as 'time-and-a-half' or 'double-time' etc.

PC 4.1.1

Paid and unpaid holidays and compulsory holidays

The contract will also clarify (as a supplement to the hours per week to be worked and number of paid weeks per year) what the employee's holiday entitlement is – both in terms of the number of days or weeks per year which may be taken (after negotiations with management as to when) as paid holiday. Such holiday leave lies outside bank holidays – those days which employees are statutorily entitled to, such as Good Friday, Easter Monday, Christmas Day and other state holidays. Note that some organisations – especially manufacturers – close down their premises for a Christmas–New Year fortnight, and may require their employees to take a number of days of their paid leave during this period as 'compulsory paid holidays'.

Sick pay and maternity leave

As a result of recent legislation, employees' sick pay is now paid by the employer, as opposed to the state. Contracts of employment have been amended in a number of business sectors, so that sick pay coincides with *but no longer exceeds* statutorily required levels and durations of payment. The *TURER Act 1993* made some improvements to statutory maternity leave and to the mother's entitlement to return to the same job after confinement.

Pensions and superannuation

Details of the pension scheme operated by the organisation (either contributory – where the employee makes a contribution, or non-contributory – where the employer pays all) must be included in the contract. As a result of recent legislation, employees may now elect whether to take their pensions with them or to leave them frozen (until the age of 65) when they change employers.

Termination and redundancy

The contract will also include details of the period of notice to be served (on either side) if the employer or employee wishes to terminate the contract of employment. Legal provisions exist either through referral to an industrial tribunal or through statute for employers to gain authorisation to terminate the contract, say, of an employee who is habitually, but intermittently, off sick. The process of making an employee redundant is carefully detailed under the *Employment Protection (Consolidation) Act 1978*.

In addition, the contract must indicate where details are to be accessed concerning the regulations which an organisation has adopted which govern some of its employment terms – say for summary dismissal in an oil refinery for smoking in a designated non-smoking area.

Grievance and disciplinary procedures

The contract must indicate who the organisation's grievance officer is, with whom an employee may register a grievance, say a complaint about unfair treatment or discrimination etc. Note that fuller details of the procedures an organisation follows in this area are usually included in its *Personnel Manual* or *Employees' Handbook*, to which reference is likely to be made in the contract.

Health and safety

Both the employer and employee have mutual responsibilities for safe working and maintaining a safe working environment. These are fully detailed in the *Health & Safety At Work Act 1974* to which reference may be made in the contract.

Supportive documents

It is important to note that, while not included in the contract of employment, supportive documents such as a job description, employees' handbook or set of company regulations etc. may play an important part in any ensuing dispute between employer and employee and may be cited by either party at an industrial tribunal as a means of demonstrating the presence or absence of a given item relevant to any action brought.

SUMMARY OF THE EMPLOYER-EMPLOYEE CONTRACT OF EMPLOYMENT

PC 4.1.1

- The contract must be written/printed and delivered to the employee within eight weeks of starting employment.
- The contract must include statements which make clear: job title, place of employment, name and address of employer, details of pay and hours of work, paid holiday and sick pay entitlement, maternity leave, pensions, termination, grievance officer and location of related company regulations.

The contract formalises the legal agreement between employer and employee, where:

- the employer agrees to pay an agreed amount for a specified amount of work carried out, undertakes to maintain a safe working environment and to abide by a body of employment law which regulates termination and redundancy, as well as statutory obligations governing sick pay, maternity leave and the collection of contributions for PAYE, NIC and state pension schemes
- the employee likewise undertakes to deliver work of a satisfactory standard during agreed the hours of employment; to work safely – both in terms of personal safety and that of co-workers and to report any dangerous or potentially dangerous equipment or situations; to remain loyal and to respect confidences – in terms of privileged information acquired from the employment about confidential aspects of the employer's business; to carry out any reasonable instruction which is not illegal.

Employee induction

PC 4.1.2

In addition to ensuring that each newly appointed employee is made aware of the legal essentials of his or her employment, many organisations provide a period of initial training and orientation called induction.

The structure of an induction period varies obviously with the type of job. A factory machinist, for example, will be introduced to:

- the person he or she reports to in the management line and the appropriate trade union representative (if applicable)
- the geography of the shop floor and works buildings and location of canteen, toilets, shower rooms, etc.
- the operation of the machinery to be worked
- HASAW safety regulations in force and explanations of company regulations arising, together with disciplinary measures taken if ignored; action to be taken in case of emergency
- works social and sports facilities and social club committee members
- the location and staff associated with issuing pay, providing welfare and counselling (i.e. personnel) and operating grievance procedures.

Similar induction processes (with varying emphases on the extent of training on equipment or administration systems) are adopted for office and managerial staff. Many developed organisations also provide induction manuals for newly appointed employees which supply helpful briefing notes on company policy and practices in:

- job rotation and job enrichment schemes
- staff development and further training opportunities
- company policy and approaches to customer care, quality management, equal (male/female) opportunities
- details of pension scheme
- special concessions (e.g. purchasing company products or access to preferential discounts on insurances or holiday packages, etc.).

The essential objectives of employee induction are to provide a specific briefing (with training if needed) on the job's requirements, an introduction to the people with whom the employee will directly work and an orientation towards the culture and practices of the organisation's working environment.

PC 4.1.2

INDUCTION PROCEDURES

A tutor-led study and discussion of the organisation's policies and procedures on:

- Conditions of service
- Training and development
- Health and safety at work
- Grievance and disciplinary procedures
- Trade unions recognised by management
- Equal opportunities/pay policies
- Sickness reporting procedures etc.
- Emergency evacuation procedures

DISCUSSION TOPICS

PC 4.1.1

1 Some organisations create specialist human resource/personnel departments which service all departments, others include the human resource function *in* specialist departments such as marketing or production. Which approach do you think more likely to prove effective? Why?

2 Which of the personnel functions listed on pages 356 and 357 do you think most important?

3 Outsourcing – contracting outside agencies to undertake work for a business – is becoming a popular option among many large organisations. Can you think of any human resource functions which an organisation could outsource? Or can you make a strong case for delivering all the functions of human resource management in-house?

4 Human resource managers sometimes regard themselves as a kind of 'piggy-in-the-middle' since they often provide an interface between management and workers. Where would you place the function? Is it a part of management, a neutral function or one which naturally represents the workers' interests?

GROUP ACTIVITIES

PC 4.1.1

It is suggested that students do these activities in pairs.

1 Research into one of the following Acts of Parliament and then give a 5–10 minute oral briefing to your class on what you discover, supported by a single side A4, bullet-point hand-out:

- The Employment Protection Act 1975 and (Consolidation Act) 1978
- The Equal Pay Act 1970
- The Sex Discrimination Act 1975
- The Race Relations Act 1976
- The Employment Acts 1980 and 1982
- The Trade Union Reform and Employment Rights Act 1993

Concentrate on those parts which influence and impact upon the human resource function in an organisation.

2 Seek to obtain 2–3 blank contracts of employment from contacts you have locally. Compare their content and layout in terms of what is included and how important parts of the contract are communicated. Brief your class in a 10 minute oral presentation and display the contracts on your base-room notice-board

3 Research into current pensions provisions – both state and private – and report back to your class in a 5-10 minute oral presentation. Include in your talk details of pension transfer and mobility.

4 Obtain via contacts a copy of: a staff handbook/personnel manual and a set of an organisation's employment regulations. Brief your class in a 5–10 minute oral presentation on what you learn about their contents.

PC 4.1.2

Beyond contractual obligations

As outlined above, the relationship of the employer and employee is based upon a contract of employment which acts as the pivot upon which balance mutual rights and responsibilities – essentially to deliver a fair amount of work for what is deemed a fair reward. It should be borne in mind, however, that, like many contracts, the employment contract is available to both parties should circumstances require, but does not cover or extend to a number of additional layers of mutual obligation which characterise many private and public sector organisations.

For example, some paternalistic employers provide a package of conditions of service which extend far beyond what they are legally required to – in order to attract and keep top-quality staff. Again, some employees give much more service and allegiance to their employers than is required of them.

Thus the functions of human resource management embrace much more than the delivery of a contractual package of employees' rights. They extend to:

- staff welfare
- social and recreational facilities
- crèche provisions
- confidential guidance and counselling
- pensions advice etc.

PC 4.1.2

CHECKLIST OF EMPLOYER RESPONSIBILITIES MANAGED BY HUMAN RESOURCES

- legally proper recruitment procedures
- employee induction into HASAW and related responsibilities
- staff training and development co-ordination
- monitoring of staff welfare and (in some organisations) co-ordination of company medical provisions
- representing management in pay and conditions of service negotiations with employees' representatives
- administering the organisation's grievance and disciplinary procedures
- acting for the organisation in matters arising over anti-discrimination laws – e.g. sexual harassment, racial discrimination, equal pay etc.
- monitoring the implementation of the HASAW Act and keeping the organisation's safety manual up-to-date

How extensive a human resource department's span of work becomes depends very much upon the nature of the organisation's business, and its internal culture. Enlightened senior managers and directors take the view that a well-cared-for staff are:

- more likely to work productively and increase output and the attainment of objectives

- less likely to leave – so reducing labour turnover
- less likely to take 'sickies' – which have the effect of decreasing output
- more likely to contribute positively to developmental ideas and proposals
- more likely to respond constructively to change etc.

In this way, a human resource function which extends beyond basic contractual obligations makes a positive and valuable contribution to the achievement of a business's corporate plan.

CHECKLIST OF EMPLOYEES' RESPONSIBILITIES AT WORK

PC 4.1.2

In order to fulfil his or her part of the 'work contract', an employee must:

- **comply with the terms and conditions of the agreed contract of employment** (provided that they are founded on current legal processes)
- **meet the requirements of the HASAW Act 1974** which places specific legal requirements upon all employees to work safely and to promote a safe working environment
- **uphold at work the anti-discrimination requirements** of the Equal Pay, Sex Discrimination and Race Relations etc. Acts
- **accept reasonable (and legal) work instructions and requests cheerfully** and make an effective contribution to the objectives of the organisation (as may be set out in its mission statement)
- **create and maintain productive relations** with: customers, co-workers, subordinates and superordinates (e.g. those below, above, alongside or external to the organisational hierarchy)
- **work within a quality management framework** which seeks to achieve a continual process of product/service improvement and customer satisfaction.

Non-discriminatory legislation: main points of the Acts

PC 4.1.2

The Equal Pay Act 1970 and Equal Pay (Amendment) Regulations 1983

The *Equal Pay Act* reached the statute book in 1970, based on the premise that employees should receive equal pay (and/or bonus, commission etc.) for equal work done. In 1983, the Act was amended to include provisions for other forms of reward or benefit, such as paid holidays or sick pay. In a nutshell, the Act and Regulations provided a recourse to an industrial tribunal (assuming a dispute could not be settled internally) if an employee – male or female – had cause to believe that he or she had been subject to discrimination by:

- not receiving the same pay and/or associated monetary reward for doing the same work as another employee
- not receiving the same pay for worked deemed to be of *an equal value* to the employer

(e.g. two managers occupying equivalent positions on the organisational chart, but doing different work, such as a sales ledger manager and a purchase ledger manager).

The Equal Pay Act 1970 does not enable comparisons of pay to be made between employees working for different companies, unless they all come under the same overarching umbrella of, for instance, a single holding company and are its subsidiaries or are wholly owned divisions. However, provided this stipulation is met, comparisons can be made of jobs in different locations – say factories, warehouses or retail stores.

The compensation provided by an *Employment Appeals Tribunal* broadly enables the successful complainant to obtain back-pay for up to two years of arrears. (For a more detailed treatment of the Equal Pay Act 1970, see *Business Law* (3rd ed.) by D Keenan and S Riches, published by Pitman Publishing.)

Note that the provisions for equal pay came to extend to other areas where employees – male or female – could suffer discrimination, such as recruitment procedures and termination/redundancy practices, ethnic origin etc. as a result of the later legislation of the *Sex Discrimination*, *Race Relations* and *Employment* Acts (see below).

PC 4.1.2

■ The Sex Discrimination Acts 1975 and 1986

Like the Equal Pay Act 1970, the *Sex Discrimination Acts 1975* and *1986* provide legal remedies for employees who have been discriminated against because of their sex – in areas such as recruitment, conditions of service, promotion, job design, training and personal development etc. For example, it is illegal to word an advertisement which refers either to a salesman or a saleswoman, or to make reference to required skills or attributes which are deemed to be slanted to one human gender or another – with a few exceptions, such as where a male or female would need to undertake certain work, such as that of a beautician or a fitter of artificial limbs etc. because of natural considerations of propriety. Indeed, many job roles formerly undertaken by either male or female employees, such as nurses, soldiers, sailors, pilots, police officers, rugby league physiotherapists etc. are now being carried out by capable employees of either sex.

Again, the industrial tribunal may find a case proven and award damages in the form of compensation.

PC 4.1.2

■ The Race Relations Act 1976

This Act came about in no small part as a result of the significant influx of immigrants to the UK in the 1950s and 1960s, when full employment created a job vacuum. The prospect of a better life and the right to enter the UK legally prompted a number of families from various former British possessions in the Caribbean, Asia and Africa to settle in the UK. Many brought with them developed skills such as textile working or small business entrepreneurial flair. Some were also, in effect, refugees from authoritarian governments. Such movements of people from one ethnic and cultural centre to another also took place during this period in other countries, such as the influx of European and Asiatic immigrants to Australia and North America.

In order to ensure that employees of differing religions, racial or ethnic origins did not suffer from discrimination, the *Race Relations Act 1976* made it illegal to penalise employees in areas like those covered by the Sex Discrimination Acts 1975 and 1986 because of their colour or racial inheritance – recruitment, training, opportunities for promotion etc. As with the above Acts, redress is normally obtained through the industrial tribunal system.

Anti-discrimination watchdogs

Note that the *Commission for Racial Equality* and the *Equal Opportunities Commission* were set up by UK governments to act as watchdogs in the areas of discrimination relating to pay, sex, race and disability in the work-place etc.

■ Summary

PC 4.1.2

As the above section indicates, the period 1970–90 saw an extensive introduction of legislation aimed at protecting employees – men or women, full or part-time – from discriminatory activities, whether from employers or co-workers. And the very existence of such legislation with its financial compensations and awards of damages does act as a deterrent.

However, it would be naive to believe that this legislation has proved completely effective in ridding the work-place of uncivilised, harassing and stress-causing behaviour. In reality some employers and some employees 'get away with it' because people need the work and are too frightened to complain. This is why it is important for *every* person joining the national work-force – and especially those studying to become managers in it – to combat discrimination wholeheartedly from Day One, since it divides an organisation and eats away at society if allowed to grow by default.

Grievance, dismissal and redundancy procedures

PC 4.1.3

Whatever the size of the workforce, large or small, disputes inevitably arise between its members. Wherever human beings interact, sooner or later an individual – or a group – will come to feel aggrieved because of a sense of injustice, unfairness or discrimination.

For this reason organisations adopt carefully worked-out procedures – agreed to by both management and trade union officers – to handle and resolve any grievances which employees may need to air

Many such problem situations are capable of being investigated and resolved at departmental or section level promptly and informally. However, where a deep sense of injustice prevails or significant interpersonal conflict has developed, a procedure needs to be in place to take the grievance to an arbitrator at a higher level.

The flow-chart in Fig. 4.2 illustrates this process.

The point at which a representative of the employee's trade union or association accompanies the aggrieved employee at a meeting depends upon the procedure which has been drawn up. All such grievance procedures are customarily produced by the organisation as a printed document which is supplied to new employees at their induction.

Because some grievances are not easily resolved, a set-down appeals procedure may – in extreme cases – allow for the intervention of a most senior figure, like a governor of a

PC 4.1.3

Fig 4.2

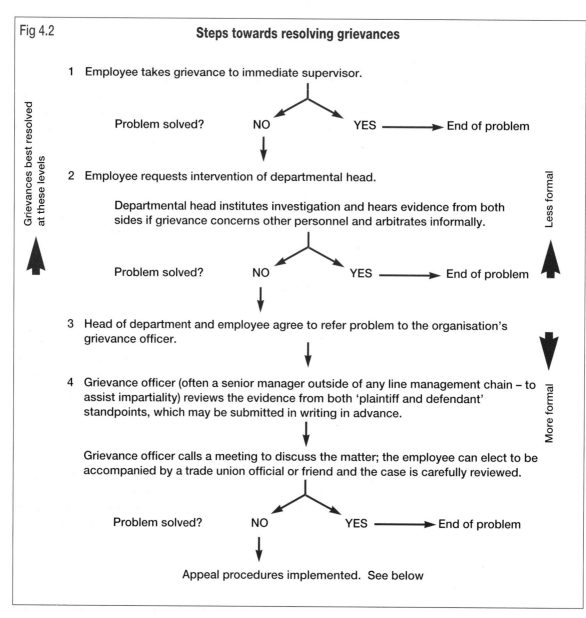

Steps towards resolving grievances

1 Employee takes grievance to immediate supervisor.

Problem solved? NO / YES → End of problem

↓ NO

2 Employee requests intervention of departmental head.

Departmental head institutes investigation and hears evidence from both sides if grievance concerns other personnel and arbitrates informally.

Problem solved? NO / YES → End of problem

↓ NO

3 Head of department and employee agree to refer problem to the organisation's grievance officer.

↓

4 Grievance officer (often a senior manager outside of any line management chain – to assist impartiality) reviews the evidence from both 'plaintiff and defendant' standpoints, which may be submitted in writing in advance.

↓

Grievance officer calls a meeting to discuss the matter; the employee can elect to be accompanied by a trade union official or friend and the case is carefully reviewed.

Problem solved? NO / YES → End of problem

↓ NO

Appeal procedures implemented. See below

Grievances best resolved at these levels ↑

Less formal ↑ / More formal ↓

school or a non-executive chairman of the board. However, good procedures are carefully designed to resolve grievances wherever possible at lower, informal levels of the hierarchy and to avoid if possible the involvement of the 'top brass'.

If what starts out as a grievance becomes an industrial dispute, then the organisation's procedures may require the calling in of conciliation officers of the *Advisory, Conciliation and Arbitration Service* (ACAS) who have developed skills and experience in arbitrating in such matters.

To work at levels within the organisational hierarchy where a grievance may be settled promptly and with least upset, procedures must be designed so as to be seen as fair and impartial by all employees. Where good industrial relations exist, management and trade union officials often work jointly to resolve a problem quickly at the informal level. Where relations are confrontational, minor grievances soon escalate because of poor communication and unwillingness to use goodwill – on either side.

■ Termination of employment

PC 4.1.3

The law surrounding the termination of an employee's contract of employment places responsibilities upon both employer and employee. The law provides for notice of termination to be given on either side (see the contract of employment on page 362). In circumstances where an employee has clearly broken the contract of employment with the employer the term dismissal is used to describe the termination. Save for instances such as summary dismissal for gross misconduct, the employee is entitled to be given notice of termination of employment in accordance with statutory provisions. The period of notice will vary from one week to 'not less than twelve weeks', depending on the number of years an employee has worked for the same employer. Employees are entitled to receive in writing a statement of the reasons for termination of contract provided that they have worked for at least twenty-six weeks for the employer prior to the set date of termination.

■ Legitimate, wrongful and unfair dismissal

PC 4.1.3

In general terms, an employee may be legitimately dismissed if the job has properly been made redundant, if the employee is in breach of contract through a form of gross misconduct (such as reckless negligence in lighting a match in a prohibited area of an oil refinery), if legal and reasonable instructions have been disobeyed, if prescribed standards of work performance have not been met or for any other significant and legally acceptable reason.

Wrongful dismissal

In law, an employee is deemed to have been wrongfully dismissed if the employer is in breach of the contract of employment because proper notice has not been given to the employee. By the same token, an employer may seek remedies in law if an employee breaches the employment contract by failing to give and work out notice according to contract.

Unfair dismissal

The *Employment Protection (Consolidation) Act 1978* makes provision for employees to obtain compensation and/or reinstatement or re-engagement if they are adjudged to have been unfairly dismissed by an industrial tribunal.

The process of securing a judgement of unfair dismissal is lengthy and complex. The Act particularly identifies the following instances where an employee would be deemed unfairly dismissed if employment were terminated because he or she had:

- elected not to join a trade union on religious grounds
- joined or intended to join a trade union
- been unfairly selected for redundancy
- become pregnant
- not been taken on again after confinement
- been discriminated against by being dismissed for striking (when others had not)

The twenty-six week qualifying period also obtains in cases of unfair dismissal, which can be claimed by employees up to pensionable age.

A formula for compensation is available to the adjudicating industrial tribunal:

For each year of employment

- Between 18 and 21 years of age: ½ week's pay
- Between 22 and 41 years of age: 1 week's pay
- Between 41 and retirement age: 1½ week's pay

The current maximum compensation available for award is approximately £5,200.

While reinstatement may be legally available as a remedy for an unfairly dismissed employee, in practice it may not always be a viable proposition, given the breakdown in relations between employee and employer. An industrial tribunal may therefore take this into account when determining the award, and provisions exist to oblige employers to make further compensatory payments in such instances.

PC 4.1.3

Constructive dismissal

A remedy in law may be sought by employees who believe themselves to have been constructively dismissed. This situation does not occur frequently, but may arise when an employee resigns from his or her job as a result of an action by the employer which effectively causes the job to be materially changed or done away with. For example, a manager might return from annual vacation to find that the significant parts of his job have been allocated in his absence to another executive and that as a result he has nothing meaningful to do. In frustration he may row with his boss and quit but later come to feel that he was effectively forced out. In such a case, an industrial tribunal may adjudge that the action of the company was in effect to have constructively dismissed the manager.

Given the hardship which many unfairly dismissed employees suffer nowadays in failing to securing other, equivalent employment within a reasonable time, the levels of compensation available may be considered inadequate. Even so, the Employment Protection Acts 1975 and 1978 have proved to be legal milestones in providing protection for employees against unscrupulous 'hire and fire' employers, and the social contract which the European Community is seeking to have adopted by all member states will undoubtedly make further progress in enforcing a civilised compact between the employing and the employed.

PC 4.1.3

■ Redundancy

In legal terms, an employee is considered to have been made redundant if his dismissal has occurred or was mainly due to:

- the employer ending or intending to end the business for which the employee was taken on
- the employer terminating the work of the business in a place where the employee is employed
- the business requirements of the employer ceasing to need (or substantially cutting down) the work which the employee was taken on to perform.

Employers have to follow procedures under various Employment Acts which require the redundancy selection process to take place fairly, without discrimination and only after consultation with appropriate trade union representatives, and unfair selection for redundancy provides grounds for action against unfair dismissal.

Many employers consider that the 'last in, first out' approach is a reasonable way to prioritise posts selected for redundancy, but other factors such as level and range of skills, length of employment service and suitability for redeployment, etc. are also used.

Progressive employers take great pains to minimise the traumatic effects which being made redundant can have on employees – especially those in middle age with many years of service behind them. Personnel departments may establish special units to counsel staff selected for redundancy and work together with local and central government agencies to help them obtain alternative employment. In addition, they may be given training while still in employment to assist them in acquiring or improving marketable skills which are in local demand.

Many organisations try to minimise the impact of enforced redundancy by offering packages to employees to encourage them to take early retirement or voluntary redundancy. Such packages may include the payment of lump sums and an addition to the number of years of pension increments to which the employee is entitled – termed pension enhancement.

Redundant employees are entitled to receive payments worked out on a scale similar to that detailed above in the section on unfair dismissal. In certain circumstances organisations may be given rebates by the government to help them meet redundancy payments.

To qualify for redundancy payments an employee needs to have worked for at least sixteen hours a week over an unbroken period of at least two years for the same employer.

ACAS and industrial relations

PC 4.1.3

The Advisory Conciliation and Arbitration Service (ACAS) was established under the Employment Protection Act 1975 to promote the improvement of industrial relations in general and, in particular to broaden the base of collective bargaining between employers' confederations and trade unions.

ACAS was also charged with the responsibility of providing a conciliation and settlement service in industrial disputes by supplying individuals or teams of conciliation officers who would act as mediators, listening carefully to both sides of a dispute and helping both parties to progress to a negotiated settlement.

As a rule, ACAS responds to invitations to assist, but it is empowered under the 1975 Act to enquire actively into the activities of an industry or organisation if it is felt that there is evidence of a pressing need to improve relations.

Since 1975, ACAS has been instrumental in encouraging companies and public sector bodies to adopt ACAS-approved codes of practice in, for example, a procedure for handling disciplinary matters. Such a code of practice emphasises what an effective and fair disciplinary procedure should be.

PC 4.1.3

ACAS – APPROVED ASPECTS OF A DISCIPLINARY PROCEDURE

A fair and impartial disciplinary procedure should:

- be written down;
- be made available to all employees;
- explain who operates the procedure and who is party to it;
- detail what disciplinary action is liable to be taken for what kind of indiscipline;
- allow individuals to be accompanied by a trade union official or co-worker/friend if they so wish at disciplinary interviews;
- avoid dismissal for a first disciplinary action, save in cases of gross misconduct;
- include a right of appeal;
- be administered fairly and without discrimination.

PC 4.1.3

Disciplinary Procedure: Example 1 (any organisation)

(1) Purpose and scope

This procedure is designed to help and encourage all employees to achieve and maintain standards of conduct, attendance and job performance. The company rules (a copy of which is displayed in the office) and this procedure apply to all employees. The aim is to ensure consistent and fair treatment for all.

(2) Principles

a No disciplinary action will be taken against an employee until the case has been fully investigated.

b At every stage in the procedure the employee will be advised of the nature of the complaint against him or her and will be given the opportunity to state his or her case before any decision is made.

c At all stages the employee will have the right to be accompanied by a shop steward, employee representative or work colleague during the disciplinary interview.

d No employee will be dismissed for a first breach of discipline except in the case of gross misconduct when the penalty will be dismissal without notice or payment in lieu of notice.

e An employee will have the right to appeal against any disciplinary penalty imposed.

f The procedure may be implemented at any stage if the employee's alleged misconduct warrants such action.

(3) The procedure

Minor faults will be dealt with informally but where the matter is more serious the following procedure will be used:

Stage 1 – Oral warning

If conduct or performance does not meet acceptable standards the employee will normally be given a formal ORAL WARNING. He or she will be advised of the reason for the warning, that it is the first stage of the disciplinary procedure and of his or her right of appeal. A brief note of the oral warning will be kept but it will be spent after .... months, subject to satisfactory conduct and performance.

Stage 1 – Oral warning (continued)

If conduct or performance does not meet acceptable standards the employee will normally be given a formal ORAL WARNING. He or she will be advised of the reason for the warning, that it is the first stage of the disciplinary procedure and of his or her right of appeal. A brief note of the oral warning will be kept but it will be spent after ...... months, subject to satisfactory conduct and performance.

Stage 2 – Written warning

If the offence is a serious one, or if a further offence occurs, a WRITTEN WARNING will be given to the employee by the supervisor. This will give details of the complaint, the improvement required and the timescale. It will warn that action under Stage 3 will be considered if there is no satisfactory improvement and will advise of the right of appeal. A copy of this written warning will be kept by the supervisor but it will be disregarded for disciplinary purposes after ...... months subject to satisfactory conduct and performance.

Stage 3 – Final written warning or disciplinary suspension

If there is still a failure to improve and conduct or performance is still unsatisfactory, or if the misconduct is sufficiently serious to warrant only one written warning but insufficiently serious to justify dismissal (in effect both first and final written warning), a FINAL WRITTEN WARNING will normally be given to the employee. This will give details of the complaint, will warn that dismissal will result if there is no satisfactory improvement and will advise of the right of appeal. A copy of this final written warning will be kept by the supervisor but it will be spent after ...... months (in exceptional cases the period may be longer) subject to satisfactory conduct and performance.

Alternatively, consideration will be given to imposing a penalty of a disciplinary suspension without pay for up to a maximum of five working days.

Stage 4 – Dismissal

If conduct or performance is still unsatisfactory and the employee still fails to reach the prescribed standards, DISMISSAL will normally result. Only the appropriate Senior Manager can take the decision to dismiss. The employee will be provided, as soon as reasonably practicable, with written reasons for dismissal, the date on which employment will terminate and the right of appeal.

(4) Gross misconduct

The following list provides examples of offences which are normally regarded as gross misconduct:

theft, fraud, deliberate falsification of records,

fighting, assault on another person,

deliberate damage to company property,

serious incapability through alcohol or being under the influence of illegal drugs,

serious negligence which causes unacceptable loss, damage or injury,

serious act of insubordination,

unauthorised entry to computer records.

If you are accused of an act of gross misconduct, you may be suspended from work on full pay, normally for no more than five working days, while the company investigates the alleged offence. If, on completion of the investigation and the full disciplinary procedure, the company is satisfied that gross misconduct has occurred, the result will normally be summary dismissal without notice or payment in lieu of notice.

(5) Appeals

An employee who wishes to appeal against a disciplinary decision should inform ...... within two working days. The Senior Manager will hear all appeals and his/her decision is final. At the appeal any disciplinary penalty imposed will be reviewed but it cannot be increased.

PC 4.1.3

Checklist for handling a disciplinary matter

This checklist sets out the key steps which employers should consider when handling a disciplinary matter. All employers regardless of size should observe the principles of natural justice embodied below:

1 Gather all the relevant facts:
- promptly before memories fade
- take statements, collect documents
- in serious cases consider suspension with pay while an investigation is conducted.

2 Be clear about the complaint:
- is action needed at this stage?

3 If so decide whether the action should be:
- advice and counselling
- formal disciplinary action.

4 If formal action is required, arrange a disciplinary interview:
- ensure that the individual is aware of the nature of the complaint and that the interview is a disciplinary one
- tell the individual where and when the interview will take place and of a right to be accompanied.
- try to arrange for a second member of management to be present.

5 Start by introducing:
- those present and the purpose of the interview
- the nature of the complaint
- the supporting evidence.

6 Allow the individual to state his/her case:
- consider and question any explanations put forward.

7 If any new facts emerge:

decide whether further investigation is required; if it is, adjourn the interview and reconvene when the investigation is completed.

8 Except in very straightforward cases, call an adjournment before reaching a decision:

come to a clear view about the facts

if they are disputed, decide on the balance of probability what version of the facts is true

9 Before deciding the penalty consider:

the gravity of the offence and whether the procedure gives guidance as to:
- the penalty applied in similar cases in the past
- the individual's disciplinary record and general service
- any mitigating circumstances
- whether the proposed penalty is reasonable in all the circumstances.

10 Reconvene the disciplinary interview to:
- clearly inform the individual of the decision and the penalty if any
- explain the right of appeal and how it operates
- in the case of a warning explain what improvement is expected, how long the warning will last and what the consequences of failure to improve may be.

11 Record the action taken:
- if other than an oral warning, confirm the disciplinary action to the individual in writing
- keep a simple record of the action taken for future reference.

12 Monitor the individual's performance:
- disciplinary action should be followed up with the object of encouraging improvement
- monitor progress regularly and discuss it with the individual.

ACAS offers further advice for handling the disciplinary process to the effect that all disciplinary matters should be carefully investigated before any hasty formal meeting is arranged, that all employees should have the right to state their side of the matter at issue and if they wish be accompanied by a trade union official. They also suggest that disciplinary codes (except in cases of proven gross misconduct) should provide for warnings and opportunities for employees to remedy any shortcomings before a dismissal letter is issued. Such opportunities are given a time-scale in which an employee may, for example, be given three months in which to demonstrate an improvement. Many disciplinary procedures provide for two orally delivered warnings and a final written one prior to dismissal. At all events, an employer's disciplinary code must be demonstrably fair and reasonable.

Where an employee considers that he or she has not had access to a just disciplinary process leading up to dismissal, the right exists in law to take a complaint of unfair dismissal to an industrial tribunal *(see below)*.

While employers are not required to adopt such codes of practice, their acceptance and use on the part of employers may go a long way towards demonstrating in industrial disputes and industrial tribunal actions that an employer has acted with due reasonable care towards a particular, aggrieved employee.

■ Industrial tribunals and appeal tribunals

PC 4.1.3

Industrial tribunals were established by parliament to operate as types of court – with legal powers – to hear cases relating to complaints made under a range of Employment Acts, such as wrongful and unfair dismissal and unfair selection for redundancy, etc.

Such tribunals work through ACAS in the first instance to seek to effect a conciliation, but ultimately have powers to require reinstatements or to award financial compensation where an employee's case is proven to the tribunal's satisfaction.

Employment Appeal Tribunals were established by the Employment Protection Act 1975 to provide both employers and employees access to a higher authority which would adjudicate on appeals lodged after industrial tribunal hearings.

Appeals heard by the Appeals Tribunal include those arising from actions taken under the following Acts:

Equal Pay Act 1970
Sex Discrimination Act 1975
Employment Protection Act 1975
Race Relations Act 1976
Employment Protection (Consolidation) Act 1978

PC
4.1.2
4.1.3

DISCUSSION TOPICS

1 What qualities would you expect to find in an organisation's grievance officer? What could be done if he or she did not possess them in the eyes of employees with grievances?

2 Do you think employees generally are sufficiently aware of their employment rights? If not, what would you propose as practical means of improving the public's levels of awareness?

3 What impact do you think periods of recession and rising job insecurity have on industrial relations? Do you think that employment legislation goes far enough in securing an employee's employment rights? Or too far? Should all employees accept that they are part of a job market for buying and selling work skills, and if they do not complain when they receive rises and promotion, nor should they if they are laid off or made redundant?

4 Have trade unions had their day? Or are they needed more than ever in organisations which provide employment?

5 Can an employee ever be adequately compensated for unfair dismissal – even if a return to the same job is made available by the judgement of an industrial tribunal?

PC
4.1.4

The role of trade unions and staff associations

Background

In 1868, at the time of the meeting of the first Trades Union Congress, the watchword among its first delegates was that they wanted each day: 'Eight hours for work, eight hours for rest and eight hours for education.' In Victorian times the working man's leaders realised that, in order to meet and to negotiate with employers on an equal footing, an education was vital. Moreover, in those days, a sixteen hour day of work in a textile mill or 'manufactory' was common, six days a week.

The creation of trade unions in the nineteenth century was bitterly resisted by employers, who feared that they would bear the brunt of paying for social welfare, the welfare state having to wait a further hundred years to be born. It was not then uncommon for pregnant, single women to be 'whipped into the next parish' nearing their confinement, so that another authority would be responsible for the cost of keeping mother and child. For the elderly and needy, the spectre of the workhouse always beckoned, where 'hard work and short victuals' accompanied their final years.

It was against this back-drop, in which there was no state welfare safety-net, and in which employed people enjoyed few if any rights, that the trade union movement began some 150 years ago.

■ Social reformes and trade union-inspired changes in the workplace

PC 4.1.4

The social conscience of the British people has changed radically since the 1840s. Services paid from taxes now fund a free education and health service; the effects of sickness and disability are nowadays softened by state pensions, grants and allowances; old age pensioners now receive a state pension, so that none need fear penury and the workhouse.

In the workplace, successive generations of trade unionists allied by enlightened employers brought about many benefits and improvements, including:

- the right to belong to a trade union or staff association without fear of discrimination
- the right to strike without the consequence of immediate dismissal
- reductions in the required number of hours an employee was obliged to work each day and week
- pro rata reductions in the hours to be worked by juveniles the eradication of child labour
- the introduction of safety regulations – notably in coal-mining, construction and agriculture and fishing industries
- access to time off and no loss of pay for maternity confinement
- payment of sickness benefit and unemployment benefits
- compulsory insurance paid for by employers in case of accidental injury or death.

■ Restoring an equilibrium in industrial relations

PC 4.1.4

Between 1960–75, the balance of industrial power swung in some industrial sectors in favour of some highly militant trade unions, and many people became concerned about the mounting number of working days and man-hours lost to strikes, many of which were unofficial and 'wild-cat', stemming at times from irresponsible leadership at local levels. As a result, between 1979–93, a number of bills were debated in Parliament, and laws enacted to restrict what successive governments saw as industrial power without responsibility. Also, because of a number of scandals surrounding the balloting of trade union members at this time, reforms were introduced to guarantee impartiality and to prevent ballot-rigging. The measures enacted included:

- requirements of postal, secret ballots of trade union members when, for example, asked to vote for or against proposed industrial action
- the counting of votes by independent scrutineers such as the Electoral Society
- the prohibition of flying pickets – sometimes trade union activists – who would picket outside the gates of businesses where industrial disputes were taking place, but who were not employed by the firm at that location
- the setting of limits upon the number of trade union members permitted to picket outside employers' premises
- written seven-day notice to employers by trade unions of an intention of its membership to strike
- the abolition of closed shops – a practice in which all employees of an organisation – say a printers – were obliged to join a single trade union
- the right of employees to elect not to join a trade union, and to remain thereafter free from discrimination or duress

PC 4.1.4

■ Recession-driven changes in work patterns and conditions of employment 1988–95

The deep recession of the late 1980s caused unemployment to rise to almost four million. During this time, membership of trade unions fell markedly, and their influence in the workplace waned. With so many people desperate for work, both local and national agreements on work practices either lapsed or were re-negotiated. Flexible working patterns were introduced under which part-time employment replaced to a significant extent its full-time equivalent, together with short, fixed-term contracts of employment.

As a result, trade unions were obliged to re-think their positions on pay and conditions. The radical changes in the market for labour brought about by the recession had the effect of swinging the pendulum of industrial power once more towards the employer, who undoubtedly took advantage of the recession-driven changes in the market for jobs. However, though trade unions are currently having to cope with a diminished membership and a reluctance on the part of their members to 'rock the boat' to the point of losing their jobs, the shift towards a more amenable and less militant workforce stems much more directly from UK industry's efforts to combat the global economic success of Pacific Rim states rather than from a desire to return to Victorian values, advocated by some right-of-centre politicians.

PC 4.1.4

■ Towards a social contract

Today, evidence is becoming visible of a move towards a productive equilibrium between employers and trade unions similar to that enjoyed in Germany since 1945. Both parties are aware of a need for stability and co-operation in order to construct work patterns and agreements which will prove lasting, yet which will not affect adversely competitiveness in home and world markets. An example of a new-found mutual respect is to be found currently in the willingness of employers' confederations and the City of London to view the prospect of a Labour government with some confidence, as opposed to customary strong reservations. The emerging confidence is prompted in no small measure by the recent changes, made by the Labour party and supported by a number of trade unions, to Clause Four of the Labour Party's constitution, which modify its commitment to public ownership and state-control of the means of production and distribution.

PC 4.1.4

■ Current trade union and staff association activities

As the above background section illustrates, the relationship between employers and the trade union representatives is never static. Depending upon the prevailing economic climate and market for jobs, the pendulum of industrial influence and power swings to and fro. Moreover, general social expectations and outlooks among the working population change in response to changes in technology and global economic trends, and these, in turn, influence the pattern of industrial relations. However, there are some major areas of trade union and staff association activities – undertaken on behalf of members – which are remain constant, as the following table illustrates:

THE ONGOING CORE ACTIVITIES OF TRADE UNIONS AND STAFF ASSOCIATIONS

PC 4.1.4

The full-time officials and their work-based members (convenors, shop stewards etc.) work constantly in their members' interests to:

- improve pay and conditions of work in annual rounds of negotiation with employers' representatives
- monitor health and safety (making improvements as necessary) by sitting on work-based committees or councils
- represent members in disciplinary or grievance procedures
- provide information, views and basic negotiating positions to ACAS etc. when industrial disputes are in a phase of conciliation and arbitration between employers and recognised trade unions
- provide advisory and counselling services for employee members in terms of their legal rights etc. in case of dispute or grievance
- mount training and development programmes in industrial relations and employment matters for work-based trade union officials
- meet with employers' confederations and associations to discuss matters of mutual interest, such as the health implications of IT equipment and systems.

DISCUSSION TOPICS

PC 4.1.2 4.1.3 4.1.4

1 Can legislation alone remove discrimination from the workplace?

2 Are women any nearer to gaining equality at work an they were, say, twenty years ago? If so, why? If not, why not?

3 To what extent is an employee who wins a case against his or her employer at an industrial tribunal in a 'no win' situation in terms of returning to work the same workplace? Should more be done to protect an employee in such circumstances? Can more be done in reality?

4 Do you think that calling in ACAS is the best way of seeking a resolution to an industrial dispute, or are there other ways which you think might prove less involved and less time-consuming?

5 Are the scales of compensation which industrial tribunals have to work to sufficient in your view?

6 Are trade unions still necessary today?

7 Has the 'industrial power pendulum' swung too far in favour of the employer today?

8 How do you think industrial relations will evolve over the coming ten years?

PC 4.1.5

Securing employee co-operation in the workplace

In quality management circles, the importance of team-work is well understood. Similarly, management specialists like Elton Mayo, Rensis Likert and Peter Drucker have demonstrated how group morale influences work output. Today, therefore, few industrialists or senior commercial managers would deny the crucial importance of securing the 'active co-operation' of their respective work-forces if organisational objectives are to be met. Moreover, in an age of increasing use of technology at work, more employees are becoming technical experts and professionals, who would react predictably to any attempt on the part of macho managers intent on 'kicking butt'!

How, then, does today's more sophisticated management gain and hold employee co-operation? The following checklist details some major strategies:

PC 4.1.5

EMPLOYER STRATEGIES FOR GAINING AND MAINTAINING EMPLOYEE CO-OPERATION

Wise employers gain and keep the co-operation of their employees by:

- **rewarding achievement with shares in the current year's profits or the allocation of company shares** (e.g. the John Lewis Partnership, merchant banks etc.)
- **the appointment of employee representatives to committees and working-parties** etc. so as to enable them to be consulted and involved and to feed back decisions to their co-workers
- **the creation of teams** which form cross-sections of staff from different positions in the organisational hierarchy: project-groups, task-forces, quality circles, etc. which advise or execute decisions through which employees generally obtain a sense of consultation and involvement
- **the dissemination of accurate information on a frequent, regular basis** – through in-house newspapers, notices, email bulletins etc. which discourage rumour and disinformation
- **enhancing perceptions of job security:** through regular consultations with trade-union officials, the publication of redundancy policy – such as 'last-in, first-out' or a points-based system which favours long-service, parents or the disabled etc. or natural wastage priority etc.
- **advertising and acknowledging individual employee's achievements** – on departmental notice-boards, in in-house newspapers, in press-releases to the local press etc.
- **recognising relevant trade unions or staff associations** and negotiating with them over pay and conditions etc.
- **providing 'fringe benefits'**, such as cheap car loans, crèches, subsidised private health care etc.

PC 4.1.5

CONSEQUENCES OF FAILURE TO SECURE EMPLOYEE CO-OPERATION

- manpower shortages in key/specialist areas
- a workforce whose skills lie at the 'trailing' as opposed to 'leading' edge of the technology they work with
- an ageing and elderly workforce resulting from a failure to introduce 'new blood' posts, and to monitor the distribution curve of employees' ages
- output and continuity of operations hampered and diminished by high levels of absenteeism or labour turnover
- a poor morale resulting from adversarial employee relations, 'M16' management cultures or a lack of effective employee representation/consultation systems
- adverse publicity arising from media reporting of industrial tribunal awards on upheld unfair/constructive dismissal complaints etc.

Failure in human resources management in areas such as those indicated above leads inevitably to the following:

- the organisation being overtaken by its competition
- the research, design, production and servicing of its products or services becoming obsolescent in terms of the technology employed and of poor quality in terms of design, build and eventual use
- a decline in overall productivity and profit levels

and ultimately to:

- take-over, buy-out, asset-stripping or bankruptcy

This being the case, intelligent company directors and senior executives go to great lengths to anticipate the dangers of poor human resource management and use these policies and practices to make quite sure that their staff – truly their greatest asset – is maintained at a peak of effectiveness and efficiency.

REVIEW TEST

PC 4.1. 4.1. 4.1. 4.1. 4.1.

1. List the major rights of both an employer and an employee.
2. Write down the names of three major Acts of Parliament affecting employment.
3. List the main components of a contract of employment.
4. What do you consider to be the main roles of the human resource function?
5. What test could a court of law apply to distinguish between an employee and a contractor in a dispute?

6 List four main purposes of an employee induction programme.

7 How do the Sex Discrimination Act 1975 and Race Relations Act 1976 impact upon employee recruitment? Give two examples for each Act.

8 What are the names of the two government-supported watchdogs which monitor discrimination in the workplace?

9 Explain briefly the difference between wrongful and constructive dismissal.

10 What circumstances must be present in order for a company to make an employee legally redundant?

11 What does ACAS stand for? What does it do?

12 Where, eventually, would an unresolved grievance be taken?

13 Give two reasons for a legitimate termination of a contract of employment by an employer.

14 List five main stages in handling a grievance procedure effectively.

15 What are the main functions of an industrial tribunal?

16 List three trade-union inspired employment law reforms which benefit employees today.

17 List three government-inspired reforms which curbed the powers of trade unions between 1979 and the present day.

18 List five main activities which trade union or staff association officials undertake on behalf of their members.

19 List four ways in which employers can encourage their employees' co-operation.

20 What advantages derive from the setting up of work-teams in areas such as safety and quality in terms of employer-employee relations?

PC
.1.2
.1.3
.1.4

GROUP ACTIVITIES

1 Find out how a firm's achieving of the *Investors in People* award benefits an organisation's employees.

2 Research into how the Sex Discrimination Act 1975 affects the recruitment process locally.

3 Find out how a case is heard in an industrial tribunal, and how both plaintiff and defendant are represented.

4 Research into the activities and effectiveness of the operations of ACAS.

5 Find out how grievances are handled in either your workplace or your study-centre.

6 Research into the types of award and levels of compensation which are currently made by industrial tribunals in cases of racial or sex discrimination and wrongful or unfair dismissal.

7 Find out the nature and scope of the role of the local branch of a national trade union in your area.

For each of the above activities, report back to your class via a 5–10 minute oral presentation.

KNOWLEDGE TEST

Element 4.1
Investigate human resourcing

1 (i) An employer is obliged to take reasonable steps to protect an employee at work.
(ii) An employee has a responsibility for his or her own safety at work.

Which of the following options best describe the above statements?

A (i) T (ii) T
B (i) T (ii) F
C (i) F (ii) T
D (i) F (ii) F

2 A contract of employment must include:

A details of pay
B details of redundancy pay and procedures
C who the grievance officer is
D who the recognised trade union convenor is

Which of the above statements is true, and which false?

3 (i) New full-time employees have to work for three years before becoming eligible for redundancy pay.
(ii) Details of an organisation's regulations manual may be used to make a case in an industrial tribunal hearing.

Which of the following options best describe the above statements?

A (i) T (ii) T
B (i) T (ii) F
C (i) F (ii) T
D (i) F (ii) F

4 A Induction of new employees is now compulsory.
B An employee must carry out any instruction from his/her line manager.
C An employee could be taken to court for revealing confidential information gained from his or her job.
D It is illegal under the Sex Discrimination Act 1975 to require an employee to wear a particular type of dress or uniform at work.

Which of the above statements is true, and which false?

5 (i) In certain circumstances ACAS has the legal power to intervene in an industrial dispute.
(ii) In current employment law, an employee has the right to be accompanied by a trade union representative at a disciplinary interview.

A (i) T (ii) T
B (i) T (ii) F
C (i) F (ii) T
D (i) F (ii) F

PC
4.1.1
4.1.2
4.1.3
4.1.4
4.1.5

PORTFOLIO OF EVIDENCE ACTIVITY

Element 4.1
Investigate human resourcing

TRAVALEZE CARAVANS LIMITED

Scenario 1

You work as an assistant to the Human Resources Manager at the head office of Traveleze Caravans Limited, a company which manufactures a wide range of caravans and campers. At present, your Human Resources Department is engaged in updating its range of informational literature which it supplies to newly appointed staff, since, with an increasingly full export order book, Traveleze is looking to make a number of new appointments - across the range of its management and work operative structure - in the run up to opening a new factory in the West Midlands.

As a result, you have been asked to research and design a pamphlet which will advise newly arrived employees at the new complex of their employment rights. For some years now, Traveleze has prided itself on its excellent record of productive industrial and employment relations between management and workforce, and your MD and owner, Bob Newton is keen to ensure that the record extends to the new factory, which expects to recruit both male and female personnel to work on a shift system. The local community from which staff will be recruited is multi-ethnic.

Recently, your line manager, Julie Vickers, briefed you as follows:

> *'I don't think the pamphlet should be long-winded, or people won't read it. On the other hand, there is an essential body of information to get across, and I'd like you to concentrate on: pay and conditions; health and safety; grievance and disciplinary procedures; our anti-discriminatory policies; what steps an employee can take if they feel they have a grievance; the part played at Traveleze by its recognised trade unions. Remember that Mr Newton wants this pamphlet to make clear (a) what rights an employee has and, most important, (b) that we fully support the legal basis of employment at Traveleze.'*

Scenario 2

Having made such a good job of the employees' rights pamphlet, Mr Newton has now requested that you undertake a further similar job for him. He is the current chairman of the West Midlands Engineering Employers' Confederation (WMEEC) and this employers' group is currently looking at employers' rights relating to employment. He wants you to design a pamphlet to be circulated to senior managers in your industry and locality which sets out clearly what their current rights are. In particular, he would like the pamphlet to include suitable diagrams which show the steps an employer can take in the case of a contravention of the HASAW Act or one of the anti-discrimination laws. As the pamphlet is likely to have a high profile Mr Newton has emphasised the need for it to be well designed and to contain up-to-date, accurate information.

Scenario 3

Two new directors have recently joined the board of Traveleze, who have been working abroad for the past five years. You understand that they inherited shares from a close relative of Mr Newton. In order to help them to obtain a 'handle' on Traveleze's operations, Mr Newton has requested – through your boss – that you compose a short factsheet (the first of a series) which highlights **two** of the following employer responsibilities:

- recruitment

- negotiations on pay and conditions
- disciplinary procedures and how Traveleze handles them
- employees' access to Traveleze's grievance procedures.

A further briefing paper has also been requested to outline how (at Traveleze) the staff work towards meeting its organisational objectives - as, for example, by participating in the quality circles system - and how the board of Traveleze could further improve employee co-operation by introducing, for example: share ownership, bonus/commission schemes, a job security policy etc.

Task 1

At the outset of this activity, make sure you compose an activity action plan and fill out the appropriate parts of you planning and review log.

Task 2

Produce the pamphlet required for Scenario 1, making sure that your information, structure and style are clear and simple. Remember that the pamphlet is intended to be distributed to new employees at all levels of appointment. Including any illustrations or diagrams etc. this pamphlet should be about four sides of A5, and be word-processed if possible, so as to make use of appropriate fonts and point sizes.

Task 3

Produce a pamphlet (using a contrasting design) of an equivalent size which satisfies the requirements of Scenario 2. Remember that this pamphlet will go to experienced, well-informed senior managers in the engineering industry. Also, the style of the pamphlet should be neutral and factual, so as to convey an impartial and fair tone.

Task 4

Having researched the topics you select for Scenario 3, produce a suitable set of factsheets and a briefing paper which meet your briefing's requirements. Each factsheet/briefing paper should be about 1–1.5 sides of A4 (printed text) long. Remember that your readership will not be entirely familiar with your subject-matter, so you will need to ensure that you explain your points clearly – but not long-windedly!

Performance criteria covered

4.1.1, 4.1.2, 4.1.3, 4.1.4, 4.1.5

Core skills covered

Communication:
3.2.1, 3.2.2, 3.2.3, 3.2.4, 3.2.5, 3.3.1, 3.3.2, 3.3.3, 3.4.1, 3.4.2, 3.4.3, 3.4.4

Information Technology:
3.1.1, 3.1.2, 3.1.3, 3.1.4, 3.1.5, 3.2.1, 3.2.2, 3.2.3, 3.2.4, 3.2.5, 3.2.6, 3.2.7, 3.3.1, 3.3.2, 3.3.3, 3.3.4, 3.3.5, 3.3.6

PC
4.1.2
4.1.3
4.1.4
4.1.5

CASE STUDY 1

Mending the cracks in Plastimould

Plastimould Ltd is a company manufacturing a range of household utensils from a chemical base – bowls, buckets, pipes, brushes etc. For the past six weeks it has had a serious industrial dispute on its hands. One of the stages in the production process has been declared 'unsafe' by the unionised factory staff.

This stage concerns the cleaning out of vats which have contained the material for moulding into the various products in the company's range. It is accepted by both management and union representatives that it is possible during the cleaning process for fumes to be generated which are dangerous to the skin and which under no circumstances should be inhaled.

Recently three men have collapsed not long after working on the cleansing of the vats and they are still off work sick. After the third man had fallen ill, the union decided after a full meeting of the factory union membership to ban any of the union's members from working on the vat cleansing process. The effect of this ban was to halt production completely.

The union want an independent enquiry into the dangers and effects to health stemming from the cleansing process. For their part, management have declared that the cleansing process is perfectly safe, provided that the protective clothing and equipment provided is worn and used as specified in company regulations.

The union's position is that the clothing is old-fashioned, having been designed more than ten years previously, and that no one to their knowledge had carried out any recent tests to confirm the effectiveness of its protection. The men have complained that it is too hot to wear, and that its bulkiness makes it impossible to work in the more inaccessible parts of the vats. The respirators are also, according to the men, inefficient, especially when any physical exertion is required.

Management has pointed out that the protective clothing and equipment conforms to the safety specifications laid down for such work in the relevant section of the industrial safety legislation. The men, says management, have been cutting safety corners to boost bonus earnings by not wearing all the equipment and clothing when there is a clear need to. If there have been instances of men becoming sick, which management will not accept as being a direct consequence of the cleansing process, then it must be the result of contributory negligence.

The union regards this last attitude of management as totally hypocritical. It claims that in the past management has turned 'a blind eye' to total adherence to factory safety regulations. Only now that the company is faced with a law-suit for damages arising from the medical condition of the three workers currently sick in hospital has the accusation of 'contributory negligence' arisen. In any case, the company has failed in its obligation to inform its factory staff adequately of the potential dangers involved in the cleansing process, and now, 'caught red-handed', was trying to prevent an independent inquiry from being set up.

The latest rejoinder from management is that unless a formula can be decided to restart production with immediate effect, there may well be a possibility that the parent company of Plastimould will divert its production to another factory in another country, thus causing widespread redundancy. The union is inclined to see this as bluff, although some members concede that the six-week lay-off must have had crippling effect on the company's financial position.

ASSIGNMENTS

1 From the management or union team viewpoint, prepare your case for a 'return-to-work' negotiating meeting and then simulate the meeting. Observers or a team member should take notes and produce narrative minutes.

2 Depending upon the outcome of the meeting draft either a 'joint communique' or separate statements for circulation to Plastimould staff.

3 As an individual student write an essay on the problems implicit in the case study and suggest how you think the management and the union should resolve their differences.

CASE STUDY 2

PC
4.1.1
4.1.2
4.1.3
4.1.4
4.1.5

The Harris Case

On Tuesday 1 February 199–, Jack Harris, a machine operator at Advance Engineering Company Limited, was summarily dismissed . . .

'D' Machines – Extract of company regulations

Extract from the Company Regulations of Advance Engineering Company Limited:

> **VI SAFETY PROCEDURES**
>
> **3 Operation of Classified Machinery**
>
> Certain production processes (specified below) are effected by machines having a 'D' (Danger) classification. Under no circumstances may such machines be left unattended by operatives while assembly-line work is in progress.
>
> (a) Relief Summoning Procedures
> Operatives working 'D' classified machines are required to summon a relief operator before leaving the machine for any reason while work is in progress.
>
> (b) Summary Dismissal
> In view of the danger to personnel working in the vicinity of 'D' classified machines, operatives who leave them negligently unattended render themselves liable to summary dismissal
>
> Revised: 1 December 199–

'Try not to worry . . .'

An extract from a conversation which took place in the surgery of Jack Harris's family doctor on Wednesday 19 January 199–:

Doctor Grant: 'Well, Mr Harris, I think I'd better put you on a course of anti-depressants. I don't think you need to stay at home – especially while your wife is in hospital – but you must take things steadily. The pills I am prescribing will help you to do just that. And don't worry about Mrs Harris – she's going to be all right. . . .'

Jack Harris: 'Thank you, Doctor, I'm very grateful. It's been a worrying time ever since the wife was taken ill. Still, they told me this morning she could be out of the intensive care unit in a few days' time, if all goes well. . . .'

'Give us a break!'

An extract from a conversation between Alec Baker, Supervisor, and Jack Harris in the works staff restroom, Tuesday 1 February 199– at 15.35 hours:

Alec Baker: 'Right, Harris, you've had it this time! This time I'm going to have to report you to Mr Watkins! You'd better put that fag out and come with me to his office – straight away!'

Jack Harris: 'Aw, give us a break, Mr Baker, I've only just . . . You see, I've had a lot . . . Well, I've not been . . .'

Alec Baker: 'Save it for Mr Watkins! Come on. It's not as if you haven't been warned about leaving a 'D' classified machine unattended. The line was clearly working when I spotted you missing! Total disregard for your workmates – that's what beats me!'

Summary dismissal

Mr Watkins' reaction on hearing of the incident from Alec Baker in the Works Manager's Office. Tuesday 1 February 199– at 15.55 hours:

'Found smoking you say. In the restroom. Well, it all seems pretty clear-cut to me! Left his 'D' machine unattended and the line in progress when you spotted his absence. You'd think they'd have more sense! Especially after my recent reminder. You'd better wheel him in, Mr Baker! . . . '

The EWA steps in

Extract of a conversation between Jack Harris and Vic Cooper, Convenor of the Engineering Workers' Association at Advance Engineering, Tuesday 1 February 199– at 16.35 hours:

Jack Harris: 'He never gave me a chance, Vic, nor did Watkins! I dunno, I just came over sort of shaky. There was a stoppage further up the line, so I thought I'd just have a quick sit-down in the restroom. I never meant to be away more than a minute or two . . . '

'D' MACHINES – NOTICE TO ALL WORKS PERSONNEL

Notice to all Advance Engineering Works Personnel posted on general works noticeboard 24 January 09.00 hours.

MEMORANDUM

To:	ALL WORKS PERSONNEL	Ref:	JK/RG HSAW 24
From:	WORKS MANAGER'S OFFICE	Date:	24 January 199–

OPERATION OF 'D' CLASSIFIED MACHINES

All Works Personnel are reminded of Section VI, Para 3, Sub-sections (a) and (b) of the revised Company Regulations issued earlier this month.

Recently instances have occurred when 'D' classified machines have been left unattended. Such acts of negligence on the part of machine operative staff could well lead to serious injury or even fatality.

All works personnel are therefore reminded that failure to comply with the above regulations will render them liable to summary dismissal.

J. K. Watkins
Works Manager

Vic Cooper: 'Absent only a minute or two you say. Line stopped again! Didn't you tell 'em you weren't feeling well? Anyway, anyone can see you're not right – not by a long chalk. Didn't give you a chance? Jack, you should have spoken up! Well, I think it's a clear case of victimisation! You'd best go home now. Charlie'll go with you. But don't you worry, you'll keep your job – or my name's not Vic Cooper! Now, I've got some telephoning to do to District Office! . . .'

'. . . on the grounds of unfair dismissal . . .'

Conversation between John Watkins, Works Manager, and Dennis Brooke, Managing Director of Advance Engineering in his office. Friday 4 February 199– at 10.15 hours:

John Watkins: 'Bad business. Not made any easier by Peter Taylor's absence (Advance's Personnel Manager, absent since Christmas because of illness). We could have done with his expertise. Of course, we had to take a firm line. If company regulations are seen to be openly flouted . . . Open and shut case I'd say.'

Dennis Brooke: 'I'm not so sure. I know things have been too lax in the Works, but by all accounts, Jack Harris was regarded as being conscientious. I hope we haven't acted hastily over this . . . I've a letter here from the EWA informing me of their intention to advise Mr Harris to take his case to the Industrial Tribunal and to claim unfair dismissal, and that they will be providing him with legal advice.

According to them, Harris was unwell at the time of the incident. Your "open and shut case" had better be as good as you think it is!'

Prior to the Industrial Tribunal's hearing, the EWA secured a written statement from Jack Harris's doctor, to the effect that Jack had been prescribed medication to alleviate anxiety caused by his wife's ill-health.

DISCUSSION TOPICS

1 How well did Alec Baker, John Watkins and Dennis Brooke handle Jack Harris's absence from his 'D' Machine? Can you detect any mismanagement in terms of your knowledge of the Health and Safety at Work Act and current employment protection legislation?

2 To what extent can the summary dismissal of Jack Harris be fairly judged to be the result of his own negligence? Was Dr Grant at fault in allowing Jack to continue to work while feeling under stress?

3 Comment on Vic Cooper's role in the dismissal process. Should he have reacted differently? If so, in what ways?

4 Given the dangerous nature of unattended 'D' Machines, has the company taken sufficient care in briefing their machine operators on procedures to be adopted when wishing to leave them?

5 What do you think – on the basis of the information available in the case study – would be the outcome at an industrial tribunal of Jack's claim for unfair dismissal?

GROUP ACTIVITIES

1 First carry out any further necessary researches into summary and unfair dismissal and industrial tribunal procedures, then role-play the industrial tribunal hearing with the following 'cast':

Industrial tribunal chairman

Two further tribunal members

A legal representative for each party

Jack Harris

Witnesses to be called

Each party to the case to produce their own supportive documents, and the panel to produce a written judgement with reasons.

2 Assume you are Peter Taylor, Advance's Personnel Manager, newly returned to work after the tribunal hearing. In the light of the recent Harris case, produce a memorandum to all company supervisors and managers explaining the company's policy on summary dismissal and how to handle potential instances in a legally correct and good code of practice manner.

Element 4.2
JOB ROLES AND CHANGING WORKING CONDITIONS

Element 2.2 examined the ways in which organisations structure themselves and how they tend to allocate authority within a pyramidic hierarchy, where a few senior executives – often directors – who inhabit the top of the pyramid possess most authority and delegate it downwards through several tiers to the operatives or support staff working at the base of the pyramid, who possess least. PC 4.2.1

Also, Unit 2 outlined how senior managers and directors tend to make decisions which affect *all* staff in a business and which have an extended life, sometimes spanning 3–5 years; whereas junior employees may work within a much narrower and shorter decision-making range – of, say, a day or a week, and extending only to the work of a small unit or section.

The following section describes the job roles of the key positions within private sector companies and public sector organisations:

PC 4.2.1

KEY JOB ROLES IN PRIVATE AND PUBLIC SECTOR ORGANISATIONS

Private sector companies

The chairman

- bestrides the top of the organisational pyramid
- is elected by the board of directors
- chairs meetings of the board of directors
- may have executive status or may leave day-to-day running of the company to the managing director

The directors

- decide on important matters at board meetings
- have legal obligations and responsibilities under the Companies Act 1985
- may exert influence on company activities by having extensive shareholdings in the company
- the board of directors presents its annual report to the shareholders for approval at the end of each trading year

The managing director

- the executive head of most organisations, with authority over all the staff
- is a member of the board of directors

The company secretary

- responsible to the managing director and board to ensure all the company's affairs are conducted according to legal requirements

- services and attends meetings of the board of directors
- attends to all correspondence involving shareholders and the calling of shareholders' meetings
- is usually responsible for fire, health and safety regulations, company contracts, trade mark registrations, etc
- acts as legal advisor to the company

The departmental manager

- is responsible to the managing director for the work of one department in the organisation
- directs the work carried out by the members of staff in the department
- ensures targets are met, eg projected (budgeted) annual sales turnover is achieved at the desired level of gross profit (profit before tax)
- is provided by the company with the human, equipment and financial resources to reach the pre-set targets

The section supervisor

- is responsible to the head of department for the work of a section or unit in the department (eg a large accounts department may have sections for the sales ledger, purchase ledger, nominal ledger, payroll, credit control, etc.)
- reviews work in progress with the head of department to ensure targets are met
- is responsible for section staff

The shop steward

- is responsible for trade union matters within the section/organisation
- represents the trade union members in negotiations with management
- is responsible to area branch secretary and trade unions' officers

The operative or support staff member

- works within a specific set of responsibilities and tasks – say, by operating a lathe, milling-machine or steel press, or by word-processing text, acting as a receptionist or switchboard telephonist etc.
- tends to work routinely on short-duration tasks under fairly close supervision (see section supervisor)
- is responsible for the all-important detail-work of the organisation

Public sector organisations

County councillor/District councillor

- is elected by those registered to vote in each local area
- usually a member of a political party
- makes decisions in full council meetings or in committees
- is responsible for setting budgets and carrying out legally imposed duties

Local government officer

- full-time official who carries out the policies of the elected members under the direction of a chief executive
- officials are divided into departments and sections covering specific areas of the work

The chairman of a public corporation

- is responsible to a central government department for the administration of a public corporation; the central government department will be headed by a Permanent Secretary responsible to a Minister – a senior Government Member of Parliament
- duties resemble those of a company chairman.

Fig 4.3 **Key 'players' in the local government public sector organisation**

PC 4.2.1

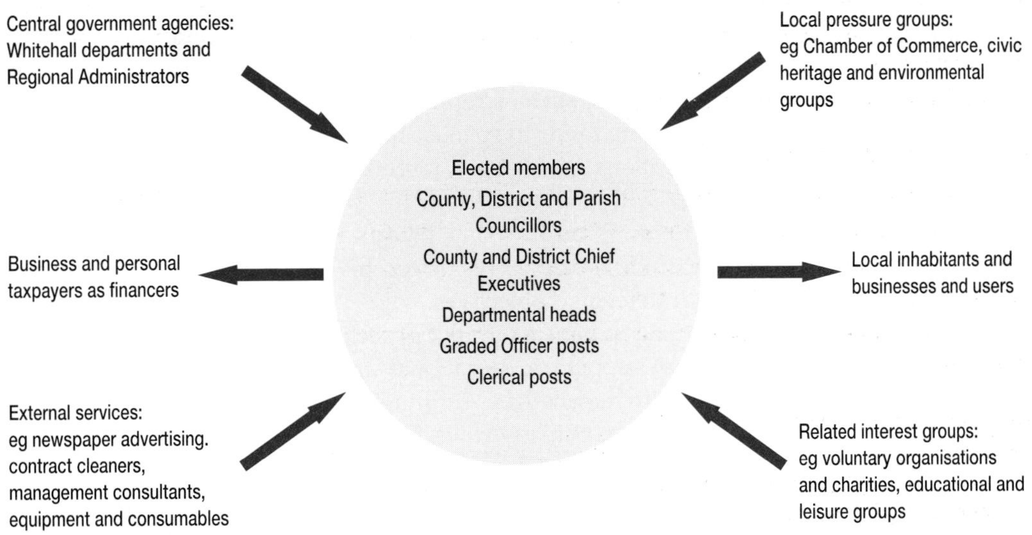
Central government agencies: Whitehall departments and Regional Administrators
Local pressure groups: eg Chamber of Commerce, civic heritage and environmental groups
Elected members
County, District and Parish Councillors
County and District Chief Executives
Departmental heads
Graded Officer posts
Clerical posts
Business and personal taxpayers as financers
Local inhabitants and businesses and users
External services: eg newspaper advertising. contract cleaners, management consultants, equipment and consumables
Related interest groups: eg voluntary organisations and charities, educational and leisure groups

Job responsibilities

PC 4.2.1

■ At senior management and officer level

At the senior level of a private or public sector organisation, managers' job roles tend to be both corporate and strategic. That is, such staff do not get over-involved in day-to-day, operational management preoccupations, since that is the role of departmental and middle managers, supervisors and support staff. Instead, they tend to: plan, develop, devise strategies to meet changes effectively, ensure the financial viability of the organisation, as well as its future security (see the marketing plan) and the effectiveness of its work-force and facilities (see manpower planning and facilities management). Essential to the job role of senior managers is a constant flow of summary information – production, accounting, sales or customer service-based etc. – to enable them to make informed decisions – especially since at their level, a wrong decision could result in redundancies into the thousands, or the loss of sales orders worth millions. Much of their performance monitoring role takes place in the form of meetings – at board of director level, or with departmental heads – at which policies are hammered out and decisions (often tricky and complex) are made by consensus if at all possible. Senior managers will also have major responsibilities, for example, as grievance officers, pay and conditions negotiators and staff welfare counsellors.

PC 4.2.1

■ At middle-management level

The managers occupying the middle of the organisational pyramid tend to be leading either specialist departments, units with a cross-company function (such as centralised filing) or smaller expert sections, such as reprographics and desk-top publishing etc. The extent of their decision-making tends to span a financial year. Usually they are allocated a budget to fund their operations, and are set targets to meet by senior management. For example, a sales manager will have to manage his or her sales team effectively, so as to deliver targeted sales revenue and arising profits within a specific budget. The all-important function of the middle-manager is to lead his or her team in such a way that they deliver – or exceed – their delegated objectives.

Middle managers also tend to have a number of section supervisors or deputy managers who coordinate the work of support or operational staff within a very specialised function, such as maintaining the purchase ledger, running sales in the north west region or the training arm of the organisation. In many ways, a middle manager is a kind of junction-box or staging post, through whom messages flow upwards and downwards – as instructions to be followed, or as operational feedback etc. They also tend to be organisational trouble-shooters within their own sphere of authority, and accountable to senior management for any glitches, errors, shortcomings or failures. Theirs is a very exposed position!

PC 4.2.1

■ At supervisory level

An organisation's supervisors occupy a most important job role, since they are closest to where the myriad of specific, detailed jobs are carried out. A major responsibility they have is to manage the work of staff on whom a great deal of responsibility rests – for meeting deadlines, accuracy, quality outcomes and so on. They also provide invaluable feedback to middle managers on aspects such as staff morale, responses to changes in work practices, operational problems (or successes) and keep middle managers generally in touch with work aspects for which they are ultimately responsible, but which they cannot oversee directly.

PC 4.2.1

■ At the operative and assistant level

Inhabiting as they do the broadest, 'ground-floor' tier of an organisation, this tier of staff might be forgiven for viewing themselves as a mixture of Samson and Atlas, holding their supervisors, managers and directors up! In many ways, theirs is a very demanding and difficult job role to undertake, since they are on the receiving end of orders, instructions and requests, but have very limited authority – and yet they are the ones who make the organisation work, by carrying out the hundreds or thousands of daily, routine tasks upon which, say, a manufacturer of motor cars, a high street chainstore or national transport system depends.

Much of the stress in their job roles stems from having to make instructions from above work, and from having to carry out routine and repetitive tasks cheerfully and conscientiously every day. Consequently, they need to be methodical, calm, patient and tolerant – especially if they come into regular contact with customers.

■ Organisational job roles and human resource responsibilities

PC 4.2.2

At each level of the above tiers of organisational activity, a number of human resource responsibilities exist, as outlined below.

At director/senior management level

- Directors and senior managers have a responsibility to ensure that the organisation has sufficient expert staff in each of its specialist departments who can keep the business 'at the leading' edge and 'meet and beat' the competition – both current and anticipated: this involves senior management and human resource executives in monitoring a manpower plan which checks continually on retirements, resignations, transfers etc. and makes suitable recruitment and staff development decisions accordingly.
- Another senior management function is to monitor payroll and conditions of service costs – so as to avoid creeping increases, but also to ensure that staff are paid enough to deter them from seeking other posts or from being head-hunted.
- They will also set the corporate policies for staff appraisal, development and training.

At middle-management level

- Middle managers tend to interface with human resources extensively in the areas of staff recruitment and their subsequent development and training (see Element 4.3).
- They may also become involved in providing information to human resources managers in cases of grievance or disciplinary action.
- Sometimes line managers carry out staff appraisal interviews and complete reports themselves, and sometimes they may work closely with HR management in this sensitive area.
- Middle managers are usually the source of detailed information about workforce performance, training, skills acquired, experience etc. which is collected and stored on HR personnel databases

At supervisory level

At this level, supervisors tend to provide information for the use of middle and HR management in areas like: absenteeism, skills development, grievance/disciplinary matters, advice on health-related staff matters such as stress, injury or accident etc; they also report upwards on practical aspects of conditions of service.

Manpower planning and skills auditing

PC 4.2.2

An organisation's personnel operations are as much concerned with the future as are its marketing activities. For instance, if a company wishes to embark successfully upon a new policy, say to export its products to EU countries following upon the creation of the 1992

Single Market, then its personnel department will need to plan for this new development well in advance. It will need to undertake, for example, employee surveys and audits so as to ascertain:

- who can speak what European language(s) and to what degree of fluency
- who has experience of European business cultures and has travelled in targeted export countries
- who would be best suited to be developed into new roles involving documentation in European languages, selling in Europe, coordinating European advertising and so on

Also, the company's directors may decide to set up a new export department to handle the extra business. This decision would in turn require the personnel department to create and implement a plan to:

- identify which staff would be offered posts in the new department
- what implications this would have for promoting or recruiting staff to the department(s) which lose personnel
- to devise in consultation with sales and marketing managers an organisational structure for the department, including the compilation of fresh job specifications and descriptions (see pages 419–23); also, to produce conditions of service and salary scales which fit in with existing company schemes and policies
- plan for the future growth of the export department in terms of additional staffing, which may in turn require in-house staff training and development programmes or further recruitment
- brief as necessary employment bureaux on the newly created posts and booking space in selected recruitment newspapers and journals, etc.

As the Fig 4.4 illustrates, implementing changes which involve either moving existing staff to other posts, or recruiting new staff cannot be undertaken effectively overnight. Furthermore, the above example is likely to be just one of many personnel projects going on side-by-side in a large organisation.

For this reason, an effective personnel team takes pains to manage the organisation's workforce as a coherent whole. That is to say, it maintains a manpower planning function which continually monitors what qualifications, skills, expertise and experience are required – currently and in the future – to enable all departments to meet their goals and objectives without staffing crises or emergencies.

Fig 4.4 **The human resources planning process**

PC 4.2.2

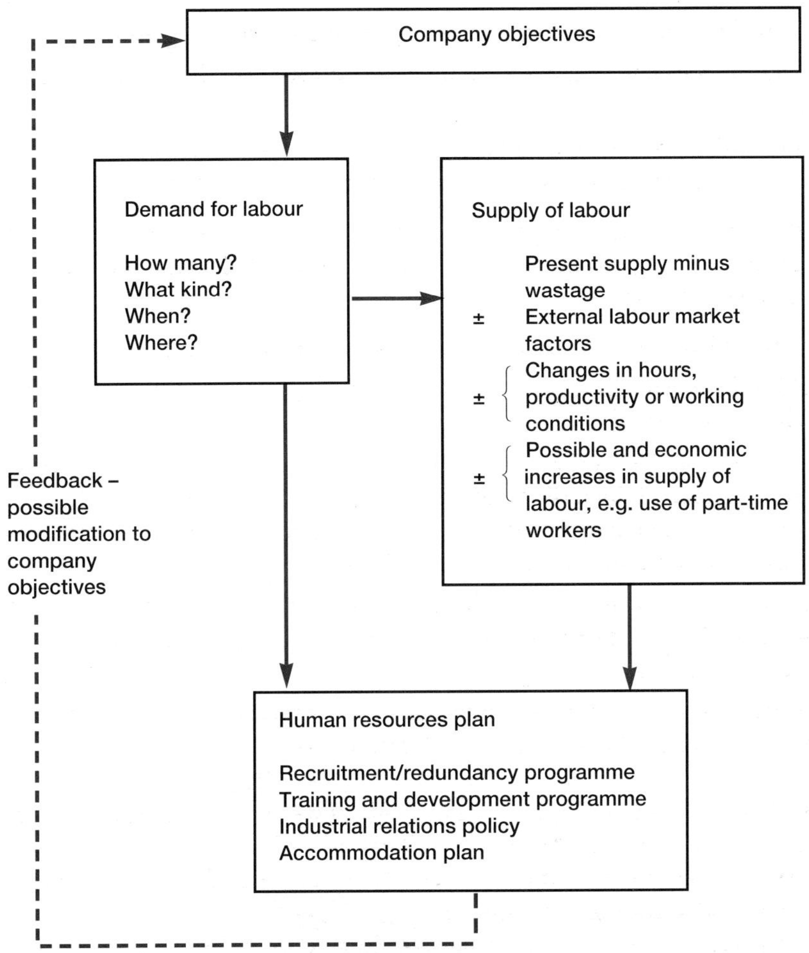
Company objectives
Demand for labour
How many?
What kind?
When?
Where?
Supply of labour
Present supply minus wastage
± External labour market factors
± Changes in hours, productivity or working conditions
± Possible and economic increases in supply of labour, e.g. use of part-time workers
Feedback – possible modification to company objectives
Human resources plan
Recruitment/redundancy programme
Training and development programme
Industrial relations policy
Accommodation plan

Reproduced from *Human Resources Management,* 7th edition, by H T Graham and R Bennett, M & E Handbooks.

TYPICAL FEATURES OF MANPOWER PLANNING

PC 4.2.2 4.2.3

Future human resource needs

Liaising with departments so as to anticipate what kind of and how many employees will be needed by when in order to maintain each department's business plan – in terms of expansion, product development, restructuring, relocation, etc.

Staff development and training

Negotiating with managers and their staff over personal career development programmes which mesh with both departmental and corporate strategic plans; commissioning suitable training courses, either in-house or from external agencies.

Age analysis

Maintaining a database of all employees broken down into departments, sections and units which shows employee distribution by age. Graphic representation of this data assists personnel managers in devising and implementing 'new blood' recruitment programmes which fit in with retirement frequencies and also voluntary redundancy or early retirement offers at timely intervals.

Failure to undertake this aspect of manpower planning can have dire consequences for companies when, say, a quarter of its R&D staff retire almost simultaneously!

Abilities, experience and skills analysis

Undertaking regular audits of all employees and keeping database records of their:

- existing qualifications
- programmes of further study leading to additional qualifications
- training courses attended
- on-the-job work experience leading to additional skills development
- updating conferences and seminars attended, etc.

Such records may be studied in order to identify specific staff with expertise which has come to be needed, such as engineers with some Russian who are familiar with Russian industry, or to help senior managers in drawing up human resource requirements in strategic plans.

Staffing costs and cost centres

A further important element of manpower planning is to monitor the costs of the workforce as divided into appropriate functions like production, direct labour, salesforce, and office administration staff. Working with departmental managers, Work Study and O & M units, the personnel team may be able to devise strategies for using the workforce more cost-effectively and undertake plant bargaining productivity negotiations based on the information they have extracted from this monitoring process.

Local and national demographic trends

Companies occupying the same industrial or commercial sector inevitably find themselves in competition for specific kinds of personnel, say, CADCAM software engineers, cost accountants or trilingual personal assistants. Therefore, an effective manpower plan undertakes systematic monitoring – not only of the salaries paid and conditions of service offered to key staff like those above but also of the pay-rates for factory operatives and shop assistants who are recruited locally.

Further monitoring activities will include areas such as: the numbers of school or college leavers coming on to the job market, the mature returners being retrained at local colleges of technology, local employment areas where skills shortages have been identified by county council planning departments, national employment trends and statistics (by industrial/commercial sector) published by HMSO, the nature and extent of local and national unemployment, regional and local pay rates, etc.

Personnel managers in large companies will also liaise with local planning authorities so as to ensure if possible that a sufficient supply of low-cost housing is available for its plant or warehouse workforce, and that their needs are being catered for in county strategic plans.

Ratios of workforce occupancies

In liaison with facilities managers, a personnel team may also maintain records of staff occupancy of, say, open office or factory floors, so as to ensure that UK and EC HASAW requirements on personal working space are complied with, and also to anticipate when additional premises may be needed to accommodate an expanding unit, and so on.

■ Why skills audits are needed

PC 4.2.2 4.2.3

Successful organisations are always changing and re-shaping their activities to enable staff to meet fresh challenges or overcome new problems. As a result, line managers may need their staff to embark upon various kinds of self-development like:

- **distance learning degree programmes** such as the Master in Business Administration or a BA in European Business
- **part-time study professional diplomas and certificates** like the Diploma of the Institute of Marketing
- **intensive two to three day short courses** in, say, desktop publishing or developments in EC legislation
- **in-house training courses for two to three hours per week** on, for example, selling a new product or how to service and maintain a new item of plant
- **home-study programmes** on, say, organisational procedures and operations techniques
- **secondment to another department or unit** for specialist training or updating

and so on.

Thus a busy organisation may have several hundred members of its workforce simultaneously undertaking a wide range of personal development activities like those outlined above. Such staff will also be enlarging their banks of skill and expertise simply by becoming experienced in new routines and working procedures. For example, an office assistant working daily on a word processing or desktop publishing package will come to master many of its features through trial and error and by swapping successes and problems with co-workers.

As a result of all this multifarious activity, a personnel department can quickly get out of touch with the developing skills and experiences of its workforce. This can be both dangerous and wasteful. For instance, new personnel may be recruited to posts which could have been filled by existing members of staff, whose relevant skills and experience had become unrecorded and thus overlooked. Moreover, failure to carry out a continual monitoring of organisational human resource needs against existing capabilities may lead a company into dire straits as its personnel become less and less able to cope with new processes, changing market conditions and technological innovations.

■ Designing and storing a skills audit database

PC 4.2.2 4.2.3

The advent of relational databases – those which can be created so as to permit various kinds of specified data retrieval – proved a boon for personnel managers wishing to create and maintain an accurate record of staff skills and abilities.

Such particulars are surveyed on a regular basis, say, by distributing questionnaires, which are then used as data entry pro formas for keying into the database. The creation of the database file into specific fields for qualifications, short courses, operation of equipment and work experience, etc. enables personnel managers to produce analyses and individual profiles in skill-specific areas such as:

- bilingual personal assistant (French and German to post-degree level) with Wordstar 7.1 word processing skills
- Doctor of Philosophy in plant sciences with diplomas in crop-spraying and marketing

Fig 4.5

PC 4.2.2

Personnel Record update

NAME DEPARTMENT DATE

In order that we may keep our personnel records up-to-date, please show below any changes since

Date of Last Update show changes only.

Address Phone Weight

Marital Status:

I have joined/left Trade union

Number of dependants including yourself

Dates of birth of children born since last update

Have you joined/left our pension scheme?

Describe any physical defects you have developed since last update

Describe any major illness you have had since last update, explain

If you received compensation for injuries since last update, explain

Do you now have a car available for your own use? Registration number

ADDITIONAL SCHOOLING OR SPECIAL TRAINING

Dates	School/college etc.	Name of course and brief description

New memberships in technical or professional societies

New professional offices or honours

Any other changes you would like us to note

Employee's signature Reviewed by

Supervisor

NOTE TO SUPERVISOR: Describe on the reverse side any special projects or assignments which you feel have aided this employee's development and increased his value to the Company.

Form 108
2/87

Reproduced by kind permission of Waterlow Business Supplies

- factory foreman with National Examining Board in Supervisory Management certificate with three years experience of robotic spot-welding and four years of car body paint-spraying techniques

Access to such a staff skills and abilities database – kept up to date by regular skills audits – provides an invaluable human resource planning and deployment tool.

CHECKLIST OF TYPICAL FEATURES OF HUMAN RESOURCES SKILLS, ABILITIES AND EXPERIENCE

PC 4.2.2

- Qualifications on joining the organisation.
- Membership of professional bodies (e.g. Institute of Chartered Engineers).
- Details of any particular abilities potentially useful to the organisation – for example:

  degree of fluency in specified foreign languages;

  levels of expertise in various computer programming languages.
- Details (in chronological order) of all in-house and externally commissioned training courses undertaken and results/reports on outcomes.
- Particulars of degree/diploma /certificate work-related programmes of study pursued.
- Records of all experience and training on specific machines and equipment – for example, which passenger aircraft a pilot is qualified to fly and how many hours he/she has logged on which jets, etc.
- Extent of experience in various particular posts both prior to joining and within the organisation with dates of transfers and/or promotions including job titles, etc.
- Notes of hobbies and leisure pursuits which could prove of value to the organisation, e.g. expert photographer or computer buff.

DISCUSSION TOPICS

PC 4.2.2

1 Given the nature of its work, what kind of problems do you think a personnel manager might have in his or her interactions with a company's senior managers?

2 What range of skills do you think a successful and effective personnel manager needs to possess?

3 What sort of problems would you expect an organisation to encounter which has not undertaken any structured manpower planning over the past 15 years?

4 How would you organise a skills audit in, say, a manufacturing and exporting company of some 800 employees? To whom would you provide what collated data?

PC 4.2.3 4.2.4

The human resource function and the management of change

A most important function of human resources in any organisation today is to support its senior staff in devising and implementing policies to manage change effectively, so that the organisation not only survives, but continues to flourish. Today, change in a business or public service context takes on a variety of forms – each presenting different challenges:

PC 4.2.3 4.2.4

TYPES OF CHANGE FACED BY BUSINESS AND PUBLIC SERVICE ORGANISATIONS

- **Technological**
  Stemming from the wide-spread use of new technologies – computer, laser, fibre-optic, genetic engineering, biotechnology, etc. which are developing fast and radically affecting people's work and private lives.
- **Economic**
  New economic and trading blocks have been created: the European Union, the Pacific Rim States, the Russian Federation, the north and south American trading bloc etc. which are creating significant changes globally – in the mobility of workers (150 million Chinese on the move in the People's Republic searching for jobs in urban areas), in standards of living, threats from imports, dumping into home markets, resource disputes, as in fishing and mining and so on.

  The impact of the 1988–94 UK recession caused profound changes in work and employment patterns, increasing fixed-term, part-time and freelance employment contracts as organisations 'down-sized' and carried out 'head-count reductions' – coded terms for shedding personnel.
- **Societal**
  Changes in people's lifestyles – the need for a married couple to work after having children, single-parent families, the high incidence of divorce (around 40% in the UK currently) long-term unemployment in some regions, the free movement of workers within the EU – all bear upon the size and shape of organisations, and how they manage their workforces.
- **Demographic**
  Across the western world, people are generally living longer; also, fewer children are being born; the workforce is therefore ageing, and increasing numbers of pensioners are putting financial and resource pressures on: health services, state pensions, local community services, the availability of housing etc.; as a result, many private and public sector organisations as well as the state are having to re-think their employment policies and state benefits; in the UK, the retirement age for women was recently raised from 60 to 65.
- **Governmental**
  Increasingly, the UK government's industrial and employment policies are impacting on business organisations – such as through the new tax on fuel, privatisations of large state utilities, the encouragement of foreign manufacturers to set up shop in the UK, the effects of membership of the EU on employment practices and regulations affected business etc.

■ The effects of change on working conditions

PC 4.2.3 4.2.4

Inevitably, changes brought like those outlined above work their way through to individual shops, factories or local government departments. The effects they have centre upon the following types of outcome:

PC 4.2.3 4.2.4

THE IMPACT OF CHANGE UPON WORKING CONDITIONS

Changes of a national significance impact upon individual organisations as follows:

- **increases in costs:** for example, by several million pounds annually for a business like ICI as a result of the fuel tax
- **changes in employment contracts and conditions:** for example by moving away from established, full-employment rights posts (which carry the costs of national insurance, redundancy payments, paid holidays etc.) to short, fixed term contracts or the hiring of freelance, self-employed contractors
- **changes in working conditions:**
  - — for example, by having to design and build dust-free work-shops and kit out staff accordingly in order to make computer chips or electronic equipment
  - — for example, by multi-skilling all the workforce so as to promote flexibility and cost-effectiveness – as did Nissan in its new (1989) car factory in Sunderland
- **changes in organisational structures and decision-making:** sometimes changes in sales and profitability cause businesses to radically restructure themselves, as did the IBM Corporation in the late 1980s, when it decentralised authority and enabled sales teams to set the prices for computers they sold etc. in order to re-establish a leading market position.

■ Planning for change

PC 4.2.3 4.2.4

Given that the end of the 20th century sees the UK and the developed world still going through a major economic revolution as a result of developments in technology and an inexorable increase in world population, forward-looking and caring business organisations are now taking serious steps to establish policies and mechanisms which enable their managers to manage change, and their workforces to cope with its effects.

The following check-list illustrates some of the major techniques used in businesses to manage change successfully:

PC 4.2.3 4.2.4

TECHNIQUES FOR MANAGING CHANGE SUCCESSFULLY

- **Establishing a senior 'think-tank':** which undertakes a role called 'futuring' – looking into the future in terms of the company's activities and trying to anticipate what will impact how upon the organisation, and how it can best be prepared for – as, for example, the economic impact of the Euro Tunnel upon the county of Kent's economic and transport infrastructure.
- **Introducing policies which deal with specific types of change:** such as IBM's decision some years ago at its UK head office to 'lead from the front' in terms of its business of making and selling computers and allied systems by first training its staff and then transforming their desk-top working environment during a pre-set transition period away from a mix of paper and terminal to a fully-fledged computerised system based on electronic mail and the creation of electronic files by scanners etc.
- **Consulting and involving staff:** if staff are to respond positively to the introduction of change, it is essential that they and their representatives are consulted and involved from the outset – so that they understand the reasons for the change and the extent of it – upon themselves as individuals; such an open policy also avoids the demoralisation of staff from wild rumour and unfounded speculation.
- **Developing affected staff:** where staff are directly affected by changes – say in having to operate equipment using a new technology – is vital that they are provided with sufficient training and time for adjustment.
- **Monitoring the effectiveness of changed systems:** introducing change almost inevitably causes unsuspected side-effects and problems; it is therefore essential that the people and systems which are affected by changed work practices are closely monitored so as to obtain either positive or negative feedback on the results.
- **Changing the changes:** to complete this loop, senior management may have to modify the changes it has introduced in the light of their impact upon organisational effectiveness, or to extend transitional periods and staff development programmes.

PC 4.2.1 4.2.2 4.2.3 4.2.4

REVIEW TEST

1 List three major job role responsibilities of: a company director, a middle manager, a shop steward and a work assistant.

2 List two major responsibilities of a county councillor.

3 In what ways do the responsibilities of managing director impact upon a business's corporate plan? Provide a brief explanation.

4 In what ways is a middle manager likely to find him or herself to be 'between a rock and a hard place' in organisational terms?

5 Give examples of two activities in which a departmental manager and a human resources manager are likely to work together.

6 List three ways in which working conditions have altered since the 1988–94 UK recession.

7 List four different types of change which business organisations have to cope with.

8 Describe briefly three changes which may affect a business organisation a) beneficially and b) adversely.

9 What is likely to happen if an organisation does not involve and consult fully with its workforce when in the process of introducing change?

10 Describe briefly four types of strategy which business managers can use to help in managing change successfully.

GROUP ACTIVITIES

PC
4.2.1
4.2.2
4.2.3
4.2.4

These activities can be done individually or in pairs.

1 Arrange to visit a medium-to-large local business or public sector organisation in order to interview **one** of the following: a company director, a departmental manager, a supervisor, a trade union employee/official, an operative or assistant. Find out what they consider to be the key responsibilities of their respective job roles. Report back to your class and compare notes, focusing on the theoretical and the actual.

2 Arrange to meet with a departmental manager and to find out how the human resource function links with his or her managerial activities – when and why. Produce a short bullet-point summary and distribute it to your co-students.

3 Working as a pair, arrange for one partner to research a public sector organisation's conditions of service, and the other those of a private sector company. Then compare your findings for similarities and differences. Give a 5–10 minute briefing to your class on what you discovered, and your rationale accounting for the differences.

4 Arrange to interview (as a pair) 3–4 middle managers – say two for a private and two for a public sector organisation and find out what type of change they are affected by and how they are managing it. In a general class discussion, compare notes on your findings.

KNOWLEDGE TEST

Element 4.2
Investigate job roles and changing working conditions

1 (i) A key job role of a middle manager is to produce a corporate plan annually.
(ii) A key role of a supervisor is to look after the interests of his/her staff.

Which of the following options best describes the above two statements?

A	(i)	T	(ii)	T
B	(i)	T	(ii)	F
C	(i)	F	(ii)	T
D	(i)	F	(ii)	F

2 Which of the following statements are true and which false?

A A shop steward will normally invite a human resource manager to trade union meetings in the capacity of an observer.

B Futuring is a technique used by organisations to identify areas of opportunity and/or threat which they may need to respond to.

C A company secretary's major role is to co-ordinate an organisation's document production, filing and records.

D Manpower planning is a technique used to ensure that an organisation always possesses an effective workforce.

3 (i) Company directors are mostly involved in making strategic policies and decisions.
(ii) A middle manager is unlikely to act as a company's grievance officer.

Which of the following options best describes the above two statements?

A	(i)	T	(ii)	T
B	(i)	T	(ii)	F
C	(i)	F	(ii)	T
D	(i)	F	(ii)	F

4 Which of the following changes is likely to cost money (C) and which save money (S) when introduced into an organisation?

A flexible working agreements
B robotics in a factory
C a systematic staff training and development programme
D outsourcing of data processing

PC
4.2.1
4.2.2
4.2.3
4.2.4
4.2.5

PORTFOLIO OF EVIDENCE ACTIVITY

Element 4.2
Investigate job roles and changing working conditions

'ALL CHANGE!'

Scenario 1

You work as a research assistant for a firm of management consultants which specialises in placing people on its register in suitable posts in both private and public sector organisations. In order for its team of 12 consultants to keep abreast of current job roles and work practices, your manager, Ranjit Singh, has asked you to research into the following job roles:

- a company director
- a middle manager
- a supervisor
- an assistant
- an operative.

Your research should concentrate on: the responsibilities they have for identifying and meeting the targets relating to their jobs, what the main features are of their work with others, what training and development they receive, what disciplinary procedures they are subject to, and what changes are affecting their work currently. This report should also examine the reasons why working conditions are prone to change and should explain a single, particular reason for change and how its has affected certain staff.

Scenario 2

Your next task is to research into one specific component of an employment contract, such as hours to be worked, the commission system employed, maternity leave entitlement etc. and to devise a plan aimed at bringing about a change in the area you have selected. For example, it could be to design a job-sharing scheme for female staff who, after having had a baby, do not wish to return in the short-term to full-time work, or it could be to introduce a fair and equitable system for selecting candidates for compulsory redundancy, or it could be a scheme for encouraging early retirement in a 'down-sizing' scenario.

Your plan should explain why working conditions are subject to change and provide an in-depth illustration of the reason for changes to working conditions. It should also explain who would have the responsibility for implementing your plan.

Task 1

Your first task is to complete the appropriate parts of your activity planning and review log.

Task 2

First arrange to research the information needed for the report detailed in Scenario 1, and then create a suitable structure for it bearing in mind its twin aspects. A suitable report is likely to be some 4–5 sides of printed A4.

Task 3

For this task, you are free to select any part of an employment contract you and your teacher consider appropriate. However, before settling on any particular topic, you should bear in mind any legal constraints – for example, that all female staff have the right to return to their posts after maternity leave, and that, therefore, a job sharing scheme would have to be voluntary and not compulsory. A suitable plan is likely to be some 3–4 sides of A4 long, including any illustrative material.

Performance criteria covered

4.2.1, 4.2.2, 4.2.3, 4.2.4, 4.2.5

Core skills covered

Communication:
3.2.1, 3.2.2, 3.2.3, 3.2.4, 3.2.5, 3.3.1, 3.3.2, 3.3.3, 3.4.1, 3.4.2, 3.4.3, 3.4.4

Information Technology:
3.1.1, 3.1.2, 3.1.3, 3.1.4, 3.1.5, 3.2.1, 3.2.2, 3.2.3, 3.2.4, 3.2.5, 3.2.6, 3.2.7, 3.3.1, 3.3.2, 3.3.3, 3.3.4, 3.3.5, 3.3.6

CASE STUDY

PC 4.2.3 4.2.4

A century of change at Flowsure Pumps Limited

New engine technology prompts business start-up

Flowsure Pumps Limited was founded in 1902 by an agricultural engineer, Henry Williams, in the southern outskirts of Birmingham. The rationale for forming the company derived from the fastgrowing need for pumps of all sorts in agricultural, engineering and motor car manufacturing companies.

Women employed at Flowsure

Flowsure made slow but steady progress until the outbreak of the First World War. Then the demand for pumps soared as the British war machine started to roll. By the time conscription was introduced in 1916, two-thirds of Flowsure's male fitters, machinists and clerks were fighting in France and their places taken by local women and young lads.

Telephone links with USA boosts business

In the 1920s, with profits secured from aiding the war effort, Henry Williams re-equipped his administration offices. Flowsure was one of the first firms to purchase electric typewriters in 1920 and to secure export orders for special marques of the 3.5 million motor cars which were manufactured in the USA in 1927 – through a deal largely effected by using the just opened Rugby – England to Rocky Point, New Jersey radio-telephone link.

New product averts closure

In the early 1930s, Flowsure was badly hit by the slump and nearly closed down. Its survival was largely due to a far-sighted product diversification introduced by James Williams, Henry's oldest son, who had recently graduated from the University of London with a BSc in Fluid Mechanics. He had spent some months in 1932 in America studying at Harvard and had been lucky enough to see an early automatic washing machine being demonstrated. He immediately spotted the enormous market potential of a machine which would do away with the regular chore of washing clothes by hand. As a result of his persuasion and determination, Flowsure set up a small production line and began to make washing machines. Initially they were sold only into the wealthiest three per cent of homes by stores like Harrods and Selfridges – much like the television receivers which sold like hot cakes to the rich when the BBCs first television service started in 1936.

As a result of the product diversification policy introduced in 1933, the name of the company was changed to Flowsure Products Limited and an appealing logo designed around the letters FPL.

Modern office equipment investment

In 1913, Flowsure's workforce had comprised an all-male complement of 23. By 1939, it had grown to 140, including 35 female factory operatives and 19 female office staff who worked on a range of modern office equipment which included:

- a jack-plug telephone switchboard;
- a teleprinter for sending and receiving telex messages within the UK and to a limited number of European cities;
- a mixture of manual and electric typewriters and dictating equipment, located in a typing pool comprising three lines of desks;
- three pencil-sharpening machines for the shorthand-typists;
- a 'multibiller' for producing copies of documents such as invoices and statements;
- a mechanical postage meter;
- a Gestetner rotary duplicator for making copies fro typewriter-cut stencils;
- several electrically operated accounting machines.

After the Second World War, Flowsure's newly demobbed Office Manager ordered a punched-card system far storing accounts and stock-control data and imported an American Xerox photocopier, which was originally used with limited access to copy confidential documents.

Work study boosts productivity at Flowsure

On Flowsure's shop floor through the 1950s output was increased by a series of work study projects which examined carefully the layout of each production-line, the ergonomics of operators' movements and the ways in which components were brought to the lines. As a result, the company invested extensively in pallet-based storage and fork-lift trucks. At the same time, the workforce became progressively more unionised as successive innovations in production made jobs look less secure.

Thin order book prompts racial tension

The 1960s full-employment boom not only brought about seven-day, three-shift working, but also the addition to the workforce of a number of immigrants from Caribbean and Asian countries. While labour relations remained generally good during the 1960s 'boom years', the recession and three-day week of the early 1970s caused orders to drop significantly for several years subsequently. In the mid 1970s, a number of racially-centered disputes blew up in the factory, and when three coloured operatives were made redundant in 1976, their compatriots staged an unofficial strike. An industrial tribunal found that the three operatives had, in fact, been unfairly dismissed under the newly introduced Race Relations Act and they were reinstated with compensation.

Information Technology transforms work patterns and job roles

The work of both the factory and adjacent offices underwent extensive change between 1980 and 1990. In order to maintain its competitive edge in both the pump and washing machine markets, Flowsure invested heavily in computer-controlled production systems, including robotic welding and paint-spraying. Entire pump mechanisms were designed using computer-aided design and manufacturing techniques (CADCAM), and casings and housings were machined automatically through the use of computer numeric control (CNC) techniques.

As a result of the widespread introduction of IT systems into the factory, Flowsure's production workforce was reduced from 652 in 1980 to 331 in 1991. Because of the complex employment protection legislation of the 1970s, Flowsure was obliged to appoint a highly experienced personnel director in 1983 and to expand its personnel function.

The changes in Flowsure's office-based departments were no less radical. In 1982 a Computer Services Department was set up to provide a comprehensive service on both production and administrative fronts. In 1985, stand-alone word processing systems were being used in most departments, and by 1990, all the firm's typewriters – save the one used by the Managing Director's PA, Mrs Nora Buxton (who had admitted to being 54 years old for several years) – had effectively been replaced by a LAN/WAN system linking all departments and all personnel down to section-leader level. In 1994 a Reprographics Resources Unit was established to undertake all printing and document production in-house using desktop publishing and laser-printer technology.

Flowsure taken over in dawn raid!

Also in 1994 Flowsure's independence came to an end. In 1986, the Board had decided to go public and had managed to sell the desired amount of shares – in this case worth £6.2 million – on the Stock Exchange. Unfortunately, the Board had not been sufficiently vigilant thereafter in monitoring who was buying its shares, and became the victim of a highly organised, hostile take-over bid in June 1994 by Burleigh Holdings plc, a multinational conglomerate.

Restructuring – redundancy hits Flowsure

There followed an extensive restructuring of the company stemming from a Burleigh decision to sell off a large part of the specialist and not very profitable pumps business. As a result, four of the 12 company's directors negotiated resignation deals and 16 middle managers along with 43 works employees and 10 office administration personnel were made redundant. Three middle managers were appointed to a reconstructed board of directors, four junior managers received promotion to departmental head level, three new foremen were appointed and five support staff became supervisors in newly designed posts.

Burleigh job boost at Flowsure

Twelve months after acquiring the company, production of a range of washing-up machines made by a Burleigh subsidiary was transferred to Flowsure as part of a rationalisation plan, and located in a factory on adjacent land which Burleigh also purchased. Once fully operational, the new factory employed some 250 personnel and 25 allied support staff.

PC 4.2.3 4.2.4

CASE STUDY DISCUSSION TOPICS

1 What do you think were the likely effects at Flowsure of the change from 66% of its workforce being male to 66% being female in 1916?

2 In what ways did Flowsure's prompt acceptance of changes in office technology in the 1920s assist its expansion?

3 James Williams almost single-handedly rescued Flowsure in 1932 by introducing product diversification. Can you think of any similar examples in today's manufacturing industries?

4 How well do you think Flowsure's senior management team planned for and managed change in the immediate post-war period 1945–51?

5 How does work study bring about change in an industrial environment? What effects is it likely to have on a factory-based workforce?

6 As Flowsure's human resources manager in 1976, what steps would you have taken to ensure that the racially-centred tensions did not recur?

7 Identify six ways in which Flowsure's moves into IT in the 1980s were likely to have affected its personnel.

8 How might Flowsure have avoided its hostile take-over by Burleigh Holdings plc in 1994?

9 How do you imagine the take-over affected Flowsure's staff? As Burleigh's board of directors, what policies would you devise to minimise any likely adverse effects of the take-over?

10 How well, in your opinion, did Flowsure respond to and manage the extensive changes it experienced between 1902–94? Can you think of anything that its directors might have done differently? If so, with what likely outcomes?

Element 4.3
RECRUITMENT PROCEDURES, JOB APPLICATIONS AND INTERVIEWS

A central function of human resource management is the process by which people are recruited into the organisation. Nowadays, there are many legal considerations (stemming from Acts like the Employment Protection Act 1978 and the Employment Act 1982) which render the process of terminating an employee's contract both involved and lengthy (see pages 371–5). For this reason, personnel and line management departments take particular pains in their efforts to recruit people who can do the advertised job well, and who are likely to become cherished, long-serving members of the workforce. PC 4.3.1

The chart on pages 416–17 illustrates some 17 steps in a typical staff recruitment process. It offers, however, only a mainstream indication of the procedure, since appointments at varying levels within an organisation require different degrees of attention and involvement. For example, a post for a supermarket baker may simply be advertised within the store under VACANCIES: BAKER, and the interview process may be informal and fairly short. Even so, whatever the level of appointment, the law underpinning recruitment remains the same in terms of what constitutes:

- a fair and non-discriminatory job advertisement
- binding letters of job offer and acceptance
- a legally satisfactory contract of employment

RECRUITMENT: FOUR KEY PHASES

PC 4.3.1

Before anyone is recruited to a given post, it will be carefully analysed by expert managers who carry out these tasks:

Job Analysis: Have the job requirements changed since the post was last advertised? If so, how?

How do the changes impact upon the person specification and job description to be drawn up (see pages 419–23)?

Person Specification: How accurately does this identify and detail the abilities, skills and personality traits needed in the ideal applicant? If it is an existing specification, how does it need changing?

Job Description: Is this still current and up to date? If not, what changes need to be made in the light of evolved: technology, work practices, company policy etc?

Interviewing Procedures: Who will select candidates' long-list/short-list (in-house personnel department or recruitment agency?)

Who will interview? Who will chair panel?

Who will 'orchestrate' the selection questions?

PC 4.3.1 4.3.2 4.3.3

THE RECRUITMENT PROCESS

1 Need for new post identified.

Line managers and personnel department consult — **Job need identified**

2 Line manager details needs: reviews post for changes if it already exists, or lists fresh requirements if a new post is to be established.

Lists the physical, educational, experience, aptitudes, skills and personality requirements needed in the person who could do the job successfully. Prioritises requirements as 'essential' or useful'.

3 *Personnel specification* is revised or a fresh one drawn up.

Personnel specification produced

Defines: who the employee reports to and who may report to him: lists in detail the duties and responsibilities of the post-holder.

4 *Job description* is revised or a fresh one devised.

Job description updated

Sells the job by briefly indicating what benefits – pay, prospects, 'perks' etc are offered in return for an applicant possessing the expertise displayed as needed in the advertisement.

5 *A classified or display advertisement* is composed for insertion in local/national press.

Advertisement placed

These may include potted history of the organisation and details of successes as well as outline of job location, duties and prospects.

6 *Duplicated particulars of the post* and application forms are made ready for posting to applicants; the job description may be included in pack to applicants.

Applicants respond

Smaller organisations sometimes ask only for 'letters of application'; large firms want the 'full application package'.

7 *Initial letters of interest* are received and application packs despatched

8 Completed applications are received which include *formal covering letter of application, completed application form(s)* and a copy of a *curriculum vitae.*

Applications sifted

Note: many organisations hire *employment consultants* to sift through initial applications and to propose candidates for shortlisting.

National and international companies receive hundreds of applications for key posts

During this period, line managers and personnel staff meet to organise interview procedures and agree who will assess what.

9 Shortlisted applicants are sent *letter invitation* to attend for interview.

Shortlist drawn up

10 *Acceptance letters* received from shortlisted applicants.

It is common practice in private sector companies for employees to make very confidential applications for new jobs. Their references will only be taken up with the candidate's permission, and usually after an oral job offer has been made and accepted – 'subject to satisfactory references being received'.

11 *Confidential references* are obtained from referees cited in application forms and copied for interview panel, along with shortlisted candidates' application forms and CVs.

References taken up

Interview panel also provided with *interviewing schedule* on which to record impressions and ratings.

This schedule gives the interviewer a means of 'marking' the candidate for aspects like:
Appearance
Alertness
Knowledge/expertise
Potential
Rapport

Usually a pro forma to detail road/rail fares, hotel and meal costs; employers usually state in application pack whether expenses for interviews attendance will be paid.

12 Interviews take place. Candidates provided with expenses claim forms to return after completion. Oral offer of appointment made and orally accepted (subject to acceptable references being obtained).

Interviews take place

Some organisations advise the successful candidate by letter after the interview process as this may take place intermittently.

It is good manners and good public relations to thank all applicants for their interest in the post.

13 Written letter confirming job offer despatched to successful candidate, and courtesy letters despatched to unsuccessful applicants.

Job offered and accepted

14 Written job acceptance letter returned.

While a contract of employment may be deemed to exist on the basis of witnessed oral offers and acceptance, the process is confirmed by the exchange of letters.

15 Letter of resignation sent to current employer by successful applicant.

Resignation submitted

This must be received by the new employee within 8 weeks of starting in the job: it will include details of pay, holiday entitlement, hours of work, sickness pay and pension agreements, periods of notice required on either side, job description details and appropriate information about company rules and regulations.

16 Written contract of employment sent to new employee and countersigned by both parties.

Employment contract issued

17 Job description also provided to new employee with company manual and prospectus etc.

Acts and statutes underpinning the recruitment process:

- Employment Protection (Consolidation) Act 1978
- Sex Discrimination Act 1975
- Equal Pay (Amendments) Regulations 1983
- Fair Wages Resolutions (House of Commons)
- Race Relations Act 1976
- Misrepresentation Act 1967
- Trade Union Reform and Employment Rights Act 1993

PC 4.3.1 4.3.2

■ Job analysis

Before making a commitment to a fresh employee, efficient organisations carry out a job analysis on the post to be advertised in order to check whether it has changed (sometimes unnoticed), whether its last occupant had undertaken additional duties informally, or whether certain functions have become obsolete etc. The departure of one employee also provides managers and supervisors with the opportunity to re-think their operations since, in a sense, they have obtained a 'wild card' temporary period of flexibility which they frequently use to modify section or departmental work.

PC 4.3.2

■ The person specification

Once the scope and range of the post has been reviewed, it is possible to draw up a revised person specification, which details the sort of abilities, skills and experience an ideal applicant would possess. This specification is frequently used by the staff who produce the recruitment advert, since it precisely describes the sort of person wanted.

PC 4.3.2

■ The job description

Once the job to be advertised has been carefully defined, it is possible compose an entirely new or a revised job description, which is a kind of schedule of the major duties and tasks which the post-holder is expected to carry out, and which clarifies to whom he/she will report and for whom (subordinates) he/she will be responsible. Both the person specification and the job description are key tools which interviewers will refer to when preparing for the interviews.

■ The interview

The interview provides that all-important opportunity for applicants and employer to meet, for faces and personalities to be put to paper applications, for chemistry to happen and for questions to be asked and answered on either side which aim to provide additional information and reassurances

The table set out on pages 416–17 illustrates in 17 sequenced steps how the key stages of recruitment are carried out.

Person specifications and job descriptions

PC 4.3.2

The difference between a person specification and a job description

Some people find it difficult to distinguish between a person specification and a job description. Essentially, a person specification is a checklist drawn up to identify what particular physical characteristics, general and/or vocational qualifications, skills, aptitudes and previous work experience **an ideal candidate for a given post should possess.**

A job description sets out clearly **the most important responsibilities and duties which make up a given job**.

The person specification

PC 4.3.2

Set out on page 421 is an example of one type of person specification. The essential features of the specification are graded into Necessary, Helpful and Optional since an organisation would be extremely lucky to obtain the services of an employee who possessed all the characteristics identified.

Depending on the type of post to be advertised, the person specification will place more emphasis on either educational qualifications, analytical and communication skills, say, for a personnel manager, or manual dexterity, conscientiousness and the ability to perform routine tasks repetitively if for a production-line operative.

In some jobs, like that of an RAF pilot, 20-20 uncorrected vision (doesn't wear glasses) is deemed essential, while physique is of little or no importance in, say, a computer programmer.

Managers use the process of designing or updating the person specification as an opportunity to reconsider how a job has changed or developed, what aspects have become more or less important and thus what emphasis should be given to the redesigned job occupant's profile. The specification also provides advertising copy writers with a stripped-out summary of the key features of the ideal applicant and thus assists the advertising process.

The job description

PC 4.3.2

The main purpose of the job description (see pages 422 and 423) is to define as clearly as possible for both its possessor and his or her line manager what the key ingredients of the job are. Compilers of job descriptions seek to identify the priority aspects of a post:

> **To meet agreed company sales turnover targets and to maintain the operations of the sales function within allocated budgets.**

and the list of job responsibilities are usually set out in descending order of priority.

The job description also places its possessor clearly into a line management hierarchy with items entitled: Responsible To: and Responsible For:

In addition to setting out main job functions, the job description may also include details of any equipment, records, security systems or parts of premises for which the possessor is responsible.

A good job description also includes the name of its compiler, approver, the date of first issue and the dates of any subsequent revised issues.

Job descriptions are helpful tools in the personnel appraisal process, but should not be taken too literally as the 'tablets of stone' which define all possible aspects of a post. The statement: 'That's not in my job description!' sometimes betrays a sign of a deteriorating manager–subordinate relationship. And in the case of staff in the higher reaches of the organisational hierarchy, the complexities of jobs and their capacity for open-ended transactions make it virtually impossible for job descriptions to cover all aspects of the work to be undertaken.

PC 4.3.2

CHECKLIST OF MAIN COMPONENTS

Person Specification

Date compiled

Location in management line

Physical characteristics
Vision, hearing, manual dexterity, etc.

Qualifications
GCSEs NVQs GNVQs GCE A-levels
BTEC/RSA/LCCI/CGLI
Professional Institute, etc.

Experience
Previous posts, full/part-time,work experience, HND sandwich blocks, etc.

Personality
Self-starter, tact/discretion, sense of humour, etc.

Interests and hobbies
Foreign travel/languages computer buff, etc.

Circumstances
When available, willing to work overtime, willing to work overseas, clean driver's licence, etc.

Job Description

Date compiled
Date of previous review

Job Title

Department
Location of post
Responsible to
Responsible for

Scope of post
Brief of summary of major features of the post.

Major responsibilities
Checklist of the main priorities of the job set out in descending order as numbered sentences.

Other responsibilities
– for, say, security, office equipment or works plant, supervision of the work of others, etc.

Education and qualifications
Some job descriptions include a summary of the education and qualifications needed for the post.

Name of Compiler
Name of Approver
Date of issue

Specimen person specification for a personal secretary

Date: Date of previous review:

Job title: Personal secretary

Reporting to: Middle tier manager

Characteristics	Necessary	Helpful	Optional
Physical:			
20-20/Corrected vision	✓		
Good hearing	✓		
Manual dexterity for keyboarding	✓		
Good carriage and well-groomed appearance	✓		
Qualifications:			
RSA/LCC Secretarial			
Diploma/Certificate		✓	
Shorthand to 100 wpm	✓		
Typewriting to 40 wpm	✓		
Word processing to NVQ Level 3	✓		
Information processing to NVQ Level 3		✓	
English to GCSE A–C	✓		
French to GCSE A–C		✓	
Experience:			
Previous personal secretarial post		✓	
Coordination of overseas travel arrangements		✓	
Working under pressure to tight deadlines	✓		
Personality:			
Tact/discretion	✓		
confidentiality	✓		
Self-starter	✓		
Sense of humour		✓	
Interests/hobbies:			
Foreign languages		✓	
European culture		✓	
Fashionwear/clothes sense			✓
Circumstances:			
Able to start work 1.5.19—		✓	
Clean driving licence			✓
Willing to travel abroad		✓	
Willing to work late at times		✓	

Drawn up by: ______________________

Approved by: ______________________

Issue Date: ______________________

PC
4.3.2

Specimen job description

Date: 12 January 199X   Previous Review Date: 15 June 199X

Job title   Personal Secretary to Deputy Sales Manager

Department: Home Sales Department

Location: Company Head Office

Responsible to: Deputy Sales Manager

Responsible for: Work of WP Assistant and Office Information Assistant

Scope of post: To provide secretarial services and informational support to the Deputy Sales Manager and to assist in administering the activities of the home sales force; to coordinate and supervise the work of the DSM's word processing and office information staff; to liaise with field sales personnel, according to DSM's briefings and requests.

Major responsibilities

1 To supervise the opening of correspondence and to ensure its prompt distribution according to house practices.

2 To transcribe and deliver as appropriate incoming fax, telex and email messages.

3 To accept, transcribe (using appropriate media) and dispatch DSM's correspondence, reports, memoranda and textual messages.

4 To maintain the DSM's electronic appointments and scheduling diaries efficiently.

5 To administer the DSM's paper and electronic filing systems effectively, and to ensure the security of all computer-stored data.

6 To supervise the operation of office equipment so as to maintain efficient, cost-effective and safe practices.

7 To make travel/accommodation arrangements for DSM and designated staff as required.

8 To administer the sales force expenses payment system and to maintain the DSM's office petty cash and purchases systems.

9 To maintain a cost-effective office stationery provision in liaison with the company's office administration manager.

10 To receive visitors and look after their comfort and hospitality needs.

11 To supervise the work of the DSM's office personnel so as to maintain good standards and timely completion of delegated tasks.

12 To monitor office practices and procedures and to advise the DSM on possible improvements and modifications in the light of changing office technology and information systems.

13 To ensure that office security is maintained and that confidences are not breached.

14 To promote an alert approach to HASAW matters at all times.

15 To undertake any reasonable task from time to time at the DSM's request as may be deemed appropriate within the scope of the post.

Equipment/Systems Responsibilities

Office computer terminals for sale operations and malfunction reporting.

Office fax, PABX extensions, photocopying and printing equipment for cost-effective and safe operations and malfunction reporting.
Office-held computer files for safe keeping and prompt accessing and liaison with company DP manager for defect/malfunctioning reporting.

Education and Qualifications
General education to GCSE standard and vocational secretarial education to LCCI Private Secretarial Certificate/NVQ Level 3 Administration.
Previous office information processing and secretarial experience essential; the post also requires developed interpersonal/communication skills and developed office applications software and telecommunications expertise as well as word processing proficiency.

Recruitment advertising and documentation

PC 4.3.1

■ Advertising the post

Two alternatives are available to a personnel department in recruitment advertising – either to undertake the work in-house, or to subcontract it to a recruitment bureau. Either way, the previously drawn-up or revised person specification and job description provide handy summaries of essential requirements and expectations which advertising copywriters can use in designing a display or classified advertisement.

The nature of the post to be advertised – managerial/professional or clerical/factory worker – will affect the decision of national or local advertising and the kind of publishing/broadcasting media employed.

MEDIA USED IN RECRUITMENT ADVERTISING

- National quality press
- National tabloid press
- Local or (district) weekly newspapers
- Free local papers
- Professional/trade journals and magazines (e.g. *Computing*)
- Regional independent television
- Local commercial radio
- Billboards and notices displayed on company premises

Note: Some jobs are never publicly advertised. Exceptionally able managers and professionals are 'head-hunted' by specialist consultancy firms working on behalf of an organisation needing to recruit. Very discreet approaches are privately made to the 'hunted' expert, negotiations ensue and, if successful, the sought-after person quietly resigns and takes up the new post. This approach is used when it is accepted that public advertising will not attract the type of person required.

■ Advertising rates

All advertising media – national and local newspapers, commercial television and radio – update regularly their advertising prices on what are called rate cards. Not unexpectedly, the costs of advertising vary according to:

- size and type of advertisement or length of commercial
- position in newspaper, time and date of commercial broadcast
- discounts given for repeated insertions or broadcasts.

As a result of their market research, commercial television and radio companies are able to advise personnel managers when specific segments of the local or national population will be viewing or listening. Similarly, newspaper advertising managers are able to provide details of the breakdown of their readership (see the Marketing Unit for details of how the public is segmented into socio-economic groupings).

■ Designing the advertisement

There is always a tension in recruitment advertising between supplying too much information in too small a typeface – which people won't read – and providing such sparse information that potential applicants fail to become interested.

Many advertisements provide a brief outline of two sets of details which complement each other:

WE ARE PREPARED TO OFFER THIS: ***(Checklist or job offer package)***

FOR THIS: ***(Checklist of abilities/experience required in successful applicant)***

Eye-catching headlines play an important part in successful advertisements:

PART-TIME GIRL OR MAN FRIDAY NEEDED ON SATURDAYS!

JOIN OUR FRIENDLY MADHOUSE IF YOU WANT A JOB THAT'S FUN!

MANAGING DIRECTOR £65,000

Some headlines capture attention by being 'zany' and humorous, others simply by the bald statement of a huge salary. The tone and style of the advertisement will depend entirely upon the nature and level of the post in the hierarchy and how the organisation likes to promote its corporate image.

ADVERTISING ASSIGNMENT

PC 4.3.1

In groups of two or three, study the two advertisements set out below and on page 426. Draw up a checklist of the features of their design and layout which you think work to make them effective. Then consider any other approaches which you would adopt in advertising the same posts.

Having completed this evaluation, compare notes with the other groups in your class.

Fig 4.6

Western Riverside Waste Authority

General Manager

£45,000 package including non-contributory leased car (Pay award pending)

We are seeking a committed senior manager to lead this progressive authority now firmly established after its inception 3 years ago which has the major task of disposing of waste from the four inner London boroughs of Hammersmith & Fulham, Kensington & Chelsea, Lambeth and Wandsworth.

The Job

- To be responsible for the operation of two major refuse transfer stations and a civic amenity site located in Wandsworth.
- To provide strategic management, with particular emphasis on planning future waste disposal arrangements for the authority.
- To be responsible for the management of over 80 staff based at two stations and civic amenity site.
- Responsible for the efficient operation of budgetary and administrative systems as well as the negotiation of major contracts.
- To actively promote the running of the operations in a safety conscious and environmentally sensitive way.

The Person

The person we are seeking would ideally possess:

- An engineering background HNC/degree level.
- Significant managerial experience within the waste disposal industry or process engineering.
- Advanced negotiating skills.
- A flair for strategic thinking and priority setting in a dynamic environment.
- The ability to assume 'hands on' control when required.

Although experience in the waste industry would be an advantage, consideration will be given to candidates with other appropriate experience.

Benefits include index linked pension, generous leave entitlement and relocation package if required.

The salary and benefits package attached to this post reflects the fact that we are looking to appoint someone with outstanding qualities which are required to lead the Authority in a period of significant change and the introduction of new developments.

If you would like an informal discussion about this post please contact the Clerk to the Authority, Mr G. K. Jones on 0181-871 6001, who should also be contacted for application forms and further details either by telephone or at the following address: Town Hall, Wandsworth High Street, Wandsworth, SW18 2PU. Closing date for applications: 6th September 199X.

W•R•W•A

Fig 4.7

'You're not flogging ad space! I thought you wanted a real job.'

'Yes, I am and it's just the job I wanted. The career prospects are real enough.'

'Don't tell me "young dynamic company . . . due to expansion you'll be a manager next week . . . retire at 30 . . ." – you've been had!'

'Well, the Company has more than doubled in size over the last 2 years, and it's been established over ten years. The average age is early 20's, five of our Publishers are under 30! By the way, they all started in ad sales.'

'Got it! You fell for the line about megabuck OTE. Bet they didn't tell you about the impossible targets?'

'No, I fell for the good basic salary plus the commission opportunity to earn nearly half as much again. My first year's training programme is good news too.'

'Where did you say you worked?'

Centaur Communications Ltd,
50 Poland Street, London W1V 4AX.
Write to the personnel and Training Manager and tell her why you're right for the U.K.'s fastest growing business publishing house.

CENTAUR
LIMITED

An equal opportunity employer.

PC
4.3.1
4.3.2

FOLLOW-UP ACTIVITIES

1 First carry out your research, then design a person specification for a trainee manager in a supermarket chain or departmental store.

2 Design a job description for one of the following, having undertaken your research:

a a college engineer;

b a school secretary or bursar;

c a college departmental secretary/personal assistant.

3 Assume that you work in the personnel department of Sentinel Insurance plc, a national company which regularly employs school and college 18-plus leavers as trainee branch managers. Design an application form which you think would capture all the information needed for effective subsequent interviewing.

4 First carry out your research, then design a suitable recruitment advertisement (publication size 12 square centimetres) for the same post for which you designed the job description in Activity 2.

DISCUSSION TOPICS

PC 4.3.1 4.3.2

1 Some organisations have poor track records in providing and updating regularly their employees' job descriptions. Why do you think this is so? What management and employee activities and relationships can you identify which are likely to be assisted by the existence of a reasonably current job description?

2 Can you anticipate any problems which may emerge from employees working strictly to the wording of their job descriptions?

3 Can a job description or person specification ever really provide sufficiently detailed information to make it a document worth producing?

4 Why do so many companies nowadays employ recruitment consultants to handle the advertising element of their recruitment needs?

Recruitment interviews

PC 4.3.4 4.3.5

Different organisations adopt varying approaches to recruitment interviews. The following table illustrates the documentation which is generally employed to assist the interview process:

INTERVIEW SUPPORT DOCUMENTATION PRODUCED BY:

THE APPLICANT

- **Curriculum vitae**
  A schematised summary of educational and job experience.
- **Completed application form**
  Set of data supplied in response to questions and information requests on the form; some forms include an opportunity for applicants to expand on certain aspects on further A4 sheets.
- **Supportive letter of application**
  Posts which are administrative or managerial usually require a supportive letter of application in which the candidate formally confirms his or her application and provides a set of statements, about qualifications and experience, etc. which seek to demonstrate a match with the advertised requirements of the post.

THE ORGANISATION

- **Person specification**
- **Job description**
- **Recruitment advertisement**
- **Factsheet/résumé about organisation and the advertised post**
  Many firms produce a briefing sheet which explains the scope of its activities and where the advertised post fits in.
- **Interview assessment form**
  Many personnel departments supply interviewing staff with a form for recording on-the-spot responses to the performance of interviewees; such forms are divided into key assessment areas (*see below*)

The recruitment interview is essentially concerned with the following two-way, exploratory process:

The employing interviewers: Seek to obtain confirmation in a face-to-face dialogue that the applicant is able to confirm and elaborate upon the data supplied previously on paper, and that, in the flesh, he or she is able to demonstrate expertise and attitudes which meet up with (or exceed) those specified. The interviewee's potential for growth and development is also evaluated.

The job applicant: Correspondingly, the applicant seeks confirmation that the terms of the advertised job offer match expectations, that the conditions of service are acceptable, and that there are apparently genuine opportunities for career development; and, in times of recession, convincing evidence that the organisation will still be trading in the long-term future!

PC 4.3.5

■ Typical sections of an interview assessment form

While there are no fixed parameters for the design of an interview assessment form, personnel departments over the years have identified the following key areas for evaluation:

- **Physical appearance and deportment**

  Does the applicant communicate the kind of personal image suited to the advertised post? Does he / she have poise and presence?

- **Attainments**

  To what extent do qualifications and previous job roles and work experience meet the needs of the post? Is there any evidence of a capacity for future growth and development from the platform of the attainments to date?

- **General intelligence**

  Can the candidate demonstrate a capacity for 'thinking on his/her feet', analytical thought, lateral and creative thinking, problem-solving and decision-making, etc? Is the candidate a 'quick' thinker, or a more reflective, methodical person?

- **Special aptitudes**

  What particular skills and aptitudes does the candidate possess which are directly relevant and advantageous, such as foreign languages, expertise in the latest software package, a recent qualification in stress counselling etc?

- **Personality/disposition**

  What are the personality traits of the candidate? Serious-minded? Light-hearted? Extrovert? Introvert? Gregarious? Loner? Short-fused? Placid? etc.

- **Interests and hobbies**

  Do the applicant's current recreational pastimes provide any insight into his or her suitability for the post? Do they reveal any capacities which would reinforce the application?

- **Circumstances**

  Are the applicant's current circumstances in harmony with the job needs such as clean driving licence for sales rep's post; length of notice to be worked if urgent need for a quick start in post?

(Adapted from the National Institute of Industrial Psychology, Seven-Point Plan)

Conventionally, interviewers use a schedule which is designed as a matrix so that a rating, say, A–E can be assigned to each of the above areas, with a value like the following:

A Greatly exceeds job requirements.
B More than matches job requirements.
C Matches job requirements.
D Does not match job requirements.
E Significantly fails to meet job requirements.

In addition, panel lists may make further notes in between interviews for later checking on aspects of the interview which were either deemed to go well or badly.

The structure of recruitment interviews inevitably varies, but the following pointers form common denominators of most recruitment interviews. Whether the interview takes a panel or sequential one-to-one form, good interviewers will have agreed beforehand who will pose what connected range of questions on areas such as:

- education and general/vocational qualifications
- experience in previous posts
- degree of expertise in 'state-of-the-art' processes and systems used in the organisation and related to the post
- outlooks and attitudes upon job-specific and general topics
- capacity for growth and development; determination, tenacity and ambition, etc.

Also, good interviewers make a point of asking the same questions at certain stages to each candidate, so as to obtain an objective assessment of each response.

USEFUL RECRUITMENT PROCESS CHECKLISTS

PC
4.3.4
4.3.5

SHORT APPLICATION FORM FOR EMPLOYMENT

Surname	Forenames
Address	Telephone Nos – private/business
Date of birth	Nationality

Detail of any physical disabilities

Current clean driving licence?

Any criminal convictions other than a spent conviction under the Rehabilitation of Offenders Act 1974?

Employment:

Position applied for:

Pay expected:

Would you work full-time? part-time? - state hours/week

If offered this post would you work in any other capacity? please detail

Have you previously worked for us?

On what date would you be available?

Note : An extended application form also asks for details of education, employment history, and personal/professional references.

THE CURRICULUM VITAE

A *curriculum vitae* may be composed by using the following framework:

Personal details
Full name and current address
Telephone number
Age, status - married/single
Nationality
Dependents - wife, husband, children

Education
Secondary school(s)
College(s) } with
University } dates
Postgraduate institution
Main subjects taken
Activities, interests
Post(s) of responsibility

Qualifications
Examination passes indicating grades, dates and examining boards.

Work experience
Usually expressed by starting from immediate past and working backwards.
Name of organisation, location, job designation, range of duties, extent of responsibilities, reasons for leaving.

Interests
Leisure activities, hobbies, indicating posts of responsibility – e.g. Honorary Secretary of Drama Club – where appropriate.

Circumstances
Period of notice required to be given.
Mobility – car-ownership, any limiting commitments.

A *curriculum vitae* is usually set out schematically, with appropriate dates and chronological structures.

THE APPLICATION FORM

The following information is generally required on an application form for a job:

Name
Address
Telephone number
Age: date of birth
Status: married/single
Maiden name if married woman
Education
Qualifications
Current/previous experience
Present designation or title
Name and address of employers
Details, with dates, of employment since leaving full-time education
Details of salaries in each appointment
Outline of hobbies, interests
Names, addresses and occupations of referees
Date of availability
Signature and acknowledgement of accuracy of data provided

PERSONNEL REQUISITION

Description of need	date needed: job title and category: recruitment salary range: permanent/temporary: full/part-time:
Reason for need	replacement or addition: if replacement, give reasons:
Requirements	education: qualifications: experience: other please specify:
Approval:	
Date vacancy filled:	Name:

INTERVIEW REPORT (extract)

Candidates are rated in this way:

Poise

- ☐ Ill at ease, jumpy and nervous
- ☐ Somewhat tense, easily irritated
- ☐ Reasonably at ease
- ☐ Self-assured
- ☐ Extremely self-assured

(Interviewers tick an appropriate box)

PC 4.3.5

The letter of application

PC 4.3.3

Candidates for jobs sometimes get the wrong end of the stick. They fail to read the all-important final section of a recruitment advertisement, and consequently send off an inappropriate letter of application. The following section identifies and explains three different types of letter used in job applications.

1 The simple request for further information and an application form

This is not, in fact, a letter of application. It is simply a means of obtaining information an employer has assembled about the advertised post, together with the application form in use. It responds to advertisement wording such as:

> *Further details about the post and application forms are available from John Smith, Human Resources Manager,* (and here follows the employer's address)

As the letter requesting this documentation is most likely to be dealt with by a clerical assistant, it needs to be short and courteous only, as shown in the example on page 432.

Example

Dear Sir

Trainee management post in sales **Your ref: ABV245**

I was most interested to read your advertisement for the above post in yesterday's *Daily Courier*, and should be grateful if you would kindly arrange for me to receive details of the appointment, together with an application form.

Yours faithfully

Julie Brown

PC 4.3.3

2 The letter which is a covering letter accompanying application form and curriculum vitae

This is indeed an important type of letter of application and a model is provided on page 434 which illustrates how a would-be personal assistant uses it to reinforce her application for the Finosa Fabrics post. Bear in mind that a curriculum vitae tends to be of a general nature, while the complete application form provides answers to questions *the employer has asked*. The covering letter, therefore provides an invaluable opportunity for an applicant to 'tailor' his or her expertise and experience *to a specific post*. It also provides an opportunity to re-state and reinforce any key attributes the applicant thinks are strong 'selling points' which the employer will read and absorb.

PC 4.3.3

3 The 'letter only' letter of application

Smaller organisations often advertise posts and conclude the advertisement with:

Apply in writing to . . .

In this case, the letter of application has to be a one-man band, and communicate key information which the applicant thinks relevant to the application. It will therefore provide information which shows how the applicant's expertise, skills and experience are relevant to the description of the post given – in a logical sequence of paragraphs. Remember, however, that there is nothing to prevent you enclosing a curriculum vitae and thus saving a lot of time – which can be devoted to emphasising and reinforcing your strongest features!

■ Model letter of application

PC 4.3.3

The post Jane Simmonds applied for:

> **FINOSA FABRICS LTD require a PERSONAL ASSISTANT to the EXPORT SALES MANAGER (EUROPE)**
>
> A knowledge of two EU foreign languages is required and experience of export sales procedures is an advantage. The successful candidate will work on his or her own initiative and be able to handle incoming telephone, fax and email messages and documentation from French or German agents. He or she must also be prepared to travel abroad.
>
> The company provides excellent conditions of service, including five weeks paid holiday per annum, subsidised health insurance and restaurant facilities. Salary negotiable: according to age and experience.
>
> Apply in writing to: The Personnel Manager, Finosa Fabrics Ltd, 4 York Way, London WC2B 6AK
>
> Applications to be received by 30 May 199—

Commentary

Jane Simmonds' letter of application (Fig 4.8) begins by acknowledging the source of the advertisement, makes a formal application statement and refers to relevant enclosures.

In her second paragraph, Jane endeavours to establish a close link between her own career aspirations and vocational education and the essential nature of the advertised post.

Jane goes on to draw particular attention to those aspects of her more recent education which she considers have equipped her with a sound preparation for the post.

In case her prospective employers may be unfamiliar with them, Jane outlines the relevant course components of the Diploma, emphasising those parts which would be most likely to interest her potential principal.

Jane endeavours to display self-confidence without immodesty, and evidence of existing achievement. Since she lacks full-time work-experience, Jane makes the best of her travels and knowledge of the countries relating to the advertisement. She also includes mention of a course of study which has provided relevant insights.

Realising that her lack of work-experience could prove a stumbling-block, Jane emphasises the practical work-experience she has had, and highlights aspects of it which she hopes will be relevant to her application.

Availability for interview is made as easy as possible.

Since she needs the job, Jane displays a willingness to start just as soon as possible after the end of her course, thus demonstrating her 'earnestness of intent'.

PC
4.3.3

Fig 4.8 **Example of a letter of application**

Recipient's name and address. Date	'Appleblossom' South Downs Way Burleys Hampshire PO23 4QR Tel: 01705–496843

Dear Sir,

I should like to apply for the post of personal assistant to your Export Sales Manager recently advertised in the 'Daily Sentinel', and have pleasure in enclosing my completed application form and a copy of my curriculum vitae.

The advertised post particularly appeals to me, since my own career aspirations and education have been specifically directed for the last two years towards an office administration appointment in the field of export sales.

In the sixth form at Redbrook High School I specialised in Advanced-level German, French and English and proceeded in September 199- to Redbrook College of Technology, where I embarked upon a bilingual secretarial course leading to the Institute of Export's Diploma in Export Studies.

The course includes intensive commercial language studies (I am specialising in German), communication, office administration and export studies with particular emphasis on E.C. procedures and documentation. In addition, the Diploma course provides shorthand, word processing and E.C. telecommunications components, including work in the special foreign language.

I expect to achieve a good pass in the June Diploma examination and to attain shorthand and typewriting speeds of 100/50 wpm, having already secured passes at 80/40 wpm.

During my full-time education, I have travelled extensively in Germany and France, and have become familiar with the customs and outlook of both countries. In August 199- I gained a valuable insight into German business methods during a month's exchange visit to a Handelsschule in Frankfurt-am-Main.

Assisting my father for the past two years in his own company has afforded me an opportunity to use my own initiative and to obtain helpful work experience in areas such as sales documentation, customer relations and the use of data processing in a sales context.

If called, I should be pleased to attend for an interview at any time convenient to you.

My course at Redbrook College of Technology finishes on 30th June 199- and I should be available to commence a full-time appointment from the beginning of July onwards.

Yours faithfully

Jane Simmonds (Miss)

Note: It is usual for letters of application such as the one above to be handwritten

GROUP ACTIVITIES

PC 4.3.3

1 In groups of two or three study Jane Simmonds' letter from the point of view of Finosa's Personnel Manager and consider the following questions:

Has Jane's letter succeeded in arousing your interest? If so, why? If not, why not? Does Jane's letter succeed in meeting the aims suggested in the commentary? Do you have any criticisms to make of Jane's letter in terms of the information supplied, its structure, its tone and style? Could it be improved upon? Does it adequately match the requirements implied in the advertisement?

2 Draft letters from Finosa to:

a call Jane Simmonds to attend an interview

b inform Jane Simmonds of her failure to obtain the post after interview

c offer Jane Simmonds the post after interview

In 3 groups consider whether the above letters could be created as mail-mergeable standard letters, and if so, how.

INDIVIDUAL ACTIVITIES

PC 4.3.3

1 As Jane Simmonds, assume that, while awaiting news from Finosa after interview, you have been offered, and accepted a post with another company as a result of an earlier application. Write a letter to Finosa appropriate to the situation.

2 As the chairperson of Finosa's interviewing panel, draw up a series of questions that you wish to be passed to each candidate. Compare your list with those produced by your co-students.

DISCUSSION TOPICS

PC 4.3.3

1 Should letters of application still be handwritten?

2 Why do so few recruitment advertisements include details of hourly or annual pay? By omitting such details do they not waste people's time?

PC 4.3.4

How to produce an effective curriculum vitae

A. The 'traditional' cv structure

A curriculum vitae following the traditional structure (which may be most appropriate for applicants yet to acquire work experience) is set out as follows:

1 Personal details:

FULL NAME AND ANY LETTERS
HOME POSTAL ADDRESS
TELEPHONE AND FAX NO (IF INSTALLED)
NATIONALITY   DATE OF BIRTH

2 Education:

Note: at post GNVQ Advanced level you need only record your secondary school(s) onwards; set down any notable achievements – e.g. headgirl, rugby 1st XV etc) Set out this section as follows:

FROM – TO   NAME OF ESTABLISHMENT(S)

DATE   ACHIEVEMENTS

3 Examinations and qualifications

Use this template to set out your results and start from most recent down to earliest:

DATE   NAME OF EXAMINATION (e.g. BTEC GNVQ Business Advanced)   GRADE AWARDED

4 Work experience

Set down here any full and/or part-time work experience you have gained:

FROM – TO   NAME OF ORGANISATION   JOB TITLE/DESCRIPTION OF WORK

Start from most recent going down to earliest: include details of any significant responsibilities and/or staff reporting to you (to indicate valuable experience gained)

5 Special skills

Set down here details of any special skills or expertise acquired – e.g. foreign languages competences, expertise with computer packages: Word Version 6, Lotus 123 for Windows etc.

6 Interests

Set down here (in one word headings) a list of hobbies, leisure, community activities etc.

7 Circumstances

Set down here further useful information e.g. notice required in present job, earliest date of availability to start a job, driving licence status, willingness to work anywhere in UK (if genuine) or abroad.

B. 1988–94 recession-onwards cv

PC 4.3.4

Since the recession brought millions of redundant and terminated adults into the job market, some out-placement specialist advisers have recommended the following cv structure:

1 Personal details

Set out as for 'traditional' cv.

2 Mission statement

This is a brief (one/two sentences) statement stating the applicant's employment goal:

Example

A product manager with five years' successful experience of managing an extensive range of fast-moving consumer durables in both the UK and overseas markets now seeks to deploy hard-won experience and team-leading skills in a more challenging marketing management post providing opportunities for personal growth in a leading-edge environment.

This mission statement is then followed by a set of bullet-point statements which exemplify the abilities and achievements suggested by it:

Example

Proven ability to promote product market development allied to profitable sales through:

- Effective market research into kitchen white goods products
- 'Hands-on' involvement in product design and field testing
- Team-leading in sales promotional activities working with a budget exceeding £300,000
- Successful market launches of advanced microwave ovens and washing machines – to a market penetration of some 25%

3 Career history and achievements

Set down here is a listing (from most recent downwards) of:

DATES ORGANISATIONS JOB TITLES RESPONSIBILITIES

Plus a sentence on reasons for leaving e.g. promotion to next entry below, or to start a family etc.

4 Special skills and expertise

Similar to 'traditional' section.

5 Interests

Similar to 'traditional' section.

6 Circumstances

As for 'traditional' cv.

NOTES: The traditional curriculum vitae tends to be more factual and less self-promotional, whereas the 'recession onwards' cv evolved from a need among applicants to promote themselves hard in an over-crowded job market – it was said that a cv among, say, 400 for a single post **had to excite its readers within 10 seconds**, or be passed over!

There is no single, right or correct way to structure a cv. The above two models represent two approaches which are currently in use. However, note that all cvs should be well set out in highly schematised layouts, using all the visually appealing resources of word-processing and laser printing – different font sizes, emboldening, italics, underscoring, bullets etc.

Your aim is to sell yourself effectively on paper – without appearing to be on an ego trip. But remember: hiding your light under a bushel in a cv ensures that someone else gets the job!

Keep your cv as short as possible – but don't write in indecipherable note-form. Make it a delight to absorb because of its excellent layout. Let facts speak for themselves – e.g GNVQ Business Advanced (Dist.), 1991–1992 Headgirl, Midchester School etc.

PC
4.3.5
4.3.6

Interviews: general introduction

The interview is used in organisations to meet the needs of many, quite different situations. Some interviews are extremely formal affairs, where a candidate for a post may be examined and evaluated by a board or panel of interviewers. Others are conducted in a much more relaxed atmosphere, in a 'one-to-one' relationship, between, say a manager and a subordinate.

In point of fact, it is very difficult to establish where conversation ends and the interviewing process begins in the work situation.

The interview process is employed to obtain information and responses in a wide variety of areas, from sales performance to accounts collection, from disciplinary proceedings to promotion selection, from counselling on personal problems to personnel appointments. The following table indicates some of the principal areas in which the interview is commonly used.

MAIN APPLICATIONS OF THE INTERVIEW

Job application
Resignation – debriefing
Performance assessment
Counselling
Disciplining
Promoting
Information seeking
Instruction giving

It is therefore important for the members of any organisation to regard the interview not as an intimidating process to be endured, but rather as a tool of communication from the use of which the interviewee has as much to gain as the interviewer. The truth of this observation becomes much more apparent if the interviewee in particular stops to consider that the process *is* two-way.

The following section examines the job application interview process. Careful preparation and probing questions on the part of the interviewee may result in his declining an offered post with a company which is performing poorly and where job prospects exist in theory rather than in practice. It is important therefore, at the outset to interpret the term 'interrogation' as 'a two-way channel for finding out'.

■ The job application interview

PC 4.3.5 4.3.6

When interview techniques are being discussed, it is usually the formal interview which is considered. It is important to remember, however, that even in informal interview situations the guide-lines which follow will still hold true in principle, if not in detail.

In any interview, the interviewee will be assessed, either directly or indirectly in these areas:

- appearance
- deportment
- manners
- speech
- intelligence
- judgement
- values
- common sense
- initiative
- resourcefulness
- assurance.

Basically, the interviewer will be seeking reassurance or information in line with the questions:

- How does the interviewee project himself?
- What has he to offer in terms of specialist skills or knowledge?
- What has he to offer in terms of personality?
- What potential to develop does he display?

PC 4.3.5

■ The interviewer's preparatory role

A practised interviewer makes use of a number of resources, tools and techniques in order to help the selection of the best available candidate for a post. These may be summarised as:

- making the time to read and make careful notes of all the short-listed applicants, so as to base questions on each individual's backgrounds and experiences, and so as to go to the interview prepared
- devising a list of questions whose aims are:
  - — to put a candidate at ease at the interview's start
  - — to encourage the interviewer to open up on a topic
  - — to delve and probe into a specific area in order to explore a strength or weakness
  - — to prompt a candidate who dries up etc.
- if part of an interviewing panel, deciding who will ask what questions in what running order
- using specially designed forms on which to log impressions and to rate candidates in areas such as: appearance, manner, subject-expertise etc.
- having copies for reference of each applicant's application form, cv, letter of application etc. and (if the chair of a panel) having details of the post's salary and conditions of service etc. to answer candidate's enquiries.

As the above list indicates, experienced interviewers come to job application interviews well-prepared and informed – since they may be making a decision which could cost a company some £170,000 during the subsequent five years, if an executive is being appointed!

PC 4.3.5

■ The interviewer's techniques

Well conducted interviews have distinct beginnings, middles and ends, which are carefully managed by the interviewer.

The outset phase

At the outset, an interviewer will invite an arriving applicant to take a seat, and depending on the formality of the interview may offer some refreshments. During this initial period, the candidate's first impressions will be being absorbed and evaluated by the interviewer.

Usually, interviewers take pains to put a candidate (who is naturally likely to be rather nervous) at his or her ease, by asking two or three 'ice-breaking' questions like:

'How was the journey?' 'Did you have any trouble finding us?' etc.

The next phase is to move gently into broad, background questions like:

'Tell me about your education.' 'What did you study at college?'
'What did you like most (or least) at school?'

Such questions are aimed at getting the candidate talking, to begin to evaluate his or her communication and self-presentation skills, and to start assessing personality traits, such as an absence of over-bearing conceit, self-confidence and so on. Notice that the interviewer's questions are deliberately *open,* that is to say, cannot be answered with a monosyllabic 'yes' or 'no'. In this way, the interviewer encourages the candidate to talk, on the basis of that ancient Chinese proverb: *'Open your mouth, that I may know you!'*

The middle phase

Some interviewers progress through the interview following broadly the structure of the curriculum vitae – from education to qualifications, to work experience etc., but others have their own approach. What all approaches have in common is a move from the general to the particular. Interviewers tend to want to check out key parts of their person specifications and job descriptions by seeking to establish, for example, whether expertise cited on an application form actually exists, or whether experience apparently gained in a relevant post was really all it was described to be etc. Thus an interviewer will move during the middle phase to asking more detailed and penetrative questions, and will often ask secondary, supplementary questions which oblige a candidate to provide more detailed explanations and answers:

'How many staff reported to you at Global Consolidated?'

'What was the extent of your operations budget?'

'Why did you leave Universal Bearings after only six months?'

'So, if you are committed, as you say, to computerised accounts systems, how would you react to moving into an accounts management post with us in a division which is still using paper-based systems?'

Interviewers ask questions which:

■ require factual answers:	*'How long did you work in electronics?'*
■ test personality and views:	*'What do you think of the process of deregulation in business?'*
■ check out alleged expertise:	*'So how would you check out the return on investment of a proposed new product?'*
■ test a candidate's ability to 'think on his feet'	*'If you were appointed to this post, how would you organise your first week here?'*

and which may require explanations, such as a gap between successive previous posts.

As an interviewee, perhaps the best means of anticipating the likely range of a interviewer's questions is:

- to break down the data of the job advertisement into person specification and job description requirements, and to frame the likely questions to be asked which will match your application to their needs
- to analyse the needs of the job description if available and to consider what questions are likely to emerge in the same way

- To use the NIIP Seven Point Plan areas: *physical make-up, attainments, general intelligence, special aptitudes, interests, disposition and circumstances* as triggers to prompt what likely questions will emerge to elicit details about your own application.

The closing phase

Usually time constraints force an interview to reach its closing phase. If the interviewer has done the job well, both he and the interviewee will feel they have achieved their joint objectives of:

a) arriving at a reasoned judgement as to the strength of the candidate's application, and

b) communicating well personal strengths in terms of the expertise, skills and experience which the post requires.

Thus the interviewer will provide an opportunity before the close for the interviewee to ask any questions about the post's development and promotion opportunities, queries about the pay and conditions package, envisaged start date and so on. Note: rightly or wrongly, the candidate who has no questions to ask always seems to appear lame and lack-lustre!

In the private sector, interviewers tend not to make immediate job offers, but to ring or write after a few days; in some public sector organisations, all candidates are asked to wait during their collective interviews, and an immediate decision is required of the person to whom the post is offered. Either way, it is important for the interviewee to move out of the interview with grace and charm, having expressed thanks for the opportunity to be interviewed etc. – because there may well be a next time!

PC 4.3.6

The interviewee's techniques

Appearance, manners, deportment

As an interviewee, whether making a first job application or an employee before a promotion panel, your personal appearance matters! Rightly or wrongly other people will make judgements about you which will be influenced by your appearance. Looking smart and well-groomed is an asset in any situation and is nowhere more important than at an interview.

The way you hold yourself, move and gesticulate will also affect the way people regard you. In professional and business life attractive people are those who temper assurance with modesty, and who behave calmly, with due consideration for others. On entering the interview room, for example, take care to do so politely but not over-hesitantly and wait to be proffered a hand to shake or to be invited to take a seat. Once seated, avoid the tendency to slouch or lounge and assume a posture which is comfortable, but alert. Also, it is sensible to hold the hands in the lap, and to return them to this position between any gestures.

It is also important to master any feelings of nervousness. Feeling nervous is natural during an interview and you may be sure that the interviewer is aware of this fact and that he or she will go to some trouble to set you at your ease. Nevertheless, allowing nerves to take over, and displaying signs of tension by hunching into the chair, wringing hands, twisting rings or biting lips not only impairs your performance, but transmits a sense of unease to the interviewer as well. The result may be that you do not do justice to yourself and that you leave doubts about your capacities in the mind of the interviewer.

PC 4.3.6

Listening before speaking

Once the interview is under way, perhaps the best advice is to listen! It is all too easy as an interviewee to attend with only half an ear to what is being said or asked. Moreover, you will need to employ all your faculties and to keep extremely alert to ensure that you anticipate, for example, where a sequence of questions is leading you, or to see the probing which may be going on beneath an apparently harmless question!

Listening attentively will also help you to prepare your answer while a question is being framed. It is amazing how fast the brain works in such situations.

Looking at the questioner

The ability to 'look someone squarely in the eye' has always been regarded as a sign of honesty and assurance. It helps in any case, during an interview to look at a speaker posing a question since facial expression, gesture or posture often provide valuable insights into what is an interviewer's mind, and shows that you are paying attention.

Similarly, when providing an answer you should make eye-contact with the questioner, but not to the extent of boring into him or her with a transfixing stare!

Think before you speak

This well-worn truism is still excellent advice to the interviewee. Blurting out a nonsense or 'gabbling' on because of nerves are traps into which the unwary often fall. Moreover, it is not possible in an interview to escape from being assessed and both the words you utter and the way in which you express yourself will reveal much about your intelligence, judgement, common sense and *nous*.

In order to answer questions successfully and in so doing to create a favourable impression, you should ask yourself these questions both before and during your answer:

- Have I understood the question?
- Do I appreciate what it is driving at?
- Are there any traps or pitfalls present in the question?
- Can I draw on my own experience to illustrate my answer?
- Am I speaking clearly and convincingly?
- Have I covered the ground and said enough?

Thinking *while* speaking

Just as the practised reader's eye travels ahead before reading a phrase aloud, so the practised interviewee's mind will be thinking ahead and monitoring what is being said. Additionally, the interviewee's eyes will be looking hard at the interviewer for signs of a favourable response to what is being said.

Sometimes the way in which the spoken word is constructed into phrases or sentences allows for 'rest' or 'pause' expressions to be uttered while the brain composes the next important point:

'... as a matter of fact I ...'

'... I accept the truth of that but ...'

'... although my initial response might be to ...'

'... in this case I would ...'

Also, there are means of delaying arrival at the explicit answer point of a difficult question by means of a sort of delaying tactic:

'I suppose it depends to a large degree upon how the term X is interpreted ...'

'I don't have an easy or quick answer to that question, but on reflection I ...'

It should be noted that interviewers are only too aware of how much easier it is to pose questions than to answer them, and make natural allowances for initial hesitancy. A word for caution, however: if an interviewee displays a frequent inability to answer questions directly, they are bound to sow in the interviewer's mind seeds of doubt regarding integrity, honesty or, quite simply, lack of knowledge.

PC 4.3.6

Measure what you say

Interviewers are skilled at posing questions which cannot be answered by a simple 'yes' or 'no'. For example, a question would not be phrased:

'Did you enjoy your previous job'

but rather,

'What did you find most satisfying about your previous job?'

In this way the interviewee is invited to expand a reply rather than to offer monosyllabic answers, which inevitably cast doubt upon fluency, knowledge and assurance. It is common, however, for inexperienced interviewees to speak rapidly at great length, as if the assessment were based on words spoken per minute and the range of unrelated topics covered! You must therefore ensure that what you are saying is relevant to the question and forms a summary of the main issues as you see them. It is good practice to pause after having made what you consider an adequate number of points to allow the interviewer either to ask you to continue or to ask another question. Try to strike a happy medium. Saying too little prevents you from demonstrating your knowledge and ability. Saying too much reveals a disorganised and 'butterfly' mind.

Ask *your* questions

Whatever the interviewing situation, the interviewer largely has control of the interview, Nevertheless you should ensure that you make an opportunity to ask the questions *you* have framed. In the context of an application for a job, you wish to establish whether you want the organisation equally as much as it may wish to decide whether it wants you! Such opportunities tend to occur at the end of the interview but clarifying questions may be put throughout. And note: it always sounds lame and lack-lustre to say, in response to an invitation to ask your own questions: 'No, actually, you seem to have answered all of my questions already'.

DISCUSSION TOPICS

PC 4.3.5 4.3.6

1 'Despite all the paraphernalia of pseudo-scientific interview techniques and document aids, the process remains one of chemistry and preferences based on personal prejudices.'

2 The job interview is more properly viewed as a sales pitch than as a two-way exchange of information and viewpoints.

3 Women still find it much harder than men to obtain promotion and advancement in organisations. Should all recruitment and promotion interview panels be required by law to include a woman?

4 What sort of questions do you think an interviewee should ensure he or she asks at a recruitment interview?

■ The legal and ethical obligations of job interviews

PC 4.3.7

Maintaining confidentiality

Recruitment procedures involve interviewing staff in having access to a large amount of data supplied by job applicants, much of which is provided on the distinct understanding that it will be treated confidentially. Similarly, employers who supply references about applying staff do so on the strict understanding that the information they contain is treated with the utmost confidentiality. At the same time, an interviewer may betray some confidential detail about his organisation's activities during an interview that is going well, which an outsider would not get to hear, and which should also be treated confidentially.

Thus on all sides, there is a need for information supplied to be handled securely, so that it does remain confidential, as for example any details of a 'timed-out' previous criminal record, or of a physical condition or disability of a sensitive nature.

Security measures

Therefore, interviewers need to ensure that the following steps are taken during a recruitment interview process.

- All applications should be handled by a responsible assistant and kept securely in a locked safe or cabinet.
- Photocopies of application documents should be handed out personally to interviewers and collected from them afterwards, with only a departmental manager and/or the human resource manager retaining master copies of the successful candidate's application.
- Application documents of unsuccessful applicants should be shredded immediately after an appointment has been offered and accepted.
- No application document sets should be left unattended on desk tops.

PC 4.3.7

Legal requirements

As already explained in this Unit, strict statutory requirements surround the recruitment process in terms of existing anti-discrimination legislation on grounds of gender, race and religion etc.

Care must therefore be taken with job advertisements, person specifications, job descriptions and allied informational literature to ensure that no lapse occurs which imply that an advertised post has been tailored to either a man, say, or to an indigenous, UK white. By the same token internal employees must have been given access to the same information as external parties, so that from start to finish, the selection process is seen to have been fair and even-handed. Otherwise, an organisation could have a grievance on its hands.

During the interview care must also be taken by interviewing staff to avoid asking questions which could be deemed to have a discriminatory bias, such as:

> *'How do you think you will manage in the advertised job as a single parent with a son aged three?'*

or

> *'How would your religious obligations fit in, do you think, with our daily hours of work?'*

Nor should interviewers allow bias or prejudice to interfere with the making of a fair and even-handed selection decision. A number of cases have been brought successfully to industrial tribunals by aggrieved people who consider themselves to have been either passed over for promotion or to have failed in applications where competitors were less well qualified and experienced. Some in senior posts have settled out of court for compensation thought to be in six figures!

The interviewer is similarly obliged to ensure that every applicant is provided with a clear understanding of the details of the proposed contract of employment. Moreover, experienced applicants confirm their acceptance of a job offer only after having perused the contract on offer, since misunderstandings are much more difficult to clear up when in post.

Many larger business organisations, proud of their track-record, state in their recruitment literature that they are *equal opportunity employers*, and all interviewers should ensure that this aspect is communicated clearly.

PC 4.3.7

Ethical considerations

Some obligations lie strictly outside existing legislation, but are nevertheless important. For example, an interviewing panel should take pains to ensure that all candidates are equally treated, and not that, say, a Robert Redford or Sharon Stone are given an easy time because of their looks. Some panels ask the same questions to each candidate as a matter of course in this respect.

Other aspects exist such as not succumbing to prejudice regarding older or disabled applicants, or rushing the interview of a candidate low down in the running order, when a strong candidate was seen earlier.

While both sides in the interviewing process naturally wish to promote their best sides, neither interviewer nor interviewee should stoop to lying or being economic with the truth. Once an untruth comes to light – whether about the running down of a factory, or about a qualification cited but not held, it can destroy a working relationship, so it is simply not worth it.

Lastly, existing staff are naturally curious to learn about a newcomer, just appointed, and so line managers etc. who took part in the interview must be on their guard not to divulge privileged information – even to long-standing colleagues.

■ Non-verbal communication and interviews

PC 4.3.5 4.3.6

Non-verbal communication (NVC) is a fascinating area of study. It concerns the many ways in which people communicate in face-to-face situations, either as a means of reinforcing or of replacing the spoken word. Sometimes people employ non-verbal communication techniques consciously, at other times the process is carried out unconsciously. In many instances, the response is involuntary. A sudden shock, for instance, may result in someone draining in facial colour, opening his or her eyes wide and becoming slack-jawed. It is particularly important to remember to read and interpret correctly the NVC signals which are transmitted during the interview, since they may provide valuable clues on how to respond to a question, or whether a question has hit a sensitive spot etc.

Non-verbal communication may be divided into three main areas, with rather technical labels for readily observable activities or responses

Kinesics

Facial expressions

Smiles, frowns, narrowed eyes transmitting friendliness, anger or disbelief etc.

Gestures

Pointing fingers, 'thumbs up' sign, shakes of the head, transmitting an emphasising focus, congratulations or disagreements etc.

Movements

Quick pacing up and down, finger-drumming, leisurely strolling, transmitting impatience, boredom or relaxation.

Proxemics

Physical contact

Shaking hands, prodding with the forefinger, clapping on the back, transmitting greetings, insistence or friendship.

Positioning

Keeping a respectful distance, looking over someone's shoulder, sitting close to someone, transmitting awareness of differing status, a close working relationship or relaxed mutual trust.

Posture

Standing straight and erect, lounging, sitting hunched up, leaning forward, spreading oneself in a chair, transmitting alertness and care, self-confidence (or even over-confidence), nervousness or ease.

PC
4.3.5
4.3.6

NVC SIGNALS: EXPRESSION AND POSTURE

Facial components which are employed to signal a wide range of NVC responses or feelings:

Forehead – upward and downward frowns
Eyebrows – raising, knitting, furrowing
Eyelids – opening, closing, narrowing
Eye pupils – dilating
Eyes – upwards, downwards gazing, holding or avoiding eye contact
Nose – wrinkling, flaring nostrils
Lips – smiling, pursing, drawn in
Mouth – wide open, drawn in, half-open
Tongue – licking lips, moving around inside cheeks, sucking teeth
Facial muscles – drawn up or down, for grinning, teeth clenching
Jaw/Chin – thrust forward, hanging down
Head – thrown back, inclined to one side, hanging down, chin drawn in, inclined upwards

Commonly used gestures

The following gestures are seen regularly in daily life, either reinforcing or substituting for the spoken word:

Head
nodding sideways to urge someone along
nodding up and down
shaking sideways
inclined briefly
cradled in one or both hands

Arms and hands
widely outstretched
jammed into trouser pockets
firmly folded across the chest
holding the back of the head with fingers laced
making chopping movements with the side of the hand
hands pressed together in 'praying' position'
one or both hands held over mouth
flat of hand patting desk-top
hand brushing something away in the air
both hands placed open upon the chest

Fingers
running through the hair
drumming on table-top
stroking mouth and chin
stabbing the air with forefinger
clenched into a fist
manipulated in an arm-wave
patting the fingertips together with the fingers of both hands out-stretched
rubbing the thumb and fingers together

Remember to read and interpret NVC signals during an interview!

REVIEW TEST

PC
4.3.1
4.3.2
4.3.3
4.3.4
4.3.5
4.3.6
4.3.7

1 List four major phases in the recruitment process.

2 Explain briefly the difference between a person specification and a job description.

3 What is the difference between a confidential reference and a testimonial?

4 Which Acts of Parliament directly affect the recruitment process?

5 List the major sections of a) a person specification and b) a job description.

6 Why is it important for both the above documents to be dated and carry the name of the person who compiled them?

7 List four different media used to advertise a technician or managerial post.

8 List five important features of good recruitment advertisement design.

9 List the type of documents used a) by an interviewer and b) by an interviewee for use in the recruitment process.

10 List the typical sections of a) a traditional cv and b) a 'post-1988' cv.

11 What would you expect to be the content of a typical covering letter of application?

12 Describe briefly the main phases of a typical job interview.

13 Explain the difference between an open and a closed question.

14 Explain the legal responsibilities of an interviewer briefly.

15 List three different types of ethical obligation of an interviewee.

16 Describe briefly the actions to be taken to keep job application particulars securely.

17 Explain succinctly how reading NVC signals can be helpful at an interview.

GROUP ACTIVITIES

PC
4.3.1
4.3.2
4.3.5
4.3.6
4.3.7

These activities can be done individually or in pairs.

1 Collect a selection of the following samples from local organisations and compare and contrast their structures and formats: a person specification, a job description, an application form. Present your findings orally to your class.

2 Collect a series of job advertisements from both local and national newspapers for posts in these areas: senior and middle management, technician, clerical, operative, Compare them and decide – for each series – which advertisement is most effective and why.

3 Arrange to talk to an experienced interviewer and ask him or her to explain the major, most effective techniques used. Draw up a bullet-point summary and distribute to your class with a brief explanation.

4 Interview a friend or relative who has recently had a job application interview. Ask him or her to explain how it was conducted and how he/she handled it. Report back to your class (anonymously) on what you discovered.

5 Arrange to interview the human resources manager of a large organisation about the legal and ethical aspects of interviewing. Make a summary of your findings and share it with your class.

Element 4.3
Evaluate recruitment procedures, job applications and interviews

1 (i) A person specification is drawn up to help a new post-holder to become familiar with the job.
(ii) A job description details precisely how a job should be done.

Which of the following options best describes the above statements?

A	(i)	T	(ii)	T
B	(i)	T	(ii)	F
C	(i)	F	(ii)	T
D	(i)	F	(ii)	F

2 Which of the following statements are true, and which false?

A An open testimonial is more valuable to an interviewer than a confidential reference.
B Requesting information about physical characteristics contravenes the Sex Discrimination Act.
C A job description may include details of its holder's line manager.
D Under existing anti-discrimination legislation, it is illegal to print an advertisement in a language other than English.

3 Which of the following are likely to be headings of sections for assessment in an interview assessment form?

A Area of residence
B General intelligence
C Leisure interests
D Ethnic origin

4 (i) There is no single, correct structure for a curriculum vitae
(ii) A personnel requisition form is used to move a new employee from induction to a place in the allocated department.

Which of the following options best describes the above statements?

A	(i)	T	(ii)	T
B	(i)	T	(ii)	F
C	(i)	F	(ii)	T
D	(i)	F	(ii)	F

5 Which of the following statements is true, and which false?

A A curriculum vitae should only be sent to an employer if it is requested.
B Some employers prefer to receive hand-written letters of application.
C A closed question is used by the interviewer to finish the interview.
D It is not ethical to interpret NVC signals during an interview.

PORTFOLIO OF EVIDENCE ACTIVITY

PC
4.3.1
4.3.2
4.3.3
4.3.4
4.3.5
4.3.6
4.3.7

Element 4.3
Evaluate recruitment procedures, job applications and interviews

TOPFLIGHT RECRUITING PLC

Scenario 1

You work in the Market Research Department of Topflight Recruiting plc, a national employment bureau and outplacement agency. At present, Topflight is seeking to improve its understanding of current recruitment procedures and trends. Your boss has therefore asked you to use your initiative and contacts to research and write a report with the following terms of reference:

'We need to find out what the current situation is in your part of the country – that's why I want you to do this report – and to get a clear handle on any perceptible trends and developments. We're especially interested in any problems which you find out about – skills shortages, need for computer literacy, problems in attracting the right kind of applicants for specific jobs etc. I suggest you concentrate either on a largish local business – or, if you can, a local recruitment agency.

We'll use your report with the others commissioned to get a national picture which will help us in our own marketing and advice to our branches.'

Scenario 2

As the personal assistant of the head of department at your study centre, you have been asked to produce the following recruitment-related sets of documents:

1 The post of deputy head of department:

- a revised and updated *person specification*, since the post-holder is about to move on a result of promotion
- a similarly revised *job description* for the same post

2 The post of departmental secretary:

- likewise updated versions of both a *person specification* and a *job description*

Note: In liaison with your teacher, you may be assigned other posts for which to produce the equivalent two sets of documents, such as: Vice Principal, Finance Manager, Refectory Manager, College Engineer, Senior Caretaker, Librarian etc.

You have also to produce a commentary, based on discussions held with the actual, existing postholders whose jobs you selected, which summarises their views on how well your documents matched a) the qualities and attributes needed to do the job, and b) the content of the job itself.

Scenario 3

In this scenario you are tasked with producing a) two letters of application and b) two curricula vitae.

The letters of application should be in response to the two advertisements printed below (Figs 4.9 and 4.10)

Fig 4.9

> # WANTED!
> ## ENERGETIC MANAGEMENT TRAINEE
>
> An able and energetic management trainee is sought in our [insert here the title of a suitable department in your first chosen sector] department, to work as assistant to the manager.
>
> **We offer:**
>
> - excellent prospects for advancement
> - in-house training leading to qualifications
> - a first-class employment package of salary, paid holidays and pension scheme
>
> **We seek:**
>
> - a keen and committed school or college leaver with suitable qualifications.
>
> **APPLY IN CONFIDENCE TO:**
>
> Mrs Jackie Winter, Personnel Manager
> Millenia Enterprises Limited
> PO Box 142
> Manchester M18
>
> *Full CV and details of education required*

Fig 4.10

> # ARE YOU READY FOR THE CHALLENGE?
>
> ONLY THE **REALLY** COMMITTED NEED APPLY!
>
> A unique opportunity had arisen in our newly set-up **Information Unit** for a smart, imaginative manager who can bring fresh and innovative ideas on inter-departmental communications to our organisation [*which is in the second sector you chose*].
>
> As a company-wide Communications Liaison Officer you will work closely with all our departments to ensure that the policies and strategies of our board of directors are fully understood at all levels. You will also work to maintain and promote effective information and communications among all our 750 staff.
>
> To convince us that you are the right person for this exciting post, write to:
>
> **Sonja Bhuni, Human Resources Manager**
> **Transglobal Corporation (UK)**
> **International House, Euston Road**
> **LONDON NW3 LS4**
>
> *Please send us full details of your education, work experience and career plan.*

Scenario 4

Next, you are tasked with producing two curricula vitaes – one for yourself, and one for someone who has been working for a number of years (say, a parent, relative or friend). For your own cv, you may choose to base it upon one of the posts advertised above, or to design one for real use. You will need to reassure the person you interview in order to produce the second cv that you will respect his/her confidences and will substitute a fictitious name and address etc.

Scenario 5

Lastly, you are to design and produce two interview appraisal forms: a) one to be used by yourself in conducting a self-appraisal after having taken part in a role-played or actual interview – either as interviewer or interviewee, and b) one to be used by others who will appraise you as either an interviewer or interviewee in a real or simulated interview.

You should also design a set of notes to support your forms which will act as a guideline for interviewers and interviewees on how they should conduct themselves in terms of legal and ethical considerations at job interviews.

Task 1

Before embarking on any of the above activities, make sure you complete the appropriate parts of your planning and review log.

Tasks 2–6

Carry out the tasks relating to Scenarios 1–5 and remember that each of the documents you are to produce must be visually appealing, easy to complete (as appropriate) and clearly set out. Liaise with your teacher on whether your documents should be word-processed or hand-written.

Note: Your class should make an opportunity to discuss together the effectiveness of the interview appraisal forms in use, and should consider producing a pair embodying the best features of the design noted.

Performance criteria covered

4.3.1, 4.3.2, 4.3.3, 4.3.4, 4.3.5, 4.3.6, 4.3.7

Core skills covered

Communication:
3.1.1, 3.1.2, 3.1.3, 3.1.4, 3.1.5, 3.2.1, 3.2.2, 3.2.3, 3.2.4, 3.2.5, 3.4.1, 3.4.2, 3.4.3, 3.4.4

Information Technology:
3.1.1, 3.1.2, 3.1.3, 3.1.4, 3.1.5, 3.2.1, 3.2.2, 3.2.4, 3.2.5, 3.2.6, 3.2.7, 3.3.1, 3.3.2, 3.3.3, 3.3.4, 3.3.5, 3.3.6

CASE STUDY

PC
4.3.2
4.3.3
4.3.4
4.3.5
4.3.6

Wanted! Trainee Sales Manager for Excel Computers Ltd

The company

Excel Computers Limited manufactures, markets and retails an extensive range of computers and ancillary equipment, selling to both public and private industry.

Among its other duties, Excel's Sales Department provides an administrative and information service to its 75 sales representatives. The service helps them to perform effectively in what is a highly sophisticated market – both in terms of advanced product technology and the presentation of technical information.

Excel has established a policy of appointing each year, as trainee managers, a number of school and college leavers. They are provided with excellent, in-service training opportunities, including day-release to higher education courses. In addition, their training programmes include experience periods in all departments before taking on specific departmental responsibilities.

The vacancy

Personnel Manager: 'I see young Sara Maxwell has just got the job she's been hoping for in Marketing. I suppose you'll be asking me to find her replacement!'
Sales Manager: 'You're absolutely right! I'll miss Sara, of course, but I suppose Sales' loss is

Marketing's gain! At all events, we ought to press on directly with the selection process in order to beat the rush at the end of June. Good college-leavers are at a premium these days! I'd better revise the person specification and job descriptions straight away! The following was Sara's job description.

JOB DESCRIPTION

TITLE:	TRAINEE SALES ADMINISTRATION MANAGER
DEPARTMENT:	SALES DEPARTMENT
HOURS OF WORK:	37.5 hour week. Flexible Working Hours: Monday–Friday Core Time: 1000–1600
RESPONSIBLE TO:	The Assistant Sales Manager
RESPONSIBLE FOR:	Designated junior clerical and secretarial staff.
AUTHORITY OVER:	Designated junior clerical and secretarial staff.

GENERAL DESCRIPTION

To become proficient in performing duties related to sales administration, with particular regard to providing a supportive service to company sales representatives. To undertake work delegated by senior Sales Department personnel. To attend in-service training courses as required. To direct the work of assigned junior clerical and secretarial staff as requested.

DUTIES AND RESPONSIBILITIES

1 To work within established company regulations and to support determined company policies.

2 To develop sales managerial skills, with particular reference to: sales administration procedures, product knowledge, marketing activities and sales information systems.

3 To assist in the provision of administration and information services provided to the company's sales representative force.

4 To liaise with Marketing Department in communicating sales promotion and advertising programmes to company sales representatives.

5 To deal with arising correspondence, memoranda, reports, meetings, documentation etc.

6 To assist the Assistant Sales Manager generally, or any other senior Sales Department staff as directed by the Assistant Sales Manager.

7 To assist as required with the data processing of sales documentation and sales statistics.

8 To supervise the work of junior staff members as required.

9 To attend courses of training as required.

EXCEL COMPUTERS LIMITED

ORGANISATIONAL INFORMATION

HEAD OFFICE: Excel House, Guildford Road, Kingston-upon-Thames, Surrey KT12 6GR
Telegrams: Excel, Kingston-upon-Thames
Telephone: Kingston 88000
Fax: 0181-639 6848

FACTORIES: Bristol, Liverpool, Leicester

RESEARCH AND DEVELOPMENT: Excel Laboratories, Harlow New Town

TRAINING HEADQUARTERS: Moorbridge Manor, Dorchester, Dorset

PERSONNEL: 16,479 (Head Office: 643)

DEPARTMENTS: Research and Development, Production, Marketing, Sales, Accounts, Office Administration, Personnel, Distribution and Transport, Training, Communication Services

CONDITIONS OF SERVICE (Head Office Staff)
The company's head office operates a flexible working hours system; staff work in accordance with a job appraisal scheme – all jobs are graded and promotion/remuneration is based upon performance assessed at regular intervals. Company subsidised meals are available in the staff restaurant. Sports and social club facilities are well catered for in the company's leisure complex adjoining head office premises.
Paid Leave: junior – training management grades: 3 weeks per annum plus usual bank holidays.
Company house mortgage loans available at preferential terms.

CAREER OPPORTUNITIES:
The Company's employees are encouraged to develop a knowledge of company activities as a whole and opportunities exist for careers to progress via a number of departments. The company promotes from within whenever possible.

TRAINING:
Excel Computers Limited maintains an ideally situated Training Centre at Moorbridge Manor, Dorchester. Residential course form a central part of management development. Applications to attend day-release higher education courses are reviewed by a standing review committee.

SALARIES:
Management salaries are reviewed annually and paid monthly in arrears. Each management post follows an incremental scale, and annual increases are zoned within defined upper and lower limits according to performance.
Example: Trainee Manager Grade 6

Entering salary:	£14,500
First increment:	£750–1500 p.a.
Second increment:	£900–1700 p.a.

All incremental scales are reviewed annually.

SALES INFORMATION
Total sales turnover last year exceeded £420 million. A new national LAN/WAN system was introduced recently. Business Computer Systems sales rose by 19% last year. Major customers included the Bestbuy Supermarket chain, Sentinel Insurance Limited, Vesco Automotive Products Limited and Harridges Stores.

FUTURE DEVELOPMENTS:
In March of this year, Sir Peter Henryson, Chairman, announced that Excel was strengthening its EU exporting position: 'The time has come for Excel, secure in its very firm UK market, to go on to the export offensive. We have the people, the products, the marketing and the sales expertise. We intend to "excel" in a number of European and transatlantic markets. Our plans are well advanced. You are all familiar with the advertisements placed in the national press reporting the recent Annual General Meeting. Well, I strongly recommend you to "Watch This Space!" '

ACTIVITIES

1 Compose a person specification for the Excel Trainee Sales Administration Manager post, shortly to be advertised.

2 Devise an application form suitable for use in Excel's appointment of the Trainee Sales Administration Manager.

3 Draft an information sheet suitable for sending to candidates who have applied for the Trainee Sales Administration Manager post, outlining the scope of the job and the main features of Excel's business and organisation.

4 Design a display advertisement for the Trainee Manager post and devise an advertising strategy based on your own locality, identifying which newspapers and other media you would use to advertise the post.

5 Make a checklist of questions as follows:

a questions which Excel interviewers would wish to ask applicants for the Trainee Manager post;

b questions which applicants would wish to ask Excel interviewers.

6 Complete the application form devised in 2 above as an applicant for the post. Compose an appropriate curriculum vitae. Write a suitable letter of application to:

The Personnel Manager,
Excel Computers Limited,
Excel House,
Guildford Road,
KINGSTON-UPON-THAMES
Surrey
KT12 6GR

7 Set up Excel interviewing panels to evaluate applications received from members of the group. Discuss constructively the strengths and weaknesses of applications.

8 Simulate the interviews for the post of Trainee Sales Administration Manager. Group members should role-play the Excel panel, comprising: the Personnel Manager, the Sales Manager and the Assistant Sales Manager. Other members of the group should role-play successive applicants. Panel interviewers should have time to study applicants. Panel interviewers should have time to study applicants' letters and forms. Applicants should also digest the information in the information sheet devised in 3. Observer-role group members should assess the performances of interviewers and interviewees. Simulations may be tape- or video-recorded for subsequent evaluation.

FURTHER SOURCES OF INFORMATION

Human Resources Management, 8th edn, H T Graham and R Bennet, M & E Business Handbooks, 1994. ISBN: 0 7121 1051 8

Personnel Management Made Simple, 2nd edn, S Tyson and A York, Made Simple Books, 1989. ISBN: 0 7506 0726 2

Business Law, 3rd edn, D Keenan and S Riches, Pitman, 1993. ISBN: 0 273 60114 8

Negotiating, Bill Scott, Paradigm, 1988. ISBN: 0 9488 25 26 X

Understanding Organisations, 3rd edn, C B Handy, Penguin Books, 1992. ISBN 0 4 009110 6

People in Organisations, 3rd edn, T R Mitchell and J R Larson, McGraw-Hill International, 1987. ISBN: 0 07 100585 4

Hiring and Firing, K Lanz, Pitman, Natwest Business Bookshelf, 1988. ISBN: 0 273 02826 X

Essentials of Employment Law, 3rd edn, D Lewis, Institute of Personnel Management, 1990. ISBN: 0 85292 447 X

Thriving on Chaos, Tom Peters, Pan Books, 1987. ISBN: 0 330 30591 3

UNIT

5

PRODUCTION AND EMPLOYMENT IN THE ECONOMY

Element 5.1
Analyse production in businesses

Element 5.2
Investigate and evaluate employment

Element 5.3
Examine the competitiveness of UK industry

PERFORMANCE CRITERIA AND RANGE

Element 5.1: Analyse production in businesses

PERFORMANCE CRITERIA

A student must: *page*

1 identify added value in production and **ways to achieve added value** 463–7
2 explain **why businesses aim to add value** 466–7
3 identify and give examples of **factors** which can contribute to change in production 468–71
4 **analyse improvements in production** 468–71

RANGE

Ways to achieve added value: quality assurance, productivity, Just-In-Time (JIT) production, using human resources effectively
Why businesses aim to add value: to meet international competition, to meet customer requirements, to improve profit,
Factors: price, technology (management information systems (MIS), robotics, automation, computer-aided-design (CAD), computer-aided-manufacturing (CAM)), contracting out, single sourcing, labour flexibility, legislation, competition, quality standards
Analyse in terms of: cause of change; impact on production, research and development needed; human resourcing changes; changing customer and supplier relations
Improvements in production: better productivity, quality assurance, investing in (research and development, training, physical resources), reducing pollution, changing working methods

EVIDENCE INDICATORS

- A report which describes ways in which businesses add value and explains why they add value through production.
- One section of the report should identify and give examples of factors which can contribute to a change in production. It should analyse at least two improvements in production explaining the causes of change and its consequences for the business, its employees, its customers and suppliers.

Element 5.2: Investigate and evaluate employment

PERFORMANCE CRITERIA

A student must: *page*

1 identify and explain **types of employment** 472–5, 483
2 **evaluate** the effects of changes in the types of employment 475
3 identify the **implications of employment trends** in the local economy 475–85
4 **evaluate** the **implications** of **employment trends** in the local and national economy 475–85

RANGE

Types of employment: self-employed, full-time, part-time, permanent, temporary, contract, non-contract; skilled, unskilled, home-working
Evaluate in terms of: employee needs (pay, benefits, career progression opportunities, job security, working conditions); business needs (to control costs, to maintain profits, to maintain levels of productivity, to maintain customer satisfaction)
Implications for: employment, unemployment; deskilling, re-training; male employment, female employment
Employment trends: national levels of employment; shift from manufacturing to service industries; full-time and part-time; permanent and temporary; skilled and unskilled; male and female; growth of the 'underground' economy, regional levels of employment; differences in pay
Evaluate in terms of: effects on individuals in employment, effects on the unemployed, effects on communities, effects on government revenue and expenditure

EVIDENCE INDICATORS

A report which identifies and explains types of employment and evaluates how at least four types of employment have changed in a business. It should evaluate the effects of changes in terms of employee and business needs.
The report should illustrate national and regional trends in:

- employment in one manufacturing and one service industry
- full-time and part-time employment
- male and female employment
- differences in pay

and explain the implications for:

- employed or unemployed people
- communities
- government revenue and expenditure.

Element 5.3: Examine the competitiveness of UK industry

PERFORMANCE CRITERIA

A student must:	*page*
1 **compare performance** of UK economy with **major competitors**	486–90
2 describe **business strategies** intended to improve competitiveness	490–5
3 describe **government strategies** intended to improve competitiveness of UK industry	495–500
4 **evaluate business and government strategies** intended to improve competitiveness	496–500

RANGE

Comparing performance in terms of: economic growth, investment, inflation, exchange rate, share of world trade, research and development, technological development, productivity
Major competitors: European, non-European
Business strategies relating to: organisational structure, human resourcing, marketing, scale of production, finance, new technology
Government strategies: exchange rate policy, control of inflation, privatisation, deregulation, reducing role of the government, investment in new technology; improving training and education; taxation to affect aggregate demand, government expenditure, European market integration, participating in the World Trade Organisation (WTO)
Evaluate in terms of: market share, sales, revenue, efficiency, productivity, product quality, service; trading conditions, standard of living, levels of employment

EVIDENCE INDICATORS

- A set of league tables supported by a summary, comparing UK economy with at least three major competitors. The tables should compare economic growth, investment, inflation, exchange rate, share of world trade and productivity. The supporting summary should explain and justify the choice of performance indicators.
- A short report describing how one business faces competition. It should describe the strategy used by the business to improve its performance in a competitive world market and evaluate the strategy in terms of its effects on employees and on the business.
- The report should also evaluate government strategies which affect the business and show how these may help or hinder business to compete.

INTRODUCTION

This unit explains production and employment in the economy. How production adds value to goods and services is identified and examined and changes in production and their effects are investigated. The main types of employment in the UK are identified and the changes in employment are evaluated. Trends in employment are examined and evaluated. The performance of the UK economy is compared to its major competitors, and business and government strategies for improving competitiveness are described.

Element 5.1
ANALYSE PRODUCTION IN BUSINESSES

Identify added value in production and ways in which added value is achieved

PC 5.1.1

■ Added value in production

Production is a term which covers all the processes of adding value by the private and public sectors in the provision of goods and services to consumers and customers. Before the production process, a chair consists of pieces of wood and a pair of jeans is just a roll of denim fabric. The construction of the chairs or jeans into a finished product means that they are worth more than the raw materials from which they were made, the production process has added value to the materials. In a similar way, people who produce services add value to the materials with which they work. The doctor uses his or her knowledge and expertise to provide a service, and their patients find this beneficial and useful. The doctor has added value to the consulting room and equipment by examining and advising the patient.

■ Ways to achieve added value

Marketing

The marketing concept suggests that all businesses start with the customer. A firm adopting this approach begins by determining what customers want and then making it for them. Marketing encompasses planning and designing goods and services that satisfy customers' needs, as well as pricing, promotion and distribution of those goods and services. Promotions such as advertising and branding aim to extol the benefits of buying and consuming the product. The jeans with a well known brand label which have been widely advertised are perceived by the consumer as having added value compared with unlabelled similar garments.

Quality assurance

Quality can be defined as how well a product does what it is intended to do – how closely it satisfies the specifications to which it is built. It is a degree of excellence on which products or services can be ranked on selected features.

Quality assurance is an operations process involving a broad group of activities that are aimed at achieving the organisation's quality objectives. An organisation's interpretation of quality is expressed in its strategies. Although the precise activities involved in quality assurance vary from organisation to organisation, activities like determining the safest system for delivering goods to customers and maintaining the quality of parts or materials purchased from suppliers are included in most quality assurance efforts.

Statistical quality control is a process used to determine how many products from a larger number should be inspected to calculate a probability that the total number of products meets organisational quality standards.

Quality assurance is a chain of activities that start when quality standards are set and end when quality goods and services are delivered to the customer. An effective quality assurance strategy reduces the need for quality control and subsequent corrective actions.

Quality assurance is best when a 'no rejects' philosophy is adopted by management. Mistakes are costly. Detecting defective products in the final quality control inspection is too late and too expensive. Emphasizing quality in the early stages – during product and process design – will reduce rejects. Getting production right first time means that the company does not have to spend a great deal on an after-sales service which is occupied with correcting defects. In the car industry it is now becoming more commonplace for manufacturers to offer 3-year warranties, as they are so confident of the quality of their product.

Many service industry products involve customer experience. Checks on this are therefore often made by an anonymous employee posing as a customer to monitor the experience a customer may have of the service provided. Retailers, such as Top Shop and Top Man, will employ people to pose as customers wishing to return an article bought earlier in the day and restaurants have inspectors posing as customers eating a meal. The anonymous 'customers' then write a report on the customer service they received and that branch of the organisation is given a rating based on the findings in the report.

PC 5.1.1

Productivity

Productivity is the relationship between costs of inputs (e.g. people, marketing, materials, finance, distribution) and revenue from outputs (income from sales, repeat sales, continuity of sales). Productivity describes how much is produced relative to the resources used to produce it. A company that uses fewer resources to make the same number of products as another firm is more efficient.

One method of improving a firm's productivity is value-added analysis, which involves the evaluation of all work activities, material flows and paperwork to determine the value they add for the customer. Value-added analysis often reveals day-to-day activities that are wasteful, unnecessary, and can be eliminated without harming customer service. The resulting savings in labour and materials raises productivity. In addition to value-added analysis, better training and equipment can boost productivity.

Just-In-Time production (JIT)

JIT systems aim to coordinate the supply of materials so that they arrive just when they are needed – just in time. The concept was developed primarily by the Toyota Motor Company of Japan and is also called 'zero inventory'. In theory, the system should lead to no stocks being held; in practice, it minimises them. JIT brings together all materials and parts needed at each production point at the precise moment that they are required. It saves money by replacing a stop-and-go production approach with a smooth movement. Everything flows from the arrival of the raw materials and parts to final completion and shipment of finished goods. JIT reduces the number of semi-finished goods to practically nothing.

JIT systems require total commitment from the workforce and its suppliers – there is no room for errors such as faulty components and delays in delivery. JIT works best in companies that manufacture relatively standardised products and that have consistent product demand. Such companies can order materials from suppliers and assemble products in several small, continuous batches. The result is a smooth, consistent flow of purchased materials and assembled products and little inventory build-up.

If implemented successfully, JIT can improve organisational performance in several ways. It can reduce unnecessary labour costs generated by products manufactured but not sold. Also it does not tie up money in the form of unsold products and it saves money on storing stocks.

Effective use of human resources

PC 5.1.1

The efficient use of personnel should reduce costs and appropriate working conditions can raise productivity. In order to use the workforce more efficiently, people should not be employed when there is little or no work for them. There is a growing trend towards the use of part-time, temporary and contract labour so that employees are taken on when needed and not as permanent full-time staff. Patterns in the use of labour now match demand for the product more accurately. Firms have increased their use of part-time and temporary staff to cover busy periods.

In addition to the use of non-standard or atypical contracts, many firms vary the numbers of staff available through hours worked. Some companies have implemented zero-hours contracts which enable staff to be called in at short notice when needed, others employ staff on annual hours so that they may work longer days or weeks during busy times of the year without having to be paid overtime rates.

Multi-skilling, or functional flexibility, entails each worker being skilled to do several jobs; this is more efficient for firms when there is insufficient work for all employees to perform one task continuously. Workers can cover for one another during absences and can train one another on-the-job whilst the work is being carried out, at little extra cost to their employer.

Human resources can also reorganise their own work more effectively. They are the ones carrying out the work and they understand the problems involved, problems can be solved by the workers at minimal cost to their employers. The workers can be organised into project teams/quality circles to study particular problems; or they can be grouped together to organise their work as they see fit. Ideas such as job rotation can increase productivity rates, particularly when the workers have conceived the idea themselves and are committed to it.

Effective use of human resources can also be achieved through continuous training. Often firms restrict the availability of training to their full-time permanent employees, and part-time and temporary staff may have to pay for and organise their own training outside of the work environment. The government encourages training by offering tax relief on tuition fees and accrediting skills through National Vocational Qualifications.

PC 5.1.2

Why businesses aim to add value

To meet international competition

It is important that UK businesses are able to compete with their foreign competitors. Firms who do not wish to compete through exporting and continue to produce in the same way as they have done for years for their home market soon find that foreign competitors take away their home market. International competition cannot be avoided. The UK used to have manufacturers of sewing machines, cars, typewriters and motorcycles, now these products are all made by foreign-owned firms. In order to compete in global markets with such firms as McDonald's, Nestlé and BMW, UK firms need to be competitive both in terms of price and quality.

Meeting customer requirements

The adding of value during the production process can be tailored to customer requirements. Products and services which match customer needs will be in far greater demand than those which are lacking in certain respects.

Jobbing production is production of single articles or 'one-off' items. These products may be small, tailor-made components, huge pieces of equipment or large single items, such as a ship. Most products are made for a particular customer or to a particular order. Jobbing production is to be found in industries such as heavy engineering (e.g. production of electricity generating plant), shipbuilding and civil engineering (e.g. bridge construction). It is also to be found in most other industries, where it is employed to produce prototype models, spare parts, modifications to existing plant and many other 'one-off' tailor-made pieces.

The production of services is very often customised to suit one particular customer's needs. Haircuts, conveyancing services from a solicitor for the purchase of a house, repairs to shoes or washing machines, dentistry, life assurance, are all tailored to meet a particular customer's needs. Even services which appear to be standardised such as air travel, a day out at a theme park or staying in a hotel, do have options within them which enable customers to fit their experience to meet their particular needs.

To improve profit

Profit consists of the difference between the cost of producing a good or service and its selling price. The greater the difference, the greater the amount of profit made from selling a single item. Total profit will also be greater if sales increase. Various methods of adding value can be used to reduce costs or to increase sales. Quality assurance, increased productivity, just-in-time production and reduced labour costs will all contribute towards keeping costs low and improving profits. Quality assurance again will help to increase sales, as will various marketing tools such as advertising and promotional offers. Added value is aimed at achieving organisational objectives such as profitability, survival and growth.

■ To survive and grow

PC 5.1.2

Added value enables organisations to make sufficient profit to remain in business and survive to trade for another year, or to grow through increased profits. Growth is a strategy adopted by management to increase the amount of business that their firm is currently generating. Management generally invests substantial amounts of money to implement this strategy and may even sacrifice short-term profit to build long-term gain.

Managers can also encourage growth by purchasing other companies, merging with other companies, or taking over other companies. BMW's purchase of the Rover Group gave them an instant increase in their share of the world car market. Acquisitions may give firms further advantages in terms of added value as they will also acquire another firm's management structure, production processes and equipment and access to their supplier network. If any aspects of the new acquisition's production system is superior to their own, this will give them increased added value.

GROUP ACTIVITY

PC 5.1.1 5.1.2

As a group of 4–6 people, form a company and decide upon a product which you could manufacture. Choose suppliers, a place to make your product, what equipment you would need, how you would sell and market the product and which group members will perform the various tasks in the company. Draw up a draft business plan to include these points. Go through the business plan and decide as a group how the following activities would achieve added value:

1 Marketing

2 Quality assurance procedures

3 The use of labour

Other points for discussion:

a) Who are your suppliers and exactly how would you receive the supplies?

b) Could this be improved upon to give added value?

c) What measures could you take to improve productivity in your company?

DISCUSSION TOPICS

PC 5.1.1 5.1.2

1 How might advertising add value to a pair of jeans?

2 Are there any products which do not meet your needs, and in what way do they fail to meet your needs? How could this be improved to increase added value?

3 Are there any problems involved with Just-In-Time production?

4 What difficulties might a supplier face whose customer had just implemented a JIT system and was insisting on small and frequent deliveries?

5 What advantages and disadvantages face people on part-time and temporary contracts?

6 Examine some of the personal belongings you have with you to establish where they were manufactured. What features of these items encouraged you to buy them? What could UK firms learn from your findings?

PC
5.1.3
5.1.4

Identify and give examples of changes in production

■ Technology (management information systems)

Management information systems (MIS) are designed to transform data into information that can be used for decision making. MIS managers must determine what information will be needed, then gather the data and provide ways to convert them into the desired information. They must also control the flow of information so that only those who need or who are entitled to certain information receive it, otherwise this could lead to information overload. Information supplied to employees and managers varies, depending on the functional area in which they work (such as accounting or marketing) and on their level in management.

Information needs of various managers differ. Sales managers supervise salespeople, assign territories to the salesforce, and handle customer service and delivery problems. To do their job well, they need current and accurate information on the sales and delivery of products to customers and accurate information on the sales and delivery of their products to customers in their branches. Regional managers set sales quotas for each sales manager, prepare budgets, and plan staffing needs for the next year. To do so, they need total monthly sales by product and by branch. Management needs sales data summarised by product, customer type, and geographic region and analysed in comparison to previous years' and competitors' sales. The wealth of information is made more readily available because of the use of computers. The ability to use information rapidly to make decisions more quickly gives businesses competitive advantage.

■ Robotics

Although Japanese companies pioneered their use, firms all over the world are interested in the construction, maintenance, and use of computer-controlled machines in manufacturing operations. Some modern car manufacturers use robots to weld, assemble, paint and inspect cars. Robots have not gained wide acceptance in many UK firms for many reasons, including their high cost, incredible complexity, and technical limitations.

Robotics are only one part of a larger manufacturing automation system called computer-integrated manufacturing (CIM). In addition to controlling robots, CIM controls the flow of materials and supplies in production. CIM can also manage material requirements planning and just-in-time production systems.

■ Automation

Automation is the performance of mechanical operations with either minimal or no human involvement. These techniques are not new. The Industrial Revolution began with huge spinning and weaving machines that rendered manual techniques obsolete. Nearly every company in the world uses some machinery in place of hand labour. Many small firms have automated at least to the degree that personal computer systems monitor production outcomes.

The Japanese have pioneered soft automation (also called flexible automation) systems that use machines that are adaptable enough to perform several functions. As a result, changing from one product design to another requires only a few different instructions to a computer, saving valuable machine set-up time and machine and labour stoppage costs. UK firms have often relied on hard automation, in which each machine is dedicated to performing just one specific function.

■ Computer-aided design

PC 5.1.3 5.1.4

CAD (also called computer-aided engineering (CAE)) uses computers to design new products. Through the use of sophisticated analysis methods and graphics, CAD allows users to create a design and simulate conditions to test the performance of the design, all in the computer. CAD systems let designers see the result of changes in design without having to create costly prototype models and test them under real-world conditions.

■ Computer-aided manufacturing

In a direct off-shoot of computer-aided design, computer-aided manufacturing (CAM) uses computers to design and control the equipment needed in the manufacturing process. For example, CAM systems can produce tapes to control all the machines and robots on a production line. CAD/CAM is useful for engineers in a manufacturing environment to design and test a new product and then to design the machines and tools to manufacture the new product.

■ Contracting out

Production costs may be reduced by employing other companies to make certain components of the product. Contracting out involves awarding a contract to a separate firm to manufacture part of the product or service. This has increased in many companies to the extent where the original manufacturer has become an assembly plant, with component parts being made by suppliers in the UK or abroad. The Amstrad company has its computers made in the Far East. The decision for managers as to whether to make all the parts in-house or to contract-out some of the production is known as the 'make or buy' decision. Contracting-out has always been used to a small extent with firms such as banks and restaurants using window cleaners, companies who specialise in plant displays, and contract cleaners as separate suppliers rather than employees of the firm. Contracting out is also suitable for short-term or specialist work.

■ Single sourcing

Purchasing parts or components from many different suppliers in different countries has been slimmed down dramatically by some companies so that they deal only with a single supplier. Single sourcing can involve one supplier shipping parts out from one location in the world to all the assembly plants of their customer, or the supplier shipping from its manufacturing plants in various countries. The idea is the same, that a single supplier will supply a part for all the customer's assembly plants worldwide.

Ford of America, the world's second largest vehicle maker, has merged its North American and European automotive operations into a single operating unit. After a global search, common component producers have been chosen to supply the European and the US and Mexican assembly plants. Ford's philosophy was to develop a part only once from supplier to the world. Ford has developed an integrated, global supply base with a drastic reduction in the total number of suppliers. Ford believes that they will gain cost advantages in the form of economies of scale and also better quality from more focused quality control efforts. A few parts are dual-sourced, so that Europe and North America each has its own supplier. The Ford Tempo/Mercury Topaz range had more than 700 suppliers, whereas the successor Ford Contour/Mercury Mystique models have only 227 suppliers, drawn from around the world.

PC 5.1.3 5.1.4

■ Labour flexibility

A further change in production methods is through multi-skilling. Each production worker is trained to perform a variety of tasks required in the production process and is therefore skilled in many jobs. This avoids production being halted through absence or demarcation disputes as each worker possesses the flexibility to undertake all tasks and does whatever is needed. Firms such as Rolls Royce Motor Cars have organised their production workers into multi-skilled teams; the teams organise their own work and are responsible for teaching one another their jobs. Each team has its own team leader and the team members themselves perform their own quality checks; there is no longer any need for supervisors on the shopfloor.

■ Legislation

Around 400 million tonnes of waste are produced annually in the United Kingdom. The sectors with the largest waste generation are agriculture with 80 million tonnes and mining and quarrying with 110 million tonnes.

There are laws governing what organisations can do in the production process. The Deposit of Poisonous Wastes Act, Pollution of Rivers Act, Health and Safety at Work Act, Clean Air Act and local by-laws create rules by which companies have to abide. Firms cannot pollute the environment and allow their employees to undertake risks at work without the threat of legal action against them. The type of legislation applicable to a producer will differ, depending on the product. Producers of chemicals will be governed by legislation which is different to that governing a night-club, say, and both are covered by strict guidelines on all their actions.

■ Quality standards

Traditional quality control has been directed towards checking the quality of the conformance of the product to the original design and ensuring that the production process produced components or finished goods which conformed to their specification (or within close tolerances). In contrast to this approach the emphasis today is more on the original design, which the customer ordered or expressed a preference for. Quality considerations are at the core of the production process, which includes the production of services as well as products. Quality control means continuously improving the product and aiming for prevention of errors rather than relying on inspection to correct mistakes and/or to reject faulty components. The benefits for this approach are claimed to be increased productivity and lower costs together with increased customer satisfaction and profitability.

DISCUSSION TOPICS

PC 5.1.3 5.1.4

1 What is the connection between management information systems and production?

2 How do the use of robots and automated plant change the nature of work for the people employed in a factory?

3 How can computers reduce costs in the production process?

4 How many tasks can you think of that need doing around your school or college, and which ones could be contracted out?

5 What are the advantages of single sourcing?

6 Think of jobs you have done in the past (part-time or full-time). Were the people you worked with multi-skilled or did everyone perform the same task all day, every day? Which system is preferable?

7 What sort of laws and regulations might be applicable to a night-club which sells alcohol and aims for a target market of 18–24 year olds?

8 How can quality assurance be applied to a service industry such as an ice cream parlour or a hairdressers?

9 How do the changes in production of goods and services affect the way firms compete with one another?

10 Do the changes in production enable firms to charge lower prices than they otherwise would?

Element 5.2
INVESTIGATE AND EVALUATE EMPLOYMENT

PC 5.2.1

Types of employment

■ Self-employed

The self-employed have traditionally constituted only a small percentage of the total labour force in the UK. The number of self-employed workers was approximately 1.8 million or about 7.4 per cent of the workforce throughout the 1970s. However, there was a growth in self-employment during the 1980s, which has continued throughout the 1990s, so that by 1994, the number of self-employed was 3.2 million, and they formed 13 per cent of the labour force. Women are less likely to be self-employed than men, 2.4 million men are self-employed (17 per cent of total male employees) and 808,000 women are self-employed (7 per cent of total female employees). There are also regional variations in self-employment with over 16 per cent of those in employment in the south-west being self-employed compared with 10 per cent in Scotland.

The substantial increase in the numbers of self-employed may not reflect a dramatic shift towards an enterprise culture in the UK. The figures might seem to indicate that more people are becoming entrepreneurs, setting up their own businesses and taking risks with the aim of making profits. The growth in self-employment occurred at a time when the UK economy was suffering the severest and most prolonged recession since the 1930s.

■ Full-time employment

The number of people employed on a full-time basis in the UK falls each month. The total workforce in September 1994 was 21.5 million and in the same month in 1990 it had been 22.7 million. In addition to the fall in total employment, the number of part-time workers, who are included in the total workforce figure, is continually increasing. Those who are employed full-time often work long hours with 58 per cent of male employees working 41 hours or more per week and 18 per cent of female employees working 41 hours or more per week. Employees in the UK tend to work longer hours than those in Europe.

Part-time work

Part-time work in the UK consists of work of 30 hours per week, or any number of hours below that. Part-time therefore consists of a great variety, from people doing one or two hours per week, up to those working 6 hours per day, five days per week. The total workforce employed on a part-time basis is just over 6 million and is increasing; over a quarter of all jobs are part-time. The increase from 1993–94 was an extra 184,000 part-time jobs. Many part-time workers are women; in Great Britain in summer 1994, while 88 per cent of male employees were working full-time in permanent positions, for women the figure was only 52 per cent.

Temporary

The number of people in the workforce employed on a temporary basis was 1.59 million in summer 1994; this was an increase of 143,000 on the previous year. Employers take on temporary staff for a variety of reasons, such as short-term cover, gaining specialist skills or to cope with the peaks in demand for labour. The nature of temporary employment varies and can take a variety of forms: employment agency staff, fixed-term contracts of usually between one and three years, whilst other temporary employees are taken on on a week-by-week basis.

Skilled and unskilled

The demand for labour in manual and unskilled jobs is expected to continue to contract during the 1990s. The growth in demand for labour will therefore be concentrated among the higher skilled occupations, and in particular among professional, scientific and technical occupations. This is shown in Fig 5.1, where growth of employment is expected in skilled occupations, but reductions are anticipated in others.

University graduates are the main source of supply for these higher skilled occupations, but higher education is also influenced by demographic factors and the need to compete with employers anxious to recruit 'A' level school leavers. While demand for graduates is generally up, there is a particular need for two specific types: the technologist, required by the electronic, electrical engineering and computing sectors, and the high-flyer, increasingly sought to meet the long-term needs of senior management. Many employers are attempting to solve their problems by broadening the entry requirements, so that now nearly half the vacancies currently advertised are open to all graduates.

Traditionally, distinctions between shopfloor workers who are skilled, semi-skilled or unskilled have been very noticeable, with different pay grades and job titles throughout the factory. More recently, five-year apprenticeships have become a thing of the past; now new technology and automation have changed the nature of jobs and reduced the need for highly skilled craftsmen, training is much more rapid, even for skilled jobs. Also, with the advent of multi-skilling and teamwork within factories, there is a greater homogeneity within the workforce.

Fig 5.1 **Occupational employment changes, 1990–2000**

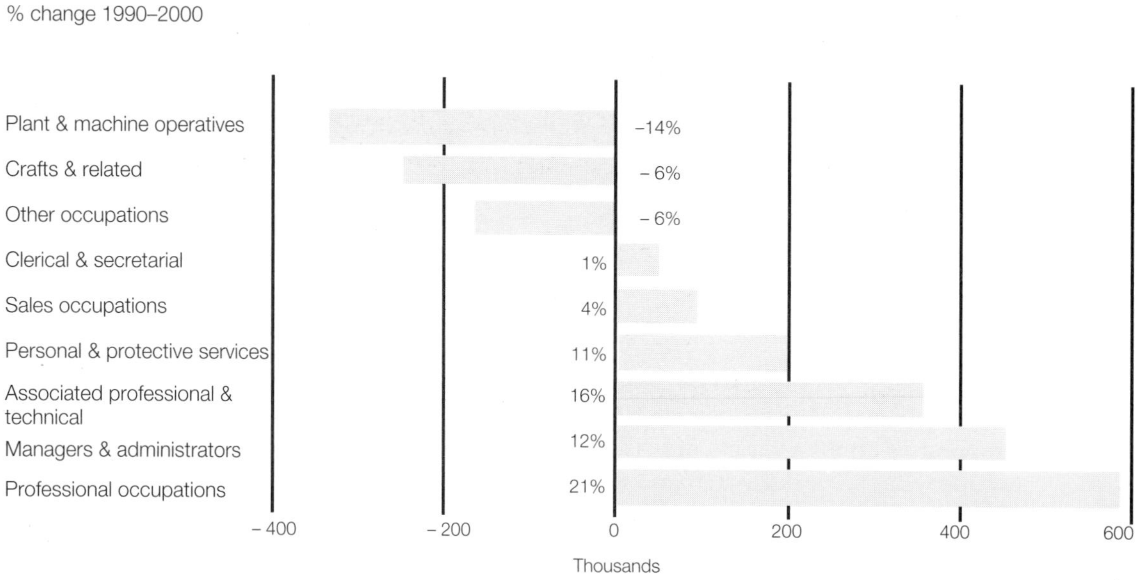
% change 1990–2000
Plant & machine operatives
Crafts & related
Other occupations
Clerical & secretarial
Sales occupations
Personal & protective services
Associated professional & technical
Managers & administrators
Professional occupations
-14%
- 6%
- 6%
1%
4%
11%
16%
12%
21%
- 400
- 200
0
200
400
600
Thousands

Source: Institute for Employment Research

■ Home-working

One in ten firms employ people who work from home, these are often craft workers doing such tasks as sewing and knitting, and they are usually low paid. One in twenty firms employ teleworkers who work from home via a telecommunications link and carry out most of their work on computer. Teleworkers are found at all organisational levels, from senior management to the lowest grade of clerical work, and in a very diverse range of occupations. The two occupational groups most commonly found teleworking are consultants and secretarial or administrative staff, followed in importance by data entry staff, computer professionals, training or education specialists, researchers and sales or marketing staff. Other telework occupations include translation, design, planning, social work, telephone counselling, inspection, legal work, accountancy, financial advice and engineering.

There are various ways of organising teleworking and these fall into two main categories. Firstly, schemes usually involving management or professional staff, in which teleworkers have employee status, work full-time, and are fully integrated into corporate culture, participating in training and staff development programmes and spending, typically, 1–2 days a week on the employer's premises. Contrasting with these schemes are those involving self-employed staff, typically engaged in data entry, typing, translation or some types of editorial and research work. People in this group are more likely to work part-time, to be paid by results and to spend virtually all of their working time at home.

DISCUSSION TOPICS

PC 5.2.1 5.2.2

1 Why might so many people be self-employed in the UK?

2 What advantages and disadvantages do you think there might be in starting your own business?

3 Does the rise of part-time employment and the fall in the numbers of full-time jobs mean that men will stay at home in future, while women go out to work?

4 Research has shown that temporary workers suffer the same type of stress as the unemployed, due to the insecure nature of their job and inability to plan for the future. Could employers do anything to reduce this stress?

5 How would you advise someone planning to leave school as early as possible, with no qualifications, who is sure they can easily get a job?

6 Why are homeworkers often badly paid?

7 What might be the disadvantages of homeworking and teleworking?

Changing trends in employment

PC 5.2.3 5.2.4

■ The changing industrial base

The main sectors of employment are referred to as:

- Primary
- Secondary
- Tertiary

Industries found in these sectors include:

- The primary sector: agriculture and the extractive industries such as coal mining and quarrying.
- The secondary sector: manufacturing and construction.
- The tertiary sector or the service sector: banking, insurance and education.

Table 5.1 **Changes in employment according to sector**

	1977 *(000)*	*1991* *(000)*
Primary	1,086	700
Secondary	839	4,846
Tertiary	12,697	16,245

PC
5.2.3
5.2.4

As a country's economy develops, so the relevant importance of each sector will change. Before the industrial revolution most people were employed in agriculture. By the 1850s the manufacturing sector of the economy was the most important sector for employment and output. From the latter part of the nineteenth century the tertiary sector grew in importance as it supported or serviced the manufacturing industry. Today the service sector is the largest employer and contributes most to the UK's economy.

The changes in the importance of the manufacturing and tertiary sectors accelerated most during the 1960s and 1980s. For example in 1960 manufacturing accounted for 39 per cent of employment and 26 per cent of output. By 1990 employment in this sector had fallen to 23 per cent and output to 22 per cent. The tertiary sector, however, was employing 70 per cent of the nation's workforce and contributed to over 65 per cent of its output.

The influence of the primary sector continued its decline during the 1980s as both coal and North Seal Oil reduced in output.

De-industrialisation

The decline in the importance of manufacturing is generally referred to as de-industrialisation. De-industrialisation means a decline in manufacturing in terms of:

- the absolute employment level
- the total share of employment in the economy
- a decline in the share of output of the economy

The causes of de-industrialisation include the lack of competitiveness of UK goods with foreign goods both at home and abroad. This lack of competitiveness can be on price, delivery and quality.

During the 1980s UK manufacturers had to contend with a high exchange rate brought about by the exporting of North Sea Oil and high UK interest rates. This made it difficult to export because the high pound made exports expensive and difficult to sell abroad. In the home market the manufacturers had to compete against cheaper imports.

The importance of manufacturing to the UK economy is that other sectors depend on it and cannot operate without manufactured goods. The catering industry needs plates, saucepans, tables and chairs. All items produced by manufacturers can be sold abroad and earn foreign currency, but this is not the case with the tertiary sector. Although the service sector makes a significant contribution to the UK's balance of payments, some services, such as rail travel or the services of firemen and traffic wardens, cannot be sold abroad.

Service industries need manufactured goods in order to provide for their customers. Hotels and restaurants are in the service sector, but they need buildings, furnishings, carpets, crockery and cutlery, cash registers/computers, stationery and a host of other manufactured goods to be able to provide a service.

The decline in the manufacturing sector means that the UK is in a weaker position for competing with countries such as Japan. However, some economists argue that de-industrialisation is just part of the natural development of the economy. The UK was the first to industrialise, so the likelihood is that the UK will be one of the first nations to move on to the next stage in economic development. Other countries such as the United States of America are experiencing similar situations with their secondary sectors.

Changes in labour

As the structure of the economy has changed so there have been changes in the make-up of the labour market. The labour market is vibrant and dynamic and many of the changes in the labour market are related to the labour force. It was stated earlier that the actual size of the labour force will depend on the size of the population, the age structure, the ratio of male to female and the activity rates of those employed.

In 1990 the civilian labour force, i.e. those people in employment plus those who are unemployed and claiming benefit but not including the armed forces, totalled, 28.2 million.

Table 5.2 **Civilian labour force: by age**

Great Britain				Millions
	16–24	25–54	55 and over	All aged 16 and over
Estimates				
1971	5.1	15.0	4.9	24.9
1976	5.1	16.1	4.5	25.7
1979	5.6	16.3	4.2	26.0
1983	5.9	16.4	3.7	25.9
1984	6.0	16.7	3.6	26.4
1984	6.1	16.8	3.7	26.6
1986	6.2	17.3	3.4	26.9
1990	5.8	18.8	3.5	28.2
Projections				
1996	4.9	20.2	3.4	28.6
2001	5.0	20.3	3.6	28.9

[1] Estimates for 1971 are based on the Census of Population. Those for 1976, 1984 are based on the GB Labour Force definitions, and from 1984 on the ILO definitions.

Source: Employment Department

Table 5.2 shows that there has been a steady increase in the total civilian labour force. Part of this change is accounted for by the relatively high birth rates in the 1960s. Within the labour force in 1990, 16–24 year olds made up 21 per cent of the civilian labour force, but by 2001 this is projected to fall to 17 per cent.

There have been an extra 2 million people who have joined the labour force since the 1970s. This has meant that more jobs have had to be created during a period of high unemployment. Between 1983 and 1990 the economy created 940,000 jobs, many of which were part-time and taken up by women.

The difference between those who had jobs and those who had not – the job deficit – gradually closed during the 1980s only to widen again with the onset of the new recession.

The self-employed

The 1980s saw a rapid growth in the number of self-employed. Between 1981 and 1990 the number of self-employed increased by 57 per cent. By 1990 almost 3.25 million people were self-employed and half of these people had work either in the construction sector, distribution, catering or the repairs sector of the economy.

Fig 5.2 **The job deficit (millions)**

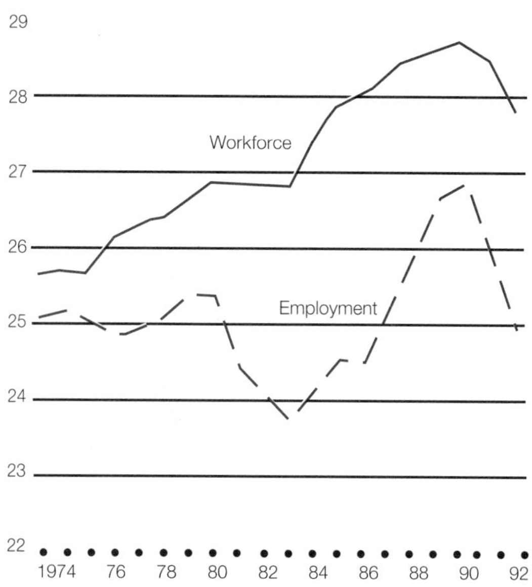

Source: Dept of Employment. *Guardian*, Friday, February 19 1993

Table 5.3 **Number of self-employed persons between 1971 and 1990 in 000's**

	1971	1981	1990
All industries	1,953	2,058	3,222
Males	1,556	1,641	2,449
Females	397	417	773
Manufacturing	129	146	272
Service	1,199	1,274	1,981
Other	625	638	969

In 1989 there was a total of 130.4 million people employed in the EC. Since 1985 over 7 million jobs had been created, while at the same time there was a change taking place to the pattern of employment. Fewer are now employed in agriculture and industry whilst more are employed in services.

Table 5.4 **Number employed by sector in the EC**

	1975	*1989*
Agriculture (000)	13,942	9,209
Percentage of employed	11.2	7.1
Industry (000)	48,395	43,138
Percentage of employed	38.8	33.2
Service (000)	62,453	77,761
Percentage of employed	50	59.8

The main reasons for the increase in the self-employed include the following:

- Those people who had been made redundant decided to work for themselves.
- Government policies encouraged the unemployed to start their own business.
- Businesses decided to contract out their work rather than employ their own workers.

The 1980s was the era of the entrepreneur.

Activity rates

This refers to the proportion of the population above the minimum school-leaving age who are in the civilian labour force. Recently there have been changes in these rates for both men and women. In 1993 the male activity rate was 74.2 whereas the activity rate for women was 52.8. This represented a fall since 1971 for male activity rates from 80.5 per cent, while women's rates increased from 43.9 per cent. Demographic factors influence women's activity rates, for example firms taking on women because of the shortage of teenage workers, the comparatively low birth rate during the 1970s and a rise in the average age at which women have children. The fall in male activity rates was due mainly to the increase in male unemployment.

The UK activity rate is above the EU average. The activity rate varies between states because of the uneven distribution of:

- employment in agriculture, industry and services
- the age structures of the country
- the percentage of women in the job market.

Table 5.5 **European Community activity rate (%)**

	Total	*Male*	*Female*
Belgium	39.6	49.7	30.0
Denmark	56.1	61.8	50.6
Germany	47.9	59.9	36.7
Greece	40.7	53.0	29.2
Spain	38.0	51.0	25.6
France	44.7	52.1	38.8
Ireland	37.9	50.5	25.0
Italy	41.4	54.1	30.0
Luxembourg	42.4	56.1	28.7
Netherlands	45.6	56.8	34.7
Portugal	46.9	56.4	38.3
UK	50.9	59.5	42.6
Eur 12	44.9	55.6	34.9

In the EC there has been a general decline in the male activity rate. This has been offset by the increase in the female activity rate. The main factor influencing female activity rates can be attributed to the number of opportunities available for part-time working.

Changes in the public sector in the UK

The employment patterns in relation to public sector and the private sector changed during the 1980s.

Table 5.6 **Changes in employment in public and private sectors**

	1970 *(000)*	*1980* *(000)*	*1990* *(000)*
Workforce in employment	24,753	25,327	26,924
Private sector employment	18,238	17,940	20,430
Public sector employment	6,515	7,387	6,071

Most of the decrease in the public sector employment since 1981 is accounted for by a fall in employment in public corporations as a result of privatisation.

PC
5.2.3
5.2.4

Women in employment

The fastest growing sector of the labour market is female employment. In 1911, women made up 30 per cent of the workforce, by 1971 this had risen to 42 per cent and by 1993 the figure stood at 48 per cent. It is projected that women will make up 50 per cent of the labour force by the mid 1990s.

Women have always made significant contributions to the labour market, but their contributions depended upon the attitudes of society and the economic climate at the time. The types of employment have also changed over time. At the start of the century women could find employment in factories or in domestic service. Today there is no barrier to the types of job available to women – women on the floor of the Stock Exchange or women Prime Ministers.

In periods of labour shortages women are actively encouraged to work. In times of conflict, such as during both the First and Second World Wars, women took the place of men in the factories or on the farms. However, when the men returned, women were expected to give up their jobs. During the inter-war years it was expected that women would work until they got married and then they would set up home and have a family. Men were the bread-winners.

Since 1970 there has been a shift in attitudes towards women and legislation relating to women in employment. It is now accepted and expected that women make a contribution to the economy. This trend for an increase in women's participation rate in employment is evident in other countries.

Fig 5.3 **Female participation rates in a selection of OECD countries, 1987-2000**

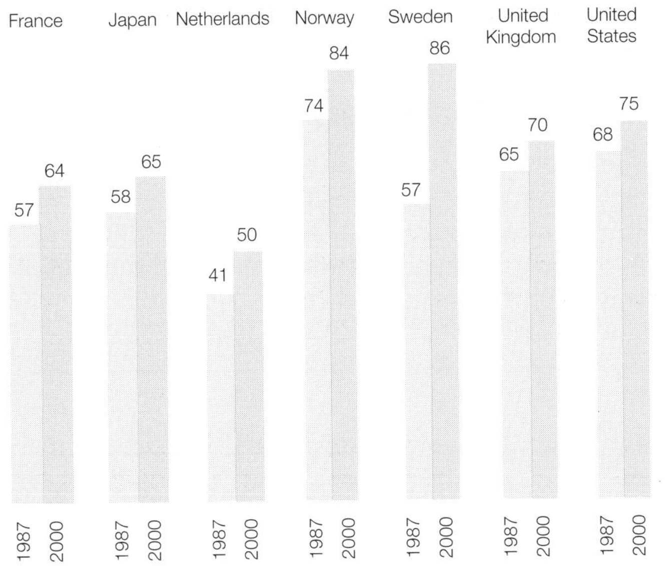

Source: ICI Paper (1987) Deomgraphic Trends

■ The reasons for the trend in female employment

PC 5.2.3 5.2.4

The rise of the tertiary sector

The growth of the tertiary sector in economic terms has meant a change in employment and employment patterns as more people are now employed in services and are part-time and temporary working has increased. The tertiary sector is now more important than the secondary sector which traditionally employed men in the staple industries of coal mining, ship-building and in the manufacturing sector. These industries have been replaced and their place has been taken by the service industries, for example, banking, insurance and retailing. Service industries are major employers of women.

The rise of part-time occupations

There has been a shift away from full employment to part-time occupations. During the 1990s it is expected that half the UK workforce will be made up of part-time workers. One of the reasons for this is that part-time workers are less costly to employ. Not only are their wages lower than full-time workers but also other employment costs are reduced, for example, sickness benefits and pension contributions.

However, part-time work is useful for married women who have young children and are able to fit working around their family commitments.

The change in the family structure

The trend this century has been for smaller families, i.e. two adults and two children or fewer. Not only has the trend been to have fewer children but to have them later in life and for the women to return to work as soon as possible. The desire is to maintain the standard of living of the family.

Another trend in families has been the rise in one-parent families which has increased the pressure on women to work. However, because mothers have to look after their children they find it difficult to find employment.

Women are cheaper to employ

Women do not earn as much as men despite changes in attitudes and legislation towards women.

Table 5.7 **A comparison of weekly wages in 1990**

	Male	*Female*
Manual	£237.20	£148.00
Non-manual	£354.90	£215.50

Among the reasons for these differences are that women tend to work in part-time occupations which do not pay the same rates as full-time work and they also tend to work in low-paid industries such as retailing and catering. Women often work in those industries or small firms which are poorly unionised.

Family commitments may mean that women do not wish to work overtime or unsociable hours. This may mean that they miss out on the higher rates of pay.

Women have breaks in their careers when starting a family. The longer a woman is out of a job, the more difficult it becomes for her to get her old job back at the same level and at the same money. For example, a systems analyst who left her job seven years ago would no longer have the knowledge or the skills to do the job now. Women have to restart their careers usually at the bottom of the ladder for pay and prospects, whereas a male colleague who was employed by the firm at the same time at the start of his career would not only be earning more but would probably have gained promotion.

Attitudes of employers

Despite legislation on equal pay there remains a gap between the earnings of men and women.

However, the Equal Pay Act 1970 has required that women performing similar tasks to men must be treated in the same way as men regarding terms and conditions of employment. The Equal Pay Amendment Regulations 1983 allowed women to claim equal pay on the basis of work of equal value if they found it difficult to make a claim based on 'like work' or 'work related or equivalent'.

The Sex Discrimination Act 1975 requires that men and women should be guaranteed equality of opportunity. Since the introduction of the Acts there has been an improvement in women's pay.

PC 5.2.4

■ Measures for bringing more women into the workforce

More women would be able to enter the workforce if constraints on them were removed and employers were more imaginative with the conditions of employment. Employers could be more flexible with their working hours to fit in with the school timetable, offer more child care facilities and give leave of absence to either parent rather than mothers only.

Changing contractual arrangements

PC 5.2.4

The tradition of getting a full-time job upon leaving school and staying with the same firm for 40 years seems to be almost gone in the UK economy. The standard full-time permanent contract is still with us, but is becoming rarer. The growth areas in employment contracts are part-time, temporary, outside contractors, agency works and the self-employed. Firms use these contracts increasingly to improve flexibility in the workforce.

Flexibility in the labour market through the use of non-standard contracts has come about as a result of recent recession, the increasingly competitive international market and uncertainty about levels of demand.

TYPES OF FLEXIBILITY IN THE LABOUR MARKET

- **Functional**
  Employees are increasingly multi-skilled and can do one another's jobs.
- **Numerical**
  Non-standard employment contracts allow employers to increase or decrease employee numbers quickly in response to changes in demand for labour.
- **Financial**
  Payment systems are becoming individual, with rewards for performance, or 'market rate' rather than 'across the board' with all employees having the same pay rates.

Numerical flexibility and the use of non-standard contracts

PC 5.2.1

Part-time employees

The main reason for the use of part-time permanent employees is to cater for tasks which require a limited number of hours to complete. Examples are cleaners, usually employed for a few hours before or after the company's opening/closing hours, and catering employees, often working from mid/late morning to mid afternoon.

Other reasons for employing part-timers are to match employment levels to peaks in demand, for example, retail trades use part-timers for busy periods during the week. Some employers grant part-time hours because job applicants do not want full-time and others because they can retain valued staff who are unable to continue working full-time.

The growth in the use of part-time staff has come mainly from the retail sector which is experiencing increasing trading hours. Part-time workers rarely get overtime rates for working beyond the standard working day, which increases their attractiveness to employers.

Temporary employees

Employers often need short-time cover for full-time employees who are on holiday or sick. Temporary workers are also used to meet fluctuations in demand, to deal with one-off tasks and to provide specialist skills. The growth area for the employment of temporary workers has been in the health, education and distribution industries. Public sector budget constraints and uncertainty about future funding levels may have influenced the choice to increase the numbers of workers on temporary contracts.

Self-employed workers

'Self-employed' in this sense describes individuals who are given work by companies but are neither employees of that organisation nor of any other organisation. The most important reason for firms to employ these people is for the specialist skills they offer. There may be an increased demand for specialist skills, or more companies trying to cut costs by buying in skills when needed. Examples of self-employed workers are builders, window cleaners, management consultants and computer specialists.

Costs of employing non-standard labour

Most companies pay the same hourly rate for full-time and part-time employees. Where there are differences, the part-time rate is lower in the majority of cases. The hourly rates paid to agency temps are likely to be higher than for full-time employees.

National Insurance is another major cost item. If employees earn more than a lower earnings limit, both employer and employee are liable for contributions based on total earnings. This provides an incentive to keep total earnings below the limit. Despite this, most part-timers earn more than the threshold.

The majority of part-time and temporary workers are not included in company pension schemes, whereas most permanent full-time workers are. Indirect costs of employing labour are caused by absenteeism (sick leave) and turnover. Part-timers have a slightly higher turnover rate than full-time workers and a lower rate of absenteeism.

The main cost saving associated with non-standard labour is in lower fringe benefit provision.

PC
5.2.3
5.2.4

Employment trends

Growth of the 'underground' economy

The underground economy is that economic activity which is undeclared. Taxes such as VAT, income tax and National Insurance contributions, and government regulations such as health and safety laws, impose a burden on workers and businesses. Some are tempted to evade taxes and they are said to work in the underground, informal or hidden economy. In the building industry, for instance, it is common for workers to be self-employed and to under-declare or not declare their income at all to the tax authorities. The size of the underground economy is difficult to estimate, but it is thought that around £12 bn of construction work is undeclared. Medium-sized construction firms are being squeezed by their competitors working on an underground basis, as they can be undercut on prices by 17.5 per cent, the value of VAT.

Transactions in the black economy are in the form of cash. Cheques, credit cards, etc. could all be traced by the tax authorities. Tax evasion is the dominant motive for working in the black economy but a few also claim welfare benefits to which they are not entitled. The amount of revenue lost by the government due to the existence of the underground economy is estimated at £14 bn per annum.

■ Regional levels of employment

PC 5.2.3 5.2.4

Northern Ireland has the highest figure for unemployment at 12.3 per cent of the total workforce for the UK in January 1995. Scotland had 9 per cent unemployed and Wales 9.2 per cent, the North of England had 11.3 per cent unemployment. Various regions of the UK have been badly hit by the closure of coal mines and manufacturing industries; in some cases whole towns have been affected by the shutdown of the major employer. Many service industries have opened, but do not offer the same type of permanent, full-time male employment which was available previously.

■ Differences in pay

PC 5.2.3 5.2.4

The average gross weekly earnings of full-time adult employees in October 1994 was £328.9. The rate of increase from the previous year was estimated to be 4 per cent. Different occupational groups earn different amounts, with managers and administrators earning £472.5 on average and of those males averaged £514.2 per week and females averaged £353.2 per week. Some of the lowest paid employees work in hotels and catering, earning on average £204 per week.

Differences in pay are directly related to the demand for labour for a particular job and the amount of supply of labour to that job. Few people will be able to offer themselves as hospital consultants if a post is advertised as most people do not possess the necessary qualifications and experience, whereas many people would be able to apply for a job as a trainee hairdresser or postal worker. If the supply of labour is great, then an employer can afford to offer lower wages for the position than for a position which requires skills and experience.

DISCUSSION TOPICS

PC 5.2.3 5.2.4

1 Can the UK economy manage without any manufacturing industry, and become a complete service economy?

2 What sort of activities could be classed as being part of the underground economy?

3 Why do people feel justified in avoiding paying their taxes?

4 How does the underground economy harm the economic activity which is taking place legally?

5 Why are people reluctant to move to a different part of the country to get a job?

6 Should everyone be paid the same wages, no matter what job they do? What would happen if the government made this a legal requirement for all employers tomorrow?

Element 5.3
EXAMINE THE COMPETITIVENESS OF UK INDUSTRY

PC 5.3.1

The competitiveness of the UK economy

The success of the UK economy in the world market can be measured by its performance in world trade. This can be done by comparing economic performance indicators such as the UK's share of world trade, economic growth and productivity with that of other countries.

Success in the world market place will be determined by the competitiveness of UK firms. Competition usually takes two forms:

1 Price

2 Non-price competition, e.g. quality and delivery of goods and services.

The ability to compete depends on the economic well-being of the country, business performance, the support of the government for business and the strength of the competing opposition.

PC 5.3.1

UK economic performance

■ Economic performance indicators

Economic growth

This refers to the percentage increase in national output. In Fig 5.4 a country can either produce capital goods or consumption goods or a combination of both.

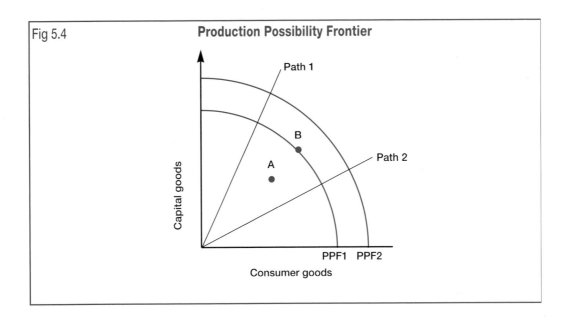

Fig 5.4 **Production Possibility Frontier**

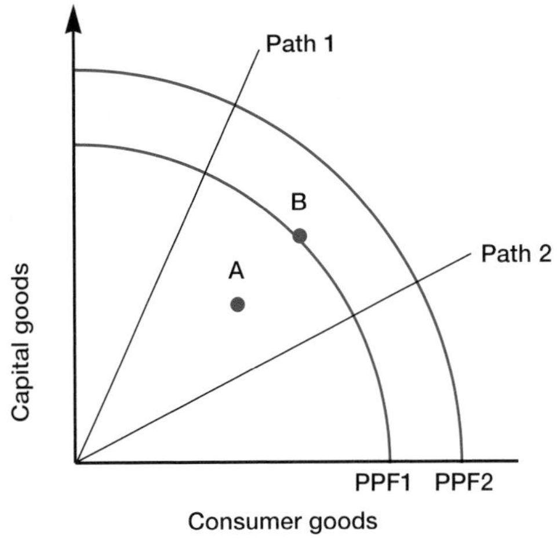

The Production Possibility Frontier shows the maximum or the potential output of a country with its given resources. If a country is producing within the boundary at point A this means that the country is under-performing; this may be because of unemployed labour or under-utilised machines. If the country increases its output to B there is said to be an **economic recovery**. If a country is able to push its boundary from PPF1 to PPF2 the country is said to be achieving **economic growth**. Enlarging the productive potential of an economy should increase real income per head.

In Fig 5.4 if a country follows path 1 (i.e. more towards capital goods) the country is making capital goods at the expense of consumer products. The country is investing in capital goods at the expense of consumer goods in the short term. This means that consumers should benefit in the future with high quality low-priced goods and the country will be able to compete in the world market. If the country is producing along path 2 the country is producing consumer goods at the expense of capital goods. The consumer would benefit in the short term but the country would face problems in the future, trying to compete with those countries producing cheaper and better products. A country adopting this approach is one whose businesses are seeking short-term rewards but will face difficulties in the future. The UK has tended to adopt the latter path, whereas the Economic Tiger countries of the Far East such as Japan have tended to follow path A.

The UK's economic growth has not been consistent. From 1979 to the mid-1980s the UK's economy went into recession where national output fell. From 1985 the UK's economy started to recover and output increased. This rise in output continued until 1987 when the economy started to overheat. Inflation became a worry and the Government slowed the economy down by increasing interest rates and taxes. The economy went into recession again which lasted until 1992. This fluctuation in output is known as the **Trade Cycle**.

Table 5.8 shows that the UK's major competitors also had the same trends in their economic growth but with the USA and Japanese economies growing at a faster rate. A point to consider is the stage of development these economies are at. If Japan's economy is more advanced than the UK's, then Japan's economic growth in real terms is faster, but also starts from a higher point.

PC 5.3.1

Table 5.8 **Economic growth (%)**

	USA	*Japan*	*Germany*	*UK*
1978–80	2.5	4.9	2.9	1.4
1981–83	1.0	3.4	0.3	1.3
1984–86	4.2	4.1	2.5	3.1
1987–89	3.7	5.2	2.8	3.7

Investment

This is the production of goods not for immediate consumption, but which will aid in the production of other goods and services, for example, industry invests in machinery, plant, equipment and vehicles. The Government invests in schools, hospitals, and roads.

Investment in capital goods is usually made because businesses have to replace worn-out equipment and buy new equipment to expand their operations. The demand for capital goods stimulates the economy and allows it to grow. Capital goods enable businesses to operate more efficiently and produce goods which are of a consistent standard, good quality and low price. Continuous investment enables businesses to compete successfully, to earn high profits for their investors and pay high wages to their employees.

Table 5.9 **Levels of investment as a percentage of Gross Domestic Product**

	UK	*West Germany*	*Japan*
1974–79	19.3	20.8	31.8
1980–84	16.3	21.1	29.6
1985–89	16.3	19.1	30.1

The European average investment is 20%. The UK does not invest as much as its major competitors. This means businesses have difficulty in competing in the domestic and foreign markets. If the UK economy is expanding, businesses soon run out of capacity and as it takes time to invest in new machines to meet the demand, businesses put up their prices and make high profits in the short term. Domestic demand will also be met by buying imports which gives foreign competitors access to the UK markets and allows them to become established. High-priced UK goods and import penetration make it more difficult for UK businesses to compete.

Reasons for the UK's poor investment record

- **Short-termism**. This refers to the requirement of institutions demanding a quick return on their investment. UK institutions are reluctant to invest over the longer term and UK businesses expect a return on their investment after three years. The average percentage of profit retained in a company in the UK is 32 per cent, whereas in the US it is 45 per cent, Japan 63 per cent and Germany 68 per cent. Countries such as Japan and Korea favour investment over the long term and are more geared to heavy investment. This will give them the competitive edge in future years.
- The range of alternative investments for the individual may encourage individuals to put their money in less risky investments such as saving schemes.

- Investment by individuals in housing rather than industry as a means of acquiring wealth.

Research and development

It is through research and development that new products and processes are developed. This enables countries to maintain their competitive edge. Japan and America spend over £300 per person on research and development, France and Germany spend over £200 per person while the UK spends less than £150 per person.

Inflation

Inflation is a consistent rise in the general level of prices over a period in time. In the UK the inflation rate is measured by the Retail Price Index (RPI). It has been the main economic objective of governments since 1979 to reduce inflation. The present Conservative government target is zero inflation. Low inflation is deemed to be important as a main criterion for being competitive by price. If inflation is higher in the UK than for her competitors UK business will have difficulty in competing against cheap imports and will have difficulty in selling abroad.

The inflation rates for the UK and her competitors are as follows:

Table 5.10

	USA	*Japan*	*Germany*	*UK*
1978–80	9.7	5.1	4.1	13.2
1981–83	6.6	3.2	5.0	8.4
1984–86	3.3	1.6	1.4	4.8
1987–89	3.7	1.2	1.4	5.7
1994	2.9	– 0.1	3.0	2.4

The UK has suffered from higher inflation than her competitors and it is only recently that the UK has been able to bring rates down to the level of her competitors.

Productivity

This is the amount of a product produced per unit of resources used, e.g. output per person. When a business improves its efficiency, productivity will rise, i.e. the business will be able to produce more with the same amount of inputs. Productivity increases through better management, more efficient equipment and better use of labour. During the 1980s UK industry downsized, i.e. reduced the amount of labour; for example in 1980, 6.8 million people were employed in manufacturing but this was reduced to 4.5 million by 1993. This reduction, and the increase in the flexibility of its workforce, has helped to reduce the productivity gap with the UK's competitors.

Share of world trade

World trade continues to increase, with the UK share of this trade in decline. It is not only the decline in the share of the trade which is a cause for concern but it is also worrying that this declining share is at the same time within an increasing market. The manufacturing sector of the economy is the wealth creating sector and in 1970 this sector was contributing 31.5 per cent of GDP. In 1977 this had declined to 29.5 per cent. During the next three years there was a rapid decline in manufacturing's share of GDP when it fell to 24.5 per cent. Since 1980 the manufacturing output as a share of GDP has been contributing a similar amount.

This fall in manufacturing output has had an impact on the UK's international trade. Until 1982 the UK had a surplus in its manufacturing trade but because of poor exporting performance and the UK's propensity to import manufactured goods, there has been a huge manufacturing trade deficit. In 1983 this deficit was £5 billion and by 1989 it had risen to £20 billion. In 1993 the deficit had been reduced to under £10 billion.

This in turn has dragged the current account on the balance of payments into deficit. The UK's share of world manufacturing exports has also altered over time:

1960: 16.3%, 1970: 10.6%, 1980: 9.6%, 1984: 7.8%, 1991: 8.3%

PC 5.3.1

DISCUSSION TOPICS

1 Are there any disadvantages to firms of competing on price?

2 How many different types of non-price competition can you think of?

3 If you were a breakfast cereal manufacturer, what competitive strategies would you use?

4 What investment should the government undertake in the UK at the moment?

5 What investment do you recommend your school or college should undertake?

6 What would be the benefits to the UK economy of government and business doing more research and development?

7 Why is inflation a disadvantage to firm's competitiveness?

PC 5.3.2

Business strategies to improve competitiveness

■ Organisational structure

Changes in organisational structure can take several forms:

- clarifying and defining jobs
- modifying organisational structure to fit the communication needs of the organisation
- decentralising the organisation to reduce the cost of coordination, increase the controllability of subunits, increase motivation and gain greater flexibility.

Many companies in the UK have been going through a period of slimming-down, or downsizing. This has involved making large numbers of the workforce redundant, which reduces the cost of the payroll and makes the profit position of the organisation look healthier very quickly. Some companies have called in business consultants who have taken the firm through a process called **re-engineering**; this is not concerned with engineering, but with taking a fresh look at what the business does and what it wants to achieve. Re-engineering programmes often result in a drastic reduction in the workforce, delayering of the hierarchy so that many managerial jobs disappear, and a new method of delivering the product or service to the customer. Sun Life Assurance Society has been through re-engineering and has managed to reduce the time an insurance policy takes to be processed from 46 days to 21 days. Teamwork and multi-skilling have been introduced, costs have been reduced and quality has improved. It is a very painful process for a business and its employees to go through and as yet has mainly been introduced in financial services in the UK.

Many companies are now de-diversifying, which means getting rid of some of their products or services and concentrating on the core business – the major product. This often involves selling off subsidiary companies, or closing them down. Recent trends in changing organisational structure have been to reduce and simplify the organisation in order to make it more competitive.

■ Human resources

PC 5.3.2

The people employed by a business are often the only source of competitive advantage – one restaurant may be much like another, one insurance policy much like another, but the service given to the customer when entering the restaurant may be so superior that the restaurant has an advantage over its competitors. Companies such as Asda Stores aim to have world class customer service and they train all their employees to give the best customer service possible. Training is the key to producing good service as well as good products.

Provision of training

Training is:

> **'Developing the necessary skills, knowledge and attitudes in the employees of the organisation.'**

Training is an investment in the employees which can be carried out in-house or externally. New recruits to a company need training in order to learn their new jobs and existing employees may need training for different or future requirements.

Training is a cost to the organisation and as such it is often cut back during hard times when it is needed most. The return on the investment in training is often difficult to see or long-term in nature, which can make it appear unnecessary. There are still many firms in the UK which do not have a training officer or a training department. This is unfortunate as an investment in training will increase the effectiveness of the organisation.

If the organisation invests money in training, it should expect to receive a return on that investment. It is important that the firm should identify the training needs, select appropriate training methods and monitor and evaluate the effects of training after it has taken place.

Identifying training needs

The following need to be decided:

- Organisational goals
- What needs to be done to achieve these goals?

- What should each employee be able to do to carry out their job?
- What gaps are there in the knowledge, skills or attitudes required by employees to carry out jobs?

The area for training is the last question; it identifies the training gap. There are indicators that there is a training gap such as low productivity, accidents, customer complaints. Another way of assessing the training gap is through the idea of competencies. The training or competency gap is identified by assessing whether the employee can perform all the tasks required to do one job. This has taken the training world by storm and is being adopted in education, vocational training and management training.

Competency-based training specifies tasks related to a job which the job holder should be able to perform. Once the employee is deemed to be competent in performing all the tasks associated with a job, he or she can be awarded a qualification. A National Vocational Qualification (NVQ) comes in various levels and is awarded by an 'awarding body' such as City & Guilds, RSA or BTEC. The Management Charter Initiative is a competency-based management qualification and is equivalent to NVQ level 3 (Supervisory Managers), level 4 (First Line Managers) and level 5 (Middle and Senior Managers).

Induction

New employees need to be familiarised with the workings of the organisation, safety matters, general conditions of employment and the work of the department in which they are employed. Many large firms have formal induction programmes which aim to integrate new employees into the organisation.

STEPS IN AN INDUCTION PROGRAMME

- History and management of the organisation
- Personnel policies and terms of employment
- Employee benefits and services
- Facilities of the organisation
- General nature of the work to be done
- Introduction to supervisor
- Rules and safety measures
- The relation of various jobs to the new job
- Details of the job
- Introduction to fellow workers
- Follow-up after several weeks.

Induction will have been successful if the new employee is confident in his or her situation.

Training for different kinds of employee

Shopfloor

Training can be carried out by a training instructor if there are large numbers of new recruits. If not, then the supervisor can be trained on how to instruct new starters.

Shopfloor or manual jobs are often specific to a particular organisation and therefore training is needed even for those who had the same job title in another establishment. These jobs seldom receive adequate training, resulting in a lower level of performance and less job satisfaction than if training had been in place.

Administrative

Computers and word processors are prevalent in office settings. Employees will usually enter the organisation with the required skills, training only being given when a new computerised system is installed. Often, the only training office workers receive is during the induction period.

Technical

Technicians and apprentices go through long periods of on-the-job training as well as part-time attendance at college to gain the relevant qualification.

Recessions have made the five-year apprenticeship scheme in companies more unusual and workers are becoming multi-skilled and able to do many jobs.

Youth training

The Youth Training Scheme (YTS) began in the 1980s as a one-year programme, and became two-year in 1986. Training and work experience was provided for school leavers on a large scale. In 1989 Youth Training was transferred to Training and Enterprise Councils (TECs) which are local bodies, with the intention of the training being appropriate to local needs.

Management style is also changing with the popularity of Japanese methods of management. Some UK managers are adopting a more hands-on approach, wearing similar clothing to the shopfloor workers, walking about on the shopfloor, and advocating the view that the entire workforce is a team, working towards one common goal. Some companies have gone over to one canteen for all, one car park for all, to emphasise the team spirit and make all employees feel valued and an essential part of the firm.

■ Marketing

PC 5.3.2

Companies are having to think globally about their marketing campaigns, researching what customers need in other countries and matching that up with their home market. They have to ensure that names, colours, logos and patterns do not mean something different in another country and that their product and its packaging is acceptable and attractive in a variety of cultures.

Companies are using their brand names to launch other products, *brand stretching*, such as Mars with their ice-cream bars and other products all bearing the Mars name. This use of brand names is a very useful business strategy for launching new products and ensuring that they are market leaders at an early stage. Often companies do not invest sufficiently in advertising and promotions to keep their brand names in the mind of the consumer, and supermarket 'own brands' are becoming increasingly perceived by consumers as quality products.

Scale of production

Companies can increase their scale of production if they have a larger market in which to sell. This will bring economies of scale – cost savings due to increasing size. They can make maximum use of their equipment and managers, buy supplies in bulk, obtain finance more easily and cheaply and the cost of advertising will be spread over a larger number of sales. Large firms targeting large markets will be able to produce their products at lower cost and therefore be more competitive. Smaller firms can target niche markets and take advantage of computer software and databases as part of their business strategy.

PC 5.3.2

Finance

Companies can obtain finance from banks and financial institutions and balance this with new issues of shares in the company. If companies use banks as their sole source of finance it may prove to be very expensive, especially if interest rates rise, as the company will have larger repayments each month. One of the better business strategies is to limit borrowings, as large loan repayments can cause cash flow problems.

Joint ventures are now becoming a popular way of reducing costs and risks. A joint venture is a collaboration between two or more organisations on an enterprise. IBM, America's largest computer company has over 40 joint ventures. One of them is with Siemens, a German microelectronics firm, and Toshiba, Japan's biggest computer company. They are all trying to develop a silicon circuit that will revolutionise consumer electronics. Ford Motors has a joint venture with Volkswagen in South America, a joint venture with Nissan in the United States, and actively collaborates with Mazda on a number of vehicle projects. Joint ventures are increasingly being called *strategic alliances*.

New technology

Companies reluctant to invest in new methods of production and new products will find themselves competed out of business in future, as new production methods enable cheaper, faster production with higher quality. More products are made right first time and there is less wastage and scrap produced. Savings are made on staff and the machinery is usually very reliable and enables modern designs to be manufactured.

New technology can act as an agent for change, the advent of one new invention or discovery can give many possibilities. Fibre optics gives the potential for all the world's telephone conversations to be channelled down a single light pipe. The information-carrying prospects for fibre optics are huge. Computer giant, IBM, is thinking of using these capacities to get rid of exchanges in networks. Just as when we use a radio receiver to pluck out any single piece of information from the airwaves, IBM's vision sees information users choosing information they want while ignoring the rest. Similar holographic communication techniques could also be used to help surgeons at one hospital receive advice from those at another. Virtual reality would become more real.

In parallel with the development of optical fibres has come the development of more efficient means of carrying information. Multiplexing is the best known. Extra information-carrying channels are squeezed into existing space either by assigning carrier frequencies, time slots, codes, or a combination of all three. Data compression is another alternative.

Personal computer software that claims to double disc capacities is an example. Another is the squeezing of full motion video recordings on to compact discs. The cost of high technology products and services on the information highway are falling all the time due to continual new developments and improvements. These are therefore bound to affect all businesses and consumers in a variety of ways.

PC 5.3.2

DISCUSSION TOPICS

1 How can a business change its organisational structure to improve competitiveness?

2 How does the customer service at McDonald's give them competitive advantage?

3 What training have you had in jobs you have had in the past, or hold at the present? Does this training help the firm's competitiveness against other firms?

4 How might the Japanese way of treating all workers as important members of a team help a firm improve competitiveness?

5 What information would you need if you were a confectionery manufacturer considering launching your best-selling chocolate bar in Spain and Italy?

6 What disadvantages might competitors experience when collaborating on joint ventures?

7 How can firms find out about new technological developments which might affect their business?

Government strategies

PC 5.3.3

The UK has a mixed economy, i.e. one with **public** and **private** sectors. The public sector involves local and central government providing goods and services for general consumption based on need and social well-being rather than an individual's ability to pay. For example, the government pays for the building of roads, hospitals and schools. Local government provides services such as refuse collection and libraries.

The government also has influence over the private sector by restricting business behaviour for example by:

- legislation regarding monopoly practices
- legislation relating to consumer protection
- legislation relating to labour and labour relations
- its taxation policy.

Government can also influence the operations of business by making markets operate more freely by reducing barriers for businesses and encouraging competitiveness.

The extent of direct government involvement in the production process has diminished since 1979. It has been the role of the government to adopt policies which enable firms in the UK to compete with the rest of the world.

PC
5.3.3
5.3.4

Government policies

■ Reducing the role of government in the economy

The governments since 1979 have adopted policies which have taken products and services out of the public sector. This process is known as **privatisation** and **deregulation** and can take different forms:

- the sale of assets, e.g. council houses
- the sale of state-owned corporations, e.g. British Gas, water companies and National Power
- the introduction of private contractors to provide services within public services, e.g. private contractors supplying cleaners for schools or caterers for hospitals
- allowing firms to compete with the public sector providers.

The government pursued privatisation because it felt that opening up these industries to market forces and the ensuing competition would lead to greater efficiency, greater growth and the industries would respond more quickly to the demands of the consumer. This in turn would lead to more choice, products of better quality and a lower price.

The industries would not be able to turn to government to pay for losses but instead would be accountable to their owners, the shareholders. Taking industries out of government control also meant that governments would not be able to use these industries for their political and economic objectives. Previous governments had used the industries as a means to reduce unemployment. For example, uneconomical coal mines were kept open because in some cases they were the only main industry in a local area. Their closure meant that there would be high unemployment in those areas.

The labour market is one area the government has had a major influence in trying to reduce distortions. For example, since 1979 the government has regarded pay as a matter for employers and employees to determine whereas previously the government had tried to set ceilings or guidelines for pay awards.

The government has abolished Wages Councils which had previously set wages and conditions of work, especially in those industries which were difficult to unionise such as catering. The government has also changed the restrictions on the working hours for women and children.

By introducing legislation which reformed industrial relations it is said that the government has produced a fairer balance between employers and employees with legislation giving more weight to the individual union member.

The support of nationalised industries by government meant that the market was distorted. For example, it was argued that nationalised industries paid high wages and would always be able to pay high wages because they were backed by the government. This not only distorted wage levels but other industries had difficulties in competing for labour because either they could not pay the same level of wages or if they did, they passed their labour costs onto the customer.

Removing government from production enabled markets to operate more freely and without too many distortions.

Controlling inflation

PC 5.3.3 5.3.4

The control of inflation has been a major government objective since 1979 and the present government has adopted a target range for inflation of 1–4 per cent as measured by the **Retail Price Index**.

Inflation causes problems to the economy and restricts the abilities of business to operate. Inflation causes uncertainty in the economy; individuals are unwilling to save because they see the purchasing power of their savings diminish. Individuals spend their income which fuels inflation. The lack of savings reduces funds for business to borrow. This, alongside high nominal rates of interest, discourages investment. Inflation may make home-produced products expensive and so encourage consumers to buy imports. The result is that firms have difficulties in competing in the domestic market and selling abroad. In the long term the economy will suffer from poor economic growth which means the standard of living in a country with high inflation will be generally lower than one with a low level of inflation.

The government will try to reduce inflation through high interest rates and reducing the money in circulation. Inflation is deemed to be a monetary phenomenon and the main policy the government has used is monetary policy. High interest rates discourage borrowing money and therefore spending. For example, if the government raised interest rates individuals who have a mortgage will find that they have to pay more. This means that unless they can obtain higher wages to pay for their extra costs, they will have to reduce their spending on other items.

Industry also faces higher cost through higher interest payments. They will have to reduce their costs or see their profits reduced. Many businesses reduced their costs by paying lower pay rises, cutting wages or reducing their workforce; some businesses were unable to manage and went into liquidation.

The government can also use **fiscal policy**, i.e. by increasing taxation and cutting its own spending which has a deflationary impact on the economy and reduces demand. The reduction in demand for goods and services can move the economy into recession. To compete for a declining demand, businesses will look at their prices to see if they can be reduced or they will look to improve on the value added to the product.

As inflation falls and the economy picks up businesses are usually more competitive and are in a stronger position than before the recession.

Fiscal policy

PC 5.3.3 5.3.4

Fiscal policy is the means by which a government can, through altering taxation and its own expenditure, influence aggregate or total demand in the economy. Taxes are paid by individuals and businesses. Individuals, sole traders and partnerships pay income tax on their earnings and profits and companies pay corporation tax on their profits.

By lowering income tax this not only increases the disposable income of employees but it also reduces the amount people in business have to pay in taxes on their profits. Therefore a reduction in these direct taxes should encourage people to start their own business or invest in business. This stimulates the economy because there are more goods and services available and more choice for the consumer.

The government has also changed the emphasis on taxation, by moving away from direct taxation to indirect taxation. By reducing income tax it is thought this will encourage people to work harder because they keep a higher proportion of their income.

The move to indirect taxation, such as VAT, taxes expenditure rather than effort and there is an element of choice for the tax payer.

Reducing the direct tax for individuals means they have more disposable income available for spending or saving. This extra demand itself increases demand through the **multiplier** effect: one person's expenditure is another person's income. Imagine a person has an extra £500 to spend and they buy a product. The person who receives that money may decide to save £50 and spend the remaining £450. The person who receives that £450 may in turn decide to save £45 and spend the rest. Someone else receives £405. The original £500 is multiplied through the economy and actually creates £2500 of expenditure.

The government itself can inject money into the economy by spending on goods and services. Therefore by altering its spending it can alter the level of demand in the economy. It can expand the economy by spending more than it usually does or it can reduce demand by spending less. The change in spending levels will impact on business.

Spending less on some services and allowing the private sector to provide as well, for example in education and health, should lead to more choice and lower costs for the consumer.

If the government's expenditure is greater than its revenue the government is forced to borrow. Government borrowing became a cause for concern because it was felt that it 'crowded out' the private sector: not only could the government be sure to get the funds it required because they are a safer bet than private industry, they could also pay a higher interest on the funds borrowed. The government reduced the ability of businesses to borrow and at the same time forced up the cost of borrowing, making it difficult for businesses who wanted to borrow to invest.

PC
5.3.3
5.3.4

■ Education and training

Governments have recognised the changing skills and abilities of the economy can be met by education and training. In education the changes which have taken place have been the introduction of the core curriculum, GCSEs and vocational courses in schools and colleges such as GNVQ. The education should be such which allows students more knowledge, skills and abilities enabling them to meet the needs of a rapidly changing world.

Training is seen as an investment for the future. Successive governments have tried to encourage training. In 1988 the government introduced the **Employment Training Programme** (ET). This was seen as the way forward to *'train the workers without jobs for the jobs without workers'*. This training was reserved for those people who had been out of work for six months or more. One of the problems with this scheme was that it was only for six months and was said to be too short. Of those people who had been trained, only one in three got a job or got a qualification.

Youth Training is targeted at 16-year-olds who are leaving school. It is a two-year programme and its aim is to place youngsters in a work environment where they will gain experience and skills for future employment.

NVQs were introduced to give accreditation and recognition to those people who had acquired skills in the workplace.

Apprenticeships were seen as the way in which people were trained. Many organisations would take on youngsters from school for training which would last for five or seven years. After 1945 the agreed schemes were administered by joint employer and union bodies. However, partly because of changes in funding, the desire to cut costs, and the decline in the manufacturing sector, apprenticeships declined; for example, in 1979 there were 367,000 apprentices but this figure had declined to 216,000 by 1994.

There is now an initiative referred to as **Modern Apprenticeships** which is employer-led and which endeavours to improve the training in craft, technical and supervisory skills. The training will lead to NVQ Level 3 or above. Each sector of industry is represented by its **Industry Training Organisation** which will set the standards for each scheme. There will be a written agreement between the employer and young person and the agreement will be underwritten by the local **TEC** (Training and Enterprise Council).

Training and Enterprise Councils (TECs)

These organisations operate the national training programme and each council is based upon areas with a working population of around 250,000. In 1990 each TEC had a budget of £20 million per year. Besides offering training schemes the TECs also operate business enterprise schemes. The TECs are also allowed to supplement their budget by selling their services to local employers who require training schemes.

■ International dimensions

PC
5.3.3
5.3.4

The Maastricht Treaty negotiated in 1991 and ratified in 1993 was for the European Union to move closer towards economic and monetary union. There are three stages to economic and monetary union.

Stage 1

The single market was to be completed by 1 January 1993 to allow the free movement of goods, labour and capital. All restrictions were to be removed by this date and most of the targets set by the Single European Act (1986) have been achieved.

Stage 2

By January 1994 Members of the European Union were to fix their exchange rates within narrow bands and not seek realignment.

The UK had had a floating exchange rate whose rate was determined by market forces. This had been seen as an effective way to operate sterling value against other currencies because it was felt that it was better to allow the currency find its own value rather than have the government try to gauge the rate of exchange and then adopt policies which would keep the value at that rate. Concentrating on the exchange rate would move the focus away from other government objectives. Trying to maintain the value would also use up the country's reserves. A floating exchange rate would also be able to accommodate any supply shocks to the economy. For example, in 1979 there had been increases in the price of crude oil which the exchange rate adjusted to and then in the 1980s with the advent of North Sea oil the pound sterling appreciated in value. The government did not have to introduce measures to hold the value. It only intervened to modify any changes.

However, during the late 1980s it was felt that volatile exchange rates caused uncertainty in international trade and was therefore undesirable. From 1987 the pound sterling shadowed the German deutschmark at around £1–DM3.00. On Monday 8th October the UK joined the **Exchange Rate Mechanism** (ERM) at a rate of £1–Dm2.95.

In 1992 speculators mounted attacks on ERM currencies and on 'Black Wednesday' (16th September 1992) the UK's membership was suspended and her currency is again floating.

Stage 3

The purpose of this stage is to determine the timing of the move towards the 'Single Currency'. The final deadline is for 1999. Britain has opted out from stage three until a government commands a majority in parliament in favour of a single currency. For the single currency to be successful there needs to be a convergence of economies in terms of inflation rates, budget deficits, public debt and interest rates.

The UK believes that it is surrendering too much of its economic policy to Europe. However, it is presumed that countries including France, Germany, Belgium, Netherlands, Luxembourg, Denmark and Ireland will join a single currency but not until the new millennium.

The UK international trade is mainly with the rest of Europe where over 60 per cent of her trade is focused, but North America is still a major trading partner. It is the emerging nations in the Far East, especially those on the Pacific Rim including countries such as Japan, Korea, Taiwan, and Malaysia, which pose the greatest threat to the UK. China is the sleeping giant whose economy is taking on more market features and is growing at a fast pace which offers both an opportunity and a threat to the UK.

To encourage free trade between nations by removing barriers such as tariffs and quotas, GATT (the General Agreement on Tariffs and Trade) has been able to get countries to agree on less restrictive measures. The negotiations, referred to as 'Rounds', take many years. The last one started in Uruguay in 1986 and was completed in 1990 and the main agreements included an overall cut in tariffs by one third and a reduction in farm subsidies.

PC
5.3.3
5.3.4

DISCUSSION TOPICS

1 Why should the government play any part in the economy?

2 How will privatisation and deregulation help the private sector?

3 Why should the government be concerned about distortion in markets?

4 Why should the government be concerned about inflation?

5 In what circumstances might inflation be a good thing?

6 Why does the government use interest rates as a tool to tackle inflation?

7 Why might the government have difficulty in controlling the money supply?

8 Why is it argued that lower income tax will make people work harder? Is this true?

9 What difficulties face a government using fiscal policy to tackle inflation?

10 What skills will students studying for their GNVQ use in their place of work?

11 Why do government training schemes come in for criticism?

12 What advantages are there for businesses in the Single European Market?

13 How does the consumer gain from international trade?

CASE STUDY 1

Images change as joblessness affects all social classes

John Arlidge considers whether there are similarities between the 1930s and present day unemployment

The images have changed. Couples slumped in front of videos on modern estates have replaced cloth-capped men hanging around slum terraces. Queues to the soup kitchens have shortened. With joblessness among men at a post-war high, however, are there similarities between the 1990s and the Depression of the 1930s?

Unemployment was much worse between the wars. In August 1932, joblessness reached 23 per cent among the insured population – those eligible for the benefits of the day. This was about 16 per cent of the total workforce, compared with 10.6 per cent last month.

The jobless were more regionally concentrated. The export-dependent industries hard hit in the slump – shipbuilding, cotton textiles, coal – were located mainly in the north of England, Scotland and Wales, which observers called 'outer Britain'. As sales collapsed, unemployment reached 36 per cent in Wales and 28 per cent in Scotland and the North-east.

Although unemployment rose to 13.5 per cent in London and the South-east in 1932 – today it is about 10.5 per cent – 'inner Britain' saw job growth between the wars. About 3.5 million jobs were created between 1921 and 1938 south of an imaginary line between Coventry and Ipswich.

Dudley Baines, senior lecturer in economic history at the London School of Economics, said: 'There was higher regional industrial specialisation than now. Northern industries lost markets and had nothing to fall back on. But in the South there were vacancies. Developments like the Hoover and Gillette factories in west London, all came in the 1930s.'

'Blue-collar' workers comprised the overwhelming majority of the Thirties' jobless while 'white-collar' workers, who formed a much smaller part of the workforce, were hardly affected. Today the spread is much wider. Half of the 1.5 million jobs lost since the summer of 1990 have been in manufacturing industry. The service sector – financial services, retailing, public service – accounted for about half of the remaining 750,000.

John Philpott, director of the Employment Policy Institute, an independent think-tank, said: 'Today, unemployment cannot be thought of as affecting just one sort of industry or worker. Joblessness extends across the social and occupational spectrum.'

Calculating the number of women who are unemployed is difficult. Mr Baines estimates there are 6 million more married women looking for work today than in the Thirties when about 10 per cent of married women worked. 'Single women worked between the wars but married women were by and large not part of the labour market,' he said.

'It is difficult to know whether married women would have worked had there been jobs. If you accept that most of them would not, then female unemployment in the thirties was far lower than today.'

Women today form half of the 'hidden' unemployed – the estimated 1 million people who are not eligible for benefits, or do not claim them. Although changes in the methods used to measure joblessness make it difficult to make direct comparisons, it is likely that the number of hidden jobless was lower in the Thirties than now.

Using 1931 census data, Charles Feinstein, professor of economic history at All Souls College, Oxford, estimates that unemployment was 'very considerably' less among the uninsured in domestic service, farming, the post office and railways than among the insured.

With high personal indebtedness, life might seem hard now but unemployment was a more devastating experience 60 years ago.

Unemployment benefit for a single man was 17 shillings (85p), when social observers calculated the required minimum income was more than 22 shillings (£1.10), plus rent. Mr Baines estimates that the 1930s benefit for a family of four, in today's money, was £30 per week, compared with £96 now, plus housing benefit of, say, £22.

Only 4 per cent of the population had private cars. The television, now in 90 per cent of homes, was not available, and few people took holidays abroad.

Some who lived through the Depression say today's more divided communities, coupled with the higher standards of living enjoyed by those in work have created a 'crisis of expectations' among the jobless greater than that 60 years ago.

Mr Baines disagrees. 'It is extremely easy to idealise the past. The idea of chumminess of working class society in adversity is a load of rubbish. When times are hard they are hard. If you are hungry, you are hungry.

CASE STUDY DISCUSSION QUESTIONS

'Images change as joblessness affects all social classes.'

1 How has the image of the unemployed changed?

2 Why was unemployment much worse during the inter-war period?

3 Why is it difficult to calculate the numbers of unemployed?

4 In money terms are the unemployed today better off than the unemployed in the 1930s?

CASE STUDY 2

Siemens Works, Congleton

The business

Siemens Works, Congleton is in Cheshire. Four hundred people are employed at the site. The site is split into two sections. Two-thirds of the workforce are employed in electronics, making a range of drives used in the automation industry, the other one-third make a range of switchgear. Siemens have been in Congleton since 1971. Their parent company is Siemens AG of Germany. A Total Quality programme was introduced two years ago aimed at continuous improvement of all work processes.

In 1992 the Congleton Works increased their turnover by 40 per cent and made a profit for the first time ever. Their German parent company had been supporting them until that time.

Features of workforce performance

Wages

There are three different wage structures:

1 Hourly paid

2 Staff

3 Management

Every July hourly paid people are involved in a collective bargaining process. The union is the Amalgamated Engineering and Electrician's Union (AEEU). All other staff are on individual contracts and they are assessed individually by their managers each October. Each manager has a budget and makes pay awards within that budget.

Managers receive a bonus related to earnings (Results Related Earnings). Everyone is paid monthly into their bank account.

Benefits and conditions of work

1 **Pension scheme:** This is contributed to by employees. 'It is one of the top ten occupational pension schemes in the country', says Personnel Manager, David Kruze.

2 **Subsidised private health care**

3 **Subsidised restaurant**

4 **Holidays:** 26 days per year, which rises to 30 days with length of service.

5 **Sickness scheme:** Employees can get up to 30 weeks on full pay, depending on length of service.

The working week is 37 hours for shopfloor workers and 36½ hours for all other employees.

Shopfloor:
8 am–4.30 pm Monday–Thursday
8 am–1 pm Friday
Office:
8.30–4.30 Monday–Friday

Health and safety record

Siemens plc have the following objectives for health and safety:

- 'The elimination of all unsafe practices and conditions of work both at our own premises and while working at client's installations.'
- 'The maintenance of high standards for health, safety and the environment at our own premises and client installations.'
- 'The development of controls to ensure safe working systems are established for all E & A (Energy and Automation) activities, with particular emphasis on off-site working.'
- 'The provision of appropriate training and information on matters of health and safety for each employee/contractor commensurate with their work activities.'
- 'The promotion of co-operation by consultation with employee representatives on health, safety and environment issues.'
- 'The development of promotional campaigns to stimulate and encourage health, safety and environmental awareness throughout E & A.'

There is a Health and Safety Manager and an Occupational Health Nurse.

David Kruze: 'The company has an excellent health and safety record. It's due to the type of work we do, it's fairly light engineering. As a major employer we have to make sure that we adhere to regulations and introduce procedures in line with the latest legislation.'

Siemens plc Energy and Automation produce a booklet on Health & Safety Policy. This states that the Health & Safety Manager:

> '...has a responsibility to the Managing Director for policy, co-ordination and audit concerning health, safety and the environment. He also advises General Managers, Departmental Managers and E & A employees/contractors on matters relating to health, safety and the protection of the environment.'

There is a Health and Safety Committee which looks at all the processes in the company and makes sure that potential problem areas are being addressed. Members of the Committee tour round the site every two months and identify problems. They then attempt to resolve those problems during committee meetings.

David Kruze: 'Health and Safety is the individual responsibility of all the managers for their area.'

Training

There is a company Personnel Development Training and Development Policy. It reads as follows:

'**Policy Statement**

1.1 The aim of Training and Development is to facilitate change within the organisation and individuals, with a view to:
    1.1.1 improving performance/productivity per head
    1.1.2 developing organisational capability
1.2 In our Corporate Mission statement, we state: "The creativity and commitment of our employees are the foundations of our success."

Management fully endorses the role of training and development as a crucial determinant of our organisational growth and profitability. Consequently, this policy document exists to identify the ways in which cost effective training and development activities will be implemented throughout Siemens plc.'

The Training and Development Policy also states that training will be by different methods:

In-house courses and workshops
External/Open Training Courses
Distance/Open Learning including Computer Based Training
Secondment/Job Rotation
Assessment/Development Centres
Performance Coaching
Mentoring

The present training consists of:

Off-site at local colleges
For example

HNC in Engineering course
HNC in Business Studies course

Open University
Siemens pay for the first 50 per cent of course fees on commencement of the course and the remaining 50 per cent on successful completion.

On-site
Corporate training and development department

- All managers do a mandatory course 'Management by Co-operation'.
- Managers immediately below the senior management team go through a modular training scheme which includes:
  1 Introduction to quality
  2 The problem solving discipline
  3 Team-work
  4 Interpersonal skills
- Hourly paid employees have all received a one-day training session on the aims and philosophy behind Total Quality.

David Kruze: 'We make sure that all the rest of our training fits in with Total Quality.'

The training course for introducing Total Quality was devised by management consultants for Siemens. Siemens Congleton Senior Management deliver the courses themselves.

Training needs are identified during the performance appraisal interview. This information is used by David Kruze to analyse training needs. *David Kruze*: 'From there we decide how we're going to address those needs over the coming year.'

Every employee on the site has been involved with training for Total Quality.

Equal opportunities

The company has an Equal Opportunity Policy. This is given to all staff in the form of a booklet and staff sign a form to say that they have received it. One of the General Statements of Policy in the booklet is:

> 'The company affirms its commitment to the development of positive policies to promote equal opportunity in employment regardless of a person's colour, race, nationality, ethnic or national origins, sex or marital status. This principle will apply in respect of all conditions of work including: pay, hours of work, holiday entitlement, overtime and shiftwork, work allocation, sick pay, recruitment, selection, training, promotion or re-deployment.'

The company states that it is an Equal Opportunities Employer.

Specialisation

David Kruze: 'We believe in multi-skilling and job rotation. This enables us to have total flexibility on the shop-floor to increase worker motivation. We try to do job rotation even on the more technical jobs.'

Employees are trained in the Company's training school for multi-skilling and flexibility. It is written into employment contracts that new employees agree to undergo training to become multi-skilled.

Motivation

There is a Suggestion Scheme to encourage employees to put forward ideas for improvements in the production process.

David Kruze: 'The Total Quality programme is aimed at motivating every employee through empowerment. People are actively encouraged to come up with ideas.'

Every employee has a Personal Action Plan – they have a chart on the wall near their workplace and they monitor their own progress. This is not checked upon by supervisors or management, it is purely the responsibility of each employee to take charge of their own planning.

Redundancy

No one has been made redundant since early 1992. Until recently Siemens has been unaffected by the recession in Britain. The German recession started in 1993, much later than in the UK, and Siemens' sales are affected by the German experience.

Siemens have a redundancy policy which states:

'Redundancy, as defined by Statute arises if:

(1) The employer has ceased, or intends to cease, to carry on the business for the purpose for which the employee was employed, or
(2) The employer has ceased, or intends to cease, to carry on that business in the place where the employee was so employed, or
(3) The requirements of that business for employees to carry out work of a particular kind, or for employees to carry out work of a particular kind in the place where he/she was so employed, have ceased or diminished or are expected to diminish, or
(4) Employees have been laid off, or kept on short time for either:
   (a) four or more consecutive weeks, or
   (b) six or more consecutive weeks within a period of thirteen weeks.
   Under (4), employees may resign and claim redundancy, provided they follow the appropriate statutory procedure.'

Selection criteria for choosing those to be made redundant is based on a points system. Points are awarded for the following:

1 Skills

2 Performance/flexibility

3 Discipline

4 Attendance

5 Timekeeping

6 Service

Weightings are designed to ensure that the best workers are kept on. 50–40 points can be awarded for 'can competently do all / vast majority of jobs', whereas one point is given for each year of service up to 30 points.

Data sources

Siemens is a member of the confederation of British Industry (CBI). David Kruze uses IDS Studies (Income Data Surveys) and liaises with local employers for information on wage rates. Information is also gained from local and national newspapers on going rates for certain professions.

David Kruze is a member of the Institute of Personnel Management and receives information from them. The company receive information from the Health and Safety Executive, Equal Opportunities Commission and they buy into various companies that offer salary surveys.

CASE STUDY 3

Halifax Building Society

The business

The Halifax is the world's largest building society. It was formed as a result of the merger of Halifax Permanent Building Society and Halifax Equitable Building Society in 1927.

There are over 700 branches in the UK and a network of almost 2000 agencies which provide a counter service. They have recently opened a branch in Spain.

Forty people are employed at their Crewe office, 10 of whom are part-time. There are six managers – the Branch Manager John Richardson and 5 deputies with functional titles such as 'Sales Manager'.

Features of workforce performance

Wages

There are 12 grades within the Halifax Building society:

1–5 Managers – Branch / Service Centre / Area, depending upon the size of the operation

6–7 Assistant Manager Level / Small Sales Outlet Manager Level / Function Manager in Service Centre

8–9 Supervisor of larger teams / Local Branch Manager level

10 First Line Supervisor / Interviewer

11 Complex Clerical / Counsellor

12 Routine Clerical / Cashier

All staff are salaried and are covered by this 12-point grading system. The pay system is performance related. All staff are assessed in an annual appraisal against targets agreed at the beginning of the year with their line manager. Pay rises are agreed 3-6 months after the

appraisal interview. If someone is assessed as being effective in their work at grade 3 and their pay is below the mid point for that grade, they receive a higher pay rise than someone who had the same assessment and whose salary was above the mid point of grade 3.

The performance related pay rises are agreed between the Halifax Building Society and the Staff Association of the Society.

There is also a profit sharing scheme which is based on the end of year results of the Society. This scheme is registered with the Government PRP office and can, up to a certain limit, be paid free of tax.

Benefits and conditions of work

1 **Pension scheme:** Occupational pension scheme which includes life assurance arrangements.

2 **Concessionary mortgage scheme:** Available when employees have been with the Society for one year.

3 **Holidays:** 22 days per annum, rising to 30 depending on level of service and grade.

4 **BUPA membership:** For management grades and those with long service.

The working week is 9 am–5.15 pm Monday–Friday and in addition branches are open on Saturdays.

The 10 part-time staff have been mainly recruited for counter service on busy days. Many of the part-time staff were full-time and have returned to work after having families.

John Richardson: 'We're delighted to accommodate them as they're already trained and know the environment.'

Staff turnover is very low: Absenteeism also is not a cause for concern. *John Richardson*: 'If someone is absent regularly, we counsel them about it and find out what the problems are. If they need further help, we can point them in the right direction.'

Health and safety record

The Society is committed to the health, safety and welfare of staff and other people.

Safety policies, guidance and instructions assist Managers in fulfilling their statutory responsibilities.

Managers carry out a quarterly inspection of their premises, accompanied by Staff Association representatives. They look for possible hazards and evaluate the risks to staff and then ensure any necessary remedial action is taken.

Managers also carry out risk assessments relating to display screen equipment and train staff in correct posture and other risk reduction measures.

Training and development

John Richardson: 'The Halifax Building Society is dedicated to training and development. Working for the Halifax is a career and someone who wants to stay with us can be developed towards a management role. We have recruited graduates and managers from other companies, but most of our managers are developed within the Society.'

The Society has a large in-house training centre in Halifax developing and delivering its own training courses. The Society divides its branch network into eight regions and there is a training office in each region. There is also a Field Trainer who is responsible for workplace training in each area. Each branch office has a Training Co-ordinator who is usually a member of the management team and is responsible for induction training and the co-ordination of the monthly training plan in the branch.

John Richardson: 'Part of our mission statement emphasises development of people, the whole operation is dedicated to it. We are selling something quite intangible. The service staff give to customers is the be all and end all of our existence. You can get a mortgage anywhere on the High Street, although not as quickly and efficiently as we can give you one.'

Promotion depends on ability and potential. People selected for promotion or 'accelerated development' (achieving promotion more quickly than is normal) may attend assessment centres. Here they take part in a range of tests such as group exercises, individual presentations, in-tray exercises, numerical and analytical reasoning tests. These assessment centres provide the staff member and the Society with information on their skills and abilities.

Staff are encouraged to take the Chartered Institute of Bankers' examinations, either at local colleges or through a correspondence course. *John Richardson*: 'People can plan their own development. We are looking for people who are self-motivated to develop.'

Managers can also study for the Diploma in Management Studies or an MBA (a Masters degree in Business Administration).

Equal opportunities

There is a statement about the Halifax being an Equal Opportunities employer in the Staff Manual. *John Richardson*: 'We are very dedicated to equal opportunities and getting more women into senior management.' John's principal assistant is a woman and there are three female supervisors and one male in the branch.

A growing number of branches are managed by women. *John Richardson*: 'Already women are running the largest branches'.

Staff are given career breaks for bringing up families. They are encouraged to return for short periods during the break. This updates them with current practice. *John Richardson*: 'The vast majority of women return after having children. We are a difficult employer to leave. We have good working conditions.'

The Halifax's North West region has won awards for their employment opportunities for disabled people. The Crewe branch employs a deaf person.

Productivity

Managers have daily review meetings for around 10 minutes at the end of each day to discuss progress of work flows in each job.

There are weekly management meetings to look at the weekly figures. These look at throughput, backlogs, work flows and anything outstanding. They focus attention on exceptions. Backlogs of mortgage applications would be a major concern and would be given urgent attention.

John Richardson: 'I know the staff who are doing well because I see them through the week. I spend very little time in my room. We try and balance the jobs out, to give everyone a fair day's work. Staff will say that they're not busy and need moving onto something else. If that is the case, I rotate their roles. Some people have lots of experience such as Sales Interviewers because they have to have done other jobs in the office before they can attain that position. Their roles are flexible.'

Specialisation

John Richardson: 'Most of the people we recruit are selected for their ability to learn and adapt. Not everyone is trained to do every job, but people are trained sufficiently so that we have good cover for absences. People are specialists in the sense that they work on an area for a period of time and gain expertise.

The Society tries to design jobs so that employees can see an end result of their work to attain a feeling of job satisfaction.

The Society also attempts to empower people by giving them decision-making authority. *John Richardson*: 'There are certain key jobs I look at – I talk to the mortgage applications team, the arrears team, the sales team, and give them recognition for their work.' Employees' achievements are recorded on charts which are displayed on the office walls. There are communication meetings every week. *John Richardson*: 'If something has gone well we'll make sure the team know about it and praise those involved.'

Redundancy

There is a Security of Employment Agreement between the Society and the Staff Association which has been in force for many years. *John Richardson*: 'We've never made anyone redundant to date. We've kept tight control of numbers we employ during boom years. We run a tight, efficient ship.'

Social activity

Staff are encouraged to get involved in social events. The branch has a Sports and Social Club and around three-quarters of the staff are members. The Society gives the Club financial support.

John Richardson: 'They tend to do things as a group, they go out together. Today they have organised fund raising for Children in Need. They decided what they wanted to do and did it, it's their idea.'

DISCUSSION QUESTIONS

Case studies: Siemens Works, Congleton and Halifax Building Society

1 Compare the Training and Equal Opportunity Policies of the two businesses.

2 What difficulties are there when evaluating the productivity of firms in manufacturing and service industries?

3 What employee benefits do the two firms provide? What other benefits could they include for their employees?

ASSIGNMENT

You are required to compile a study of two business sectors (e.g. travel sector and textiles sector) using a data set for the UK and the EC. The study will investigate differences in employment generally and within the specific business sectors.

Research

Use a variety of sources (some suggested sources are listed at the end of this chapter). For example, the *Employment Gazette*, November 1993 shows:

8.1 TOURISM

Employment in tourism-related industries in Great Britain

Employees in employment (000s)

	Restaurants, cafes, etc.	*Public houses and bars*	*Night clubs and licensed clubs*	*Hotels*	*Libraries museums art galleries and sports*	*All*
1991						
March	291.2	322.6	142.7	286	358.9	1401.3
September	287.7	338.6	141	313.1	402.4	1482.8
1992						
March	283.4	315.3	138.7	270.9	382.5	1390.6
September	298.1	329.1	137.9	304.9	399.8	1469.8

CSO provides an abstract of statistics which shows all aspects of the UK economy, e.g. industries, output, employment.

Eurostat provides information on European countries.

You should show that you know and understand:

a general trends in UK and EU employment

b trends in employment within different business sectors

c economic relationships which influence employment trends

CASE STUDY 4

Energy policy in relation to coalmining and demand for fuel

The UK has always had a strong coal industry as this was once the major source of power. It fuelled the ships that carried British goods to her trading countries and coal was a major export. Factories needed coal for their power plants. Every town in Britain had its own gas supply as gas was extracted from coal. Trains, the major means of transport until the 1960s, were driven by steam locomotives using coal as their fuel. People used coal fires in their homes as a means of heating. Electricity was generated by coal.

However, the demand for coal has gradually fallen away. UK export markets were lost to other countries, especially during the Second World War as the country concentrated on winning the war. In other situations UK coal became too expensive. During the 1950s and '60s there were changes in the types of fuel used for transport, ships and trains. People travelled less by train because as they became better off, they bought cars. Owning a car gave people the freedom and flexibility that a train could not give them. The flexibility of the road systems and the low running costs of lorries moved freight off the railways.

Oil became a major competitor of coal when cheap oil was imported from the Middle East, and in the 1970s oil from the UK's own oilfields in the North Sea came on stream. Electrical power stations started to convert to oil as a fuel to generate electricity. The use of coal for burning in homes from the 1950s was restricted by the Clean Air Acts. This legislation was introduced after people had died during winters from the effects of smog, a potentially lethal concoction of fog and smoke from coal. Gas companies looked for a less dangerous and cleaner gas. Originally, liquified natural gas was imported from North Africa, but again the UK was discovered to have large reserves of its own natural gas. Houses were converted to use natural gas, and because gas was cheaper than coal more people used it for their heating.

Table 5.11 **Coal output in million tonnes**

	1947	*1950*	*1960*	*1970*	*1980*	*1990*	*1992*
Deep mines	187.5	205.6	186.8	135.5	110.3	72.3	61.8
Opencast	10.4	12.4	7.7	8.1	15.3	17.0	15.0
Licensed	2.1	1.5	2.3	2.2	1.1	2.3	4.0
Total	200.0	219.6	196.7	144.7	126.6	91.6	80.8

As the demand for coal fell, the coal industry had to look at ways in which it could compete in the energy market. Uneconomical mines were closed down and the miners were either made redundant or they were encouraged to work in another coalfield. The coal industry also opened 'Super Pits', those which could use more efficient machines. Technology increased the productivity of each miner and the unit cost of coal fell. However, another consequence of introducing machines was the need for fewer miners. The total number of miners has fallen in the last 25 years and especially during the last 10 years.

While coal was important, miners could expect to negotiate high wages. As coal lost importance, so miners' wages fell behind those of other workers. However, in 1973 the price of oil quadrupled and as a consequence energy derived from that source became expensive. Coal again was seen as the important fuel for generating electricity. It was recognised to be unwise to depend on one fuel as the source of power. The miners were able to demand a substantial pay increase in 1974.

Coal as an energy source not only had competition from other fossil fuels but the government, until the mid 1980s, saw nuclear energy as the natural successor to finite fuels and embarked on a policy to produce electricity by nuclear power. The research and development costs were subsidised by governments as were the heavy costs of building the power-stations. The government's aim to generate a substantial amount of electricity by nuclear power was called into question by nuclear incidents in other countries. One occurred in America at a nuclear plant on Five Mile Island and during the 1980s a serious incident occurred at Chernobyl in Russia. The safety of nuclear power plant was called into question. At the same time the nuclear energy industry was struggling with the problem of waste disposal.

This should have been an opportunity for coal. However, during the 1980s the government decided to speed up its closure of uneconomical mines, cutting the cost of subsidies to coal to reduce government spending and taxation. The result was a year-long miners' strike which lasted until 1985. The strike was not about increased wages but saving miners' jobs. Not all miners agreed with the National Union of Mineworkers' approach to the strike and miners in the Nottingham coalfield broke away from the NUM to form another union called the Democratic Union of Mineworkers. The split in the miners' ranks reduced its power.

Privatisation of the electrical companies meant that government control was relinquished and the electricity companies no longer had to buy from British Coal but could seek supplies from the cheapest source e.g. Australia and Poland. The demand for British coal gradually fell as it could not compete with the cheaper, cleaner coal from abroad. Mines were forced to close. At the same time mines were closed the industry was prepared for privatisation.

By December 1993 there were 22 deep-mine collieries employing 15,000 workers earning an average £350 per week.

Energy policy

The President of the Board of Trade is responsible for energy matters in the UK.

The UK's energy policy is to ensure the secure, adequate and economic provision of energy to meet Britain's requirements. The government encourages the exploitation of Britain's energy resources. It wants all economic forms of energy to be produced, supplied and used as efficiently as possible without endangering the environment. The government sees the profitable development of the UK's oil, gas, coal and nuclear energy as important to the country's economic future.

European Energy Charter

In 1991 Britain signed the European Energy Charter

The main objectives are:

- An open competitive market for trade in energy, including a framework for investment promotion and protection.
- Co-operation in the energy field through the co-ordination of energy policies.
- Promotion of energy efficiency and environmental protection

Data

Table 5.12 **Inland energy consumption (in terms of primary sources) million tonnes oil equivalent**

	1981	*1986*	*1989*	*1990*	*1993*
Oil	65.2	66.2	69.5	71.3	71.1
Coal	69.6	66.8	63.6	63.8	63.3
Natural gas	42.2	49.2	47.4	49.0	52.8
HEP	1.4	1.4	1.4	1.6	1.4
Net imports of electricity	–	3.1	3.0	2.9	3.9
Total	186.6	199.2	200.2	202.7	207.7

Table 5.13 The coal industry

	1947	1950	1960	1970	1980	1990	1993
Output (million tonnes)							
Mines	187.5	205.6	186.8	135.5	110.3	72.3	61.8
Opencast	10.4	12.4	7.7	8.1	15.3	17.0	15.00
Licensed	2.1	1.5	2.2	1.1	1.1	2.3	4.0
Total	200.0	219.6	196.7	144.7	126.6	91.6	80.8
Number of pits							
At year end	958	901	698	292	211	65	50
Output							
Per man year (tonnes)	267	298	310	471	479	1,181	1,611
Per manshift (tonnes)							
Production					9.09	22.62	30.39
All underground			1.81	2.92	10.92	29.24	43.39
Employees (000s)							
Colliery manpower	718.4	688.6	588.5	286	230.7	57.3	31.7
Other			42.6	70.3	62.2	17.0	12.5
Accidents							
No. of fatalities	–	476	316	92	39	11	3
Disputes							
Lost tonnage (millions)	1.7	1.0	1.6	3.1	1.5	0.2	0.1

Accidents	1992/3
Fatal	3
Major	326
Others (over 3 days absence)	1,711
Total	2,040
Number of operating pits end of March year 1992/93	
Scottish	1
North-East	5
Selby	8
South Yorkshire	12
Nottinghamshire	12
Midland/Wales	12
Total	50

ASSIGNMENT

Using the case study on energy policy, or a case study of your own, explain the external influences on business employment practice using economic relationships.

Other business employment practice cases may include:

- food subsidies in relation to farming and the single market for food, labour supply and labour reducing technology
- the introduction of compulsory competitive tendering or deregulation to local authority services and the effect on the demand and supply of labour
- Sunday trading and late shopping trends in retailing and the effect on the demand for labour

You should demonstrate that you know and understand:

a How business actions concerning employment are influenced by external forces

b Current examples of employment practice

c Actions taken by business, using economic relationships in terms of demand for the product and the demand for and supply of labour

CASE STUDY 5

The UK car industry

The British car industry at one time was a major force in the world market. However, during the 1960s and '70s, the car industry was troubled by producing cars of poor quality, the firms tended to be product-led rather than customer-orientated, there was lack of investment, overmanning and poor industrial relations. Car firms merged to form larger businesses to take on foreign competitors. However, the mergers tended to be unsuccessful. Some Biritsh firms were taken over by foreign companies and eventually the sole remaining British car manufacturer, British Leyland, was taken into public ownership. Later this company was sold to British Aerospace and sold cars under the Rover badge. In January 1994 British Aerospace sold the Rover company to the German car manufacturer BMW.

During the 1980s and early '90s, the car industry went through radical changes. Japan invested heavily in Britain, opening car factories in Washington, Derby and Swindon. They introduced Japanese methods of production, and their British competitors soon followed these working practices. Production is leaner than previous operations – fewer people are employed, and productivity is higher. New methods included just-in-time, zero buffer stocks and quality built into the production process. There is a delegation of responsibility. For example, workers are responsible for the quality of parts produced. In other aspects of quality control, workers join quality circles to help each other to solve problems relating to quality. The attitude now is 'getting it right first time' rather than 'that will do'. Quality is not sufficient, the processes must be 'continuously improved'.

In Japanese-owned companies, people are encouraged to identify with the company. Although there is no guaranteed job for life, as in Japan, there is greater job security. Recently Nissan in Britain were suffering from a drop in world demand for cars. No worker has been threatened with compulsory redundancy and the firm is not asking for voluntary redundancy. However, the workforce has recognised that there needs to be a reduction in their numbers. The companies believe job security helps to motivate the workers.

Team spirit and single status are an important part of Japanese working practices. Managers and workers share a common goal rather than work against each other in an 'us and them' situation. Everyone is referred to as an associate. Everyone wears the same uniform, eats in the same canteen and there are no reserved parking spaces for managers. There is no grading between workers, but each worker is a member of an identifiable team and all workers are expected to be multi-skilled and able to move between jobs. Managers and everyone else, including office workers, are expected to work on the production line if the need arises. Managers do not have offices and often have experience on the shop-floor so that they are technically competent and are available if the workers need to contact them.

To help reduce internal demarcation disputes and to help negotiations on wages and working conditions, car firms are moving to a reduction in the number of unions they will deal with. The Japanese companies tend to have single union agreements.

The production targets the British car industry are aiming for are those set by the Japanese in Japan. The time needed to produce a car in Japan is 13.2 hours while in North America it is 18.6 and Europe 22.8. Rover Cars produced 500,000 per annum in 1992, which is equal to 35 cars per man employed per year, compared with the European average of 31 cars per man employed per year.

There are potential problems with the Japanese methods of production. The type of work could be stressful because of the demand by management for constant innovation, quality improvements and the need to intensify workers' efforts. Just-in-time puts greater dependency of workers on each other. The pressure is on the workers to keep the production line moving. In Japan, workers are expected to make up lost production in their own time. Managers, for example, who are called to work on the line, are expected to do their managerial tasks later in the day. Labour is just part of the production process and their major function is to increase productivity, quality and profit.

The introduction of Japanese working practices in the British car industry is enabling it to compete with the rest of the world, especially Japan. The problem facing the car industry is that it is introducing the practices now, but by the time they have fully implemented Japanisation, the Japanese will be further down the road of increasing productivity!

ASSIGNMENT

Arrange to visit two different businesses, such as local factories, retailers, banks, travel agents, building societies and compare the businesses' policies in one of the following areas for a new employee aged 16–18.

Wages

- What is the basic wage? Are there any regular bonuses?
- How do they compare with the national/regional average?
- How does the employer calculate the wages?
- How are the employees paid (cash, cheque, bank account)?
- Does the payment system improve business performance?

Benefits and conditions of work

- What benefits (pensions, holidays) does the organisation provide for the new employee?
- Do the benefits increase with length of service?
- Where will the new employee be working? Is it comfortable and well heated and ventilated?
- What hours is the new employee expected to work? Are weekends and evenings involved?

Health and safety record

- Ask to see the written health and safety policy.
- What actions has the organisation taken to implement this policy?
- Does the policy mention particular hazards and how they should be dealt with?
- How is the workforce informed about health and safety policies?
- What training do employees receive in safety procedures?

Training

- Is there an induction programme? How long does it take and what does it consist of?
- How many different jobs in the organisation have training programmes? (Does the organisation have a policy of employing people who are already qualified?)
- How long would the training last for the new employee?
- What is involved in the training? Does the new employee have the opportunity to have off-the-job training, such as college courses? If so, does the organisation pay for these or give the employee any time during working hours to attend the courses?

Equal opportunities

- What is the proportion of the workforce who are: female, from ethnic minorities, handicapped?

  Are these groups represented in the organisation?
- Compile a breakdown of the numbers of each group within: managerial, administrative, operational jobs.

  What proportion of the people doing these jobs is female, from ethnic minorities or handicapped?
- What proportion of the total workforce is over 50?

Productivity

- How is this measured?
- Does the business measure the productivity of its competitors' workforces?

Using evidence presented in a variety of forms (statistics, video, transcripts of interviews, written report, documentation from the organisations), critically review the organisations as employers. Contrast the two organisations studied and present an argument, supported by the evidence you have gathered, as to whether you believe the organisations to be good employers to work for or not. Make recommendations as to how they could improve their performance.

SOURCES OF INFORMATION

Central Statistical Office, Great George Street, London SW1P 3AQ

Central Statistical Office, Cardiff Road, Newport, Gwent, NP9 1XG

HMI Customs and Excise (monthly trade statistics), Tariff and Statistical Office, Unit 51, Room 711, Portcullis House, 27 Victoria Avenue, Southend on Sea, Essex SS2 6AL

Employment Department (employment census), Headquarters Building, PO Box 12, East Lane, Halton, Runcorn WA7 2DN

Employment Department (labour force survey), Caxton House, Tothill Street, London SW1H 9NF

Department of Employment (training), Moorfoot, Sheffield S1 4PQ

Department of Environment, 2 Marsham Street, London SW1P 3EB

Health and Safety Executive, Daniel House, Stanley Road, Bootle, Merseyside L20 3LZ

Department of Health, Hannibal House, Elephant and Castle, London SE1 6TE

Office of Population Censuses and Surveys, St Catherine's House, 10 Kingsway, London WC2B 6JP

Department of Trade and Industry (overseas trade analysed in terms of industries), 151 Buckingham Palace Road, London SW1W 9SS

Department of Trade and Industry (fuel and energy statistics), 1 Palace Street, London SW1E 5HE

The Scottish Office Library, Publication Sales, Room 1/44, New St Andrew's House, Edinburgh EH1 3TG

The Scottish Office (Scottish economic statistics), Alhambra House, 45 Waterloo Street, Glasgow G2 6AT

Welsh Office, Economic and Statistical Services Division, Crown Building, Cathays Park, Cardiff CF1 3NQ

Northern Ireland Departments (economic statistics), Stormont, Belfast BT4 3SW

Northern Ireland Departments (employment and manpower statistics), Netherleigh House, Massey Avenue, Belfast BT4 2JS

Eurostat (information office), Jean Monnet Building, L 2920 Luxembourg (tel. 352 4301 4567)

Eurostat (data shop), Rue de la Loi 120, B 1049 Brussels (tel. 32-2 235 1504)

British Broadcasting Corporation, Broadcasting House, London W1A 1AA

Central Office of Information, Hercules Road, London SE1 7DU

Office of Fair Trading, Room 306, Field House, 15 Bream's Buildings, London EC4A 1PR

Society of Motor Manufacturers and Traders, Forbes House, Halkin Street, London SW1X 7DS

Sports Council, 16 Upper Woburn Place, London WC1H 0HX

Sports Council for Wales, Sophia Gardens, Cardiff CF1 9SW

Trades Union Congress, Congress House, 23-28 Great Russell Street, London WC1V 3LS

House of Commons, London SW1A 0AA

Independent Television Commission, 70 Brompton Road, London SW3 1EY

Low Pay Unit, 27 Amwell Street, London EC1R 1UN

Channel 4, 124 Horseferry Road, London SW1P 2TX

Confederation of British Industry, Centre Point, 103 New Oxford Street, London WC1A 1DU

Equal Opportunities Commission, Overseas House, Quay Street, Manchester M3 3HN

For local information, try local offices of organisations. The local Chamber of Commerce and local authority may help with information in your area. For European information, there are a number of publications and you can also try the relevant embassy.

FURTHER SOURCES OF INFORMATION

Priest and Coppock's *The UK Economy, A Manual of Applied Economics*, M J Artis, Weidenfeld and Nicolson. ISBN 0 297 79691 7

Industrial Relations in Britain, G S Bain, Basil Blackwell. ISBN 0 631 15859 6

Economics, A Student's Guide (3rd edn), J Beardshaw, Longman (1992) ISBN 0 273 03777 3

Economics Theory & Practice, D J Browne, Edward Arnold Publishers. ISBN 0340 49664 9

Understanding Industrial Relations, D Farham and J Pimlott, Cassell Publishers (1990) ISBN 0 304 31794 2

Law of the European Union (2nd edn), M & E Handbooks, Penelope Kent, Pitman Publishing (1995) ISBN 0 7121 0851 3

Economics, M Parkin and D King, Addison-Wesley Publishing Co (1992) ISBN 0 201 41611 5

Introductory Economics, G F Stanlake, Longman ISBN 0 582 03695 X

Personnel Management A New Approach, D Torrington and Laura Hall, Prentice Hall (1991) ISBN 0 13 658667 8

The National Economies of Europe, D Dyker, Longman (1992). ISBN 0 582 058813

Europe in Figures (3rd Edn), Eurostat, HMSO

European Economic Integration, F McDonald and S Dearden. Longman (1994). ISBN 0 582 25141 9

The Economics of the Common Market (7th edn), D Swann, Penguin Books. ISBN 0 14 014497 8

Economic Trends, CSO

Social Trends, CSO

Employment Gazette, the official journal of the Employment Department, published monthly by HMSO, Subscription enquiries HMSO, Tel. 0171-873 8499

Newspapers, *Financial Times*, *The Independent*, *The Guardian* and *The Sunday Times*.

UNIT

6

FINANCIAL TRANSACTIONS, COSTING AND PRICING

Element 6.1
Explain added value, distribution of added value and the money cycle

Element 6.2
Explain financial transactions and complete supporting documents

Element 6.3
Calculate the cost of goods or services

Element 6.4
Explain basic pricing decisions and break-even

PERFORMANCE CRITERIA AND RANGE

Element 6.1: Explain added value, distribution of added value and the money cycle

PERFORMANCE CRITERIA

A student must: *page*

1 explain the **trading cycle** of goods or services in a business and their **added value** 523–6
2 explain the **distribution of added value** 526
3 explain the **money cycle** 527
4 explain **factors** for consideration **when selling** 527–9
5 explain **factors** for consideration **when buying** 529

RANGE

Trading cycle: order, supply, payment; process raw materials or components for a service to meet customer requirements, charge for goods or services; make a return on investment, make a trading profit or loss
Added value: value of goods or services supplied; cost of goods or services bought from others; added value created
Distribution of added value: wages and salaries, taxes, interest paid to lenders, money required to pay off debts, dividends paid to shareholders, profit retained in the business
Money cycle: initial cash, purchase materials, produce goods, sell goods on credit, goods are paid for, residual cash
Factors when selling: cash, credit, credit worthiness, payment terms, credit control, bad debt
Factors when buying: assessing suppliers, specification, quantity, price, delivery date

EVIDENCE INDICATORS

- A diagram which illustrates the trading cycle of the goods or services produced by one business. The diagram should be supported by approximate annual figures for the business. These figures should show the accumulated costs of goods or services bought from other businesses, the final value of the goods or services when sold to the customer and the resulting added value (profit). The figures should be supported by a commentary which suggests how the profit could be distributed and explains why it might be retained in the business, used to pay off debts or paid to shareholders.
- A spreadsheet which shows how the money cycle for the same goods or services mirrors the trading cycle and starts and ends with cash.
- Notes explaining why the finance department in the same business would have to consider the credit worthiness and payment terms which they offer to customers, and why the quantity ordered, price paid and delivery date are significant in terms of both the trading and money cycles.

Element 6.2: Explain financial transactions and complete supporting documents

PERFORMANCE CRITERIA

A student must: *page*

1 explain the **purposes** of financial transactions and documentation 533–9
2 explain the use of **purchase documents** and complete them clearly and accurately 539–46
3 explain the use of **sales documents** and complete them clearly and accurately 547–59
4 explain the use of **payments documents** and complete an example clearly and accurately 560–70
5 explain the use of **receipts documents** and complete an example clearly and accurately 560–70
6 explain why it is important to complete documents correctly and give possible **consequences of incorrect completion** 571–3
7 identify and explain **security checks for business documents** 571–3

RANGE

Purposes: monitoring performance, recording purchases and sales, generating accounts, meeting legal requirements, confirming mutual understanding between buyer and seller
Purchase documents: orders placed, purchase invoice, credit note, goods received note
Sales documents: orders received, sales invoice, delivery note, sales credit note, statement of account, remittance advice
Payments documents: cheque (cheque, bank giro form, remittance advice and petty cash voucher), Banking Automatic Credits Systems (BACS), Electronic Data Interchange (EDI), debit cards, credit cards
Receipts documents: receipt, cheque, paying-in slip, bank statement
Consequences of incorrect completion: incorrect purchases, incorrect sales, incorrect payments, incorrect receipts; incorrect accounts, incorrect information about business performance
Security checks for business documents: authorisation of orders, invoices against orders and goods received notes, authorised cheque signatories, segregation of duties

EVIDENCE INDICATORS

- a set of purchase documents (purchase order, goods received note, purchase invoice) clearly and accurately completed
- a set of sales documents (sales orders received note, delivery note, invoice, credit note, statement of account) clearly and accurately completed
- a set of payment documents (cheque, bank giro form, remittance advice and petty cash voucher) clearly and accurately completed

- a set of receipts documents (receipt, bank paying-in slip, cheque and bank statement) clearly and accurately completed
- each set of documents should be supported by notes which explain the purposes and functions of the documents, the need for clarity and accuracy in their completion and the importance of security checks.

Element 6.3: Calculate the cost of goods or services

PERFORMANCE CRITERIA

A student must:	*page*
1 explain **direct costs** and **indirect costs** of businesses	590–2
2 identify correctly a **unit of production or unit of service** from given data	593
3 calculate the **direct costs** of the production or service for a **time period**	604–7
4 calculate **indirect costs** of the production or service for a **time period**	604–7
5 calculate the total (absorption) cost of a unit of the production or service	592–602
6 explain **variable and fixed costs** in terms of their relationship with production	598–601
7 calculate the **variable costs** of a unit of the production or service from given data	604–7
8 calculate the marginal cost of a unit of the production or service	604–7

RANGE

Direct costs: production materials, machine or assembly wages
Indirect costs: other wages, depreciation, power, management, administration, marketing, other running expenses (rent, rates, telephone)
Time period: monthly, quarterly, annually
Variable costs: raw materials, power
Fixed costs: rent, rates, management, administration

EVIDENCE INDICATORS

- A set of calculations from given data, showing the breakdown of the total cost and marginal cost of a unit of production or service for an organisation. Evidence may be computer-generated using spreadsheets or manually-generated, but must include a commentary in the student's own words explaining the thinking behind the numbers.
- A summary explanation of a business's direct and indirect costs which shows that the student understands the different components of costs, and knows which costs vary with production levels.

Element 6.4: Explain basic pricing decisions and break-even

PERFORMANCE CRITERIA

A student must:	*page*
1 identify **basic factors** which determine price and describe **related pricing strategies**	608–10
2 explain **break-even point**	611–12
3 draw and **label** a break-even chart from given data	614–16
4 **analyse** the break-even chart	614–16
5 explain **reasons** for using a break-even chart	614–16

RANGE

Basic factors: need to make a profit, prices of competing products, under-used capacity
Related pricing strategies: cost plus pricing, market lead pricing, marginal cost/contribution pricing
Break-even point: the profit or loss of a business, the relationship between total cost and sales over a range of output levels, the relationship between fixed costs and variable costs
Label with: sales and costs, units of production, fixed costs, variable costs, total costs, sales, break-even point, profit, loss, selected operating point, margin of safety
Analyse: units of production, value of sales, the profit or loss at given levels of production and sales, margin of safety
Reasons: starting a business, measuring profits or losses, examining 'what if?' scenarios

EVIDENCE INDICATORS

A short report which

- explains the basic factors which influence the pricing of goods or services
- describes a related pricing strategy for one good or service
- explains the significance of break-even point for a business
- includes a break-even chart annotated with the labels ranged (produced from given business information), with notes which analyse the chart and giving at least one reason why a break-even chart might be used in the context of the given business information.

INTRODUCTION

Unit 6 explains the cycle which occurs when businesses trade, how in the process of trading value is added to goods and services and how that added value is distributed. It goes on to explain the workings of the money cycle in business and financial factors which affect both buying and selling.

Next, Unit 6 explains in detail how the document systems work which are used in financial transactions – purchases, sales, payments and receipts etc. – and why the correct completion of such documents is so important, as well as the consequences of incorrect completion.

The Unit also examines how direct and indirect costs are incurred by businesses, as well as fixed and variable costs, and how these aspects impact upon pricing policies.

Unit 6 lastly surveys the factors which determine price and various pricing strategies (see also Units 1 and 3), as well as the use of break-even analysis in financial planning and monitoring.

Element 6.1
EXPLAIN ADDED VALUE, DISTRIBUTION OF ADDED VALUE AND THE MONEY CYCLE

[See also Element 1.1]

The trading cycle of goods and services

PC 6.1.1

In Unit 1, the cycle of business activity in the economy was explained at a macroeconomic level. The thrust of Element 6.1 is to carry this examination further at a micro level, in the context of an individual business's financial transactions and rolling business operations.

In terms of an individual business, the trading cycle looks like Fig. 6.1 on page 524.

■ Key sequences in the trading cycle

PC 6.1.1

The following are the key sequences in the trading cycle:

Opening phase: injecting finance into the business

The cycle starts either with the start up of the business, or with a further trading period (often of a calendar month in length, which corresponds with credit agreements granting 30 days in which to pay up after the receipt of a statement for goods sold/purchased on credit). This phase requires money to be spent, essentially on purchasing something to sell on.

Second phase: turning cash into goods/services to sell on

Depending upon the nature of the business, the injection of cash will be used to purchase goods or services to sell on – whether as raw or semi-fashioned materials to manufacture into products, as finished goods to stock shelves or gondolas, or as intangibles such as insurance policies or services such as cleaning or child-minding.

Note that the cash is needed because some bills will come in earlier than others. In an ideal trading environment, a business will seek to defer paying for materials or stock until it has sold them on, thus turning over relatively small amounts of capital twelve or more times each year. However, some stock may 'stick', and some staff may need to be paid weekly etc.

PC 6.1.1

Fig 6.1 **The trading and money cycle**

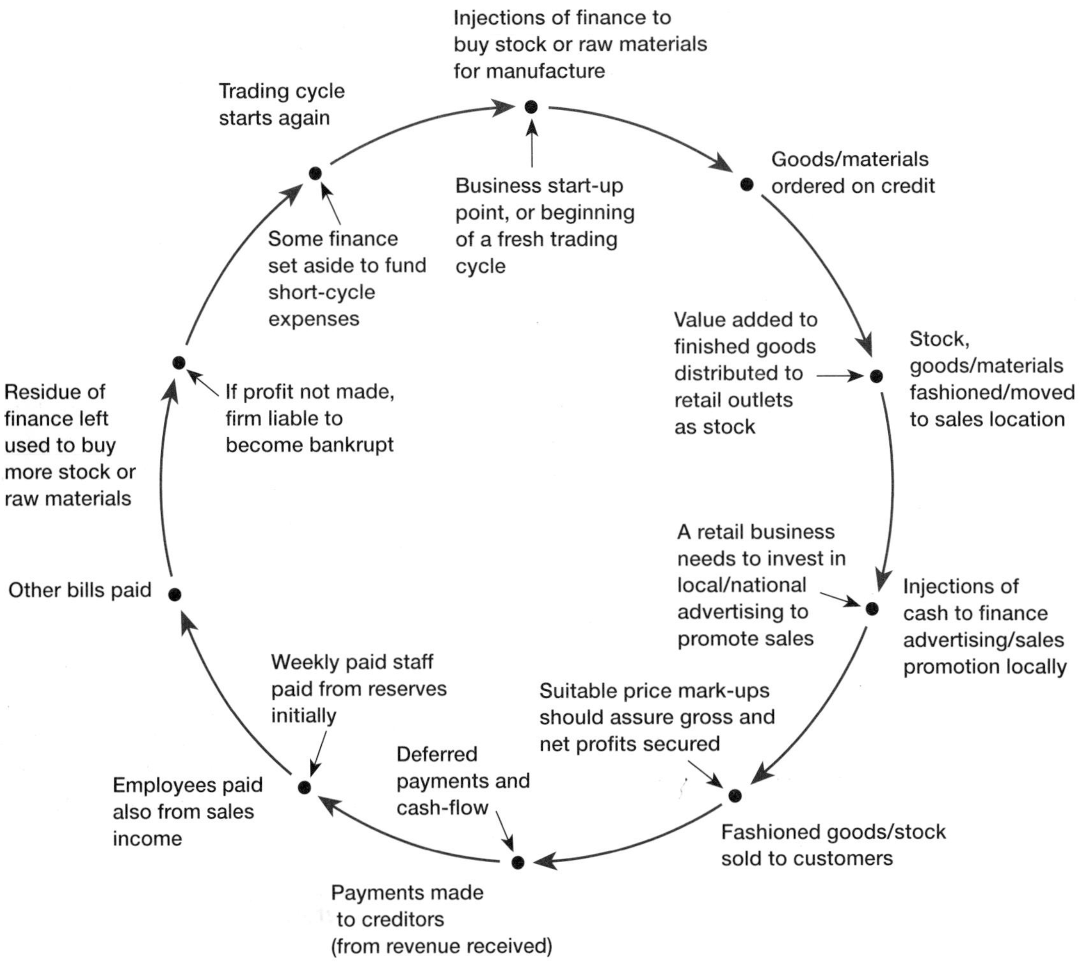
Injections of finance to buy stock or raw materials for manufacture
Trading cycle starts again
Goods/materials ordered on credit
Business start-up point, or beginning of a fresh trading cycle
Some finance set aside to fund short-cycle expenses
Value added to finished goods distributed to retail outlets as stock
Stock, goods/materials fashioned/moved to sales location
Residue of finance left used to buy more stock or raw materials
If profit not made, firm liable to become bankrupt
A retail business needs to invest in local/national advertising to promote sales
Other bills paid
Injections of cash to finance advertising/sales promotion locally
Weekly paid staff paid from reserves initially
Suitable price mark-ups should assure gross and net profits secured
Deferred payments and cash-flow
Employees paid also from sales income
Fashioned goods/stock sold to customers
Payments made to creditors (from revenue received)

The trading cycle relies on value-added goods or services being sold at a sufficient profit.

Third phase: sales are generated

All being well, the goods or services acquired will be sold on at a profit – value being added to them by reason of their availability, warranty, appeal and so on. The level of profit generated (see Units 1 and 3) will depend on a range of variables, but must be sufficient to cover all operating costs and still to provide a surplus – see below.

Fourth phase: paying for goods and services received

The goods (or services) purchased to sell on have to be paid for; employees have to be paid, as do various operating costs, such as rent, rates and services. Sufficient profit has therefore to be generated on a weekly and monthly basis to enable a business to pay its way.

Fifth phase: generating a sufficient surplus to re-invest

This is the crucial phase – it makes or breaks. For the business to move on into its next trading cycle, it must have generated enough profit – after paying for its operational or 'cost of sales' expenses – to replace sold stock or to purchase fresh supplies of raw material. Additionally, the directors of the business will need some income to live on in the form of 'drawings'.

Opening phase: take two

If all has gone well, and the business has made enough money, a subsequent trading cycle begins and progresses in the same way.

The consequences of making a loss

In the short term, a business may survive a poor trading cycle (during which sales proved sluggish) by drawing upon its financial reserves (always assuming it has some) to pay its bills. Alternatively, it might seek to obtain a fresh loan from, say, its bank, to tide it over.

However, as night follows day, unless successive trading cycles generate sufficient profits, a business will fail and the receivers will be called in.

■ The trading cycle and added value

PC 6.1.1

The trading cycle is perhaps best considered as a spiral – a successive series of connected loops or circles which move forward, usually on a calendar monthly basis, to form a business's financial or trading year. At various points along each loop, value is added to a good or service as Fig. 6.2 illustrates.

PC 6.1.1

Fig 6.2 **The trading cycle, added value and generated profits**

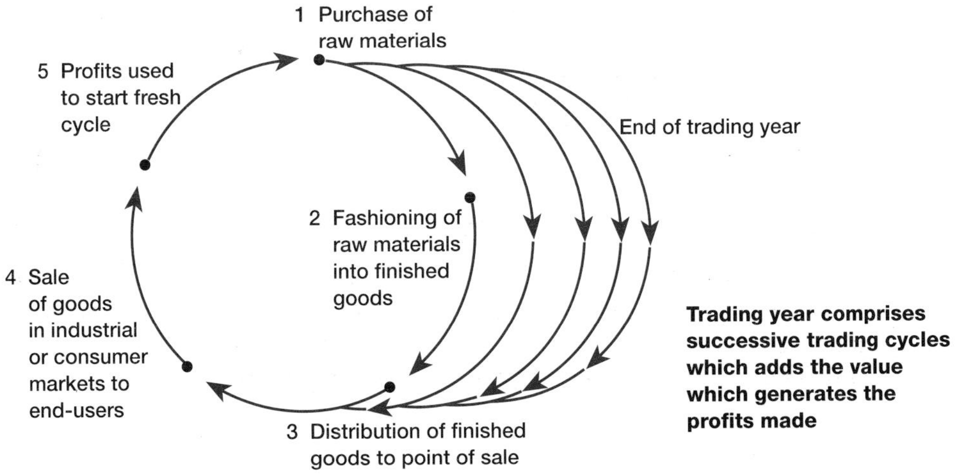
1 Purchase of raw materials
2 Fashioning of raw materials into finished goods
3 Distribution of finished goods to point of sale
4 Sale of goods in industrial or consumer markets to end-users
5 Profits used to start fresh cycle
End of trading year
Trading year comprises successive trading cycles which adds the value which generates the profits made

It is interesting to note that value is frequently added at the boundaries of the three economic sectors – primary, secondary and tertiary. For instance, iron ore is first extracted from the ground, then given added value by its transformation into steel rolls or plates; it is then fashioned into, say, a motor car or boiler and sold on to distributors who break the bulk and deliver goods to points of sale and thus create further added value; once at its sales point, a final value is added to it when the industrial purchaser or consumer pay a price which subsumes all the earlier stages of added value.

It is also important to remember that a good passing through a number of production phases in a factory is subject to careful scrutiny by the firm's cost accountants, who calculate both the value added to the good as it nears completion, and the costs it progressively bears (see direct and indirect costing).

Again, in this context, in order to create added value, a manufacturer may either purchase raw materials to fashion or process, or may buy in finished or semi-finished components, such as batteries, pumps, switches, thermostats, engine castings and so on.

PC 6.1.2

The distribution of added value

The above section explains how added value is the source of all profits generated in a business's trading cycle, and it is also important to understand how accumulated profits are distributed in a typical company. Fig 6.3 on page 527 illustrates how acquired profit is used within a business:

- to pay its way
- to purchase goods or materials to re-start the cycle
- to pay out stake-holders such as share-holders and directors
- to set aside financial reserves as an insurance for the unexpected.

PC 6.1.3

The money cycle in businesses

The money cycle is a term which refers to the process of:

1 Obtaining supplies of cash initially to 'pump-prime the cycle' – either in the form of a bank loan, investment from shareholders or sleeping partners or from directors etc.

2 Using such cash – either to buy the raw materials outlined above, or to purchase stocks of goods for re-sale, or to purchase rights (such as agency or franchise rights) to sell a service, such as insurance or training. Note in Phase 2, the cash may buy finished goods for instant resale or may buy raw materials and components for use in the manufacturing process.

3 Selling finished goods, stock or services to customers in either the industrial or consumer market – *at a profit*. Note that a manufacturer may sell on to a wholesaler or distributor. Such sales may be made on a credit or cash sale basis; credit sales require involved administration to collect the money at the end of agreed credit periods.

4 The sale of goods or services at a profit will secure surpluses (after the distribution of added value has been allowed for (see above)) which enable the money cycle to re-start. When insufficient profits are generated, the business is heading for the financial rocks!

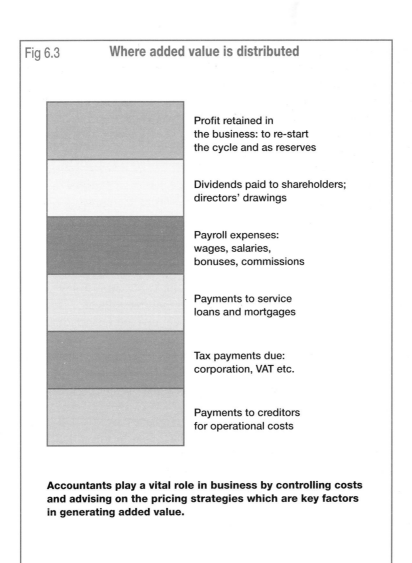

Fig 6.3 **Where added value is distributed**

PC 6.1.2

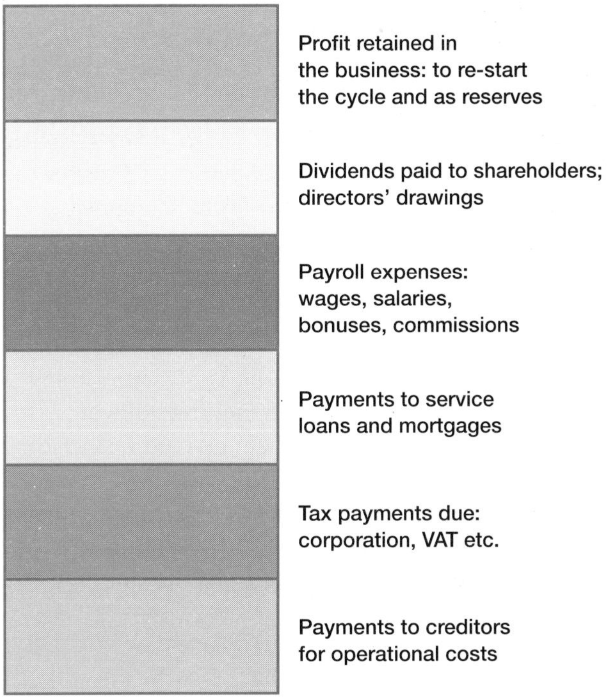
Profit retained in the business: to re-start the cycle and as reserves
Dividends paid to shareholders; directors' drawings
Payroll expenses: wages, salaries, bonuses, commissions
Payments to service loans and mortgages
Tax payments due: corporation, VAT etc.
Payments to creditors for operational costs

Accountants play a vital role in business by controlling costs and advising on the pricing strategies which are key factors in generating added value.

Factors involved in buying and selling

PC 6.1.4 6.1.5

One particularly important task of the many which accounts departments carry out is to check out the credit-worthiness of customers who wish to open accounts so as to be able to pay for goods or services on credit. If credit is allowed mistakenly and a debt incurred becomes a bad debt, it proves very costly for a business, Consider, for example, that a company may be operating on the basis of generating 10% net profit from the total cost of a good sold. If a debtor reneges and does not pay for the good, the business will have to sell an additional ten items of the same good to recover its lost investment.

For this reason, businesses invariably require various forms of credit reference – from a customer's bank, from other traders with whom business is transacted and so on – in order to obtain reassurance that the customer is 'credit-worthy'. It is also worth noting that, today, when a business gains a reputation of being 'non-credit-worthy' it will find it extremely difficult to obtain credit anywhere, since national credit reference agencies provide (at a cost) on-line computer data about such risky would-be customers – especially those which have had a county court judgement against them for non-payment of debts.

A systematic watch is kept in the accounts departments of businesses with significant credit sales on the time debtors take to pay, and the ratio of bad debts incurred, so as to avoid problems of ultimate profitability and also intermittent cash-flow difficulties. When customers fail to pay promptly within agreed time limits, accounts put stops on their accounts, thus preventing them from running up higher bills on account.

PC
6.1.4
6.1.5

■ Financial incentives and selling

Selling

For reasons of administrative costs involved and the risk factor, many businesses offer financial incentives – lower prices, discounts, additional free gifts etc. – to woo customers into paying cash for goods, as opposed to buying them on credit, since this aids their cash-flow and reduces administrative costs.

Where credit sales form part of a business's sales strategy, it will offer various forms of incentive to secure prompt payment, such as settlement discounts on monthly statements paid promptly of some 3–5%, and also year-end additional discount rewards for prolonged prompt payment etc.

Also, it is worth remembering that, where businesses supply extensive credit to customers – especially those using credit cards or charge cards, the annual percentage rate (APR) charged on a loan may be as high as 34%. In other words, a consumer may pay an *additional third of the sales value* of a good (over a 12 month period) for the benefit of the loan provided.

Buying

An equally important but different set of procedures and checks is applied when a company sets out to purchase goods or services. A preliminary action often taken is to vet or audit a business which might, say, supply parts to a manufacturer in terms of its: quality and specifications standards, stability and long-term viability stemming from a sound financial basis, delivery records, responsiveness to requests for modifications and so on. Indeed, today, many businesses like Marks & Spencer plc, Ford UK and Sainsburys etc. provide suppliers with detailed specifications on quality and product standards which they have to satisfy in order to remain suppliers.

For costly, larger items – constructing buildings or supplying heavy plant and so on – purchasers produce offers for tenders which are, in effect, detailed schedules specifying exactly what standards, quality and delivery dates etc. a company has to meet in order to be given the work. Such tenders take the form of contracts, and many include penalty clauses for, say, late completion.

Not unexpectedly, purchasers shop around seeking to secure an item at the most competitive price available. For this reason, central purchasing managers and buyers keep in close contact with regular suppliers and hold catalogues and price lists which suppliers regularly update. In times of recession, a purchasers' market is created, and extended haggling goes on, where purchasers look for 'knockdown' prices – and get them! For instance, between 1988 and 1993 many printing firms were taking on jobs at breakeven prices, simply to keep going, pay employees and hold out until better times arrived.

Lastly, as well as needing to secure top quality, extended guaranteed supply, and bargain-basement prices, purchasers seek to negotiate favourable delivery times, such as just-in-time deliveries to factories which enable them to hold almost no buffer stocks and therefore to save on warehousing costs.

REVIEW TEST

PC
6.1.1
6.1.2
6.1.3
6.1.4
6.1.5

1 List the main stages of the trading cycle.

2 Explain briefly where added value is most commonly distributed in a business.

3 What happens if insufficient profit is secured during a given trading cycle?

4 List the main stages of the money cycle. Explain how the money cycle relates to added value.

5 What is the cost accountant's role during the production of a good in a factory?

6 List the main factors which are involved from a financial point of view in controlling the selling process in a business. Explain briefly the purpose of each factor you identify.

7 Similarly, list the main factors for purchasing and explain also the purpose of each.

8 How do accountants seek to avoid bad debts in a business?

9 What is an invitation to tender? How does it work? What advantages does tendering have for the tender-giver?

10 How do large manufacturers exercise control over the quality of the components they buy in?

INDIVIDUAL/PAIR ACTIVITIES

PC
6.1.1
6.1.2
6.1.3
6.1.4
6.1.5

1 Arrange to visit a manufacturing company and interview some of its cost accountants on their job roles and functions. Report to your class on what you discover.

2 Make arrangements to interview a small trader–retailer and find out how he or she manages the monthly trading cycle of the business. Brief your class in a 5–10 minute oral presentation.

3 Arrange to interview a company accountant and find out the areas in which added value is distributed and in what ratios or percentages of the whole. (Note: naturally, such accountants will be reluctant to impart any sensitive or confidential data.)

4 Interview an accountant in a private or public sector enterprise and find out how the money cycle works in the sector you investigate. Report back orally to your class.

5 Find out how accountants in a local business handle their bad debts and what legal rights they have to obtain payment. Report back accordingly to your class.

6 Find out what your local Small Claims Court does, and how it may aid businesses.

7 Arrange to interview a purchase manager in a manufacturing company and find out what he or she is responsible for. Brief your group on what you discover.

KNOWLEDGE TEST

Element 6.1
Explain added value, distribution of added value and the money cycle

1 Which of the following are, and which are not, components of the trading cycle?

A Obtaining raw materials for processing.
B Seeking new customers.
C Making a trading profit.
D Researching new products.

2 (i) The payment of corporation tax is a common distribution item of added value.
(ii) Payments of dividends to shareholders fall outside the distribution of added value.

Which of the following options best describes the two above statements?

A	(i)	T	(ii)	T
B	(i)	T	(ii)	F
C	(i)	F	(ii)	T
D	(i)	F	(ii)	F

3 Which of the following statements is true, and which false?

A Credit sales made by account customers are more profitable than cash sales.
B Investments made by shareholders can be used to start the money cycle.
C Procurement is an alternative term for purchasing.
D Clearing banks provide credit references about their customers who seek to open credit accounts with a business.

4 A settlement discount is:

A a discount given when a customer's complaint about a purchase is settled
B a discount provided by a supplier to an account customer who decides to settle a bill with cash
C a discount given by a supplier for goods billed on a monthly statement
D a discount given in the financial services sector when an erratic account period has settled down.

5 (i) An age analysis of debtors is carried out to identify younger purchasing managers who are expected to be more prone to 'soft-selling' techniques.
(ii) Just-in-time is a term used in the distribution industry to describe an automatic telephone ordering system which records orders at any time during a 24-hour period.

Which of the following options best describes the two above statements?

A	(i)	T	(ii)	T
B	(i)	T	(ii)	F
C	(i)	F	(ii)	T
D	(i)	F	(ii)	F

PORTFOLIO OF EVIDENCE ACTIVITY

PC
6.1.1
6.1.2
6.1.3
6.1.4
6.1.5

Element 6.1
Explain added value, distribution of added value and the money cycle

ADDING VALUE TO ACCOUNTANTS!

Scenario

You work as a researcher and writer for *Business Training Limited*, a medium-sized organisation with training centres in Northern Ireland, northern England, Liverpool, Manchester and the Midlands, London and the southern counties. In your Research & Development Department, *BTL* produces most of the learning materials it uses in its training programmes, and as *BTL* enjoys a good reputation nationally, with some household names among its clients, it is always careful to ensure that the materials produced are: lively, topical, accurate and well-presented.

Your current brief involves you in producing training materials for an accounting technician course – that is to say for employees who are engaged to work mostly at the accounts processing end, where the details are attended to. At present, you are engaged in producing a training pack for the early part of an accounting technician programme entitled:

> *THE MONEY-GO-ROUND: WHERE THE FINANCE COMES FROM, HOW IT IS USED AND WHERE IT ENDS UP*

For part of the training pack, you have to research (basing your data on a single, easily understood and typical business) a business trading cycle and produce a diagram which details clearly its major phases. Additionally, the diagram should include approximate value for the items you specify – the goods or services bought in, and the retail (or final) value of the goods or services when sold, which will produce total value added (equivalent to the profit generated).

The diagram should be accompanied by a set of notes which suggest where the profit is likely to be distributed by the business and why.

The training pack is also to include a section in the form of a spreadsheet (the trainees will be given disk copies of it) which illustrates how the trading and money cycles cover the same trading ground where both begin and end with a sum of money.

A further section of the pack is to include an illustrated explanation of the way in which the surveyed business's accounts department would need to handle requests for and the monitoring of credit account applications and credit-worthiness; how it would handle payment terms and conditions offered to its customers, as well as explanations of the importance of: quantities ordered, prices paid and delivery dates in both the trading and money cycles.

Your boss has suggested that you focus on a smallish business and the cash-flow situations it has to manage in order to survive and prosper.

Task 1

At the outset, make sure you complete the appropriate sections of your planning and review log.

Task 2

Making use of your local network of contacts, locate a suitable small business to research. Make sure you convey to your contact the fact that no confidential information will be used or imparted, and that he or she will see and authorise your final draft etc. Then, obtain the raw data needed to inform your diagram. Note: you may find your centre's bookshop or refectory a helpful business to research.

Liaise with your teacher with a view to using DTP/reprographics media, such as graphics software and colour printers or plotters etc. with which to produce a high-quality diagram.

Task 3

Next, produce suitable notes to explain the aspects of distributed and retained profit. Such notes are likely to be some 3–4 sides of printed A4 in length.

Task 4

Using financial data either obtained from the local small business you researched or from other means, such as an annual shareholders report etc., produce a suitable spreadsheet detailing how finance in the trading/money cycles begins and ends with cash sums, and how the initial investment is spent, together with details of the added value it creates.

Task 5

Produce a set of notes, based on your private study reading, recent researches and other sources of information which explains the roles and responsibilities of a finance department as outlined in the above scenario. Remember that these notes are to form part of a training pack, and so they should be simple, clear and appealingly presented. A suitable length for the notes is about 3–4 sides of printed A4.

Performance criteria covered

6.1.1, 6.1.2, 6.1.3, 6.1.4, 6.1.5

Core skills covered

Communication:
3.2.1, 3.2.2, 3.2.3, 3.2.4, 3.2.5, 3.3.1, 3.3.2, 3.3.3, 3.4.1, 3.4.2, 3.4.3, 3.4.4

Information Technology:
3.1.1, 3.1.2, 3.1.3, 3.1.4, 3.1.5, 3.2.1, 3.2.2, 3.2.3, 3.2.4, 3.2.5, 3.2.6, 3.2.7, 3.3.1, 3.3.2, 3.3.3, 3.3.4, 3.3.5, 3.3.6

Application of Number:
3.1.1, 3.1.2, 3.1.3, 3.1.4, 3.1.5, 3.3.1, 3.3.2, 3.3.3, 3.3.4, 3.3.5

Element 6.2
EXPLAIN FINANCIAL TRANSACTIONS AND COMPLETE SUPPORTING DOCUMENTS

Every business – from the humblest sole trader's to the mighty multinational's – needs to keep careful 'books' or accounts, for a number of compelling reasons:

PC 6.2.1

THE KEY PURPOSES OF THE BUSINESS ACCOUNTING SYSTEM

Businesses are obliged to keep careful bookkeeping and accounting records so as:

- to meet legal requirements to present audited accounts (by an independent chartered accountant) at the end of each trading year or period to the Inland Revenue for the purposes of calculating the taxes due from the business
- to ensure that the selling, purchasing and payments transactions which the business undertakes are free from error (billing mistakes can quickly lose customers' goodwill and paying too much for goods bought in can erode or eradicate profits just as quickly)
- to provide continuous feedback both in terms of the minutiae of individual transactions and of summarised financial analyses (called management accounting reports) which inform management in a variety of ways on how the business is doing, and which are used extensively in the production of corporate and business plans
- to ensure that financial processes, especially those involving cash and items which might be converted into cash (such as an open cheque), are securely handled and not liable to misappropriation or theft
- to form the source data for the production of year end or final accounts, which provide feedback on how the business has performed overall; this information is also legally required to be made available to the shareholders of both private and public limited companies, and is naturally desired by the business's owners and/or directors; again, the potential purchasers of a business will undoubtedly request details of, say, the last five years of trading to inform their decision.

Authors note: The following section – up to page 539 – provides a clear and easy-to-absorb overview of the double-entry book-keeping system commonly used in financial departments. Students do not need to acquire a knowledge of double-entry book-keeping in pursuit of the GNVQ Advanced Business Award, but it is felt that the following section will much assist students in understanding the rest of Unit 6 and also Unit 7.

In his excellent text *Bookkeeping & Accounts* (3rd edition), Frank Wood explains the fundamental accounting equation upon which the double-entry bookkeeping system is based as the need to demonstrate the relationship or balance between the assets or capital (which its start-up directors have put into it) with the liabilities (or monies owing to others) who have lent out finance etc. to it.

In other words,

ASSETS ALWAYS EQUAL CAPITAL + LIABILITIES

Frank Wood explains this simply this way:

Resources: what they are (Assets)	=	Resources, who supplied them (Capital + Liabilities)

Essentially, the assets of a business represent all its sources of wealth, either in the form of premises, land or machinery, or money due to the business from customers who owe it for goods or services purchased on credit or account, or money balances (in credit as opposed to being overdrawn) being held on behalf of the business in its bank.

A business's liabilities, on the other hand, comprise all the debts it owes to others – its suppliers of stock, its stationery suppliers, its accountants, its insurance company etc. the various expenses incurred in its business operations – payroll, heat, light, cleaning etc. and the debts incurred by borrowing money from a bank, building society or finance house in the form of business premises mortgages, money to finance expansion or to purchase new and expensive equipment.

PC 6.2.1 (back-ground)

The double-entry system: debiting and crediting – DR and CR

To avoid any confusion – which commonly occurs – between the everyday meaning of **debit** and **credit** and the quite separate and specific, double-entry bookkeeping meaning, commit the following table to memory:

THE KEY RULES OF DEBITING AND CREDITING

Accounts	To record	Entry in the account
Assets	an increase	Debit
	a decrease	Credit
Liabilities	an increase	Credit
	a decrease	Debit
Capital	an increase	Credit
	a decrease	Debit

Source: *Frank Wood's Bookkeeping & Accounts*, 3rd edn, Pitman Publishing 1992

The following table provides some helpful examples of how the debiting and crediting system works with regard to assets, capital and liabilities:

EXAMPLES OF DEBITING AND CREDITING

Transactions		Effect	Action
199– May 1	Started an engineering business putting £1,000 into a business bank account.	▲ Increases *asset* of bank. ▲ Increases *capital* of owner.	Debit bank account. Credit capital account
May 3	Bought works machinery on credit from Unique Machines £275.	▲ Increases *asset* of machinery. ▲ Increases *liability* to Unique Machines.	Debit machinery account. Credit Unique Machines account.
May 4	Withdrew £200 cash from the bank and placed it in the cash box.	▼ Decreases *asset* of bank. ▲ Increases *asset* of cash.	Credit bank account. Debit cash account.
May 7	Bought a motor van paying in cash £180.	▼ Decreases *asset* of cash. ▲ Increases *asset* of motor van.	Credit cash account. Debit motor van account.
May 10	Sold some of the machinery for £15 on credit to B Barnes	▼ Decreases *asset* of machinery. ▲ Increases *asset* of money owing from B Barnes.	Credit machinery account. Debit B Barnes account.
May 21	Returned some of the machinery, value £27 to Unique Machines.	▼ Decreases *asset* of machinery. ▼ Decreases *liability* to Unique Machines.	Credit machinery account. Debit Unique Machines.
May 28	B Barnes pays the firm the amount owing, £15, by cheque.	▲ Increases *asset* of bank. ▼ Decreases *asset* of money owing by B Barnes.	Debit bank account. Credit B Barnes account.
May 30	Bought another motor van paying by cheque £420.	▼ Decreases *asset* of bank. ▲ Increases *asset* of motor vans.	Credit bank account. Debit motor van account.
May 31	Paid the amount of £248 to Unique Machines by cheque.	▼ Decreases *asset* of bank. ▼ Decreases *liability* to Unique Machines.	Credit bank account. Debit Unique Machines.

Source: *Frank Wood's Bookkeeping & Accounts,* 3rd edn, Pitman Publishing 1992

In the middle ages in Europe, when the double-entry bookkeeping system was invented by merchants, a single book or ledger was sufficient to record the transactions which took place. Today, however, in an age of national chainstores, supermarkets, conglomerates and multinationals, businesses would need an articulated lorry to carry such a book to its various accounts department staff!

Therefore, it has become common practice to separate the books and ledgers which make up the modern double-entry accounting system in this way:

1 **Books of Original Entry,** into which every transaction is recorded on a daily basis, or as and when it occurs. These books are also referred to as journals, e.g. the Sales Journal, the Purchases Journal. Books of Original Entry record these data:

- the date of the transaction
- its details
- the money totals involved

The journals which make up the books of original entry in a business are:

- Sales
- Purchases
- Returns Inwards
- Returns Outwards
- Cash Book
- General Journal
- Petty Cash Book

Fig 6.4 **Diagram of books used in a double-entry bookkeeping system**

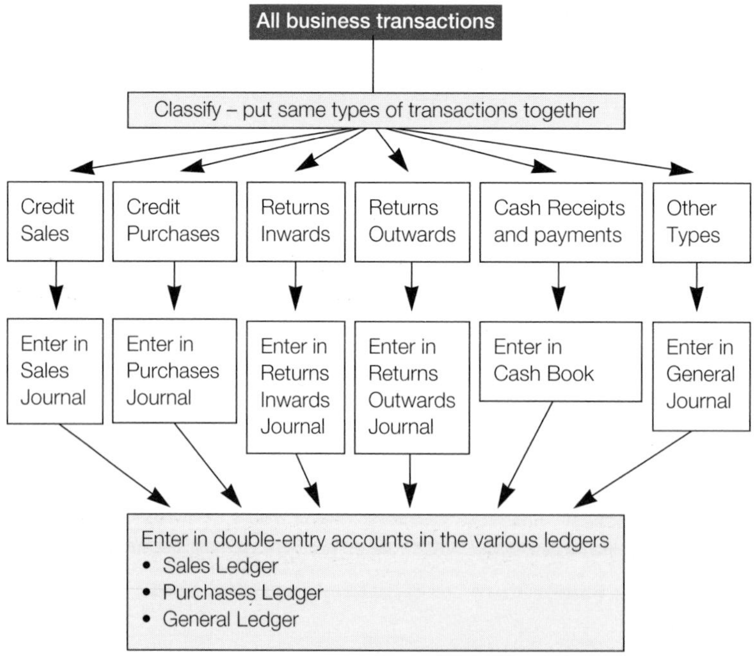

Source: *Frank Wood's Book-keeping & Accounts*, 3rd edn, Pitman Publishing 1992

Note that both the sales and purchase journals record credit transactions only, while the cash book records receipts and payments for cash, and that the general journal picks up other types of transaction.

2 **Ledgers** which summarise transactions in specific sectors:

- **Sales Ledger**
- **Purchase Ledger**
- **General Ledger**

Thus every transaction which increases or decreases a business's assets, capital or liabilities is entered as a debit or credit, first into a book of original entry (journal) and thence into the appropriate ledger as Fig 6.4 (above) illustrates.

DISCUSSION TOPICS

1 The two sides of Frank Wood's 'accounting equation': assets = capital + liabilities need to balance in the double-entry bookkeeping system.

What help does this necessity provide to the business owner in the effective running of his or her business?

2 Can you think of any advantages which might stem from managing a double-entry bookkeeping system by means of a computer software application? Would there be any disadvantages?

3 Is there a danger in a large business of its accountants becoming too preoccupied with the processing of number-based information, and too divorced from direct interactions with suppliers and customers?

4 Why do so many managing directors of limited companies have accounting backgrounds do you think? Do you consider that an accounting route is the most appropriate to achieve this type of post?

■ The basic structure of double-entry bookkeeping

PC 6.2.1 (background)

The diagram shown in Fig 6.5 on page 538 shows clearly the overall structure of the double-entry bookkeeping system and the relationships in debiting and crediting terms which interconnect the various books and ledgers.

■ Types of accounts

The accounts which hold the detailed transactions of the double-entry bookkeeping system are also given specific names, and these are explained in the checklist on page 539.

PC 6.2.1 (background)

Fig 6.5 **The basic structure of double-entry bookkeeping**

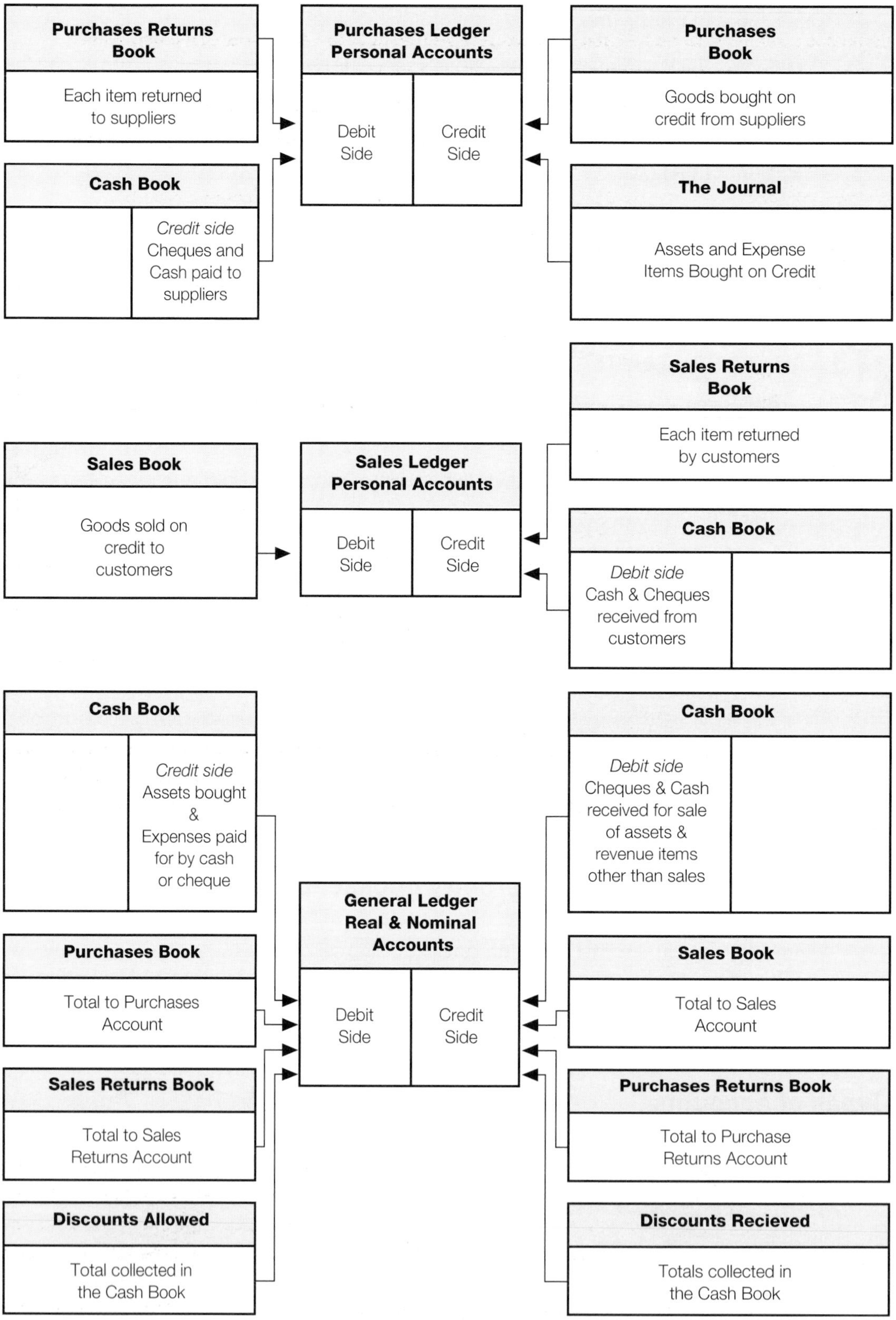

Source: *Frank Wood's Book-keeping & Accounts*, 3rd edn, Pitman Publishing 1992

TYPES OF ACCOUNTS

Some accountants describe all accounts as **personal** accounts or as **impersonal** accounts:

- **Personal accounts** – These are for debtors and creditors.
- **Impersonal accounts** – Divided between real accounts and nominal accounts.
- **Real accounts** – Accounts in which property is recorded. Examples are buildings, machinery, fixtures and stock.
- **Nominal accounts** – Accounts in which expenses, income and capital are recorded.

A diagram may enable you to understand it better:

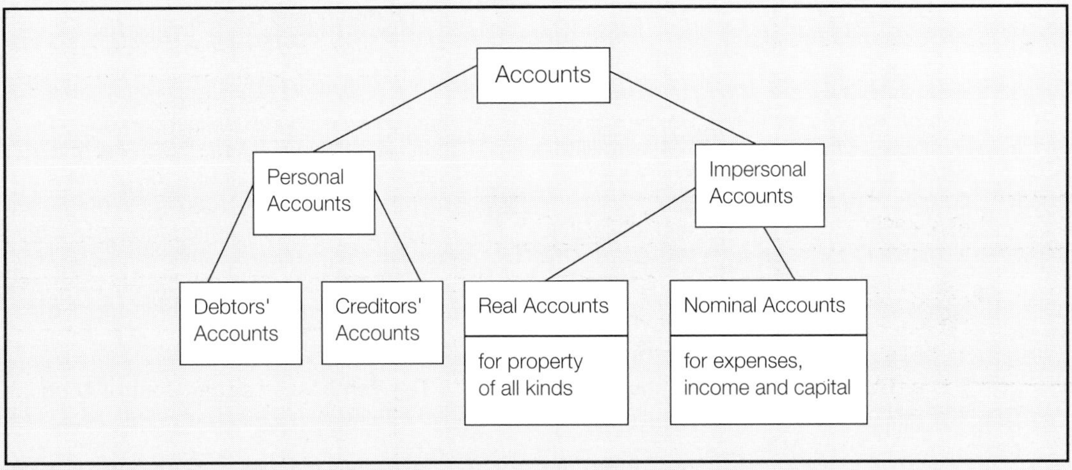

Nominal and private ledgers

The ledger in which the impersonal accounts are kept is known as the **nominal** (or general) **ledger.** Very often, to ensure privacy for the proprietor(s), the capital and drawing accounts and similar accounts are kept in a **private ledger**. By doing this office staff cannot see details of items which the proprietors want to keep a secret.

Source: *Frank Wood's Bookkeeping & Accounts*, 3rd edn Pitman Publishing 1992

Documenting purchases

PC 6.2.2

At the outset of this section it is worth remembering that, in an accounting context, both the sales and purchasing processes are closely connected in that the supplier's sale is the customer's purchase. And so the information you acquire about the sequence of account sales documents will stand you in good stead when studying the sequence of purchase-related documents, and vice versa.

Figure 6.6 illustrates the monthly cycle through which purchases are documented and paid for.

PC 6.2.2

Fig 6.6 **The monthly cycle of purchases documentation**

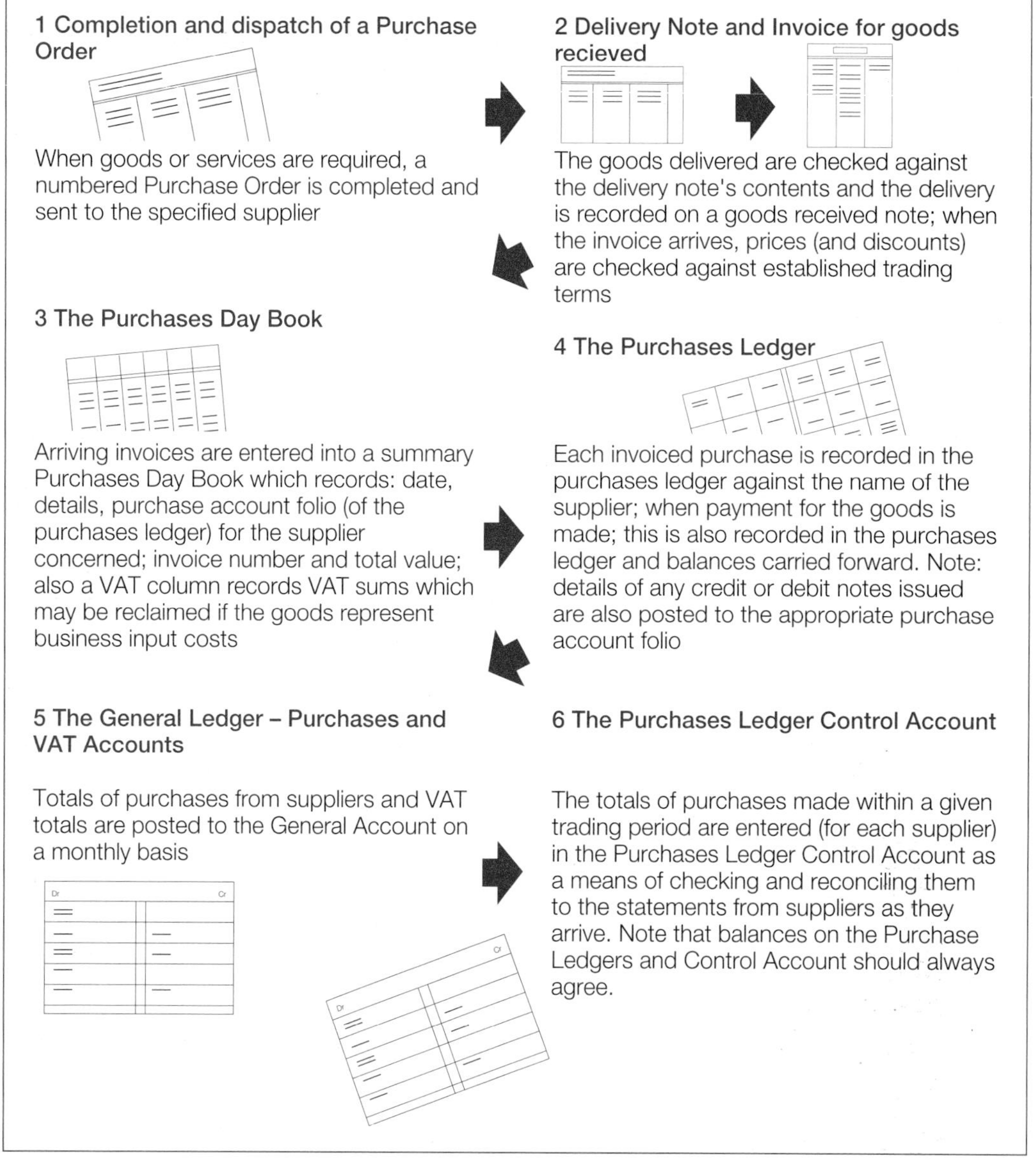
1 Completion and dispatch of a Purchase Order
When goods or services are required, a numbered Purchase Order is completed and sent to the specified supplier
2 Delivery Note and Invoice for goods recieved
The goods delivered are checked against the delivery note's contents and the delivery is recorded on a goods received note; when the invoice arrives, prices (and discounts) are checked against established trading terms
3 The Purchases Day Book
Arriving invoices are entered into a summary Purchases Day Book which records: date, details, purchase account folio (of the purchases ledger) for the supplier concerned; invoice number and total value; also a VAT column records VAT sums which may be reclaimed if the goods represent business input costs
4 The Purchases Ledger
Each invoiced purchase is recorded in the purchases ledger against the name of the supplier; when payment for the goods is made; this is also recorded in the purchases ledger and balances carried forward. Note: details of any credit or debit notes issued are also posted to the appropriate purchase account folio
5 The General Ledger – Purchases and VAT Accounts
Totals of purchases from suppliers and VAT totals are posted to the General Account on a monthly basis
6 The Purchases Ledger Control Account
The totals of purchases made within a given trading period are entered (for each supplier) in the Purchases Ledger Control Account as a means of checking and reconciling them to the statements from suppliers as they arrive. Note that balances on the Purchase Ledgers and Control Account should always agree.

PC 6.2.2

■ 1 Drawing up and despatching the purchase order

Most organisations have established procedures which preface the drawing up of a purchase order. These usually involve obtaining estimates or quotations (if goods are priced below an agreed ceiling, or going out to tender if goods (or services) exceed, say, a four-figure sum.

Once it has been satisfactorily established that a potential purchase is available from a given supplier at an acceptable price, then the purchase order may be drawn up for the signature of a manager or director with the assigned authority.

The key data comprising a typical purchase order is shown on page 544.

■ 2 The delivery and goods received notes

The ordered goods will arrive in due course and the supplier's driver will require a signature on his delivery note as proof of safe delivery. In turn, the recipient of the goods will make out a goods received note for the assistance of the appropriate accounts, purchasing and stockroom staff, each of whom will require such information as part of their record-keeping systems.

■ 3 The purchases day book

Every day, in medium to large organisations, hundreds of invoices arrive in twice-daily postal deliveries to accounts departments. These invoices may relate to stock purchases, stationery supplies, laundry costs for overalls, the redecoration of branch premises and so on.

In order to create some order out of the multi-coloured, multi-sized bunch of newly arrived invoices, they are carefully entered into a purchases day book (Fig 6.7).

Fig 6.7

PC 6.2.2

PURCHASES DAY BOOK

Date	Details	Folio	Invoice	Total	Goods	VAT
Nov 1	Bould & Co. Motor oil	C1	SR2103	104.26	88.75	15.51
" 3	Hambleton's: Sparking plugs	C12	SR2114	140.57	119.63	20.94
" 7	Monktons Ltd: Swarfega	C24	SR2123	29.14	24.80	4.34

The purchases day book ensures that a prompt and accurate detail is kept of the essential details of all incoming invoices:

- date of arrival
- invoice details, i.e. name of supplier and details of goods
- purchase ledger folio reference of supplier concerned
- the organisation's unique purchase order number
- the combined total value of the invoice (goods and VAT)
- the total value of the goods excluding VAT
- the VAT total for the goods supplied

The purchases day book entries may then be posted to the purchases ledger. Note that daily totals need only be posted to the purchases and VAT accounts, and that some firms organise their purchases day books to reflect their principal purchase areas (Fig 6.8).

PC 6.2.2

Fig 6.8

PURCHASES DAY BOOK

	Date	Supplier	Inv. No.	A/c No.	Total	Electrical	Motor	Office	Telephone	Sundries	VAT
	A	B	C	D	E	F	G	H	I	J	K

PC 6.2.2

Posting credit purchases to the purchases ledger

1 The credit purchases are posted one by one, to the credit of each supplier's account in the purchases ledger.

2 At the end of each period the total of the credit purchases is posted to the debit of the purchases account in the general ledger.

Fig 6.9 **Posting credit purchases**

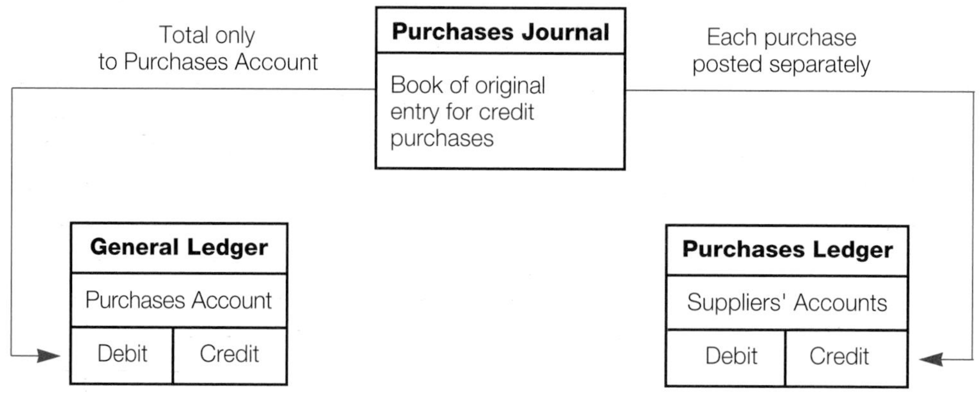

Total only
to Purchases Account
Purchases Journal
Book of original
entry for credit
purchases
Each purchase
posted separately
General Ledger
Purchases Account
Debit
Credit
Purchases Ledger
Suppliers' Accounts
Debit
Credit

Source: *Frank Wood's Book-keeping & Accounts,* 3rd edn, Pitman Publishing 1992

Fig 6.10 **Example of posting credit purchases**

Purchases Journal

	Invoice No	*Folio*	*(page 49)*
199X			£
Sept 2 R Simpson	9/101	PL16	670
8 B Hamilton	9/102	PL29	1,380
19 C Brown	9/103	PL55	120
30 K Gabriel	9/104	PL89	510
Transferred to purchases account		GL63	2,680

Source: *Frank Wood's Book-keeping & Accounts,* 3rd edn, Pitman Publishing 1992

Fig 6.11 **Example of a purchase requisition**

THE BODY SHOP

PURCHASE REQUISITION

Date: 17 AUGUST 1993

Raised By: G RAINHAM Dept: MATERIALS

Suggested Supplier's Name: (address if applicable):

MIMICK MANUFACTURING

MANCHESTER

Purchase Order No.: (if apllicable): 570157

Confirmation Order: Yes [X] No [ ]

FOR ANY SINGLE CAPITAL ITEM OVER £250 A CAPITAL EXPENDITURE PROPOSAL FORM IS REQUIRED.

Delivery Date: ASAP

DELIVERY DETAILS:

SPECIAL PACKAGING/LABELLING:

N/L CODE	QUANTITY	FULL PRODUCT DESCRIPTION	STOCK CODE	UNIT PRICE	TOTAL (excl VAT)
022-476-002-30	2	CENTRIS 610E 4/80			
		(INCLUDING 2 X 14" COLOUR SCREENS			
		FROM RESERVED STOCK)		956.00	1,912.00

Note
This requisition is produced in a set of three attached copies, colour-coded white, pink, and blue (for distribution) and employs NCR technology

SPEC IAL INSTRUCTIONS TO PURCHASING DEPT:

Authorised Signatory: [signature] Date: 18/8/93

Courtesy of Body Shop Supply Company

PC 6.2.2

Fig 6.12

Example of a purchase order

THE BODY SHOP
SUPPLY COMPANY

THE BODY SHOP SUPPLY COMPANY
WATERSMEAD, LITTLEHAMPTON, WEST SUSSEX BN17 6LS
TELEPHONE: LITTLEHAMPTON (0903) 731500
TELEX: 877055 BODYSH G FAX: (0903) 726250

PURCHASE ORDER No. 570157
REVISION
LH — Page: 1
G RAINHAM — Buyer: MJ
Date: 19/8/93

VAT REGISTRATION NO. GB 543 9386 15
REGISTERED IN ENGLAND NO. 1284170

PLEASE ENSURE OUR PURCHASE ORDER NUMBER APPEARS ON ALL DELIVERY NOTES AND INVOICES

SUPPLIER
Mimick Manufacturing Ltd
Unit 12, Cresswell Industrial Estate
Kings Way
MANCHESTER
M60 9NL

DELIVERY ADDRESS
The Body Shop International plc
Watersmead Bussiness Park
LITTLEHAMPTON
West Sussex BN17 6LS
Tel: 0903 731500

STOCK CODE	DESCRIPTION	QUANTITY	DUE DATE	UNIT COST	VALUE
022-476	CENTRIS 610E 4/80 (INCLUDING 2 X 14" COLOUR SCREENS FROM RESERVED STOCK)	2.000	9/9/93	956.00	1912.00
	F.A.O. G RAINHAM – MATERIALS				
	Please mark invoice/statement for the attention of:- The Body Shop Supply Finance Department				
				Total	1912.00

DELIVERY INSTRUCTIONS

For and on behalf of
The Body Shop International PLC..

Authorised Signature: ____________

Courtesy of Body Shop Supply Company

■ 4 The purchases ledger

PC 6.2.2

The purchases ledger includes the details of purchase transactions with a company's suppliers in the form of summarised financial data extracted from invoices, credit and debit notes received, together with any amendments needed to remedy any input errors.

A data source for the nominal ledger

Also, the purchase ledger provides a source of data needed for the purchases and purchases returns accounts in the nominal ledger (in which are recorded general summaries of income and expenditure of a business – rents received, sales, purchases returns, incoming fees, dividends etc., and also wages, heat and light, purchases, sales returns and so on.

Documents generated from purchase ledger data

Other accounting operations (and their documentation) which derive from purchase ledger entries include:

- summarising monthly purchases per supplier
- producing data for the purchase control account as a means of preparing to reconcile incoming suppliers' statements against in-house purchasing records
- producing the documentation relating to the payment of goods purchased on account
- remittance advices, cheques and cash book entries for goods paid for by cash
- management accounting information in the form of reports or analyses of purchases

■ 5 and 6 The nominal ledger and purchase control account

PC 6.2.2

The purpose of the general ledger (sometimes also referred to as the nominal ledger) is to record in summary form those transactions which go to make up the income and expenditure activities of a business's operations – sales, purchases, income or profits from various sources, running expenses, and so on. This ledger also holds details of the company's assets and liabilities.

In terms of purchase transactions, the nominal ledger holds summary details of the purchase control (or creditors') account for ease of reference, unencumbered by masses of detailed, daily purchase transactions such as receiving and cross-checking the details of delivery notes, invoices, debit and credit notes and statements etc.

■ Summary

The accounts documents which record the sales and purchasing operations of a business form in essence its lifeblood, circulating as they do around each month's trading period. So important is it to exercise control over both the sales and purchasing operations that larger firms employ accounting personnel called cost and management accountants, whose primary role is to set up systems which provide regular reports on sales and purchasing activities such as:

- sales to target charts (weekly, monthly, quarterly, annually)
- break-downs on costs of sales – direct and indirect costs attributable, including the purchase of stock and contribution to overheads.
- trading and profit and loss accounts – to monitor profitability, which will include the cost of goods and services purchased

A natural follow-on from documenting sales and purchasing operations is, of course, to record just as carefully the resultant flow of cash and other forms of money in and out of the business, and this topic is examined in the next section.

PC 6.2.2

DISCUSSION TOPICS

1 What advantages to a business do you consider stem from setting up a centralised purchasing department and system?

2 The practice of pilferage and petty theft – in the form of taking home items of office stationery, small items of office equipment, products manufactured, pirated copies of computer software applications etc. has been considered by some employees in organisations as part of the 'perks which go with the job'.

What types of security checks and processes can you think of which an accounts (and other involved departments) manager could introduce into a purchasing process to minimise endemic petty theft?

3 'One organisation's sale is another's purchase.' Can you think of any ways in which an ongoing supplier–customer relationship could be streamlined so as to simplify and speed up the credit sale/purchase process for both parties?

PC 6.2.2

ACTIVITIES

In pairs, carry out one of the following activities:

1 Make arrangements to visit the accounts department of a medium to large local firm so as to obtain an expert briefing on how the credit sales and purchasing accounting operations are carried out in practice.

Give your class an (authorised) oral briefing of about 10 minutes.

2 Make arrangements to visit the offices of a company purchasing manager and find out what makes up his or her job role.

Report back to your class with an oral briefing of about 10 minutes.

3 Find out if any local companies in your locality (likely to be manufacturers) are using the electronic data interchange (EDI) system to manage their purchasing from suppliers.

If so, make arrangements to obtain a briefing from the manager responsible on how the system works and what advantages it possesses. If no local operation is on hand, research into the subject with the help of your school/college/public reference library.

Brief your class orally (with illustrations) on what you discover in about 10 minutes.

Documenting credit sales

PC 6.2.3

Most private sector organisations need to generate sales constantly in order to survive – hence the need for mail-order catalogues, calls by sales representatives, direct selling door-to-door or by phone and so on.

However, the most persistent and energetic sales efforts invariably prove futile if they are not accompanied by a well-designed and painstakingly monitored sales documentation system, which records each step of the sales process clearly and free from errors (as far as is humanly possible). Without such a system being in place and vigilantly monitored, a company can soon run into cash-flow problems and ultimately into bankruptcy, since its account customers may be encouraged to defer payment endlessly and to sell on goods wrongly priced in their favour and so on.

The chart in Fig 6.13 on page 548 illustrates the main stages in the sales process which need to be documented in a sequence if the initial purchase order from an account customer is to be delivered and paid for within a previously agreed time-frame.

■ Eight key stages in documenting credit sales

PC 6.2.3

1 Receiving the purchase order

Today customers order goods or services in a wide variety of ways: by phone (*not recommended – no written record*), by letter, or by mailing a purchase order with a unique reference (*much better*), by faxing a purchase order (*quicker than the post but not a legal record)* and by electronic data interchange (EDI) – the buyer's computer 'talks' to the supplier's computer and orders goods directly; this expensive but fast ordering system is used by large manufacturers such as Ford UK Limited and Lucas plc.

Naturally enough, the key data on a purchase order will include the details shown in the following checklist.

KEY DATA ON A PURCHASE ORDER

- the purchaser's name and address for both delivery of the order and for the receipt of the associated accounts documentation (which may not be the same)
- name and address details of supplier, including any named person under 'for the attention of' who normally deals with such orders (to speed up the ordering process)
- date and accounting system references e.g. the purchase order number, say: JUN/1234/ABC
- quantity of items ordered: 100 cubic metres...
- key specification details: make, type, brand name, specifications, model number, unit price, extension price (i.e. total being ordered, reference to VAT rate payable etc.
- clear instructions on whether order is to be delivered or collected, or, if urgent, deadline date for delivery etc.

PC 6.2.3

Fig 6.13 Sales documentation: manual system – monthly cycle

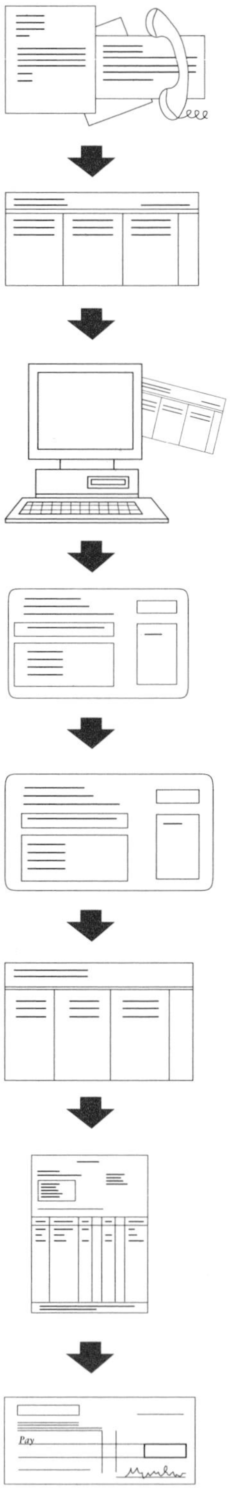

1 **Order received**
This may be by letter, telephone, fax or sales representative's order book

2 **Stores requisition raised**
This authorises the movement of the goods ordered from the warehouse to the dispatch department

3 **Stock record is amended**
The record may be kept on computer database or in a manual system using cards. The stock record is amended to show the reduced balance

4 **A sales invoice is issued**
The sales invoice shows the quantity and description of the goods supplied, price, customer's account number and the amount of VAT due

5 **A delivery/advice note is made out**
This is usually a copy of the invoice but without the pricing information. The delivery-man obtains a signature on one copy as evidence of receipt by the customer

6 **The transaction is recorded in the sales ledger or in the computer record**
The customer's account is brought up to date by adding the total of the invoice to the existing balance

a) **A credit note** is raised if the customer reports that the goods received are faulty or damaged in transit, and are returned to the supplier.

b) **A debit note** is raised if a pricing error is made on a sales invoice in favour of the customer in order to correct the pricing

7 **A statement of account is issued**
This is sent to the customer at the end of the trading period (usually monthly). The statement lists all invoices and credit notes raised during the month and shows the balance payable by the customer and the payment terms, discounts etc.

8 **The customer settles the account**
The customer sends a cheque with a remittance advice note. The payment will be entered in the sales ledger or computer record and the balance owing amended accordingly. Note: subsequent invoices will have been raised before the statement in 7 is due for payment

THE PROCESS BEGINS AGAIN

Most purchase orders indicate the agreed purchase price per item. This is normally the retail price before any deduction for discounts allowable, since such discounts are usually only shown at the later invoicing stage.

The examples shown in Fig 6.14 below illustrate two typical ways of organising the key data of a purchase order:

Fig 6.14 **Two styles of purchase order** *PC 6.2.2 6.2.3*

PURCHASE ORDER Order No. 1079

BURGESS & SON
27 Frith Street
Birkenhead B21 3RZ

Tel: (0601) 41732 VAT Reg. No. 632 117381

Roberts Suppliers Co.
Liverpool Road
Liverpool

Date: 3rd Sept 199X

Quantity	Cat. No.	Description	Price
2	LM713	Easi-ride mowers complete with collection boxes Delivery included	£1,527.30 each plus VAT

PURCHASE ORDER Order No. KT27

RUDKINS SUPERSTORES
Market Place, Runcorn

Tel: 0631 233152

Roberts Suppliers Co.
Liverpool Road
Liverpool

27th August 199X

Please supply:	Price £
6 Garden Forks (Aluminium)	22.30 each
10 Wheelbarrows	67.95 each
2 x 24" Quickmow Machines (Electric) with cable	324.00 each
Will collect, please advise	Plus VAT

Source: *Frank Wood's Business Accounting AAT Student's Workbook*, Sheila Robinson, Pitman Publishing 1993

2 and 3 The stock requisition order and stock control system

Once a purchase order has been received by the supplier, the next stage is for a stock requisition order to be made out. This order gives authorisation for goods to be moved from the place where they are being stored (warehouse or stockroom) to dispatch (a point from which they may be loaded on to vans or lorries for delivery).

The stock control system (whether on paper cards or computer) maintains records of stock movements (of a given item) in and out and the current resulting balance of stock-in-hand.

The stock requisition order and stock control systems carry out these important functions:

- they enable a close record to be kept of levels of stock being held, thus ensuring that re-ordering takes place before a 'stock-out' situation arises where orders cannot be promptly met
- they help to prevent stock losses from pilferage, theft or unauthorised movement of goods
- they aid the tracking of goods ordered (if a customer calls to complain of non-delivery of ordered goods, their progress along the sales order / delivery chain can be monitored).

PC 6.2.3

Fig 6.15

STOCK CONTROL CARD

DESCRIPTION	Grade A Tent Cloth (Gold)	BAY NO	13
		MAXIMUM	500 metres
CODE NO	60 TC A/G	MINIMUM	100 metres
		REORDER LEVEL	150 metres

Date	Receipts		Issues		Balance in stock	Remarks Goods on Order and Audit check
	Goods Rec'd Note No.	Quantity	Reqn. No.	Quantity		
199-		metres		metres	metres	
July 1					300	
" 4			734	100	200	
" 14			823	100	100	15/7 Order No. 97324
" 28	7629	200			300	

Minimum stock level reached (→ balance 100 on July 14)

Re-ordering process activated (→ 15/7 Order No. 97324; 200 received on July 28)

Source: Adapted from *Finance, First Levels of Competance*, John Harrison, Pitman Publishing 1990. By kind permission of the author.

Fig 6.16 PC 6.2.3

STORES REQUISITION FOR STOCK

NO. 734

MATERIALS REQUIRED FOR: DATE 4/7/9-

JOB NO .... RUN NO 4321

Quantity	Description	Price per unit £	p	Cost £	p	Notes
100 metres	Code No. 60 TC A/G Grade A Tent Cloth (Gold)					

Works Foreman P. Long Operative S. Hills	Storekeepers Initials	Cost Office Ref: ....

Source: *Clerical Accounting*, J Harrison & R Dawber, Pitman Publishing 1976

Note that, today, most medium to large firms have their sales systems fully computerised. A computerised system will ensure that, once a purchase order has been entered (into an integrated accounting software system), the stock control details and requisition authorisation will be automatically passed on to the stock-room personnel and the appropriate deductions made to stock levels and printout documents raised etc. The advantages of an integrated computerised accounting system include:

- fewer data entries, therefore less risk of error
- faster administration resulting in customers' orders being delivered and recorded much more quickly
- fewer sheets of paper clogging the administrative system.

4 The delivery/ advice note PC 6.2.3

Once authorisation has been given for the goods ordered to be moved, they are taken to the organisation's dispatch point. In the case of a regional warehouse servicing a national supermarket chain, this is likely to be a covered (secure) area with loading bays raised some 1 – 1.5 metres above ground level to allow pallets to be loaded directly on to backed-up articulated lorries by means of fork-lift trucks. In a book distribution company, for example, goods which comprise various books ordered by booksellers are first 'picked' by staff moving along shelving set out in a computerised sequence of book sets, and then packed into cardboard boxes for moving to despatch, where a national carrier collects them and delivers them according to a route masterminded (again!) by a computer.

In order to ensure that security requirements are satisfied and to obtain a record of prompt delivery, most suppliers provide the delivery driver with an advice or delivery note for the receiving customer to sign. This note provides the same information as the purchase order (unless some goods on the order are omitted because they are out of stock, in which case this fact will be advised under a reference like: 'to follow'), and is, to all intents and purposes, a version of the invoice to come but with all pricing details omitted. The omission of such details is to prevent confidential buying terms from becoming common knowledge and perhaps being leaked to the customer's competitors.

While the delivery driver may only want to obtain his signatures and date (in order to speed off to his next drop, the prudent receiver of the goods is well advised to check all deliveries for breakage or damage in transit before accepting delivery (which may limit his ability to obtain recompense for goods later found to be faulty). Often, the receiver – especially in a small business – is occupied with customers when a delivery occurs, and so signs for the delivery with the added reservation: 'goods received uninspected' in order to reserve the right to return faulty goods and thus to obtain a credit note for them.

PC 6.2.3

5 The invoice

Before examining the invoicing stage of account sales documentation, it is important to recall that, before any account sales transactions are begun, a business supplier will have obtained satisfactory financial references (from, say, a would-be account customer's bankers or other existing suppliers). The supplier of goods or services on account will then have agreed a ceiling amount for orders placed within any trading period (four weeks, a calendar month etc.), as well as the period of credit extension (for example 30 days) immediately following the receipt by the account customer of the statement relating to goods purchased in a given trading period. In this way an account customer is expected (under the terms of the agreed credit given) to pay for goods delivered say, during March by the end of April. Note that during periods of rapidly rising inflation or when high interest rates make money 'dear', traders may shorten significantly the length of credit time given to account customers.

The examples shown in Fig 6.17 on page 553 provide some typical examples of current invoicing layouts.

Just as for a purchase order, there are a number of key data entries required on a sales invoice in order for it to prove an effective accounts document.

PC 6.2.3

KEY DATA ON A SALES INVOICE

- the customary postal address details for both supplier and customer
- the account customer's unique account number
- a unique reference number for each individual invoice (for ease of later reference or query); note that some invoices also include a reference to the trading period in which they were issued
- entries for: quantity and description (model, make, specification etc.) of the goods
- a catalogue or goods stock number if appropriate
- the gross (i.e. retail or pre-discount price) price of a single good – its unit price
- the extended price of the total number of goods of an identical type ordered (for example 3 × Gardenade Rustless Wheelbarrows)
- an entry for the combined total value of the goods appearing on the invoice (Total: £149.99) before the addition of VAT
- an entry showing the deduction of agreed discounts – for example 'Less 30% trade discount... £130.50'
- an entry for the VAT (at its current rate, say, 17.5%) in £s to be added to the invoice total
- the unique VAT registration number of the supplier: e.g. VAT 863 2730 33

Fig 6.17

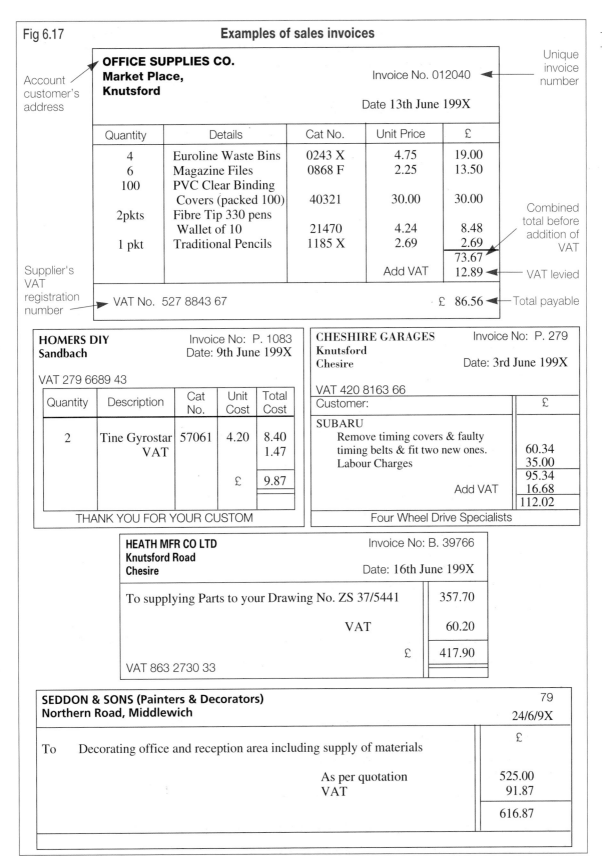

Examples of sales invoices

OFFICE SUPPLIES CO.
Market Place,
Knutsford

Invoice No. 012040

Date 13th June 199X

Account customer's address → OFFICE SUPPLIES CO.

Unique invoice number → Invoice No. 012040

Quantity	Details	Cat No.	Unit Price	£
4	Euroline Waste Bins	0243 X	4.75	19.00
6	Magazine Files	0868 F	2.25	13.50
100	PVC Clear Binding Covers (packed 100)	40321	30.00	30.00
2pkts	Fibre Tip 330 pens Wallet of 10	21470	4.24	8.48
1 pkt	Traditional Pencils	1185 X	2.69	2.69
				73.67
			Add VAT	12.89

VAT No. 527 8843 67 — £ 86.56

Combined total before addition of VAT → 73.67

VAT levied → 12.89

Supplier's VAT registration number → VAT No. 527 8843 67

Total payable → £ 86.56

HOMERS DIY
Sandbach

Invoice No: P. 1083
Date: 9th June 199X

VAT 279 6689 43

Quantity	Description	Cat No.	Unit Cost	Total Cost
2	Tine Gyrostar	57061	4.20	8.40
	VAT			1.47
			£	9.87

THANK YOU FOR YOUR CUSTOM

CHESHIRE GARAGES
Knutsford
Chesire

Invoice No: P. 279

Date: 3rd June 199X

VAT 420 8163 66

Customer:	£
SUBARU Remove timing covers & faulty timing belts & fit two new ones.	60.34
Labour Charges	35.00
	95.34
Add VAT	16.68
	112.02

Four Wheel Drive Specialists

HEATH MFR CO LTD
Knutsford Road
Chesire

Invoice No: B. 39766

Date: 16th June 199X

To supplying Parts to your Drawing No. ZS 37/5441	357.70
VAT	60.20
£	417.90

VAT 863 2730 33

SEDDON & SONS (Painters & Decorators)
Northern Road, Middlewich

79
24/6/9X

	£
To Decorating office and reception area including supply of materials	
As per quotation	525.00
VAT	91.87
	616.87

Source: Adapted from *Frank Wood's Business Accounting AAT Student's Workbook,* Sheila Robinson, Pitman Publishing 1993

Note: In some account sales transactions the deduction of any allowed discounts is taken from the payment due for an issued monthly statement; this practice keeps the details of net buying terms confidential – between the accountants of the supplier and accounts customer.

PC 6.2.3

■ Posting credit sales to the sales ledger

1 The credit sales are posted, one by one, to the debit side of each customer's account in the sales ledger.

2 At the end of each period the total of the credit sales is posted to the credit of the sales account in the general ledger.

Fig 6.18 **Posting credit sales**

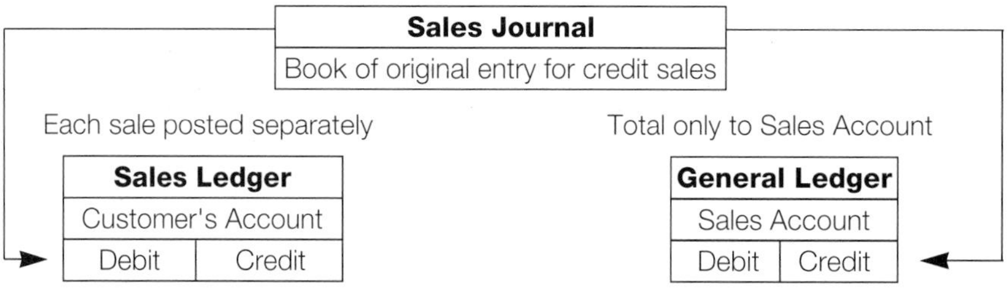

Source: *Frank Wood's Book-keeping & Accounts,* 3rd edn, Pitman Publishing 1992

PC 6.2.3

Fig 6.19 **Example of posting credit sales**

Sales Journal

			Invoice No	Folio	(page 26) £
199X					
Sept	1	D Poole	16554	SL 12	560
"	8	T Cockburn	16555	SL 39	1,640
"	28	C Carter	16556	SL 125	200
"	30	D Stevens & Co	16557	SL 249	1,100
		Transferred to Sales Account		GL 44	3,520

Source: *Frank Wood's Book-keeping & Accounts,* 3rd edn, Pitman Publishing 1992

PC 6.2.3

6 The sales ledger entry

Just as documents need to be raised to provide records of delivery and pricing details for credit customers, so they need to be entered into the supplier's accounting system – in this case into the sales ledger – before being passed on in summary form (via sales journal or sales returns books) to the nominal or general ledger.

In the accounting system, it is the sales ledger which records against individual account sales customers' entries the financial details of goods sold to them on credit (in the left-hand Dr column) and payments received for goods purchased by them (in the right-hand Cr column:

Fig 6.20 PC 6.2.3

Sales ledger

Dr			Halshaw Printing Co. A/c			SL1	Cr
Date		Fol	£	Date		Fol	£
31 July	Balance	b/d	117.90	13 July	Bank	CB7	57.90

Source: *Frank Wood's Business Accounting AAT Student's Workbook,* Sheila Robinson, Pitman Publishing 1993

In this way, the supplier maintains careful records of what is owed and what is paid for at any time for any account customer.

The details of each invoice issued will be retained on a sales ledger card (or its computerised equivalent) in order to enable the monthly statement to be compiled, printed and delivered.

6A and B Credit and Debit Notes

PC 6.2.3

Sometimes, despite every effort to avoid them, mistakes occur, or goods prove faulty at the delivery stage. For example, a clerical error may result in 21 and not 12 identical stock items being charged for on an invoice. This mistake, having been picked up by a vigilant accounts clerk or sales assistant, is pointed out to the supplier, who therefore needs to rectify it by reducing the items charged for by 9. Such a transaction is accomplished by the issue of a credit note for the amount. In order for the sum involved to be credited (so as to prevent any ensuing overpayment by the account customer) the sum will also be shown as a credit in the Cr column of the monthly statement and be deducted from the gross total amount shown as due for payment. Note also that when credit notes are issued, there will be a corresponding reduction due in the amount of VAT payable.

When, on the other hand, a mistake occurs in the account customer's favour – perhaps this time spotted by an equally alert accounts clerk working for the supplier, then a debit note is issued in the same way as for its credit note counterpart. The debit note amount will also be clearly shown on the relevant statement as an extra item of expenditure incurred. Both credit and debit notes will supply cross-references to the issued invoices to which they refer.

E & OE: Errors and Omissions Excepted

In order to enable mistakes in arithmetic or textual reference to be rectified at a later date, many firms include the abbreviation E&OE at the foot of their account sales documents (invoices, credit/debit notes and statements) so as to avoid a customer claiming that the issued document represented a firm, contractual price for goods received and accepted.

PC 6.2.3

7 Statements of account

A statement of account is 'rendered' or sent to each account customer on a regular basis. Usually, the basis employed requires that statements are sent to account customers a week to a fortnight after the end of the trading period, say, four weeks or a calendar month, to which they refer. The reason for this particular timing is two-fold:

Batch runs of computerised statements
First, suppliers need some time after the closing of the trading period to produce (usually on computer by means of an integrated accounts software package) the summary details (the invoice references and billed totals) of all the invoices relating to a single customer's account on to the statement, including any issued credit or debit notes. In large companies, the calculations for each statement and the statements themselves – which may run into thousands – are processed in a series of batches through the computer, starting with customers' trading names A–E and so on. Naturally this takes some time to achieve, added to which is the time taken for statements to arrive through the post.

Customer checks on statements received
By the same token, customers' accounts departments need some time to check that the statements' details and totals coincide with their own records (in their purchase ledgers) before authorisation is given for the account to be paid. This can mean cross-checking each received invoice against the statement manually in many small businesses – hence the need for strict care and attention to be paid to delivery acceptance procedures. In larger firms, the computer handles much of this work and concentration is paid to reconciling totals – the statement's total, minus any credit notes raised for goods returned, plus any debit note amounts which rectify suppliers' errors.

Settlement discounts

In order to assist the prompt payment of an account within the agreed settlement period (for example: *twenty-eight days after the end of the related trading period*) suppliers often include at the foot of a statement a calculation of a settlement discount which the customer may deduct from the bill if payment is made within, say, the stipulated twenty-eight days:

Total:	£1545:55
Less Settlement Discount 3.75%	£ 57:95
Net:	£1487:60

Note that in times of high inflation suppliers tend to shorten the settlement time for accounts to be paid and increase the 'carrot' of settlement discount deductible (which is probably built into the agreed account sales price terms in the first place!)

The following example (Fig 6.21) illustrates what a typical statement looks like:

Fig 6.21

PC 6.2.3

STATEMENT OF ACCOUNT

STARCELL OFFICE SUPPLIES

UNIT 8 HANDYWELL INDUSTRIAL ESTATE, NORTHTOWN NO6 1EU

Tel: 039 843 3291 Telex: 986243 Fax: 039 2196743

VAT Registration No. 2538758 32

Date: 31 March 199X

To: Pitman Publishing
128 Long Acre
London WC2E 9AN

Terms; 5% 7 days
2½ 28 days
Otherwise net

Date 199-	Details	Ref No.	Dr £	Cr £	Balance £
1 Feb	To account rendered Jan				460.27
9 Feb	To invoice	10862	103.80		564.07
12 Feb	By credit note	566		24.20	539.87
15 Feb	To invoice	10876	91.40		631.27
23 Feb	To debit note	195	11.60		642.87
28 Feb	To invoice	10933	84.32		727.19
28 Feb	By cheque			500.00	227.19
	Amount outstanding				227.19

E & O E

Statements and overdue accounts

Some companies take the opportunity on monthly statements to draw attention to any invoices which remain unpaid from earlier trading periods. Also, if payment proves tardy, copy statements may be sent to slow-paying customers as the first of a series of strategies aimed at securing overdue payment for goods or services sold on account. If this proves ineffective, then the accounts department will activate its debtors' collection system (usually 2–3 letters in total), which tend to culminate in terse warnings such as:

> *...Unless payment is received within seven days of the receipt of this letter,* [which is sent by recorded delivery] *the company will have no hesitation in taking legal actions to recover the debt.*

Such sentiments represent the final effort to recover an overdue debt, when retaining the customer's goodwill is no longer deemed necessary, since once payment has been received, the account will be closed.

Age analysis of debtors

An important part of the management of credit sales is to keep a watchful eye on the time taken by account customers to pay for goods or services received. Failure to collect monies due can quickly lead to cash-flow problems and, if the business is heavily reliant upon account sales, to crises. It is common practice, therefore, for an age analysis of credit sales debts to be undertaken – preferably automatically by an accounts package computer program, or manually from the sales ledger.

PC 6.2.3

8 Remittance advice and cheque in payment

Having received the supplier's statement and checked it out against its own internal purchase account documentation, payment is authorised by accounts and a remittance advice note raised detailing precisely what payment is being made for, along with a cheque (crossed a/c payee for security) for the agreed amount.

The account sales cycle begins again ...

By the time the payment has been received, recorded and processed, it will not be long before it is once more time to batch and run the statements for the succeeding month's sales...!

PC 6.2.3

DISCUSSION TOPICS

1 What dangers exist for a business which has, say, 75 per cent of its turnover in credit sales?

2 What parts of the credit sales process can you think of (or add to) which help to make the 'sale on account' a financially safe and secure transaction for the seller involved?

3 Do you think that legislation is needed to ensure that firms pay for the goods or services they have bought on credit within a set time? Note that at present many firms deliberately hold back on payments due in order to assist their own cash flow etc.

ACTIVITIES

PC 6.2.3

In groups of two or three, carry out one of the following activities and report back suitably to your class:

1 Draw up a flow chart (relating to a medium-sized company) which shows the sequence of actions taken in order to process a credit sale from start to finish, including the activities of the salesperson, the accounts staff, and the stockroom and delivery personnel. Indicate which documents are issued at each stage, and which department or section receives which top or copy item.

When you have completed your flow chart, copy it to other groups in your class and hold a discussion to see how it might be improved so as to cut down on activities and time taken without sacrificing reliability and security.

2 Find out what legal support a company can rely upon when seeking to recover debts owing from a 'bad account customer' who refuses to pay for goods or services received.

Design a factsheet to record your findings and circulate it around your class.

REVIEW TEST

PC 6.2.1 6.2.2 6.2.3

1 List five key purposes of a business accounting system.

2 Write down the accounting equation upon which the double-entry bookkeeping system is based.

3 Set down the table which illustrates the key rules of debiting and crediting account entries which increase or decrease: assets, liabilities and capital.

4 State what debit and credit actions you would take if your business purchased a motor-van for cash which cost £180.

5 What information is stored in books of original entry?

6 List the books which make up the full set of books of original entry.

7 List the ledgers commonly used in the double-entry accounting system.

8 Explain briefly the difference between a personal and an impersonal account.

9 What is a private ledger?

10 Set down the main steps in the processing of a credit sale and list the accounting documents involved at each step.

11 What key data would you expect to find on a typical purchase order?

12 How does a delivery note differ from an invoice?

13 List the key data you would expect to find on a typical credit sale invoice.

14 Set down a typical entry for an individual account customer's purchase of goods in a sales ledger.

15 Explain the difference between a credit note and a debit note and how they affect the statement to which they relate.

16 What does E & OE stand for? What is it used for in credit sales documentation?

17 Why are credit sales statements batch run through the computer in a large business?

18 What is a settlement discount and what is its purpose?

19 What is a letter of collection? How is it used in the documentation of accounts?

20 What is meant by 'age analysis of debtors'. How does this concept impact upon an accounting system?

21 Why do firms send remittance advice notes with cheques paying for goods or services received?

22 List five advantages of employing an integrated accounts software application package to process a company's accounts.

23 What is meant by EDI? How does it assist the accounting process?

24 List the key steps in sequence of a credit purchase and state which document is used at which step.

25 What is the purpose of a purchases day book? What information does it record?

PC 6.2.4 6.2.5

Payments and receipts documents

In most businesses, payment for goods or services received is made either by cash or cheque. And it is upon these two forms of income that this section concentrates.

However, it should not be overlooked that payment for goods or services can take other forms than cash or cheque:

PC 6.2.4 6.2.5

NON-CASH/CHEQUE FORMS OF PAYMENT

- postal/money orders purchased at a post office or bank
- banker's draft (a safe form of payment for large sums which the clearing bank guarantees to honour); a banker's draft cannot 'bounce' like a cheque issued against an empty account.
- purchase by credit card/switch card or other forms of 'plastic money'
- direct debits and standing orders made out in the company's favour, by which purchases can be paid for by transferring money directly from the customer's to the seller's bank account

PC 6.2.4 6.2.5

■ Processing cash and cheques

During the course of daily trading a host of organisations large and small – supermarkets, newsagents, football clubs, leisure centres, departmental stores, market stallholders etc. – accept both cash and cheques as payments for goods or services sold.

Accepting cash today may seem the least of a businessman's problems, except that counterfeit money is increasingly in circulation, and many firms pass notes through scanning machines especially designed to identify counterfeit notes.

Similarly, clearing banks circulate among bona fide traders details of chequebooks and cheque guarantee/credit cards recently stolen in order to minimise the effects of cheque fraud. Currently the clearing banks undertake to honour cheques issued by their customers to whom they have supplied a cheque guarantee card up to amounts of either £50 or £100, and the appropriate amount is shown clearly on the customer's card.

Paying into the bank

Prudent business proprietors and branch managers pay their takings of cash and cheques into their banks daily by means of a night safe facility and a paying-in book. This avoids the need to keep money overnight in empty premises.

Nevertheless, businesses such as departmental stores with large daily turnovers still feel it worthwhile to purchase a safe into which to transfer takings hourly from their various sections and floors, and to make regular daily deposits at the nearest branch of the company's bank.

■ Recording and processing money paid in to the business

PC 6.2.4 6,2,5

Each organisation evolves its own system for receiving, recording and banking money flowing into the business. In the following section the major stages in a typical system are illustrated.

Key stages in receiving, recording and banking incoming monies

PC 6.2.4 6.2.5

■ 1 In the small business

Cash sales

When a cash sale transaction takes place, customers are provided with a written/till receipt detailing the item(s), cost and VAT (if applicable). The small trader retains a copy of the receipt (note that most cash registers record and analyse all transactions to aid cashing up at the end of daily trading.

The coins, notes and cheques received in payment are kept in a cash register (till) until the end of the day's trading. They are then totalled and after leaving aside for the next day a 'float' or small amount of mixed coins and notes for change etc. the total money taken during the day is entered on a Takings Summary Form (Fig 6.22 on page 562).

Some small businesses, say a garage family business, may use a payments received analysis sheet on a daily basis to record the payment (by individual invoice) of, for example, a service to a delivery van. Since payment has been either by cash or cheque, such transactions need to be set down separately and by account customer (Fig 6.23 on page 562).

Accounts documents and audit trails

Such an analysis sheet provides a record of individual payments of account and may also serve as a source document in any audit trail. The audit trail is a documented system or

PC
6.2.4
6.2.5

Fig 6.22

TAKINGS SUMMARY FORM			
ASSISTANT'S NAME *Peter Jones*		DATE 4-5-9X	
			£
1	Opening Float		15.90
2	Total of Payments Rec'd Analysis Sheet (re: Customers' Accounts)		245.25
3	Total of Cash/Cheque Petrol Receipts		642.80
	TOTAL	£	903.95
4	Deduct Opening Float		15.90
	TOTAL AMOUNT TAKEN	£	888.05
ANALYSIS OF CASH/CHEQUES			
Cheques Total			392.15
Cash Total			495.90
		£	888.05
DISCREPANCIES (if any)			

Source: Adapted from *Frank Wood's Business Accounting AAT Student's Workbook,* Sheila Robinson, Pitman Publishing 1993

PC
6.2.4
6.2.5

Fig 6.23

PAYMENTS RECEIVED ANALYSIS SHEET Date 10-5-9X

Customer	Total amount received £	By cash £	By cheque £	Invoice No.
B. Simpson	14.62	14.62		06931
Ace Taxis	32.50		32.50	06932
K. Stone	7.00	7.00		
H White & Son (Builders)	24.95		24.95	0693
TOTALS	£ 245.25	£ 86.20	£ 159.05	

Source: Adapted from *Frank Wood's Business Accounting AAT Student's Workbook,* Sheila Robinson, Pitman Publishing 1993 route through which an accounting activity may be checked, so as to ensure that each step in the accounting process is error-free. *PC 6.2.4 6.2.5*

For example, should an account payment cheque become mislaid prior to being banked, the fact that it was received is evident on the payments received analysis sheet. Both internal accountants, a company's chartered accountants and the Inland Revenue may need to sample a company's accounting systems and procedures by using the audit trail approach in order to be satisfied that the summarised totals on, say, a trading and profit and loss account are correct. This is especially the case when a firm makes extensive use of a computerised accounts package.

Fig 6.24(i) **Example of a bank paying-in slip** *PC 6.2.4 6.2.5*

Counterfoil:

Date 4-5-9X
Credit BLACKWALL Gge

£50 Notes	50	00
£20 Notes	120	00
£10 Notes	100	00
£5 Notes	85	00
£1	93	00
50p	21	00
20p	6	00
10p, 5p	3	00
Bronze	17	90
Total Cash	495	90
Cheques etc. see over	392	15
£	888	05

Slip:

Date 4-5-9X **bank giro credit**

Cashier's stamp and initials

Code No 77 - 05 - 13
Bank OAK
Branch BUXTON

Credit BLACKWALL GARAGE

Account No. 69345651

Number of cheques *8*

Paid in by P. Jones

£50 Notes	50	00
£20 Notes	120	00
£10 Notes	100	00
£5 Notes	85	00
£1	93	00
50p	21	00
20p	6	00
10p, 5p	3	00
Bronze	17	90
Total Cash	495	90
Cheques etc. *see over*	392	15
£	888	05

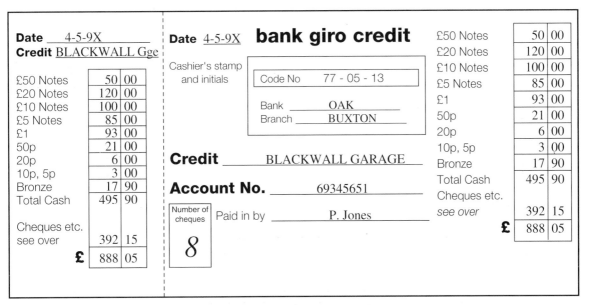

Fig 6.24(ii) Reverse

Cheques etc.

£	125	94	brought forward **£**	264	01
	32	50		56	83
	24	95		22	45
	80	62		42	60
				6	26
Carried forward **£**	264	01	Carried over **£**	392	15

Counterfoil Carried over £

392 15

Source: Adapted from *Frank Wood's Business Accounting AAT Student's Workbook*. Sheila Robinson, Pitman Publishing 1993

Paying money into the bank

Once the day's takings have been summarised and details noted of any account payments made, the cash and cheque takings (less the float) may be banked. It is good practice to use a night safe, money pouch/sack and plastic coin bags (provided by the bank) in order to deposit a day's takings in the bank' vaults rather than in a shop or filling-station till etc.

The clearing banks provide paying-in forms in book sets to this end. Note that the retained counterfoil provides the trader's record of what has been deposited (see Fig. 6.24 on page 563).

The components of a business cheque

Each of the cheques received by a business displays a set of key information – for its issuer, recipient and the two banks involved in debiting and crediting it to the respective interested parties (see Fig. 6.25).

PC
6.2.4
6.2.5

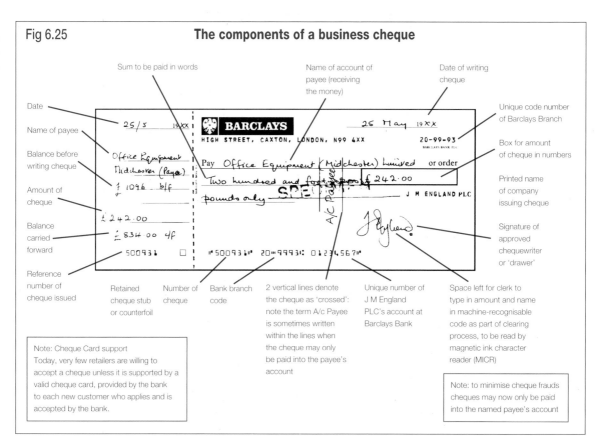

Fig 6.25 The components of a business cheque

Note: Cheque Card support
Today, very few retailers are willing to accept a cheque unless it is supported by a valid cheque card, provided by the bank to each new customer who applies and is accepted by the bank.

Note: to minimise cheque frauds cheques may now only be paid into the named payee's account

The alternative to paper cheques: 'smart' plastic shopping cards

In the UK, millions of cheques are processed by the clearing banks each working day. However, bank guarantee cards like those using the Switch system and so-called smart cards, which store electronically in a built-in micro-chip the current balance of a person's account (so as to ensure that enough money is in the account to pay for goods or services about to be purchased) are replacing the issuing of paper cheques. Not everyone likes the instant debit/credit transfer of funds which the Switch systems operates, but then, not everyone liked at first the introduction of self-service in petrol stations in the early 1970s!

The bank statement

PC 6.2.4 6.2.5

Unless requested at more frequent intervals, a small company is likely to receive a monthly statement of account from its bank (see Fig 6.26).

PC 6.2.4 6.2.5

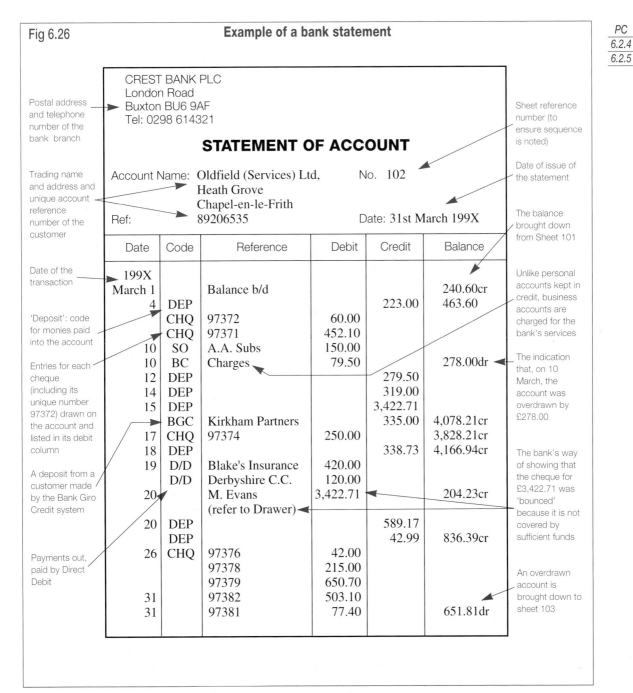

Fig 6.26 **Example of a bank statement**

CREST BANK PLC
London Road
Buxton BU6 9AF
Tel: 0298 614321

STATEMENT OF ACCOUNT

Account Name: Oldfield (Services) Ltd, Heath Grove, Chapel-en-le-Frith — No. 102

Ref: 89206535 — Date: 31st March 199X

Date	Code	Reference	Debit	Credit	Balance
199X March 1		Balance b/d			240.60cr
4	DEP			223.00	463.60
	CHQ	97372	60.00		
	CHQ	97371	452.10		
10	SO	A.A. Subs	150.00		
10	BC	Charges	79.50		278.00dr
12	DEP			279.50	
14	DEP			319.00	
15	DEP			3,422.71	
	BGC	Kirkham Partners		335.00	4,078.21cr
17	CHQ	97374	250.00		3,828.21cr
18	DEP			338.73	4,166.94cr
19	D/D	Blake's Insurance	420.00		
	D/D	Derbyshire C.C.	120.00		
20		M. Evans (refer to Drawer)	3,422.71		204.23cr
20	DEP			589.17	
	DEP			42.99	836.39cr
26	CHQ	97376	42.00		
		97378	215.00		
		97379	650.70		
31		97382	503.10		
31		97381	77.40		651.81dr

Annotations:

- Postal address and telephone number of the bank branch
- Trading name and address and unique account reference number of the customer
- Date of the transaction
- 'Deposit': code for monies paid into the account
- Entries for each cheque (including its unique number 97372) drawn on the account and listed in its debit column
- A deposit from a customer made by the Bank Giro Credit system
- Payments out, paid by Direct Debit
- Sheet reference number (to ensure sequence is noted)
- Date of issue of the statement
- The balance brought down from Sheet 101
- Unlike personal accounts kept in credit, business accounts are charged for the bank's services
- The indication that, on 10 March, the account was overdrawn by £278.00
- The bank's way of showing that the cheque for £3,422.71 was 'bounced' because it is not covered by sufficient funds
- An overdrawn account is brought down to sheet 103

Source: Adapted from Frank Wood's *Business Accounting AAT Student's Workbook*, Sheila Robinson, Pitman Publishing 1993

This statement shows clearly each inflow and outflow of money by means of individual entries in either the credit or debit column and the resultant balance. The bank statement also indicates whether an account is in credit (CR) or overdrawn (DR) as a result of more cheques having been issued than money paid in at a given point in time.

The clearing banks provide a range of abbreviations to help the customer to interpret the statement:

CR	credit	CP	card purchase
DR	debit	BGC	bank giro credit
OD	overdrawn	CC	cash or cheques
SO	standing order	AC	automated cash withdrawal (e.g. Cashpoint)
DD	direct debit	EC	eurocheques etc.
DV	dividend		

The takings of a business paid into a bank's night safe deposit will be checked by a bank cashier the following morning and the pouch and paying-in book will be ready for collection at the start of the next daily paying-in cycle. The cash and cheques (once processed and safely cleared against their issuers' bank balances) will be credited to the paying-in firm's account and the banked total will appear as a credit entry on the statement.

PC 6.2.4 6.2.5

■ In the large business

The sequence of steps explained above are followed by larger companies, which also employ some additional procedures and security practices.

The cash book

In order to avoid cash being lost or misappropriated on its way to the bank, large organisations use a cash book to record and track precisely its progress within the accounting system in use. The cash book is also used to record the routine deposits of cash and cheques into a company's bank account (see Figs 6.27 and 6.28).

PC 6.2.4 6.2.5

Handling payments received in large companies

An apocryphal story about one particular branch of a famous High Street clothing retailer recounts that, as the nearest branch of the plc's bank was some distance away and the tills were too small for the current boom in sales, the floor supervisors used to hide various parts of the day's takings in brown paper bags stuffed into the pockets of ladies' and gents' overcoats. These would then be retrieved at the end of the day for checking and banking!

Nowadays, large firms pursuing whatever business activity are much more systematic and careful about the ways in which they process their payments received. In large stores, accounting staff remove takings from tills for banking at regular intervals during the day. Firms with large numbers of account customers have all associated payments routed either to a regional or head office accounts department which employs specialist staff to handle them and nothing else.

Such payments are processed as explained earlier in this Unit via the sales account day journals and postings to the sales and nominal ledgers. It is worth noting, however, that large firms usually introduce stringent internal security systems to forestall the accidental loss or theft of cash or convertible money orders etc. For example in some organisations *all* incoming mail (save that for the most senior executives) is opened by trusted mailroom/

Fig 6.27 **Example of a two-column cash book** PC 6.2.4 6.2.5

Cash Book

199X			Cash £	Bank £	199X			Cash £	Bank £
Aug	1	Capital		1,000	Aug	7	Rates		105
"	2	T Moore	33		"	8	Rent	20	
"	3	W P Ltd		244	"	12	C Potts	19	
"	5	K Charles	25		"	12	F Small Ltd		95
"	15	F Hughes	37		"	26	K French		268
"	16	K Noone		408	"	28	Wages	25	
"	30	H Sanders		20	"	31	Balance c/d	49	1,204
"	30	H Howe	18						
			113	1,672				113	1,672
Sept 1		Balances b/d	49	1,204					

Source: *Frank Wood's Book-keeping & Accounts*, 3rd edn, Pitman Publishing 1992

Fig 6.28 **Example of bank column cash-book layout** PC 6.2.4 6.2.5

CASH BOOK (Bank Column Only)

Dr Cr

Date	Details		Folio	Bank	Date	Details		Folio	Bank
199X					199X				
March 1	Balance		b/f	240.60	March 3	Wage	371		452.10
3	C. Mellor	161.00							
	M. Bennett	25.00			4	Post Office Counters			
	E.Proudlove	37.00		223.00		M/Van Tax	372		60.00
12	Cash Sales Banked			279.50	6	J. Ashton	373		121.42
14	F. Ball	134.00			8	Rent–			
	B. Green	185.00		319.00		Sims & Co.	374		250.00
15	M. Evans			3,422.71	12	Fountains			
						(Stationery)	375		102.63
16	Sales			589.17					
					17	S. Brown	376		42.00

Source: *Frank Wood's Business Accounting AAT Student's Workbook,* Sheila Robinson, Pitman Publishing 1993

accounts staff. All cheques and other monies despatched as payment for goods and services are carefully extracted from postal envelopes and recorded on to a type of payments received schedule and signed for by the clerk responsible for accepting the payments. In this way, the likelihood of any incoming payments being 'lost' internally is minimised.

PC
6.2.4
6.2.5

Processing payments for purchases

In large organisations, the staff responsible for paying for all goods and services are likely to be just as busy as their account sales counterparts. Therefore systematising the process is just as important:

1 Departmental personnel requiring a good or service start the process by filling out and submitting to, say, the purchasing department **a purchase requisition order.**

2 This order is routed to the purchase department for scrutiny and authorisation. (Remember that in many large organisations the cheapest and best buying terms result from centralised purchasing, so the requesting department's requisition is checked so as to ensure that it specifies the approved stockist and the correct buying terms and discounts etc.) From the purchase requisition order **a purchase order** is made out.

3 The next steps may be viewed as a kind of mirror image of the steps explained in the sales accounting process, in that the purchasing company despatches the purchase order to the supplier and awaits the receipt of:

- **a delivery note**
- **a sales invoice**
- **any debit or credit notes issued**
- **a statement**

4 These incoming documents are checked against the company's own purchase accounts system – goods-in docketing, entries in the purchases day book and postings to the purchases and nominal ledgers.

5 Once the purchase accounts section is satisfied that a supplier's statement agrees with its own records of what has been received (allowing for any purchase returns arising from incorrect or faulty goods supplied etc.) payment will be authorised for the account rendered by the incoming statement.

PC
6.2.4
6.2.5

Payment for goods or services received

In a large organisation, a section of its accounts department is likely to handle all payments due, including any expenses claims by its own salesforce, petrol purchased by maintenance staff etc. This role is undertaken by a cashier, who will also issue 'top-ups' for imprest petty cash accounts kept in departments (see below).

Where payments are processed against purchase orders placed with established suppliers, then (just as for the issue of sales account statements) a batch run will be undertaken with the aid of specialised purchase account software which automatically computes, prints and records the cheques issued against each individual account. Similarly, a printed remittance advice note will be produced to accompany the cheque (see Fig. 6.29).

PC 6.2.4 6.2.5

Fig 6.29

REMITTANCE ADVICE

TO: Gripsure Trainers Ltd
41 South Street
London SW4 6AJ

SQUIRES SPORTS
Booth Avenue
Birmingham

Account Ref: JC 102 | Date: 12.1.9X | Page: 25

DATE	DETAILS	INVOICES	CREDIT NOTES	PAYMENT AMOUNT
4.12.9X	Cross-Country JX	G42193		124.92
7.12.9X	Jogger JT3	G42241		96.82
12.12.9X	Ladies' Badminton	G43211		130.25
16.12.9X	Circuit Trainers		F4 321	–24.95
28.12.9X	STATEMENT		BALANCE DUE	£327.04

Source: Adapted from *Frank Wood's Business Accounting AAT Student's Workbook*, Sheila Robinson, Pitman Publishing 1993

The petty cash account

PC 6.2.5

While the cash book is used to record the principal inward and outward flow of cash and cheque monies of a business, it has been found much more convenient in larger organisations to 'delegate' the purchase of and payment for a host of small cost consumables to its various departments and cost centres. The procedure employed to facilitate this is called the petty cash imprest system.

The imprest system works upon the principle of the accounts cashier making available to each department a type of float – say of £100:00 – to finance the intermittent purchases of tea, milk and sugar, postage stamps, inking pads, air-freshener and the like.

A petty cash book in each department is used to record each individual purchase transaction (including the totalling of VAT in a separate column where applicable). When the departmental clerk responsible for managing the petty cash sees that the balance being brought down in the book is running low, he or she requests and obtains another £100:00 top-up, and the cycle starts again. Note that the employee who buys any item through the petty cash system must obtain a petty cash voucher from the departmental petty cash clerk describing the purchase and its cost, and pass over the receipt relating to the purchased item. This procedure helps to keep the system secure from abuse.

Each time an imprest (of say £100:00) is made to a department, the accounts cashier will credit the sum to the cash book so as to maintain the balance of the company's cash holdings and appropriate debit entries will be made to nominal and personal accounts. The receipts obtained from petty cash purchases are also retained to satisfy any arising auditing needs.

PC 6.2.5

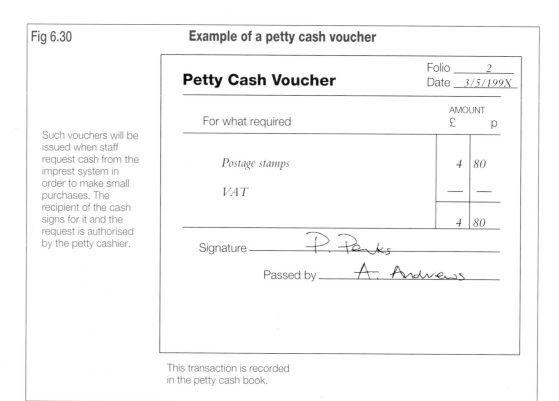

Fig 6.30 **Example of a petty cash voucher**

Petty Cash Voucher

Folio *2*
Date *3/5/199X*

For what required	AMOUNT £	p
Postage stamps	*4*	*80*
VAT	—	—
	4	*80*

Signature P. Perks

Passed by A. Andrews

Such vouchers will be issued when staff request cash from the imprest system in order to make small purchases. The recipient of the cash signs for it and the request is authorised by the petty cashier.

This transaction is recorded in the petty cash book.

PC 6.2.5

Fig 6.31 **Example of a petty cash book**

PETTY CASH BOOK (Dr / Cr)

Received	Date	Fo	Details	V No	Total paid out	Travel £	Postage £	Stationery £	Sundries £	VAT £
50 00	Jan 1	38								
			Fares	1	1 75	1 75				
	3		Stamps	2	4 80		4 80			
			Envelopes	3	5 60			4 87		0 73
	5		Coffee	4	3 20				3 20	
			Staples	5	4 49				3 91	0 58
	6		Pencils	6	3 99			3 47		0 52
	7		Fares	7	5 70	5 70				
			Milk	8	3 45				3 45	
					32 98	7 45	4 80	8 34	10 56	1 83
			Balance c/d		17 02					
50 00					£ 50 00					
17 02	Jan 8		Balance b/d							
32 98		39								

'Injection' of an imprest of £50 to start the petty cash funds

Ledger page or folio number

A fresh imprest is drawn from the cashier in order to restore the petty cash imprest to its original £50 'float'. Thus £32.98 is needed.

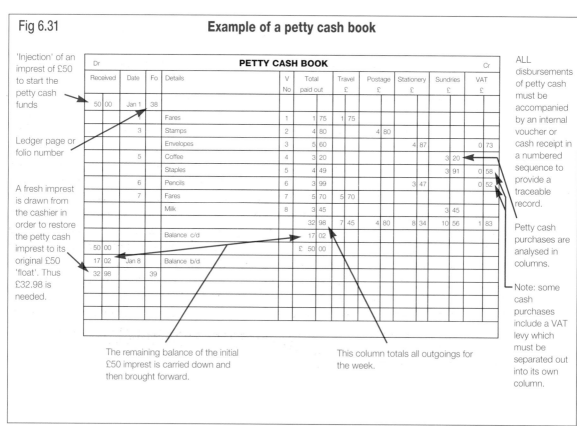

The remaining balance of the initial £50 imprest is carried down and then brought forward.

This column totals all outgoings for the week.

ALL disbursements of petty cash must be accompanied by an internal voucher or cash receipt in a numbered sequence to provide a traceable record.

Petty cash purchases are analysed in columns.

Note: some cash purchases include a VAT levy which must be separated out into its own column.

Accounts documents and security

PC 6.2.6 6.2.7

A major advantage that a sole trader of a small business enjoys is that of being personally responsible for the financial security of the business. He or she alone handles all the payments received, effects all banking activities and makes all outgoing payments for purchases.

Contrastingly, in a national chainstore group this activity may involve literally hundreds of employees. Given such numbers of staff involved, it is statistically very probable that at the 'least trustworthy' end of any related distribution curve a number of employees will exist who would be 'on the fiddle' where movements of cash are concerned – if given the chance. Each clearing bank, for example, employs a division of inspectors who visit branches – sometimes without warning – to carry out spot checks on their transaction systems and routines. Large national chains and conglomerates do likewise.

Also, the managers of both private and public sector organisations are constantly aware of their accountability – to shareholders, building society members, elected councillors and governors etc. – for the finance left in their charge.

As a result, a number of key security practices have evolved to protect the integrity of that part of the organisation's operation which is responsible for the stewardship of its financial transactions (see checklist on page 572).

■ The consequences of incorrect accounting actions

PC 6.2.6

The liability for prosecution under one of the various Companies Acts for having committed an illegal act in an accounting context is not the only danger that may face a company with lax accounting procedures which seduce staff.

Other serious consequences may accompany the distribution of account sales statements which are all GIGO (garbage in, garbage out) as a result of an error in data processing. Once good account customers become aggravated by the involved process of having to put right incorrect accounts documentation, they may well move across to another supplier – especially if there is little to choose in terms of quality and net buying-in prices. Customer goodwill takes a long time to earn and may be lost for good and all in a trice!

Not only can a good account be lost as a result of unspotted, uncorrected accounting errors, the senior management of a company may make calamitous wrong decisions on a strategic scale if the source data employed in a management accountant's financial reports and analyses is wrong. For example, an error in the costing of a prototype product which is subsequently successfully test-marketed may result in production being authorised on a national sales scale which results in millions of pounds of income failing to materialise. Again, a failure to back up the personal sales accounts in a computerised accounts system has resulted in many companies being bankrupted, since, in the absence of a firm's ability to send out statements for accounts rendered, few customers bother to pay up, and an irretrievable cash-flow crisis ensues.

PC
6.2.6
6.2.7

KEY PRACTICES WHICH ASSURE FINANCIAL INTEGRITY

1 The double-entry bookkeeping system and its accompanying regular production of trial balances and reconciliations prevent errors being compounded and misappropriations going undetected.

2 Bookkeeping and accounting systems employ carefully sequenced checks on the movement of money around the organisation through the maintenance of, for example, the purchase control ledger, the cheque requisition form and the petty cash voucher procedures.

3 Both paper-based and computerised accounts systems have to be capable of sustaining audit trails through which sample checks may be undertaken to follow an individual sales or purchase transaction from start to finish.

4 Apart from the requirement for signatures and authorisations to accompany the movement of monies, use is made of safes' alarm-systems and allied security measures to protect cash and valuable documents – both in house and at the bank.

5 Recording mechanisms, inward and outward such as goods inward dockets, stock requisition orders, purchase orders, etc. are cross-checked to appropriate external source documents, such as incoming invoices and despatch notes to ensure that no unauthorised activities have occurred.

6 The centralisation of the accounts function – which controls all financial activities within large organisations – limits the number of employees handling money and facilitates the effective management of accounting systems.

7 Similar centralisation (on a smaller scale) of the opening of incoming mail and the recording of payments in an inward remittance book etc. prevents potential accidental loss or theft of money.

8 The commissioning of external chartered accountants (together with the work and responsibilities of the company accountant) helps to ensure that a company's accounts are audited by a professional, disinterested third party. Any temptations a chartered accountant may have to connive at illegal financial practices in the company which retained him or her are quickly dispersed by the thought of being struck off the practising register by the Inland Revenue.

9 The scrutiny of the accounts and performance of public limited companies by their shareholders.

PC
6.2.6
6.2.7

DISCUSSION TOPICS

1 Is an organisation justified in setting up a procedure which requires that *all* incoming mail – even that marked confidential or personal – addressed to staff below the level of, say, director, be opened in the mailroom so as to ensure security in the case of payments being made to it?

2 What steps would you introduce into your own business to ensure that daily cash takings were not subject to pilferage by your employees?

3 Do you think that the clearing banks currently provide sufficient services in terms of the banking and paying-in activities of traders? How would you extend or improve them?

4 Have Switch cards made paper cheques obsolete? If so, why are millions still being processed by banks daily?

5 Why is 'telebanking' from home or office taking so long to arrive? Will it catch on, and should it?

ACTIVITIES

PC
6.2.4
6.2.5
6.2.6
6.2.7

As an individual, carry out one of the tasks below and report back to your class:

1 Find out what the range of services are which a clearing bank typically provides to a local business, which ones are free, and how much is charged for the others. Collect some of the brochures and leaflets which banks employ to promote their services and display them in your base-room.

2 Research into the ways in which a company may make or receive payment for goods or services, *other* than by cash or cheque.

Brief your class on your findings with a suitable factsheet and examples.

3 Design an imprest petty cash system (for your department) which employs a computer spreadsheet application.

Arrange to field test your system for two weeks and report back to your class on the outcomes.

4 Find out how an audit trail system works within an integrated accounting software system and report back to your group on your discoveries.

5 Interview a practising accounts manager and find out what techniques are available to ensure the integrity of a system in operation. Brief your class on your findings.

REVIEW TEST

PC
6.2.4
6.2.5
6.2.6
6.2.7

1 List the key information which appears on a crossed cheque.

2 What information is recorded on a payments received analysis sheet?

3 What information would you expect to input on to a bank paying-in slip?

4 What do these abbreviations (taken from a bank statement) stand for:
OD SO DD BGC EC ?

5 What role does the cash book play in a double-entry accounting system?

6 Explain briefly how an imprest petty cash system works, and the documentation it employs.

7 Explain briefly five procedures you would adopt as an accountant in your accounting system to ensure the integrity and security of its operation.

8 Give three examples of serious problems which can ensue if incorrect accounting actions go unspotted and uncorrected

KNOWLEDGE TEST

Element 6.2
Explain financial transactions and complete supporting documents

1 Which of the following are key purposes of financial transactions and documentation?

A To meet legal requirements.
B To maintain security where money is involved.
C To enable stock holdings to be kept at the right level.
D To provide feedback information for competitors.

2 (i) A delivery note is another term for an advice note.
(ii) A purchase requisition must be completed to authorise the removal of goods from a stock-room.

Which of the following options best describes the two above statements?

A	(i)	T	(ii)	T
B	(i)	T	(ii)	F
C	(i)	F	(ii)	T
D	(i)	F	(ii)	F

3 Which if the following statements is true, and which false?

A A credit note is raised in order to refund money due to a purchaser.
B A delivery note will not include price details of goods.
C Statements sometimes include settlement discounts.
D E and OE stands for Enquiries and Orders Entered.

4 (i) A remittance advice is sometimes sent with a cheque in payment for goods received.
(ii) A letter of collection is written by accountants seeking to obtain overdue payment for goods sold on credit.

Which of the following options best describes the two above statements?

A	(i)	T	(ii)	T
B	(i)	T	(ii)	F
C	(i)	F	(ii)	T
D	(i)	F	(ii)	F

5 (i) Large firms will not accept delivery of goods without an accompanying delivery note referring to their purchase order number.
(ii) The general and nominal ledger are two terms for the same thing.

Which of the following options best describes the two above statements?

A	(i)	T	(ii)	T
B	(i)	T	(ii)	F
C	(i)	F	(ii)	T
D	(i)	F	(ii)	F

6 Which of the following forms part of the set of payments and receipts documents?

A A takings summary form.
B A bank giro credit form.
C A petty cash voucher.
D A bank paying-in slip.

7 (i) Two signatures are sometimes needed on a cheque when one of the signatories is under eighteen.
(ii) Banks prefer to deal with cheques that are uncrossed.

Which of the following options best describes the two above statements?

A	(i)	T	(ii)	T
B	(i)	T	(ii)	F
C	(i)	F	(ii)	T
D	(i)	F	(ii)	F

PORTFOLIO OF EVIDENCE ACTIVITY

PC
6.2.1
6.2.2
6.2.3
6.2.4
6.2.5
6.2.6
6.2.7

Element 6.2
Explain financial transactions and complete supporting documents

Task 1: Purchase requisition

You work as Administrative Assistant to the Production Manager of Vulcan Engineering Limited, manufacturer of engine castings for the motor trade. Part of your job role is to order cleaning and hygiene materials used in the production process. Your teacher plays the role of your Production Manager, who authorises your purchase requisition forms.
Use the purchase requisition form on page 579 to order the following goods:

> 10 five-gallon drums of Kleenahand cleaning gel which has a retail price of £35.50 per drum; 20 tins of Skincare protective skin ointment priced at £3.95 per tin; 12 bales of cotton waste priced at £12.50 per bale; 2 dozen bottles of lavatory disinfectant priced at £1.95 per bottle and 10 packs of paper towels priced at £3.45 per pack.

Task 2: Purchase order

Your role has now changed to that of Assistant Purchasing Officer for Vulcan Engineering Limited. You have before you the purchase requisition from your Production Department. Your task is to complete the purchase order on page 580 which is to be sent to:

> Industrial Cleaners Limited
> Cleaner House Waythorpe Industrial Park
> Waythorpe Lancs. BT15 3RG

The Production Department is in urgent need of the order you are to process and so you have instructions to advise your supplier that it be considered urgent and sent on the first available delivery van.

The next purchase order number in your running sequence is: AX 46572. When you have completed your purchase order, it has to go to your Chief Purchasing Officer for signature – a role played by your teacher.

Task 3: Sales order book

The scenario shifts, and you now find yourself playing the role of a sales ledger clerk working for Industrial Cleaners Limited. You have before you the purchase order numbered AX 46572. Your task is to enter its particulars on to your Sales Order Book schedule (page 581). The first column entitled 'Our Order Number' is used to contain a sequence of the company's own order numbers, the next of which is S 4582. Your sales catalogue reveals the following references for the products ordered:

[Product]	[Sales Catalogue Number]
Kleenahand cleaning gel	C239
Skincare protective ointment	H45
Cotton waste bale	I 375
Lavatory disinfectant	T278
Paper towels	I 29

Any particular delivery requirements are to be entered into the column marked: Delivery Comments, and the delivery date in the final column.

Task 4: Delivery note and invoice

Your next task is to make out both the delivery note and invoice for the order from Vulcan. On pages 582–3 are the simulations of the two forms. In reality, they are likely to be printed in contrasting pastel colours as NCR or 'no carbon required' sheets, where the delivery note lies on top of the invoice and is lightly affixed to it at its head. This enables the details of the order to be filled out once only and for the pricing – including the all-important discount allowed – to be printed on the invoice only (which is sent directly to the accounts department). On many delivery notes – as is simulated below – the pricing components are obliterated on the delivery note.

The next delivery and invoice number on your NCR pad is: KB 12684 and your internal transaction number is 12 4 9X. Vulcan's account number is: IND 23692. Note that Industrial Cleaners uses the alphabetical letters which form part of its Sales Catalogue reference numbers as its product codes – e.g. H and C, standing for hygiene and cleaning products. Also, all the products ordered by Vulcan are standard rated for VAT purposes.

Make out first your delivery note using the above information, and then, using the following terms negotiated with Vulcan produce the associated invoice:

VULCAN ENGINEERING LIMITED
Credit purchase sales discount allowable:
12.5% off retail prices for purchase orders over £300:00
15.0% off retail prices for purchase orders over £600:00
Terms: strictly 30 days Settlement discount: 3.75%
Credit limit: £3,000 per calendar month

Task 5: Goods received note

The scenario moves back to Vulcan Engineering's Goods Inwards Department, where you are now working as a clerk. Your next task is to check the goods which have just been delivered by Industrial Cleaners and to complete the next goods received note on your pad, the reference number of which is F 1383. The goods have been delivered by van and your teacher is role-playing its driver and must therefore sign for their delivery to you as your – and his/her – proof of delivery.

On inspection, you find that one of the drums of Kleenahand gel has been damaged – apparently in transit – and is leaking pink gel.

Use the Industrial Cleaners Limited delivery note and the goods received note on page 584 to complete this task.

Task 6: Statement of account

Your role for this task is Sales Ledger Clerk at Industrial Cleaners Limited. Among your responsibilities is the administration of a number of customer credit sales accounts, including that of Vulcan Engineering Limited. You are therefore currently tasked with producing the statement of account for Vulcan in respect of last month's credit sales transactions. Employing the information you have acquired in undertaking the above five tasks, make out the appropriate statement of account to send to Vulcan Engineering using the statement form on page 585. Remember that Vulcan's account number is: IND 23692. The following data relate to last month's account sales transactions:

Invoices issued

Date	Invoice No	Amount £
03/5/9X	KB11892	321:39
12/5/9X	KB11992	95:45
17/5/9X	KB12236	409:26
21/5/9X	KB12684	664:46
28/5/9X	KB13468	102:89

Credit and debit notes issued

On 24 May 199X, a credit note, number FG 3489, to the value of £35:45 was issued to Vulcan in respect of a damaged drum of Kleenahand gel. On 27 May 199X a debit note number XC 4591 was issued to rectify an undercharge on invoice KB12236. The debit note was issued against a pack of 25 medium-size rubber gloves and amounted to £12:63.

Balance carried forward

Note that a carried forward balance of £12.86 is shown on Vulcan's account as still outstanding and should be shown as the first item on your May statement of account.

Task 7: Payment by cheque

Assume that you work as the Senior Purchase Ledger Clerk at Vulcan Engineering Limited, and that part of your job role is to verify, authorise and effect account purchases, including those made from Industrial Cleaners Limited. Using the cheque on page 586, make out the payment due from the rendering of their account which you produced in Task 6.

Task 8: Paying-in slip

As Chief Cashier of Industrial Cleaners Limited, your next banking transaction involves you in paying the following amounts into your bank, using the paying-in slip on pages 586–7:

			£
Cheques			128:93
			45:80
			2396:35
			346:72
			15:84
			1015:99
Cash:	Notes:	£50	250:00
		£20	320:00
		£10	610:00

Cash (*contd*):

			£
	Coins:		
		£1	296:00
		50p	29:50
		20p	14:80
		10p	16:30

Note: Before completing your paying-in slip, find out what multiples of coins a typical clearing bank will accept in its pre-printed plastic coin bags. Then make out your paying-in slip accordingly, leaving your balance of coins in your safe for your next banking.

Task 9: Completing a receipt

For this task, assume that you work part-time as a voluntary assistant in Vulcan Engineering's Social and Welfare Club. Among the many facilities which the club offers are reduced prices for tickets to shows and pantomimes etc at various times of the year, when numerous employees go together on a Club Outing.

At present you are busy issuing tickets and providing receipts for the next Club Outing, which is to a Saturday evening performance of *Phantom of the Opera* at the Adelphi in London's West End. The performance starts at 7.30p.m. on Saturday 21 September 199X, and Bill Tomkins wishes to pay you for four tickets, priced £32.50 each, including return coach fare.

Using the receipt form on page 587, make out a suitable receipt.

Task 10

For your set of purchase documents, produce a set of notes to submit with them, which explains for each: its purpose and function, why it is important to complete the forms accurately and clearly, and why security checks are important during the purchase process.

Task 11

For your set of sales documents, produce a set of notes which similarly explains the purpose and function of each, and the importance of clarity, accuracy and security checks during the sales process.

Each set of notes should be some 3–4 sides of A4 long

Performance criteria covered

6.2.1, 6.2.2, 6.2.3, 6.2.4, 6.2.5, 6.2.6, 6.2.7

Core skills covered

Communication:
3.4.1, 3.4.2, 3.4.3, 3.4.4

Application of Number:
3.1.1, 3.1.2, 3.1.3, 3.1.4, 3.1.5, 3.1.6, 3.1.7, 3.2.1, 3.2.2, 3.2.3, 3.2.4, 3.2.5, 3.2.6, 3.2.7, 3.2.8, 3.2.9

FORMS TO BE USED IN ELEMENT 6.2 TASKS

Use this form for Task 1

Fig 6.32

PURCHASE REQUISITION

Date...../...../.....   Ref No..............

Department:..

Quantity	Descripton of goods	Unit price	Supplier's reference	Supplier

Requisition raised by:...   Authorised by:..............................
Purchase Order No..(to be completed by Purchasing Dept.)

Use this form for Task 2

Fig 6.33

VULCAN ENGINEERING LIMITED
Bramshott Works Foundry Way
BRAMSHOTT Lancs OLD14 6AJ
Tel: 0902 653291 - 4 Fax: 0902 372985

PURCHASE ORDER

To:

____

----
post code: ___________

Date: / /

Purchase Order No:____________
(to be quoted in all correspondence)

Please deliver to the above address unless otherwise instructed

Quantity	Description	Your Cat No.	Unit price £	Extension £
			Total:	

For and on behalf of:
VULCAN ENGINEERING LIMITED

signed:____________________ Chief Purchasing Officer

Use this form for Task 3

Fig 6.34

SALES ORDER BOOK

Date: / /

Our Order No.	Customer	Qty	Cat No.	Delivery	Comments	Delivered

Source: Adapted from *Finance, First Levels of Competence*, John Harrison, Pitman Publishing 1990. By kind permission of the author.

Use this form for Task 4

Fig 6.35

INDUSTRIAL CLEANERS LIMITED
Cleaner House Waythorpe Industrial Park Waythorpe Lancs BT15 3RG
Tel: 0864 678341 Fax: 0864 658362
VAT REG NO. 204 9975 42

DELIVERY NOTE

To: ____________________

Date: / /

Delivery Note No. ____________

Transaction No.	Your Order No.	Delivery No.	Invoice Date	Account No.	

Product Code	Description	Unit Price	Quantity	VAT Code	

Use this form for Task 4

Fig 6.36

INDUSTRIAL CLEANERS LIMITED
Cleaner House Waythorpe Industrial Park Waythorpe Lancs BT15 3RG
Tel: 0864 678341 Fax: 0864 658362
VAT REG NO. 204 9975 42

INVOICE

To: ____________________
____
____
____

Date: / /

Invoice No. ____________

Transaction No.	Your Order No.	Delivery No.	Invoice Date	Account No.	

Product Code	Description	Unit Price	Quantity	VAT Code	Price £

Gross:	
Less Discount:	
Nett:	
Plus VAT at %:	
Total Payable:	

Terms: Net 30 Days E & OE
VAT Code: V = added at standard rate Z = zero rated
E = exempt

Use this form for Task 5

Fig 6.37

VULCAN ENGINEERING LIMITED

GOODS RECEIVED NOTE

Date: / / *Ref No.*________________

Goods Supplied By: ____

Our Purchase Order No. ____________________

Supplier's Delivery Note No. ____________________

Name, signature and company of delivery person:

Name__________________ Signed:____________________

Company: ____

Quantity	Description of Goods

Inspected By:

Name__________________ Signature:____________________

Enter below details if found damaged on inspection:

Use this form for Task 6

Fig 6.38

INDUSTRIAL CLEANERS LIMITED
Cleaner House Waythorpe Industrial Park Waythorpe Lancs BT15 3RG
Tel: 0864 678341 Fax: 0864 658362
VAT REG NO. 204 9975 42

STATEMENT OF ACCOUNT

To: ____________________
____
____
Post code: __________

Date: / /

Customer Account No.
____

Date	Invoice / Credit / Debit Ref.	Cr £	Dr £	Balance £
			Total: £	
			Less settlement discount: £	
			Balance due: £	

Cr: Amount credited
Dr: Amount debited

E + OE

Use this form for Task 7

Fig 6.39 **Business cheque**

Date ______________

Pay ______________

Bal. Bt Fwd ___ _____

£

Other items ________

Bal. Cd Fwd ________

02451

NATIONAL WESTCHESTER BANK 65–34–56

Bramshott Branch
31 High St. Bramshott, Lancs BT4 9KL

________19___

Pay ______________ Account Payee

£

VULCAN ENGINEERING LIMITED

Cheque No.	Branch Sort Code	Account No.	Transaction Code
02451	65–34–56	64431192	03

Use this form for Task 8

Fig 6.40a **Paying-in slip (front)**

Date ______________

A/C ______________

Cashier's Stamp

Cash ______________

Cheques ______________

£

01692

________19___ Paid in by:______________ bank giro credit

Cashier's Stamp

NATIONAL WESTCHESTER BANK

2 65 34 56

Bramshott Branch

Cheques ☐

Fee box ☐

VULCAN ENGINEERING LIMITED

Notes £50		
£ 20		
£ 10		
£ 5		
Coins £ 1		
Other coins		
Total Cash		
Cheques etc.		
£		

01692 65 34 56 95567342 98

Use this form for Task 8

Fig 6.40b **Paying-in slip (back)**

Details of cheques			Sub-total Brought forward				
Carried fwd.	£		Total carried over	£		£	

Please do not write or mark below this line

Use this form for Task 9

Fig 6.41

RECEIPT

VULCAN ENGINEERING LIMITED
SPORTS & SOCIAL CLUB
Bramshott Works Foundry Way
Bramshott
Tel: 0902 687453

No.

Manager: Jack Bastow

Date: / / 199X

VAT REG NO. 347 9857 23

To ______________________________

Description	£	p
Total		
Plus VAT		
Price		

Received with thanks ______________________________ Chief Cashier

PC
6.2.1
6.2.2
6.2.3
6.2.7

CASE STUDY

'Open all hours!'

Arun and Lata Patel's lives had been 'open all hours', ever since they first bought their business – a minimarket in a suburban shopping precinct – some five years ago. Then, the 150 houses on the Westbury Park development had been only half completed and business had been slow and hard to build. Thanks to the Patels' relentless hard work and willingness to rise at the crack of dawn and retire well after midnight, the minimarket had prospered, as the Westbury suburb of Grafton, a busy industrial town, had rapidly expanded. The store, called the Minimax Grocers & Newsagents, was in the middle of five shops in a parade lying back from a busy through-route to the A6. The Patels, with their 16-year-old daughter, Sonal and 10-year-old son, Naresh occupied a flat over the store.

Minimax had started out as a run-of-the-mill general stores, specialising in those small order items which local shoppers had forgotten to buy at the supermarket or did not want to make a special journey for. With a bus-stop into town just opposite, and room for parking out front, Arun quickly realised, however, that there was ample scope for selling newspapers, magazines and sweets, etc. Before much longer, he was employing six newspaper delivery youngsters. They also picked up orders for home-delivered groceries, which Arun delivered mid-mornings around the adjacent estates in his elderly but trusty van. The delivery side of the business expanded rapidly to a point where Arun had to stop taking on new customers - much against his will.

About a year ago, with the completion of the up-market Westbury Park development, customers who had acquired a taste for exotic micro-oven ready meals, gave Arun and Lata the idea of making room for another open freezer which would stock the spicy and different dishes which innovative food manufacturers were marketing under Chinese, Indian, Mexican and Indonesian brand names.

By this time, the Patels badly needed more helping hands. As luck would have it, two of Arun's nephews moved into the district looking for work in Grafton's textile industry. Both in their early twenties, they were just the trustworthy help that the shop urgently needed. Nor did they need much persuading, when Arun outlined his longer term plans for acquiring additional outlets. Ramesh, the elder brother took over the newsagency and confectionery side, while his brother Raj delivered the grocery orders and with his easy humour and persuasive ways quickly extended business.

Soon after, an incredible stroke of luck occurred – the butcher's shop next door came on to the market. The sitting tenant had been content to provide a mediocre service, and as a consequence could not afford the new lease's increased rents. Arun was quick to see his chance and had clinched the deal before the local estate agent had even displayed the particulars in his front window!

This time it was Mrs Patel who had her say. 'You know,' she had said, 'what Westbury needs is a really good fast-food takeaway!' Always with an eye to market trends, she had overheard snippets of conversation among teenagers and young married couples about the nearest fast-food outlet some two miles away which had a good reputation for ample portions and really tasty dishes. 'If they'll drive over there, they'll walk in here,' she observed shrewdly. 'We could also fit in a few tables for people who want to eat here, too,' she added. After meeting some demanding requirements, Arun obtained planning permission for the change of use and early in November, the grand opening of Arun's 'Tandoori Takeaway' took place, with Mrs Patel in charge!

* * *

Some eight weeks earlier, Sonal had started working towards a GNVQ Business (Advanced) Award at Grafton College of Technology. From day one, with business in her bones, she had never looked back. She seemed to devour the Units and Elements – especially those parts dealing with business accounting.

She had a natural flair with software and had achieved a Grade A in her Business Information Studies GCSE.

One evening, having just finished an assignment, she poked her head round her father's upstairs office in the flat. He was almost buried under paper! It bulged out of cardboard wallets, ring-binders and box files; it was festooned around the walls, suspended from rows of bull-dog clips, it littered his desk and window sills. Advice notes, invoices, handwritten orders, catalogues, price-lists, special offers and bank statements! It seemed as though Arun had kept every single piece of paper since the first day's trading. Sonal scooped up a handful and let it drop back on to the desk.

'Stop that you silly girl!' shouted Arun. 'Now look what you've done. I'd just sorted those invoices into sequence!'

'Daddy, look at you! You're drowning in a sea of bumf!'

'What do you mean, bumf – I know exactly where everything is kept – or did until you interfered – now go away and let me finish!'

'Not until you make me a promise you'll keep.'
Sonal paused dramatically, for she well knew she was the apple of her father's eye.

'Certainly not! What promise?'

'That first thing tomorrow you go down to Computerama and get fixed up with a decent PC set-up and some suitable accounting software – before you go down for the third time and all your past flashes before your eyes! I don't know how you've managed up till now, but with the new shop and the deliveries expanding, soon you won't need to stop for sleep – you won't have time!'

* * *

For several days Sonal's words echoed around Arun's brain like an advertising jingle that wouldn't go away. Eventually he brought the matter up with Lata. 'I think she's probably right. You should move with the times,' Lata responded. 'How can you even think of new outlets when you're drowning in the paper from just two!'

Outnumbered and out-argued, Arun was waiting the next morning outside the front door as they opened up Computerama for business!

GROUP ACTIVITIES

In pairs, first carry out your fact-finding and then undertake the following tasks.

1 Basing your approach and decision-making on the information in the case study, research into the types of bookkeeping/accounting software currently on the market which you consider would best meet the needs of the Patel's business – both currently and allowing for likely future developments.

Brief your class with an illustrated oral presentation on the package(s) you selected and why.

2 Using the information in the case study and your knowledge of small business trading, draw up a checklist of the input data which would need to be collected systematically and keyed into the Patel's computer in order for them to be able to interpret and analyse what you believe would be useful management accounting information.

3 Using the knowledge you have gained from the Element 6.2 Activity above, draw up a factsheet of what you consider to be the advantages (to the Patels) of using a computerised bookkeeping/ accounts system, as opposed to a manual, paper-based one. Compare your list with those of your co-students.

Element 6.3
CALCULATE THE COST OF GOODS OR SERVICES

PC 6.3.1

It has become a truism to say that businesses exist to make profits. However, what is not so widely acknowledged is that, without controlling their costs, businesses are not only unlikely to generate profits, they may soon find themselves making an early acquaintance with the Official Receiver!

This section, therefore, concentrates upon the key role in financial management of efficient and effective costing in all its aspects:

- direct and indirect costs
- fixed and variable costs
- absorption costing
- marginal costing
- break-even analysis
- budgetary control

Whether your career takes you into manufacturing, a service industry or the public sector, a sound grasp of the principles of costing and cost control allied to an ability to produce associated charts and schedules will always stand you in good stead.

PC 6.3.1

Costing in a manufacturing environment

As a manufacturing business makes rather than buys finished goods we need an account which will enable us to calculate the cost of the finished goods produced. This is known as a manufacturing account and for Dudley Manufacturing Ltd would look like the following example:

PC 6.3.1

DUDLEY MANUFACTURING LIMITED
Manufacturing Account for the Year ended 31 December 1992

	£	£
Cost of Raw Materials Used		
Opening Stock	3,250	
Purchases of Raw Materials	52,185	
	55,435	
Closing Stock	1,565	
		53,870
Manufacturing Wages		35,625
Prime Costs		89,495
Factory Overheads		
Factory Rent and Rates	6,480	
Factory Light, Heat and Power	7,935	
Machinery Repairs	1,575	
Other Factory Expenses	3,250	
Depreciation of Plant and Machinery	3,765	
		23,005
		112,500
Work in Progress		
Opening Value	1,575	
Less Closing Value	3,890	
		(2,315)
Factory Cost of Goods Produced		110,185

You will see that the above is simply a list of all the expenses incurred in the factory.

- The cost of the raw materials used and the manufacturing wages have been added together to give prime cost.
- Factory overheads have been listed including the depreciation of machinery subtotalled and added to prime cost.
- As a factory has a continuous production line in operation at any one time there are partly finished goods in it. At the end of the year an adjustment has to be made for the change in work-in-progress for the beginning to the end of the year.
- The final figure is the factory cost of the finished goods produced and is transferred to the Trading Account. It is used instead of the purchases figure for a retail firm.
- The Trading Account on page 592 calculates the gross profit as usual; you can see how the factory cost of goods produced has been substituted for purchases.

For example, the Trading Account for Dudley Manufacturing Ltd might look like the following:

PC 6.3.1

DUDLEY MANUFACTURING LIMITED
Trading Account for the Year ended 31 December 1992

	£	£
Sales		180,835
Cost of Sales		
Opening Stock of Finished Goods	7,590	
Factory Cost of Goods Produced	110,185	
	117,775	
Closing Stock of Finished Goods	8,910	
		108,865
Gross Profit		71,970

- The Profit and Loss Account and the Balance Sheet will follow in the usual way. The only item to remember is that in the Balance Sheet the stock figure will show the stock of raw material, work-in-progress and finished goods.

Elements of cost

For a long time, manufacturing firms have found it necessary to analyse their costs in order to control them and thus make their businesses more competitive and profitable. In more recent times all types of businesses have understood the necessity of analysing and controlling costs. There are three main elements of cost:

- Raw materials: The cost of the materials used in the production of goods.
- Direct labour. The cost of the work force directly engaged in the production of goods.
- Overheads. All other costs involved in operating the business.

PC 6.3.1

Classification of costs

Costs can be categorised in two basic ways either because of their type or because of their behaviour.

If we define costs by type we get direct and indirect costs.

Direct costs. These are the raw materials and direct labour

Indirect costs. These are overheads such as rent, rates, light heat and power, etc.

If we define costs by behaviour we get fixed and variable costs.

UNIT MEASURES USED IN COSTING

PC 6.3.1 6.3.2

It is important in costing to be aware of the various major measurements (in terms of units) which are commonly used in costing techniques:

Units of production

In a manufacturing environment, these are likely to be individual product items: a refrigerator, a fuse, an electric motor etc.

Units of service

In the service industry, a unit of production (in a costing sense) might be: a life insurance policy, a seat at a theatre or cinema performance, a cover (a consumed meal) in a restaurant, a service call-out, a passenger mile etc.

Units of labour

Measured in: man-hours, vehicles produced per operative per year, per total of employees etc.

Time periods

Measured, say, per second, per minute, per hour, day, month, quarter, year etc.

Fixed costs. These are costs which do not vary with the level of activity of a firm. A good example is the rent paid for the use of premises. The landlord will expect the rent to be paid whether a firm has manufactured and sold 500 or 5,000 widgets. A fixed cost will alter in time, the landlord will review the rent at the end of a set period.

Variable costs. These are costs which vary in direct proportion with the level of activity of a firm, for example, raw materials. If you produce 500 widgets you will need twice as much material than if you produce 250 widgets.

Semi-variable costs are costs which contain a fixed and a variable element. Many costs are like this but we assume that they can be split into their fixed and variable elements.

If we look at simple graphical representations of fixed and variable expenses they would appear as shown in Figs A and B. This is a simplistic way of looking at the costs since if a firm wishes to expand beyond a certain point, it will need to rent bigger premises. At the same time a supplier of raw materials is likely to give a discounted price if more than a certain quantity of goods is purchased.

In such cases the graphs shown in Figs A and B would need to be amended as shown in Figs C and D.

PC 6.3.2

Fig A

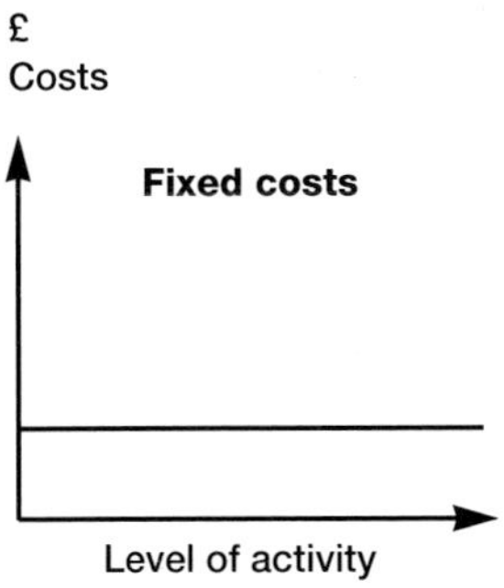
£
Costs
Fixed costs
Level of activity

Fig B

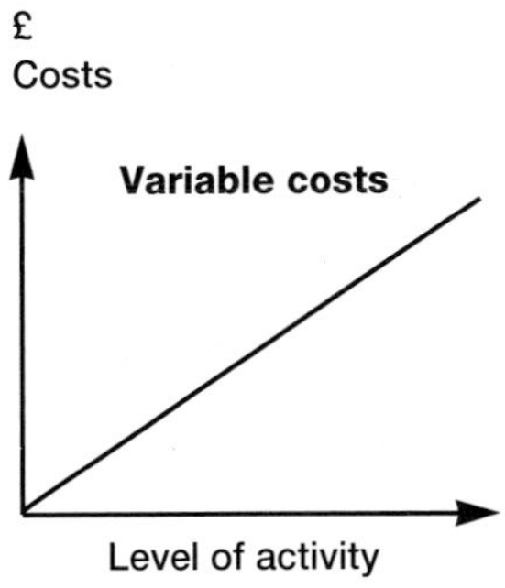
£
Costs
Variable costs
Level of activity

Fig C

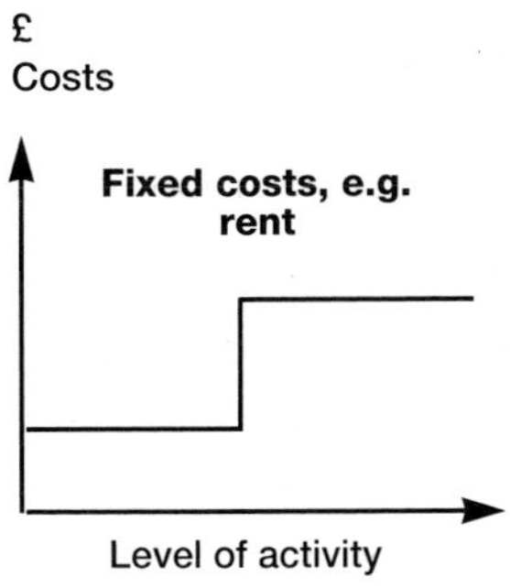
£
Costs
Fixed costs, e.g. rent
Level of activity

Fig D

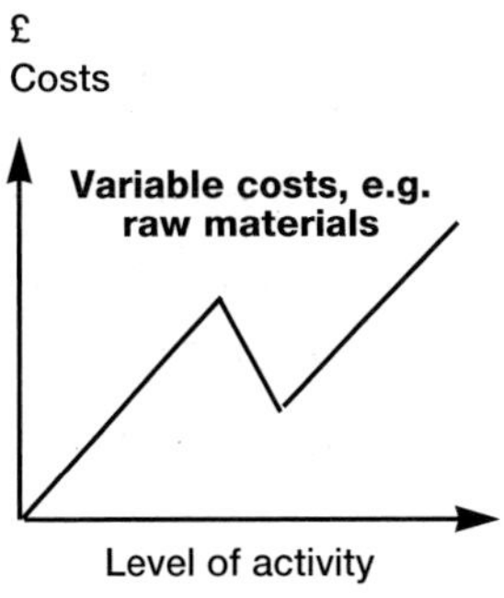
£
Costs
Variable costs, e.g. raw materials
Level of activity

PC
6.3.1
6.3.2
6.3.3
6.3.4

■ Absorption costing

If a firm which produces several different types of product wants to know what a particular item 'costs' to produce, it needs to identify the direct costs and then to add on an appropriate proportion of the overheads of the firm. When the firm has calculated the cost of an item, it will then be able to decide how many it needs to sell in order to make a reasonable profit.

Unfortunately, if a firm has several departments such as machining and finishing departments, it is not always easy to see how to split manufacturing costs between them and thus at times arbitrary divisions are made. Absorption costing does not claim to apportion overheads accurately to each department, it attempts to split overheads between revenue-producing departments and thus finds a 'cost' of a product.

Cost centre

A factory is split into specified sections/departments to which costs are allocated. These could be a service or a manufacturing section of a firm. Expenses are allocated or apportioned to each cost centre in a predetermined way.

The varying stages in absorption costing are as follows:

- The overheads for the next period are estimated as accurately as possible.
- The overheads which are specific to a department are allocated to that section.
- Overheads which cannot be specifically allocated are apportioned to departments in a particular way. There are several methods of apportionment including:

  1 On the basis of floor area.

  2 On the basis of the direct wages allocated to the departments.

- If there are any service areas in the factory, their costs must be apportioned between the production departments. This is usually on the basis of the average time spent by the service department in each of the production departments.

  The total overheads of each production department are now known and these are used to calculate an overhead absorption rate for that department. Again there are many methods of calculating overhead absorption rates, some of the most common are:

a machine hour rate $= \dfrac{\text{Department overheads}}{\text{Estimated no. of machine hours}}$

b labour hour rate $= \dfrac{\text{Department overheads}}{\text{Estimated no. of labour hours}}$

c labour rate $= \dfrac{\text{Department overheads}}{\text{Estimated cost of labour}}$

The cost of a job can then be calculated:

Cost of job = raw materials + direct labour + overheads using the appropriate rate

The required selling price of the job can be calculated by adding a suitable mark-up to the cost price.

These stages can be shown diagrammatically as follows:

Fig 6.42 **Absorption costing**

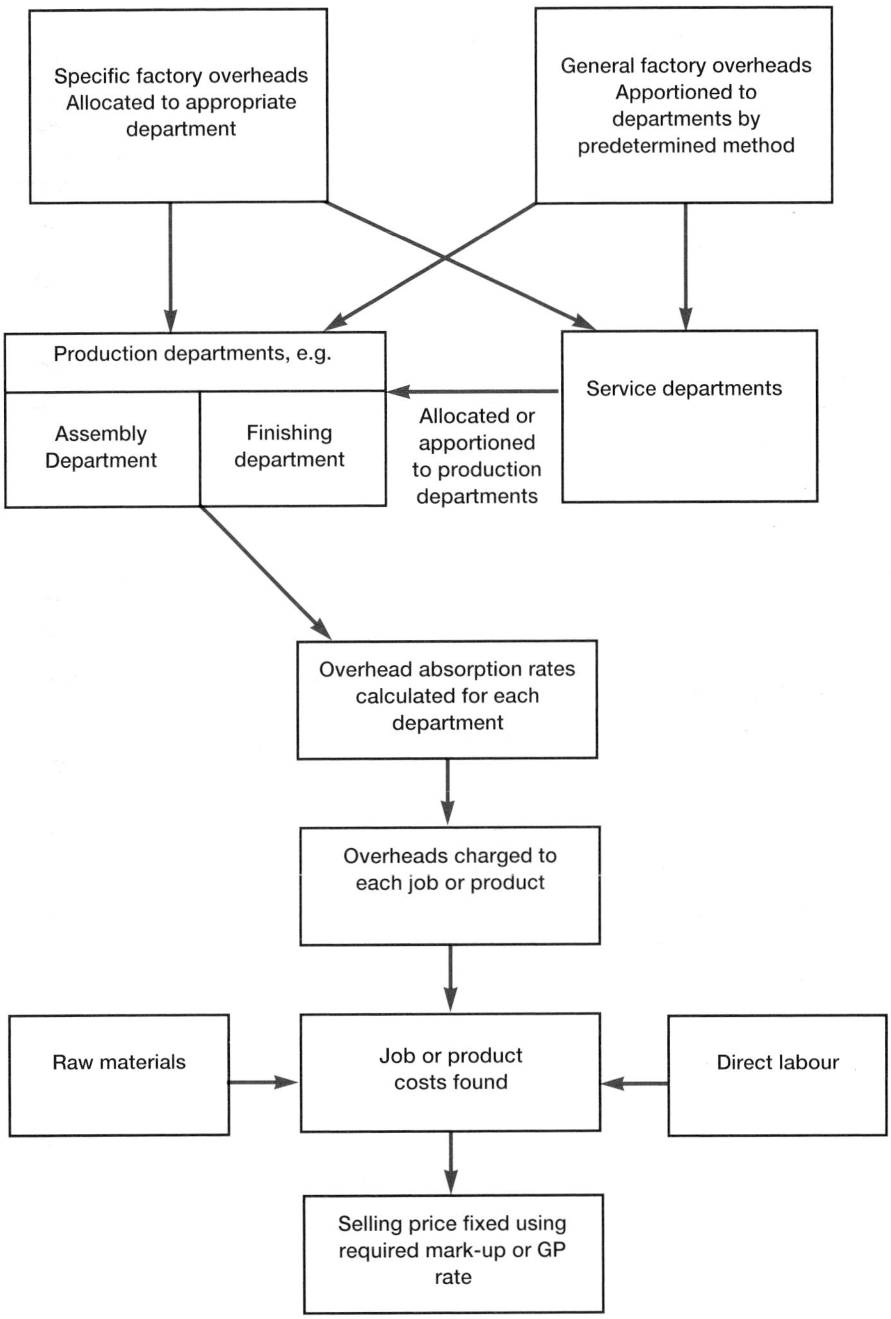
Specific factory overheads Allocated to appropriate department
General factory overheads Apportioned to departments by predetermined method
Production departments, e.g.
Assembly Department
Finishing department
Service departments
Allocated or apportioned to production departments
Overhead absorption rates calculated for each department
Overheads charged to each job or product
Raw materials
Job or product costs found
Direct labour
Selling price fixed using required mark-up or GP rate

PC
6.3.1
6.3.2
6.3.3
6.3.4

Limitations of absorption costing

The first limitation is that the figures that are used to determine the cost of an item are estimates and will not be the actual costs incurred by the firm. This is true of any costing system used and is a general problem.

The other main drawback is that the method of apportioning overheads is purely a matter of choice of the managers of the firm and may become outdated with time. Unfortunately firms are very lax over the updating of their costing system. With the change in production from labour orientated methods to machine methods there is a need to update traditional labour rate methods.

PC 6.3.4 6.3.5

EXAMPLE OF FIXING A SELLING PRICE USING ABSORPTION COSTING

Helmsley Ltd is a small manufacturing company producing a variety of equipment for the hotel and catering trade. It operates from a factory which is divided into three sections, assembly, finishing and service.

The costs for the coming period are estimated to be:

Specific overheads	Assembly	£50,000
	Finishing	£20,000
	Servicing	£7,500
	General administration	£150,000

It is the company's policy to allocate the administration expenses to departments on the basis of floor area. These are:

assembly: finishing: service   8 : 3 : l

During the period it is estimated that the machines in the assembly department will operate for 50,000 hours and the labour force in the finishing department will work 12,500 hours.
The service department, on average, charges the assembly department for 1,500 hours and the finishing department for 500 hours of work.
A regular customer has asked for a quote for a customised product. It is estimated that it will take 12 machine hours and 4 labour hours in the finishing department to complete the product. The direct materials and labour will cost £130.
The firm usually requires a gross profit of 40 per cent on sales.
Calculate the selling price that should be quoted to the customer.

Stage 1

Produce a chart of overhead distribution to find the overheads of each production department.

Cost centre	*Assembly*	*Finishing*	*Service*	*Total*
	£	£	£	£
Specific costs	50,000	20,000	7,500	77,500
General admin. apportion (8 : 3 : 1)	100,000	37,500	12,500	150,000
Subtotal	150,000	57,500	20,000	227,000
Apportion service area (ratio 1500 : 500)	15,000	5,000	(20,000)	–
Total Production Dept. overheads	165,000	62,500	–	227,500

Stage 2

Calculate overhead absorption rates for each department.

a Assembly Department. This would be based on the machine hours of the department as the assembly is, basically, a machine intensive process.

$$\text{i.e. overhead absorption rate} = \frac{\text{department overheads}}{\text{estimated no. of machine hours}}$$

$$= \frac{165{,}000}{50{,}000}$$

$$= \text{£3.3 per machine hour}$$

b Finishing Department. This would be based on the labour hours of the department as the finishing is usually a labour intensive process.

$$\text{i.e. overhead absorption rate} = \frac{\text{department overheads}}{\text{estimated no. of labour hours}}$$

$$= \frac{62{,}500}{12{,}500}$$

$$= \text{£5.0 per labour hour}$$

Stage 3

Calculate the total cost of the product.

Total cost = raw materials + direct labour + overheads

Raw materials and direct labour	£130.00
Overheads for assembly dept. (£3.3 ph × 12 hrs)	39.60
Overheads for finishing dept. (£5.0 ph × 4hrs)	20.00
Total factory cost	£189.60

Stage 4

Calculate the required selling price.

If a gross profit on sales of 40 per cent is required then the factory cost is 60 per cent of required selling price.

$$\text{Thus the required selling price} = \frac{\text{Total factory cost}}{60\%}$$

$$= \frac{189.60}{60\%}$$

$$= \text{£316.00}$$

PC 6.3.6

Marginal costing and break-even analysis

Marginal costing considers costs under the headings of fixed costs and variable costs. It does not try to find the cost of production in terms of raw materials, direct labour and overheads. Rather it considers the variable costs of production and what profit or loss would be made if varying levels of production and sales were achieved.

Marginal costing uses a few simple mathematical ideas.

Contribution

This is defined as: selling price less variable costs. It can be expressed as a contribution per unit or as a contribution from producing and selling a number of units.

It is the contribution that is made towards meeting fixed costs and making a profit.

Break-even point

The break-even point is where a firm makes neither a profit nor a loss, the point where income and expenses are equal.

This is defined as: $\dfrac{\text{Fixed Costs}}{\text{Contribution per unit}}$

It tells us how many units must be sold before the business breaks even.

If you want to know how much the sales income must be before the firm breaks even, then you must multiply the break-even point by the selling price per unit, i.e.

$$\text{Break-even point in £} = \text{Break-even point in units} \times \text{selling price per unit}$$

Margin of safety

This tells us how 'safe' a scheme is by looking at how far our estimated sales can fall below the estimated maximum before the scheme is no longer viable, that is before we would be in a loss-making situation.

$$\text{Margin of safety} = \frac{\text{Maximum Estimated sales} - \text{break-even point}}{\text{Maximum Estimated sales}}$$

This gives the answer as a percentage. For example the sales can be 10 per cent lower than expected before the firm is no longer profitable.

Example

Assume that a firm makes widgets which it expects to sell for £15 each. The material costs will be £4.50 and the labour £5.50 per widget. The maximum sales are estimated to be 6,000 units and the fixed costs £22,500. Then:

Total variable costs = raw material + labour cost

= £4.50 + 5.50 per unit

= £10.00 per unit

Contribution = Selling price – variable costs

= £15.00 – £10.00 per unit

= £5.00 per unit

$$\text{Break-even point} = \frac{\text{Fixed costs}}{\text{Contribution per unit}}$$

$$= \frac{\text{£22,500 units}}{\text{£5}}$$

= 4,500 units

Break-even point in £ = Break-even point in units × Selling price per unit

= 4,500 × £15

= £67,500

$$\text{Margin of safety} = \frac{(\text{Estimated sales} - \text{Break-even point})}{\text{Estimated sales}} \times 100\%$$

$$= \frac{(6{,}000 - 4{,}500)}{6{,}000} \times 100\%$$

= 25%

■ Break-even charts

PC 6.3.6 6.3.7 6.4.2

It is often useful to present break-even information in the form of a graph. If we wish to draw a break-even chart for the above example the first step would be to produce a small table of calculations as follows:

Units	*Variable costs (£10 per unit)*	*Fixed costs*	*Total costs*	*Sales income (15 per unit)*
	£	£	£	£
0	0	22,500	22,500	0
3,000	30,000	22,500	52,500	45,000
6,000	60,000	22,500	82,500	90,000

We assume that there is a linear relationship between units and costs and units and sales income. Thus the total cost line and the sales income line will appear as straight lines on a graph and it is only necessary to plot two points on each line. However, as a safety precaution it is suggested that three points are plotted. If the points are not in a straight line you have made a mistake!

The break-even chart from the above information would look like the one shown in Fig 6.43.

PC
6.3.6
6.3.7
6.4.2

Fig 6.43 **Break-even chart**

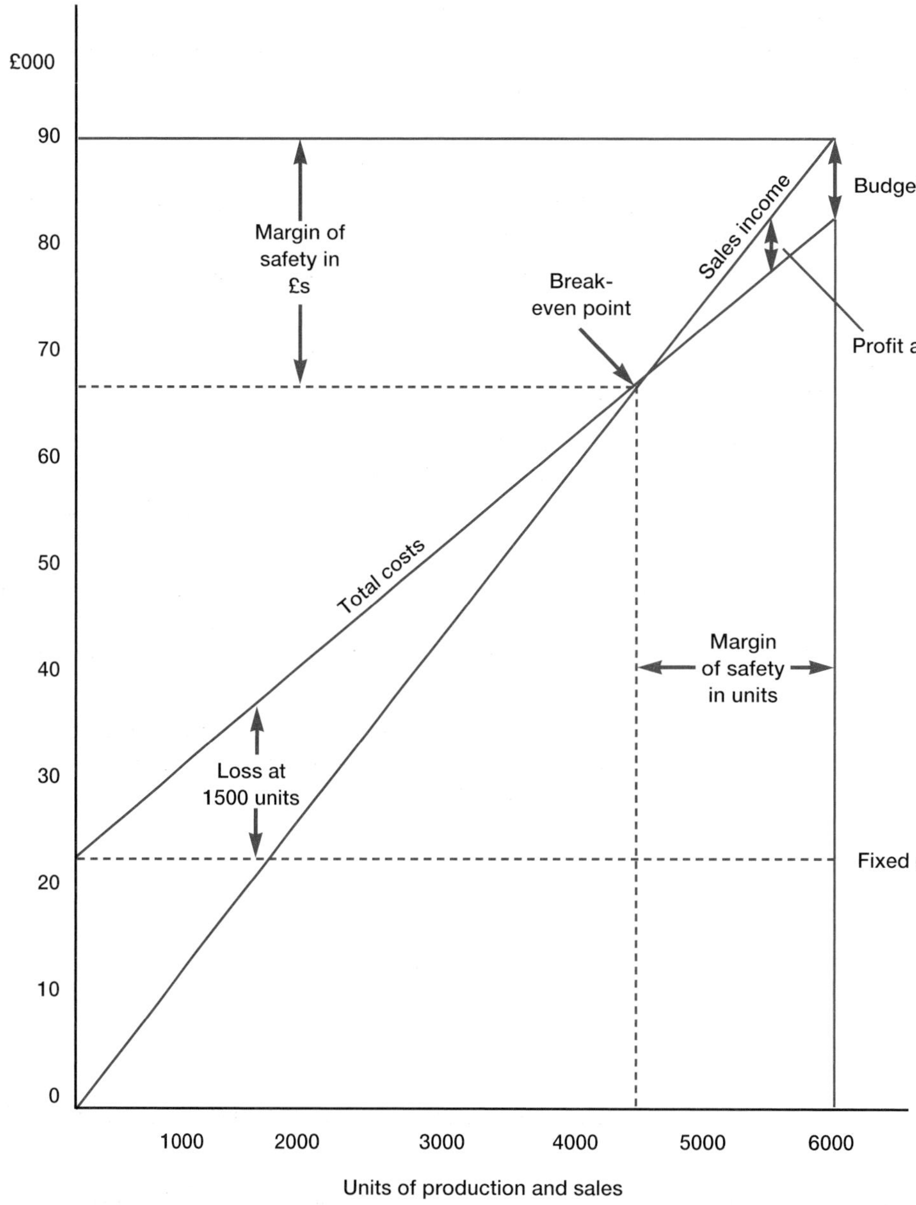

From a study of the break-even chart you will see that:

- the horizontal axis represents units of activity. This axis needs a scale that starts at zero and extends as far as the maximum level of activity.
- the vertical axis represents money. This axis needs a scale that starts at zero and extends as far as the maximum amount of sales (or total costs if the break-even point has not been reached).
- the sales line starts at the origin as no income is received if nothing is sold.
- the fixed costs line shows that these costs are constant at all levels of activity.
- the variable costs are superimposed on the fixed costs line to give total costs.

- the point where the total costs line and the sales line cross is the break-even point. This is because at this point total costs equal sales income and thus no profit or loss is made.
- the margin of safety is represented by the distance between the break-even point and the maximum expected sales. It is not expressed as a percentage here as it is possible to see how large it is compared with the maximum estimated sales.

Other uses of a break-even chart

Although it is often argued that the principal use of a break-even chart is to find the break-even point in a given situation, there are other uses of these charts.

It is possible to find the expected profit or loss at any particular level of activity, e.g. using the above chart it can be seen that:

a If 1,500 units are sold then a loss of £15,000 will be made.

b If 5,500 units are sold then a profit of £5,000 will be made.

It should be obvious that below the break-even point a loss will be made, but this is confirmed as the total cost line is above the sales line.

Break-even charts are also used in 'what if' situations. It is possible to use a break-even chart to find relevant information to answer such problems as:

a Would it be better if we sold goods at £15 each when then the estimated sales would be 6,000 units or to reduce the price to £13.50 when the estimated sales would be 8,000 units? By drawing a third line on the break-even chart it will be possible to compare the two schemes.

b Would it be better to make the product in-house or to subcontract the work to another firm? Again by adding another line to the break-even chart to represent the costs of subcontracting the work it will be possible to make a comparison.

Absorption costing *v* marginal costing

PC 6.3.8

It will probably be useful at this stage if these two traditional methods of costing are compared.

- Businesses which use absorption costing do so because they wish to attempt to find the total 'cost' of manufacturing a product. Thus they hope to be able to set their selling price at such a level that it will not only be attractive to potential purchasers but generate sufficient volume of trade to cover all their expenses and produce an acceptable profit.
- Businesses which use marginal costing do so because they believe that it is more realistic and assists the decision-making process. Marginal costing is useful in quickly assessing the position for situations such as, what happens if we change our selling price? Would it be better to make or buy one of our products?

  As marginal costing does not attempt to allocate fixed costs to a product, some argue that it is a more accurate method of costing, it does not rely on some arbitrary method of apportioning overheads.
- Additionally, as fixed costs relate to a period not to the level of activity, some people

argue that it is fairer to set all fixed costs against revenue of the period and not to carry any fixed costs forward in stock valuation.

It is up to a company to choose which method of costing to use. It should not change the method to suit a particular set of circumstances. One of the basic principles of accounting is consistency.

PC
6.3.1
6.3.2
6.3.5

DISCUSSION TOPICS

1 What sort of *external* factors are currently most likely to impact upon a manufacturing company's operational costs?

2 Of all the kinds of costs which a manufacturing company incurs during its operations, which do you consider to be the least difficult and which the most difficult to control? Give reasons for the choices you make.

3 What advantages do you consider derive from dividing an organisation's departments and units into individual cost centres? Can you think of any disadvantages?

4 As the manager of, say, the production department of a large engineering firm, what action could you take if you felt that your department was having to bear too large a proportion of allocated service department overheads? How would you ensure that absorption costing is objectively carried out?

5 What advantages do you consider marginal costing possesses compared with absorption costing? Is the former better suited to manufacturing and the latter to retail and service industries? If so, why?

PC
6.3.1
6.3.2
6.3.6
6.3.7

ACTIVITIES

Undertake in a group of two or three **one** of the following activities and share your findings with your class:

1 Arrange to visit a local factory and to interview its available cost accountant and production managers in order to ascertain the principles (but not the necessarily confidential costings) which it uses to monitor the value and costs being added to its products in the course of their manufacture.

Your teacher may need to help you obtain an 'entree' for this activity.

2 Find a visiting speaker (say from one of your local management accountants' professional institute branches) who would come and speak to your class on the links between costing, budgeting, pricing, marketing and profit. Brief him or her on what approach you would like the talk to take.

Arrange for notes to be taken of the talk and circulated.

3 In liaison with your school/college refectory manager, produce a break-even analysis chart to calculate sales and profit for a new snack or beverage to be introduced.

REVIEW TEST

PC
6.3.1
6.3.2
6.3.6
6.3.7

1 Explain briefly the difference between direct and indirect costs.

2 List three ways in which units of labour may be identified.

3 Explain briefly what absorption costing is and how it works.

4 Explain what marginal costing is and how it is used.

5 What is a break-even point?

6 What is a margin of safety in a break-even calculation?

KNOWLEDGE TEST

Element 6.3
Calculate the cost of goods or services

1 (i) Direct costs are those which are passed directly on to the customer.
(ii) Indirect costs include overheads such as rent, administration and insurances.

Which of the following options best describes the above two statements?

A	(i)	T	(ii)	T
B	(i)	T	(ii)	F
C	(i)	F	(ii)	T
D	(i)	F	(ii)	F

2 (i) Fixed costs remain the same during an accounting period such as a year.
(ii) Variable costs differ according to the number of units of a good produced.

Which of the following options best describes the above two statements?

A	(i)	T	(ii)	T
B	(i)	T	(ii)	F
C	(i)	F	(ii)	T
D	(i)	F	(ii)	F

3 Absorption cost is a technique which:

A allocates direct costs only to a given product to calculate its manufacturing cost
B allocates both direct and variable costs to calculate its manufacturing cost
C allocates direct costs and a proportion of indirect costs (overheads) to calculate its manufacturing cost
D allocates indirect costs only to a given product to calculate its manufacturing cost.

4 A cost centre is:

A a small department in a manufacturing company which monitors production costs
B any department or unit in a business which incurs costs

C the term given to the department or unit in which cost accountants work
D that part of a product or services which is most costly to produce.

5 (i) A break-even chart is used primarily to calculate the point at which the sales revenue of goods sold equals the costs of production.
(ii) A break-even chart is used mainly in connection with marginal costing.

Which of the following options best describes the above two statements?

A	(i)	T	(ii)	T
B	(i)	T	(ii)	F
C	(i)	F	(ii)	T
D	(i)	F	(ii)	F

PC 6.3.1 6.3.2 6.3.3 6.3.4 6.3.5 6.3.6 6.3.7 6.3.8

PORTFOLIO OF EVIDENCE ACTIVITY

Element 6.3
Calculate the cost of goods or services

PLASTIKA PRODUCTS LIMITED

Scenario

For the past two years you have worked as Assistant Cost Accountant for *Plastika Products Limited*, a company with an annual turnover of some £5 million, which manufactures a range of products – all constructed in plastic from various types of polyesters and resins. At the current time, you are closely involved with *Plastika*'s Marketing Department in carrying out a costing exercise on a single product, a plastic, locking box for 3.5 floppy disks. These boxes, product coded PCB 010 are sold on to a range of wholesalers and retailing multiples who affix their own brand names to them by means of self-adhesive labels (which you also manufacture for them).

Set out below is a costs schedule for product PCB 010 which you have obtained as a print-out from your computer:

COSTING DETAILS:
COMPUTER DISK STORAGE BOX

Product Code: PCB 010	**Design Ref No.:** 17/8/93
Information current at:	15/6/9– (i.e. at present time)
Production started:	4/1/95
Current estimated annual production:	50,000 Units

The rest of the costing schedule, along with a lot of other information, was irretrievably lost a week ago when a violent electrical storm effectively erased a number of cost accounting files held on the firm's mainframe computer. Luckily, only five files were lost, not having been backed up in time, and your boss, Jo(e) Walters, Chief Cost Accountant is currently engaged in discussions with your Computer Services Unit to ensure that such a calamity cannot happen in the future. Meanwhile, you have been tasked with re-capturing the costing data which will enable you to provide the Marketing Department with much-needed information, since demand for the product is significantly increasing in the post-recession economic recovery. So far, you have assembled the following data:

Direct costs

1 The production wages attributed to the disk-box are: proportion of salaries of works managers: £18,000; line foreman £12,000; 6 operatives earning a total of £64,000

2 Unit costs for the materials to make the boxes (based on buying terms for an annual product run of 50,000 units) are currently priced at: plastic materials for moulding: 50p, metal lock and two keys: 80p, material to make two plastic hinge buttons: 8p, four self-adhesive, circular rubber stand cushions: 6p, one self-adhesive brand label: 3p.

3 Referring to past quarterly bills, you discover that the average power costs allocated to the manufacture of the boxes was £685 per quarter.

4 About fourteen months ago, a new production line was constructed for the boxes from plant and equipment costing £124,550. *Plastika* operates a reducing balance depreciation system on such plant, and has followed the Inland Revenue's regulations in that 40% of the purchase cost was depreciated at the end of year one, with a further 25% to be written down this year.

Indirect costs

As a result of time-consuming sleuthing, you have managed to secure copies of files in your offices and those of Marketing and Central Administration which revealed the following information on the indirect costs which were apportioned to the manufacture of PCB 010:

1 An annual apportionment of £19,500 was set against PCB 010 to cover the managerial and administrative work associated with the manufacture and marketing of the product.

2 Similarly, Marketing is currently budgeted to spend £10,450 on marketing sales support and promotional activities relating to the computer disk boxes.

3 Your Transport Manager has checked his files and confirmed that, on the basis of a 50,000 units being produced annually, he has allocated £15,375 as the anticipated distribution costs. Further apportionments to the production and sale of the boxes are: rent and rates £4,755 annually, insurances £3,850 and professional services £4,445 p.a.

4 Discussions with production managers confirm that the plant manufacturing the PCB 010s is running at about 60% of its capacity at present.

Marketing Policy and Trends

When the boxes went into their second year of production, confident predictions were made of an annual demand for some 60,000 units. Eventually, a commitment was made to gear up for a production run of 50,000 units for year two (of which two months has so far elapsed). So far, the order flow suggests that the total of 50,000 may be exceeded, but it is early days. At present the boxes are being sold on to wholesalers and national multiples at an average price of £5.95. Their mark-up results in a general retail price of between £9 and £12:00.

Before starting Task 1, remember to organise yourself to submit your *Planning and Review Log* with your evidence for this activity.

Task 1: Producing a break-down of costs schedule

All being well, your computer is back up and running, so if it is available, use your spreadsheet software to produce a break-down of the costs of making and selling the PCB 010 computer disk boxes. If your computer is still down, produce your schedule by hand. Your schedule should show direct and indirect costs separately, and should also indicate for each cost heading what the cost is per unit of manufacture (based on the current scheduled production of 50,000 units p.a.). If using a spreadsheet, make sure that you create cell formulae which will enable the spreadsheet to show correctly the result of any changes in unit costs or quantities of production per annum. One completion of your spreadsheet/manual costing schedule, arrange to demonstrate it to your teacher. who will role-play Mr/Ms Jo(e) Walters, Chief Cost Accountant, who wishes to ensure that your calculations are correct before releasing your data to other departmental staff.

Task 2: Producing a break-even chart

Once Mr/Ms Walters has checked that your calculations are correct (or you have made any necessary adjustments), you are to undertake a further job as an aid to the work your Marketing Department are currently undertaking. You have been asked to produce a break-even chart for the PCB 010 computer box product. Your brief includes the following requirements:

Sales are to be plotted along a production quantity axis extending to 100,000 units, and are to be shown in four separate prices: £5:45, £5:95, £6:95 and £7:95. Your costs axis is to extend to £1 million. For your break-even chart, you have been requested to deem your fixed costs as: management/administration, rent and rates, insurances, professional services and depreciation. The production wages bill is fixed in that the figures you have were calculated to cover the cost of producing 50,000 units per annum. However, your manager has worked out that an additional wages cost of £8,500 p.a. must be added for each additional 5,000 of box units manufactured over 50,000. In terms of power, an additional 0.5p should be added to each unit of manufacture over 50,000. Your Marketing Department reckons that an allocation of 18p should be added to unit costs to cover marketing expenses for units in the production range of 50,000–75,000 per annum, and 14p between 75,000 and 100,000. By the same token, your department has worked out that because of better buying terms coming on stream, raw material costs for between 50,000 and 100,000 units will be £1.31 per unit. Lastly, your Transport Manager has calculated that for an annual production total of between 50,000 and 100,000 a contribution of 25p per unit should be included in costs.

Using this information, construct an appropriate break-even chart. When you have completed your chart, work out the answers to the following:

1 What profit should be generated from the sale of 85,000 units at: £6:95 and at £5:45?

2 What will be the total fixed and variable costs for a production run of a) 65,000 and b) 100,000?

3 In order to help the Marketing Department, advise them whether Plastika would earn more profit from selling 60,000 boxes at £5.95 or 70,000 boxes at £5.45, and what the respective profits would total.

4 Your Sales Department has just received a firm enquiry for an export order of 25,000 units (to be collected 'ex works', with no distribution or marketing costs attached). The order would come on stream in 8 months' time, when you calculate you should have reached your target of 50,000 units. Thus the export order would be for the units of production 50,001–75,000. The potential customer is looking to buy the boxes at a unit price of £2:75.

What advice would you give your Sales Department?

Task 3

Your final task is to produce a summary of a business's direct and indirect costs – such as might be used by

Joe Walters as part of a training package for GNVQ students on work experience placements. In particular, your summary should indicate clearly which costs vary with production costs.

A suitable summary is likely to be about 1.5–2 sides of A4 long.

Performance criteria covered

6.3.1, 6.3.2, 6.3.3, 6.3.4, 6.3.5, 6.3.6, 6.3.7, 6.3.8

Core skills covered

Communication:
3.2.1, 3.2.2, 3.2.3, 3.2.4, 3.2.5, 3.3.1, 3.3.2, 3.3.3, 3.4.1, 3.4.2, 3.4.3, 3.4.4

Information Technology:
3.1.1, 3.1.2, 3.1.3, 3.1.4, 3.1.5, 3.2.1, 3.2.2, 3.2.3, 3.2.4, 3.2.5, 3.2.6, 3.2.7, 3.3.1, 3.3.2, 3.3.3, 3.3.4, 3.3.5, 3.3.6

Application of Number:
3.1.1, 3.1.2, 3.1.4, 3.1.5, 3.1.6, 3.1.7, 3.2.1, 3.2.2, 3.2.3, 3.2.4, 3.2.5, 3.2.6, 3.2.7, 3.2.8, 3.2.9, 3.3.1, 3.3.2, 3.3.3, 3.3.4, 3.3.5

Element 6.4
EXPLAIN BASIC PRICING DECISIONS AND BREAK-EVEN

Note: this section should be followed in conjunction with:

PC3	**Element 1.2**
PC2	**Element 3.2**
PC6 and 7	**Element 6.3**

PC 6.4.1

Basic factors which determine price

Prices are set in business as the result of a number of market factors and organisational objectives, principal among which are:

- to make a targeted profit,
- to achieve a pre-set volume of sales by unit or income,
- to penetrate a market,
- to milk an obsolescent product, and so on.

Other determinants of price, however, may lie outside of the control of a business:

- the number of competitors in the market and pricing trends due to fierce competition
- the imposition of a government tax which affects demand
- the arrival on the market of an 'all singing, all dancing' highly innovative competing product.

However, some additional determinants may well lie within a business's control:

- additional capacity on a production line which thus supplies marginal costing benefits and economies of scale by enabling additional products to be made at little extra cost
- falls in the costs of: raw materials, labour or transportation (as may occur during a recession).

Additional capacity may ultimately enable a company to make a profit by selling additional numbers of a product at very little above its rate of fixed costs for that product.

This is how hotels are able to make special offers on unsold rooms and suites, once they have recovered their fixed costs on an occupancy basis of, say, 65%. It is also why package holiday tour operators can – through travel agencies – sell last minute holidays well below holiday brochure advertised costs.

In short, it is important to keep in mind that prices rarely remain static for long, are susceptible to both internal and external changes, and are a very important tool in both the marketing mix, and in the financial function of husbanding a business's resources in order to generate desired profits.

Pricing strategies

[See also Unit 1 and Unit 3]

PC 6.4.1

■ The in-house approach: cost-plus pricing

Where, say, a manufacturer holds a dominant position in a given market, it may arrive at a price structure through its internal monitoring of the costs incurred from the start to the end of the manufacturing process, which will be both direct and indirect, and encompass:

- materials used in manufacturing
- bought-in components and semi-finished goods
- labour
- depreciation on plant and equipment
- operating costs: heat, light, water services etc.
- allocated costs of general management and administration
- distribution costs etc.

When all such cost components have been added together, a total cost price emerges. To this is added a further sum, which will embody the profit the business wishes to make, and from which will be deducted:

- corporation taxes
- shareholders' dividends
- finance for the next money / trading cycle round
- reserves finance etc.

The final cost which results will become the price to be charged for the product. This process is called *cost-plus pricing*.

PC 6.4.1

■ External, market-driven pricing

Cost-plus pricing may work well enough in a market with few competitors and where high profit margins are available. It tends not to work where competition is fierce, driving prices down, and where profit margins are thin, requiring high volumes of sales. In such a market-led pricing situation, firms tend to 'make goods to a price'. That is to say, they start from the other end from cost-plus pricing, and first determine what price a market will bear for a good. From this point, the business will decide upon the product's specification, design, type of materials and components etc. on the basis of manufacturing the product 'to a price', and to a pre-set profitability. In a market-driven situation, products tend to use simple design techniques, cheap materials and low-cost production processes. Thus the end product tends to be 'cheap and cheerful'. Examples of such products include self-assembly furniture, plastic toys and garden furniture, entry-level hi-fi and radios etc.

PC 6.4.1

■ Marginal cost/contribution pricing

As indicated above, a business may find itself in a position – say through under-employed production capacity – to produce goods above and beyond planned production costs, where targeted fixed costs and projected variable costs have already been recovered. The additional costs – marginal costs – of making more goods in this situation is very small:

unit sales price – unit marginal cost = contribution

Where a business is able to reach a total contribution level in excess of its total fixed costs, it will make a profit. Moreover, once that business has reached the point in the same production run or product life-cycle where both sales and profits have already been generated to a satisfactory level, it has two pleasant options:

a) either to sell additional goods at the established market price and so earn a much greater profit (than it did earlier in the product run)
b) or to sell the products made in the marginal cost zone at a lower price (say under a retailer's own label) and thus stimulate further demand etc.

PC 6.4.1

■ Price and product positioning

In this way, manufacturers position the same product at different price levels in the market-place, where, say, the *same* pullover commands a high, premium product price when sold with its famous maker's label prominently displayed, a mid-market price when sold under, say, a High Street clothing chain-store's label, and a low market price when sold unlabelled through small traders and markets.

Break-even point

PC 6.4.2

As already explained in Unit 3 and in Element 6.3, the break-even point is reached when the income generated from the sales of a product or service equals both the fixed and variable costs incurred. Fixed costs will include items such as rent and rates for premises, insurances, depreciation on plant for a given year etc. Variable costs will include items like labour (where additional shifts may need to be worked or more people taken on if production expands), raw materials (where additional output requires additional input) and energy (where introducing an additional shift will cause plant to be worked for longer hours) etc.

Once the break-even point has been reached, a business has the potential to move into profit with a given product, assuming more sales will be made, and as the break-even chart on page 600 illustrates, a margin of safety can be attained. The margin of safety is that amount or percentage of sales which lies between the break-even point and the overall maximum targeted sales to be achieved. Within the margin of safety, as the chart shows, lies the budgeted profit, which can be exactly forecast.

When a business arrives at a point where sales flag soon after the break-even point having been reached, it is faced with making serious decisions:

a) to get out and transfer investment into another product

b) to invest more in terms of a promotional campaign aimed at increasing sales

c) to lower the price – but accept a much slower move towards profitability and the dangers of making a loss etc.

Sometimes in large businesses with an extensive product range, a decision may be made to continue to sell a particular product within the margin of safety zone at just above a break-even level in order to keep competitors out of the given market – especially if a replacement new product is in development.

■ Break-even charts and start-up businesses

PC 6.4.2

A break-even chart is also a helpful management and planning tool for the new business owner or planner, since it enables him or her to work out how much sales turnover will need to be generated at a given level of price in order to first reach and then progress beyond breaking even. It can also be used to project various levels of profitability by plotting various pricing levels or, alternatively, fixed and variable costing levels, and to answer questions like:

- What happens if sales increase by 15%?
- What is the effect of cutting fixed costs by 7.5%? etc.

For this reason, break-even charts are used to illustrate such aspects in business plans submitted to, say, a bank as part of a loan application.

PC 6.4.1 6.4.2

■ Production strategies and the break-even point

Larger companies employ various production strategies aimed at securing either increased profits or higher volume sales. Where, for example, a product range is well-established and accepted, a manufacturer may well elect to site factories making the range in areas of low-cost labour – as evidenced by the construction of factories over the past ten years in the UK by both Japanese and German companies. Alternatively, where labour costs are high, a manufacturer may elect to go for a long-term plan of, say, introducing robotics and computerised production methods via sophisticated equipment. While installation costs would be high, they would be offset by low running costs and deliver an overall cheaper production cost during a period of, say, ten years, than would be the case if its existing labour force were retained.

Also, high levels of fixed and variable costs inevitably demand either long sales runs and/or high prices. In such cases, multi-nationals may seek, for example, to manufacture computers in countries where both cost elements are low and to sell them in countries where prices secured are high.

PC 6.4.1 6.4.2

REVIEW TEST

1 Supply three basic factors which determine price.

2 Explain how cost-plus pricing is determined.

3 What is a market-driven price? How does it differ from a cost-plus price?

4 What is the break-even point in a graph plotting sales, cost of sales and profit?

5 What is the margin of safety in a break-even chart?

6 Explain how marginal costing can work in a business's favour when selling goods.

7 Explain clearly the difference between fixed and variable costs.

8 How can a break-even chart be used in starting up a new business?

9 What production strategies can be determined with the aid of a break-even chart?

10 How does a break-even chart make it possible to forecast profit levels of a given product?

PC 6.4.1 6.4.2 6.4.3 6.4.4

INDIVIDUAL/PAIR ACTIVITIES

1 Arrange to interview a small trader, such as a greengrocer or newsagent, and find out what factors determine for the business how retail sales prices are determined. Report back orally to your class on what you discover.

2 Make an appointment to talk to both a production manager and a cost accountant in a medium-to-large manufacturing business and find out how costs are calculated and controlled in production runs, and how the production costing element links to eventual sales pricing. Report back to your class in an oral briefing.

3 With the help of your teacher, design a break-even chart on student recruitment for your department, and explain your findings to your class.

KNOWLEDGE TEST

Element 6.4
Explain basic pricing decisions and break-even

1 Which of the following basic factors determine price?

A The need to make a profit.
B The need to undercut competitors.
C The need to reduce production capacity.
D The extent of fixed and variable costs.

2 (i) Cost-plus pricing is a method of pricing arrived at by adding the costs of making a good to the costs of distributing and marketing it.
(ii) Market-driven pricing occurs when a large number of competitors drive down prices in an attempt to increase sales.

Which of the following options best describes the above two statements?

A	(i)	T	(ii)	T
B	(i)	T	(ii)	F
C	(i)	F	(ii)	T
D	(i)	F	(ii)	F

3 Which of the following statements is true, and which false?

A Goods sold in excess of their marginal costs make a contribution to fixed costs.
B By selling enough goods to produce a total contribution in excess of total fixed costs, a firm will make a profit.
C A variable cost is one which is subject to change, such as seasonal variations in demand, the weather or production capacity.
D A fixed cost is one which remains the same during a trading period, production run or other unit of similar measurement.

4 (i) A margin of safety is that which occurs when enough units of a product have been made so as to reach the break-even point.
(ii) A break-even chart can assist the planning of a start-up business.

Which of the following options best describes the above two statements?

A	(i)	T	(ii)	T
B	(i)	T	(ii)	F
C	(i)	F	(ii)	T
D	(i)	F	(ii)	F

5 Which of the following scenarios would be likely to generate a profitable sales run?

A High fixed costs and variable costs and a low sales price.
B Low fixed costs and variable costs and a low sales price.
C Low fixed costs and variable costs and a high sales price.
D High fixed costs and variable costs and a high sales price.

PC
6.4.1
6.4.2
6.4.3
6.4.4
6.4.5

PORTFOLIO OF EVIDENCE ACTIVITY

Element 6.4
Explain basic pricing decisions and break-even

BUSINESS TRAINING LIMITED

Scenario

You work as a researcher and writer for *Business Training Limited* (see Element 6.1) in a department which produces learning materials and training for accounting staff in business organisations.

You are currently engaged in producing a briefing pack for your trainers, part of which aims to explain how pricing decisions are made in businesses and also how break-even analysis can assist this activity.

Accordingly, your manager has asked you to research and write a short briefing for the pack which explains clearly:

a) the nature of the basic factors which influence the prices of goods and services arrived at by different types of supplier
b) and describes in detail the pricing strategy adopted by a business for a specific, single product or service
c) the importance and use of break-even analysis in business including an illustrative break-even chart which includes explanatory labels for each its components – using data from a given business. Note: the chart should also be accompanied by brief explanatory notes.

You have also been asked to keep in mind the nature of your recipients – trainers who need to be able to follow information easily and to absorb it quickly, aided by clear structures and visually appealing formats.

Task 1

Fill out at the start of this activity the appropriate parts of your planning and review log.

Task 2

Research carefully into the areas of pricing and break-even analysis and produce your notes based on business data you have been able to acquire. In case of any difficulty, discuss with your teacher the possibility of using simulated data which he/she may be able to make available.

Task 3

Produce a briefing which is structured suitably, according to the components listed in the scenario above. Your briefing is likely to be 5–6 printed sides of A4 long. Seek to use a graphics software package to produce your break-even graph if possible.

Performance criteria covered

6.4.1, 6.4.2, 6.4.3, 6.4.4, 6.4.5

Core skills covered

Communication:
3.2.1, 3.2.2, 3.2.3, 3.2.4, 3.2.5, 3.3.1, 3.3.2, 3.3.3, 3.4.1, 3.4.2, 3.4.3, 3.4.4

Information Technology:
3.1.1, 3.1.2, 3.1.3, 3.1.4, 3.1.5, 3.2.1, 3.2.2, 3.2.3, 3.2.4, 3.2.5, 3.2.6, 3.2.7, 3.3.1, 3.3.2, 3.3.3, 3.3.4, 3.3.5, 3.3.6

Application of Number:
3.3.1, 3.3.2, 3.3.3, 3.3.4, 3.3.5

TWO SKILLS-BUILDING ASSIGNMENTS

ASSIGNMENT 1

PC
6.4.2
6.4.3

Your firm sells a product for an average cost of £50 each. You have identified the following variable costs:

Labour £10

Materials £15

Variable overhead £5

Your monthly production is 95 units and the attributable fixed costs are £1,500.

Calculate:

1 the normal monthly profit for the product

2 the break-even point in units

3 the margin of safety in units

4 the profit that would result if a further 15 units could be made and sold for the same price/cost structure

ASSIGNMENT 2

PC
6.3.8

Your firm makes just one product and its costs, profit and selling price have been estimated as follows for a production/sales run of 10,000 per annum.

	£ (000)	£ (000)
Sales		1,000
Less costs		
Labour	500	
Materials	100	
Overheads	300	900
Net profit		100

You estimate that 80 per cent of the labour is a variable cost, all of the materials are variable and 40 per cent of the overheads are variable.

Calculate:

1 a profit statement using a marginal costing layout,

i.e. Sales less Variable Cost = Contribution

Total Contribution less Fixed Cost = Net Profit

2 the contribution per unit

3 the profit or loss of *a)* an increase of 20 per cent in sales and *b)* a decrease of 20 in sales.

FURTHER SOURCES OF INFORMATION

Frank Wood's Book-keeping & Accounts, 3rd edn, Pitman Publishing, 1992. ISBN: 0 273 03770 6

Book-keeping Made Simple, G Whitehead, Heinemann, 1987. ISBN: 0 434 98484 1

Frank Wood's Business Accounting AAT Student's Workbook, Sheila I Robinson, Pitman Publishing, 1993. ISBN: 0 273 60188 1

Book-keeping & Accounting, 2nd edn, G Whitehead, Pitman Publishing, 1991. ISBN: 0 273 03516 9

Commerce, D T Williams (revised by M Pincott), Pitman Publishing, 1985. ISBN: 0 273 03279 8

Business of Banking, D Wright and W Valentine, 2nd edn, Northcote House Publishers Ltd, 1988. ISBN: 0 7463 0535 4

Finance for BTEC National, J Hopkins, Pitman Publishing, 1988. ISBN 0 273 02877 4

UNIT

7

FINANCIAL FORECASTING AND MONITORING

Element 7.1
Explain sources of finance and financial requirements of business organisations

Element 7.2
Produce and explain forecasts and a cash flow for a small business

Element 7.3
Produce and explain profit and loss statements and balance sheets

Element 7.4
Identify and explain data to monitor a business

PERFORMANCE CRITERIA AND RANGE

Element 7.1: Explain sources of finance and financial requirements of business organisations

PERFORMANCE CRITERIA

A student must: *page*

1 explain the **financing requirements** of a business 621–3
2 explain **assets** and **working capital** 621–3
3 explain **common methods of finance** appropriate to the financing requirements 623–6
4 explain **usual sources of finance** appropriate for different methods of finance 626–34
5 explain **characteristics** of common methods of finance 626–34
6 explain **usual sources of finance** for different **types of business organisations** 626–36

RANGE

Financing requirements: asset finance, working capital finance
Assets: land, buildings, production machinery, transport, office machines, fixtures and fittings
Working capital: current assets (stocks of raw materials, work in progress, stocks of finished goods, debtors, cash), current liabilities (creditors)
Common methods of finance: trade credit, overdraft, factoring, leasing, hire purchase, loan, mortgage, profit retention, venture capital, equity, grants, gifts
Usual sources of finance: sellers, banks, factors, leasing companies. hire purchase companies, building societies, the business, venture capital investors, owner's savings, partner's savings, share issues, government grants, membership fees, charities
Characteristics: short-term, long-term, unsecured, secured
Types of business organisations: profit-making (sole trader, partnership, public limited company (plc), private limited company (Ltd.)), non-profit making (trades unions, charities)

EVIDENCE INDICATORS

- An explanation of the financing requirements of business organisations demonstrating an understanding of the difference between asset finance and working capital finance.
- An explanation of the different methods of finance including their usual sources, their characteristics, their appropriateness to different types of asset finance and their appropriateness for different types of business organisations

Element 7.2: Produce and explain forecasts and a cash flow for a small business

PERFORMANCE CRITERIA

A student must: *page*

1 explain the **purposes and components** of **forecasts** 637–45
2 produce a capital budget and trading forecast for a twelve-month period for a small business See Unit 8
3 explain **capital budget headings** and **trading forecast headings** 651–2
4 explain the **purpose of a cash flow** as a component of a forecast to a business seeking finance 638–42
5 explain the **significance of timing** in a cash flow forecast 638–9
6 explain **cash in-flow** and **cash out-flow headings** 646
7 collect data for each heading to support informed forecasts 643–4
8 produce feasible forecasts of cash in-flow and cash out-flow for one twelve-month period See Unit 8
9 produce monthly and cumulative net balances for a twelve-month period See Unit 8
10 explain the **consequences of incorrect forecasting** 646–7

RANGE

Purposes of forecasts: to predict what the business thinks will happen; to create opportunities to appraise alternative courses of action, to support business plan, to set targets, to monitor performance
Components of forecasts: capital budget, trading forecast, cash flow forecast
Capital budget headings: premises, machines, vehicles
Trading forecast headings: sales, raw materials, wages, water rates, telephone, other running costs
Purpose of a cash flow: to highlight the timing consequences of a capital budget and trading forecast, to support an application for finance, lender's confidence, owner's confidence, monitoring of performance
Significance of timing: credit periods for: purchases and sales, VAT payments, VAT recoveries, wages
Cash in-flow headings: start-up capital, loan receipts, sales receipts, VAT recoveries
Cash out-flow headings: payments for assets, raw materials, wages, water rates, telephone, other running costs, interest payments, loan repayments, VAT payments
Consequences of incorrect forecasting: incorrect working capital, cash flow problems (liquidity, insolvency)

EVIDENCE INDICATORS

A capital budget, trading forecast and cash flow forecast for a twelve-month period for a small business. These should be computer-generated using a spreadsheet package. The capital budget and forecasts should be supported by a commentary which explains the thinking behind the budget and forecast figures; the significance of in-flow and out-flow timing; the consequences of a net outflow of cash over successive periods of the forecast; and the use of a cash flow to support the seeking of finance.

Element 7.3: Produce and explain profit and loss statements and balance sheets

PERFORMANCE CRITERIA

A student must:	*page*
1 explain a **basic accounting system** suitable for a small business	663, 664–70, 690–2
2 identify and explain **accounting periods**	664
3 extract a **trial balance** from given accounting records	660–2
4 identify each account on the trial balance correctly in relation to **profit and loss** or **balance sheet** items	662, 671
5 produce and explain **profit and loss** and **balance sheet** in vertical form from the trial balance figures	664–74
6 explain the **purposes** of balance sheets and profit and loss statements	674–88

RANGE

Basic accounting system: documents, accounting records (ledgers, sales ledger, purchase ledger, cash book, general or nominal ledger), trial balance, financial statements or final accounts

Accounting periods: monthly, quarterly, annually

Trial balance: owing to creditors, owed by debtors, sales, purchases, money (cash, bank), expenses, drawings, fixed assets (premises, machinery; owners' capital, loans)

Profit and loss: sales, cost of sales, gross profit, overheads; net profit

Balance sheet: assets, current assets, current liabilities; owners' capital, profit and loss brought forward, profit and loss for period

Purposes: inform owners, inform managers; secure finance, maintain finance; monitor performance; fulfil statutory obligation, assess taxation liability

EVIDENCE INDICATORS

- A brief summary which explains a basic accounting system and how it could be used by a small business.
- A trial balance, profit and loss statement and balance sheet for a small single product business such as a sole trader running an ice cream kiosk or a self-employed decorator. (They should be produced from accounting records given to the student.) The trial balance, profit and loss statement and balance sheet should be supported by a commentary which explains how profit and loss statements and balance sheets are used to secure and maintain finance from lenders.

Element 7.4: Identify and explain data to monitor a business

PERFORMANCE CRITERIA

A student must:	*page*
1 identify **users** of accounting information	698–700
2 explain the **reasons for monitoring** a business	698–700
3 explain the use of **comparisons and variance** in monitoring a business	700
4 identify and explain **key components of information** required to monitor a business	700–1
5 explain the implications for the **performance of a business** from a given set of accounting information	709–12
6 explain the use of **solvency ratios, profitability ratios** and **performance ratios** in the interpretation of accounting information	702–5

RANGE

Users: owners, managers, providers of finance, tax authorities, general public, employees

Reasons for monitoring: solvency, profitability, taxation, maintaining finance, comparison with targets, improving performance

Comparisons and variance: actual with forecast for the business, actual with previous years for the business, inter-firm comparison

Key components of information: forecasts (balance sheet, profit and loss account, cash flow), actual (balance sheet, profit and loss account, aged debtors, aged creditors), previous year's (balance sheet, profit and loss account, aged debtors, aged creditors)

Performance of a business: solvent, profitable, achieving targets, better or worse than targets; establish tax liability, minimise tax liability, maintain funding, in comparison with others

Solvency ratios: current (current assets, current liabilities); acid test (liquid assets – current assets less stock/current liabilities)

Profitability ratios: return on net assets (%) (net profit/net assets); profit margin (%) (net profit/sales); gross profit (%) (gross profit/sales)

Performance ratios: selling (admin/sales (%)): (overheads/sales (%)); asset turnover: (sales/net assets); stock turnover (sales/stock); debtor collection period (debtors/(sales/365))

EVIDENCE INDICATORS

- A description of the key components of information used to monitor a business which explains who would want to use such information, why they would want it, and why comparisons and variances can be useful when monitoring the performance of a business.
- A summary of two given sets of accounting information for two comparative businesses which explains, and uses ratios to illustrate, the profitability (gross and net), solvency and performance of the two businesses.

INTRODUCTION

Unit 7 examines the dual roles of financial forecasting and monitoring in business. It identifies and explains the financing requirements of a business, focusing upon both assets and capital. The Unit goes on to explain currently common methods for financing a business, the sources of this finance and their various characteristics and usefulness in terms of different types of business.

In addition, Unit 7 explains how forecasts and cash flows may be produced to assist in managing a business and monitoring its performance, centring upon the customary range of money inputs and outputs, as well as upon the consequences of inadequate forecasting.

The Unit also provides detailed coverage of the production of profit and loss statements and balance sheets, explaining how they are constructed and the uses to which they are put as financial management tools.

Lastly, Unit 7 puts the production and analysis of financial information into the context of monitoring a business's performance and of supplying key data to its senior managers at regular intervals. The key accounting ratios are also explained in this section.

Element 7.1
EXPLAIN SOURCES OF FINANCE AND FINANCIAL REQUIREMENTS OF BUSINESS ORGANISATIONS

The financing requirements of business

PC 7.1.1

In straightforward terms, a business needs finance for four main reasons:

- to start up at the very outset of trading
- to maintain the trading and money cycles by generating enough surplus finance to 'kick-start' the next round of trading
- to finance additional, new projects once a business is under way
- to act as saved financial reserves and insurance against the proverbial rainy day or the unexpected.

The two-way financial split

PC 7.1.2

When a business entrepreneur starts to put together a financial plan for a new business, it very soon emerges that the finance available will be routed into two quite different areas of spending:

- assets
- working capital.

Spending money on assets

A group of business directors or partners are likely to allocate a significant part of the finance available to them into the acquisition of:

- **land** – on which to erect business premises
- **buildings** – the cost of erecting the buildings themselves, or of acquiring them

- **plant** – the cost of acquiring and installing plant and equipment to be used by the business
- **fixtures and fittings** – shelving, counters, display cases, lighting etc.
- **office equipment** – computers, printers, copiers, fax and telephone equipment etc.
- **vehicles** – articulated lorries, vans, sales force cars etc.

Of course, if an existing business is purchased most of the above items will already exist, but will still need to be paid for.

PC 7.1.2

Working capital: money spent on running the set up business

Once the business base (the fixed assets of the business) has been established the directors or partners will need to turn their attention to buying in those items needed to operate the business in order for it to begin its trading and money cycles. This will involve them in spending money on:

- **raw materials, semi-finished goods or components** – if the business is in manufacturing
- **stock** – if the business is in retailing
- **advertising and sales promotion** – in order to gain customers
- **payroll** – to pay for work done for the business
- **services** – heat, light, water, rates, insurance etc.

A business's working capital will also be needed to finance a host of other running costs, from instant coffee to paper-clips. In accounting terms, working capital finance is divided into:

- **current assets** – money owed to the business – usually by credit customers; cash in the bank or in the till; stocks yet to be sold; semi-finished goods in manufacture
- **current liabilities** – money the business owes to its creditors for goods or services etc. purchased on account.

Note that the finance used to start up a business is sometimes referred to as risk capital, since it is by no means certain that the business will prosper and provide a regular return on the money put into it by directors, shareholders or partners. For this reason, relatively high returns are paid out to such investors in terms of annual dividends.

As Fig 7.1 on page 623 illustrates, all businesses basically need two forms of finance:

1. **Start-up, pump-priming capital**, which may come from directors' investments, loans or the issue of shares etc.
2. Money earned in the form of an **operating profit** – stemming from the profitable sale of goods or services.

Additionally, it may be that a company invests some of its profits and derives income from interest payments or dividends from time to time.

Fig 7.1 **Working capital and cash-flow forecasting in the operating cycle** PC 7.1.2

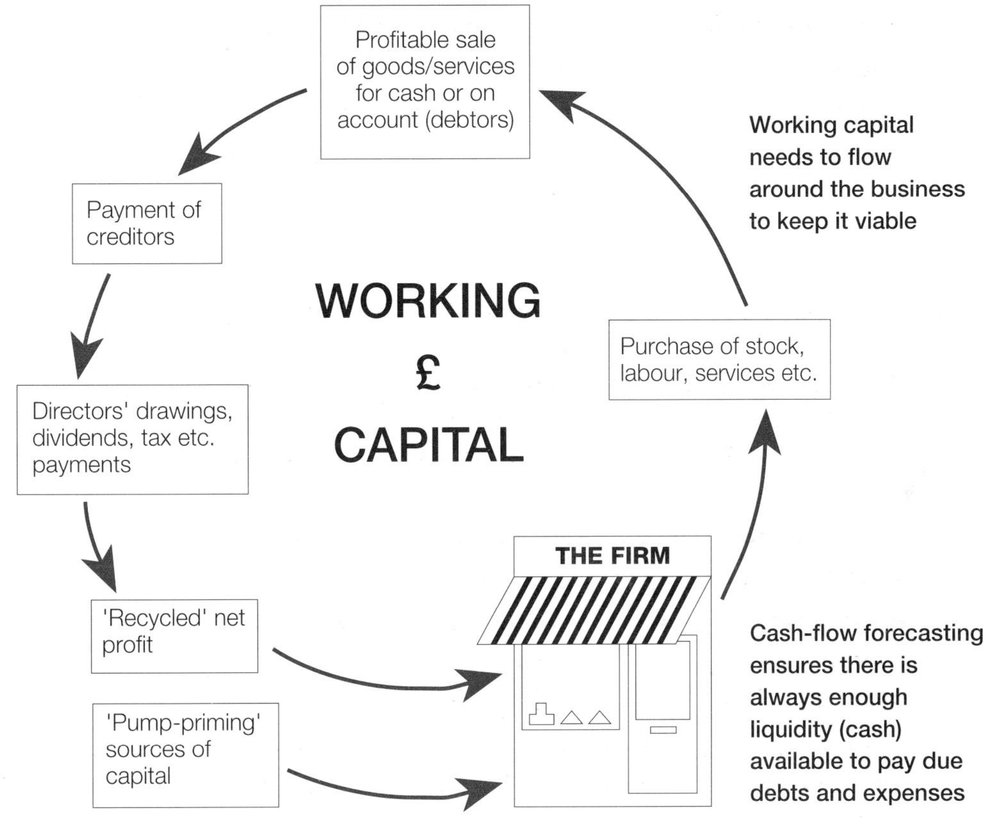

Profitable sale of goods/services for cash or on account (debtors)
Payment of creditors
Directors' drawings, dividends, tax etc. payments
'Recycled' net profit
'Pump-priming' sources of capital
WORKING
£
CAPITAL
THE FIRM
Purchase of stock, labour, services etc.
Working capital needs to flow around the business to keep it viable
Cash-flow forecasting ensures there is always enough liquidity (cash) available to pay due debts and expenses

Common methods of financing a business

PC 7.1.3

The methods employed to finance a business vary according to two main factors:

- the amount of money needed (large or small)
- the time required to repay any money loaned to finance the business.

Not unnaturally, business people tend to want longer time periods within which to repay large loans.

■ Large loans over long periods

Extensive finance in a business tends to be needed to pay for items like:

- premises
- farming or industrial land

- complex plant and installations
- acquiring existing businesses
- opening new branches or outlets.

As a result, a number of specialist lenders have emerged over the past two hundred or so years to meet the needs of would-be borrowers of large sums:

- the High Street clearing banks
- building societies
- merchant banks
- finance houses.

Occasionally, wealthy people will provide loans to business people whom they know and can trust, or use such investment as a means of securing a place on a board of directors or sleeping partner status.

All businesses which lend out money tend to require essentially two things:

a) security against the loan
b) as high a return of interest on the loan as they can secure.

In the case of security against the loan, few if any banks or financial houses would risk lending out, say, £100,000 as an unsecured loan, since if the borrower defaulted (by being, for instance, a sole trader with unlimited liability who has gone bankrupt), the bank could 'kiss its money goodbye'! Thus banks tend to require some tangible asset – such as a paid-for private residence – to serve as security or collateral for any loan. Thus the loan becomes secured, since if the borrower defaults, the bank can take over the asset (since it will require to hold the deeds of the residence in any case). In this way, a would-be start-up business entrepreneur may find him or herself in a Catch 22 situation in which it is not easy to secure start-up capital.

Building societies operate in a similar way, and will retain the deeds of any property on which a loan has been taken out, until the borrower has paid both capital and interest completely.

While lenders naturally prefer to charge high levels of interest on any loan given, they inhabit an extremely competitive market in which interest charges are watched with eagle eyes by both would-be borrower and finance provider. Thus a long-term loan to finance bricks and mortar tends to be only a few points above the prevailing bank rate of the time.

However, erecting bricks and mortar in the UK is one thing, but seeking to establish a business to import goods from North Korea or to develop a car-engine which runs on water quite another! For such high-risk business ventures alternative lenders are needed, such as a merchant bank or finance house. Such lenders have been known to charge up to 100% interest rates per annum for very high risk ventures, and 'venture capital' is never cheap – simply because of the risks involved. However, high risks can – and have – brought in high returns, as Richard Branson's creation of Virgin Airlines has demonstrated.

PC 7.1.3

■ Small loans over short periods

All types of business need to make small loans over short periods – say up to two years – in order to finance equipment or, say, a small extension or addition to the business, such as a photocopier, a new shop-front, a delivery van or a lock-up shed.

Where loans of, say, between £2,000 – £20,000 are concerned, the following methods of finance may be used:

- a loan from a clearing bank or building society
- an agreed overdraft from a bank or building society on an existing account
- a hire-purchase agreement with a finance house or supplier
- the issue of credit from the supplier (usually for smaller sums).

Such loans tend to require comparatively high levels of interest. Many hire-purchase agreements impose a level of 20–30% plus per annum on money loaned out. Banks similarly make high charges. In both instances this is because such loans are unsecured. The popularity of HP stems largely from the fact that, at no initially large outlay of money, after making, say, thirty-six payments (including interest) ownership of the good passes to its 'hirer'.

Other methods: renting and leasing, self-funding, factoring

PC 7.1.3

Other financing methods are available to businesses other than using up precious capital to purchase a good or service. Instead, a business may elect to rent – say premises – on a monthly basis, thus avoiding the need to find extensive finance. Needless to say, rents charged include margins of profit which reflect the opportunity cost of, say, not selling the premises, as well as the costs of maintenance, if this is the landlord's liability.

Premises or motor-vehicles may be leased as an alternative to outright purchase, in which case the lessee acquires the right to use the item leased for the period of the lease, but does not own it. The absence of freehold ownership of premises, purchased, say, on a 30-year lease is generally reflected in the lower price of the lease.

Whenever possible, a set of business directors or partners may opt to finance a project out of retained capital set aside for the purpose, since this is usually the cheapest form of loan available, no interest charges being required. However, in this instance, a firm's accounts director may ask pointed questions about opportunity cost. Could the money used to finance the item be used more profitably in the business elsewhere? What will be the return on the investment? Will it be higher than that obtainable from putting the sum involved in, say, gilts?

Factoring

Another means of financing a business project is through factoring, although this method of finance is normally to be counted among those 'of last resort'. This is because factoring involves another business in purchasing a firm's outstanding account customers' debts, but at a price much reduced from their face value. Thus the seller obtains ready cash, but loses out on the profits represented in the sums due from credit sales. These go to the factoring business.

Gifts and grants

In order, say, to encourage a business to construct a factory in an area of high unemployment, the UK government may provide a gift or grant to such a business, or it may facilitate a tax holiday, by waiving an amount of corporation tax payable. Similarly the UK government and the European Union provide grants and subsidies for certain types of business development in areas designated as in need of economic development.

Share issues

A very popular method of financing projects and developments among public limited companies is through the issue of a new tranche of shares, sometimes referred to as a rights issue, when existing shareholders are given preferential purchasing opportunities.

PC
7.1.1
7.1.2
7.1.3

DISCUSSION TOPICS

1 What steps could a person who wishes to set up a small business take to obtain a start-up loan?

2 What are the pros and cons of outright purchasing as opposed to HP, leasing or renting?

3 Are APR charges for unsecured loans too high these days? Can anything be done?

4 What techniques could be adopted by a small trader to check whether the costs of a business loan were affordable in business terms?

5 It is said that many small businesses fail through being under-capitalised. What would be the best advice to give to a small trader seeking to expand his or her business?

PC
7.1.1
7.1.2
7.1.3

INDIVIDUAL/PAIR ACTIVITIES

1 Find out what three clearing banks currently charge for: a) unapproved overdrafts, b) agreed overdrafts, c) business mortgages, d) loans to buy business equipment.

2 Do the same for three national building societies. Compare notes on your discoveries in a class discussion.

3 Find out what the current charges are in your locality for: a) purchasing a motor-car or van on HP, b) leasing a lock-up shop of about 13m × 10m per annum, c) renting a photocopying machine, d) leasing a delivery van. In an oral presentation to your class, compare the above charges with the costs of outright purchase for each a) – d) item.

4 Find out how a shares issue provides working capital for a plc and explain what you discover to your class.

PC
7.1.4

Sources of finance available to business

The above section on methods of financing businesses has already outlined some of the major players in the financial services market for lending and borrowing money. The following section identifies more closely methods of finance with their customary sources.

■ Long-term assets

PC 7.1.4

As you are aware, long-term assets in a business include land, premises, plant and machinery, equipment and fixtures. While such assets are essential in order to run a business, they are not always readily turned into capital which might fund a start-up business or fresh business initiative.

However, assets of the above type may well be employed to provide sources of finance in one or more of these ways:

- surplus land may be sold or leased to provide cash
- premises owned by the organisation may be 'leased back' to, say, an insurance company or bank, thus releasing cash for investing in the business plan
- surplus expensive equipment could be sold or leased
- a loan could be secured from a bank or finance house using the organisation's assets as security for it. (For example, a mortgage could be taken out on premises owned by a company.)

■ Venture and investment capital

PC 7.1.4

Very often the entrepreneur wishing to start up a business has insufficient capital with which to do so. Some (reckless) would-be entrepreneurs offer their own private houses up as security for, say, a bank loan, and run the risk of finding themselves and their families 'out on the street' if the business fails.

However, as there has been an expanding market for several hundred years in the business of lending money to entrepreneurs (medieval merchants financed speculative voyages of sea-captains seeking gold, silver, silks, spices etc.), it is no wonder that, today, there exist numerous private and merchant banks clustering around the financial centres of the world – London, Zurich, Frankfurt, Hong Kong, New York and Tokyo – whose main purpose is to lend out risk or venture capital to those entrepreneurs who can convince them that a particular business venture's 'likely return on capital invested' balances with an acceptable degree of risk. Such sources of finance do not, however, come cheap and may levy up to 70–80 per cent interest charges per annum or loan period.

■ Other sources of finance

PC 7.1.4

Other sources of business lending include:

- clearing banks
- building societies
- finance houses
- private, individual investors (e.g. sleeping partners)
- hire-purchase companies (if the finance is needed for plant, vehicles or equipment etc.)
- government agencies (which may on occasion provide grants or loans to assist business start-ups as a means of regenerating a depressed regional or local economy).

■ Interest charges – the costs of servicing a loan

A main factor in deciding which source of loan finance to accept is, of course, the charges (interest) which are required to service the loan. These will vary from time to time, depending upon the level of the base interest rate imposed on clearing banks by the Bank of England, and thus the extent of the supply of money in the economy. It is not uncommon for start-up and business project interest rates to exceed 30 per cent annual interest charges. For this reason, business directors continually clamour for decreases in prevailing interest rates, so as to make borrowing for capital investment less expensive.

PC 7.1.4

■ Internal equity

Because borrowing money from external sources is so expensive, many companies prefer – if they can manage it – to provide investment capital from within. There are a number of ways in which this may be achieved:

- as outlined above, from the sale or lease of long-term assets – land, premises etc.
- by drawing upon reserves: many larger organisations (especially public limited companies) retain significant proportions of their post-tax profits in the form of reserves and thus do not usually distribute all their generated profits as dividends to shareholders
- by making use of accumulated finance which has been set aside to replace depreciated equipment (thus giving themselves, in effect, an interest-free loan)
- by the company directors providing interest-free loans to the business from personal sources in the form of a cash injection (though this source is bound to have strings attached in some form or other)

PC 7.1.4

■ The offer of shares for sale

A popular way of obtaining capital for business expansion is to offer for sale shares in the company concerned. Smaller, private limited companies may achieve this by inviting one or more people to purchase shares in the firm and to join the board of directors. While this may promptly provide welcome cash to finance a business plan, it may well also alter the balance of control by redistributing the available shares among an enlarged board of directors, giving overall control to whichever grouping holds more than 50 per cent.

The issue of shares is more commonly undertaken for public limited companies by national and international issuing houses via stock exchanges and market makers, which will quote a new share issue at a specific, opening price. Depending upon the degree of interest shown in the shares, they will, thereafter, float up or down. New shares offers are often advertised through prospectuses (which provide relevant details of the company's track-record, financial strength and other reassuring data) published in financial newspapers and journals.

Sometimes – as with some government privatisation share flotations – financial houses, pensions organisations and banks etc. are invited to tender for sets of shares which are then sold to the highest bidders. At other times, existing company shareholders are given a 'first-refusal' of buying freshly marketed shares in what is termed a rights issue, where they may be enabled to purchase newly offered shares as a percentage of their existing holding, and sometimes more cheaply than the general public in a subsequent open offer.

Types of share issued

Ordinary shares

These are most generally issued and will be given a (nominal) face value price at the time of issue. What they subsequently cost to buy and sell (including the stock-broker's commission) will depend on what value is placed upon them by the money market at a given time. For example, the original shares of the privatised British Telecom were issued at £1.00 and are currently trading at £4.30. Ordinary shares tend to appreciate most dramatically in value in a buoyant economy, but are last in the queue for paying out if a company goes into receivership, and neither automatically qualify for the payment of an annual dividend.

Preference shares

As their name suggests, preference shares enjoy superior benefits, which (in the form of debentures) include the payment of a fixed rate of dividend each year (e.g. Harridges 8%). Preference shares are entitled to be paid out during a receivership before any ordinary shares.

Short-term finance (up to 3 years)

PC 7.1.4

Bank overdraft

This is usually the simplest type of finance to arrange and often the cheapest. Interest is only charged on the overdrawn balance, but the rate will vary according to current interest rates. It must be remembered that technically an overdraft is repayable on demand and this can occasionally prove a problem.

Traditionally overdrafts have been used to finance stock and work in progress as the sale of the finished goods will generate funds which will repay the loan. Many seasonal businesses rely on overdrafts to finance periods when sales are low.

Today, however, some firms have an almost permanent overdraft which is used to finance the purchase of fixed assets.

Creditors

It is often forgotten that this is a way of obtaining finance. Most companies obtain their stock on credit and pay within agreed credit periods.

Factoring or invoice discounting

Factor agencies will give a firm around 80 per cent of the value of invoices as soon as they are sent. The balance will be paid as the money is received, less the charges of the factor company.

PC 7.1.4

■ Medium-term finance (3–10 years)

Bank loans

This is a more formal arrangement with a bank than the overdraft facilities. The bank agrees to a loan at a fixed rate of interest. Repayment of the loan and interest payments are scheduled at the beginning and are usually directly debited from the current account to the loan account.

Hire purchase

This has been described earlier in the section, but it is worth noting here that the interest is an allowable expense for tax purposes and that other tax allowances can be claimed in the year in which the goods were bought, even though the full cost has not been made to the finance company.

Leasing

A company may choose to lease fixed assets rather than buy them. The ownership of the assets remain with the finance company and the rent charged is sufficient to cover the cost of the asset and to provide the finance company with a reasonable return on their investment.

PC 7.1.4

■ Long-term finance

Bank and other loans

In these cases the institution will usually require security for the loan. This is often by a charge over the company's property even though the loan is not being used to buy the property.

Debentures

Debentures are loans and their characteristics are similar to preference shares described earlier in this section.

Share capital

Share capital is sometimes put in a separate category known as permanent capital as a company must have some issued share capital to exist.

Other sources

There are many other sources of finance available in particular circumstances including:

- Venture capital and export finance available through banks.
- Grant Aid Schemes initiated by the Government. These include Assisted Area Grants, Regional Development Grants and others.
- European Economic Community Funds provided by the Community's budget to

promote the Community's objectives by providing finance for suitable projects. These funds include the social and regional development funds. Additionally the European Investment Bank will provide finance for projects in industrial, energy and infrastructure fields.

- Local forms of assistance

  Many local authorities will give assistance for particular projects. The assistance given will vary from authority to authority and full information can be obtained on local schemes from the relevant body.

- Department of Trade and Industry

  One of the functions of this government department is to encourage research and development into new uses of, for example, computers, microprocessors and fibre optics. It will provide expertise and financial assistance towards equipment and development costs.

The advantages and disadvantages of the common types of finance available to small businesses can be summarised as shown on page 632.

REVIEW TEST

PC 7.1.2 7.1.3 7.1.4

1 List four long-term assets a business is likely to possess.

2 Explain briefly how these assets might be employed to provide the finance needed for a new business project.

3 Explain briefly what is meant by the term 'venture and investment capital'.

4 List the main sources of finance available to a small trader wishing to expand his or her business, and to a public limited company wishing to do the same.

Capital gearing

PC 7.1.5

As we have seen, long-term finance can be satisfied by issuing shares or raising loan capital. The relationship between equity and loan capital is termed the *gearing ratio.* There are various ways gearing can be measured, but generally a company will be described as *highly geared* when it has a high proportion of fixed interest capital compared with ordinary share capital. Low gearing occurs when a company makes little use of fixed interest capital. The effect of gearing on a company is shown by the example in Table 7.1 on page 633. Companies A and B have raised the same amount of capital but in different ways. Company A makes little use of fixed interest capital – we can say it is low geared with a ratio of 1:9. Conversely Company B, with its greater use of loan capital, is highly geared having a ratio of 9:1.

In situation 1, both companies – after paying the debenture interest – have a residue available for ordinary shareholders which is equivalent to a 10 per cent return on capital.

In situation 2, profits have increased by £10,000. The impact on Company A with its greater use of equity capital is to raise the return to shareholders by 1 per cent to 11 per cent. However, in Company B the profits have to be spread between far fewer

PC
7.1.2
7.1.3

Types of finance available to small business

	Advantages	*Disadvantages*
Short term		
Bank overdraft (from clearing	Usually cheapest finance available; flexible; quickly obtainable; no minimum sum; interest paid on usage only; normally renewable.	Technically repayable on demand; vulnerable to change in government and banking policy; temptation to use for wrong applications (because of cheapness and convenience); may require personal guarantees.
Short-term loan (from clearing banks and finance houses, often owned by clearing banks)	Term commitment by lender; often quickly obtainable; can often roll over; improves overdraft flexibility.	Dearer than overdraft (except in special circumstances); uneconomical if funds not really required; may involve some restrictions.
Credit factoring (from specialist finance houses, often owned by clearing banks)	Can save costs if properly used – but often doesn't; credit linked to sales; used properly can be very convenient over a bridging stage; flexible; factors may carry bad debt risk (for extra payment); high percentage advance.	Can be some loss of contact with customers; difficult to terminate; regarded by some financiers as sign of weakness; might reduce overdraft facilities; dearer than it looks at first glance; minimum invoice/account value £100/£1,000 puts it beyond reach of some who need it most.
Invoice discounting (from specialist finance house)	No loss of contact with customers; can be ended easily; credit linked to sales; flexible; inexpensive and fairly quick to arrange can be great help in tight liquidity situation.	Might reduce overdraft facilities; dearer than overdraft facilities; regarded by some financiers as a sign of weakness.
Medium term		
Hire-purchase (from specialist finance houses, mostly owned by clearing banks)	Quick and inexpensive to arrange; ideal for short life, heavy use assets with guaranteed return, costs and repayment terms fixed for period; does not normally affect bank overdraft; capital allowances available straight away	Fairly expensive; default may be prosecuted over-vigorously; interest expressed as flat rate can be misleading (a rough rule of thumb is to double the flat rate to get the true rate).
Leasing (usually from same finance houses as hire-purchase)	Same advantages as hire purchase except since ownership does not pass, tax allowances are not available to leases but they are reflected in a lower cost.	Ownership does not pass, therefore no tax allowances.
Medium-term loans (from specialist financial institutions, clearing banks, merchant banks, government and EC sources)	Term commitment by lender – costs and repayment known; ideal for financing fixed assets; low minimum sum from some sources; inflation lessens real cost.	Might involve borrowing and other restrictions; dearer than shorter period finance; early repayment may involve additional interest charges.
Long term		
Long-term loans (from specialist institutions, insurance companies, government and EC sources)	Improves financial flexibility; other advantages same as for medium-term loans; improves balance sheet; cumulative effect of inflation makes it highly economic in real terms.	Same disadvantages as medium-term loans; insurance company loans dearer than they look when linked to life policies; lengthy to arrange (allow four months); may be partly convertible into equity.
Share capital (from specialist institutions, venture capital funds, merchant banks, pension funds)	Improves the platform on which borrowings can be raised. No repayments.	Can be expensive and, if in equity form, will reduce the owner's stake.

Reproduced from *Starting a Business* by Hargreaves, published by Heinemann.

shareholders. Thus the impact of this profit rise is far greater. The return on capital has doubled from 10 per cent to 20 per cent.

In situation 3 though, where profits fall by £10,000 the return to ordinary shareholders in Company A falls from 10 per cent to 9 per cent. However, for Company B, the reduction in profit means that the shareholders will receive no return on their capital this year. Summarising, we can say that profit fluctuations will have a smaller impact on a low-geared firm than a high-geared firm. High gearing benefits firms in prosperous times, but in a recession, when sales and profits fall, the very existence of the firm may be at risk through an inability to service (pay interest on) its loans.

PC 7.1.5

Table 7.1 **The impact of gearing upon profitability**

	Company A (£'000)		*Company B* (£'000)	
Ordinary shares	900		100	
Debentures (10%)	100		900	
Total long-term finance	1,000		1,000	
Situation 1				
Profit	100		100	
Debenture interest	10		90	
Residue available to equity shareholders	90		10	
As a % return on ordinary share capital	10%	$\frac{(90)}{900}$	10%	$\frac{(10)}{100}$
Situation 2				
Profit increases by 10%				
Profit	110		110	
Debenture interest	10		90	
Residue available to equity shareholders	100		20	
As a % return on capital	11%		20%	
Situation 3				
Profits decline by 10%				
Profit	90		90	
Debenture interest	10		90	
Residue available to equity shareholders	80		Nil	
As a % return on capital	9%		Nil	

Source: *A-Level Business Studies*, M. Buckley *et al.*, Longman 1992

DISCUSSION TOPICS

PC 7.1.2 7.1.3 7.1.4 7.1.5

1 What do you see as the dangers in running a business which is heavily indebted to a bank or finance house?

2 Is there any such thing as a 'reasonable' interest rate to charge in return for lending out sums of money? Or should the extent of the interest rate be limited only by 'what the market will bear'?

3 What do you see as the consequences in an economy of 'expensive money'?

4 It has been said by financial commentators that obtaining cash injections from the issue of shares by large companies enables their managers to gain extensive (even unbridled) control, since shareholders rarely attend annual shareholders' meetings in any significant numbers. Should shareholders be given more power and rights? If so, of what kind?

5 How does high and low gearing affect a company's security?

PC
7.1.2
7.1.3
7.1.4
7.1.5

ACTIVITIES

In pairs, undertake *one* of the following activities:

1 Find out the current interest charges levied by a local clearing bank on a loan to start up a small business, and what kind of planning documentation is required from the would-be entrepreneurs.

2 Find out the going rate for a medium-to-large company to secure a loan of, say, £250,000 to finance a business project, and what sort of securities a bank or finance house might require.

3 Find out what type of financial support is currently being made available by your local Training & Enterprise Council (TEC) and/or Department of Trade and Industry to assist business start-ups, expansion or development.

4 Research into three to five sets of published company accounts and find out what proportion of profits is retained in the form of reserves, and what proportion of turnover is paid out in the form of shareholders' dividends – seek to provide a rationale for your findings.

5 Research into the issue of shares as a means of obtaining additional injections of capital.

Report back to your group on your findings in the form of a 5–10 minute oral presentation and summarise your key data as a factsheet for distribution to your class as a revision support tool.

PC
7.1.1
7.1.2
7.1.3
7.1.4
7.1.5

REVIEW TEST

1 List four main reasons for a business needing finance.

2 List the principal types of fixed asset in a business.

3 Do the same for a business's current assets.

4 What are current liabilities?

5 Explain briefly how working capital flows around a business.

6 List three common methods of long-term finance.

7 Similarly, list three for short-term finance.

8 How does leasing differ from freehold purchasing?

9 What is hire-purchase? How does it work?

10 Explain how factoring works.

11 What is a rights issue? What is it used for?

12 What is meant by the term 'internal equity'?

13 Explain the difference between an ordinary share and a debenture.

14 What is meant by the term 'capital gearing'?

15 How does gearing affect a business's profits?

KNOWLEDGE TEST

Element 7.1
Explain sources of finance and financial requirements of business organisations

1 Which of the following are fixed assets?

A semi-finished goods
B land
C stock
D business premises

2 Which of the following are current assets?

A cash-in-hand
B outstanding credit sales
C delivery vans
D raw materials

3 (i) bank overdrafts do not have to be secured
(ii) a bank will require security for a large business loan

Which of the following options best describes the above two statements?

A	(i)	T	(ii)	T
B	(i)	T	(ii)	F
C	(i)	F	(ii)	T
D	(i)	F	(ii)	F

4 Which of the following statements is true, and which false?

A Venture capital is the source of finance for overseas projects.
B When leasing, the lessor does not own the leased item.
C Trading credit is needed before a new business may commence trading.
D Internal equity is a term used to describe finance a business possesses which it can use to fund development.

5 (i) A building society's rules prevent it from making small-scale loans.
(ii) A clearing bank may provide business mortgage services.

Which of the following options best describes the above two statements?

A	(i)	T	(ii)	T
B	(i)	T	(ii)	F
C	(i)	F	(ii)	T
D	(i)	F	(ii)	F

PC
7.1.1
7.1.2
7.1.3
7.1.4
7.1.5
7.1.6

PORTFOLIO OF EVIDENCE ACTIVITY

Element 7.1
Explain sources of finance and financial requirements of business organisations

MIDCHESTER BUSINESS CLUB

Scenario

You are the assistant manager of the *Midchester Business Club,* an organisation established in 1990 with Midshire TEC and Midshire County Council support, to provide support and advice to local people who had recently or were about to open small businesses.

Your manager, Jo Verghesi, is currently revising an informational booklet which provides Business Club members with up-to-date information and advice on the financial requirements of businesses, and also how and where to obtain financial support.

You have therefore been detailed to produce some sections of the booklet. In particular you have been asked to research and produce a clear explanation of:

What are the finance needs and requirements of businesses?

Jo Vherghesi has asked you to focus on assets and working capital for this section. She has further tasked you with producing an explanation of the different methods and sources of business finance, together with an explanation of their pros and cons for different types of business, to be produced under the heading:

Business finance: What do I need? Where do I get it? What is right for my business?

Task 1

Remember to complete the appropriate part of your planning and review log before starting this activity.

Task 2

First research and produce a suitable brochure entry on business finance requirements, bearing in mind the recipients of the Business Club brochure, some of whom are not at all familiar with business or finance jargon.

Task 3

Next, produce the explanation of finance methods and sources section of the brochure in a similar way.
Note: If at all possible, produce your brochure sections via PC and word-processing software. The combined length of your entries is likely to be between 4 and 6 sides of printed A4 long.

Performance criteria covered

7.1.1, 7.1.2, 7.1.3, 7.1.4, 7.1.5, 7.1.6

Core skills covered

Communication:
3.2.1, 3.2.2, 3.2.3, 3.2.4, 3.2.5, 3.3.1, 3.3.2, 3.3.3, 3.4.1, 3.4.2, 3.4.3, 3.4.4

Information Technology:
3.1.1, 3.1.2, 3.1.3, 3.1.4, 3.1.5, 3.2.1, 3.2.2, 3.2.4, 3.2.5, 3.2.6, 3.2.7, 3.3.1, 3.3.2, 3.3.3, 3.3.4, 3.3.5, 3.3.6

Element 7.2
PRODUCE AND EXPLAIN FORECASTS AND A CASH FLOW FOR A SMALL BUSINESS

[See also Unit 8]

Cash-flow forecasts

PC 7.2.1

■ The role of the cash-flow forecast

Prudent companies employ accountants to monitor continually the relationship between money flowing out of the enterprise (in the form of payments for raw materials, stock purchases, support services, payroll etc.) and revenue coming in from debtors (in the form of payments for goods or services sold to them), as well as any income from any investments. If income received always preceded in time payments out, there would be little or no need for cash-flow forecasting and analysis. Problems arise, however, when there is insufficient hard cash (liquidity) at the bank or in the safe to pay bills which have become due.

For this reason, management accountants tend to look for a ratio of 2:1 for current assets against current liabilities as a measure of a firm's financial viability or robustness in its business operations. (*Note:* current assets are those assets which can be readily converted into cash within, say, one year – payments for goods/services sold, finished goods ready for sale, stock in hand etc.; current liabilities represent the monies owed to creditors.) The 2:1 ratio reassures interested parties that the enterprise is most unlikely to fail as a result of a cash-flow problem.

Since 1992, companies have been required to include a cash-flow statement in their presentation of accounts, an example of which is shown in Table 7.2 on page 638.

■ Producing and interpreting a cash-flow forecast

PC 7.2.1

The following section (reproduced by kind permission of the National Westminster Bank plc from *Profit by Planning*) provides an excellent illustration of the way in which methodical cash-flow forecasting helps a new business through its all-important first twelve months of trading. *Note:* the following section has been written to address directly a would-be business start-up entrepreneur.

PC 7.2.1

Table 7.2 **Example of a cash-flow statement**

Sandal PLC
Cash flow statement for the year ended 30 April 1992

	£000	£000
Net cash inflow from operating activities		4,765
Returns on investment and servicing of finance		
Interest received	2,435	
Interest paid	(56)	
Dividends paid	(1,890)	
Net cash inflow from returns on investments and servicing of finance		489
Taxation		
Corporation tax paid	(1,546)	
Tax paid		(1,546)
Investing activities		
Payments to acquire fixed assets	(857)	
Receipts from sales of fixed assets	280	
Net cash outflow from investing activities		(577)
Net cash inflow before financing		3,131
Financing		
Issue of ordinary share capital	200	
Repayment of debenture loan	(40)	
Net cash inflow from financing		160
Increase in cash and cash equivalents		3,291

Source: *Business Studies* (Longman Revise Guides), M. Buckley *et al.*, Longman 1992

PC 7.2.1

Completing cash-flow forecasts

Once you have completed your operating budget you are ready to move on to your cash-flow forecast. Again, there are two forms enclosed, one for you, and, if appropriate, one for your bank manager.

Completing a cash-flow forecast is not just a question of transferring the figures from your operating budget. We will discuss some of the differences a little later on. First though, let's consider the objectives of a cash-flow forecast:

Cash is the life-blood of the business and neglecting to give attention to this vital element is one of the main reasons for business failures.

Time spent assessing the cash requirements and monitoring cash-flow is time well spent because it can:

- identify potential cash shortfalls before they occur
- enable potential surplus cash to be identified and used efficiently
- ensure that adequate cash is available for any necessary capital expenditure

- encourage more efficient use of resources and reduce costs
- lead to soundly-based decisions

How do you complete a cash-flow forecast?

PC 7.2.1 7.2.2 7.2.3

Like your operating budget, your cash-flow forecast will be based on assumptions. Again ensure these are realistic and make a note of all the assumptions used.

Unlike your operating budget, your cash-flow forecast is not concerned with profit and loss. It merely represents your best estimate of the timing of cash receipts and payments, through your bank account, over a period.

Please bear in mind:

a) The period of credit you give to your customers or take from your suppliers. If, for example, you allow 30 days credit, your operating budget could show invoiced sales in say January, which should not feature in your cash-flow forecast until February, and then only if you have adequate systems in place to ensure that customers pay on time.

If yours is a new business without a track record, you may well have to settle with your suppliers immediately. This will obviously have a material effect on your cash-flow.

b) You should show all cash to be paid and received, including capital expenditure, and loans received and repaid. These items are not in the operating budget. Conversely, remember that depreciation should not be included in a cash-flow forecast as it is purely a book entry and does not involve cash going in or out of the business.

c) VAT will be included in a **cash-flow forecast**, although it is excluded from an **operating budget** as it is not a charge against profit or loss but is a cash settlement with H M Customs and Excise.

NB. Where the business is not registered for VAT – and therefore not charged on sales – include as part of expenses figures shown in operating budget. The reason for this is that since you will be unable to claim tax back from H M Customs & Excise, it will have an effect upon your projected profit.

To help you to complete the form, let's run through some of the headings in more detail. Again, it will be helpful if you have the form in front of you while reading the next section. See page 643 for the form referred to.

Line 4 Exclude your Bank overdraft, but include all other loans, including those from the Bank.

Line 5 Show all money of a permanent nature that you or your fellow directors/partners are putting into the business.

Line 7 Show such items as grants, selective financial assistance and so on.

Line 10 Show all remuneration and withdrawals from the business.

Line 13 All items should tie in with the information shown in your business plan.

Line 16 Include items such as electricity, gas, oil, water, telephone, insurance and so on.

Line 21 Include such items as Solicitor's fees, Accountant's fees, Consultancy fees and so on.

Lines 23-25 Include any other appropriate items.

Line 29 Show the opening current account balance in the Bank's book, but exclude Bank loans.

Monitoring

Now you've completed your forecasting, you may feel that all the hard work is over. Far from it. Although you've given a lot of thought already to the future of your business, monitoring your performance is probably more important.

You must now use the information you have compiled in an effective way and compare your actual performance against your projections.

If there is a difference, you need to find the reason and decide whether you need to take any corrective action.

Let's look at some figures for a possible cash-flow forecast and compare the actual performance with the projections. While we will concentrate on just the 6 and 12 monthly accumulated figures, you should be looking at your performance on a monthly basis to ensure you have the earliest possible warning of any difficulties. In practice the 6-monthly figures will not appear on your cash-flow forecast form but the 12-monthly will be your total column.

PC 7.2.2 7.2.3

		Trading Periods			
		6 months to June		*12 months to December*	
Line	*Receipts*	*Projected* £	*Actual* £	*Projected* £	*Actual* £
2	Sales (inc VAT) debtors	41,400	41,400	103,500	92,000
5	Capital introduced	10,000	10,000	10,000	10,000
A	Total receipts	51,400	51,400	113,500	102,000
	Payments				
8	Cash purchases	32,200	40,250	59,800	58,850
11	Wages /salaries (Net)	13,000	13,000	26,000	26,000
12	PAYE/NI	2,500	2,500	5,500	5,500
13	Capital items	5,000	5,000	5,000	5,000
15	Rent	2,250	1,500	3,750	3,750
15	Rates	240	240	480	480
16	Light and heat	450	475	900	1,000
16	Telephone and post	210	190	440	420
16	Insurance	400	400	400	400
19	Interest	680	750	940	1,465
20	Bank/finance charges	200	300	400	500
21	Bookkeeper	1,000	1,000	2,000	2,000
21	Professional fees	400	400	950	950
23	General expenses	400	500	800	1,000
26	VAT	1,000	800	5,500	4,375
B	Total payments	59,930	67,305	112,860	111,690
C	Net cash-flow (A–B)	(8,530)	(15,905)	640	(9,690)
29	Opening bank balance	Nil	Nil	Nil	Nil
D	Closing bank balance (C + or – Line 29)	(8,530) Overdrawn	(15,905) Overdrawn	640 In credit	(9,690) Overdrawn

Reproduced by kind permission of National Westminster Bank from *profit by planning – Services for the Smaller Business*

Comments on actual figures for the first six months

PC 7.2.3 7.2.4

a) Cash from sales at £41,400 is as anticipated, following a firm order.

b) Wages, PAYE, rates, insurance, book-keeping, professional fees and capital expenditure are as predicted.

c) Light, heat, telephone, general expenses, interest and Bank/Finance charges: these differ from the projection which, without previous experience to suggest likely expenditure, is hardly surprising. Still, there's no significant difference so, now the accounts are settled, there's no need to worry.

d) Although rental payments seem reduced, this is only because the June payment of £750 was put off until early July.

e) However, the purchases differ significantly from the forecast: not £32,200 but £40,250!

Here are some (but not all) of the possible reasons for the difference with comments on potential remedies:

Possible reasons	Possible remedies
(i) More material has been used than originally estimated. Result: a reduction in gross profit margin.	(i) If the contract is to continue, you might try and renegotiate the price to allow for use of more materials or look for means of reducing wastage. Otherwise you have to shop around to buy them more cheaply.
(ii) Suppliers have raised the price of materials. Result: once again, a reduction in gross profit margin.	(ii) As above you have learnt the hard way that you must allow for price rises when quoting for a contract of several months. Another time you won't underestimate on materials. You might buy more materials in advance but see (iii) below.
(iii) Stock is building up because buying and production are out of line.	(iii) While this does not affect the gross margin, is it wise to carry stock surplus to immediate needs? True it avoids price rises, but with stock possibly financed by bank borrowing, the interest costs may cancel out any savings.
(iv) In a business where credit is taken from suppliers, the increase in purchase payments could mean a shorter credit period allowed by the supplier.	(iv) You need to balance prompt payment to the supplier with the impact on bank borrowing.

Of course, there are many more possibilities. The same lesson will emerge from all of them: comparison of actual performance against original projection is the best way to identify potential problems and possible solutions to them.

PC
7.2.3
7.2.4

Comments on actual figures for 12 months to December

a) At the end of 12 months we now see that cash from sales is £11,500 down; this difference has only arisen in the second half year.

Possible reasons	Possible remedies
(i) You did less business after finishing an initial contract in June.	(i) You should try to get more work. During this time your workforce would not have been at full stretch and with no promise of more work, you might have to consider some cuts in staff. Likewise cuts in overheads, although it is unlikely to yield significant savings at this stage.
(ii) Your customers took more than the originally projected credit period.	(ii) You should be tougher. You should strengthen credit control, and press customers to honour your terms of business.
(iii) While production continued as forecast, invoicing and deliveries fall behind.	(iii) You deliver on completion and invoice promptly.

b) Even when the payment-for-purchases figure is virtually as projected, it is a good idea to ensure that this is for the right reasons as there may be compensating differences. In this instance, purchase payments were:

	12 months	*1st 6 months*	*2nd 6 months*
Forecast	£59,800	£32,200	£27,600
Actual	£58,850	£40,250	£18,600

You can see from the record, that the second half of the year is also very different from the forecast. This example shows what might have happened:

Because sales in this period were lower than forecast, payments for purchases were reduced by, say, £4,400.

Having got on good terms with your suppliers over the first six months, you persuaded them to give you credit terms during the second six months. Result: goods delivered from August on were not paid for until September or later. Hence a once and for all cashflow benefit

£4,600

£9,000

This £9,000 is the difference between the forecast and the actual figure for the second six months. It shows why you should always analyse the reasons behind such differences.

Other differences

VAT is down because sales are down offset in part by the reduction in buying.

Interest is up because, during the second half year, the overdraft has been running at a higher level than was originally forecast.

These examples illustrate what might happen to your cash-flow forecast. Similarly you should monitor your performance through your operating budget to ensure that your profit projections are on course.

Example of a cash-flow forecasting schedule

PC 7.2.2 7.2.3 7.2.4 7.2.5

Enter Month													
Figures rounded to £ 's		Budget	Actual	Budget	Actual	Budget	Actual	Budget	Actual	Budget	Actual	Budget	Actual
1	**Receipts** Sales (inc VAT) – Cash												
2	Debtors												
3	Other Trading Income												
4	Loans Received												
5	Capital Introduced												
6	Disposal of Assets												
7	Other Receipts												
A	**Total Receipts**												
8	**Payments** Cash Purchases												
9	Payments to Creditors												
10	Principals Remuneration												
11	Wages/Salaries (net)												
12	PAYE/NI												
13	Capital Items												
14	Transport/Packaging												
15	Rent/Rates												
16	Services												
17	Loan Repayments												
18	HP Leasing Repayments												
19	Interest												
20	Bank/Finance Charges												
21	Professional Fees												
22	Advertising												
23													
24													
25													
26	VAT												
27	Corporation Tax etc												
28	Dividends												
B	**Total Payments**												
C	**Net Cashflow (A–B)**												
29	Opening Bank Balance												
D	**Closing Bank Balance (C ± Line 29)**												

Basic Assumptions – Please specify the following assumptions used in completing this form and list any other relevant ones overleaf

– Credit Taken – the average period taken from creditors. Days

– Credit Given – the average period given to debtors. Days

Note. The cash-flow forecast normally spans 12 months

Reproduced by kind permission of National Westminster Bank from *profit by planning – Services for the Smaller Business*

PC
7.2.2
7.2.3
7.2.4
7.2.5

Example of an operating budget schedule

Enter Month													
Figures rounded to £ 's		Budget	Actual	Budget	Actual	Budget	Actual	Budget	Actual	Budget	Actual	Budget	Actual
	Sales												
1	Home												
2	Export												
A	**Total Sales**												
	Direct Costs												
3	Materials – purchases												
4	Wages and Salaries												
5	Stock Change (Increase)/Decrease												
B	**Cost of Goods Sold**												
C	**Gross Profit [A – B = C]**												
D	**Gross Profit as % of Sales [C ÷ A x 100 = D]**												
	Overheads												
6	Production												
7													
8													
9													
10													
11													
12	Selling & Distribution												
13													
14													
15													
16													
17													
18	Administration												
19													
20													
21													
22													
23													
24	Other Expenses												
25													
26													
27													
28													
29													
30	Finance Charges												
31	Depreciation												
E	**Total Overheads**												
F	**Net Profit before Tax [C – E = F]**												
G	**Sales required to break-even [E ÷ D x 100 = G]**												

Note. The operating budget schedule normally spans 12 months

Reproduced by kind permission of National Westminster Bank from *profit by planning – Services for the Smaller Business*

Why cash-flow forecasts are needed in business

PC
7.2.4
7.2.5

As the above example from Natwest's *Profit by Planning* amply illustrates, a clearing bank will usually want to see a carefully compiled cash-flow forecast (and overall business plan) before advancing any start-up business loan to a would-be entrepreneur. Correspondingly, in order to assist the process of preparation and decision-making which precedes the commencement of trading, banks like Natwest go to much effort in order to design and distribute sets of schedules and supporting notes. In this way, the prospective borrower gives confidence to the potential lender by demonstrating that his or her original business idea has been strengthened by a professional, business-like approach to planning and financing.

The following checklist illustrates the ways in which a cash-flow forecast support the business operation:

HOW A CASH-FLOW FORECAST SUPPORTS BUSINESS OPERATIONS

PC
7.2.4
7.2.5

A cash-flow forecast supports business operations by:

- reassuring prospective lenders of finance of the viability and likelihood of success of the business planning process (especially in start-up situations)
- providing a means of measuring on a continuous month-by-month basis the degree to which actual performance is mirroring forecast or targeted performance (so that prompt corrective action may be taken if needed)
- enabling the forecaster to better schedule the payment of creditors and to plan for large items of expenditure such as quarterly VAT payments
- allowing the forecaster to focus attention on possible danger areas, such as an increasing time-lapse between the issue of account statements and their payment
- monitoring the amounts and frequency of directors' drawings
- monitoring the sales turnover month on month and comparing this with totals of monthly payments

Cash-flow forecasts, operating budgets and opportunity costs

PC
7.2.4

In large, established companies, the cash-flow forecast, together with a proposed operating budget may be demanded by management accountants working for enthusiastic managers who put up project proposals, say, to introduce a new product or service. Careful analysis by the management accountants of the submitted forecast and budget will enable them to decide whether the new project is likely to generate a demanded level of profit, or whether the concept of opportunity cost will come into play – whether the finance to be used up in the proposed project might yield a better return on investment from a deployment elsewhere in the company's operations.

PC
7.2.5
7.2.6

CHECKLIST OF KEY FACTORS NEEDED TO PRODUCE AN EFFECTIVE CASH-FLOW FORECAST

When undertaking the production of a cash-flow forecast, the following are the key factors which need to be checked out carefully:

Receipts

Realistic projections of the amount of sales turnover and how it is likely to build, given factors like seasonal demand, customers' likely cash availability (e.g. immediately after Christmas) etc.

Accurate data on the levels of available start-up capital

Prudent projections of any income (and its timing) from investments made with any available capital

Payments

Prudent projections on the number of staff needed and how much they will be paid (including any bonuses or commission). Remember how cost-effectively Marks & Spencer plc deploy their full and part-time staff)

Up-to-date calculations on the levels of PAYE and NIC which will be levied weekly/monthly

The timing and amounts of the purchases of capital items – fixtures, equipment, vehicles etc.

Sufficient allowance for heat, light, telephones and postage and office consumables such as photocopying

Correct calculations for monthly rentals such as PCs, printers and copiers, and the costs of associated materials

Correct calculations of the amounts of interest and service charges payable to: banks, building societies, hire-purchase companies etc.

Close forecasts on fees charged by accountants (note that some companies now ask chartered accountants to tender for auditing the year's accounts

Provisions for emergencies or reserves which may be deemed necessary to cover a potentially slow trading period (say January or February) so as to avoid cash-flow problems

And, most important, *realistic provisions for bad debts*; in today's tough business world, many otherwise sound firms fail early because of bad debts incurred or giving credit to exceedingly slow paying account customers

Realistic projections of how much directors will need to take (and the frequency) in the form of drawings from the business

PC
7.2.10

The consequences of incorrect forecasting

The compilation and monitoring of a cash-flow forecast has saved many a small and new business from potential disaster. Unfortunately, the same cannot be said for those forecasts produced which communicate incorrect information!

If errors are made in either the cash input or output sections of the forecast, problems are bound to occur, as for example where an incorrect computation of VAT collected results in an insufficient sum having been set aside for the quarterly payment which is due. Again, errors in computing payroll costs can result in cash-flow problems when such payments are to be made.

All kinds of errors are possible on the input side also, where errors in calculating gross profit margins result in goods being priced too low, and thus too little sales revenue being generated.

For this reason, it is essential to check and double check calculations from which extrapolations will be made – for instance, where monthly apportionments of rent and rates are made from a single figure to be divided by twelve.

PC 7.2.1 7.2.4 7.2.5

DISCUSSION TOPICS

1 What do you consider to be the most useful features of a well drawn up cash-flow forecast in terms of aiding a newly established business?

2 What sort of business eventualities does the cash-flow forecast **not** cater for?

Can you provide examples and suggest other ways of managing their impact?

3 What items in a cash-flow forecast would **you** monitor most carefully in your own, new business over 6-12 months? Provide a rationale for the items you select.

4 Many small businesses fail in their early stages of development because they fail to get in fast enough the money which is owed to them for goods or services sold on account. What strategies can you think of which could be used to secure prompt payment from a firm's account customers?

PC 7.2.1 7.2.2 7.2.3 7.2.4

ACTIVITIES

In groups of two or three, research into one of the following activities and then produce a set of briefing notes for circulation around your class:

1 Find out how a debt factoring service can assist a business with cash-flow problems.

2 Find out how and why management accountants use opportunity cost calculations as a means of evaluating the viability of proposed new business projects.

3 Find out what techniques a company's accountants employ to ensure that its cash-flow remains in a healthy state.

4 Find out some of the ways in which a company's working capital may be used most cost-effectively in, either, say, a manufacturing or retailing business environment.

PC
7.2.1
7.2.2
7.2.3
7.2.4
7.2.5
7.2.10

REVIEW TEST

1 Explain briefly the role of the cash-flow forecast in a business plan

2 What is the purpose of a capital budget?

3 Why is timing important in forecasts?

4 Explain the difference between a cash-flow forecast and a cash-flow statement

5 How can a cash-flow forecast help a business manager to avoid a situation where net outflows exceed net inflows in successive months of trading?

6 Why is it important to log VAT receipts and payments in a cash-flow forecast?

7 Explain briefly the nature and purpose of an operating budget

8 Describe briefly the main components of the in-flow and out-flow sections of a cash-flow forecast

9 What are the likely consequences of incorrect forecasting?

KNOWLEDGE TEST

Element 7.2
Produce and explain forecasts and a cash-flow for a small business

1 (i) A cash-flow forecast plots estimated in- and out-flows of money over a trading period.
(ii) A cash-flow statement is an historical accounting document.

Which of the following options best describes the above two statements?

A	(i)	T	(ii)	T
B	(i)	T	(ii)	F
C	(i)	F	(ii)	T
D	(i)	F	(ii)	F

2 Which of the following statements are true, and which false?

A Introduced capital is shown as a receipt in a cash-flow forecast.
B Net cash flow derives from receipts minus payments.
C Brackets around a figure indicate that it is an estimate.
D VAT payments received are included in the receipts/inflow section.

3 (i) The term operating schedule is an alternative for cash-flow forecast.
(ii) An operating schedule includes a breakdown of direct and indirect costs.

Which of the following options best describes the above two statements?

A	(i)	T	(ii)	T
B	(i)	T	(ii)	F
C	(i)	F	(ii)	T
D	(i)	F	(ii)	F

4 Which of the following statements is true, and which false?

A A cash-flow forecast may be used to persuade prospective lenders to provide loans.
B Timing is more important in operating statements than it is in cash-flow forecasts.
C Incorrect calculations on a cash-flow forecast could lead to the early failure of a young business.
D A well-produced cash-flow forecast removes the necessity of providing reserves of finance for the unexpected or an emergency.

5 (i) A bank manager would expect a cash-flow forecast to show a profit by the end of trading month three at the latest.
(ii) As long as a cash-flow forecast shows a business to be breaking even, a bank manager will be inclined to authorise a loan.

Which of the following options best describes the above two statements?

A	(i)	T	(ii)	T
B	(i)	T	(ii)	F
C	(i)	F	(ii)	T
D	(i)	F	(ii)	F

PORTFOLIO OF EVIDENCE ACTIVITY

Element 7.2
Produce and explain forecasts and a cash-flow for a small business

It is recommended that this activity be undertaken as part of the business planning activity of Element 8.2 (PC 8.2.5 refers) in order to support an integrated approach to finance, marketing and business planning.

Two further activities are provided below to provide skills development opportunities in forecasting and budgeting.

SKILLS BUILDING ASSIGNMENTS

PC 7.2.2

ASSIGNMENT 1

You are required to complete a cash-flow statement for a new firm 'Smith & Co.' which starts business on 1 April. Use the Cash Budget Form on page 651 to fill in your responses.

1 Smith will put £35,000 into a business bank account on 2 January.

2 Later that week Smith draws cheques to pay for the following:

a) Premises £20,000 for the purchase of a lease

b) Fixtures and fittings £5,000

c) Motor vehicles £9,000

3 All stock purchases will be on credit. Smith will purchase stock costing £5,000 at the beginning of January that must be paid in February. Other purchases will be at the rate of £4,000 per month including

purchases for the rest of January. Other than the initial £5,000 purchase all goods will be paid for two months after their purchase.

4 Sales are estimated to be at a rate of £6,000 for January and £8,000 thereafter. All sales are on a credit basis and debtors will pay their accounts in the month after the sale.

5 Salaries will cost £1,000 per month payable in the same month.

6 Other expenses will average £400 per month, payable one month in arrears.

7 Insurance will cost £800 payable in February and rates will cost £500 per quarter payable in March and June.

8 Smith will take £1,000 per month as personal drawings.

9 A bank loan of £10,000 will be received in February.

PC 7.2.2

ASSIGNMENT 2

From the following information you must use the Cash Budget Form on page 652 to record the following receipts and payments:

a) Opening bank balance £5,000

b) Production in units:

Nov	Dec	Jan	Feb	Mar	Apr	May	Jun	Jul
460	540	700	640	560	500	420	380	400

c) Raw materials used in production cost £6 per unit. Of this one-third is paid one month before production and two-thirds in the same month as production.

d) Direct labour costs of £8 per unit are payable in the same month as production.

e) Variable overheads are £16 per unit payable three-quarters in the same month as production and one-quarter in the month following production.

f) Sales at £32 per unit:

Oct	Nov	Dec	Jan	Feb	Mar	Apr	May	Jun
240	360	480	580	620	620	680	520	360

Debtors to pay their accounts: one-fifth as a deposit in the month of the sale and the remainder two months later.

g) Fixed overheads are £900 per month payable each month.

h) Extensions to the premises costing £15,000 are to be paid for in February.

i) A loan of £18,000 will be received in February.

C
3.1

CASH BUDGET FORM

Months	Jan	Feb	Mar	Apr	May	Jun
Receipts						
(1) Capital						
(4) Sales Receipts from debtors						
(9) Loan						
Total receipts	£	£	£	£	£	£
Payments						
(2) Fixed assets						
(a) Premises						
(b) Fixtures						
(c) Motor Vehicles						
(3) Stock purchases						
(5) Salaries						
(6) Other exps						
(7) Insurance Rates						
(8) Drawings						
Total payments	£	£	£	£	£	£
Receipts less payments	£	£	£	£	£	£
Balance at bank	£	£	£	£	£	£

CASH BUDGET FORM

Months						
Total receipts	£	£	£	£	£	£
Payments						
Total payments	£	£	£	£	£	£
Receipts less payments	£	£	£	£	£	£
Balance at bank	£	£	£	£	£	£

Element 7.3
PRODUCE AND EXPLAIN PROFIT AND LOSS STATEMENTS AND BALANCE SHEETS

The accounting system used in the UK and Europe has evolved over the past five hundred years or so. In medieval times, it was often the reeve, a kind of estates manager, who kept the books of the lord of the manor; in Renaissance times, when Venetian, Elizabethan, Portuguese, Spanish and Dutch merchant venturers financed fleets of galleons to seek out spices, gold, silks and exotic carvings etc., their business accounts were kept in bound books or ledgers; hence the terms *the books of account* and *sales/purchase ledger*. *PC 7.3.1.*

Today, business transactions have become so enormous, especially those undertaken by national conglomerates, chainstores or multi-nationals, no books of account would be large enough to cope and so the advent of computer technology has proved very timely in terms of integrated software packages which can process and store vast amounts of data keyed in from, say, a chainstore's 500 UK branches.

The following section explains in detail how a business accounting system works in terms of logging all its sales and purchase transactions in respective ledgers, monitoring its cash levels and payments to banks – with all being checked for accuracy, by the drawing up on a regular basis of a trial balance; how trading profits (or losses) are recorded and how at the end of each financial year a business's balance sheets are drawn up.

This section also explains the purposes for such detailed accounting work in terms of providing data for financial management reports, meeting statutory obligations (such as the annual production of final accounts for Inland Revenue scrutiny), and to ensure the overall financial health of the business.

Sole trader

A sole trader is someone who set up a business for himself. He may employ people to work for him, but he is responsible for the decision-making in the firm.

Partnership

A partnership is a group of people working together in a business. Usually all partners put money into the business and take on responsibilities for various aspects of the running of the firm.

Company

A limited company is a separate legal entity. It is owned by its shareholders who appoint directors to run the company. A company can be a Public Limited Company (a PLC) or a Private Limited Company (Ltd).

The basic differences between the three types of firm are shown in the chart on page 654.

Main features of typical businesses

	Limited companies	Partnerships	Sole traders
Type of ownership possible	Dividend into 'shares'. There may be any number of shares from two (public companies seven) upwards. Each share carries certain defined legal rights and duties. Shares may be divided into classes with different legal attributes. Any share of a given class is identical with any other as respects legal attributes. A shareholder may hold from one share upwards. Hence very great subdivision of ownership is possible	There normally may be no more than 20 partners. Rights and duties are fixed by agreement. Each partner may have different rights and duties. Subdivision of ownership interest requires agreement of all partners	One owner
Risk to personal estate of owners if business becomes insolvent	Limited to a fixed amount per share, usually paid when the share is first issued	Unlimited. Any partner is responsible for all the debts of the business	Unlimited
Management	In hands of directors elected by shareholders at annual meetings	By agreement between partners	As owner wishes
Information about business available to public	A good deal of information, including annual accounting information, must be registered with the Registrar of Companies and / or sent to shareholders, etc. The public can inspect registered information. The Registrar exercises some supervision over information registered. There must be an annual audit of the accounts, in most cases by qualified accountants	None, except that partners' names must be registered publicly if they are different from the business name	As for partnerships
Withdrawal of funds from the business	Dividends may be paid to shareholders only out of profits. A special legal procedure, involving the consent of the courts, is necessary to repay shareholders' capital	By agreement between partners	At discretion of owner
Financing possibilities	Limited risk, the subdivision of interest, and the law relating to borrowing on the security of 'debentures' makes financing simpler and cheaper than is the case with partnerships and sole traders	Relatively restricted (*see* Companies)	Relatively restricted (*see* Companies)
Constitution	Embodied in formal legal documents copies of which are registered. Alteration requires a special legal procedure, involving the consent of a specified proportion of the shareholders	As agreed between partners. May be informal and need not be in writing	None
Tax on income	Corporation Tax on profits	Income Tax (Sch. D Case I or II)	As for partnerships
Termination	Perpetual succession unless liquidation	By agreement	At will

Reproduced from *Accounting*, R J Bull, published by Butterworth

Using a full double-entry system: and producing a trial balance

While Unit 7 concentrates on examining the structure of company accounts, it is important that you also gain an insight into the 'nuts and bolts' of the double-entry bookkeeping system.

[*Note:* GNVQ Advanced Business does *not* require students to demonstrate any knowledge of the double-entry book-keeping system. However the following section is supplied as a useful grounding in the system – which underpins all modern accounting systems.]

■ Nature of the full double-entry system

The double-entry system is the basis of all bookkeeping systems, whether they are manual (handwritten) systems or computerised systems. To be able to '*think in double entries*' is a great advantage, because it can answer every problem that ever presents itself in accountancy. The whole layout is illustrated in Fig 7.2 on page 656. The numbers 1–5 guide us through the system and you should look at the part numbered 1 and study the illustration and then read the notes which begin with section 1 below. Having followed that section, proceed to part 2 of the illustration and so on.

1 Every transaction has a business document related to it

A '*transaction*' is a business arrangement of any sort whatsoever. The most common transactions are listed below. At the end of each is the document related to it.

- *Purchases* of goods for resale or to be worked into a finished product for resale. (The document is an invoice; the top copy of the invoice from the supplier who sold us the goods.)
- *Sales* (the document is the second copy of our invoice – the top copy having gone to the customer).
- *Purchase returns* (the document is the *credit note*, the top copy of the supplier's credit note which is sent to us when the supplier receives back the returned goods).
- *Sales returns* (this time it is the *second copy of our credit note*, the top copy having gone to the customer who returned the goods to us).
- *Purchases of consumables* (there will usually be an *invoice* or *bill* for the supply of these items. It will be the top copy of the supplier's invoice. If there is no invoice for a small item the till receipt or some other *petty cash voucher* – perhaps an internal petty cash voucher made out and signed by the proprietor – will be used.)
- *Purchase of capital items* (there will always be an invoice from the supplier of the capital item, and it will be the top copy). With some items there may be a *deed* (premises) or a formal *hire-purchase document*, etc.
- *Payments in cash and by cheque.* Here the receipt we obtain (the top copy) or give (the duplicate copy) or the *cheque* (inwards or outwards) will be the valid document. If we use a petty cash book, these receipts will become *petty cash vouchers.*

Fig 7.2 **How the double-entry system works**

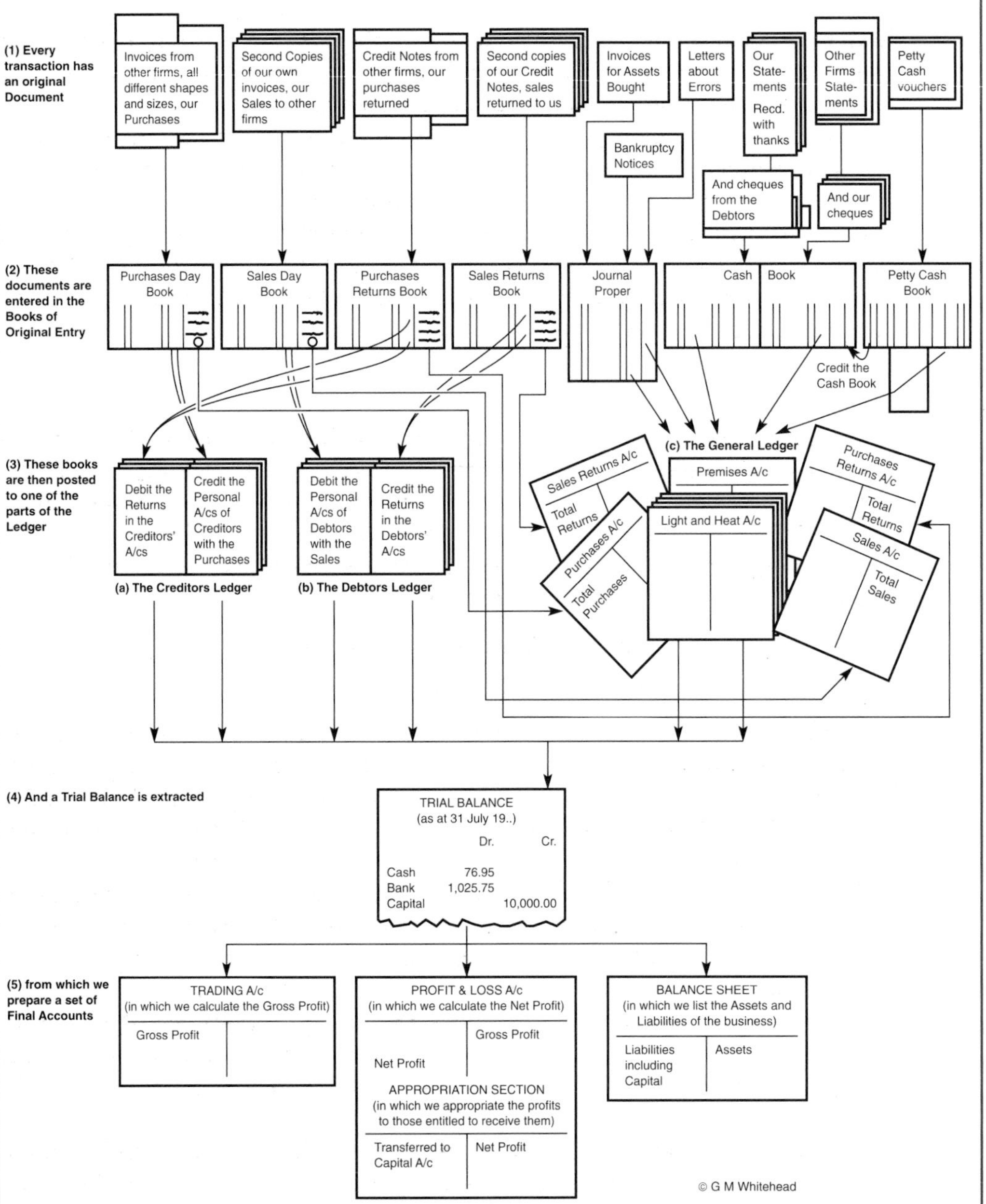
(1) Every transaction has an original Document
Invoices from other firms, all different shapes and sizes, our Purchases
Second Copies of our own invoices, our Sales to other firms
Credit Notes from other firms, our purchases returned
Second copies of our Credit Notes, sales returned to us
Invoices for Assets Bought
Letters about Errors
Our State-ments Recd. with thanks
Other Firms State-ments
Petty Cash vouchers
Bankruptcy Notices
And cheques from the Debtors
And our cheques
(2) These documents are entered in the Books of Original Entry
Purchases Day Book
Sales Day Book
Purchases Returns Book
Sales Returns Book
Journal Proper
Cash Book
Petty Cash Book
Credit the Cash Book
(3) These books are then posted to one of the parts of the Ledger
Debit the Returns in the Creditors' A/cs
Credit the Personal A/cs of Creditors with the Purchases
(a) The Creditors Ledger
Debit the Personal A/cs of Debtors with the Sales
Credit the Returns in the Debtors' A/cs
(b) The Debtors Ledger
(c) The General Ledger
Sales Returns A/c
Total Returns
Premises A/c
Light and Heat A/c
Purchases Returns A/c
Total Returns
Purchases A/c
Total Purchases
Sales A/c
Total Sales
(4) And a Trial Balance is extracted
TRIAL BALANCE (as at 31 July 19..)
Dr. Cr.
Cash 76.95
Bank 1,025.75
Capital 10,000.00
(5) from which we prepare a set of Final Accounts
TRADING A/c (in which we calculate the Gross Profit)
Gross Profit
PROFIT & LOSS A/c (in which we calculate the Net Profit)
Gross Profit
Net Profit
APPROPRIATION SECTION (in which we appropriate the profits to those entitled to receive them)
Transferred to Capital A/c
Net Profit
BALANCE SHEET (in which we list the Assets and Liabilities of the business)
Liabilities including Capital
Assets
© G M Whitehead

2 These documents are entered in books of original entry

Originally, in the Middle Ages, there were only two books: a book of original entry called the Journal, or day book, and the main book of account which was called the Ledger. Later it was found that having only two books was inconvenient, as only two bookkeepers could work on the books at any one time. It was therefore found to be helpful if the journal was divided into five parts. These were:

- The Purchases Day Book
- The Sales Day Book
- The Purchases Returns Book

- The Sales Returns Book
- The Journal Proper

Note that the first four are all to do with the things we buy and sell; activities which repeat themselves many times every day. The Journal Proper was kept for rarer items, such as the purchase of capital items, bad debts and depreciation, etc.

The other two books of original entry are the Cash Book and the Petty Cash Book, which as their names suggest, refer to incoming cash and cheques and outgoing cash and cheques. The chief idea of books of original entry is to make a permanent record of documents which can easily be lost. Keeping books of original entry in this way does give a great deal of work for very little benefit, and it is chiefly in this field that short-cut systems are widely used today. Computers do all such things with effortless ease, and this explains why computerised systems are so popular.

3 The books of original entry are then posted to the Ledger

The Ledger is the main book of account in the double-entry system. An account is a page in the ledger, or rather a leaf in the ledger, because both sides of a page are devoted to each account. If we open up an account with someone it simply means we give them a page in our ledger, with their name and address, telephone number etc., at the top. Every transaction with them goes on the page, either on the left-hand side (the debit side) or the right-hand side (the credit side). The rules are:

- *Debit the account that receives the goods, or services, or money*
- *Credit the account that gives goods, or services, or money*

This rule is usually shortened to: *Debit the receiver, credit the giver.* So if we supply Catherine Timms with envelopes worth £28.50 we debit her account with £28.50, because she is receiving value. She is now our debtor (she has an unpaid balance of £28.50 on her account). Later, if she sends us a cheque for £28.50 we credit her account – credit the giver. This leaves her account clear; there is no balance on her account.

Note that because there are so many accounts (one firm in the United Kingdom has over 8 million debtors alone) the ledger is split into sections. We have a *Creditors' Ledger* (with all our suppliers' accounts in it) a *Debtors' Ledger* (with all our debtors' accounts in it) and a *General Ledger*, with the rest of our accounts. More of this later.

It will not detract from our understanding of Fig 7.2 if we consider for a moment the layout of a traditional ledger account, such as would be found in all the sections of the ledger illustrated in Fig 7.2. You can see this layout in Fig 7.3 on page 658 and it is described in the notes below it.

It is when we make entries in the ledger accounts that the term 'double-entry' comes into use, for every accounting transaction requires two entries not one. Imagine a transaction in which we purchase a piece of furniture worth £100 from A. Trader, on credit, payable in one month's time. A. Trader gives us a piece of furniture worth £100. Can you think in double entries? Which account will receive a piece of furniture worth £100? Obviously it must be the Furniture Account. Debit Furniture Account with £100!

Which account is giving us £100 worth of value? Clearly it is A. Trader. Credit A. Trader's account with £100! A. Trader is now one of our creditors, and we owe him £100 for furniture received.

Later, of course, we shall pay A. Trader £100, probably by cheque. Who will receive the £100 cheque? Clearly it is A. Trader, so we debit A. Trader's account, and that wipes out the debt and leaves his account clear The bank account has given the cheque. Credit the giver, so we credit Bank account, which loses £100 of the money in the bank. The first of these double entries is shown in Fig 7.4.

Fig 7.3 **The layout of a traditional ledger account**

Dr							Cr
Debit Side				*Credit Side*			
Date	Details	Folio	Amount	Date	Details	Folio	Amount

Notes to Fig 7.3

- The page is divided down the middle.
- The left-hand side is called the debit side, or debtor side, and often has the abbreviation Dr printed at the top.
- The right-hand side is called the credit side, or creditor side, and often has the abbreviation Cr printed at the top.
- Columns are drawn on each side for the date, details, folio numbers (to be explained later) and the amount received or given.

Fig 7.4 **A double entry**

Dr			Furniture Account				L.1 Cr
199 Aug. 17	A.Trader	L2	£ 0.00				

Dr			A. Trader				L.2 Cr
				19 Aug. 17	Furniture	L1	£ 0.00

Notes to Fig 7.4

- The two accounts affected are Furniture account and A. Trader's account.
- Each account (page in the ledger) has a reference number written in the top right-hand corner. It is called a 'folio number' (Latin: *folium* = leaf).
- When the entries are made it is usual to record the folio number of the other account in the folio column. This tells anyone looking at an account where to find the other half of the double-entry.
- Note that the Furniture account received value and so it is debited, but A. Trader gave value so his account is credited. Remember the rule: debit the account that receives value, credit the account that gives value.
- Later, when A. Trader is paid by cheque, A. Trader's account will be debited and Bank account (which is giving the money) will be credited.

4 A trial balance is extracted

PC 7.3.3

Under the double-entry system entries are being made in accounts all the time, some on the debit side and some on the credit side. The busiest accounts are probably the Cash account and the Bank account, which are separated out in a special book, the *Cash Book,* kept by a bookkeeper who is fairly high in the accounting team, and called the *Cashier.* Other busy accounts are the Purchases account and the Sales account; like dealings in cash and by cheque, purchases and sales take place all day, every day in many businesses.

As a result of all these efforts we find it helpful to check up on all our entries at least once a month, and this is done by taking out a *Trial Balance.* As the name implies we try the books to see if they balance, because if they do we must have made all our double entries correctly. To draw up a trial balance we balance off each account in the ledger, including the Cash account and Bank account in the cash book. The final balance on any particular account will be on either the debit side or the credit side. If we make a list of these balances and total them, we should find that the two sides reach to the same figure.

In Unit 6 we have only a very brief indication of what the trial balance looks like, so it is helpful now if we look at one more closely. Before we do so, look at the three accounts shown in Fig 7.5 on page 660 to see how the balancing-off procedure is done. For simplicity the accounts have been shown without the full rulings.

Notes to Fig 7.5

- The first account has only one entry on the debit side. Clearly this is a debit balance and we can see at once what the figure is. There is no need to tidy up this account at all – we just record it on our list of balances as a debit balance of £137.56.
- With Commission Received Account there are several entries all on the same side, the credit side. You might think, with a name Commission Received Account these would be debit entries, because of the rule that we debit the account that receives goods, or services, or money. In fact, this money has been received but it will be debited in the Cash account (or in the Bank account if we received the money as a cheque). This account is the other half of the double entry – the one that says: 'Who gave this money to the business?' The answer is that it has been given by 'Commission Received Account' – though that may be a number of individuals who pay us for the service we rendered them. For example, garages often allow people wishing to sell a car to exhibit it on the forecourt and take 10 per cent of the sale price as commission. This is a profit of the business and goes on the credit side of the account.

  Do we need to tidy up this account? Yes – but we need not balance it off. All we do is add it up in pencil and enter the figure on our trial balance – a credit balance of £136.59.
- The third account is the Land and Buildings Account and it has items on both sides of the account. What do we do here? The answer is that we balance off the account. One side is clearly larger than the other. There is £160,407.15 on the debit side, and only £38,250.00 on the credit side. Taking the smaller side from the larger we have a difference of £122,157.15. This is the balance on the account; the value of the buildings owned when we balance the books on the last day of the month. Note that we add this balance to the credit side, making both sides equal at £160,407.15, but immediately bring the balance down on to the left-hand side, where it shows clearly in a single figure the balance on the account.

PC
7.3.3

Fig 7.5 **Balancing-off accounts before taking out a trial balance**

Mrs M Jones A/c, 2173 Camside, Cambridge CB4 1PQ L 32

199–	£		
27 January	137.56		

Commission Received A/c L 199

		199–	£
		4 January Motor-car sale	25.00
		11 January Motor-car sale	38.94
		23 January Finance contract	72.65

Land & Buildings A/c L 252

199–	£	199–	£
1 January Balance b/d	147,256.55	19 January Sale of Pett St.	38,250.00
14 January Garages	8,285.60	31 January Balance c/d	122,157.15
29 January Shop front	4,865.00		
	£160,407.15		£160,407.15
199–	£		
1 February Balance b/d	122,157.15		

Personal accounts, nominal accounts and real accounts

There is one further point to make about these accounts. They show us the three types of account we have in every business.

Mrs M Jones's account is obviously a personal account, an account with one of the persons we deal with in business. Personal accounts are always either debtors (people who owe us money) or creditors (people to whom we owe money). There is one rather special personal account, and that is the *Capital Account*, the account of the proprietor. Since we owe back to the proprietor everything he or she has put into the business, it is almost always a creditor account, with a credit balance.

Land and Buildings Account is a *real account*; that is an account which tells us about some real asset the business owns. Thus land and buildings, motor vehicles, plant and machinery, furniture and fittings and cash are all real things you can actually touch and handle. This business has land and buildings worth £122,157.15. Assets are always debit balances, and appear on the debit side of the trial balance.

Commission Received Account is not a real account. It is a record of money received, but the real money is in the cash box, or in the bank. It is said to be a *nominal account*, because the money is there 'in name only'. All nominal accounts are either profits or losses, and we keep a record of them only until the end of the year so we can work out the profits of the business.

Figure 7.6 on page 662 shows a trial balance. This one has been taken out at the end of the year, although trial balances are always done monthly. Written alongside each item are notes showing whether the item is an asset, a liability, a profit or a loss. Some items are called 'trading account items' because they appear in the trading account; don't forget that to prepare a trading account we also need the closing stock figure, which is given separately at the end. One special item is the 'drawings' of the proprietor. This trial balance is worked into a set of final accounts in the next section.

5 A set of 'Final Accounts' is prepared

The final stage in double-entry bookkeeping is to prepare a set of final accounts to discover *a*) the net profit of the business and *b*) the financial situation of the business at the start of the new financial year. This is done by producing a Balance Sheet. Since we have already learned how to produce a Trading Account and a Profit and Loss Account it is relatively simple to use the Trial Balance given in Fig 7.6 to produce a set of Final Accounts which can be submitted to the Inland Revenue.

Practical requirements to keep a full set of double-entry books

We now come down to the crucial point about keeping a full set of double-entry books: what books do you need, and where do you get them? The answer is that you need:

- A Journal Proper
- Four day books: a Purchases Day Book, a Sales Day Book
- A Purchases Returns Day Book and a Sales Returns Day Book
- A Four-column Cash Book (which used to be a Three-column Cash Book but now that VAT is a constant feature of our lives you need an extra column for the VAT)
- A Petty Cash Book (for small cash outgoings)
- A loose-leaf Ledger, divided into sections for debtors and creditors, and a 'General Ledger' section

PC 7.3.3

Fig 7.6

A typical trial balance

T SANDERSON

Trial Balance as at 31 December 199–

Ledger Accounts	*Notes*	*Dr* £	*Cr* £	*Notes*
Premises account	Asset	86,000.00		
Capital account			130,675.70	Liability
Debtors:				
R Green account	Asset	394.00		
P Colne account	Asset	426.00		
Creditors:				
M Shah account			872.50	Liability
P Driver account			729.30	Liability
Plant and machinery account	Asset	38,240.50		
Office furniture account	Asset	7,246.38		
Cash account	Asset	249.72		
Bank account	Asset	13,825.60		
Bad debts account	Loss	238.60		
Advertising account	Loss	3,294.60		
Commission paid account	Loss	25.60		
Discount allowed account	Loss	128.54		
Discount received account			236.35	Profit
Business rates account	Loss	894.56		
Carriage out account	Loss	328.70		
Salaries account	Loss	27,925.50		
Motor expenses account	Loss	1,727.36		
Rent received account			1,850.00	Profit
Stock at 1 January 199–	Trading account item	9,275.50		
Purchases account	Trading account item	29,312.65		
Sales account			98,325.50	Trading account item
Purchases returns account			2,275.56	Trading account item
Sales return account	Trading account item	2,425.50		
Drawings	Special item	12,960.00		
		£234,964.91	£234,964.91	

At 31 December stocktaking revealed that the closing stock figure was £13,925.60.

Fig 7.7 **A set of sole trader's accounts**

PC 7.3.4

T SANDERSON

Trading Account for year ending 31 December 199–

		£		£
Opening stock		9,275.50	Sales	98,325.50
Purchases	29,312.65		*Less* returns	2,425.50
Less returns	2,275.56		Net turnover	95,900.00
		27,037.90		
Total stock available		36,312.59		
Less closing stock		13,925.60		
Cost of sales		22,386.99		
Gross profit		73,513.01		
		£95,900.00		£95,900.00

Profit and Loss Account for year ending 31 December 199–

	£		£
Bad debts	238.60	Gross profit	73,513.01
Advertising	3,924.60	Discount received	236.35
Commission paid	25.60	Rent received	1,850.00
Discount allowed	128.54		75,599.36
Community charges	894.56		
Carriage outwards	328.70		
Salaries	27,925.50		
Motor expenses	1,727.36		
Total Losses	34,563.46		
Net profit	41,035.90		
	£75,599.36		£75,599.36

Balance Sheet as at 31 December 199–

		£			£
Capital (at start)		130,675.70	*Fixed assets*		
Add net profit	41,035.90		Premises		86,000.00
Less drawings	12,960.00		Plant and machinery		38,240.50
		28,075.90	Office furniture		7,246.38
		158,751.60			131,486.88
Long-term liabilities		–	*Current assets*		
			Closing stock	13,925.60	
Current liabilities			Debtors	820.60	
Creditors		1,601.80	Bank	13,825.60	
			Cash	294.72	
					28,866.52
		£160,353.40			£160,353.40

PC 7.3.3

Trial Balance: key features

Note (page 662 refers)
In abbreviated form these notes can be condensed into the following groups

Trial Balance	Dr	Cr
	• Assets	Liabilities
	• Losses	Profits
	• Three trading items	Two trading items
	• Drawings	

■ Conclusions about the double-entry system

What can we say in conclusion about the double-entry system? The chief points seem to be:

- It is the only perfect bookkeeping system, which will answer every difficulty that arises.
- There is everything to be said for getting to know the full double-entry system and being able to think in double entries.
- At the same time it is too cumbersome to be used by a person who is a 'one-man (or one-woman) band'. It really needs a specialist bookkeeper and is thus most suitable for the slightly larger business that has reached the stage where it can afford one. Smaller firms should use one of the simple systems, either Simplex or one of the more advanced systems.
- Even the firm that does have a specialist bookkeeper should consider the use of simultaneous record systems for purchases, sales, wages, etc.
- In the last analysis the true answer to accounting problems is a computerised system. The computer *does* work on a perfect double-entry system built into the programs provided by the systems analyst. The computer operator is not aware of what the computer is doing, and must ensure only that the data keyed in is correct.

This excerpt has been adapted from *Book-keeping and Accounts*, 2nd edition by Geoffrey Whitehead and published by Pitman Publishing 1989.

PC 7.3.4

Producing the annual balance sheet and trading profit and loss account

The two documents that all firms need to produce at the end of a year are a Trading Profit and Loss Account and a Balance Sheet. A trading profit and loss account looks at establishing whether a profit or loss has been made in the accounting period and the balance sheet is a financial statement which lists the assets and liabilities of a firm at the balance sheet date.

An asset is an item owned by a firm, such as motor-car or stock for sale. A liability is an amount owed by a firm for, say, stock which has been bought on credit.

If you look at pages 665 and 666 you will see a set of accounts for G Campbell who is trading at The White Hart public house. We will examine these in detail.

G CAMPBELL – THE WHITE HART
Balance Sheet as at 30 September 1995

	£	£
Fixed Assets		
Fixtures and Fittings		12,925
Motor Vehicle		5,100
		18,025
Current Assets		
Stock	9,125	
Debtors	180	
Prepayments	365	
Bank Balance	1,175	
Cash in Hand	790	
	11,635	
Current Liabilities		
Creditors	5,480	
Accrued Expenses	1,725	
Bank Overdraft	285	
	7,490	
Net Current Assets		4,145
Total Assets Less Current Liabilities		22,170
Long-Term Loan		
Bank Loan		3,000
		£19,170
Capital		
Balance at the beginning of the year		18,190
Net Profit for year	15,055	
Drawings	14,075	
		980
		£19,170

PC 7.3.4

G CAMPBELL – THE WHITE HART
Trading and Profit and Loss Account for the Year ended 30 September 1995

	£	£
Sales		142,240
Cost of Sales		
Opening Stock	10,630	
Purchases	72,460	
	83,090	
Closing Stock	9,125	
		73,965
Gross Profit		68,275
Expenses		
Wages	18,245	
Rent and Rates	14,460	
Light and Heat	4,945	
Motor Expenses	905	
Repairs and Renewals	1,665	
Telephone	385	
Printing and Stationery	675	
Bank Charges and Interest	1,755	
Loan Interest	450	
Accountancy and Stocktaking	1,900	
Insurance	1,535	
Laundry and Cleaning	680	
Entertainments	900	
Bad Debts	100	
Sundries	1,485	
Depreciation of Motor Vehicles	1,700	
Depreciation of Fixtures and Fittings	1,435	
		53,220
Net Profit		£15,055

PC 7.3.4

■ The White Hart Balance Sheet

This Balance Sheet shows the financial state of the pub at the Balance Sheet date, 30 September 1995. Hence it is important that the title of the document is correct. The White Hart Balance Sheet shows the assets and liabilities of the pub as at 30 September 1995.

Assets are items which are owned by the firm and which have at some time been bought by that firm. They are split into two categories, *fixed assets* and *current assets*.

Fixed assets

These are items which are owned by a firm which it expects to keep for some years. They are necessary for the firm to trade, but do not form part of the normal trading stock. In our case the pub owns fixtures and fittings such as bar stools and kitchen equipment and a motor car. The last mentioned is probably used for visits to the cash-and-carry and the bank etc.

Other firms would have different types of fixed assets, in general these would be categorised under four headings: land and buildings, plant and machinery, fixtures and fittings and motor vehicles. These titles can be adjusted to suit a particular situation. The purchase of these assets is known as Capital Expenditure.

Current assets

These are items owned by the firm whose value changes on a regular basis. They can be divided into five main categories:

Stock. In the case of our pub this would be the food stock for bar snacks, etc. and the wet stock (the stock of drinks).

Debtors. This is the amount of money owed to a firm from credit sales. In a pub there are very few credit sales and thus the figure for debtors is low.

Prepayments. Although a firm might have to pay some of its expenses in advance, for example, insurance is usually paid before the period covered, these are not included in a Profit and Loss Account until the relevant time. Thus they are a current asset at the balance sheet date.

Bank balances. Current or deposit account balances that can be withdrawn at short notice.

Cash in hand. The notes and coins that form the cash float and any takings not yet banked.

Current liabilities

These are amounts that are owed by a firm that must be paid within the next twelve months and usually much sooner.

Creditors. This is the amount owed by a firm to the suppliers of its stock. In our case this would be the amount due to the brewery and its food suppliers.

Accrued expenses. The amount due to the supplier of services – for example, the amount due to British Telecom for telephone calls since the last bill was paid. This is irrespective of whether an invoice has been received and paid as the service has been given.

Bank overdraft. This is shown as a liability and not as a negative asset. Technically it is repayable on demand from the bank.

Net current assets

This is the difference between the current assets and the current liabilities. It is sometimes called the working capital of a firm.

Total assets less current liabilities

This is the sum of the fixed assets and the net current assets.

Long-term loans

These are loans which are repayable at least one year after the Balance Sheet date.

The final total of the 'top section' of the Balance Sheet is calculated by subtracting the long-term loans from the total assets less current liabilities.

Capital

This represents the amount of money that the owner has put into the firm either directly or indirectly by trading, making a profit and leaving some of that profit in the firm. Drawings are the money or goods taken from the firm by the owner.

Important note: A Balance Sheet must Balance!

Note that the final figure in the Balance Sheet is the same as the total of the 'top section'. This is no coincidence. If the bookkeeping has been completed correctly and the accounts have been properly prepared, then the balance sheet will balance.

PC 7.3.4

■ The Trading and Profit and Loss Account for The White Hart

We will now look at the Trading and Profit and Loss Account. This is a summary of the income and expenditure of a firm over a period of time. Again take careful note of the title of the document. It tells you that it summarises the transactions for the year from 1 October 1994 to 30 September 1995.

Sales

This is the total value of all the sales, cash and credit, made during the year. It is irrelevant at this stage whether the cash has been received for the credit sales. A sale is considered to have taken place when the customer is invoiced.

Cost of sales

This is the amount of money that the sales have cost a firm. It is calculated by taking the stock at the beginning of the year, adding the purchases of goods for the year and subtracting the closing stock. Purchases include cash and credit purchases. It is not relevant whether the goods have been paid for.

Gross profit

This is the difference between the sales and the cost of sales.

Expenses

These are the day-to-day running expenses of the firm. They must relate to the period under review and thus consideration must be given to prepayments and accrued expenses mentioned before. Most of the expenses are self-explanatory, but one or two need further explanation and this is given below.

Net profit

This is the difference between the gross profit and expenses of the firm. It is the profit that the firm has made after all expenses have been taken into account.

Bad debts and depreciation

Bad debts. Unfortunately not all customers are honest. It is likely that in the course of a year a few cheques will 'bounce' or one or more debtors will 'vanish' without settling their accounts. These amounts will be written off as an expense of the business.

Provision for doubtful debts. The majority of business people expect that some debts, not yet identified, will eventually become bad debts. These will probably be associated with sales made in the last few weeks of a financial year. A prudent trader will make an allowance for these in his accounts and update the provision each year.

There is no provision in the accounts of The White Hart as debtors are a relatively minor sum.

Depreciation. This is defined by accountants as 'the measure of the wearing out, consumption or other reduction in the useful economic life of a fixed asset, whether arising from use, effluxion of time or obsolescence through technological or market changes. Depreciation should be allocated so as to charge a fair proportion of cost or valuation of the asset to each accounting period expected to benefit from its use.'

In calculating depreciation the following factors should be taken into account:

- the cost of the asset
- the expected useful economic life of the asset to the business
- the estimated residual value of the asset

METHODS OF CALCULATING DEPRECIATION

PC 7.3.4

(*See Trading and Profit and Loss Account, Page 666*)

The straight line method

This method simply spreads the net cost of an asset to a firm equally over the life of that asset.

Example

A firm buys a car for £12,000. It expects to keep the car for 3 years and then to trade it in for £3,000.

The net cost to the firm is £12,000 – 3,000 = £9,000

The annual depreciation is £9,000 ÷ 3 = £3,000

Some people do not like the straight line method, although it is easy to understand and calculate, because they feel that an asset loses more of its value in the early years of its life than in the later years. These people prefer to use the reducing balance method which addresses this problem.

The reducing balance method

Under this method the value of the asset is reduced by a fixed percentage each year. The loss in value gives the depreciation charge for the year.

Example

A firm buys a car for £12,000. It is the firm's policy to depreciate its cars at the rate of 25 per cent per annum using the reducing balance method. The charges for depreciation are as follows:

Year 1	
Cost of car	£12,000
Depreciation 25% of £12,000	3,000
Written-down value at end of year	9,000
Year 2	
Depreciation 25% of £9,000	2,250
Written-down value at end of year	6,750
Year 3	
Depreciation 25% of £6,750	1,688
Written-down value at end of year	£5,062

Note: As depreciation is only an estimate, calculations are made to the nearest pound.

You will have noticed that two of the three factors are estimates and thus the depreciation charge itself is only an estimate of the amount of the cost used in a particular accounting period.

An additional complication is that there are several methods of calculating depreciation. The two methods most widely used are the straight line method and the reducing balance method.

As depreciation is counted as an expense in the Profit and Loss Account, the Balance Sheet shows the written-down value of the asset at the end of the year.

PC
7.3.1
7.3.2
7.3.4

DISCUSSION TOPICS

1 What financial advantages do you see in a firm electing to become a private limited company as opposed to remaining a partnership? Can you identify any disadvantages?

2 Since a balance sheet represents only a 'frozen frame' picture of a company's finances on a given day, at a given time (for The White Hart, midnight on 30 September 1995), why is it that so much importance is attached to it by: directors, managers, shareholders, would-be purchasers of the business, and the Inland Revenue?

3 Assuming you were the owner of The White Hart, with a newly appointed resident managing couple, how often would you want to receive a trading and profit and loss account for the business done? What measures might you introduce to ensure that the account was an accurate reflection of what business took place (given that the business is largely cash-based and you are an absentee proprietor)?

PC
7.3.4
7.3.5

SKILLS DEVELOPMENT ASSIGNMENT

From the following Trial Balance produce the firm's Trading and Profit and Loss Account for the year to 31 December and a Balance Sheet as at that date.

Notes

1 Use the answer sheet provided

2 Appreciate that the closing stock figure given after the trial balance is used both in the Trading Account and the Current Assets section of the Balance Sheet.

Trial Balance as at 31 December

Account	*Debit* £	*Credit* £
Capital		115,400
Sales		150,400
Stock b/fwd	10,800	
Purchases	80,200	
Rent and rates	21,000	
Vehicle running costs	4,000	
Insurances	1,000	
Wages and salaries	15,000	
Telephone and postage	1,800	
Premises	120,000	
Fixtures	10,000	
Vehicles	20,000	
Debtors	16,000	
Creditors		20,000
Bank	11,000	
Drawings	20,000	
Loan		50,000
Loan interest	5,000	
	335,800	335,800

Note that the value of the Closing Stock at the end of the year was £14,100. Ignore depreciation of fixed assets

Assignment Answer Sheet 1

Trading and Profit and Loss Account for the Year ended 31 December

	£	£
Sales		☐
Less the cost of sales		
Stock brought forward	☐	
Add Purchases	☐	
	☐	
Less Stock carried forward	☐	☐
Gross profit		☐
Less Expenses		
Rent and rates	☐	
Insurances	☐	
Wages and salaries	☐	
Telephone and postages	☐	
Vehicle running costs	☐	
Loan interest	☐	☐
Net profit		☐

Assignment Answer Sheet 2

Balance Sheet as at 31 December

	£	£
Fixed assets		
Premises		☐
Fixtures		☐
Vehicles		☐
Current assets		
Stock	☐	
Debtors	☐	
Bank	☐	
	☐	
Less current liabilities		
Creditors	☐	
Working capital		☐
		☐
Long-term liabilities		
Loan		☐
		☐
Financed by		
Capital		☐
Add net profit		☐
		☐
Less drawings		☐
		☐

PC 7.3.4 7.3.6

INDIVIDUAL ACTIVITY

Working individually, undertake the following activity and then share your findings with your class:

Read through again carefully the balance sheet and trading and profit and loss account of The White Hart (on pages 665 and 666).

Assume you are a financial consultant working for Hooper & Downland (a national business consultancy firm). The directors of Wheatsheaf Brewery plc have asked you to produce for them a financial analysis and report on the performance and worth as a going concern of *The White Hart* which is on the market.

Produce a suitable report which justifies the recommendations you give, bearing in mind that the asking price for the pub is £200,000 freehold.

PC 7.3.6

Major types of accounts

■ Partnership accounts

What you have learned about the accounts of a sole trader are true for the accounts of a partnership. It is, however, necessary to amend the accounts to allow for the fact that more than one person owns the business

ACCOUNTING REQUIREMENTS OF THE PARTNERSHIP ACT OF 1890

Partnerships are governed by the Partnership Act of 1890. This states that in the absence of any agreement to the contrary profits and losses are to be shared equally.

Most partners will ask a solicitor to draw up a partnership agreement for them in which the following would be included:

- The amount of capital to be contributed by each partner.
- The annual rate of interest to be allowed on this capital, if any.
- The amount of salary to be paid to each partner, if any.
- The division of the profit and losses between the partners.

To account for the above a Profit and Loss Appropriation Account is drawn up after the preparation of the Profit and Loss Account and before the Balance Sheet is completed.

This account shows how the net profit is to be split between the partners.

For example, Alan and Jane are in partnership. Their Partnership agreement includes the following:

a Alan will contribute £50,000 as capital and Jane £25,000.

b Interest will be allowed on capital at the rate of 8 per cent per annum.

c In recognition of her particular skills Jane will receive a salary of £16,000 per annum.

d Residual profits and losses are to be split equally.

If in the year ended 30 June 1992 the partnership made a net profit of £42,000, then the Profit and Loss Appropriation Account would be as follows:

Alan and Jane

Profit and Loss Appropriation Account for the Year ended 30 June 1992

	£	£
Net Profit for year		42,000
Interest on Capital:		
Alan 8% × £50,000	4,000	
Jane 8% × £25,000	2,000	
Salary Jane	16,000	
		22,000
		20,000
Residual Profit		
Alan 50% × £20,000	10,000	
Jane 50% × £20,000	10,000	20,000

The Balance Sheet also needs to be adjusted as each partner has a fixed amount of capital and in addition they will want to know how much profit each has retained in the firm since this is theoretically the amount that he or she can withdraw from the firm.

The facts that you have learned about fixed and current assets and current and long-term liabilities are as true for a partnership as for a sole trader. It is the bottom section of the Balance Sheet that needs alteration. The Sole Trader's Capital Account is replaced by the Partners' Capital and Current Accounts.

The Capital Accounts show the fixed capital of each partner.

The Current Accounts show the retained profit of each partner:

- the balance brought forward from the previous year;
- the interest on capital, if any;
- the salaries, if any;
- the residual profit;
- the drawings for the year;
- the balance carried forward.

For Alan and Jane their Balance Sheet might be summarised as follows:

Alan and Jane

Balance Sheet as at 30 June 1992

			£
Fixed Assets			80,000
Net Current Assets			10,000
Total Assets less Current Liabilities			90,000
	Alan	*Jane*	
	£	£	
Capital Accounts	50,000	25,000	75,000
Current Accounts			
Opening Balance	1,000	2,000	
Interest on Capital	4,000	2,000	
Salary	–	16,000	
Residual Profit	10,000	10,000	
	15,000	30,000	
Drawings	12,500	17,500	
	2,500	12,500	15,000
			90,000

Note that in practice the details of the fixed assets and net current assets would be shown as for a sole trader.

PC 7.3.1 7.3.6

Company accounts

As with the accounts of partnerships, the rules for preparing the accounts of a sole trader apply to those of a limited company but need to be adjusted to account for the different type of business.

There is the additional complication that a company's accounts are controlled by the provisions of the Companies Act 1985 as amended by the 1989 Act.

A company is owned by its shareholders and you need to know a little more about shares before we look at the actual accounts.

When a company is formed it needs to prepare a *Memorandum and Articles of Association. The Memorandum of Association* is the document forming the constitution of the company and defines its objectives and powers. The *Articles of Association* contains the rules and regulations for conducting the business of the company, and define the rights of the members and the powers and duties of the directors.

The memorandum will contain a statement of the shares that the firm can issue, i.e. the authorised share capital. A company can issue as many shares as it wishes up to this limit.

The authorised and issued share capital will be divided into one or more different classes of shares. The principal types are ordinary and preference shares. A company must issue ordinary shares, it need not issue preference shares. Each share has a nominal or face value which may be 25p, 50p, £1 or any other amount that the company decides.

Types of company shares

Preference shares

These shares will carry a fixed rate of dividend. For example a company may authorise and issue 200,000 8 per cent Preference Shares of £1 each.

For every such share that a person holds he will receive a dividend of 8p (8% of £1) per year. In practice this may be paid in two instalments of 4p each. Preference dividends are paid before any proposed ordinary dividend but only if the company has retained profits.

In the event of the company failing and being wound up the preference shareholders will be repaid the nominal value of their shares before the ordinary shareholders receive any money. This is after external creditors have been paid.

Thus preference shares are considered 'safer' than ordinary shares.

Ordinary shares

As the name suggests these are the most common type of shares. Ordinary shareholders take the greatest risk in a company but when a company is making high profits there is the potential for large dividends to be paid.

Ordinary shareholders normally have voting rights in a company unlike preference shareholders.

Debentures

A debenture is a loan made to a company in exchange for a debenture certificate issued by the company acknowledging the debt. The debenture will carry a fixed rate of interest and this is an expense of the Profit and Loss Account.

Debentures are often 'secured' on one of the assets of the company, e.g. the freehold property. This means that if the company is wound up then the property will be sold and the proceeds used to repay the debenture holders.

Remember debentures are not shares, they are a loan to a company.

Limited company accounts

PC 7.3.1 7.3.6

A limited company will prepare a trading and profit and loss account in the same way as a sole trader. There are two expenses that may be found in its accounts which will not appear in sole trader accounts.

Directors' remuneration. This is the amount paid to the directors. Directors are employed by a company in the same way as any other employee and thus their pay is a legitimate expense of the Profit and Loss Account.

Debenture interest is shown in the Profit and Loss Account in the same way as any other interest paid.

Profit and Loss Appropriation Account

In a similar way to that of a partnership there is the need to prepare a Profit and Loss Appropriation Account for a company, this time to show how the net profit has been shared amongst the owners, i.e. the shareholders.

If we assume that a company makes a net profit of £250,000 after all expenses have been taken into account then its appropriation account might be as follows.

Profit and Loss Appropriation Account for the year ended 31 December 1992

	£	£
Net Profit for year before tax		250,000
Corporation Tax		60,000
Net Profit after tax		190,000
Dividends paid and proposed:		
Ordinary interim paid	40,000	
Ordinary final proposed	70,000	
		110,000
Retained Profit for year		80,000
Retained Profit brought forward		45,000
Retained Profit carried forward		125,000

If you examine the above account you will see that:

- the Company estimates that it will have to pay corporation tax on this year's profit of £60,000.
- this leaves a profit for the shareholders of £190,000.
- the company has not issued any preference shares. If any had been issued, the shareholders would be entitled to a dividend which would have been shown in the Appropriation Account.
- during the year the Company paid a dividend of £40,000 to its ordinary shareholders. This was probably based on the half-year accounts which would have shown that the company could expect a profit for the year.
- the Company propose to pay a final dividend for the year of £70,000. This would be paid shortly after an annual general meeting of the shareholders.
- this leaves an undistributed profit for the year of £80,000. A company will very rarely pay a dividend equal to the profit for the year. It needs to retain money in the firm to meet the problems of inflation and to allow the firm to expand.
- there is undistributed profit from previous years of £45,000 which gives a retained profit to be carried forward of £125,000.
- retained profits are called Revenue Reserves which can be distributed in future years as dividend or used to give the shareholders more shares. Such an issue of shares is known as a scrip issue.

PC 7.3.1 7.3.6

■ Limited Company Balance Sheet

The Balance Sheet of a company has the same basic structure as that of a sole trader. Obviously it is adjusted to meet the needs of the shareholders.

A Balance Sheet of a company might look as follows:

Moorgate Ltd

Balance Sheet as at 31 December 1992

Fixed Assets	Cost	Acc. Depreciation	
	£000	£000	£000
Tangible Assets			
Land and Buildings	500	50	450
Plant and Machinery	1,993	620	1,373
Office Equipment	330	162	168
	2,823	832	1,991
Current Assets			
Stock		1,589	
Debtors		1,152	
Prepayments		74	
Cash at Bank and In Hand		24	
		2,839	
Creditors: amounts falling due within one year			
Bank Overdraft		518	
Creditors		709	
Accrued Expenses		12	
Proposed Dividend		110	
Corporation Tax		255	
		1,604	
Net Current Assets			1,235
Total Assets less Current liabilities			3,226
Creditors: amounts falling due after more than one year			
8% Debentures			500
			2,726
Capital and Reserves			
Called-up Share Capital			1,575
Share Premium Account			350
Profit and Loss Account			801
			2,726

If you look at the above Balance Sheet you will see the following:

- The cost and total depreciation to date of the fixed assets are shown. This is a legal requirement.
- Current assets are the same as for a sole trader.
- The heading 'Creditors amounts falling due within one year' is used instead of current liabilities. This leaves the reader of the accounts in no doubt what a current liability is.
- Note the introduction of two new short-term liabilities; corporation tax and proposed dividends.
- Net current assets and total assets less current liabilities are calculated as before.
- The heading 'Creditors amounts falling due after more than one year' is used instead of long-term loans.

- Debentures are included in long-term liabilities.
- Share capital shows the nominal value of the issued share capital.
- If shares are issued at more than their nominal value, then the excess must be shown in a Share Premium Account. This is a Capital Reserve and cannot be used to pay a dividend.
- The Profit and Loss Account shows the retained profit carried forward as calculated in the Profit and Loss Appropriation Account.
- The total of the share capital, the capital reserves and the revenue reserves represents the shareholders' interest in the company and is known as the shareholders' equity.
- Note that the Balance Sheet balances!
- The authorised share capital is shown as a note to the Balance Sheet and gives the shareholders an indication of how much money the company could raise by the further issue of shares.

PC
7.3.1
7.3.6

Published final accounts

The accounts shown above would be those available to the management of a company. The financial information that would be available to the shareholders and other interested parties would come in the form of a set of published final accounts. These would contain:

- The Balance Sheet
- The Profit and Loss Account
- The Cash Flow Statement
- The Notes to the above Statements
- The Directors' Report
- The Auditors' Report

The Balance Sheet would summarise some of the information that has been detailed on the face of our Balance Sheet. The details required to be shown according to the Companies Acts would be shown in the Notes to the Balance Sheet.

The Profit and Loss Account would not show details of the cost of sales and expenses. The cost of sales would be shown as one figure, the expenses would be grouped under the headings of selling and distribution costs and administration expenses. Again certain details would be shown in the notes as required by the Companies Acts.

The Cash Flow Statement is explained below.

Notes to the Financial Statements would contain the details required above and other information such as details of the accounting policies used by the company such as the method of depreciation used. If any important events have happened since the Balance Sheet date and before the accounts have been completed, these would be detailed in the notes.

The Directors are required by law to issue a report containing:

- a statement of the principal activities of the company
- a summary of the company's performance during the financial year
- a summary of the expected performance for the coming year
- a list of the directors and their shareholdings
- details of the proposed dividend

The Auditors are appointed by the shareholders to report on whether the accounts give a true and fair view of the company's state of affairs at the year end and of its profit and cash flow for the year and whether the accounts have been prepared according to the requirements of the Companies Acts.

■ Summary Financial Statements

PC 7.3.1 7.3.6

It was recognised that the majority of shareholders of public companies did not examine the accounts that were sent to them. This is partly because accounts can appear to be very complicated to the untrained mind. To produce a full set of accounts for every shareholder is an expensive exercise, especially if they end up in the waste-paper basket unread. The government recognised this problem and public companies are now allowed to send their shareholders Summary Financial Statements rather than a full set of accounts.

Summary Financial Statements contain:

- **a statement by the company's auditors of their opinion as to whether the statement is consistent with the accounts**
- **a summary of the Directors' Report**
- **a summary of the Profit and Loss Account and the Balance Sheet**

■ Cash Flow Statements

PC 7.3.1 7.3.6

Cash Flow Statements were introduced in September 1991 by the Accounting Standards Board. Their objective is to report on their 'cash generation and absorption for a period'.

The problem with the traditional financial reporting basis is that the Balance Sheet shows the position of the company at one point in time and the Profit and Loss Account shows the income arising in a year and the expenses relating to that year. Neither statement shows the movement of cash in or out of the business during the year.

An accountant is frequently asked 'if the company has a retained profit for the year of £25,000 why have the bank balances decreased by £2,000? There could be numerous answers to this question and a Cash Flow Statement should supply the correct one.

The main headings in a Cash Flow Statement are:

- Operating activities
- Returns on investments and servicing of finance
- Taxation
- Investing activities
- Financing

The final figure in the statement gives the increase (or decrease) in cash and cash equivalents. It is the net cash inflow or outflow of the business for the year.

'Cash' means cash in hand or bank balances.

'Cash equivalents' means short-term investments that are very easy to turn into cash.

The following illustration (pages 682–3) has been issued by the Accounting Standards Board and shows all the main headings.

PC 7.3.6

FINANCIAL REPORTING STANDARD CASH FLOW STATEMENTS

XYZ LIMITED
Cash flow statement for the year ended 31 March 1992

	£'000	£'000
Net cash inflow from operating activities		6,889
Returns on investments and servicing of finance		
Interest received	3,011	
Interest paid	(12)	
Dividend paid	(2,417)	
Net cash inflow from returns on investments and servicing of finance		582
Taxation		
Corporation tax paid (including advance corporation tax)	(2,922)	
Tax paid		(2,922)
Investing activities		
Payments to acquire intangible fixed assets	(71)	
Payments to acquire tangible fixed assets	(1,496)	
Receipts from sales of tangible fixed assets	42	
Net cash outflow from investing activities		(1,525)
Net cash inflow before financing		3,024
Financing		
Issue of ordinary share capital	211	
Repurchase of debenture loan	(149)	
Expenses paid in connection with share issues	(5)	
Net cash inflow from financing		57
Increase in cash and cash equivalents		3,081

Notes to the cash flow statement

1 RECONCILIATION OF OPERATING PROFIT TO NET CASH INFLOW FROM OPERATING ACTIVITIES

	£'000
Operating profit	6,022
Depreciation charges	893
Loss on sale of tangible fixed assets	6
Increase in stocks	(194)
Increase in debtors	(72)
Increase in creditors	234
Net cash inflow from operating activities	6,889

2 ANALYSIS OF CHANGES IN CASH AND CASH EQUIVALENTS DURING THE YEAR

	£'000
Balance at 1 April 1991	21,373
Net cash inflow	3,081
Balance at 31 March 1992	24,454

3 ANALYSIS OF THE BALANCES OF CASH AND CASH EQUIVALENTS AS SHOWN IN THE BALANCE SHEET

	1992 £'000	1991 £'000	Change in year £'000
Cash at bank and in hand	529	681	(152)
Short-term investments	23,936	20,700	3,236
Bank overdrafts	(11)	(8)	(3)
	24,454	21,373	3,081

4 ANALYSIS OF CHANGES IN FINANCING DURING THE YEAR

	Share capital £'000	Debenture loan £'000
Balance at 1 April 1991	27,411	156
Cash inflow/(outflow) from financing	211	(149)
Profit on repurchase of debenture loan for less than its book value		(7)
Balance at 31 March 1992	27,622	–

The notes must accompany the statement as they give details of the figures used in the example.

You should note the following:

- There must be a reconciliation between the operating profit reported in the Profit and Loss Account and the net cash flow from operating activities. This should be shown as a note to the statement and can be calculated in one of two ways.
- *The 'direct' method* shows cash receipts and payments for the year aggregating to the net cash flow from operating activities. It includes cash receipts from customers, cash payments to suppliers and cash payments to and on behalf of employees.
- *The 'indirect' method* starts with the operating profit and adjusts it for non-cash charges and credits to reconcile it to the net cash flow from operating activities.

The indirect method is shown in the statement and could be compared with the direct method.

The principal advantage of the direct method is that it shows operating cash receipts and payments. Knowledge of the specific sources of cash receipts and the purposes for which cash payments were made in past periods may be useful in assessing future cash flows.

The principal advantage of the indirect method is that it highlights the differences between the operating profit and the net cash flow from operating activities. Many users of financial statements believe that such a reconciliation is essential to give an indication of the quality of the reporting entity's earnings.

PC 7.3.6

Direct method

	£000
Cash received from customers	24,765
Cash payments to suppliers	(11,480)
Cash paid to and on behalf of employees	(5,386)
Other cash payments	(1,010)
Net cash inflow from operating activities	6,889

Indirect method

	£000
Operating profit	6,022
Depreciation charge	893
Loss on sale of tangible fixed assets	6
Increase in stocks	(194)
Increase in debtors	(72)
Increase in creditors	234
Net cash inflow from operating activities	6,889

■ Examination of the calculations of net cash inflow from operations

PC 7.3.6

Direct method

The items used in the direct method are available from the financial records kept by a company. However, when companies were asked about the proposed standard, some stated that they did not currently collect information in the required form directly from their accounting systems. Thus it has been agreed that at the moment companies do not have to give the information required by the direct method.

It is possible to calculate the required figure using the Profit and Loss Account and the Balance Sheet.

The cash received from customers is: debtors at the beginning of the year + sales for the year – debtors at the end of the year.

The cash payments to suppliers is: creditors at the beginning of the year + purchases for the year – creditors at the end of the year.

Cash paid to and on behalf of employees and other cash payments can be calculated in a similar way.

Indirect method

A company is required to give this information in a note to the statement. The following should be noted:

- Depreciation must be added back to the net profit as it does not represent cash paid during the year. It is a 'book transaction'.
- The loss on sale of a tangible asset is the difference between the written-down value of the asset and the sale proceeds. Like depreciation it is not a cash transaction.
- The increase or decrease in stock is calculated by comparing the balances in two adjacent Balance Sheets.
- An increase in stock is deducted from operating profit. It represents a purchase that has not been set against the current operating profit. It must either have been paid for in cash or bought on credit and thus represents an actual or potential cash outflow.
- An increase in debtors is deducted from the operating profit. During a year an entity collects outstanding debts from the previous year and some of the money relating to this year's sales. If debtors have increased, then the company has not collected cash equal to its sales for the year.
- An increase in creditors is added to the operating profit. During a year an entity pays its outstanding debts from the previous year and for some of this year's purchases. If creditors have increased, then the company has not paid cash equal to its purchases for the year.

Returns on investments and servicing of finance

Interest received and paid are self explanatory.

Dividends are those paid during the year and would be last year's final proposed dividend and this year's interim dividend.

Taxation

The corporation tax paid this year would be based on last year's profit.

Investing activities

This shows the amount paid to acquire new fixed assets and the amount received from the sale of surplus assets.

Financing

A company can finance its activities by the issue of shares and debentures. Similarly it can be required to repay its long-term loans or, occasionally, to redeem some of its shares.

Increase in cash and cash equivalents

This should show the change in the cash position during the year.

PC
7.3.1
7.3.6

Accounts of non profit-making organisations

A club will usually want to keep a record of its financial transactions and to present accounts to its members once a year. As a club is not in business, it exists 'for the mutual benefit of its members', and so it is not suitable to prepare trading accounts in the normal way.

Receipts and payments accounts

A very small club would be content to summarise its cash and bank transactions at the end of the year. Such a summary would be called a receipts and payments account and would look like the following:

REGIS CHESS CLUB
Receipts and Payments Account for the Year ended 31 March 1995

	£	£
Receipts		
Bank and Cash Balances at 1 April 1994		483
Subscriptions		750
Competition Fees		125
Donations		50
		1,408
Payments		
Rent	200	
Light and Heat	375	
Secretarial Expenses	107	
Printing	46	
Competition Prizes	100	
New Chess Sets	294	
Sundries	33	
		1,155
Bank and cash balances at 31 March 1995		£253

Income and Expenditure Accounts

A larger club would want a more formal set of accounts and an Income and Expenditure Account would meet this need.

This is similar to a Trading and Profit and Loss Account prepared by a business. It looks at the income due for the year and the expenses relating to that year. Thus it takes into account accruals and prepayments and accounts for depreciation of fixed assets.

PC 7.3.1 7.3.6

THE ACCOUNTS OF CHAMBERS SOCIAL CLUB

Bar Trading Account for the Year ended 31 March 1995

	£	£
Bar Takings		71,165
Cost of Takings		
Opening Stock	3,765	
Purchases	54,785	
	58,550	
Closing Stock	3,595	
		54,955
Profit transferred to the Income and Expenditure Account		16,210

Income and Expenditure Account for the Year ended 31 March 1995

	£	£
Income		
Subscriptions		2,500
Profit from Bar		16,210
Fruit Machine Income		12,345
Hall Hire		1,500
Juke Box Income		1,030
New Year Dance: Income	2,530	
Expenses	1,985	
Profit		545
		34,130
Expenditure		
Wages	19,925	
Rent and Rates	3,775	
Light and Heat	2,460	
Printing and Stationery	450	
Cleaning	750	
Secretarial Expenses	615	
Accountancy and Stocktaking	1,575	
Repairs and Renewals	630	
Sundries	795	
Depreciation of fixtures	2,900	
		33,875
Surplus for Year		255

If the club holds a specific event the income and expenses will often be grouped together so the members can see whether a profit or loss was made.

Similarly if the club has a bar or sells refreshments on a regular basis with a view to making a profit then a trading account would be prepared for that activity so that the profit or loss can be determined.

If you examine the above accounts you will see:

- From the Bar Trading Account that the bar made a profit of £16,210. This is transferred to the Income and Expenditure Account.
- From the Income and Expenditure Account that the club had a New Year dance which made a profit of £545. Overall the club had a surplus for the year of £255.
- A club does not talk about a net profit; as has been said it is not in business.

PC 7.3.1 7.3.6

The Club Balance Sheet

If the club is sufficiently large then it will want to prepare a Balance Sheet to show its financial position at its year end. This takes on the same structure as that of a business, the Capital Account of the sole trader is replaced by an Accumulated Fund showing the accumulated surpluses for the club.

The Balance Sheet of Chambers Social Club might look as follows:

Balance Sheet as at 31 March 1995

	£	£
Fixed Assets		
Fixtures and Fittings at Cost		
less Depreciation		11,600
Current Assets		
Stock	3,595	
Prepayments	505	
Subs in Arrears	120	
Bank Deposit Account	10,050	
Cash In Hand	1,485	
	15,755	
Current Liabilities		
Creditors	4,560	
Subs in Advance	375	
Bank Overdraft – Current Account	5,320	
	10,255	
Net Current Assets		5,500
Net Assets		17,100
Accumulated Fund		
Balance at the beginning of year		16,845
Surplus for year		255
		17,100

Note: the only items that need some explanation are the subscriptions.

Subscriptions in arrears are a current asset as one or more members owe the Club money for their subscriptions for the past year.

Subscriptions in advance are a current liability as members have paid in advance of receiving a service, i.e. the right to use the club's facilities during the year to 31 March 1995.

SKILLS DEVELOPMENT ASSIGNMENT

The Chambers Social Club keeps its records in an analytical cash book during the year. The Honorary Treasurer provides you with a list of all the analysis columns for the club's receipts and payments. You have to use last year's balance sheet (see page 688) and the list of receipts and payments in order to produce:

a) this year's Bar Trading Account

b) an Income and Expenditure Account

c) a Balance Sheet for the end of the year

Receipts	£	*Payments*	£
Bar takings	79,140	Bank overdraft b/fwd	5,320
Subscriptions	2,600	Bar purchases	59,100
Fruit machine income	13,190	New Year Dance exps	2,070
Hall hire	1,500	Wages	21,010
Juke box income	1,110	Rent and rates	3,975
New Year Dance income	2,700	Light and heat	2,915
		Printing and stationery	590
		Cleaning	790
		Secretarial exps	585
		Accountancy and stocktaking	1,490
		Repairs and renewals	1,900
		Sundries	1,010
		New fixtures and fittings	1,000
Bank overdraft c/fwd	1,515		
	101,755		101,755

Notes

a) The purchase of new fixtures and fittings is not an expense and it needs to be added to the balance sheet balance of £11,600. You must treat the depreciation of fixtures and fittings as an expense. Use a figure of £3,150 for this year's depreciation (your balance sheet value for fixtures and fittings will then be £11,600 + £1,000 – £3,150 = £9,450.)

b) The closing stock at the bar was valued at £4,095 (this value is used in the Bar Trading Account and the Current Assets in the balance sheet).

c) The prepayment in last year's balance sheet of £505 refers to rent and rates. At the end of this year the equivalent figure is £530. The calculation of this year's expense is therefore:

	£
Amount paid	3,975
Add Prepayment b/fwd	505
	4,480
Less Prepayment c/fwd	530
This year's expenses	3,950

d) The subscriptions income has to be calculated taking into account last year's Subscriptions in Arrears and Subscriptions in Advance as well as their values at the end of this year. At the end of March 1995 the club has £100 of Subscriptions in Arrears and £450 of Subscriptions in Advance. The following calculations of the income from subscriptions has to be made.

	£
Subscriptions received in year	2,600
Less subscriptions in arrears b/fwd	120
	2,480
Add subscriptions in advance b/fwd	375
	2,855
Add subscriptions in arrears c/fwd	100
	2,955
Less subscriptions in advance c/fwd	450
	2,505

e) The Bank Deposits Account now stands at £10,955. No payments out of or into this account have been made during the year and the difference of £905 between this year's balance and last year's figure is due to the interest added by the bank. This figure of £905 must be treated as income in the Income and Expenditure Account

f) The creditor's value of £4,560 in last year's balance sheet relates to Bar Purchases. At the end of this year the equivalent value is £3,950. The calculation of the actual bar purchases for the year is thus:

	£
Amount paid in year	59,100
Less Creditors b/fwd	4,560
	54,540
Add Creditors c/fwd	3,950
	58,490

PC 7.3.5

■ Preparation of a set of sole trader's accounts

A detailed examination of the preparation of final accounts is not undertaken in this unit, but one example follows on page 693 which will give you an idea of the processes which must be undergone in order to prepare a set of final accounts for a sole trader.

During a year Colorado completed his double entry bookkeeping effectively and at the end of the year, 31 March 1995, the following balances were extracted from his books:

	£
Sales	200,000
Purchases	131,400
Stock 1 April 1994	18,000
Bad Debts	2,028
Wages and Salaries	24,216
Admin. Expenses	30,172
Selling Expenses	5,688
Bank Charges	1,306
Plant and Equipment	76,000
Office Furniture	18,000
Debtors	38,075
Creditors	18,963
Cash at Bank	2,584
Cash In Hand	372
Capital	141,514
Drawings	12,636

It was also known that at 31 March 1995:

1 The stock was £45,308.

2 £2,200 was owed for wages and salaries.

3 £240 was owed for bank charges.

4 Included in admin. expenses was £2,000 for insurance for the year to 31 March 1995.

5 Colorado provides for depreciation at 10 per cent per annum on plant and equipment and 20 per cent per annum on office furniture.

The accounts that would be prepared from these figures would be as follows:

Workings:

1 As wages are outstanding at the end of the year the total incurred during the year is:

From the trial balance	£24,216
Owing at end of year	2,200
Due for the year (P+L)	£26,416

2 Similarly for bank charges:

From the trial balance	£1,306
Owing at end of year	240
Due for year (P+L)	£1,546

3 Total owing at end of year, to be shown in the Balance Sheet

£2,200 + 240 = £2,440.

4 As insurance has been paid this year for next year the total of administration expenses for the year are:

From the trial balance	£30,172
Prepaid at end of year	2,000
Due for the year (P+L)	£28,172

5 The depreciation for the year is:

On plant and equipment 10% × £76,000 = £7,600
On office machinery 20% × £18,000 = £3,600

The Final Accounts can now be prepared and will look as follows on page 693.

PC
7.3.1
7.3.6

DISCUSSION TOPICS

1 If you were in a position to start a business would you prefer to be a sole trader or a member of a partnership?

2 Do you think that published accounts give the right amount of information to shareholders? If not, what changes (more or less) would you make?

3 Accounts are prepared on an historical cost basis. Do you think that a supplementary set of accounts should be prepared to account for inflation? If so, what problems do you envisage in the preparation of such a set of accounts?

4 To compare a set of company accounts with those of another company is not a very meaningful exercise as companies can use different accounting policies for items such as depreciation. Do you agree?

PC
7.3.1
7.3.6

SUMMARY OF THE PURPOSES OF BALANCE SHEETS AND PROFIT AND LOSS STATEMENTS

The main purposes of balance sheets and profit and loss statements may be summarised as follows:

- to inform business owners and/or their managers of the nature of its performance: whether hitting, exceeding or missing targeted levels of – sales turnover, gross profit and net profit, as well as ratios of operating costs to overall sales turnover etc
- to form the basis of submission documents to a finance lender when seeking a business loan
- to serve as monitoring documents when checking on business performance month by month
- to serve as part of the statutory set of documents which are produced by the business, vetted by a chartered accountant and used by HM Inland Revenue when charging corporation tax etc.
- to inform legitimately interested stakeholders – shareholders, directors, partners etc.

COLORADO: SOLE TRADER

Trading and Profit and Loss Account for the Year ended 31 March 1995

	£	£
Sales		200,000
Cost of Sales:		
Opening Stock	18,000	
Purchases	131,400	
Available Stock	149,400	
Closing Stock	45,308	
		104,092
Gross Profit		95,908
Expenses		
Bad Debts	2,028	
Wages and Salaries	26,416	
Admin. Expenses	28,172	
Selling Expenses	5,688	
Bank Charges	1,546	
Depreciation of:		
Plant and Equipment	7,600	
Office Furniture	3,600	75,050
Net Profit		20,858

Balance Sheet as at 31 March 1995

	£	£
Fixed Assets		
Plant and Equipment		68,400
Office Furniture		14,400
		82,800
Current Assets		
Stock	45,308	
Debtors	38,075	
Prepayment	2,000	
Cash at Bank	2,584	
Cash In Hand	372	
	88,339	
Current Liabilities		
Creditors	18,963	
Accrued Expenses	2,440	
	21,403	
Net Current Assets		66,936
Total Assets *less* Current Liabilities		149,736
Capital		
Balance at beginning of year		141,514
Add Profit for year		20,858
		162,372
Less Drawings for year		12,636
		149,736

PC
7.3.1
7.3.2
7.3.3
7.3.4
7.3.5
7.3.6

REVIEW TEST

Note: GNVQ Advanced Business students do not need to acquire any knowledge of double-entry book-keeping, and corresponding questions below are set on the basis of testing general, background knowledge to inform trial balance and profit and loss accounts aspects etc.

1 Name the five books which make up the accounts journal.

2 What are the two accounting rules governing whom to debit and whom to credit?

3 Explain simply how the double-entry system works.

4 What is a trial balance? How is it extracted?

5 What is a personal account? What is a real account? What is a nominal account?

6 What is the difference between gross and net profit?

7 What makes up a set of final accounts?

8 What is the purpose of drawing up a profit and loss account?

9 What is the purpose of drawing up a balance sheet?

10 How is the cost of sales calculated?

11 What is a bad debt? How are bad debts allowed for in a balance sheet?

12 Explain briefly the difference between straight line and reducing balance methods of depreciation.

13 What would you expect to find in a set of published final accounts of a plc?

14 What would you expect to find in a set of club accounts?

15 List the main balances you would expect to be extracted from a typical sole trader's books which would enable a trading and profit and loss and balance sheet to be drawn up.

KNOWLEDGE TEST

Element 7.3
Produce and explain profit and loss statements and balance sheets

1 (i) A trial balance is produced at regular intervals in business in order to check if detailed accounting entries have been made correctly.
(ii) If the trial balance fails to balance it is because income has exceeded expenditure for a given trading period.

Which of the following options best describes the above two statements?

A	(i)	T	(ii)	T
B	(i)	T	(ii)	F
C	(i)	F	(ii)	T
D	(i)	F	(ii)	F

2 Which of the following are ledgers which inform the production of a profit and loss account?

A Nominal
B Returns
C Sales
D Purchase

3 Which of the following statements are true and which false?

A Semi-fixed assets are those which can be converted into cash within three months.
B Gross profit is what is left over after the cost of sales has been deducted from sales.
C Net profit emerges from gross profit after all expenses have been deducted.
D Bad debts do not form a part of expenses.

4 (i) Depreciation of fixtures and fittings, vehicles and equipment form legitimate items of expense.
(ii) Stock purchases form a legitimate part of expense.

Which of the following options best describes the above two statements?

A	(i)	T	(ii)	T
B	(i)	T	(ii)	F
C	(i)	F	(ii)	T
D	(i)	F	(ii)	F

5 Which of the following statements are true, and which false?

A Current liabilities are amounts owed by a business which must be paid for within twelve months.
B The purchase of fixed assets is termed capital expenditure.
C A trial balance need not necessarily conclude with the same sum on the debit and credit sides of the sheet.
D Sole traders and partnerships are not obliged to submit annual accounts to the Inland Revenue because of their unlimited liability.

PORTFOLIO OF EVIDENCE ACTIVITY

PC
7.3.1
7.3.2
7.3.3
7.3.4
7.3.5
7.3.6

Element 7.3
Produce and explain profit and loss statements and balance sheets

TUV PLC

Scenario

You work as an assistant to the accounts manager of TUV plc, which is a small manufacturing company. Unfortunately, he has recently fallen sick, and you have been left 'holding the fort'. Your boss's illness has come at a bad time, since you are in the middle of producing the firm's profit and loss account and balance sheet.

From the data of the trial balance shown below, you have been tasked with:

a) preparing a profit and loss account

b) drawing up a balance sheet.

TUV plc Trial Balance as at 31 December 19X7

	Debit £000	*Credit* £000
Sales		1,000
Machinery – Cost	588	
Machinery – Depreciation		180
Computer – Cost	250	
Computer – Depreciation		50
Warehouse – Cost	700	
Warehouse – Depreciation		96
Delivery Vehicles – Cost	230	
Delivery Vehicles – Depreciation		80
Disposal		10
Stock at 1 January 19X7	20	
Purchases of Materials	250	
Repairs to Machinery	27	
Rent – Factory	28	
– Offices	32	
Manufacturing Wages	49	
Directors' Salaries	35	
Clerical Staff Salaries	18	
Office Heating and Lighting	9	
Sales Commission	68	
Road Tax and Insurance on Vehicles	30	
Bad Debts	50	
Provision for Bad Debts		1
Loan Interest	20	
Debtors	84	
Bank	105	
Creditors		26
10% Debenture Loans		400
Interim Ordinary Dividend	30	
8% Preference Shares		250
Ordinary Shares		310
Profit and Loss Account		220
	2,623	2,623

Notes

1 Stock was counted on 31 December 19X7 and valued at £25,000.

2 The company's auditors have discovered that the acquisition of a piece of machinery costing £12,000 has been posted incorrectly to the repairs account. No adjustment has been made in respect of this error.

3 The balance on the disposals account represents the proceeds of the disposal of a delivery vehicle which had originally cost £30,000 and which had been depreciated by £13,000. No other entries have been made in respect of this transaction.

4 Depreciation has still to be charged as follows:

Machinery	10% straight line
Computer	20% straight line
Warehouse	2% straight line
Delivery Vehicles	25% reducing balance

5 The computer is used mainly for accounting and payroll purposes.

6 The following expenses have been incurred but not recorded:

Manufacturing Wages	£1000
Factory Rent	£2000
Clerical Salaries	£2000
Office Heating	£4000

The company paid £10,000 during the year in order to insure the delivery vehicles for the 12-month period from 1 July 19X7 to 30 June 19X8.

7 The provision for bad debts has to be increased to £4,000.

8 The directors propose to pay the preference dividend in full and to make a final ordinary dividend payment of £50,000.

Reproduced from: *Accounting – An Introduction for Professional Students* by John Dunn, published by Pitman Publishing.

Scenario 2

Having produced the profit and loss account and balance sheet, your board of directors has asked you to provide them with a briefing paper on how profit and loss accounts and balance sheets can be used to secure and maintain loans from finance lenders.

Task 1

First produce your customary entries for your planning and review log on how you will tackle this activity.

Task 2

Produce the profit and loss and balance sheet from the data provided on the trial balance, making sure you employ a currently accepted format for each.

Task 3

Produce the required commentary, ensuring that it is free from jargon. Your commentary should be about two sides of printed A4 long.

Performance criteria covered

7.3.1, 7.3.2, 7.3.3, 7.3.4, 7.3.5, 7.3.6

Core skills covered

Communication:
3.2.1, 3.2.2, 3.2.3, 3.2.4, 3.2.5, 3.3.1, 3.3.2, 3.3.3, 3.4.1, 3.4.2, 3.4.3, 3.4.4

Information Technology:
3.1.1, 3.1.2, 3.1.3, 3.1.4, 3.1.5, 3.2.1, 3.2.2, 3.2.3, 3.2.4, 3.2.5, 3.2.6, 3.2.7, 3.3.1, 3.3.2, 3.3.3, 3.3.4, 3.3.5, 3.3.6

Application of Number:
3.2.1, 3.2.2, 3.2.3, 3.2.4, 3.2.5, 3.2.6, 3.2.7, 3.3.1, 3.3.2, 3.3.3, 3.3.4, 3.3.5

Element 7.4
IDENTIFY AND EXPLAIN DATA TO MONITOR A BUSINESS

This section explains why it is so important to monitor financial activity in a business, who uses what accounting information, what that information consists of and what ratios are available to accountants and managers to aid them in evaluating performance.

PC 7.4.1

The reasons for monitoring a business

A business consultant once caused mayhem in a hectic open-plan office on the 15th floor of a City of London office block. He did so by arriving on the final day of his audit of the business's activities with a large plastic dustbin and a pair of tailor's shears. Wordlessly, he proceeded to cut the phone lines of office staff who were in busy conversations, to sweep papers off desks into his dustbin, and to dump files – being used by staff – into black plastic bags. Needless to say, within about 2 minutes, the company's managing director was in the office demanding to know what was going on. The consultant explained calmly that work was being initiated in one corner of the large office, processed in another corner and filed in a third. Not a thing ever left the room!

While the above anecdote may convey an over-dramatic way of making a point, it does illustrate how a business can be frantically busy doing meaningless tasks. In a similar way, a business can become so bogged down in the minutiae of sales and purchase transactions that it fails to notice that it stopped making a profit several weeks ago, or that operational expenses have risen beyond any safe ceiling over the past six months.

For such reasons, senior managers and their accounts advisers in efficient, effective organisations set up various management accounting reports, analyses and extrapolations which supply information in summary form which casts vital light on how a business is performing.

PC 7.4.1 7.4.2

SUMMARY OF MAIN AREAS OF FINANCIAL MONITORING

- **Sales turnover:** this week against last week, this month/last month, this quarter/last quarter, this year/last year
- **Gross and net profit:** analysis of performance ratios over similar timescales
- **Operational expenses:** monthly, quarterly, annually, this year/last year
- **Cash flow:** the forecast totals of cash outflow to be covered by what estimated cash inflow; monitoring projected to actual balances
- **Tax liabilities:** forecasting from known performance what year end or quarterly tax bills are likely to be for corporation tax, VAT, tax on dividends received etc.
- **Levels of financial reserves:** monthly from bank statements
- **Interest accruing from investments:** monthly, quarterly, annually
- **Interest due on loans taken out:** monthly, quarterly, annually

Senior managers will also be interested to vet departmental budgets – actual spending to allocated budgets, so as to keep running costs under control. They will also want to know how sales are going: by product, by product range, in terms of most profitable products in the range and so on.

Essentially, such information is required across various timescales so that a business can monitor its performance in terms of profitability and financial viability, but also so that it has a solid, factual platform of performance from which to improve – monthly, quarterly and annually. It is worth recalling in this regard that rolling corporate plans and departmental business plans almost always include targets to be achieved which exceed those set for last year, last quarter, last month etc.

The users of accounting information

PC 7.4.2

Naturally, the managers of a business's accounts department will be among the prime users of accounting information, since they are directly charged with monitoring its financial health in many different ways. They are also charged with producing financial reports and analyses both for a business's board of directors as well as for its specialist departmental managers. For example, a board may require monthly trading and profit and loss accounts to be produced to supply an overall picture, while a sales manager may be more interested in how much his or her sales force sold in the past month, in what product areas and at what profit, so that 'actual sales to target sales' can be analysed and appropriate action taken if need be.

Other interested parties within the larger organisation will be its shareholders, who are entitled to receive at the least a copy of the annual accounts in the annual shareholders' report. If a business has taken out a large loan, then its bankers or lending agency will almost certainly want to see regular analyses of performance, so as to remain assured of the business's ongoing ability to service the loan.

In public sector organisations such as county and district councils, local council tax and business rate payers will want to see how their taxes are spent, and they usually receive such a break-down when they receive their annual rate demands.

As already referred to, the inland revenue's teams of local inspectors will work through documents passed on to them from a company's chartered accountants in order to calculate the business's levels of taxes and allowances.

In many organisations, performance figures are released to interested sets of workers – sales representatives, production operatives, budget-holders etc. – to enable them to see how their contributions have turned out. Such information, when positive, is an important morale and productivity booster.

PC 7.4.3

■ Comparisons of performance

As the above summary illustrates, businesses tend to make sets of comparisons over periods extending from one week to the next to one year to the next. Many employ the moving total Z-chart to do so (see Unit 3).

Companies with multiple factories, branches or outlets may seek to compare individual performance centres and district or regional groupings, and provide weightings for them as a means of creating a level performance playing-field. Almost certainly, by accessing information in the public domain or by means of market intelligence, larger organisations will seek to monitor the performance of their competitors.

■ Key financial information areas

The following chart summarises the key financial information areas (usually recorded on documents with format conventions) in which important data is collected and presented:

PC 7.4.4

KEY COMPONENTS OF FINANCIAL INFORMATION

- **Forecasts and actual out-turns:** cash-flow, trading and profit and loss account, balance sheet
- **Debtors and aged debtors:** by analysis of days elapsing between the issue of statements and payments made
- **Creditors and aged creditors:** by analysis of purchase ledger totals due by supplier
- **Days of stock:** by analysis of the number of days' worth of sales being held at any time as stock
- **Rate of stock turn-over:** by analysis of how many times a year a business's holdings of stock are turned over

Note: See below for other important accounting ratios.

■ Performance of a business

By setting up the above range of financial reporting requirements at appropriate time intervals, a business's senior managers seek to ensure that they receive the right information at the right time to inform and influence the important decisions they make, which affect the entire business.

The problem senior managers must avoid in this respect is becoming too swamped and bogged down in detail. Thus they tend to require summaries, tables of totalled information in classified groups, as well as graphs and charts which are easily absorbed.

In large concerns such summary information may be maintained on a real-time basis on computer, so that a director may see how, for example, total company sales across 450 branches are performing hour by hour!

Profitability, performance and solvency ratios

PC 7.4.6

It is insufficient in today's competitive business world just to be able to understand a set of accounts. It is also necessary to be able to interpret them and to answer such questions as:

- Has my business performed better than last year?
- Is my business as profitable as my rivals?
- If I present these accounts to my bank manager will he continue my overdraft facilities?
- Will the Inspector of Taxes be happy with these results?

In order to interpret a set of accounts it is necessary to calculate a number of accounting 'ratios' and to draw suitable conclusions from these calculations. Although the calculations are given the name of 'ratios', many of them are expressed as a percentage or as a period of time.

It is possible to calculate many ratios. Here we will look at the most important ones under three main headings:

Profitability. Whether a firm is making a reasonable profit for its size.

Liquidity. Whether a firm has sufficient resources available to pay its debts as they fall due.

Activity. Whether a firm has good control over its assets.

Profitability

There are three main ratios in this category.

1 Gross profit rate

This is calculated as follows:

$$\text{Gross profit rate} = \frac{\text{Gross profit}}{\text{Sales}} \times 100$$

This expresses the gross profit as a percentage of the sales.

If we take the accounts for The White Hart, the calculation would be:

$$\frac{68{,}275}{142{,}240} \times 100 = 48.00\%$$

This tells us that for every £100 of sales we make a profit before running expenses of £48.00

In practice you would compare this percentage with the corresponding figure for previous years. If there had been a considerable change then it would require further investigation. The reason for the change could be:

a *There has been a change in the 'sales mix'* In our case perhaps more food and less alcoholic drink was sold. As these goods have different individual gross profit rates the overall rate would have changed.

b *There was an increase in the cost of goods sold* which was not passed on to the customers. If this was a deliberate policy to retain customers, a further question must be asked. Has the volume of sales been maintained?

c *There has been a cut in price of some goods,* for example, bar snacks. This would be done to maintain or improve the volume of trade.

d *Theft by members of staff or customers.* This is a problem in all businesses and a lasting solution to it has never been found.

PC 7.4.6

2 Net profit rate

This is calculated as follows:

$$\text{Net profit rate} = \frac{\text{Net profit}}{\text{Sales}} \times 100$$

This expresses the net profit as a percentage of sales.

If we look at our pub again the calculation would be:

$$\frac{15{,}055}{142{,}240} \times 100 = 10.58\%$$

This tells us that for every £100 of sales we make a profit of £10.58 after all expenses have been taken into account.

Again a firm would compare this with its results for previous years and investigate any major difference. The reasons for a change could include:

a *A change in the gross profit rate.*

b *A comparatively large change in one or more of the expenses.* In the case of our pub it could be that there has been an exceptionally large increase in the rent payable due to a renegotiation of the rental agreement.

3 Return on capital employed

This can be subdivided into two ratios:

3.1 $$\text{Return on owner's equity} = \frac{\text{Net profit}}{\text{Capital employed}} \times 100$$

This expresses the net profit made by the owner as a percentage of the money that he has invested in it.

The Capital Employed is taken as the opening balance on the capital account or, if preferred, the average capital account balance for the year.

For The White Hart the calculation would be:

$$\frac{15{,}055}{18{,}190} \times 100 = 82.76\%$$

This tells us that for every £100 that the owner has invested in the pub a profit of £82.76 has been made. This is an extremely high percentage return but it must be remembered that the profit has got to support Mr Campbell's personal financial requirements.

In addition to comparing this year's figure with previous years etc., a sole trader could look at the return that he could get if he invested the money in, say, a building society. In comparing the two percentages the additional risk involved in running a business and the extra work involved must be taken into account.

3.2 Return on long-term capital employed = $\dfrac{\text{Net profit before interest}}{\text{Long-term capital employed}} \times 100$

This expresses the profit made on the money invested in a firm as a percentage of the money invested in it on a long-term basis. Interest must be added back to the profit in order to arrive at a figure for the money earned for people who have invested in the business on a long-term basis.

For our business the calculation would be:

$$\frac{15{,}055 + 450}{18{,}190 + 3{,}000} \times 100 = 73.17\%$$

This tells us that for every £100 invested in the pub a profit of £73.17 is made.

Liquidity

PC 7.4.5 7.4.6

There are two main ratios in this category.

1 Current or working capital ratio

This is calculated as follows:

$$\text{Current ratio} = \frac{\text{Current assets}}{\text{Current liabilities}}$$

This ratio measures that relationship between the current assets and current liabilities.

For our pub the calculation is:

$$\frac{11{,}635}{7{,}490} : 1 = 1.55 : 1$$

There is no ideal current ratio. However, for a retail business a figure of 2:1 is sometimes quoted. Many firms will have a ratio much lower than this and manage to survive quite happily. If a firm has had a current ratio of 1.5:1 for the past 5 years then it is reasonable to assume that it will continue to survive with a ratio of 1.5:1. A sudden change in a ratio is cause for concern as it suggests that it might not be financially viable.

2 Liquid ratio or acid test

This is calculated as follows:

$$\text{Liquid ratio} = \frac{\text{Current assets excluding stock}}{\text{Current liabilities}}$$

This ratio compares the liquid or near liquid funds of a firm with the liabilities which will be due for payment shortly after the balance sheet date.

For our pub the calculation is:

$$\frac{(11{,}635 - 9{,}125)}{7{,}490} : 1 = 0.34 : 1$$

As a general rule this ratio should be about 1:1. If it is very much lower than this, there is a danger of the business being unable to pay its debts on time. If it is very much larger than this, the danger is that the business is not making the best use of its funds.

The White Hart's liquidity ratios are low, but they might be acceptable. The business is a cash business and it is likely that Mr Campbell will be able to sell his stock in time to pay his creditors. If there is doubt, Mr Campbell could see if the bank will allow him sufficient overdraft facilities.

PC 7.4.6

Activity

In this section we will consider three ratios.

1 Rate of stock turnover

This is calculated as follows:

$$\text{Rate of stock turnover} = \frac{\text{Cost of goods sold}}{\text{Average stock}}$$

If we only have a set of final accounts the average stock is:

$$\frac{\text{Opening stock} + \text{Closing stock}}{2}$$

The answer tells us how many times per year the stock is 'cleared'. For The White Hart the calculation is:

$$\text{Average stock} = \frac{(10{,}630 + 9{,}125)}{2} = 9{,}877.50$$

$$\text{Rate of stock turnover} = \frac{73{,}965}{9{,}877.50} = 7.49$$

This means the same as saying that 7.5 times per year the stock is sold and then replaced. Obviously in practice the pub is never empty, there is always drink in the cellar and food in the kitchen.

Alternatively the rate of stock turnover can be expressed as:

$$\frac{\text{Average stock}}{\text{Cost of goods sold}} \times 12 \text{ or } 52 \text{ or } 365$$

This tells us how long, on average, an item is in stock. The answer is given in months, weeks or days. For The White Hart the calculation is:

$$\frac{9{,}877.50}{73{,}965} \times 52 = 6.94 \text{ weeks}$$

This means that an item is in stock approximately 7 weeks.

Any business will wish to have as high a rate of stock turnover as possible, within reasonable limits.

This ratio taken with the gross profit rate will give some indication to the pattern of trading of the firm. If the firm has a comparatively low gross profit rate and you believe this is because it hopes to have a high volume of trade then the rate of stock turnover should be comparatively high.

2 Debtors collection period

This is calculated as:

$$\text{Debtors collection period} = \frac{\text{Debtors}}{\text{Credit sales for year}} \times 52 \text{ weeks}$$

This will tell how long, on average, the firm's debtors take to settle their accounts. You should compare this with the firm's credit control policy.

As the vast majority of a pub's sales are for cash, it is not appropriate to calculate the debtors collection period in this case.

3 Creditors payment period

This is calculated as:

$$\text{Creditors payment period} = \frac{\text{Creditors}}{\text{Credit purchases for year}} \times 52 \text{ weeks}$$

This will show how long, on average, the firm takes to pay its creditors. Obviously it does not want to pay its bills any earlier than necessary but equally it does not want to antagonise its suppliers. They may withdraw their credit facilities which will not be to the firm's advantage!

For The White Hart the calculation is:

$$\frac{5{,}480}{72{,}460} \times 52 = 3.9 \text{ weeks}$$

General points to note

The interpretation of accounts is a complex issue. The ratios that are calculated can be compared with results for previous years, with budgeted figures or with results of similar firms. If the latter is undertaken, remember that there may be different accounting policies in different firms, for example, a different method of calculating depreciation.

If you are required to write a report comparing the results of two different firms, remember to use the correct format for a report. An informal style will probably suffice. Your detailed calculations are best attached as an appendix to the report and a summary of your calculations should be included in the body of the report. Students usually find it easier to write about each category of ratios and then to draw an overall conclusion.

GLOSSARY OF FINANCE TERMS

PC 7.4.

Accrued Expense An expense which has not been paid before the end of the accounting period to which it relates.

Authorised Share Capital This refers to the value of shares that a company is authorised to issue as stated in their Memorandum of Association.

Balance Sheet A financial statement showing the assets and liabilities of a firm at a particular point in time.

Break-even Point The level of activity at which a firm makes neither a profit nor a loss.

Budget A financial and/or a quantitative plan of operation for the coming accounting period.

Budgetary Control The continuous comparison of actual with budgeted results and institution of the necessary corrective action.

Business Plan A complete plan for a business including financial forecasts.

Capital Expenditure Money spent on the purchase or improvement of fixed assets.

Cash Budget An estimate of the money that will be received and paid during the following accounting period, and the effect that this will have on the cash held by the company.

Contribution The difference between the selling price and the variable costs of sale.

Creditors The people and organisations who are owed money by a business.

Current Assets Amounts owed to a business and other assets which will be converted into cash within 12 months.

Current Liabilities Amounts owed by a firm which require payment within the next 12 months.

Debenture An acknowledgement of a debt, binding a limited company to pay interest at a specified rate.

Debtors Those who owe money to a business, usually as a result of the firm selling goods on credit.

Depreciation The amount that is written off the book value of a fixed asset and charged as an expense in the profit and loss account.

Dividends The payment to shareholders from the profits of the company.

Fixed Assets Permanent assets held in an organisation which are needed for the firm to be able to function. Firms do not normally trade in their fixed assets.

Fixed Costs The costs of running a firm which do not vary with the level of activity of the firm.

Gross Profit The difference between the sales revenue and the costs of those sales.

Insolvency The condition when external debts exceed the value of assets of a business. This means that the company will be unable to pay its debts as they fall due. It is an offence to trade when knowingly insolvent.

Issued Share Capital This is the nominal value of the shares that have been issued by a company.

Mortgage This is a loan given to an individual or an organisation which is secured against a specific property.

Net Profit The profit made by an organisation after all expenses have been taken into account. It can be expressed as Net profit = Gross Profit – Expenses.

Ordinary Share Capital This is often called 'risk' capital, as the shareholders only receive a dividend if profits are made and after preference shareholders have received their dividend. Ordinary shareholders normally have voting rights in the company.

Partnership Two or more people carrying on a business with a view to making a profit from the business.

Preference Shares Shares which are paid a fixed dividend in priority to any dividend payable to ordinary shareholders. In the liquidation of a company they will receive the nominal value of their shares before the ordinary shareholders receive any money back.

Prepayments Expenses paid for in advance of the accounting period to which they relate.

All expenses must be 'matched' to the income of the same period.

Ratio Analysis A technique used for the interpretation of accounts. A comparison is made between the results of a firm in a given accounting period with those of the previous period, the budgeted figures or those of a similar firm.

Sole Trader A person who is self-employed, who is operating a business alone and has sole responsibility for its management.

Stock The goods which a firm purchases with the specific intention of selling or raw materials which it converts into goods to sell.

Variable Costs Costs which vary in direct proportion to the level of activities of a firm.

Variance The difference between a budgeted and actual figure.

REVIEW TEST

PC: 7.4.1, 7.4.2, 7.4.3, 7.4.4, 7.4.6

1 List four main purposes of financial monitoring.

2 Explain briefly who the principal (legitimate) users are of accounting information.

3 List four main components of financial information.

4 Explain simply and clearly how a gross profit and a net profit rate are calculated.

5 Why is return on capital returned an important accounting ratio?

6 What information does a liquid ratio or acid test provide?

7 Is it better to have a higher or lower rate of stock turnover? Why?

8 How can an analysis of debtors' collection periods and creditors' payment periods aid a business?

INDIVIDUAL/PAIR ACTIVITIES

PC: 7.4.1, 7.4.2, 7.4.6

1 Arrange to interview a business's accounts manager or director and find out what he or she sees as the most important financial information to be monitored and analysed and why.

2 Find out what financial information is provided in the annual report of a public limited company and assess (by examining 3–5 reports) how informative are the financial data provided.

3 Arrange to interview a partner of a local chartered accountants' practice and find out what the annual auditing of a business's accounts involves.

4 Make arrangements to visit your local Inland Revenue offices and to interview a tax inspector on his or her job role and its interface with chartered accountants.

Report back orally on the above activities to your class, and make notes of the presentations you observe for your revision notes.

KNOWLEDGE TEST

Element 7.4
Identify and explain data to monitor a business

1 Which of the following are among the main reasons for monitoring financial information?

A To check on levels of profit being generated.
B To provide data for HM Customs & Excise.
C To check on cash flow in and out.
D To ensure sufficient liquidity for directors' drawings.

2 (i) County and district councils are not obliged to publish annual accounts.
(ii) A company's shareholders are legally entitled to receive copies of annual accounts.

Which of the following options best describes the above two statements?

A (i) T (ii) T
B (i) T (ii) F
C (i) F (ii) T
D (i) F (ii) F

3 Which of the following statements are true, and which false?

A Aged debtors are (as officially designated by the Inland Revenue) a) 65 and over if male b) 60 and over if female.
B Rate of stock turnover is a measure of how many times in a trading period a business sells and replaces its stock.
C Return on capital employed is:

$$\frac{\text{Net profit}}{\text{Working capital}} \times 100$$

D Liquidity ratio is an alternative term for solvency ratios.

4 (i) A liquidity ratio is used to check whether a business has sufficient resources to pay its debts.
(ii) An activity ratio checks on whether a business has its assets under control.

Which of the following options best describes the above two statements?

A (i) T (ii) T
B (i) T (ii) F
C (i) F (ii) T
D (i) F (ii) F

5 Which of the following have a legitimate interest in a business's financial information?

A Its customers.
B Its directors.
C Its shareholders.
D Its debtors.

PORTFOLIO OF EVIDENCE ACTIVITY

PC
7.4.1
7.4.2
7.4.3
7.4.4
7.4.5
7.4.6

Element 7.4
Identify and explain data to monitor a business

Scenario 1

You work at the Central London Teacher Training College, in its Business & Management Department, where you are studying to become an accounts lecturer. You have been recently given an assignment, which is to produce a set of teaching materials to enable students (at GNVQ Business Advanced level) to understand the following:

- The key components of financial information which are used to monitor business performance.
- The range of legitimate users of such information and why they would want it.
- Why comparisons and measures of difference such as ratios are helpful in measuring a business's performance.

Your tutor has briefed you on the need to structure and present your materials in a visually appealing and easy-to-digest manner.

Scenario 2

You have been given another assignment at College, which is this time to explain from the information provided below the profitability, solvency and performance of two companies, using accepted accounting ratios:

Charlie Ltd and Bravo Ltd are both manufacturing companies in the same industry. Calculate the ratios described above for the two companies. Comment on the effectiveness of each company's management. (Hint: when calculating the liquidity ratios, think carefully about the treatment of the recoverable ACT.)

Profit and Loss Accounts for the Year Ended 30 June 199X

	Bravo Ltd		Charlie Ltd	
	£	£	£	£
Sales		700,000		1,200,000
Cost of Sales		(420,000)		(660,000)
Gross Profit		280,000		540,000
Other Operating Expenses	(32,000)		(46,000)	
Interest	(60,000)		(24,000)	
		(92,000)		(70,000)
Net Profit for Year		188,000		470,000
Tax	(37,600)		(84,600)	
Dividend	(28,200)		(103,400)	
		(65,800)		(188,000)
		122,200		282,000
Retained Profit b/fwd		147,000		158,000
Retained Profit c/fwd		269,200		440,000

[Note: ACT stands for Advance Corporation Tax]

Balance Sheets as at 30 June 199X

	Bravo Ltd		Charlie Ltd	
	£	£	£	£
Fixed Assets		900,000		1,513,000
Current Assets				
Stock	70,000		93,500	
Debtors	93,333		140,000	
Recoverable ACT	9,400		34,467	
Bank	87,000		78,000	
	259,733		345,967	
Current Liabilities				
Creditors	(45,500)		(140,000)	
Tax	(47,000)		(119,067)	
Proposed Dividend	(28,200)		(103,400)	
	(120,700)		(362,467)	
Working Capital		139,033		(16,500)
		1,039,033		1,496,500
Debentures		(500,000)		(200,000)
		539,033		1,296,500
Share Capital		269,833		856,500
Reserves		269,200		440,000
		539,033		1,296,500

Reproduced from *Accounting: An Introduction for Professional Students* by John Dunn (1992), Pitman Publishing.

You should write up your analysis of the two sets of accounts in a summary analysis, stating your reasons for preferring the performance of one of the companies.

Task 1

For (possibly!) the last time, fill out the appropriate parts of your planning and review log before starting this activity.

Task 2

Produce as requested the analysis of the performance of the two companies, taking care to double-check your calculations.

Then compose a suitable summary in about 3 sides of printed A4 which compares and contrasts their respective performances and supply a rationale for preferring the performance of one of the two firms.

Performance criteria covered

7.4.1, 7.4.2, 7.4.3, 7.4.4, 7.4.5, 7.4.6

Core skills covered

Communication:
3.2.1, 3.2.2, 3.2.3, 3.2.4, 3.2.5, 3.3.1, 3.3.2, 3.3.3, 3.4.1, 3.4.2, 3.4.3, 3.4.4

Information Technology:
3.1.1, 3.1.2, 3.1.3, 3.1.4, 3.1.5, 3.2.1, 3.2.2, 3.2.3, 3.2.4, 3.2.5, 3.2.6, 3.2.7, 3.3.1, 3.3.2, 3.3.3, 3.3.4, 3.3.5, 3.3.6

PC
7.4.5
7.4.6

Application of Number:
3.2.1, 3.2.2, 3.2.3, 3.2.4, 3.2.5, 3.2.6, 3.2.7, 3.2.8, 3.2.9

SKILLS DEVELOPMENT ACTIVITY

Caledonian Ltd

Caledonian Ltd is a medium-sized company which wishes to expand its activities. The board of directors has heard that the directors and shareholders of Goodwin Ltd are considering retirement and may be open to an offer to purchase the company.

You work for the accountants to Caledonian Ltd and are assigned the task of analysing the accounts of Goodwin Ltd. You are given the accounts of the last three years and these are summarised below:

Profit and Loss Account
for the year ended 31 December

	1990	1991	1992
	£000	£000	£000
Sales	1,700	1,950	1,900
Cost of Sales	900	1,030	1,050
Gross Profit	800	920	850
Selling and Distribution Costs	80	90	95
Administration Expenses	500	575	600
Financial Charges	10	10	10
	590	675	705
Net profit for year	210	245	145

(Note: the Appropriation Account is not available)

Balance Sheet as at 31 December

	1990	1991	1992
	£000	£000	£000
Fixed Assets	550	575	500
Current Assets			
Stock	100	110	170
Debtors	210	245	395
Balance at Bank	50	60	5
	360	415	570
Creditors: amounts falling due within one year	160	225	395
Net Current Assets	200	190	175
Total Assets *less* Current liabilities	750	765	675
Capital and Reserves			
Share Capital	500	500	500
Reserves	250	265	175
	750	765	675

You are to draft a report to the directors of Caledonian Ltd in which you are to:

a use suitable accounting ratios to analyse the accounts in terms of profitability, liquidity and activity;

b make a recommendation to the directors on whether the firm is suitable for purchase.

The draft report will be considered by the partner dealing with Caledonian Ltd and will form the basis of the report which will be sent to the directors of the company.

FURTHER SOURCES OF INFORMATION

Frank Wood's Book-keeping & Accounts, 3rd edn, Pitman Publishing, 1992. ISBN: 0 273 03770 6

Book-keeping Made Simple, G Whitehead, Heinemann, 1987. ISBN: 0 434 98484 1

Frank Wood's Business Accounting AAT Student's Workbook, Sheila I Robinson, Pitman Publishing, 1993. ISBN: 0 273 60188 1

Book-keeping & Accounting, G Whitehead, Pitman Publishing, 1991. ISBN: 0 273 03516 9

Commerce, D T Williams (revised by M Pincott), Pitman Publishing, 1985. ISBN: 0 273 03279 8

Business of Banking, D Wright and W Valentine, 2nd edn, Northcote House Publishers Ltd, 1988. ISBN: 0 7463 0535 4

Finance for BTEC National, J Hopkins, Pitman Publishing, 1988. ISBN 0 273 02877 4

UNIT

8

BUSINESS PLANNING

Element 8.1
Prepare work and collect data for a business plan

Element 8.2
Produce and present a business plan

Element 8.3
Plan for employment or self-employment

PERFORMANCE CRITERIA AND RANGE

Element 8.1: Prepare work and collect data for a business plan

PERFORMANCE CRITERIA

A student must: *page*

1 explain the **purposes of a business plan** 717–24
2 identify the **business objectives** and collect **supporting information** for the business activity for which a plan is to be prepared 725–6
3 identify the **legal and insurance implications** of the business objectives 726–8
4 discuss the feasibility of proposals with others 732–4
5 estimate **resource requirements** to design, produce, promote and sell the goods or service 729–30
6 produce a flowchart illustrating estimated **time-scales** 730–2
7 identify **potential support** for the plan 732–4
8 prepare an action plan identifying actions to be taken to finalise the business plan for presentation 732–4

RANGE

Purposes of a business plan: to seek sources of finance, to gain finance, to monitor progress
Business objectives: to make a profit, to break-even, to be subsidised; to make goods, to provide services
Supporting information: competing products, demand for the product, estimated number of customers, likelihood of repeat business, likely volume of sales, possible value of turnover, possible profit
Legal and insurance implications: employment law, health and safety regulations, environmental regulations, Trades Descriptions Act; age limits
Resource requirements: human (own skills, others' skills), physical (materials, equipment), financial (capital requirements)
Time-scales for: planning, production, marketing, selling, distribution; lead time to break-even
Potential support: own organisation, other organisations; specialists (financial, legal, marketing, production)

EVIDENCE INDICATORS

A first draft business plan outlining the goods or services to be provided and relevant supporting marketing and financial information. The draft plan should set out:

- the planned time-scales
- its legal and insurance implications
- first estimates for resource requirements
- possible support for the plan from financial, legal, marketing or production specialists
- action points identifying next steps to complete the business plan.

The draft business plan should be supported by a statement which explains the purpose of producing a business plan.

Element 8.2: Produce and present a business plan

PERFORMANCE CRITERIA

A student must: *page*

1 describe and explain **business objectives** for a business enterprise 717–24
2 outline a **marketing plan** for a business enterprise 735–42
3 outline a **production plan** for a business enterprise 743–6
4 outline the **resource requirements** for marketing and production 746–51
5 produce **financial data and forecasts** to support the business plan 752–8
6 identify monthly profit and loss and balance sheet monitoring and review procedures for the business plan 759–60
7 present and explain business plan to an audience 761–71

RANGE

Business objectives: supply of goods or service, achieve sales volume, achieve sales value, make profit, break-even, meet time scales
Marketing plan: demand for product or service, naming, pricing, packaging, promoting, distributing, merchandising, selling (targets, volume, income, turnover), timing, marketing communications, after-sales support
Production plan: design, product development, production process, production levels, premises, machinery, raw materials, labour, quality assurance, timing
Resource requirements: human, physical, financial, time
Financial data and forecasts: time period, cash flow forecast, start-up balance sheet, projected profit and loss and balance sheet

EVIDENCE INDICATORS

A presentation of a business plan, supported with visual aids, to an individual or group representing a potential sources of finance. The presentation should express clearly the five part plan (as shown below). To support the presentation there should be a question-and-answer session to demonstrate understanding of the marketing, production and financial implications of the plan in greater depth.
A five-part business plan for a small business enterprise, presented on paper or electronically, including:
Part one: Introduction and objectives – explaining the key objectives of the plan
Part two: Marketing – stating how, where and to whom the plan's products or services will be marketed and sold to achieve planned objectives.
Part three: Production – stating production intentions and schedules.
Part four: Resource requirements – stating the resources required for marketing and production.
Part five: Financial data – providing for a given time period cash flow forecast, start-up balance sheet, projected profit and loss and balance sheet, and monthly profit and loss and balance sheet for monitoring and review.

Element 8.3: Plan for employment or self-employment

PERFORMANCE CRITERIA

A student must:	*page*
1 identify and give examples of **types** of employment or self-employment	772–3
2 identify **statutory requirements** for employment or self-employment	774–7
3 identify **sources of information** and collect information for employment or self-employment	778–80, 785
4 identify opportunities for employment or self-employment	780–2
5 analyse and discuss **skills** to support employment or self-employment	783–4
6 propose a **personal plan** for employment or self-employment	786–90

RANGE

Types: paid (private sector, public sector), voluntary; own business (family business, business start-up, government enterprise scheme), partnership, franchise

Statutory requirements: income tax (individuals, small business), Value Added Tax (VAT), National Insurance, pension arrangements, company registration, benefits (for low paid, to people starting a business)

Sources of information: Job Centres, employment/recruitment agencies, media (newspapers, TV, radio), Federation of Self-Employed, Chambers of Commerce, banks, Training and Enterprise Councils (TECs), Department of Trade and Industry (DTI), charitable organisations

Skills: evaluating own strengths and weaknesses, working with others, working independently, planning, time management, setting targets, reviewing progress, decision-making, problem-solving, information seeking and handling, communicating, applying number, using information technology, occupational skills

Personal plan: time-scales (short-term, long-term), statutory considerations, sources of help and support, information needed, actions to be taken

EVIDENCE INDICATORS

A summary of at least three types of employment which should be selected by the student on the basis of their potential interest. For one type of employment a list of opportunities with relevant sources of information and statutory requirements.

A record of a discussion which analyses personal strengths and weaknesses in relation to skills for their selected employment or self-employment opportunities.

A personal plan in four sections which propose:

- time needed for the student to realise employment or self-employment intentions
- information needed, including sources
- actions to be taken for the student to become employed or self-employed
- statutory requirements for identified employment or self-employment opportunities.

INTRODUCTION

Unit 8 enables students to use a great deal of the knowledge and skills gained from studying Units 1–7: the economic environment, business administration and systems, marketing, employment law, financial procedures and monitoring techniques etc.

In particular, Unit 8 provides an overview of the role of planning in business – from corporate to start-up planning levels. It is practically based, since Unit 8 requires students to produce a draft business plan, then a five-part business plan for a small business enterprise and lastly, a survey of employment opportunities geared to an individual student's inclinations, a discussion of personal skills, and a personal plan aimed at actions to be taken to secure potential employment – either as an employee or self-employed person.

Unit 8 covers the aims and purposes of business plans, their component parts, including legal and insurance aspects, resource needs, and support required to implement a business plan. It further examines the marketing and production aspects of a business plan, as well as the vital part played in financial forecasting and operational monitoring.

This Unit finally examines the knowledge and skills needed to enable a student to secure employment and provides an opportunity to produce a considered personal employment plan.

Unit overview: business planning at the corporate level

■ Mission statements and company goals

Over-arching all business planning functions in an organisation is its mission statement. Effective mission statements express simply and briefly what the organisation has been set up to achieve. Many organisations include a set of company goals with their mission statement as a means of supplying more detail to explain their mission. Such goals aim to be ongoing and act as markers for all staff as they work – in daily or yearly cycles – towards achieving the organisation's mission.

In his well-known set of guidelines, '*Up The Organisation*', Robert Townsend refers to one of the goals which Avis, the USA car-rental company, set itself when he was running it:

> 'We want to become the fastest-growing company with the highest profit margins in the business of renting and leasing vehicles without drivers.'

Townsend goes on to stress the importance of defining goals which force all employees to concentrate on the crucial and central activities of the organisation. In the case of Avis, the definition emphasises growth and profits. It also cuts out involvement in any activities not associated with the car rental/leasing business. Avis at the time owned sightseeing and chauffeur-driven limousine hire companies; and it vetoes the future purchase of companies operating outside the given remit.

Today many North American (and European) companies devise mission statements which set out their essential reasons for being what they are and doing what they do. References to such statements are frequently published in their annual reports, public relations literature and in-house bulletins in order to engrave them upon the minds of customers, staff and the public at large.

A typical mission statement for a public limited company might look like this:

NATIONAL COURIERS (UK) PLC

MISSION STATEMENT
JANUARY 1994

- The company aims to provide a fast, reliable national courier service which keeps its delivery promises, no matter what.
- National Couriers is fully committed to the concept and processes of Total Quality Management and is continually seeking to improve the quality of its operations by putting its customers first.
- A commitment has been made to doubling sales turnover in the next five years – thus rendering the company 'Number One' in the UK courier business while maintaining existing net profit ratios.
- The company genuinely believes that its employees are its most precious resource and is committed as an equal opportunities employer to their personal and career development.
- National Courier appreciates the importance of the environment to the communities around its depots and centres and strongly supports the work of its Community Liaison Groups with local residents.

As the above example illustrates, mission statements seek to provide all-embracing statements of purpose and intent which are meant to stand the test of time. However, good mission statements avoid lapsing into worthy, over-general, abstract ideas. One of the best – of an organisation making and distributing parts to manufacturers is:

'Just In Time – With Us, Not Just A Concept!'

This statement became a painted slogan on the company's fleet of lorries and obliged all involved to ensure that delivery schedules were kept to – so as to avoid becoming a laughing-stock, hoist with their own petard.

National Courier makes the same commitment to customer service and then details its expansion plans – not to increase profit ratios, but to dominate the UK market by doubling sales turnover within five years. Notice also that National Courier takes pains to ensure that its role as a caring employer is given a high profile – both inside and outside the organisation. Lastly, in an era of environmental concern, NC emphasises its commitment to maintaining good relations with the communities around its distribution depots and garages.

In a nutshell – taking only some 135 words – National Courier's mission statement manages to encompass:

- **Its commitment to delivering on time, as promised.**
- **The importance attached to the reliability and quality of its operations.**
- **That it is a customer-oriented company.**
- **That it intends to be UK number one within 5 years.**
- **That profits (and shareholders' dividends) will be maintained.**
- **That it cares about the development of its staff and espouses equal opportunities.**
- **That it is environmentally and local-community conscious.**

As a result, National Courier staff – from directors to drivers – will be able to interpret correctly and carry out the detailed objectives and plans which senior management will tease out of the mission statement and cascade as weekly, monthly and annual targets for achieving.

The components of strategic planning

The directors and senior managers who inhabit the top-most tier of the organisational pyramid spend a great deal of their time in planning the future directions and activities of the company.

The plan they devise and update on an annual, rolling basis is called a strategic plan, since it is concerned with events and operations some three to five years into the future, which will affect and involve all the company's resources. For this reason such plans are sometimes called corporate plans, as they embrace the whole body of the organisation.

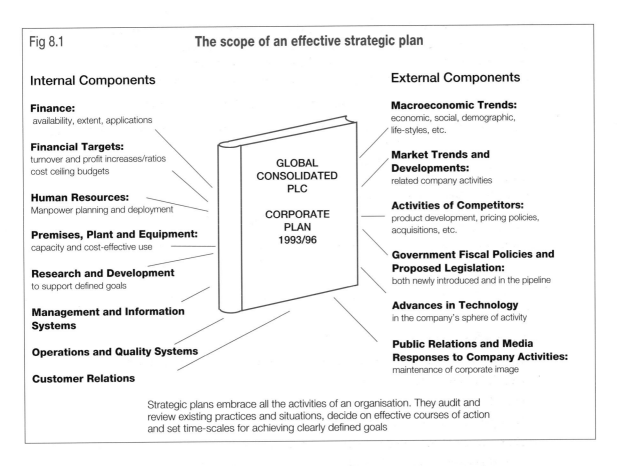

Fig 8.1 **The scope of an effective strategic plan**

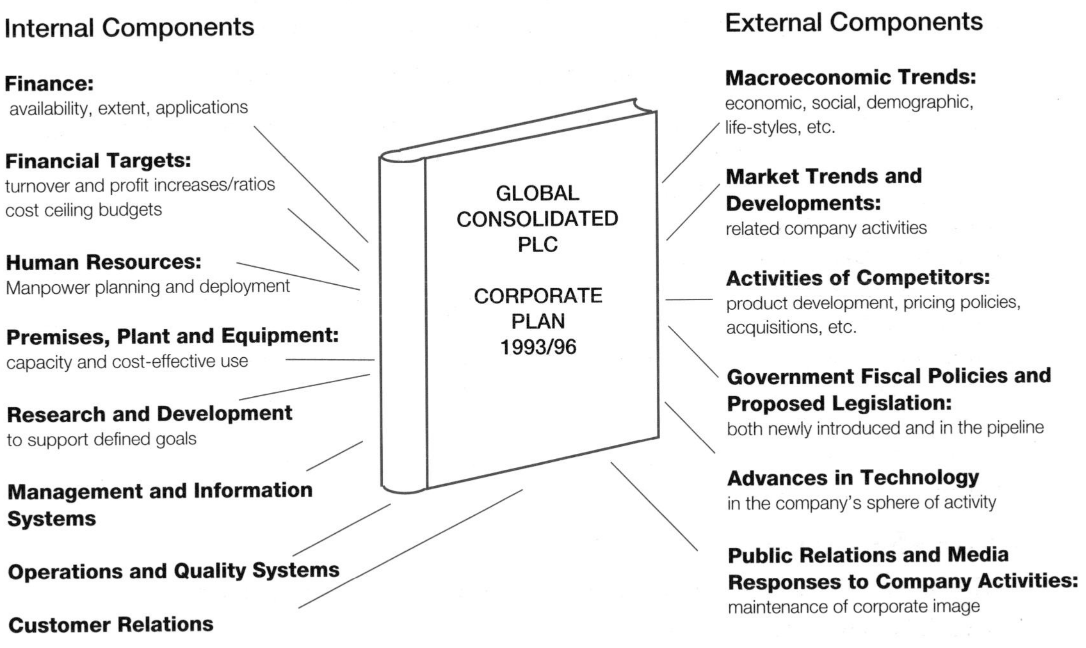
Internal Components
Finance:
availability, extent, applications
Financial Targets:
turnover and profit increases/ratios
cost ceiling budgets
Human Resources:
Manpower planning and deployment
Premises, Plant and Equipment:
capacity and cost-effective use
Research and Development
to support defined goals
Management and Information Systems
Operations and Quality Systems
Customer Relations
GLOBAL CONSOLIDATED PLC
CORPORATE PLAN 1993/96
External Components
Macroeconomic Trends:
economic, social, demographic, life-styles, etc.
Market Trends and Developments:
related company activities
Activities of Competitors:
product development, pricing policies, acquisitions, etc.
Government Fiscal Policies and Proposed Legislation:
both newly introduced and in the pipeline
Advances in Technology
in the company's sphere of activity
Public Relations and Media Responses to Company Activities:
maintenance of corporate image

Strategic plans embrace all the activities of an organisation. They audit and review existing practices and situations, decide on effective courses of action and set time-scales for achieving clearly defined goals

Fig 8.2 **Scope and time-scale of principal business plans**

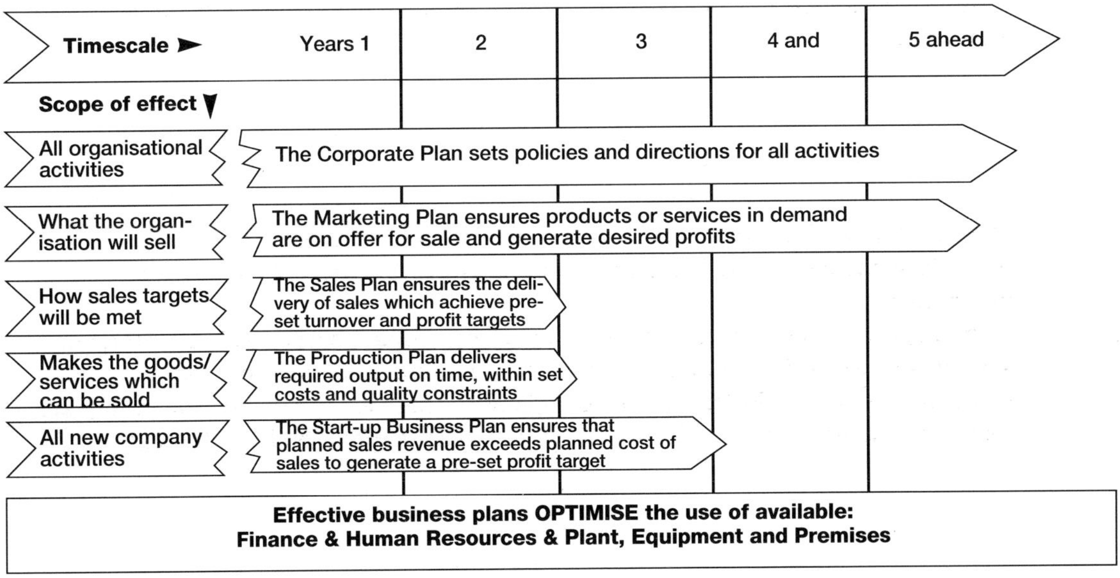
Timescale
Years 1
2
3
4 and
5 ahead
Scope of effect
All organisational activities
The Corporate Plan sets policies and directions for all activities
What the organisation will sell
The Marketing Plan ensures products or services in demand are on offer for sale and generate desired profits
How sales targets will be met
The Sales Plan ensures the delivery of sales which achieve pre-set turnover and profit targets
Makes the goods/services which can be sold
The Production Plan delivers required output on time, within set costs and quality constraints
All new company activities
The Start-up Business Plan ensures that planned sales revenue exceeds planned cost of sales to generate a pre-set profit target
Effective business plans OPTIMISE the use of available:
Finance & Human Resources & Plant, Equipment and Premises

CHECKLIST OF A STRATEGIC PLAN'S COMPONENTS

The following checklist illustrates the principal components which will be included in a business company's strategic planning:

Elements within the organisation

Finance – its likely availability and extent; its planned uses expressed as estimates and forecasts and its distribution within the organisation.

This section will also make a commitment to profit targets – either in pounds sterling or as a percentage of turnover and will set sales targets together with ceiling expenses budgets for company cost-centres.

Human resources – a review of the age, skills, experience and deployment of the company's employees; a forecast of what particular skills and experience will be needed where, in order to achieve the plan's goals and targets; the creation of staff development plans to meet future operational needs.

Premises, plant and equipment – the ability of existing buildings and equipment to meet the future needs of the organisation, and thus the need to plan for constructing, say, a new factory, re-tooling a production-line, or replacing obsolescent computer networks etc.

Research and development – the ability of the organisation's R&D arm to provide the kind of products or services which the company wishes to market in the future, and the possible need to diversify, invest more extensively in R&D or to slim out a product range etc.

Purchasing policies – the need to review the cost-effectiveness of buying-in arrangements and the review of existing suppliers and their terms.

Management and information systems – the ability of existing management structures, methods and communication systems to meet future demands, in say, a period of rapid expansion, relocation or company restructuring; the impact of new office information technology on existing practices and procedures.

Operations – a review of existing business operations – product range, manufacturing techniques, or services; factory/office/distribution/sales administration, customer and technical services etc. in order to reshape them so as to meet future needs.

Quality systems – a review of the standards being achieved and the next steps to be taken towards, say, achieving a total quality management system or 'just in time' production with 'zero defects' etc.

Customer relations – an audit of the extent and nature of customer complaints and the means of their elimination.

The development of policies to improve and develop good customer services in pre- and post-sales phases.

External factors affecting the organisation

Macro-economic trends in the Company's field of activity – surveys and analyses of social, demographic, business-cycle and consumer/industrial activities and future trends which will impinge on the future operations of the company both in national and international contexts.

Markets and market research – analyses and evaluations of current and future behaviour in the company's markets, and from this decisions as to the necessary future markets the company should plan either to develop further or to enter, and from this a detailed analysis of the segments and niches to be targeted

Activities of competitors - a detailed survey of the current and likely future activities and developments to be expected from the competition, and from this the development of strategies for forestalling them with counteractions and developments

Developments in Government Legislation – an examination of current and planned UK laws, regulations and EC directives and their likely impact on the company's activities.

Technological advances – an examination of those technologies related to the activities of the company and how likely future innovations will impact upon the company.

Public relations and environmental factors – a consideration of how future company activities are likely to be regarded by the public and the media and what steps need to be taken to ensure the continuance of 'a good press' and a respected corporate image.

A GOOD STRATEGIC PLAN

- **audits the current situation inside and outside the Company**
- **identifies key trends and opportunities**
- **and makes clear-cut decisions for action**

THE PLANNING PROCESS – FROM MACRO TO MICRO

The applications of the disciplines and skills needed to produce effective business plans are many and varied in the world of business. The following table illustrates some of the most frequently employed:

- **The corporate or strategic plan:** Larger organisations produce 3–5 year forward-rolling plans which frame policy and embrace all aspects of business activity; from the corporate plan's guidelines, shorter-term tactical and operational plans – in divisions, departments and sections are devised.
- **The marketing plan:** The marketing plan forms part of the total strategic plan and plots the future directions of the enterprise in terms of what products or services it will develop and sell – and by what means; the plan extends some 2-5 years into the future, depending upon the nature of the business; accurate interpretation of market trends and purchasing habits forms an essential part of the plan, along with timely and well-judged product development.
- **The sales plan:** Once the marketing plan is in place, the sales department produces a sales plan the aim of which is to secure the overall sales needed to generate the levels and volume of turnover and arising profit stipulated in the corporate plan and given direction by the marketing plan. In national companies, such a sales plan will be methodically broken down by region, district and branch or outlet, thus sub-dividing sales targets to be achieved and sales expenses not to be exceeded.
- **The production plan:** Manufacturing companies need to plan and synchronise their production of goods to match closely what has been ordered by regular customers, or what will directly be sold on. Just-in-time production management techniques ensure that precious capital is not tied up in materials waiting to be processed or in finished goods languishing in adjacent warehouses. Production planning also aims to minimise waste and defective products, secure the most cost-effective operating periods and systems and integrate essential plant maintenance with production as smoothly as possible.
- **Project planning** In all kinds of organisation and at all levels of activity, teams of staff are continually working on projects which are undertaken in the process of meeting the organisation's goals and objectives. Effective project planning requires a logical and methodical approach in which key activities are identified and set into the most practical and least time-consuming chronological sequence.

DISCUSSION TOPICS

1 Is it worth a small business's owners devising a mission statement, or would this be 'O.T.T'?

2 How helpful is a knowledge of strategic planning to a business start-up entrepreneur?

3 What do **you** consider to be the most important areas of business planning?

4 Given the endless stream of unexpected and unanticipated events in any business, is planning a waste of time and energy? Or can the unexpected be planned for?

5 Are mission statements merely 'window-dressing waffle', or do they make a genuine and important contribution to corporate communication?

6 Why bother to paint 'Just-in-time – with us, not just a concept!' on the side of an articulated lorry?

■ Typical business goals

- To expand the business by x per cent in y years
- To increase net profit by x per cent in the next trading year
- To increase market share by x per cent per year over a fixed period until the company becomes the market leader with a dominant hold on the market (short of arousing the interest of the Monopoly and Mergers Commission)
- To cut operating costs by x per cent in the next trading year
- To acquire x number of additional factories, branches, shops etc. over the coming y years by purchase of existing firms in order to grow and establish a regional or national coverage
- To move into the export market and develop turnover of £x in y years
- To become 'green' and secure an improved corporate image among customers and general public
- To 'give something back' by developing community service roles and commitments
- To move consciously into another economic sector so as to develop the company and improve its long-term profitability
- To make a significant increase in research and development investment in order to 'stay in the game' *and so on*

REVIEW TEST

1 Explain briefly what a mission statement is, and why an organisation needs one.

2 What is a corporate plan? Explain what it covers and why it is drawn up by a business organisation.

3 List five areas which you would expect to find included in a corporate plan.

4 In terms of business planning, explain the difference between a strategic and a tactical plan.

5 List four different kinds of plan which would be devised in the course of a year in a large private sector organisation.

Element 8.1
PREPARE WORK AND COLLECT DATA FOR A BUSINESS PLAN

In today's business world the practice of planning – whether for starting up a new business, expanding into a new market or directing the overall development of a large company – has become far more sophisticated than it was some 5–10 years ago. PC 8.1.1 8.2.1

For example, in the boom period of the mid-1980s, when finance was readily available to any would-be entrepreneur, many sole trader businesses were set up on 'a wing and a prayer' by small traders, whose success or failure were governed more by 'gut-feeling' intuition than by the assembly of key factual and numerical data. Moreover the majority of clearing banks were far more 'laid back' when vetting new business proposals and plans than they are in the much harder business world of today.

■ 'Start right, stay right!' – why planning is an essential business tool

PC 8.1.1 8.2.1

Many would-be successful small traders fail early on because of basic shortcomings in their start-up strategies. They make fatal basic errors like these:

- under-valuing the expertise and know-how needed in the selected business field
- over-estimating the size of the market to be traded in
- exaggerating the size of the market share they will win
- selecting a poor location from which to trade
- mistaking the extent of the profit margins to be secured in highly competitive markets
- under-estimating the challenge represented by established and experienced competitors
- failing to respond in time to significant shifts in market trends and patterns of demand
- failing to start with and to maintain sufficient financial reserves to enable a 'bad trading patch' to be survived
- failing to monitor closely monthly income and expenditure in a detailed cash-flow forecast

Faced with such a developed and sophisticated market-place, expert and detailed business planning forms a vital activity for every starting-out small trader and established business wishing to expand and consolidate its position. In today's competitive business world, no trader is too small to ignore these central planks of his or her business

- **an in-depth knowledge of the chosen market and its customers**
- **a continuous monitoring of the business's financial status**

- **a rolling forward business plan which 'sets the course' for the business and steers it through storm and fair weather alike.**

Acquiring and updating such vital information may be laborious, but 'you can't beat knowing', and having ready access to extensive statistical and factual data from which to devise sound future action plans.

PC
8.1.1
8.2.1

KEY FACTORS IN EFFECTIVE BUSINESS PLANNING

Whatever the sector of the economy a business occupies, and notwithstanding whether it supplies goods or services to meet defined needs or wants, it must address a common set of questions when starting to frame a business plan:

- What business do we *want* to be in?
- What business *were* we in, and *are* we in at present?
- Who are our customers? Who will they be?
- What is it – precisely – that they want now? And what are they likely to want in the future?
- How much of what is wanted can we sell in any given trading period ?
- What will be our cost of sales – both in the short and longer terms ?
- Will the sales we achieve generate profit levels sufficient to enable us to pay out adequate dividends (or directors' remunerations) and to re-invest in plant, stock and other renewals?
- Can we beat our competitors in our chosen market(s) and either increase or maintain our market share?
- Do we possess the financial, physical and human resources needed to deliver the business plan we are devising?

PC
8.1.1
8.2.1

Fig 8.3 **The eight-stage start-up business plan**

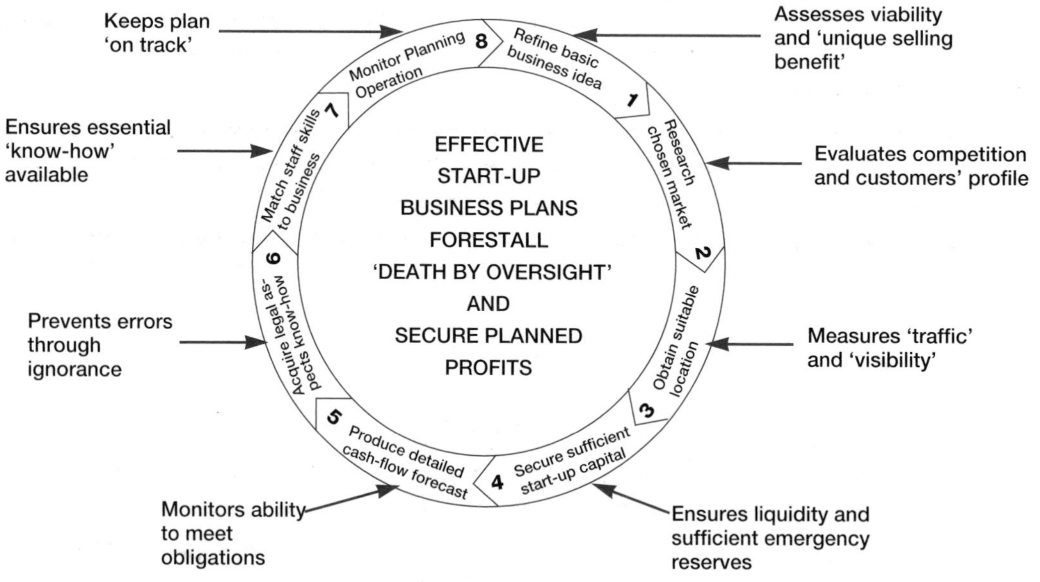
Keeps plan 'on track'
Assesses viability and 'unique selling benefit'
Ensures essential 'know-how' available
Evaluates competition and customers' profile
Prevents errors through ignorance
Measures 'traffic' and 'visibility'
Monitors ability to meet obligations
Ensures liquidity and sufficient emergency reserves
1 Refine basic business idea
2 Research chosen market
3 Obtain suitable location
4 Secure sufficient start-up capital
5 Produce detailed cash-flow forecast
6 Acquire legal aspects know-how
7 Match staff skills to business
8 Monitor Planning Operation
EFFECTIVE START-UP BUSINESS PLANS FORESTALL 'DEATH BY OVERSIGHT' AND SECURE PLANNED PROFITS

Devising a draft start-up business plan

PC 8.1.2

No business plan is more important than the start-up business plan. A good plan will result, ultimately in the evolution of a Marks & Spencer or Boots plc, but a poor one will quickly dispatch its creator into the massed ranks of the would-be but failed entrepreneurs.

There are eight main components of an effective start-up business plan:

PC 8.1.2

KEY COMPONENTS OF AN EFFECTIVE START-UP BUSINESS PLAN

- **A basic business idea** – which is imaginative, realistic, viable and achievable.
- **Thorough market research** – which supplies accurate and up-to-date information about the market to be targeted.
- **An affordable but attractive location** – whether the business is to be in manufacturing, distribution or the service industry sector; where it makes, sells or works from is a vital ingredient in its eventual success.
- **Sufficient, available start-up capital** – most new companies which fail do so because they ran out of money prematurely – often as a result of underestimating the extent of the finance required.
- **Careful and detailed financial forward planning** – both the cash-flow forecast and operating budget are highly dependent upon prudent financial estimates and detailed monitoring of income and expenditure on a regular basis.
- **A clear understanding of the legal obligations involved in setting up a business** – both sole traders and small business employers accept extensive legal obligations when setting up a business involving company, employment, health and safety and trading law; and ignorance of the law is never an excuse when things go wrong!
- **A realistic evaluation of the skills and abilities of the people to work in the business** – if there is a mismatch between the expertise needed to run the business and the level of that which is available, the enterprise may well fail while its owners are 'learning by experience', and there are usually few second chances.
- **Ongoing monitoring of the plan in action** – it is essential that sufficient time is given to monitoring 'actual' performance against 'planned' targets and estimates; in a young business there is little margin for error and limited financial reserves to call upon.

■ The purposes of a draft business plan

PC 8.1.2

Most draft business plans have two main aims:

1 To provide a briefing paper when seeking a loan from a bank or other lender, which outlines the plan's key features and approaches.

2 To act as a thinking discipline, where creative business ideas may be transformed into realistic and achievable objectives, given the extent of available start-up resources.

A fully-developed business plan (see Element 8.2) will also provide a mechanism for monitoring the performance of a business in its crucial first trading year.

Note that most lending banks today expect business entrepreneurs to produce detailed start-up business plans, and most provide pro formas and guidelines in booklet form to assist this all important process. Such booklets aid the planner in clarifying the extent of likely start-up capital, working out likely operational costs – including the servicing of any loan, and thus the earliest likely break-even date, and then the levels of anticipated profit month-on-month.

PC 8.1.2

■ From basic business idea to the plan's key objectives

It is one thing to come up with a sizzler of a basic business idea, but quite another to transform it into a realistic draft business plan. In order to do so, careful and hard-nosed rational thinking needs to be given to what, in precise terms, the key objectives of the business are to be.

The key objectives of a business plan will vary according to the needs and expectations of its devisers. A young married couple with children will need their new business to generate profits pretty quickly, whereas a retired, successful business person may wish to start up a business as an interest and, with a 'back-stop' pension, may well afford to be able to wait much longer for profits to arrive, and may settle for a more modest profit level.

Thus key objectives may be identified by asking questions like these:

- Is the business solely intended to provide a comfortable income for, say, a husband and wife or two-partner team for the foreseeable future?
- Is the core business objective for the business to expand, where 'the sky's the limit'?
- Will the business be restricted to a single outlet in a local shopping or industrial area?
- How many employees are envisaged in the business – by the end of Year One, in five years time?
- Are the business owners content to take little if any drawings in the business's early years, in order to plough profits into expansion? Or is a good income needed as quickly as possible?

Other, more detailed business objectives will seek to determine:

- the number and type of targeted customers
- the range of products or services to be sold
- the corporate image to be transmitted etc.

PC 8.1.3

■ Legal and insurance aspects

Legal implications

A key part of the early business planning process is to obtain an informed appreciation of the current national – and local – legal implications which will impact upon the business idea.

For example, it is extremely unlikely that a county council planning department will give authorisation to an application for change of use of business premises if someone wanted to convert a village shop and post office in an area of 'outstanding natural beauty' into a fast-food take-away!

The following checklist provides illustrations of the typical legal considerations which a business start-up entrepreneur would need to take into account:

Business premises

What are the current planning consents and authorised uses to which the premises may be put? Are there any restrictions in local county council planning by-laws or covenants in a leasehold agreement which the entrepreneur would have to abide by? Are there any parking restrictions, one-way traffic systems – or *proposed* changes in traffic routing which might affect the value to the entrepreneur of the proposed site for trading?

Health and safety at work

Do the premises under consideration meet HASAW requirements in terms of lavatories, rest-room and personal space requirements, along with safe walkways, general structures and electrical wiring etc? Would it be prudent to have a surveyor's structural report commissioned?

Fire and emergency evacuation requirements

Do the premises meet current fire and emergency evacuation requirements – in many instances a current fire safety certificate will be needed, issued by the county council Fire Brigade Office after a site inspection.

Proposed product or service range

Do the products which will be taken into stock conform to UK Weights & Measures, Trading Standards Office and Environmental Health Office requirements? Especial care is needed, for example, in vetting imported toys from Third World manufacturers, or garments from any foreign (or UK) supplier source so as to ensure they meet legal safety standards. Where services are concerned, can the legal requirements required of, for example, financial services, estate agency, chiropractice, or rest/nursing homes etc. be met?

Environmental protection

Is there any likelihood that the proposed business will fall foul of any environment protection laws ? For example, will outflow from a proposed manufacturing process into a river or stream cause pollution, or will work processes, such as the fitting and testing of car alarms, cause noise pollution?

Advertising and Sales Promotion

While detailed planning in this area will be done when drawing up a later marketing plan, it is important to consider – at the outset – whether any problems are likely to arise from Trade Descriptions, Sale of Goods or Consumer Credit Acts etc. relating to how products or services will be advertised and offered for sale.

Employment law

If employees are to be taken on, it is essential for prospective employers to be fully aware of their legal obligations well in advance for providing:

Employee accidental injury/ death insurance
National Insurance contributions
HASAW safety, clothing, hygiene and rest-room requirements
Contracts and conditions of service details etc.

Public, third party liability (see below)

Legal requirements must also be complied with in order to ensure that any person visiting or shopping in business premises (or liable to be injured by any falling masonry or fixture on the outside pavement etc.) is insured against any arising claim for injury or death.

Insurance implications

As the above listing illustrates, legal and insurance requirements often merge. The following listing indicates some major additional considerations:

Insurance of business premises

If premises are to be purchased freehold, the bank or building society providing any mortgage will insist that the premises be insured at least to the level of the loan in case of fire, flood or accidental damage etc. If they are to be purchased leasehold, the lessor will invariably include in the lease tightly written stipulations about structural and other building related insurances which the lessee will have to pay for.

Product liability

Similarly, it is prudent for business people to take out third party liability insurance in case a sold good causes injury or death through a defect in its manufacture and the aggrieved parties sue both manufacturer and retailer.

Vehicle insurances

It almost goes without saying that all motor-vehicles must be insured in line with the business in which they are used – whether heavy goods vehicle, light van, courier motor-cycle etc.

Private health insurance

An area of business insurance often overlooked, but essential for the small business entrepreneur is personal health insurance which also provides an income (or a lump sum in case the business fails) if he or she becomes ill and therefore unable to direct daily business operations over an extended period.

You would be forgiven for concluding that the above listings of both legal and insurance obligations might daunt the most enthusiastic would-be business person.

And indeed, one of the down-sides of current business management lies in the heavy burden imposed on business entrepreneurs by the requirements of our contemporary society. Given such a burden, not to mention the risk of losing all the invested venture capital, you might also come to appreciate the justification which such business people offer for obtaining a fair – or even handsome – profit from their business labours!

Resourcing the business plan

The obvious resources required to 'fuel' any business plan are:

- money
- human
- physical
- entrepreneurial 'get-up-and go'.

The money resource

In other words, a successful business plan needs to consider how much finance will be needed – to acquire premises, to install fixtures, fittings and equipment or plant, to pay employees, to advertise, to purchase stock or raw materials and so on. Finance will also be needed to pay for services, telephone bills, transport, packaging, stationery and a host of other operational necessities.

The human resource

The people dimension of the enterprise needs careful thought in terms of the expertise, determination, stickability and cheerfulness they will bring to it. Crucial in this regard is the business nous or flair of its owners or directors, since many businesses fail because newcomers under-estimated the trading know-how of established competitors, say in the antiques or catering markets. Also, employees cost money to appoint and to retain!

The physical resource

One wise commercial estate agent affirmed that, in his view, a retail business's success could be put down to three simple factors: '*Location, location, location!*' Certainly where a retail business elects to trade and in what kind of premises is crucial to its ability to attract customers. Indeed, some chain-store estate managers will count the volume of shoppers walking along a high street (on either side) and past a potential acquisition as part of a decision-making process. Factors when evaluating physical resources (including fixtures, fittings, plant and equipment etc.) are:

- whether to purchase outright, to lease or to rent
- whether opportunities exist to expand within premises
- maintenance and insurance costs
- the likelihood of obtaining planning permissions for change of use
- suitability for the proposed business venture.

Note also that the sellers of existing businesses tend to over-value the worth of the physical resources they include in a sales package when disposing of commercial premises, and that wise prospective purchasers of physical resources pay the cost of expert surveys and valuations, which are almost always worth the expenditure in terms of the expert feedback they provide, which can inform a reduced purchase offer.

The entrepreneurial resource

Though difficult to quantify or measure, this resource is ultimately the most important, since it supports all the decisions to be made when starting up a business. Being self-employed can certainly be most enjoyable in terms of the freedom it brings, the personal ability to make the big decisions and the sense of achievement stemming from a successful deal etc. However, there is no assured payroll cheque or direct credit awaiting the self-employed business person at the end of each week or month. So business proprietors need to possess or develop quickly a bottomless reservoir of optimism, lateral thinking, street-wise opportunism as well as endless determination. They must also be willing to take calculated risks: *'Nothing ventured, nothing gained!'* is the timeless motto of business entrepreneurs.

As the above section illustrates, effective resource planning forms a mix of handling factual quantities: amounts of money, periods of time or square metres of space etc. But it also requires the making of wise value judgements – about people's abilities and potential to grow, and about degrees of risk.

PC 8.1.6

■ Time-scales and the business plan

Getting the timing right is central to the successful delivery of any plan, and is particularly important in business planning. So also is the sequence in which individual activities are carried out – as by now you must be well aware, having undertaken many activities in the pursuit of your GNVQ award!

A number of useful techniques exist, to help project planners to manage effectively a complex series of interacting operations or activities, notable among which is the Gantt chart, which is also helpful in business planning.

The Gantt chart

This chart provides a simple yet highly effective means of displaying visually the necessary sequence of events which needs to be followed in order to complete a project on time and without incurring the costs of wasted effort. The example in Fig. 8.4 illustrates the use of a Gantt chart in constructing a garage.

Using a Gantt chart like the one illustrated obliges the planner to consider carefully:

- The sequence in which tasks have to be undertaken.
- What preparatory and/or assembly work can be carried out to save time, prior to installation.
- Where bottle-necks and delays may occur if deadlines are not met – where, say, electrical installation cannot start until the floor, walls and roof have been constructed.

Note that the Gantt chart also shows areas where a start can be made before another phase has been entirely completed.

Fig 8.4 **Gantt chart for planning construction of a garage**

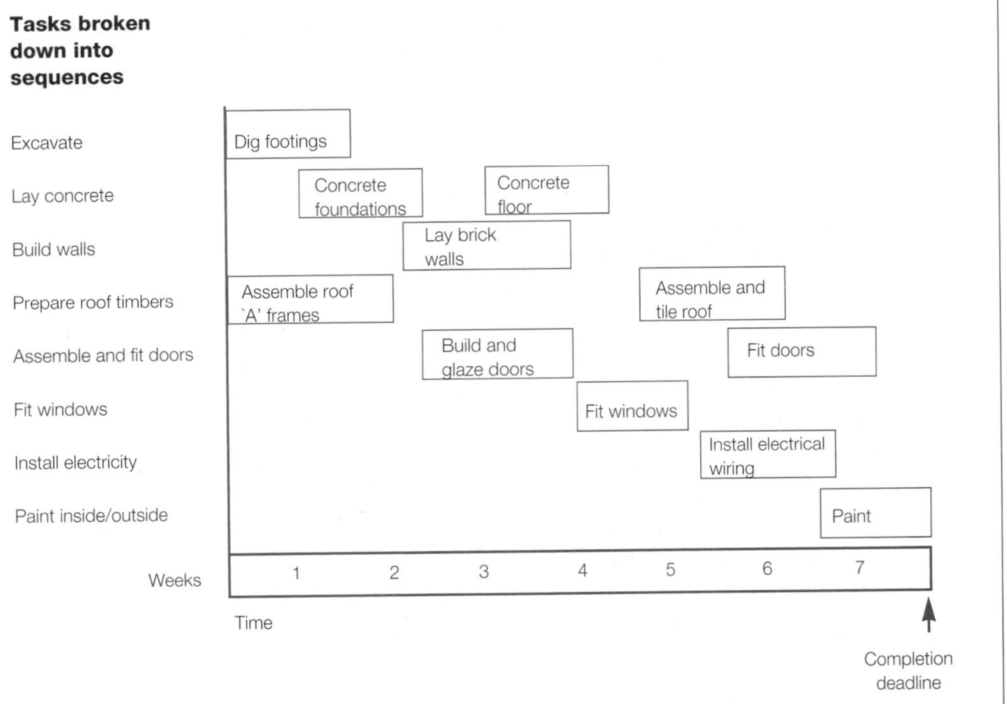
Tasks broken down into sequences
Excavate
Lay concrete
Build walls
Prepare roof timbers
Assemble and fit doors
Fit windows
Install electricity
Paint inside/outside
Dig footings
Concrete foundations
Concrete floor
Lay brick walls
Assemble roof 'A' frames
Assemble and tile roof
Build and glaze doors
Fit doors
Fit windows
Install electrical wiring
Paint
Weeks
1
2
3
4
5
6
7
Time
Completion deadline

A particularly useful feature of the Gantt chart is its see-at-a-glance visual appeal. Bottlenecks or wrongly sequenced steps are quickly noticed and changes made. Another tool in planning a series of inter-related steps is that of Project Evaluation and Review Technique (PERT). This technique is used a great deal in project planning by managers, and establishes networks or pathways throughout the successive phases of a project, indicating which activities are primary and which secondary, and which dependent upon the completion of others etc. In this way, PERT network designs reveal a *critical path*, which is the master route or sequence of the key activities.

A simpler form of such a planning approach is to employ a flow-chart which indicates the key stages of the project in a chronological or prioritised sequence.

Thus in meeting time deadlines, it is important to:

- set a realistic goal – say for the opening day of a business
- work out a set of steps or phases (working backwards from the opening day) which follow a chronological sequence – e.g. fit shop and erect shelves before taking delivery of stock
- allow time for slippages and let-downs and to catch up on missed target dates etc.
- focus on key aspects – obtaining finance, acquiring premises, hiring staff, launching start-up sales campaign etc.
- design an easy-to-read chart on which to monitor the completion of each phase of the plan.

PC 8.1.7

■ Obtaining support for the plan

Few people work well in isolation, and the old adage, *Two heads are better than one* remains true. Just as marketing managers arrange for new products to be field-tested, so an effective planner should arrange for the plan to be 'bounced off' the brains and experience of experts in order to secure feedback, possible improvements or alternatives.

The most useful advice to be sought is likely to be from specialists in:

- Financial resourcing
- Small business law
- Marketing/advertising and sales promotion
- Employment
- Premises management etc.

Such advisers are most likely to be found among: relations, family friends, tutors, local bank managers and TEC executives, youth leaders and personal contacts etc.

PC 8.1.1 8.1.2 8.1.3 8.1.5

DISCUSSION TOPICS

1 Given the associated costs of taking on an employee, what monitoring activities could be introduced to evaluate whether he or she is 'paying their way'?

2 What are the pros and cons of buying outright, leasing or renting business premises?

3 What can a self-employed person do to protect himself against loss of earnings, say when falling sick, or in planning for old age?

4 Is entrepreneurial 'get-up-and-go' *really* an important business resource, or just a myth?

5 Can business planning be taken too seriously?

PC 8.1.1 8.1.2 8.1.3 8.1.5 8.1.6 8.1.7

REVIEW TEST

1 What areas would you need to cover in the insurance section of a business plan?

2 Similarly, what legal areas need to be covered?

3 What four key resources would a business plan normally cover?

4 What is a Gantt chart? How can it assist in the production of a business plan?

5 Explain briefly why timing and deadlines are an important feature of a business plan.

6 Who are likely to provide expert advice on a draft business plan? List three types of expert.

PORTFOLIO OF EVIDENCE ACTIVITY

PC
8.1.1
8.1.2
8.1.3
8.1.4
8.1.5
8.1.6
8.1.7
8.1.8

Element 8.1
Prepare work and collect data for a business plan

DRAFT BUSINESS PLAN

Scenario 1

This activity is directly associated with that for Element 8.2, and is based upon the production of a preliminary, first draft business plan which forms the basis for the more detailed and developed business plan required for Element 8.2. The area of research will therefore be the same for both activities.

For this activity, assume that you have decided to open a small business as a means of providing for your living. This will entail you in deciding upon a basic business idea – the form your business is to take, whether in retailing, direct mail, as an office services bureau or as a driving instruction enterprise etc.
This draft plan requires you to outline your central ideas and proposals in a summary plan, which examines these areas:

- a clear explanation of the objectives of the business
- a treatment of the legal and insurance implications
- initial estimates of resource requirements
- details of who would provide support and advice on the plan
- details of its financial, legal, marketing and production* dimensions
- the key next steps and time-scales of the main stages of your plan.

* if you elect to make products

Remember that your plan should be clearly set out and easy to absorb by support contacts.

Scenario 2

You are tasked in this scenario with producing a written commentary or statement which explains why would-be business entrepreneurs produce a business plan (and also with including a section on how a business plan is used in a mature business in terms of an annual trading period).

Task 1

As usual, remember to complete the appropriate part of your planning and review log before beginning the above two activities.

Task 2

Make a thoughtful and considered choice of business idea, and remember that it should be both realistic and realisable in terms of your own expertise and knowledge. Base your plan's data on actual local expenses and charges – say to rent a lock-up shop, or a typical business rate etc.

It is important in this type of activity to rely on *real* factual, researched data as much as possible, rather than guesstimates or imagined costs etc. in order to give your plan credibility and so that you work within the disciplines of the real business world.

A suitable draft business plan is likely to be about 3 sides of printed A4 long, and to make its points succinctly, without 'padding'.

Task 3

The accompanying statement should outline clearly and factually the role and purpose of a business plan, bearing in mind that such plans are used a) to prepare for the start of a new business and b) as a planning tool for an existing business – as drawn up annually by all specialist departments, or arising from a fresh project within the mature business.

Your statement should be between 2 and 3 sides of printed A4.

Performance criteria covered

8.1.1, 8.1.2, 8.1.3, 8.1.4, 8.1.5, 8.1.6, 8.1.7, 8.1.8

Core skills covered

Communication:
3.2.1, 3.2.2, 3.2.3, 3.2.4, 3.2.5, 3.4.1, 3.4.1, 3.4.3, 3.4.4

Information Technology:
3.1.1, 3.1.2, 3.1.3, 3.1.4, 3.1.5, 3.2.1, 3.2.2, 3.2.3, 3.2.4, 3.2.5, 3.2.6, 3.2.7, 3.3.1, 3.3.2, 3.3.3, 3.3.4, 3.3.5, 3.3.6

Application of Number:
3.1.1, 3.1.2, 3.1.3, 3.1.4, 3.1.5, 3.1.6, 3.1.7, 3.2.1, 3.2.2, 3.2.3, 3.2.4, 3.2.6, 3.2.7, 3.2.8, 3.2.9, 3.3.1, 3.3.2, 3.3.3, 3.3.4, 3.3.5

Element 8.2
PRODUCE AND PRESENT A BUSINESS PLAN

The marketing plan

PC 8.2.2

The marketing plan, while an essential tool in coordinating the overall marketing function over a three- to five-year rolling period, should also be regarded as a central part of an organisation's corporate plan.

This is because its main value lies in auditing the strengths and weaknesses of the organisation's past and present situation and, from an informed position, devising detailed policies and strategies for ensuring that appropriate products or services will come on stream – sometimes four or five years into the future. Appropriate in marketing terms means:

Products or services that will:

- take the place of mature and obsolescent lines in the product life cycle
- sell because they meet the expectations of targeted customers and are deemed to be up-to-date and appealing
- capture a targeted market share
- generate levels of gross and net profit specified in the marketing and corporate plans
- ensure the development of the organisation and its survival in a competitive business world

Given the importance of an effective marketing plan to the future of the organisation, it is not surprising that it should be based upon careful research and analysis of 'hard' factual data, rather than the intuitive finger in the air to catch the wind.

Set out below is a chart which lists in chronological order the key stages which are undertaken in producing an effective marketing plan. These stages are as valid for the small, local business as for the globally based multinational.

PC 8.2.2

KEY STAGES IN PRODUCING AN EFFECTIVE MARKETING PLAN

1 Restatement and clarification of the mission

Before embarking upon any collection and analysis of data, it is important that the organisation's mission statement and goals are reviewed. For example, is the company still seeking to win market share at a modest profit, or has the basic strategy changed so that it now wishes to generate profits – say to finance expansion? Such a shift in corporate strategy would fundamentally change the shape and structure of any marketing plan.

2 The internal audit of the strengths and weaknesses of the products/services on offer

An audit to be undertaken early on in the planning period analyses the condition of each product or service which is being offered for sale. Such an audit will examine and evaluate:

- the position of the product in its life-cycle – is it young and thriving, or elderly and waning?
- what is the degree of acceptance for the product? Is it hard or easy to sell ?
- What contribution does it make to company sales revenue and profits? What is its forecast future life and projected contribution to overall sales and profits during the life of the marketing plan? What has it cost and what will it cost to bring to the market? Are these costs acceptable?
- How effective is the organisation's packaging, merchandising, advertising and sales promotion of the product compared with that of principal competitors?

3 The review of product/ service development

All successful enterprises rely on a vigorous and innovative research and development function – to ensure that new products or services are continually being invented, developed and tested as potential new members of the range to be offered for sale. A crucial element, therefore, of the marketing plan is an objective appraisal of the strengths and weaknesses of the products/services under development:

- How do they compare with products/services already being sold and in competitors' pipelines?
- Has test marketing shown that customers will buy the new product/service in sufficient quantities?
- What features does the prototype embody which the sales force will be able to capitalise upon?
- Are enough products/services in development to ensure that smooth transitions will occur as obsolescent ones time out?
- Is R & D matching (and beating!) the efforts of main competitors?

Many established companies go out of business every year through failing to maintain a strong R & D function. They end up with a tired range of products or services which fail to match, say, the technological features of competing ones or fail to meet changed customer expectations.

4 The external audit: researching the market

A particularly important stage in producing a marketing plan is the undertaking of a conscientious and detailed survey of two major – indeed key – influencers upon the business:

the customers
the competition

The market research stage is mainly concerned with checking out:

the customers in a consumer market

- whether the organisation's customers are still made up of the same socio-economic groupings, having regard to age, gender, location, education, spending power etc. if the market is a consumer market – and if not, how the customer base is changing and evolving, and what impact this will have upon aspects like product design, cost, packaging, merchandising in the future; mapping trends in customers' tastes and preferences is crucial to the market research stage.

the customers in an industrial market

- whether changes in manufacturing processing and technological advances are forcing updates and improvements upon product design and working, and what effect, for example, this is likely to have on the pricing structure the organisation devises.
- whether structural changes in the market oblige the organisation to undertake a radical re-think on its marketing strategy; for instance, whether because of the continual erosion of profit margins from selling through wholesalers – such as agrochemical suppliers to farmers – to embark upon a strategy of direct selling and cutting out the middle man.

the competitors: in a consumer market

- whether the organisation's market position is safe, or being threatened by competing firms on the basis of:

  superior products, more competitive pricing strategies, superior advertising, sales promotion and merchandising, more effective (at the time) strategies such as forgoing profit margins by selling premier products cheaply in order to secure significant increases in market share, or by enticing customers by appealing discounts, free gifts or enhanced warranties etc.

the competitors: in an industrial market

- whether the organisation's market position is under threat from the introduction of an innovative and technically superior product
- whether irresistible, supportive financial plans are being offered to manufacturers or distributors to enable them, say, to purchase a new production line or a new fleet of articulated lorries.

In all market research planning, the eventual key factor is:

What do we need to do in order to either:

a ensure we continue to hold our dominant position?

b overcome the threats we have identified in competitors' activities in the market-place?

Summary
The market research stages comprise an external audit and analysis of aspects such as product innovation and design features, pricing strategies, advertising ploys, promotional offers and 'special deals', supportive financial arrangements, product positioning (say of a family saloon car just launched by a competitor) and so on.

5 Auditing the available resources needed to deliver the plan
Sometimes socially ambitious consumers are referred to as having: 'champagne tastes, but beer money!' Similarly, prudent consumers are advised to 'cut their cloth according to their purse'.

In other words, there is little point in devising any marketing plan strategies which cannot be afforded either in terms of:

- the extent of *finance* available to underwrite the plan
- the skills and abilities of the *workforce*
- the capacities and facilities of *existing plant and equipment*

Clearly, in many organisations sufficient reserves of capital may exist to buy in expert personnel, sophisticated new equipment or meet the costs of designing major new products.
Indeed, effective organisations plan for just such eventualities in their corporate plans. However, for a marketing plan to be effective, it must also be realistic. Sometimes compromises need to be made in the light of the resources which can be directed to the plan's delivery.

Thus the marketing plan of a well-managed organisation will maintain continual contact with:

- the manpower planning of the personnel department
- the equipment replacement and renewal policies of production or retail branch management
- the manipulation of funds by the senior accountant so as to provide available capital for research and development of new products and overall support for the marketing function

6 Costing the plan

An old but true production engineering motto is:

'All change costs!'

This could be extended to include – in a marketing plan context: 'All activity, and especially changed activity costs!' Thus any marketing plan worth its salt will include a summarising stage in which all the activities and operations which go to make up the marketing plan are costed in a detailed schedule.

This schedule will include cost projections for existing and new products (or services) of:

- research and development
- production
- distribution/warehousing
- market research and marketing administration
- advertising, sales promotion and merchandising
- sales support: the sales force and sales administration
- customer and after sales services

Some organisations have established formulas which enable marketing staff to calculate *for each product or service* what proportion of the total income it is expected to generate should be written down against items such as those listed above, and what contribution it is expected to make to net profits. Such an approach is also helpful when it comes to formulating a pricing strategy for the product or service.

7 The marketing plan summary

In large organisations, as you will have realised, the marketing plan is usually a lengthy and complex document. It is therefore customary for a summary section to be included – often at the front of the plan – which lists the plan's key points and issues.

This summary helps managers to gauge the overall thrust and direction of the plan before having to take in extensive factual and statistical data.

■ The monitoring function

PC 8.2.2

Clearly, there is little point in expending the time and costs of producing a marketing plan if no one then takes the trouble to set up mechanisms and systems for providing feedback on how the plan is being followed and implemented.

Thus the marketing department will hold regular meetings with colleagues in R & D, production, sales, personnel, accounts etc. in order to check, say, whether products under development will come on stream according to due deadlines or whether sales are generating the projected gross and net profits.

DISCUSSION TOPICS

PC 8.2.2

1 'The problem with producing good marketing plans is that so much of their content is based on estimates, forecasts, projections and futuring.' What types of 'hard information' can you list which would help to make a marketing plan more specific and less speculative?

2 Establishing likely customer buying trends is always a problem. What techniques can you suggest, say, for a retail ladies' fashions boutique?

3 What would you suggest as the major differences of emphasis and approach between an industrial and a consumer marketing plan?

4 Should a marketing plan be produced, separately and in addition to a strategic plan, or not? If so, why?

5 What would you cite as the key components of a marketing plan for a small business?

Key components of a marketing budget

PC 8.2.2

Naturally, no two marketing budgets will be the same. Not only will they vary from industry to industry – manufacturing to retailing – but they will also vary according to the size and age of the business. For instance, a start-up venture may need to spend a far higher proportion of its marketing budget on advertising and sales promotion in order to achieve market penetration and to publicise the trading name, type of business and its locations.

Nevertheless, it is possible to identify a listing of key marketing budget areas which will form components of the whole.

PC 8.2.2

KEY MARKETING BUDGET AREAS

Research & development

No business can exist for long without some investment in the developing of new ideas for products or services, which will be needed to replace obsolescent ones.

Prototype testing and test marketing

A company's board of directors may well decide that testing potential products – in the factory as well as in a limited but representative market – should fall entirely within the marketing budget.

Market research and intelligence

These crucial areas are central to the maintaining and effective marketing function and should therefore be sufficiently funded.

Advertising, packaging and merchandising

All the aspects of bringing a product or service to a potential buyer's attention falls within the marketing budget, which will include estimates for all advertising agency work.

Below-the-line promotional and public relations activities

The 'soft-sell' activities such as sponsorship of musical or sports events, the creation of newsworthy press-releases and allied activities all fall within the marketing budget.

The costs of maintaining a sales force

It depends, where sales are concerned, on whether the directors view sales as an integral part of marketing, or an entirely separate function. If the former, then sales workforce costs and expenses alongside allied staff development about products and market trends etc. will fall within the marketing budget.

Development of marketing staff

Another key element to be funded is the development of individual staff within a comprehensive marketing staff development policy.

Equipment, fixtures and fittings etc.

Needless to say, the marketing plan will include an element to cover acquisition or replacement of work tools, texts, reference journals, office furniture etc.

PC 8.2.2

■ Marketing budget or corporate budget?

In terms of a company's overall corporate budget, the marketing budget component may also include costings and estimates for the relocation of staff and the acquisition and fitting out of premises – if, for example, a retail chainstore group is operating to a policy of expansion, where twenty-five new stores are due to be opened across the UK within a calendar year.

In such instances, it is most likely that the expansion – though planned for by the marketing department – will be funded from a 'development pot', such as a shares rights issue or from retained profits or from a bank loan, rather than from an annual marketing budget, which is usually restricted to paying for the forward planning and daily routines of the department.

■ Financing the marketing budget PC 8.2.2

The amount of finance allocated depends entirely upon a number of variable factors like:

- the amount of profit generated by a business, from which funds may be drawn
- the level of competition and the position of the organisation in it; a well-established market leader may not feel it necessary to devote as much money to a marketing budget as, say, a young, thrusting company wishing to acquire a larger share of the market in a hurry; however, in a fiercely competitive market all players may feel it necessary to market aggressively and to divert financial resources to this activity
- the degree of complexity or sophistication of the product/service range which may require continuous explanation and support; alternatively – say in the sweet snack market – a constant development of simple but new products may require a continuous, high level of marketing

GROUP ACTIVITY PC 8.2.2

In pairs, carry out the following activity and then write it up for circulation and discussion among your class:

With the help of your teacher or a personal contact, make arrangements to visit a local company, voluntary or charitable organisation which possesses a marketing department and interview one of its senior marketing managers. Seek to establish what kind of elements and aspects inform its marketing plan and budget – in general terms. Bear in mind that both items will be confidential in other than broad-brush terms, and concentrate, therefore, on the 'ingredients' rather than the 'costs and prices'.

■ The marketing plan and market research PC 8.2.2

No marketing plan can be devised successfully, without its originators having first carried out an in-depth research programme into the market which it is proposing to enter (see also Unit 3). This is as true for a small, local business, as for a national conglomerate! The market research is likely to concentrate on:

- **The size and extent of the local potential market.**

  In terms of: numbers of potential customers, estimated sales turnover, density of likely customers, such as the number of people who walk past a main-street shop in a range of given hours, or who inhabit a large housing estate.
- **The spending power of targeted customers.**

  Successful businesses are those which reach a sufficient number of customers possessing enough disposable income to afford the goods/services on offer. (See Unit 3 Marketing, on the services of companies providing data on local socio-economic groups.)

- **The strength and size of the competition.**

  When too many sellers enter into a given market it is said to have become saturated or over-supplied; in such circumstances, available custom becomes highly segmented – broken up into small sections – and all the traders suffer from insufficient sales income and arising profits. Furthermore, the presence of nearby competitors who are well established, with a loyal customer base, are likely to 'strangle the newcomer at birth' by temporarily sacrificing gross profit margins to a devastating series of undercutting special offers and 'unbeatable' discounts.

- **Pricing structures that the market will bear.**

  The prices for given products and services which can be obtained relate very directly to the extent of demand and numbers of direct competitors. In a market in which demand is low and in which competition is fierce, prices obtained are unlikely to generate sufficient margins to cover the cost of sales and still provide an adequate net profit. In this context, obtainable profit margins are also very closely related to how well a trader can buy his stock – 'you have to buy right to sell right'.

- **Local prospects for economic prosperity and growth.**

  Start-up market research also needs to address the likely future economic trends within the selected locality; this will involve researching into the performance of large employers, the extent of inward investment and the improvement of infrastructure elements such as inner city redevelopment or green field site factory building; negative data, such as the imminent closure of a large works, or relocation of a government agency etc. is also important – there is little point in setting up a business in a locality which is 'dying on its feet'.

PC 8.2.2

MARKET RESEARCH AND SWOT

A very helpful approach to undertaking the market research part of the start-up business plan is to analyse the **Strengths, Weaknesses, Opportunities and Threats (SWOT)** of both the start-up business itself and the businesses which make up the perceived competition. Such a SWOT analysis will include:

- the 'marketability' of the basic business idea;
- the 'sellability' of own and competing product ranges (or range of services on offer);
- the sales prices for the product or service range likely to be obtained;
- the projected arising gross and net profit margins;
- the effectiveness of advertising and sales promotion activities – own and competition's;
- 'draw' and density of customer traffic which the business location enjoys – own and competitors';
- likely impact of competitors' responses to the newly opened business;
- likelihood of 'doom scenarios' such as the construction of a bypass or a new one-way traffic system or widespread car-parking ban which could wreck the business in one fell swoop!

The production plan

PC 8.2.3

The design of the production plan is part of the essential triangular link between the marketing, sales and production processes. It is important to understand that each of these business functions is inextricably entwined with the other two:

THE RELATIONSHIP BETWEEN MARKETING, SALES AND PRODUCTION

PC 8.2.3

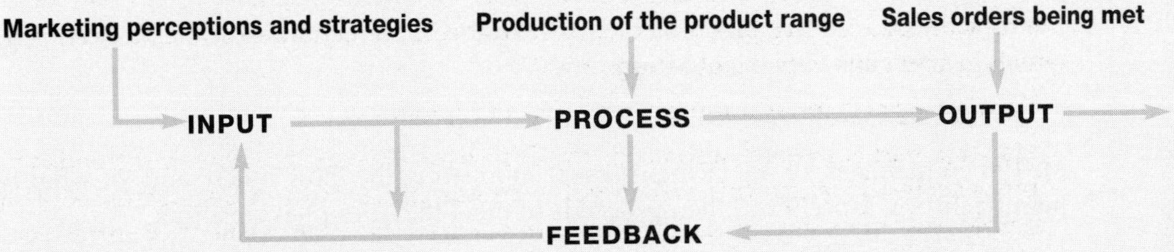

Monitoring checks: levels of stocks of produced products, ratios of production-line idle times, percentage of defective products, lead-times in meeting sale orders etc.

Fig 8.5 **How manufacturing resource planning (MRP) works in manufacturing**

PC 8.2.3

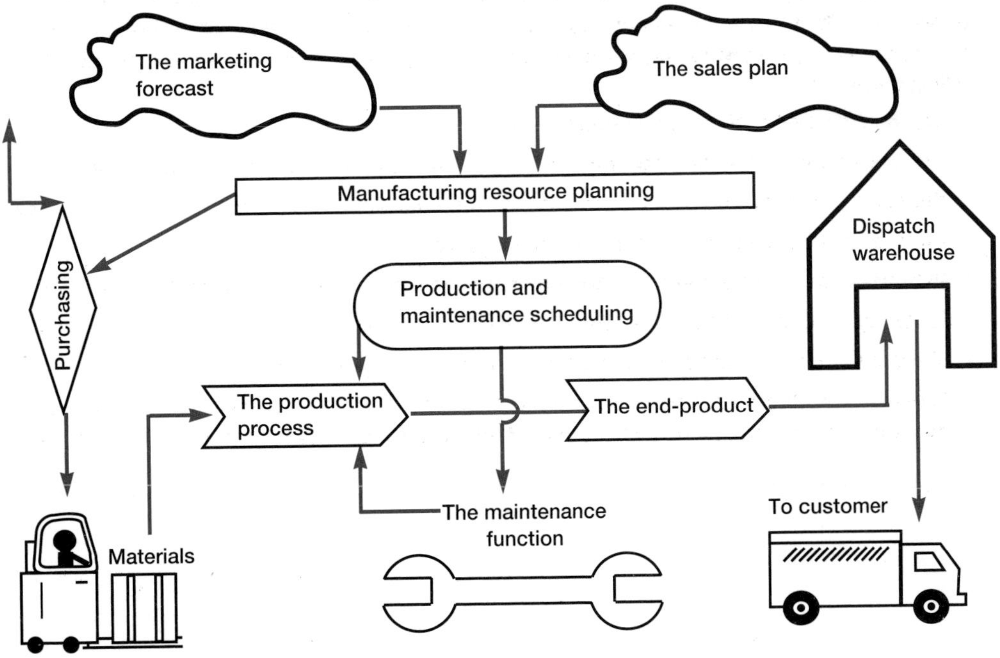

Effective manufacturing integrates: market forecasting, JIT buying, MRP planning, maintenance scheduling, storing and distributing

Manufacturing resource planning (MRP) is a system which integrates the processes of marketing, production and sales. MRP relies upon a fully integrated process and is usually coordinated by a master scheduler, whose role is to ensure that each of the three phases is most efficiently and cost-effectively managed. The diagram in Figure 8.5 on page 743 illustrates the MRP process.

PC 8.2.3

Manufacturing resource planning techniques

Manufacturing resource planning begins with the implementation of the marketing plan, which in effect answers the question:

How much do we want to manufacture?

MRP then manages all the factors present in meeting the 'how much' and 'of what type' manufacturing aspects and then proceeds to meet the sales plan question:

By when?

In other words, all the projections, estimates and forecasts have to be synthesised in a production plan into concrete ranges and mixes of products, the manufacture of which has to be scheduled as cost-effectively as possible, using just-in-time and electronic data interchange (EDI) systems. In MRP, each production stage is given a part coding.

Thus all arriving raw materials or bought-in parts are checked for quality and may not be moved on until set standards have been met. Similarly, finished goods may not be moved to the warehouse until quality checks have been fulfilled. At every stage all materials and items are given unique production batch codings to aid tracking and subsequent identification in case of a defect occurring. In this way a computerised database is built up of each and every production run. In the case of the dreaded product recall newspaper advertisement, any defect problems may be quickly located and the PR damage limited.

For a production plan to be effective, the manufacturing process must be standardised as far as possible in terms of:

- the quality of materials accepted for processing
- the stages of the production process
- the quality standards administered
- the time taken to complete the production process
- the periods of maintenance and safety checks (well within set limits)

Fig 8.6 **The cycle of integrated manufacturing resource planning**

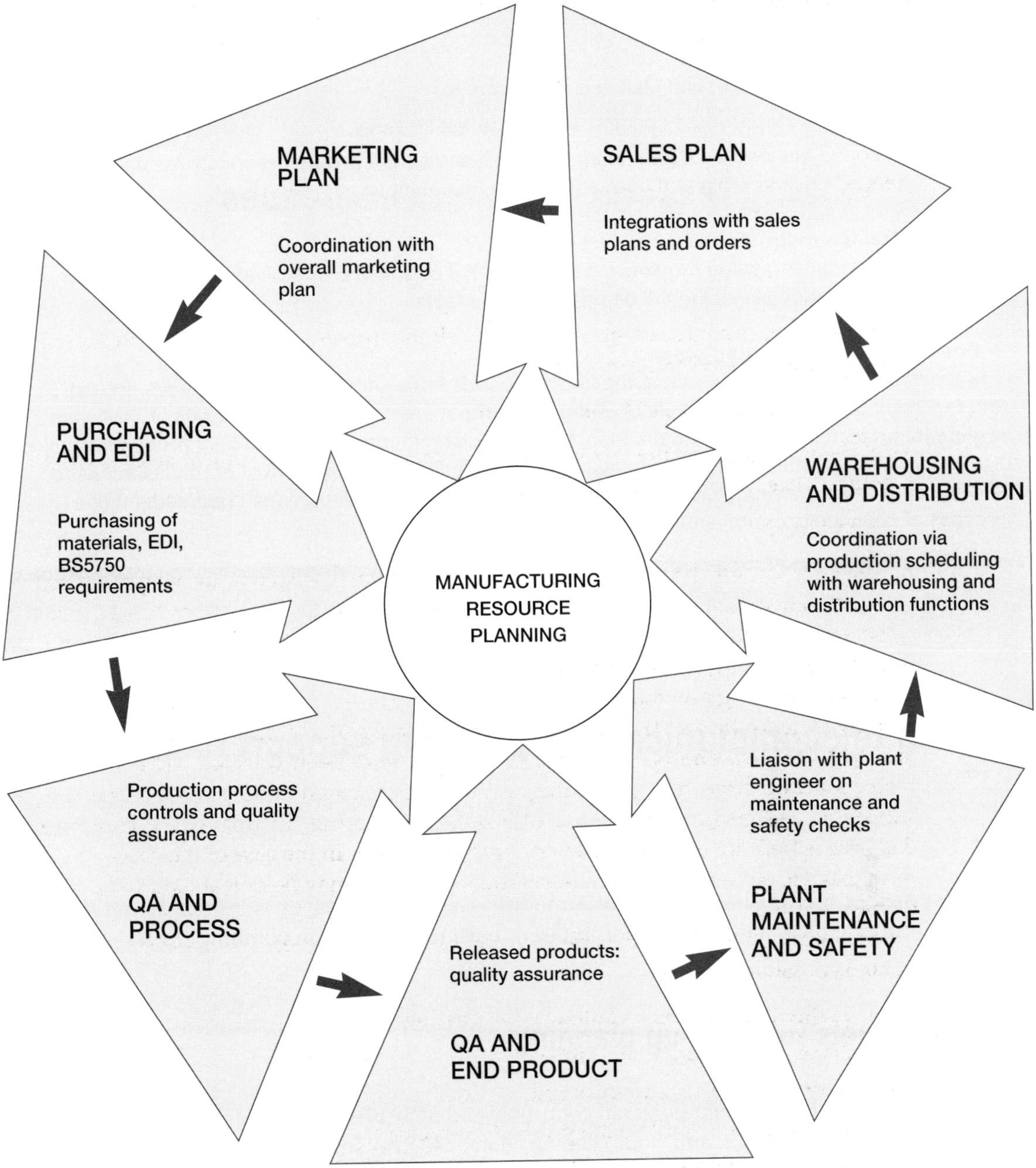
MARKETING PLAN
Coordination with overall marketing plan
SALES PLAN
Integrations with sales plans and orders
PURCHASING AND EDI
Purchasing of materials, EDI, BS5750 requirements
MANUFACTURING RESOURCE PLANNING
WAREHOUSING AND DISTRIBUTION
Coordination via production scheduling with warehousing and distribution functions
Production process controls and quality assurance
QA AND PROCESS
Liaison with plant engineer on maintenance and safety checks
PLANT MAINTENANCE AND SAFETY
Released products: quality assurance
QA AND END PRODUCT

Effective MRP relies on continuous liaison and teamwork

PC 8.2.3

KEY STAGES IN PRODUCTION PLANNING

The following are the key stages in production planning:

1 Pre-plan requirements

Prior to the design of a production plan, it is necessary to:

- have agreed the basic product concept and marketing strategy
- have developed the idea via R&D into an accepted and tested prototype, which designers and toolmakers agree is feasible and cost-effective to manufacture.

2 Production planning stages

The production planning stage requires close, sequential liaison and coordination with a number of involved process functions as Fig 8.6 on page 745 illustrates.

3 Post-production planning stages

The production planning cycle – once the finished goods have left the factory – includes evaluation and feedback phases in which levels of production output are compared with targets, actual waste levels with projected levels and so on. Also, the triangular relationship – marketing, production, sales – results in wash-up meetings at which, say, the introduction of a new product or modifications to existing ones are reviewed in order to meet, say, the total quality management requirement of a process of continuous improvement.

PC 8.2.4

IT and telecommunications planning support tools

Whether the business plan is of a modest, start-up nature, or is a mighty, multinational corporate plan, a number of helpful tools exist to support the planning process:

PC 8.2.4

■ Support tools for start-up planning

Nowadays the cost of a personal computer and a multi-software package embracing word processing, accounts and bookkeeping, database and spreadsheet applications – even in windows mode – costs hundreds rather than thousands of pounds. Such a tool is invaluable in enabling the sole proprietor to manipulate textual, number and graphic data, to keep records which are promptly retrievable, and with a printer to produce hard copies at will. Such a personal PC system provides at a low cost all the features of a capable office – in the hands of a trained user.

Now becoming obsolescent – but still helpful for 'technophobics' – are the paper-based booklets and ledgers which have turnkey business systems, from purchasing to inventory, already set out in blank form mode with helpful notes to aid completion and analysis by the small trader.

■ Aids to producing the marketing plan

PC 8.2.4

IT hardware and software applications are similarly available to the marketing personnel of a medium to large organisation. In addition to the applications listed above, marketeers make much use of computer software which models market trends and answers a wide range of 'what if' questions.

The marketing plan is also supported by a wide range of information providers, such as *JICNARS (Joint Industry Committee for National Readership Survey)* and such regular publications as *Phillips and Drew's published monthly forecasts.*

■ The production plan

In terms of the all-embracing use made of information technology, of note in the production planning process are:

- *Electronic Data Interchange (EDI)* computerised systems, through which purchasing and supplying computers 'talk' to each other and synchronise just-in-time manufacturing systems.
- *Computer-Aided Design and Manufacture IT systems* which enable designers and machine operators to perform complex design and manufacturing operations with the benefits of features like three-dimensional, rotating electronic drawings, computerised design modelling and optimum build routes and processes.

■ Telecommunications

Advances in telecommunications technology have made it possible for architects and builders – on different continents – to amend blueprints and plans electronically through the use of wide area network software. In-house confravision and video-telephones now support planning meetings and the visual examination of diagrams and charts by personnel in remote locations.

■ Support agencies

In addition to technological support, business planners can nowadays call upon a wide range of public and private sector experts, ranging from staff in the Department of Trade and Industry, the local Training and Enterprise Council (TEC), and the Chamber of Commerce, national professional institutes such as the Institute of Marketing and a host of entrepreneurial management consultants.

Local public and college libraries also now stock a broad selection of 'do-it-yourself' planning handbooks, and all the clearing banks offer comprehensive financial support services to starting out business people.

■ The best support

Underpinning the most conscientiously gathered data and statistics, forms, schedules, software and flowcharts is the most important planning tool of all – that inner determination to venture out and to succeed! And the successful business entrepreneurs find that conviction and self-belief from within, rather than from without.

PC 8.2.4

The resource requirements for marketing and production

As the above sections indicate, producing effective marketing and production plans is a demanding process. In an ideal world, a business always has enough of the right resources to call upon. But not in reality. In the real business world, people with particular specialist skills may be difficult to recruit; after a middling trading year or two, there may be precious little available finance to devote to developing a business, and lending rates may be high; plant or equipment in a business may be like the curate's egg, good and bad in parts.

Thus all business marketing and production plans tend to make compromises on their respective resource requirements – of money, human and physical resources. However, one resource can always be made better use of, and that is of course time.

Also, a realistic marketing plan may limit the introduction of new products and instead give a (cheaper) facelift to existing ones; market research methods may be made more cost-effective, by undertaking more in-house thus saving the cost of employing an agency; a marketing plan may elect to trim a sales force or to merge close-by outlets and so on.

Similarly, a production plan may require the relocation of a factory to an area where pay-rates are lower and employees easier to find who will do shift work; the installation of expensive new plant may be deferred, or a purchase plan revised to secure a cheaper alternative item of plant.

In these ways, marketing and production managers are constantly seeking to get the proverbial quart out of a pint pot, by shaving costs, devising more effective working methods and introducing simpler ways of operating. Indeed it is such effective management of resources in a business which enables it to sell its products or services competitively, to the benefit of its customers.

PC 8.2.4

■ Finance and the business plan

One of the most important financial planning tasks to be undertaken early is a calculation of the business's projected break-even point. This is the point at which sufficient goods or services have been sold to cover the cost of sales by the profit they generate. The example on page 749 shows simply and clearly how the break-even point is calculated.

The break-even point for any business's sales can also be calculated with the aid of a graph. Figure 8.7 on page 750 illustrates how sales income is plotted against fixed and variable costs. Where the rising volume of sales intersects the plotted rising track of

How to calculate the break-even point

Working out your break-even point

Break-even is the level of sales you need to cover all of your costs. Let's see how to work it out, using an imaginary manufacturer. The same calculation applies to any business. Let's say you have stock valued at £38,000 and you are projecting the following over the next 12 months.

	£
Sales	108,000
Purchases	60,000
Closing stock	50,000
Wages or salaries	32,000
Overheads	10,360

From these figures, you can work out your projected gross and net profit. That is to say, your profits before (gross) and after (net) you allow for your overheads.

Sales		108,000
Purchases	60,000	
Wages or salaries	32,000	
Stock (increase) or decrease	(12,000)*	
Less cost of goods sold		(80,000)
Gross profit (profit before overhead costs)		28,000
Less overheads		(10,360)
Net profit		17,640

* Your opening stock is £38,000, and your closing stock is £50,000. The Stock Change figure is always the opening amount with the closing stock taken off.

Now you need to work out your gross profit margin. This is your gross profit, which is your profit before allowing for overheads. It is written as a percentage of sales.

$$\frac{\text{Gross profit} \times 100}{\text{Sales}} = \frac{£28{,}000 \times 100}{£108{,}000} = 25.9\%$$

If you can reach the gross profit margin and your overheads do not change, the break-even turnover is worked as follows:

$$\frac{\text{Overheads} \times 100}{\text{Gross profit margin}} = \frac{£10{,}360 \times 100}{25.9} = £40{,}000$$

Therefore, this business will need a turnover of £40,000 to cover all overheads, as long as it keeps the gross profit margin.

Looked at another way...

£40,000 turnover at 25.9% gross profit margin = £10,360

This is just enough to cover the overheads.

There are 2 other useful calculations you can do:

First if the business keeps its present level of turnover, but its margins are reduced for some reason, perhaps because of rising costs, you can work out how much the margin can fall by, and still cover your overheads.

$$\frac{\text{Overheads} \times 100}{\text{Sales}} = \frac{£10{,}360 \times 100}{£108{,}000} = 9.59\%$$

This is the break-even gross profit margin.

Second work out the amount you need to sell every month just to break even. This figure is important because you can use it to check whether or not you are on target, or need to make some adjustments. But remember that this calculation does not take into account any seasonal changes which might affect your business.

To work out monthly targets, simply take your break-even sales figure for the year and divide by 12.

$$\frac{£40{,}000}{12} = £3{,}333 \text{ per month}$$

This model is reproduced with the kind permission of National Westminster Bank from their *The business start-up guide* 1993 variable plus fixed costs, enough revenue has been obtained to cover all associated outgoings – a break-even point has been reached. The shaded segment indicates the subsequent move into profit from the sustained increase in sales:

Whether calculated as a table or a graph, it is essential to produce a projection of sales income, cost of sales, gross and net profit early in the planning process in order to establish whether, for example, a high level of costs and overheads would result in the need for an impossibly high revenue from sales in order to generate sufficient profit. If this were to prove the case, then the would-be entrepreneur would need to 'go back to the drawing-board' to see how the components of his break-even chart might be massaged in order to produce a more realistic relationship between projected sales income and profit.

PC 8.2.5

Fig 8.7 A tool for calculating sales needed to generate a profit from given costs

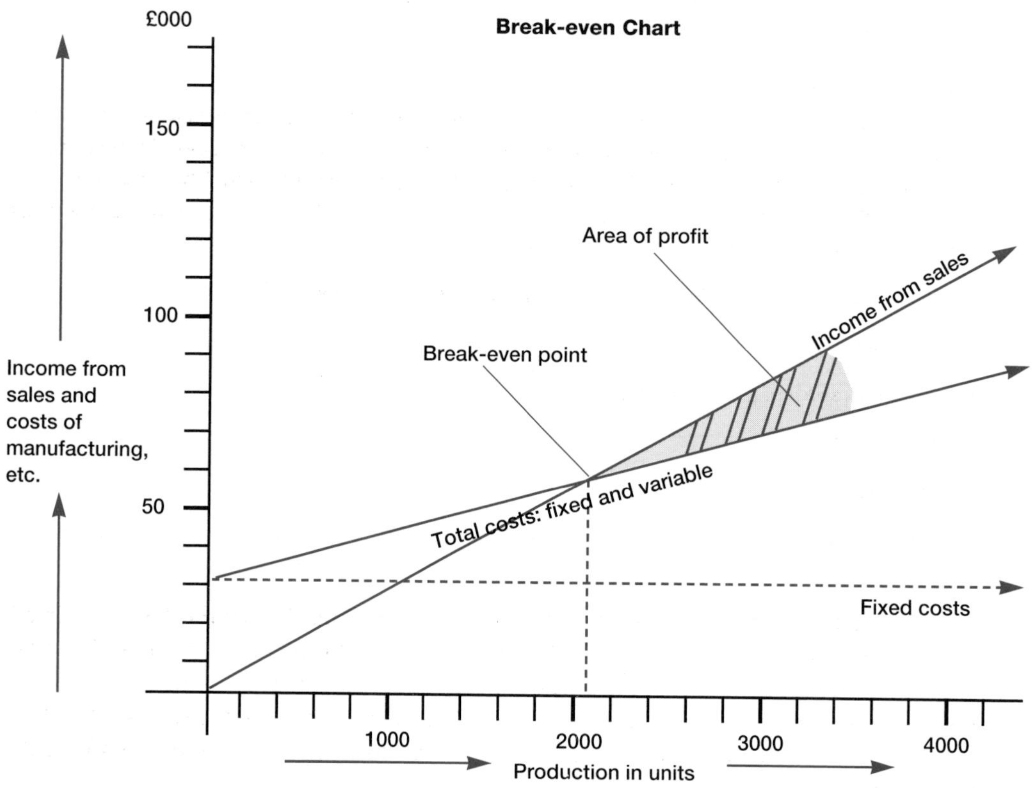

PC 8.2.5

DISCUSSION TOPIC

Given the above scenario – of a situation in which the volume of sales needed to generate enough income to cover cost of sales looks impossibly high – how could the would-be small businessman adjust his or her plan to make it more likely to succeed? What components of the plan could be trimmed most readily do you think?

PC 8.2.5

EXAMPLES OF FIXED AND VARIABLE COST ITEMS

Fixed Costs
Fixed costs are those which can be expected to remain unchanged for the duration of the trading period. Typical fixed costs in a small business include:

- Rent of premises
- Business rates
- Insurances
- Heating
- Lighting

(Remember that energy costs may be variable if, say, a firm introduces overtime and thus works equipment for longer periods to make more goods.)

Variable Costs
Variable costs are those which rise pro rata – at a rate which stems from an increase in business activity or increases in operational costs. For example, a successful business may need to employ additional sales personnel to cope with demand. Thus the firm's salary bill will increase. Or, a manufacturer may have to cope with an increase in the cost of raw materials during the trading period.

Typical examples of variable costs in a small business include:

- Salaries
- Raw materials/Bought in stock
- Fuel/energy
- Packaging

In the first months of a business the continuous monitoring of the levels of fixed and variable costs is crucial for, if their total creeps up unnoticed, a business may fail despite a high level of sales, since the profits needed to sustain it will have been eroded and insufficient profit made. Similarly, if sales fall back from projected levels, swift action will be needed to reduce cost of sales correspondingly in order to maintain a sufficient cash-flow (see below).

The following chart illustrates what trading information a prudent proprietor monitors in the course of a trading year:

PC
8.2.5

Example of a business plan monitoring schedule

		Trading Periods			
		6 months to June		12 months to December	
Line*	Receipts	Projected £	Actual £	Projected £	Actual £
2	Sales Debtors (including VAT)	41,400	41,400	103,500	92,000
5	Capital introduced	10,000	10,000	10,000	10,000
A	Total receipts	51,400	51,400	113,500	102,000
	Payments				
8	Cash purchases	32,200	40,250	59,800	58,850
11	Wages or Salaries (Net)	13,000	13,000	26,000	26,000
12	PAYE and NI	2,500	2,500	5,500	5,500
13	Capital items (for example equipment or vehicles)	5,000	5,000	5,000	5,000
15	Rent	2,250	1,500	3,750	3,750
15	Rates	240	240	480	480
16	Light and heat	450	475	900	1,000
16	Telephone and post	210	190	440	420
19	Interest	680	750	940	1,465
20	Bank and finance charges	200	300	400	500
21	Book-keeper	1,000	1,000	2,000	2,000
21	Professional fees	400	400	950	950
23	Insurance	400	400	400	400
24	General expenses	400	500	800	1,000
26	VAT	1,000	800	5,500	4,375
B	Total payments	59,930	67,305	112,860	111,690
C	Net cashflow (A-B)	(8,530)	(15,905)	640	(9,690)
29	Opening Bank Balance	Nil	Nil	Nil	Nil
D	Closing Bank Balance	(8,530)	(15,905)	640	(9,690)
	(Net cashflow + or − your opening balance)	Overdrawn	Overdrawn	In Credit	Overdrawn

This schedule is reproduced with the kind permission of National Westminster Bank.
(*See also the Cash-flow Forecast example on page 755)

Note that in the above planning/monitoring schedule the monitoring periods are shown as six months for illustration purposes. In reality, a business proprietor would monitor the items listed above at weekly and monthly intervals.

DISCUSSION TOPICS

1 What led in your view to the actual overdrawn as opposed to the in credit position at the end of 12 months' trading period?

2 Can you suggest what timely steps might have been taken to retrieve the situation?

Cash-flow forecasts and operating budgets

PC 8.2.5

■ Estimating and monitoring the cash flow forecast

Another essential financial aspect of start-up business planning – and indeed, just as important in a mature business – is the rolling cash flow forecast. This forecast is usually set down in a planning schedule which totals each month's flow of money into and out of the business. The trading period may be from January to December or from April to March, depending upon the one chosen for the business. Bear in mind that the Inland Revenue's financial year follows the latter monthly sequence.

In essence, a cash flow forecast is a table of those items which go to make up the component parts of all receipts (money flowing in to the business), and all payments which go out.

Typical composition of receipts

The items termed receipts include:

- payment for goods received as cash
- money owed for goods purchased on account
- injections of capital or personal investment into the business at the outset
- money received from selling any assets (equipment, unwanted stock etc.) belonging to the business

Typical composition of payments

The items termed payments include:

- money paid out as cash or cheques for goods purchased – notably stock to sell
- money paid out for items purchased as an essential part of the business's running costs – advertising, cleaning, insurances, fuel, heat and light etc.
- payroll for all employees and directors' withdrawals and all associated NIC payments etc.
- rent, rates and associated physical resources costs such as service charges relating to a lease

- all the repayment charges associated with hiring, leasing or renting plant, equipment, machinery, overalls, indoor plants etc.
- all financial charges such as bank charges, annual accountant's fees, interest and service charges on loans etc.
- all payments made in the form of taxes such as corporation tax, VAT, any shareholders' dividends etc.

PC 8.2.5

DISCUSSION TOPICS

One of the 'dark sides' of the business world is that today many large enterprises dispatch many small ones into receivership because they deliberately defer and delay for as long as possible paying the small trader for goods or services purchased on account. Contrastingly, the large firms seek to obtain payment for the goods or services they sell on account as promptly as possible. Such a practice, of course, helps to assure the future of the larger company through a manipulation of its cash flow which ensures that there is always a positive balance in favour of moneys flowing in.

1 Should a business law be enacted to provide small traders with stronger protection in this area?

2 What actions could the small trader take to obtain prompter payment for goods or services sold on account?

3 What rule of thumb would you suggest to a small trader as the safest ratio or mix of selling of goods *a*) for cash and *b*) on account?

What a good cash flow forecast makes possible is the anticipation of potential times when the business's financial viability – indeed its very existence – may be put at risk by the proprietor having to pay out money to meet due bills when there is an insufficient inflow of cash to do so, and for taking preventative action in the case of account customers who are very slow payers.

Mr Micawber in Charles Dickens' *David Copperfield* well knew that 'Annual income twenty pounds, annual expenditure twenty pounds ought and six' resulted in misery. For the new small business it often results in bankruptcy, even though assets may exist of a greater value than the debts incurred, but which are unrealisable in time to save the business.

Set out below is an example of the listing of items which comprise a cash flow forecast schedule. Note the straightforward arithmetic (a – b = c) for calculating the net cash flow and the final position for each month after opening and closing bank balances have been taken into consideration.

Example of a cash-flow forecasting schedule

Business name:

Cash-flow forecast [Note: schedule extends for 12 months] ⟶

Enter month					
Figures rounded to £'s		**Budget**	**Actual**	**Budget**	**Actual**
	Receipts				
1	Sales (including VAT) – Cash				
2	– Debtors				
3	Other trading income				
4	Loans you have received				
5	New capital				
6	Selling of assets				
7	Other receipts				
a	Total receipts				
	Payments				
8	cash for goods you have bought				
9	Payments to creditors				
10	Owner or directors' withdrawals				
11	Wages and Salaries (net)				
12	PAYE/NI				
13	Capital items (for example equipment and vehicles)				
14	Transport and packaging				
15	Rent or rates				
16	Services				
17	Loan repayments				
18	Hire or leasing repayments				
19	Interest				
20	Bank or finance charges				
21	Professional fees				
22	Advertising				
23	Insurance				
24					
25					
26	VAT				
27	Corporation tax and so on				
28	Dividends				
b	Total payments				
c	Net cashflow (a – b)				
29	Opening bank balance				
d	Closing bank balance (c ± Line 29)				

Basic assumptions – please give details of the assumptions you use
Credit taken – the average time your creditors give you to pay.
Credit given – the average time you give your debtors to pay.

Table of useful monitoring calculations

PC 8.2.5

You need to monitor how well your business is doing and keep track of performance. You can spot changes by using the following quick calculations

- Gross profit margin:

$$\frac{\text{Gross profit} \times 100}{\text{Sales}} = \%$$

- Net profit as a percentage of sales:

$$\frac{\text{Net Profit}}{\text{Sales}} = \%$$

- Profit azs a percentage of the capital used:

$$\frac{\text{Net Profit}}{\text{Net Assets}} \times 100 = \%$$

- Rate of stock turnover:

$$\frac{\text{Cost of stock sold}}{\text{Average stock at cost}}$$

- Net working capital (current assts – current liabilities) as a percentage of sales:

$$\frac{\text{Net working capital}}{\text{Sales}} \times 100 = \%$$

- Working capital ratio:

$$\frac{\text{Current assets}}{\text{Current liabilities}}$$

Any ratio below 1 means that your business is currently insolvent.

- Quick ratio:

$$\frac{\text{Debtors}}{\text{Current liabilities}}$$

This calculation shows whether it would be easy to sell your business using only assets which could be quickly sold or realised. It also shows whether your business can pay debts as they are due. Your debtors should only be trade debts which you will receive within a few months. In this calculation, do not include any stock unless you can sell it quickly for cash.

PC
8.2.5

Example of a start-up cash-flow forecast for a retail shop selling ladies' fashions

Cash-flow forecast

		CASH IN	**MAY**	**JUN**	**JUL**	**AUG**	**SEP**	**OCT**	**NOV**	**DEC**	**JAN**	**FEB**	**MAR**	**APR**	**TOTALS**
(1)	1	Sales (inc VAT)	1000	1500	2000	3000	3000	2750	4000	8000	1500	1750	2750	3250	34500
	2	Bank or other loans		2000											2000
	3	Owner's Capital	6500												6500
	4	Other Money in													
	5	Total	7500	3500	2000	3000	3000	2750	4000	8000	1500	1750	2750	3250	43000
		CASH OUT (INC VAT)													
(2)	6	Stock/Raw materials	5000	3000	1500	1250	1500	1375	2000	4000	750	875	1375	1625	24250
	7	Advertising & Promotion	200						200						400
	8	Bank Charges/Interest			44			38			9				91
	9	Business Insurance	350												350
(3)	10	Drawings/Salaries/NI		300	300	300	500	500	500	800	700	700	700	700	6000
(4)	11	Electric/Gas/Heat		75		75		75		125		125		100	575
	12	Fees (eg Accountant, Lawyer)	300											400	700
	13	HP/Lease/Loan Payments		80	80	80	80	80	80	80	80	80	80	80	880
	14	Motor – Fuel													
	15	Motor – Other Expenses													
	16	Postage/Carriage													
	17	Rent & Rates	1000	250	250	1250	250	250	1250	250	250	1250	250		6500
	18	Repairs & Maintenance		50			50			50			50		200
	19	Staff Wages													
	20	Staff PAYE/NI													
	21	Stationery/Printing	20						20						40
	22	Sundries	80	50	30	20	10	10	10	10	10	10	10	10	260
	23	Telephone/Fax	250	50			100			100			100		600
	24	Travelling					100							100	200
	25	VAT													
	26	Other Expenses													
	27	CAPITAL EXPENDITURE	1450												1450
	28	TOTAL	8650	3855	2204	2975	2590	2328	4060	5415	1799	3040	2565	3015	42496
	29	Net Cashflow	(1150)	(355)	(204)	25	410	422	(60)	2585	(299)	(1290)	185	235	504
	30	Opening Balance	0	(1150)	(1505)	(1709)	(1684)	(1274)	(852)	(912)	1673	1374	84	269	0
(5)	31	CLOSING BALANCE	(1150)	(1505)	(1709)	(1684)	(1274)	(852)	(912)	1673	1374	84	269	504	504

Figures in brackets are negative i.e. the business bank account would be in overdraft.

START-UP LADIES' FASHIONS RETAIL SHOP
CASH-FLOW FORECAST

PC 8.2.5

Commentary

1 *Sales*

Note that the sales forecast allows for peaks in spring, autumn and Christmas trading

2 *Stock*

Similar buying-in peaks occur as well as an initial opening stock purchase of £5,000

3 *Proprietor's drawings*

The sole trader owner is careful to minimise drawings in the early months of June–August

4 *Electricity/Gas/ Heat*

Due weighting is given to additional costs during winter months

5 *Cash-flow balances*

Note that a planned deficit in the closing balances from May to November has been allowed for and that the projected closing balance for the first 12 months of trading is a modest £504.

Erring on the side of caution
It is better in drawing up a cash flow forecast to err on the side of caution. This forecast indicates a break-even first year which is likely to move steadily into growth and increased trading profits in the second and third years of trading.

■ The operating budget

PC 8.2.6

Another helpful financial monitoring tool is the operating budget. This is similar to the cash flow forecast in that it extends monthly listings for both projected and actual financial totals over twelve months. However, the items listed and compared in an operating budget are sales and cost of sales – broken down into their component sub-headings.

Sales

The operating budget first totals the turnover value of all sales as each calendar month ensues:

(a) Income from all sales

Cost of sales

It then facilitates the calculation of a gross profit total by:

(b) totalling the cost of all goods purchased (in the month)
(c) adding the value of the opening stock
(d) deducting the value of the closing stock
(e) also deducting direct labour costs

Gross profit

The gross profit (or loss) figure, (f) is:

$$f = a - (b + c - d - e)$$

or, Gross profit = sales minus: opening stock, plus goods purchased less closing stock, less direct labour costs

Net profit

The operating budget then provides a listing of all the expenses for each month which are incurred as costs arising from the sales operation. In a manufacturing organisation these will centre upon production costs; in a service industry, they will derive mainly from mounting the sales operation and include the cost of running a sales force, advertising and sales promotion, office administration, the monthly bills for payroll, heating, light, rent, an allocation for equipment and vehicle depreciation and so on.

Thus the calculation for arriving at a net profit total is:

Gross profit:	f
less Total expenses:	g
equals Net profit:	h

Such a comprehensive and detailed business start-up plan is needed, not only to present to a bank manager as a prerequisite for obtaining a loan and overdraft facilities, but also as an essential analysis of the overall business proposal.

Regrettably, each year thousands of businesses fail – in 1991–2 some 440 were failing each week – and too many fall into the category of those which should never have been started up. That they were and failed in their first year – as about one-third do – is almost certainly due to the failure of their owners to carry out sufficient preplanning and investigation, before a commitment is made and precious assets put at risk.

For this very reason, risk-taking entrepreneurs who first plan carefully and then work 'all hours' to build up a successful business enterprise feel (rightly) entitled to the affluence and high standards of living which may come from their hard work and the initial risks they were prepared to take.

PC
8.2.4
8.2.5

DISCUSSION TOPICS

1 What do you consider the most risky aspects of starting up a business?

How might the risks you identify be minimised by the entrepreneur?

2 To what extent is a start-up business plan worth the time and effort put into its production, if the 'proof of the pudding' is always in the eating?

3 According to accepted theory, it is crucial to monitor operations closely and frequently during the first months of opening a business. Yet at such a time, its proprietor(s) are likely to be devoting all their time and energy to selling and promoting sales. What advice on the effective management of time could you offer to such small traders? How would you suggest their working week should be organised to ensure that essential data is captured and scrutinised? What IT systems could you recommend which might help?

■ The trading and profit and loss account

PC 8.2.6

The trading and profit and loss account for any given trading period – say monthly, quarterly or annually is simply the presentation of the above summarised totals, as the following example illustrates:

Specimen trading and profit and loss accounts

Trading Account

Sales		£37,500
Opening stock	£4,500	
+ Purchases	£15,000	
	£19,500	
– Closing stock	£4,600	£14,900
		£22,600
– Direct labour costs		£10,000
GROSS PROFIT		£12,600

Gross Profit Margin

$$\frac{\text{Gross profit £12,600}}{\text{Sales £37,500}} \times 100 = 34\%$$

Profit and Loss Account

Gross profit		£12,600
Business salaries (including your own drawings)	£3,000	
+ Rent	£1,000	
+ Rent	£250	
+ Light/heating	£250	
+ Telephone/post	£250	
+ Insurance	£250	
+ Repairs	£1,000	
+ Advertising	£750	
+ Bank interest/HP	£750	
+ Other expenses	£900	£8,400
NET PROFIT		£4,200

Note: for simplicity all figures shown are exclusive of VAT.

Reproduced by kind permission of Midland Bank PLC

The start-up business plan: summary

PC 8.2.1 8.2.6

While there is no single, correct way to structure a start-up business plan, the following checklist provides a suggested list of key topics in a logical sequence.

PC 8.2.1 8.2.6

CHECKLIST OF KEY SECTIONS OF A START-UP BUSINESS PLAN

1 Reference details of the business:

Owner's(s') personal details: e.g. directors, partners or sole proprietor

Business trading name

Trading address and registered office address

Date of proposed commencement of trading

2 Details of capitalisation – value and allocation of shares among directors or sums invested by partners

3 Details of basic business idea and the rationale for it

4 Market research SWOT analysis and any test marketing undertaken

5 Details of proposed location and business premises, including particulars of cost (e.g. freehold, leasehold or rental) and rates

6 Particulars of goods/services to be sold, including likely suppliers, trading margins (buying in and selling out prices) and likely extent of stocks needing to be held to provide a viable range

7 Breakdown of the costs of start-up plant, equipment, fixtures and fittings needed in order to open up convincingly

8 A detailed cash flow forecast for the first 12 months of trading supplemented by an outline forecast for years 2 and 3

9 A summary trading and profit and loss account projection for year 1

10 Details of the financial support needed to start the business:

a from personal resources

b as loans from a bank or similar source

This section will also indicate the extent of any government start-up grants or loans.

Note: This section should also include proposals on how any requested loan will be secured (say against assets in any property owned which is free of any mortgage or similar financial constraint)

PC 8.2.1 8.2.2 8.2.3 8.2.4 8.2.5 8.2.6 8.2.7

REVIEW TEST

1 List the main stages of producing a marketing plan.

2 What principal areas would an internal marketing audit cover?

3 What does SWOT stand for? How is it used?

4 List four major areas of cost for a marketing plan.

5 List five of the main marketing budget areas.

6 What does MRP stand for? How does it work?

7 List and explain the three key stages in production planning.

8 List the resources which are audited in producing marketing and production plans.

9 What is a break-even chart? How does it work as a planning tool?

10 Explain the difference between fixed and variable costs.

11 List the major components of a cash-flow forecast.

12 What items would you expect to make up the receipts of a cash-flow forecast?

13 List also the items for a payments forecast.

14 Explain how an operating budget differs from a cash-flow forecast.

15 If a cash-flow entry is shown in brackets, what does this mean?

16 Write down the formulae for calculating: gross profit margin, rate of stock turnover, net profit as a percentage of sales.

17 Why is it important for a business to produce regular trading and profit and loss accounts?

GROUP 'BUILD-UP' PRACTICE ACTIVITY

PC 8.2.2 8.2.5 8.2.7

The New College Bookshop

The Board of Governors/Corporation of your school/college has recently given permission for a new bookshop to be established as part of a policy of securing income and surpluses (profits) from enterprises which also help the students.

- The location of the bookshop has been left for a Planning Group to decide, but it must be readily accessible and ideally capable of expansion if the venture proves a success.
- Also, the hours of opening have been left to the Planning Group to decide upon after a suitable survey of customers' needs has been made.
- While it is felt that textbooks are likely to be the largest item of stock, the Governors/ Corporation are keen for the bookshop to be innovative and to meet customers' needs as comprehensively as possible.
- The bookshop must be fully self-funded, so projected turnover and profits must be sufficient to pay for running costs and payroll etc.
- The Governors/Corporation are prepared to lend the bookshop £10,000 as start-up capital and for the closing balances for the first 6 months of operation to be in the red!
- With your teachers' help, decide on an actual (prospective) location and allocated costs of: rent, rates, heat and light.

1 First undertake your researches as the Planning Group of two or three people and then produce a start-up business plan for the bookshop.

2 Using suitable AVA support, deliver your plan to your class in an oral presentation of some 10 minutes and field any arising questions.

3 Invite your Head Teacher or Vice Principal to discuss your plans with your class and to evaluate them from the point of view of their financial soundness and viability.

4 Devise a suitable advertising campaign to excite students' awareness of the new facility and include a sample poster, public-address system commercial and notice-board A4 advertisement in your advertising plan.

PC
8.2.1
8.2.2
8.2.3
8.2.4
8.2.5
8.2.6
8.2.7

PORTFOLIO OF EVIDENCE ACTIVITY

Element 8.2
Produce and present a business plan

DETAILED BUSINESS PLAN

Scenario 1

You are now tasked with undertaking what is, perhaps, the major activity of your programme of study as, in all probability, you approach its end. The task is to produce a detailed, five-part business plan, using the information you researched for the Element 8.1 draft plan activity. This business plan is to be presented to an invited audience using appropriate audio-visual aids. Your presentation is also to include a question and answer session, in which your audience will appraise your understanding of the marketing, production and financial aspects of your plan.

The following checklist indicates the key sectors which you should include in your business plan:

1 **Introduction:** key business goals and objectives

2 **Marketing:** an analysis of how you will market the goods or services you will sell

3 **Production:** how the costs of obtaining raw materials or finished goods will be met; how the manufacturing process will be carried out, and how quality will be assured (Note: if your business is not engaged in a production function, you should liaise with your teacher to substitute for this area a section detailing how your business will acquire, merchandise and display your stock, and how quality will be assured in the business)

4 **Resources:** an analysis of the type and extent of the resources you will need to start the business (see sections 2 and 3)

5 **Financial Data:** a set of forecasts and estimates using a cash-flow forecast, start-up balance sheet, projected profit and loss and balance-sheet and their monthly counterparts used to monitor performance; this section should focus on how the plan will be financed and by whom, as well as how progress will be monitored – using what techniques and at what frequency; it should also indicate who would receive what financial reports.

Scenario 2

Having produced your material – cue-cards, AVA material, hand-outs etc. – for your oral presentation, you are now tasked with preparing for the question and answer session. You should consider the precise nature of your five-part plan, and seek to anticipate the sort of questions you are likely to be asked, which will aim to probe any weaker points or to seek further explanations etc.

This being the case, you may find it useful to record the essential factual data of your plan on an easy-to-read prompt sheet. Alternatively, you may wish to prepare several OHP foils which you can use in answering questions.

Task 1

Before beginning this activity, remember to complete the appropriate parts of your planning and review log.

Task 2

Using your Element 8.1 draft plan as a starting point, research and structure your oral presentation. Remember that a picture (diagram, chart etc.) is often worth a thousand words, and also saves time. Decide how many and what kind of audio-visual aids you will employ. Too few and you may become boring; too many, and your audience may suffer from information overload. Also, remember that the most successful presenters – actors, politicians, tv personalities etc. – *rehearse* beforehand!

Note: You will need to liaise with your teacher before embarking on Task 2, in order to get a clear briefing on how long your presentation is to take, including the question and answer session, since this will directly affect the amount of information you impart – and how.

Task 3

Produce a personal prompt sheet/factsheet which will assist you in answering anticipated questions.

Performance criteria covered

8.2.1, 8.2.2, 8.2.3, 8.2.4, 8.2.5, 8.2.6, 8.2.7

Core skills covered

Communication:
3.1.1, 3.1.2, 3.1.3, 3.1.4, 3.1.5, 3.2.1, 3.2.2, 3.2.3, 3.2.4, 3.2.5, 3.3.1, 3.3.2, 3.3.3, 3.4.1, 3.4.2, 3.4.3, 3.4.4

Information Technology:
3.1.1, 3.1.2, 3.1.3, 3.1.4, 3.1.5, 3.2.1, 3.2.2, 3.2.3, 3.2.4, 3.2.5, 3.2.6, 3.2.7, 3.3.1, 3.3.2, 3.3.3, 3.3.4, 3.3.5, 3.3.6

Application of Number:
3.1.1, 3.1.2, 3.1.3, 3.1.4, 3.1.5, 3.1.6, 3.1.7, 3.2.1, 3.2.2, 3.2.3, 3.2.4, 3.2.5, 3.2.6, 3.2.7, 3.2.8, 3.2.9, 3.3.1, 3.3.2, 3.3.3, 3.3.4, 3.3.5

CASE STUDY 1

PC
8.2.2
8.2.3
8.2.4
8.2.5
8.2.6
8.2.7

The Tops Shop: a case study in devising a marketing plan

Pat Roberts, Sarah Williams and Winston Wright were all final-year students at Weston College in Dorset when they decided to form a business partnership. Pat and Sarah were following a business studies diploma programme and Winston was pursuing a fashion design course.

One day in the spring term of their second year at Weston, the three were drinking Coke in the college refectory and Winston was explaining how he and his classmates were designing sweaters, cardigans and jumpers and producing them on knitting machines.

'It's a really great way of expressing your own ideas!' Winston enthused. 'The machines are incredibly versatile, once you get to know how to drive them. Look, I've made this one,' he went on, pulling a chunky sweater out of a plastic bag which was made up of a swirling abstract pattern in pastel shades.

'It's beautiful!' said Sarah. 'I've never seen anything like it – can I try it on?'

'Help yourself,' replied Winston.

Sarah pulled it on over her shirt and pirouetted around the table. 'What do you think?' 'Really something else,' answered Pat, the quiet one of the trio, 'and it's got me thinking. It really is different from anything else I've seen – in a boutique or M & S. How much would a sweater like that cost to make, Winston?'

* * *

Pat's thinking led to a number of off-campus meetings of the three students. At the first Pat briefly outlined his proposal.

'Look, I think Winston's design genius on the knitwear machine could be a real money-spinner. I've had a good wander round town and there's nothing – absolutely nothing – like the sweaters and pullovers his group are producing on the market. If we could sell them at the right price, I reckon they'd go like a bomb!'

'Hold on a minute,' cut in Winston, 'those knitting machines don't come cheap, and what about premises and a retail outlet ...'

'Just let me finish and then I'll listen,' replied Pat. 'Look, I've just received a legacy of £15,000 from my grandma. At the moment it's sitting in a building society and the interest it's earning is just about keeping pace with inflation – it's not **working for me at all!** Why don't we three set up a business making and selling sweaters and jumpers and pullies?'

'Come to think of it,' mused Sarah, who had been looking into the distance, 'my dad's got a small barn he doesn't use now that the EU are cutting back on food production. I wonder if the upstairs could be turned into a workroom?'

'Yeah, well, I have to say the job market's pretty dead at the moment,' added Winston. 'I'm game, but I haven't got £150 quid, never mind about £15,000.'

'My dad might be interested in backing me – us,' said Sarah. 'He's like a bear with a sore head nowadays. Always moaning about not having a real job any more.'

'Are we all in?' asked Pat. 'If so, first we've got a lot of fact-finding to do – devising a marketing plan and so on.'

* * *

The facts which the trio established were set down as follows:

- The business would be a partnership – at least initially – and would be called 'The Tops Shop'. The three students would be active partners, and Sarah's father, Jack Williams, a sleeping partner with a contribution to start-up capital of £30,000 – £15,000 of which he gave to Sarah and £15,000 he put up as his own contribution.
- As Winston had the manufacturing know-how but no money, Mr Williams agreed to service a loan from the bank made to Winston for £15,000 and also put up the required security. Thus the four partners had each put into the start-up capital for the partnership an equal sum, the total being £60,000.
- Repaying the loan and interest on behalf of Winston would cost the business £9,350 per annum over three years; Winston would have to repay this amount before taking any share of the profits – unless his partners agreed to an alternative 'pay-back' arrangement.
- Pat found a small shop to let at the end of the High Street in Westbridge for £750 per calendar month on a self-repairing lease for three years with an option to renew. It was set between a popular up-market café and a busy chemist's shop. The business rate for the premises was £2,000 per year. Heat and light and water bills were said to be some £150 per quarter.
- Sarah's father said it would cost about £ 5,000 to turn the upstairs of the small barn into a warm and efficient workshop and that he'd secured permission for a change of use. Mr Williams thought a fair rent for the workshop would be £80 a week, and that rates, heat, light and power would add another £50 weekly.
- Winston found a bankrupt knitwear business in the Midlands whose machines and ancillary equipment were up for auction. In the event, all the partners went to the auction and picked up five machines and allied equipment for £4,000. Winston also found a wholesaler who could supply wool and other yarns competitively. Winston's best estimate was that, on average, the raw materials cost for a garment would be £20, if

quality was important, which all said it was. But then there was the cost of labour and overheads, etc.

- Mr Williams said he knew of some farmworkers' wives who'd probably be keen to work for the business as machine operatives – if they could be trained up – at about £3.50 per hour. The average time it took said Winston to make a garment by hand was four hours.
- Pat and Sarah did some market research work in Westbridge and district. The most similar types of product to the ones Winston was keen to design were being sold by Briony's Boutique at the other end of the High Street. Sold as 'one-offs', sweaters were retailing at £85–£95, V-necked pullovers at £60–£70, and cardigans at £75–£99. Two national multiples were selling a range of garments of a similar appearance, but manufactured entirely of man-made fibres at prices some £15 cheaper per type than Briony's; they were also mass-produced, not unique models.
- There were three other retail outlets which appeared to sell garments similar to Winston's design concept – one relied on occasional supplies from home-workers and the other two were addressing the 'down market' end, with prices at some £50 for sweaters, £30 for V-neck pullovers and £45 for cardigans in unisex designs; these two were observed by Pat and Sarah to be doing most business locally.
- Rather ominously, a sign over an empty shop by the town-centre cross announced: Acquired By Highland Fashionwear Limited.

Local advertising rates are:

- Display advertisements Westbridge Gazette: £3.80 per column centimetre; circulation: 45,000; Westbridge Freemail (a free advertising weekly): £2.99 per column centimetre; circulation: 22,000; Radio Western: £350 for 30 15-second 'plugs' per week (outside of peak listening times) plus £100 to make commercial.

(All other rates are as for your own locality.)

ASSIGNMENTS

In groups of three or four, study the above case study carefully. Where prices are not given for items you wish to know, assume them to be at the costs existing in your locality.

1 On the basis of the information provided by the case study, plus any other current prices/costs relevant to it taken from your own locality, devise a marketing/business plan which you think most likely to prove successful in your first year of trading. The marketing aspects of your plan should take into account:
   - Fixing the retail sales price of the three garments you will make – sweater, V-neck pullover and cardigan – bearing in mind the development, production, promotional and overhead costs to be born.
   - What production capacity your workshop will have *a*) initially, and *b*) after a period of one year's trading.
   - What the local competition is likely to do once you enter the market.
   - What sort of image you will give your business and its products, and who will be your targeted customers.
   - How your human resources will be organised.
   - What amount of profit before tax you will need to secure in order to cover all operational costs, loan servicing and a suitable return on the partners' investments.

2 Assuming your business survives Year 1 and is successful, the second part of your marketing/business plan should consider how best you might seek to expand the business in Years 2 and 3.

For example, would it be worth selling as a wholesaler to the retail fashion trade beyond Westbridge?

How could expansion best be financed?

For this planning activity, assume that Westbridge is where you live and its surrounding districts are your surrounding districts.

3 Present your group's plans to your class in turn and decide which is most likely to succeed and why. In a general class discussion, identify and agree upon what the most important factors are in launching a small business successfully.

Off-shoot activities

As part of the wider issues addressed by this case study, make a point of finding out about:

- The legal procedures for establishing a business partnership.
- The current costs of securing a business loan for a clearing bank.
- The various current advertising charges in your local media which a small retailer might use.
- How a business plan seeks to control its monthly cash flow.
- What tax bills The Tops Shop would face.

PC
8.2.2
8.2.4
8.2.5
8.2.6
8.2.7

CASE STUDY 2

'I want you to market our GNVQs in business!'

With these words Mrs Frances Richardson began a briefing session for the students in the Business and Computing Department of Midchester College who were pursuing a second year of study for the GNVQ Advanced Award in Business.

Sue Crane whispered to a fellow-student, Stuart Wilson, 'I bet she's just winding us up! They'd never let us do it for real!' 'Oh yes they would!' responded the sharp-eared Mrs Richardson, 'But first I want to brief you on the current market situation and background, so you can then decide for yourselves whether you want to accept the challenge.'

Mrs Richardson's subsequent briefing covered the following points:

- The College's mission is to provide a relevant range of programmes aimed mainly to meet the needs of the students, their parents and local employers throughout the local community.
- Seventy-three per cent of the local economy is service-industry based; the remainder is concentrated in several high-tech industrial parks and in agriculture. Midchester possesses an affluent number of retired people who use the banking, building society, shopping mall, leisure centre and theatre complex facilities extensively.
- Midchester is also the seat of the Midshire County Council, which employs over 1,400 staff.
- GNVQs at Intermediate and Advanced Levels in Business were first introduced into the Department in September 1993, having been especially designed to promote a practical route into either a business career or higher education. However, because they are still comparatively new, many students, parents and employers in the Midchester

district know very little about them – they still need widespread publicising in a language free from educational jargon.

- At present recruitment to the GNVQ programmes in the Department is as follows:

	Intermediate	Advanced
Third Intake:	23	24 (Sept 1995)
Second Intake:	18	19 (Sept 1994)
First Intake:	17	15 (Sept 1993)

- The reason for the lower than expected recruitment to the 1995–6 programmes has been put down to increasing competition from the three all-through 11–18 schools in the Midchester district, and to a lack of suitable information about the courses communicated in the right media.
- Some students also have expressed the view among themselves that the choice of Option Units is based on subject areas more in tune with the teachers' existing expertise than with the needs of the local economy.
- The current edition of the College's Corporate Plan has targeted an increase in recruitment across the College of 25 per cent over the coming three years. The next academic year has been set to achieve a growth of 8 per cent, and the equivalent target for the large Department of Business and Computing at 12 per cent, since the three-year target for the Department is for a 35 per cent growth rate. Mrs Richardson and her senior colleagues believe this target could be readily exceeded with the right marketing approach.
- Currently, the College publishes a full-time and a part-time prospectus once a year in March. To keep costs down, the print is small and the paper inexpensive. It is left to the Departments to produce additional leaflets and brochures.
- The local advertising media include: a weekly *Midchester Chronicle*, a commercial radio station, 'Wessex Sound', two free, home-delivered advertising papers and the usual spaces for renting on buses, at the railway station and on roadside hoardings.
- The study facilities in the Department comprise: 100 networked PCs, including 25 in an open access suite; major software applications for wp, dtp, spreadsheet, database and graphics work, an electronic training office, 3 CCTV mobile units with video playback, a select business studies library and classrooms equipped with OHP and audio recording equipment. The College Resource Centre and Library provides extensive support and is well stocked.

'Well,' concluded Mrs Richardson, 'that's about it. It's all set down on this handout (*which she circulates*). My staff and I are most eager to receive your help, since we feel that our marketing may have lost touch with the views and needs of Midchester's 16-plus teenagers. So here's what I'd like you to do . . .'

DISCUSSION TOPICS

1 What marketing strategies do you think most likely to succeed in your locality for spreading information about GNVQ Business programmes?

2 The case study refers to the competition for students between Midchester College and local secondary schools. Do you think competition is 'a good thing' in a public service educational context?

3 What do you see as the major differences in marketing a service as opposed to a product?

4 How would you monitor the effectiveness of the case study's marketing plan?

CASE STUDY ACTIVITIES

1 In groups of three or four, reread the case study carefully and then make notes of the points you consider most helpful to your group as data for *a marketing plan* (limited to the academic year of the next intake of students) which Mrs Richardson has asked you to produce. With your teacher's guidance, you may extend the data available to you by using some drawn from your school/college and locality – especially in the areas of financial costs and resources and local advertising media and charges.

2 As part of your data collecting for the marketing plan you have been asked to *design a questionnaire* to survey GNVQ Business students on their views on how they were recruited, how they rate their course of study and what improvements might be made, and so on.

3 Mrs Richardson is particularly anxious to communicate effectively the major features of the GNVQ Intermediate and Advanced Business Programmes and has asked your group to *devise a suitable brochure* in a style and English you think 16-plus prospective students will find appealing.

PC
8.2.2
8.2.4
8.2.6

CASE STUDY 3

Turner Power Tools

Cyril Turner, a former Sales Manager with Brent Power Tools Ltd, decided in 1993 to set up his own business, Turner Power Tools, situated not far from his previous employer. He began his work supported only by administrative help from a business student as part of his industrial training with the aim of promoting certain power tool brand names, becoming a recognised distributor for suppliers, and dealing mainly with account customers. Initial operations were centred on retail premises.

Constraints

Cyril Turner was severely hampered by his previous employment at Brent Power Tools and by the existing power tools distribution system.

a Power tool companies and fixing suppliers generally only trade through distributors. Brent Power Tools Ltd already acted as the local distributor for many firms in the area and the manufacturers were unwilling to cause disruption and uncertainty in the market by encouraging an unknown factor in the shape of Turner Power Tools. The contacts that Turner had made while at Brent Power Tools were therefore effectively closed at the time of setting up his business.

b Turner had signed an agreement with Brent Power Tools undertaking not to approach their customers with the same products for a period of six months.

c The more reputable, well-established companies in the North London area already had distributors in the area; those manufacturers willing to sell through Turner Power Tools were unknown even in the trade with a product quality that was also unknown.

d Turner's intention of dealing with reputable power tool companies required greater cash outlay in holding stocks.

Options

a Many start-up businesses in the power tools market begin by buying and selling to order, depending on picking up any item and make of goods available. This, however, would affect the company's initial intention of dealing with reputable power tool manufacturers.

b The prospects for Turner Power Tools beginning by operating as a retail outlet was extremely limited since the equipment concerned consisted essentially of industrial tools made of hard-wearing parts to withstand heavy duty use on building sites or as part of a hire fleet. They are therefore about four times the price of an equivalent DIY tool.

c The Japanese manufacturer Sanaa was a newcomer to the UK power tools market. The company had made its name in electronic equipment, was well known and had a high reputation for reliability. Their power tools were proven excellent but as yet this section of the company had no distributor in the north and west of London. Turner Power Tools secured this Sanaa distributorship adding substantially to its image. As part of the agreement, Sanaa passed on to the distributor any enquiries about power tools in the area; in return Turner actively promoted the Sanaa equipment. Initially the company stocked about £5,000 of Sanaa tools; this subsequently increased to about 120 tools with a net value of about £15,000. By holding stock of Sanaa equipment Turner Power Tools soon found itself in a position to supply its competitors with Sanaa goods for them to resell.

Finding customers

Cyril Turner's potential customers included local government bodies, building and construction firms, joiners' shops, electricians, and maintenance departments. The trade tends to demand on-site personal service, being on hand to take orders and arrange the delivery of goods when required.

The demand for personal selling was reflected in an initial experiment. Turner's assistant sent a mail shot to all of the 40 names of approved builders on a list supplied by the council. They reasoned that most of those on the list were small firms working from home who would be difficult to contact otherwise and could ideally be canvassed through the post. They were also locally based so the mail shot would at least supply them with information about the new company. However, the mail shot generated no direct response. A similar result came from placing an advert in two local newspapers in consecutive weeks.

The trade was found to be a close-knit one in which personal relationships with clients are very important. The price of goods is often less significant than the quality of the personal service offered: being on hand, supplying a good service including the willingness to supply goods at short notice, sometimes on the day the order is placed. In any case, customers expected deliveries within one to two days, with the sales representative often taking the goods to his own customers. Turner Power Tools were in addition willing to supply customers' requests for goods like specialist engineering tools which are not normally stocked. For those customers, such as the local authority which is only interested in price, the company was willing to match the prices quoted by competitors.

Progress

In the first three months of trading sales were double the figures expected (*see* Table 8.1). By the beginning of the fourth month of trading Turner found more and more of his time spent in the office dealing with customer enquiries and telephoned orders. As the enquiries became more complex it was essential that someone with good knowledge of the tool and fixing trades should be on hand to deal with telephone sales enquiries. It had become necessary to recruit a sales representative, someone to deal with telephone enquiries, and a clerk was hired on the Jobskills Scheme to process orders and take in suppliers' deliveries.

Table 8.1 Turner Power Tools sales and purchases, 1993–1994

Month	*Sales*	*Purchases*
November '93	5 458	3 961
December	6 728	10 198
January '94	17 534	8 484
February	30 204	14 752
March	24 424	22 271
April	22 570	16 313
May	34 755	18 821
June	32 311	11 470
July	49 836	17 384
August	33 915	53 423*
September	44 028	7 301
October	45 223	17 633
November	44 653	56 761*
December	25 401	32 328
Total	417 040	291 100

*Distortion caused by payments made for VAT quarter.

Paperwork

As sales increased so did the paperwork:

a Turner's customers placed small orders frequently. There were about 120 account customers and at the end of the month a statement was drawn up for each account. With no ledger system the statements were based on the sales day book and the difficulty in balancing the total outstanding at the end of each month had been increasing. It took between three and four days to prepare the balance statement each month.

b Turner's supplied a very wide range of goods, many of which were not held in house but subsequently ordered from suppliers. The increased use of this mechanism also greatly increased the number of delivery notes, invoices, and statements coming in from a large number of different suppliers – the company dealt with about 70, the majority of which would be involved in each month's trading.

Invoices had to be matched to delivery notes and all prices, discounts, and mathematical extensions checked; these all had to match the statements. As with sales there was no purchase ledger, but neither was there a purchase day book. To ensure that all payments for a certain month were made reliance was placed on memory and checking through all the invoices in the files.

c Each month's sales were based on the sales day book and this supplied the company's VAT analysis for sales. As there was no purchase day book the monthly VAT was calculated on the basis of cheque stubs and invoices marked paid for the month in question.

ASSIGNMENTS

In groups of three or four produce your answers to the following questions as a series of written presentations. In a class discussion, compare your answers to those produced by other groups and decide on the overall most suitable responses.

1 What important factors did Cyril Turner overlook or underestimate in planning his business start-up? Should he have foreseen them? How might they have been taken into account?

2 What do you see as the current Strengths, Weaknesses, Opportunities and Threats (SWOT Analysis) facing Turner Power Tools?

3 Assuming that it is now December 1994 and you have access to the figures shown in Table 8.1, produce the following parts of a business plan for 1995:

a An organisational structure capable of enabling the business to grow.

b A company development strategy for the coming two years.

c A marketing strategy likely to prove effective given the circumstances of the business environment of Turner Power Tools.

d A sales strategy for the coming year.

e A policy for handling the increasing paperwork.

This case study was adapted from Turner Power Tools in Alan West's *A Business Plan* and is reproduced by kind permission of Longman Group UK Limited.

Element 8.3
PLAN FOR EMPLOYMENT OR SELF-EMPLOYMENT

Choosing a specific career path is undoubtedly one of the most important decisions that people ever make – whether in terms of a first full-time job, or because of a need to make a career change. Some lucky people have no difficulty in this regard – *'I've always wanted to teach . . .'*, *'I knew I wanted to be an accountant in my teens . . .'* – while others anguish and sometimes go with the tide – *'John and Karen applied to Azco Supermarkets, so I decided to as well . . .'* – and still others drift into whatever job – never mind career – that happens along – *'Well, the dosh was getting a bit low and so I had to find something quick! S'all right I suppose, but not much prospect for promotion . . .'*. Given that deciding upon a career route is so important, it is surprising that so many people embark on the process so casually, when long-term personal fulfilment, job satisfaction and income level all depend on making a suitable set of decisions. This section provides the know-how and guidance needed to support you in devising your personal plan for employment or self-employment. Making the time to plan wisely and carefully will almost certainly result in your creating a springboard to long-term success, instead of having to settle for the sort of work which people describe as: *'Well, its only a job!'*

PC 8.3.1

Types of employment and self-employment

For the career-planner there is currently a wide range of types of employment to consider:

Working as an employee in the private sector:

- small, localised private limited companies or partnerships
- medium-sized limited companies operating within a district
- large, national public limited companies with outlets spanning the UK
- multi-nationals with divisions spread across the world.

Working as an employee in the public sector:

- in local government in the form of a borough, district, unitary or county council or authority

- as a civil servant in a government department such as the Department of Employment, Inland Revenue or Department of Trade and Industry etc.
- as a member of HM armed forces or police force
- in one of the many types of public sector agencies: health, care, tourism, leisure etc.

Working in the voluntary sector:

- for a local branch or head office of a national charity such as *Oxfam, Mind, Help The Aged* etc.
- for one of a wide range of charitable trusts, such as *The National Trust* or *Wild Life Trust.*

Working for yourself:

- as a sole trader or partner in a small, local business
- as a freelance sub-contractor in advertising, desk-top publishing or office services for business users
- as an owner or partner of a franchised outlet such as a *Body Shop, Kwik Print* or *Bolloms* dry cleaners
- as a director or partner in an existing family business.

■ Decisions, Decisions . . . !

PC 8.3.1

What type of career path you embark upon – private, public, voluntary, own or family business etc. will depend upon the nature of your own personality and working-life needs. Some of the most important questions you will need to answer are:

Q Do I want to stay close to my home environment or am I happy to move away?
Q Will I enjoy the cut and thrust, 'hire and fire' culture of a highly competitive private company, or would I prefer a more stable career dedicated to serving the public?
Q Do I want to work in a small business, with its limited range of activities, or a large organisation, with its layers of bureaucracy and armies of staff?
Q Are status and salary important to me or is helping others in need what I want to do?

Employment conditions and cultures have changed radically since the 1988–93 major recession in the UK, and job security – in any sector – is not what it was. On the other hand, entrepreneurial opportunities abound nowadays for people willing to take a chance and 'have a go'. So whether you decide on a career in a sales-driven company, a local government department, a charity or in your own business depends in part on key aspects of your individual personality. Are you a risk-taker, entrepreneur, and determined 'shot-caller'? Or are you a team-player, comfortable in a routine and ordered work culture? Or a caring person to whom status symbols and a high disposable income mean very little? Later in this section, you will have an opportunity to undertake a personal audit in this regard.

PC 8.3.2

The statutory requirements for employment and self employment

■ Working as an employee

All employees are bound by specific statutory obligations during their working lives. [See also *Unit Four: Human Resources* on contracts of employment.] Notably, these include making payments through their employer to the state for:

- PAYE: Pay As You Earn income tax
- NIC: National Insurance contributions

PC 8.3.2

Pay As You Earn (PAYE)

Instead of requiring lump-sum payments of tax relating to employment earnings at the end of a financial year, the Inland Revenue's PAYE system enables employees to meet their annual tax obligations on a weekly or monthly basis – rather like a direct debit or standing order system. In a nut-shell, a weekly or monthly tax payment is deducted from the pay of each employee after tax-free allowances and reliefs have been taken into account. Note also that contributory superannuation payments made are not taxed under *PAYE*. Employers' have to calculate on a regular weekly or monthly basis the payroll for the workforce they employ. To assist them, the Inland Revenue issues sets of tax tables at the start of each tax year. It also issues every UK employee with a code number which enables employers to calculate the levels of taxable pay after personal and married couple allowances etc. have been taken into account.

The PAYE code

Each employee is given a prefix letter as part of his or her code:

- L: for personal allowances for employees under the age of 65
- H: as for L, but also showing that the married couple's allowance has been taken into account
- P: for allowances due to employees aged 65–74
- V: as for P, but also showing that the married couple's allowance has been taken into account for employees aged 65–74.

The numbers which immediately precede the letter code stand for the first three numbers of the total allowances and reliefs which the Inland Revenue deems allowable. For instance, a code number of 352 L would indicate that the individual concerned is entitled to have £3525 tax free pay (his or her personal allowance) before *PAYE* deductions begin to come into force. The individual is also categorised as being under 65 years old. A code number of 516 H would indicate that both personal and married couple's allowances had been taken into account.

The notice of coding issued by the Inland Revenue may also include deduction entries which amend the code downwards – say for tax due but not yet paid or other changes made in the latest budget to collect additional *PAYE* taxes.

The issue of an individual *PAYE* code and regular deductions of *PAYE* tax enables employees to know (within close limits) how much tax they will pay week-on-week or month-on-month during the year, and so that they can budget accordingly in their personal and family lives. To arrive at the correct amount of *PAYE* to deduct, employers use a set of tables which shows the total *PAYE* tax due, according to the amount earned, bearing in mind that *PAYE* is currently calculated in three tax bands:

- Lower: 20% up to £ 3200 of earned income
- Basic: 25% between £3201 and £24,300
- Higher: 40% above £24,300.

Having calculated each payroll run and retained the *PAYE* tax due from employees, each employer is obliged to make regular payments to the Inland Revenue in respect of the *PAYE* taxes collected on its behalf.

Inland Revenue PAYE forms

A first-time employee will fill out a P46 form in order to obtain his or her first code number, and a person changing jobs will take a P45 form (completed by the former employer) to the new employer so as to avoid paying tax at a higher, temporary rate under emergency tax code arrangements. Obtaining a P45 when moving jobs is therefore most important! At the end of each financial year every employee receives a P60 form which supplies a summary of: total pay for the year, total *PAYE* tax deducted and confirmation of code number used, so as to be able to check personally that the correct amounts of tax have been levied.

Tax and company cars

For some years the government has also taxed employees for the benefit of having access to a company car for private use. Employees are eligible to pay tax on an amount equivalent to 35% of the price of the car (up to £80,000). Reductions in tax liability are allowed for business miles up to 2500 (one third), or up to 18,000 business miles (two thirds) driven each year, or if the vehicle is over five years old. Tax liabilities are also reduced if the employee has made a financial contribution to the running of the car. Employees who receive free fuel from their employer for private mileage must also pay a tax each year based on the size of the vehicle's engine.

National Insurance Contributions

PC 8.3.2

In addition to *PAYE*, employees also have to pay to the state a regular *National Insurance Contribution* which is related to levels of pay. This NIC payment is for:

- Unemployment Benefit
- Sickness and Invalidity Benefit
- Maternity Allowance
- Basic Retirement Pension
- Widowed Mother's and Widow's Pension
- State Earnings Related Pension (SERPS).

There are currently four *NIC* classes:

- Class 1 paid by employees
- Class 2 paid by self-employed people

- Class 3 voluntary contributions
- Class 4 paid in addition to Class 2.

Class 1 contributions

Both employees and their employers make contributions to *NIC Class 1* on an earnings related basis between £59 and £440 per week at present. Each pays about 10% of the total pay earned. But of course, only the employee's contributions are deducted from his or her pay-packet!

Class 2 contributions

At present, self-employed people pay a flat rate of £5.85 per week for *NIC Class 2*. It is important for such business owners to maintain their *NIC* payments in order to be eligible to receive a full basic state pension.

Class 3 contributions

Anyone may elect to make *Class 3* contributions in order to make good past under- or non-payments of *NIC*, so as to become eligible for full benefits.

Class 4 contributions

The Inland Revenue collects *Class 4* contributions on profits over a certain amount from self-employed business people. Some regard *Class 4* as merely income tax levied under another name.

PC 8.3.2

Statutory obligations and the self-employed

Corporation tax

Instead of paying *PAYE*, self-employed business owners pay taxes on the profits they make from their enterprises after operating costs have been deducted. Such payments are often made twice yearly, or more frequently by arrangement with the Inland Revenue. Self-employed people, therefore, need to be self-disciplined – so as not to spend the money they hold in the form of tax due to the government! Shareholders are similarly liable to pay tax on the dividends paid to them, which is usually taxed at the 25% level at source. Limited companies are currently liable to pay a corporation tax of 33% at a standard rate on profits, and small companies pay at a 25% rate on profits up to £300,000.

National Insurance Contributions

As already outlined above, self-employed business people pay a standard £5.85 *Class 2 NIC* weekly and are also liable to pay additional amounts of *Class 4 NIC* at 7.3% on profits between £6640 and £ 22,880.

The employer's obligations when running a business

As well as paying a tax on profits made and NIC contributions, a self-employed person accepts a number of additional obligations when starting up a business:

- keeping accurate records of accounts – including *PAYE* and *NIC Class 1* records for all staff employed

- keeping VAT records for all appropriate goods or services sold on and all appropriate goods or services purchased in order to operate the business; making prompt payments of VAT collected from sales to *HM Customs & Excise* quarterly
- insuring all employees against accident or death while at work
- insuring the business against any claims from third parties (customers, passers-by etc.) who may be injured or killed while in or near them – say as a result of an explosion, fire or falling masonry (note: a bank or other lender of start-up finance etc. will always be keen to see that a business's assets (which in effect may still belong to them in whole or part) are sufficiently insured)
- complying with such statutes as the Health and Safety At Work Act, the Race Relations Act and the Employment Protection Act etc.

While it is certainly true that starting up one's own business does put a good deal of responsibility upon the owner's shoulders, it should be borne in mind that not all the statutory obligations have to be discharged at the same time. Most new small businesses are run for one or two years before their owners feel able to take on employees. Also, a number of agencies – clearing banks, chartered accountants, insurance companies, *Training & Enterprise Councils*, the *Department of Trade and Industry*, local chambers of commerce etc. – exist to provide guidance and support to the would-be business person.

PC 8.3.2

Self-employment and a personal pension

While employees have access to the *State Earnings Related Pension Scheme* (SERPS) and may also make contributions to either a company or public sector pension scheme (to which the employer also may make contributions), self-employed business people have to make their own arrangements if they wish to have a secure, regular income upon retirement. Fortunately, a number of reputable life assurance companies exist which provide various types of personal pension schemes for the self-employed. Moreover, the Inland Revenue makes what is in effect a free contribution to such personal pensions by waiving tax liabilities on such pensions payments.

A self-employed person can make personal pensions payments amounting to between 17.5% and 40% of annual profits, depending upon age. Such pensions may be paid out from the age of 60 partly in the form of an annuity (where the sum saved is passed over to the assurer in return for a guaranteed annual income for the rest of the person's life), and partly as a lump sum for reinvestment to provide income.

PC 8.3.1 8.3.2

DISCUSSION TOPICS

1 What do you see as the plus and minus factors of working in either the private, public or voluntary sectors?

2 Should *PAYE* be done away with in favour of increased indirect taxes?

3 Do you agree with the current levels of the *PAYE* tax bands? If not, how would you change them?

4 Is it right that an employee should pay tax for the benefit of having a company car which can be used privately?

5 Should a shop-keeper be obliged to take out third party insurance to cover accidents etc. to customers in his shop? Or should individuals be responsible for their own accident and life insurance?

PC 8.3.3

Sources of information

Having made a decision to seek either a first post or the next job stepping-stone of your career path, the next move is to carry out a survey of:

- the commercial, industrial, public or voluntary sector in which your chosen work area is located
- the various local, national or international advertising media – newspapers, journals, magazines, radio/tv commercials, job centres and employment bureaux etc. – which regularly publish details of the type(s) of post you seek.

Before surveying the work sector you wish to move into – accounting, sales, publishing, local government or civil service – you should first draw up a list of key questions for which to find answers as you evaluate your selected career field:

PC 8.3.3

CHECKLIST OF CAREER SECTOR SURVEY QUESTIONS

Q What is the likely work culture of the sector – individualistic, closely supervised, easy-going, highly regulated, entrepreneurial, regulations-bound? In other words, will I feel at home in this work sector?

Q What are the likely promotion and personal development prospects – excellent for high-flying self-starters or time-serving and 'dead man's shoes'? Is there a high degree of structured training or merely 'learning on the job'?

Q Where is the sector going in the next ten years – upward and ever onward (say as telecommunications develops further), or downward and ever backward (say as the fishing or steel-producing industries continue to decline)? In other words, will I still have career prospects in this sector in 5–10 years' time?

Q How are the pay and conditions of service packaged? Does a pay rise occur annually via a series of stepped increments or only after a positive appraisal? Is pay related to productivity – as in 'on target earnings' (OTE) which include commissions and bonuses? Or is there no apparent progressive pay structure other than from occasional promotion? What are the conditions of service? How long are daily/weekly working hours? As a manager would you be expected to work daily 'until the job is done'? Are there unsocial hours to be worked? Will you receive generous paid holidays and expense allowances, a company car, opportunities for overseas travel and a stylish working environment? Or will the 'work be its own reward'?

Q How will you need to develop your personal qualifications (say through a flexi-study degree, HNC or professional qualification such as the Institute of Marketing's Certificate or an NVQ 3 or 4 in Management Studies) in order to support your career advancement in your chosen sector?

Q And if you have decided to set up in business on your own account, you will need to draw up a series of feasibility study survey questions such as: Is my business idea realistic given the size of my targeted market and the existing competition already selling it? Will the demand for my business product(s) grow or falter in future years? What are the start-up and year one/year two financial running costs likely to be?

By crystallising such questions – and others important to you as an individual – you will create a very helpful checklist to evaluate your selected career field *before you commit yourself to it!*

■ Job finding – 'stick or twist'?

How easily you find jobs to apply for depends on another set of factors over which you will not always have control. For instance, if you happen to live in a region of the UK where the local economy has been in decline for some time, circumstances may oblige you to seek further afield for a worthwhile career start or change. If you decide to move away from your home patch for such reasons, you will certainly need to research your likely living costs in terms of lodgings or house-sharing, food and daily commuting. Such a survey may result in your finding that a lower paid, local post which enables you – for a time – to continue to live at home will actually provide you with more disposable income.

PC 8.3.3 8.3.4

CHECKLIST OF AGENCIES SUPPLYING WORK-RELATED INFORMATION

The following organisations and agencies (whose address and phone details are to be found in your local public reference library) provide detailed help and advice for the job-seeker and business starter:

For local, travel-to-work employment:

- the local Training & Enterprise Council e.g. *Heart of England TEC*
- the local careers agency (formerly operated by the county council but currently being operated via competitive tender)
- the local *Job Centre* which is one of a national network run by the *Department of Employment*
- the local *Citizen's Advice Bureau* which among its many services is an excellent source of *'Where can I find out about . . .'* leads
- the local public reference library which keeps extensive current publications and back-numbers of local newspapers, bulletins and databanks of career and job-finding data
- local colleges of FE and sixth form colleges also provide excellent computerised applications (such as TAPS, MICRODORS, JOBFINDER etc.) which provide either careers informational databases or up-to-date details of jobs locally available; many localities run such software as a consortium of further education, careers and local employer networks.

For local self-employment:

- the local Chamber of Commerce
- the local clearing banks (which provide free business start-up packs and free advice)
- the local *TEC* (which may be able to provide a pump-priming business start-up loan or grant, and which may also be able to assist in subsidising the cost of trainee employees taken on in a young business)
- *The Federation of Self-Employed* which provides help and information across a wide range of self-employment issues
- the local *Business Club*: in many UK districts business clubs have been established (with the help of national government agencies) to bring small business people together to discuss aspects of common interest and to obtain useful advice and information

- the local *County*, *District*, *Borough* or *Unitary Councils* provide invaluable (free) help to the would-be business person through their local economic intelligence units, planning and commercial services departments.

For voluntary and charity work:

- the *Voluntary Service Overseas* (VSO)
- various national charity head and local offices: *NSPCC, RSPCA, Oxfam, British Heart Association* etc.
- the *Social Services Department* of the local county council – for details of work relating to *meals on wheels* and hospital driving etc.
- The Prince's Youth Business Trust.

When exploring local information sources about employment or business start-up opportunities, it is also important not to forget *your existing network of parents, relatives, tutors, neighbours and friends etc.* some of whom are bound to be mines of local information about the current job market and business trends and opportunities.

PC
8.3.3
8.3.4

■ Job finding and the media

The second audit or survey you will need to undertake when seeking employment is that of the local, national and possibly international advertising media which publish situations vacant advertisements and associated background information on a regular basis. The checklist on page 781 illustrates some of the major types of media currently publishing such data. Bear in mind that, for instance, in your area a weekly 'freebie' advertising newspaper will go by a suitable name such as: *The Cotswolds Advertiser*. Virtually all the types of job advertising media listed in the checklist are likely to be kept by your local public reference library, and local FE and community colleges are also likely to hold helpful stocks of specialist magazines and periodicals.

Most UK job-seekers tend to want to find employment at home, close to family, friends and familiar surroundings. However, the more adventurous, those with developed linguistic expertise, and young adults wishing to see something of the world before settling down, choose to work abroad.

PC
8.3.3
8.3.4

■ Working in the European Union

UK citizens (with British passports) are also *de facto* citizens of the European Union, and, under various EU treaties – Rome, Single Market, Maastricht etc. – are entitled to find work, live in and move freely around any member state, under freedom of movement and job-finding rights. Moreover, moves are being made currently to require such workers to be paid at the salary levels which exist within the state they work in, even though they may be Britons employed by a UK firm, but working, say in Germany. Today, job advertisements in French, German, Spanish or Greek are not uncommon in national UK daily newspapers, seeking staff to work in mainland Europe.

PC
8.3.3
8.3.4

CHECKLIST OF JOB ADVERTISING MEDIA

Local:

- daily and weekly newspapers e.g. *Birmingham Evening Mail*, *West Sussex Gazette*
- weekly free advertising papers e.g. *Durham Advertiser*, *Wilmslow Messenger*
- local computerised jobs databases held in local public and FE/schools libraries
- local specialist situations vacant newspapers e.g. *Adscene* (Dover/Deal), windows and displays of local *Job Centres* and private sector employment bureaux
- regional commercial radio and television station advertisements e.g. *Ocean Sound*, *Granada Television.*

National:

- national daily and Sunday newspapers e.g. *The Times*, *The Daily Mail*, *The Daily Telegraph*, *The Guardian*, *The Sunday Times*, *The Observer* (note that national, broadsheet dailies publish supplements for specific job sectors on specific days of the week)
- occasional advertisements on networked commercial television
- specialist professional and trade magazines and journals published weekly, fortnightly or monthly e.g. *Accounting World*, *The Bookseller*, *Opportunities* (local government), *Career Secretary* etc.
- advertisements on national computer on-line networks such as *Internet*.

International:

- newspapers with an EU focus such as *European* or, more widely, the international edition of the *New York Herald Tribune* (note: many larger newsagent chains either sell such newspapers or will obtain them against a regular order).

Also, employment agencies exist which specialise in bringing together job-seeker and EU job-giver.

While working in the EU may sound attractive, care should be taken to evaluate beforehand how far a proposed salary will go in, say, Germany or Italy, what local employment laws may be enforceable, what the conditions of employment will be and the extent of employee rights etc. since a British citizen working in mainland EU, though subject to many of the same Brussels directives as other EU citizens, will also be subject to respective state laws and business regulations.

Also, prior research will need to be undertaken in areas such as tax payments – to whom, how much, single or double tax liabilities etc. – and possible effects on pensions/superannuation payments. Further, long-term absence from the UK may diminish UK citizens' rights in areas such as free schooling for their children etc.

■ Working abroad

PC
8.3.
8.3.

Little by little, the European Union member states no longer seem to qualify as being 'abroad', so closely-bound are they becoming.

However, while working 'further abroad' may definitely have its exotic attractions, it is not without a series of disadvantages which must be carefully researched before any decision is made:

- susceptibility to diseases: tropical zones especially embody diseases to which a northern resident has little or no immunity and so vaccination and preventative dosing may be needed to avoid, say, malaria, yellow fever or bilharzia, etc.
- widely differing perceptions of: justice, personal freedom, citizens' rights, the role of women in society, etc.
- the impact on a European of differing cultures, religions and lifestyles; a number of Middle Eastern states prohibit the drinking of alcoholic drinks, and the 'chatting-up' of indigenous females by foreign young men seriously contravenes permitted social practice.

However, there are advantages, such as freedom from paying income tax on a fixed term contract, perks in the pay and conditions of service packages, the appeal of the different and unfamiliar, and not least, sunshine as opposed to damp, grey, UK skies! The key to working happily abroad is: prior research, careful evaluation and balancing of pros and cons, and taking a short taster before committing to a long-term contract.

PC 8.3.3 8.3.4

Working in the UK

As a result of regional unemployment, an increasing number of UK citizens are having to move around the British Isles to find worthwhile employment. While no simple solutions exist, prior research and evaluation again pays off. Living costs vary significantly in different UK regions, as does the extent of leisure facilities. Moreover, while it is sometimes easy to move into a job in a given area, it may be much more difficult to move out of it if, say, the scope of the work is limited, and little opportunity for personal development exists.

It may therefore be prudent for the mobile job-seeker to look for a career in a national company – High Street chainstore, clearing bank or local government department etc. – where opportunities to move upwards are linked to moving to other locations, and where the learned systems and business culture move with the employee.

PC 8.3.1 8.3.2 8.3.3

DISCUSSION TOPICS

1 What do you regard as the main influencing factors which would prompt you to choose to work in one organisation as opposed to another?

2 How would **you** set about finding a worthwhile job locally?

3 What do you see as the pros and cons of deciding to become self-employed?

4 What do think are the most effective job advertising media in your locality? Why?

5 What do you see as the up- and down-sides of working in a) mainland Europe and b) abroad outside the EU?

Analysing and discussing employment and business start-up skills

PC 8.3.5

A further part of your personal preparation for a career as either an employee or business-owner is to carry out an audit of the particular skills which are likely to be required – so that you gain a clear idea of:

- the useful skills you already possess, developed already to a sufficient level
- the skills you possess but need to develop further
- the skills you do not yet possess and will need to acquire.

The following section provides a set of headings – all core or key working skill areas in business – which you should expand and review in a structured series of class discussions (see below):

People skills

PC 8.3.5

Sometimes referred to as interpersonal skills, the ability to interact with and handle the various types of people you come into contact with in your business life – your senior managers, your immediate boss, your co-workers, your customers and the network of people in external organisations you deal with – *will prove crucial to your career success*. The following short list of questions will help your discussion group to focus on some of the most important skills needed in this area:

Q Do I tend to 'rub people up the wrong way' through impatience, aggression, self-centredness or intolerance? If so, how do I change my approach?

Q Am I a good and attentive listener? Can I make other people feel good as they talk? (Remember the old Chinese proverb: *'Open your mouth, that I may know you!'*)

Q Am I able to control my non-verbal signals and responses when I receive face-to-face communications I don't like at all?

Q Am I able to convey a sincere impression of wanting to help a customer and meet his/her needs? Or do I communicate that it's all too much of an effort?

Q Can I lead and manage other people effectively and motivate them to *want* to perform well?

Q Am I effective at relaying messages and passing on information? Or do I tend to hoard it?

Money skills

PC 8.3.

Q How developed are my 'number-crunching' skills? Can I estimate accurately? Is my mental arithmetic good enough to spot a good deal in a meeting and respond accordingly?

Q Am I able to interpret key accounting documents (e.g. *Trading & Profit and Loss Accounts* and *Balance Sheets*) correctly?

Q Do I know enough about the range of banking services locally available and am I confident about interacting with managerial banking personnel?

Q Could I draw up effective cash-flow and operating plans for a small business?

Q Do I know where to shop around in order to obtain the most competitive financial loan (say to start up a small business)? Would I recognise a stunningly good offer when I came across it?

Q Am I sufficiently informed about the range of financial services I could tap into from: a chartered accountant, an insurance company manager, a building society manager, the local TEC manager?

Q Could I exploit effectively a particular supplying market for stock I wish to sell so as to secure the best buying deal my business circumstances would allow?

PC 8.3.5

■ Self management skills

Q How effective are my administrative skills? (e.g. Can I undertake and deliver a project successfully and on time – especially one involving others?)

Q Do I manage my working time effectively? Can I define and set targets with achievable outcomes (e.g. in terms of quantifiable results – number totals, percentages, ratios etc) and timescales?

Q How good am I at chairing meetings at which individuals have to report on progress they have made and results they have achieved?

Q How confident am I about my decision-making and problem-solving skills? Do I know of any models or formulae which provide support in this regard?

Q How developed are my IT and computer-driving skills? Are there any important types of software application that I ought to 'bone up' on?

Q How developed are my information-finding skills? Do I have a sound appreciation of what services local public libraries, county/district/borough council departments, TEC offices and colleges supply? What do I know about locally available on-line databases relevant to business?

PC 8.3.5

■ Entrepreneurial skills

Q How good am I at spotting a worthwhile opportunity, going after it and achieving a positive outcome? (Audit yourself in areas of your past experience such as going in for and doing well in competitions, sports or recreational activities, personal objectives you have set yourself etc.)

PC 8.3.5

GROUP/CLASS ANALYSIS AND DISCUSSION ACTIVITY

In your ensuing group activity, make out a personal audit sheet which lists the questions discussed and summarises your self-evaluation under: 1. Satisfactory skills possessed 2. Skills development needed 3. New skills to be acquired. Then include this aspect in your personal plan for employment or self-employment (see below).

Sources of information for designing an employment or self-employment plan

PC 8.3.3

The following lists will assist you in drawing up your own sources of information to research and tap into before designing your own employment/self-employment plan:

1 *Local people with expert, specialist knowledge:*

- Careers officers and managers (both council and private sector based)
- Personal and subject teachers
- College and public librarians
- TEC personnel
- Advertising managers of local newspapers
- Committee members of the local: chamber of commerce, institute of personnel and development branch, job club etc.
- Officers working in council economic development, planning and personnel departments
- Citizens Advice Bureau staff

2 *Reference texts and journals*

The following are commonly held in local public reference libraries and most are re-published on an annual basis. This list is by no means exhaustive, but will give you a good idea of the sort of information you can readily obtain and browse in:

- *Careers Encyclopaedia* (Cassell)
- *Prospects Directory* (CSU Manchester)
- *Getting A Job In Europe* (P Riley, Northcote House)
- *A Guide To Working In Europe Without Frontiers* (Commission of European Communities)
- *Focus At 18* (Newpoint Publications)
- *The Careers Counsellor's Job Book & FE/HE Guide* (CRAC)
- *Handbook of Free Careers Information* (publ. Trotman)
- *Trade Associations and Professional Bodies UK* (publ. Millard)
- *Municipal Year Book*
- *Social Services Year Book*
- *Health Services Year Book*
- *The Insurance Directory*
- *Directory of Publishing*
- *Directory of Community Care*
- *Benn's Media UK, Europe and World*

Note that reference libraries carry many more directories relating to many more specific areas than those listed above, which provide a ready source of addresses for unsolicited job application letters or requests for careers information etc. *Making an exploratory visit to your public reference library is therefore a 'must' in your plan!*

PC 8.3.6

Designing a personal plan for employment or self-employment

Having considered the kind of work you would like to do, whether as an employee or business-owner, together with an overview of the respective statutory obligations, and having also undertaken a personal audit of your work-related skills in a group discussion, you are now in a position to design your own job-finding or self-employment plan. The following checklist will help you to identify the main aspects your plan will need to take into account:

1 **The duration of the plan:** in other words, how long will you give your self to meet your work-finding objectives?

2 **A schedule of key activities** to be carried out by when during the delivery of your plan – e.g. key people to see, letters to write, information to obtain etc.

3 **A list of people who will provide help and guidance** as you develop your plan.

4 **A list of advertising publications** which regularly include job advertisements relevant to your proposed work sector.

5 Or, a **list of local agencies and specialists on self-employment** whom you can contact for advice if drawing up a self-employment plan.

6 **A checklist of the legal, financial and employee-recruitment considerations** relating to your proposed employment/self-employment.

7 **A checklist of essential documents to be produced/obtained** by when, such as: *curriculum vitae, draft letter of application, any open testimonials, portfolio of work,* completed *National Record of Achievement* etc. or if opting for self-employment: *Year One Business Plan, Cash Flow Forecast, Marketing Plan.*

You should consider, in designing your plan, how you will structure its sections. For example, you may wish to use a structure which starts from the general and progresses to the particular, for example, from *Basic Business Idea* to, say, *Promotional Advertising*, or which starts with a brief outline of a chosen employment field and then progresses to address a prioritised plan on how to obtain a specific post within it.

PC 3.5 3.6

DISCUSSION TOPICS

1 What do you consider to be the common skills required of all employees in a technical/managerial post?

2 How would you advise someone who had identified the following personal skills weaknesses: a) with number calculations, b) with using written English language correctly, c) difficulty with working as a member of a team (e.g. tends to want to take over), d) shyness and nervousness when asked to make a presentation.

3 How important in job-finding is it to be competent at using the resources of a reference library? How would you advise someone whose skills in this area were weak?

4 What in your opinion are the key elements in a plan for securing employment or self-employment?

5 To what extent is finding a decent job a matter of luck – 'in the right place, at the right time'?

REVIEW TEST

PC
8.3.1
8.3.2
8.3.3
8.3.4
8.3.5

1 List four different types of each of private, public and voluntary sector types of employment.

2 List five major statutory requirements for employment.

3 What do the following stand for: *PAYE*, *NIC*, *SERPS*?

4 What are the three bands of income tax payable by an employee?

5 What is an Inland Revenue code number? How does it work?

6 Do an employee's state insurance contributions pay for unemployment, health and social security benefits?

7 What is corporation tax?

8 List four main employer's obligations when running a business.

9 How can a self-employed person obtain a retirement pension? What assistance is available?

10 List five agencies which supply information about jobs and careers on a local basis.

11 List three voluntary sector agencies which offer employment.

12 List four local communications media which advertise jobs.

13 List similarly four different types of national job advertising media.

14 Describe briefly the advantages for finding employment of being a citizen of an EU state.

15 List three main aspects to take into account when seeking foreign (non-EU) employment.

16 What advice would you give to someone thinking of moving away from home to find work in the UK?

17 List five basic skills required in someone seeking a trainee manager post.

18 List five reference sources relating to employment seeking.

19 Outline briefly the main sections of a plan to find personal employment or self-employment.

20 Outline briefly the main skills needed by a person intending to become self-employed.

PORTFOLIO OF EVIDENCE ACTIVITY

PC
8.3.1
8.3.2
8.3.3
8.3.4
8.3.5
8.3.6

Element 1.1
Plan for employment or self-employment

Scenario 1

For this activity, you should choose carefully three types of employment which appeal to you and which you could envisage yourself choosing from in a real career decision-making situation.

One of the types of employment you select should embody opportunities for working in the United Kingdom, the European Union and internationally – say as a translator, a sales person, a civil servant or a factory manager.

For each of the three types of post you select, you should produce a summary which outlines:

- the major functions associated with the job role
- the attractions of the work in areas like job satisfaction, promotional opportunities, employment package etc.
- what specific expertise, skills and experience are needed to do the job well
- what a typical career path in the selected sector is likely to be.

You should also indicate what sources of information exist about each of the three types of employment (say as an appendix), and what the statutory requirements are for each, for example 20–20 uncorrected vision for an RAF fighter pilot.

Scenario 2

Choose one of the types of employment you selected in Scenario 1, and, after having produced suitable notes and prompts, carry out a discussion with 2–3 other students in which you analyse and evaluate the personal skills you currently possess in terms of strengths and weaknesses in relation to those needed for the chosen employment. Note: you may discuss a self-employment opportunity or an employed post.

Scenario 3

Lastly, you are tasked with producing a four-part personal plan which would assist you in obtaining a suitable job as an employee in a private sector, public service or voluntary organisation, or as a self-employed person in business. Your plan should comprise:

1 a realistic estimate of the time you would need to find the employment you select

2 what information you would need, and where you would obtain it

3 what actions you would need to take, and in what sequence

4 what statutory requirements relate to the chosen employment.

Task 1

As usual (and perhaps for the last time!) complete the appropriate parts of your planning and review log before beginning the following Tasks.

Task 2

First research the employment posts and then produce the summaries required in Scenario 1. Take care to set them out attractively and for ease of assimilation. An appropriate summary is likely to be about 2 sides of A4 printed text long.

Task 3

Having prepared yourself, work with 2–3 partners and record successively your discussions about personal strengths and weaknesses relating to the skills of the employment you chose. Each discussion should last between 7 and 10 minutes. As a respondent in the discussion, check out the field of employment of your partner, and prepare suitable questions to ask before the discussion starts.

Note: The partners for the discussion may be: co-students, tutors, counsellors, advisers etc. at the discretion of your teacher. Also, it may be useful for each participating student to produce after the discussion a summary of those skills areas in need of further development.

Liaise with your teacher on the medium to use to record the discussion and to store it in your portfolio of evidence.

Task 4

Having assembled sufficient data, produce a suitable plan which meets the needs of Scenario 3. Bear in mind that it may well service as an invaluable aid in your actual job search, and is therefore worth taking especial pains with. A suitable plan is likely to be about 3–4 sides of printed A4 long.

Performance criteria covered

8.3.1, 8.3.2, 8.3.3, 8.3.4, 8.3.5, 8.3.6

Core skills covered

Communication:
3.1.1, 3.1.2, 3.1.3, 3.1.4, 3.1.5, 3.2.1, 3.2.2, 3.2.3, .3.2.4, 3.2.5, 3.4.1, 3.4.2, 3.4.3, 3.4.4

Information Technology:
3.1.1, 3.1.2, 3.1.3, 3.1.4, 3.1.5, 3.2.1, 3.2.2, 3.2.3, 3.2.4, 3.2.5, 3.2.6, 3.2.7, 3.3.1, 3.3.2, 3.3.3, 3.3.4, 3.3.5, 3.3.6

CASE STUDY

PC
8.3.4
8.3.5

'Gis a job!'

Kim Grey is almost 18 and is urgently in need of a full-time job. She is the eldest of four children and has been under some stress lately, since her father moved out of the family home leaving Kim and her mother to cope.

As a result of her personal situation, Kim is now earnestly looking for a full-time post, the salary of which will be needed to enable her to support herself and to contribute to what is a seriously reduced family income.

Kim is currently pursuing a GNVQ Business Advanced programme of study at Midchester College, located in a large county town in Wessex, some 70 miles south-west of London. Her course is due to finish in about ten weeks' time; Kim has worked hard, and expects to be awarded a Merit grade.

At present she is in two minds. She applied for an HE degree course via UCAS last autumn, but now doubts whether she will be able to finance herself through a three year degree course. However, at the moment, the option is still open to her.

In terms of full-time employment, Kim has a preference for some kind of administrative work, since she has particularly enjoyed the information technology aspects of her course. She is also very much an outdoor person keen on sports such as long-distance running and represented the county in the under-18 women's hockey team.

As a person, Kim is rather quiet and introspective; she prefers to listen to others and when speaking, tends to give short and to the point utterances. She is very methodical in her work and takes pains to present it neatly and clearly.

When roused, Kim has a rather short fuse, but usually calms down quickly and quickly forgets whatever it was that riled her. She is supportive of co-workers in a team context and has a lot of 'stickability' when faced with a difficult undertaking, refusing to be beaten.

So far, Kim has had some success in getting as far as three job interviews for short-listed applicants, but did not get any of the posts. One was of a fixed-term duration of six months, so she didn't mind too much not getting it. The other two would have suited, but Kim felt she did not come over too well at interview, since some of the questions 'fazed' her.

At present, Kim is feeling rather dispirited, with as she puts it *'the days ticking away until the end of June like a time-bomb!'*

CASE STUDY QUESTIONS

1 If you were one of Kim's friends, what advice would you give her, in terms of both full-time job and university education alternatives?

2 What practical steps could you suggest Kim takes in the coming ten or so weeks?

3 Assuming Kim lived in your locality, where would you suggest she went for expert advice on:

a) finding a full-time job

b) financing an HE course of study in her circumstances

c) obtaining financial support.

4 Given your understanding of the job market in your locality, where you may assume Kim lives, what type of job in what type of organisation would you recommend Kim to focus on in her job search?

5 Do you think young adults in Kim's kind of situation are able to access sufficiently supportive and helpful sources of advice? If there is room for improvement in your locality, what sort of initiatives can you suggest which might be taken by public sector, voluntary, careers and associated organisations?

FURTHER SOURCES OF INFORMATION

The Greatest Little Business Book, 5th edn, P Hingston, Hingston Associates, 1991. ISBN 0 906555 10 8

The Business Start-Up Guide, National Westminster Bank, 1992.

The Business Planner, I Maitland, Butterworth-Heinemann, 1992. ISBN 07506 0136 1 (deals mainly with financial aspects)

A Business Plan, A West, Pitman/Natwest 1991. ISBN 0 273 02824 3

Modern Business Administration, 6th edn, R C Appleby, Pitman Publishing, 1994. ISBN 0 273 60282 9

Managing Growth, M Bennett, Longman–Natwest, 1989. ISBN 0 273 03103 1

Marketing: An Introduction, 3rd edn, P Kotler & G Armstrong, Prentice Hall, 1993. ISBN 0 13 555244 3

How To Prepare A Marketing Plan, 4th edn, J Stapleton, Gower, 1989. ISBN 0 566 02723 2 (includes sales forecasting/planning)

Production Management Systems, J Browne, J Harhen, J Shivnan, Addison-Wesley, 1988. ISBN 0 201 17820 6

INDEX